THE COP
AND
THE STALKER

Based on a True Story and Actual Events

VINCENT DAVIS

PAGE PUBLISHING, INC.
Conneaut Lake, PA

First originally published by Page Publishing 2019

ISBN 978-1-64584-191-3 (pbk)
ISBN 978-1-64584-192-0 (digital)

Printed in the United States of America

CONTENTS

CHAPTER 1

As surely as summers come and go, so, too, did a new group of lifeguards assuming their jobs on the beaches and municipal pools of New York. One of them was young Vincent Davis. Eighteen years old and recently graduated from high school. His mind was filled with the serious goals and nebulous dreams so many young people have. His adolescence slipped away, replaced ever so quickly by adulthood.

High in his lifeguard chair, he reflected on his childhood between scanning for beautiful young girls and watching the water for any swimmers in distress. Adult reality, he thought, comes to everyone at different times and in stages that affect the way a child grows and matures. Enjoying his freedom from school books and final exams, Vinny wondered about the past lives of the people he was watching over but winced when the painful memory of his mother's death gripped him. For the past eight years, he'd never been able to escape it. He wondered if he'd ever be free of it.

When Vinny was aged ten, he, his mother, and a friend ran a spontaneous footrace along the block where they lived in Bay Ridge, Brooklyn. Vinny's mother stumbled and fell, striking her head against the base of a metal lamppost. Helpless and apprehensive, all Vinny could do was watch as a neighbor relentlessly performed CPR in a failed effort to save his mother's life.

He closed his eyes for a moment and saw his mother's lifeless body being loaded into an ambulance. Scanning the beach, he remembered when he, his mother, and George, his best friend at that time, watched an episode of *Ironside*. He recalled how beautiful and full of life and love she was. She took a keen interest in their every activity and loved to watch them play ball games and march in the ragamuffin parade at Halloween. His mother was a lunchtime monitor at Our Lady of Angels, the Catholic school he and his two younger brothers attended. No matter what they were involved in, she was there to encourage and support them.

When his mother died that July night, he could not understand why God had taken a loving mother whose four children needed her so very much. He asked himself that question over and over. It was cold comfort to learn that the cause of her death was a rare disease called Marfan syndrome, a condition that affects the valves and lining of the heart's arterial walls. Today, if detected in time, it can be corrected by surgery, but sadly, for her family and friends, it was not to be.

The loss to a child of his mother, at any age, cannot be measured by counting tears or the number of prayers beseeching God for answers.

What happened that tragic night changed his life forever. His mother's death matured him in an instant: he vowed to become a policeman. Never again would he stand helplessly by and watch someone die. That night, he swore to himself he would make a difference. Life teaches us all valuable lessons we never forget. They become a part of our character, and from this, Vinny learned that life was important indeed.

Being the eldest child, he tempered his anguish for the sake of his brothers and Maria, his baby sister. He repeatedly assured them of better times ahead and was there to comfort them as only siblings can do among themselves.

The death of his mother had other repercussions within the family. Vinny's paternal grandmother, Margaret, widowed on Vinny's second birthday, gave up her apartment and moved in to help his father raise the children.

Vinny had always admired and respected his honest, honorable, and hardworking father. To help make ends meet, his father worked two jobs. First and foremost, he was a New York City policeman, but his salary was insufficient to pay all the bills and feed his family.

By his working a second job as a mailer for the *New York Times*, the family managed to survive. His grandmother moving in with them was a blessing in disguise. Not only did she help with the kids and the housekeeping, but also, as Vinny later came to realize, she kept the children together. Before her arrival, there were discussions about parceling out the children among relatives on their mother's side. His grandmother's arrival saved the family by keeping it intact. If it weren't for her sacrifice, they wouldn't have grown up together and remained close. Vinny didn't know if it was because of his mother's death, but he and his siblings became inseparable and were always there for one another. Their familial bond was something Vinny never saw in any of his friends' families.

A year after his mother's death, his father unexpectedly began dating Mary McGonigle, a traditional Irish singer and aspiring actress, and less than two years later, they married. This was her first marriage, and she had no children, nor did she desire to have any children of her own, which suited Vinny's father. At that stage of his life, he had no desire to take on any additional responsibilities.

He couldn't afford to, and now Mary found herself with an instant family, but she never complained. She was always there for all the children, but especially for Maria. Only four years old when her mother died, she, perhaps easier than her older brothers, accepted Mary as her mother, and they quickly developed a loving mother-daughter relationship.

Hoping to start a new life and ease the memory of their past tragedy, the Davis family moved in to a two-and-a-half-story center-hall colonial in Yonkers, New York.

Moving to a new neighborhood was rough at first, but Vinny had a knack, even then, of getting along with people. It didn't take long for him to make new friends, one of whom was Tommy Cascione, nicknamed TC. He was a kid whom, at first, Vinny could relate to. Later, he came to idolize him as a big brother he never had. TC was the opposite of Vinny and everything he wanted to be, from the way he dressed to his mannerisms and finesse with girls. Although he was of Irish Italian descent, he looked more Italian, and with an Italian surname, everyone took him for one.

There were three types of kids and cliques in Yonkers. There were the Italians, who were the greasers. They wore black or blue jeans, white T-shirts, black boots, and of course, black leather motorcycle jackets. To Vinny, these guys looked cool, and they were rarely seen without good-looking girls on their arms. Next were the geeks. Vinny was a geek at first. Geeks dressed like mama's boys, studied hard, and got good grades. Instead of girls, they were more interested in books. Last were the potheads, who emulated the hippy era and Woodstock by wearing tie-dyed shirts, bell-bottomed jeans, and sneakers with writing all over them. Of course, the potheads bore the brunt of many attacks by the greasers, who would have nothing to do with drugs.

At first, it was difficult for Vinny to leap the chasm from geek to greaser. Although his playclothes, with the exception of the motorcycle leather, were greaser clothes, he had to get around his father and new mom's strict edict about the school's dress code. When he attended Catholic school, it was easier to fit into any group, because everyone wore the school uniform. Now that he was at a public school, his parents insisted he dress properly for school. His father would always say, as every father has said to an insubordinate child, "I don't care what the other kids are wearing! You are my son, and as long as you live under my roof, you will do as I say." Whenever his father announced his decrees, he would end the debate by saying, "Case closed!"

Thinking back, Vinny had to admit that, for a kid, he was quite inventive, and sometimes ingenious, when it came to subverting his father's edicts. It wasn't long before he began ruining his good clothes by playing in them at school. With the family's tight budget, it became cheaper for his father to send him to school in jeans. Still, his father wouldn't budge and allow Vinny to wear a T-shirt to school, but that was easy to get around. He wore one under his dress shirt, which he'd remove a half-block from home.

It wasn't long before he began hanging out with TC, who, by that time, owned, fixed, and restored old Chevys, with the other greasers. To become one required an initiation, which consisted of the kid being initiated putting his motorcycle jacket on backward and zipped up so he couldn't move, and then he would be beaten about the jacket—quite a painful experience. It was the price one paid to be a greaser.

Vinny had great times hanging out with TC and the others. In a way, they were reliving what it was like growing up as a teenager in the New York City of the 1950s. All the guys listened to oldies music. *American Graffiti* and *The Lords of Flatbush* were their two favorite movies, and of course, they were always ready to wreak havoc in a neighboring town or be ready to rumble at a moment's notice. Those were the days, unlike today, when kids fought with their hands. They didn't resort to knives, guns, or other weapons. There was, however, an occasional chain or bat, but the ground rules for a large fight were discussed and agreed upon before any fights took place. Vinny, like most young boys, had a few fights growing up on the streets of Brooklyn and rarely lost. He was naturally good with his hands but would rarely fight unless he was provoked. He didn't necessarily go looking for trouble, but if it came looking for him, he was ready, willing, and able.

No matter how hard Vinny tried to be like TC and fit in with the greasers, he couldn't master the art of picking up girls as easily as TC could. He was an expert and always had a fine-looking girl with him or sporting a fresh hickey on his neck, a testimonial to his latest female conquest. Vinny didn't have the experience yet, but it wasn't long before he had absorbed enough of TC's repertoire to make a few moves of his own on the unsuspecting girls at school.

One female in particular was TC's younger sister, Corinne. Although she wasn't a wild girl, being TC's sister, she knew the games boys played. Being TC's friend, Vinny didn't stand a chance with her, but that didn't stop Vinny from admiring Corinne. He just did so discreetly, because TC was highly protective of her. He'd warned Vinny of the consequences if he chased his sister, and to make sure he got the message, he threw Vinny off his parents' front porch when he caught Vinny just talking to her. Corinne was gorgeous, with long black hair, stunning bedroom eyes, a fantastic, bright smile, and a body to die for. Vinny tried for years to gain her affection, but she thought he was a pretentious flirt and an aspiring playboy like her brother.

As Vinny sat thinking about his tomorrows, reality knocked loudly on his door. It was the knock of a beautiful brunette. As she walked past Vinny's lifeguard chair, he was mesmerized by her figure. Her bikini clung to her, outlining every curve. As he stared at her, it dawned on him that he knew her. He hadn't seen her since the summers he'd spent at Sprain Ridge Pool. Debbie—yes, that was her name. The last time they'd talked, he departed with the feeling she thought he was a geek. Perhaps she had. But that was then, and Vinny wasn't the shy geek he once was. He'd learned a lot about women since then, and his experiences gave him the confidence to ask her out on a date.

He called down to her with a quick, "Hey, good-looking, remember me?"

She turned toward him but didn't immediately recognize him. "Are you talking to me?" she asked curiously.

"Yes!" he said.

"Take off those mirror sunglasses so I can see your face," she said. As soon as he did, she said, "Vinny Davis?" and looked at him in total disbelief.

"Yes, Debbie, it's me," Vinny said confidently. "Where are you sitting?"

As she pointed to her spot on the beach, he told her he'd stop by when his shift was over.

When he walked over and sat on her blanket a few minutes later, he was no longer afraid, shy, or lost for words. They talked for hours that day, recalling when they were children and expressing how amazed they were by how much they'd changed physically in just a few short years.

He asked if she were involved with anyone. She said she'd broken up with her boyfriend the previous April. Sensing the way forward was clear, he then asked if she'd like to go out one night. When she said yes, he became excited, not just at her answer, but also at how well he'd handled himself.

After several months of dating, he knew he was in love with her. Thinking back, he realized he'd loved her from the first time they'd met as kids. In high school, he had his share of sexual relationships, from the girls in his school to his art and English teachers. Bur that was just sex. This was, for the first time in his life, love, not just sex. Whatever goals he set for himself, he vigorously pursued them, and now he was in hot pursuit of Debbie. He wanted her for his wife, and he was going to have her. The only thing he overlooked was the fact that sometimes you have to accept rain to get green grass.

With his brief playboy life behind him, he settled down with Debbie. They were seen everywhere together. The entire package was there: family meeting family, friends meeting friends. Then came the darkness, a long darkness, like a December's night with bone-chilling sleet and freezing rain.

As Vinny sat reading a magazine, the telephone rang. He picked up the receiver. The voice on the other end asked for Vinny. "Speaking!" Vinny said. "Who is this?"

"I'm Richard Sabol, Debbie's boyfriend," the voice on the other end declared.

Vinny's first thought was that it was a sick joke, but his anger increased until it hit the red zone. If this was a joke, it'd taken a wrong turn.

Vinny quickly shot back, "I've been dating her for three months, and your name's never come up."

"That's because I'm in prison for attempted armed robbery. And I'll tell you something else—if you don't stop seeing her, not only will you be dead, but your entire family will be dead also."

Vinny had no idea who this moron was, but he knew alarm bells when he heard them. He knew how to handle threats from people he knew, but Vinny didn't know this lowlife. And to threaten the lives of his family, that was the touching of swords. Vinny responded with a barrage of profanities, ending with, "I'll meet you anytime, anyplace. When you see me, you'll wish you were still in prison, because I'll kill you! In the meantime, kiss your boyfriend Bubba for me." Vinny said the last part sarcastically. Not exactly words the bishop of Our Lady of Angels would expect to hear out of the mouth of one of his altar boys. But by then, Vinny's blood was boiling. His first thought was to get to Debbie's house as quickly as possible. Vinny's father was a cop—he could protect his family—but Debbie's family had no such security.

He got in his car and raced to her parents' house. The instant she opened the door, he knew she, too, had heard from Sabol. Her parents were visibly shaken as well.

Debbie sat Vinny down and told him about the animal Sabol. She described what sounded like an evil character out of a Stephen King novel. Sabol had been arrested in Queens for attempted murder, after he shot a drug dealer in the head during an attempted robbery. He'd been arrested numerous times but never went to trial because the witnesses against him had "memory loss" due to threats he made against them. Although never proved, when a potential witness, a woman, answered her doorbell, a man whose head was concealed under a ski mask took a 12-gauge shotgun from his coat and blew the door off.

Debbie felt she needed to justify her involvement with Sabol to Vinny. She explained how young she was at that time and that Sabol was her first love. He was very clever in concealing his devious and evil life from her, she said, and she didn't know about it until he went to jail. She cried as she told Vinny how Sabol would go to gay bars and let himself get picked up by unsuspecting males, go home with them, perform sex acts with them, then assault and rob them of their money and jewelry. Afterward, he would threaten to kill them if they called the police.

Local police knew about the crimes he committed, but knowing who committed them and being able to arrest the suspect are two different things. Without the victims' testimony, there was no case. On the rare occasions when victims came forward, he was picked up by the police but quickly released on bail. After getting out, he would return to terrify his victims to the point where they just wanted the whole incident to just go away.

Oddly, Debbie went on to explain that she felt sorry for Sabol. He'd had a bad childhood, and his parents were divorced. His mother was an alcoholic, and he never saw his father, who was a retired

NYPD sergeant. She thought she could help him change while he was in jail by keeping in touch with him and being supportive. He promised he would change, but only if she would wait for him to get out of prison, so he would have a life to look forward to with her.

"All that changed," she said with tears in her eyes, "when I fell in love with you. I tried telling him it was over and that I found someone new and was very happy, but he had other ideas. When he called me, he told me he was going to marry me when he got out of prison, whether I liked it or not! His parting words were a threat: 'I'll cut your fingers off and mail them to your parents.' He added another one: 'I'll throw acid in your face and make you so ugly nobody would want you!'"

Still visibly shaken and with tears in her eyes, she warned Vinny that Sabol was a monster and would not think twice about killing him. As he held her close in his arms, he assured her that wouldn't happen. Vinny told her his father would get in touch with the Department of Corrections and would make Sabol's life inside more difficult. She had no idea Vinny would buy a small-caliber gun and would never leave home without it.

As she sobbed in his arms, he thought of Sabol. Vinny had heard of men like Sabol, men with no redeeming qualities. They use fear and intimidation to achieve their criminal ends. Those tactics might work with others, but they sure as hell wouldn't work on Vinny. Maybe he should tell him about the "Don't Tread on Me" flag, the Gadsden flag, of our Revolutionary War his brother bought.

Vinny's father made the call to the Department of Corrections. It worked. No more threatening phone calls were made to Debbie or her family. The corrections supervisor informed Vinny's father that Sabol's outgoing mail would be censored for any written threats, but his letters to Debbie continued, with Sabol pleading and begging for forgiveness. And one more chance. Debbie never responded, and eventually, the letters stopped.

A long, anxious year passed, during which he'd passed his medical and psychological examinations, until Vinny completed all the remaining NYPD tests. Then a background investigator was assigned to review his life. People who have endured background checks can attest to the intrusive scrutiny they undergo. The investigator seemed to know everything about Vinny, almost back to the day he spoke his first words until the moment he was introduced to him. Vinny was astounded at the insignificant events of his life the investigator had discovered. Events that had slipped from his memory long ago were resurrected and probed. It seemed as though everyone who'd ever set eyes on him had blabbed something to the investigator. In addition, he had to submit a report on his excessive absences from school and another on any and all traffic violations he'd committed. It had nothing to do with his father being a police officer or any of his relatives, and everything to do with his past. The NYPD wanted to know him inside and out. He didn't like it—no one does—but it was just another of the many steps it takes to become a police officer. Many give up during this process, but Vinny was not a quitter.

People he knew who had served in the military repeated an old expression: "Hurry up, then wait."

And Vinny waited.

CHAPTER 2

I t was a cold and rainy night, but Vinny wasn't going to let that, or anything else, interfere with what he had planned. That night set in motion events that would change his entire life. He planned to propose marriage to the woman he'd grown to love more than life itself.

Although they were both only nineteen years old and statistics were stacked against them, they felt they were mature enough to make marriage work. Vinny couldn't help but think of how young and in love his mother and father were when they married. People said times were different when his parents married. Family values were stronger, too, and couples worked harder and stayed together. Another common belief was that young couples were too quick to turn and run at the first sign of trouble and that they didn't make time to communicate. Instead, they'd run home to their parents, who'd willingly take them in with open arms. Rather than advising and encouraging them to return home to their spouse to sort things out, they would offer shelter, were quick to take sides, and would offer the name of a divorce lawyer used by a close friend's son or daughter.

However, as with most young couples blinded by love, Vinny and Debbie were willing to challenge the odds and work as hard as their parents had to make their marriage work.

Vinny had worked hard and saved every cent he could so he could afford the purchase of "the rock," which was what the women of the eighties called their diamond engagement rings. In the nineties, they put it in the form of a question: "What better way to make two months' salary last a lifetime?" He thought the whole ring thing was ridiculous, and he didn't like the idea that his love was being judged by the size of the diamond he bought, but that was a standard by which Italian American families judged men, and he was marrying into one. When a man plans to marry an Italian American girl, he must buy her a ring the same size, or bigger, than that of any of her female relatives, living or dead. This custom has led to a generational increase in the size of the rock. What began as a small diamond chip will soon reach Liz Taylor proportions. God help the man who's not 100 percent Italian, because then the ring must pass not only the size test but also the closest scrutiny of every female member of her family. Vinny was what Italians call a mutt, and they weren't hesitant to say that to his face. Being a mutt made marrying a full-blooded Italian more difficult. His mother's parents, on her father's side, were from La Coruna, Spain, and on her mother's side, from Naples and Genoa. Vinny's father's parents, on his father's side, were from Ireland, and, on his mother's side, from England and Ireland. With that blood, Vinny had to work extra hard to gain the acceptance of Debbie's family.

He thought it best to start out on the right foot with his future father-in-law, a man similar to his own father. Greasing the skids, he did the expected by asking her father for her hand in marriage.

Mr. Manzo had fallen in love with his wife, Fran, at a young age. They married and immediately started a family that grew with the addition of two boys and four girls. Like Vinny's father, Mr. Manzo worked two jobs to support them and saw to it that they had a good life. His day job was with the Department of Sanitation for the city of New York, which, before the modernization of garbage trucks, was backbreaking work. At night, he delivered milk off an old truck. A hard day's work never bothered him. He was more than happy and extremely content providing and caring for his family.

This view on family life was something with which Vinny empathized, because his father was the same. Working as hard as you can to provide a better life for your family was a value that Vinny's father instilled in him when he was young. If that meant working two jobs and sacrificing free time to provide for one's family, then so be it. No sacrifice is too great when it comes to loved ones. A man must do whatever is necessary to provide for and to protect his family. Those were the core values Vinny's father, his future father-in-law, and Vinny all held. And someday, it would be the way Vinny planned to raise his own children.

But first, Vinny had to pop the big question to Debbie.

He carefully planned to surprise her. Soon, everything was in place. Debbie had taken a second job as a waitress at a local restaurant, so he decided to catch her unawares there. He brought a girl-friend she worked with into his scheme. He instructed her to set up the booth at the rear of the restaurant and place flowers and a bottle of Dom Pérignon, which he provided, on it. Vinny also told her friend to lie to Debbie and tell her a man had been in earlier and left the flowers and champagne because he was returning with his girl-friend. Just to be sure, Vinny slipped the manager $20. At 9:30 p.m., Vinny sneaked in and sat in the booth. Debbie didn't catch on and, when she saw him, was totally surprised. She thought his proposal was romantic. Her answer was yes.

Take all the minute planning that went into Operation Overlord (the invasion of Normandy in 1944), add to that the effort it took to put Neil Armstrong on the moon, then double it, and you'll have some understanding of what it takes to arrange an Italian wedding.

The women of Debbie's family, with some friends sprinkled in, charged into planning her wedding with the same vigor Spartan warriors had going into battle. The guest list soon reached three hundred, most of whom were her relatives. The only logical place for the reception was the Marina del Rey. The wedding factory in the Bronx money was no object, or so it appeared. Only the most expensive, top-shelf liquor would do for the cocktail hour and rolling bars; flaming, baked Alaska Dance hors d'oeuvres; a Venetian coffee hour; a white Rolls-Royce to haul away the eager newlyweds; three silver stretch limos for the eighteen people in the bridal party; and of course, the band had to be summoned from Prince Charles and Princess Diana's wedding to play at theirs. When Vinny told Debbie he was a manager for Jack LaLanne, he hoped she got it right—he was only a manager, not LaLanne himself. They were already working two jobs to pay for their gala wedding, in which poor Vinny had absolutely no input.

Vinny remembered his future mother-in-law telling him, "It only happens once in a woman's life."

Thank God, he thought.

Shortly after Valentine's Day, two short months before their big day, Vinny was at his future in-laws' house, waiting for Debbie to return home from work. While sitting in the kitchen, he was forced to go over a checklist with Debbie's mother, a strict, off-the-boat Italian. She left no stone unturned as she oversaw wedding preparations. Vinny sat at the table, at ease, knowing all the bills were paid, and they had money to cover any incidental wedding expenses. They breathed easily, knowing that all their hard work had paid off. It appeared to be smooth sailing ahead.

He suddenly felt a draft of cold air as the front door opened. Debbie!

He rose and went to greet her, but when he saw her, his heart nearly stopped. She had tears in her eyes and looked as though she'd been crying for a long time. His first thought was that she'd been in an accident. When she calmed down enough to tell them what had happened, it wasn't a car accident that set her to crying, but an accident of nature.

The beast was loose.

Richard Sabol was out of jail again.

That night, he waited for her to get off work, sneaked up behind her with a shotgun, and pointed it at her head. He ordered her to get in his car, and when she did, he drove off.

She was terrified and not sure what this monster would do. He grabbed her left hand and looked at her engagement ring, then thrust it away.

"I'd have given you a huge engagement ring and all the money you could ever use."

Although petrified, she explained she would never go back to him and that she was going to marry Vinny.

"Nobody steals my girl!"

He warned her not to marry Vinny, because he was going to be dead.

Hearing that final threat, in a litany of threats, Vinny erupted with volcanic fury. His instinct was a desire to beat the beast beyond recognition. Vinny needed release, and having his hands around Sabol's throat would be that release.

As Vinny grabbed his coat and put it on, Debbie's parents blocked his way. "Do you still want to be a cop?" her father asked cautiously.

Not waiting for a response to his own question, he explained in a frightened and barely audible voice, "He did this to make you come after him. Everything you've worked for your entire life, for everything you hold close to you, will be gone if you go after him. You'd be no different from him, except you'd have less of a record."

Vinny stared into the eyes of a very wise man and knew he was absolutely right. The realization that he could not jeopardize his future with Debbie and his dream of becoming a cop was sobering. He mentally sheathed his sword. There would be better day, a better situation, when the circumstances would be more advantageous. Vesuvius was temporarily becalmed.

After calming down, too, and having something to eat, Debbie remembered that her car was still parked at her job and she needed it. Vinny offered to drive her to pick it up. Although she appeared composed, he knew she was still worried. As he backed out of his parking space, a car unexpectedly pulled up and stopped next to them. The passenger window was down, and the driver yelled, "You're both dead!"

The car sped off, and Vinny instinctively gave chase. Debbie started screaming to stop the car, but Vesuvius was again erupting. He was determined to catch this demon and end his reign of terror, something that should have been done by the legal system a long time ago.

As Vinny raced over the streets of Yonkers in hot pursuit, Debbie continued to yell at him, "He has a gun! He'll kill us!"

She had no idea Vinny had a .25-caliber pistol in the glove compartment. He'd bought it when Sabol first threatened their families.

She was also unaware Vinny was an expert shot, a skill he'd learned from his father, who was an instructor at the NYPD's Firearms and Tactics Unit. Knowing Vinny was on the list to become a cop, he took Vinny to a range and gave him the proper instructions in the use and safety of firearms.

Chasing Sabol was a reckless disregard of his father's advice, but it wasn't a case of being rebellious. He held most of the values his father had instilled in him, though he would never admit it. As he raced along, the high regard and respect for the law, which Vinny was now breaking, began a struggle with his rage. Back and forth it went. What choices did he have? Kill or be killed? Obey the law or break it? To his right, Debbie was wigging out. In his head, thought upon thought ricocheted about. Here he was, a policeman's son, speeding, with a gun in the glove compartment, attempting to catch, and possibly injure or kill, someone who he believed deserved it.

The reality of what he was doing hit him with the force of a freight train. He began to slow down. He would surely disappoint his father. The words of his future father-in-law, "You will be no better than him," crossed his mind again. As he slowed further, the red taillights of Sabol's car disappeared into the night.

Vinny glanced in his rearview mirror. Fuck!

He saw the flashing red lights of a police car.

He panicked like he'd never panicked before. As he pulled over, his mind raced with a thousand possible outcomes as the officer screwed his gun into Vinny's ear. He attempted to explain why he was driving like a maniac. Fortunately, the officer noticed his father's PBA card in the windshield and asked to whom it belonged. When Vinny told him, the officer relaxed and holstered his weapon. He then asked for Vinny's license and registration. As Vinny produced his license, Debbie thought she'd be helpful. Before Vinny could stop her, she opened the glove box to retrieve his registration and insurance card. That was when his pistol fell out. The officer immediately confiscated it. Thinking quickly, Vinny told him his father had borrowed his car and must have left the gun there. The officer accepted his explanation but decided to verify it at the station house.

Damn!

After a call, his father soon arrived, disappointment on his face. Being a police officer does have its perks, but his father never took advantage of them. Vinny couldn't recall his father committing so much as a traffic infraction. Without saying a word, he identified himself by showing his shield to the desk officer. After the brief conversation his father had with the officer, Vinny saw the officer hand his father the gun. He was free to go, and they left the station house.

His father didn't say a word, but when Vinny tried to explain, he stopped him. With a face contorted by pain and disappointment, he said, "Don't come home tonight! You want to be a man, get married, and carry a gun? Live with her family, because you're no longer my son!"

Vinny tried to explain again, but his father held up his hand in a motion to stop him and said, "Case closed."

His relationship with his father had just suffered a devastating blow. As ordered, he didn't return home that night.

He sadly realized the enormity of what he had done. By telling the cop the pistol in his car was his father's and not his, he had put his father in a precarious position that might have cost him his job. It was the most selfish thing he'd ever done. He felt guilt, humiliation, and shame for what he'd done. In his own eyes, it was unforgivable, and he didn't expect to ever be forgiven. Vinny was ashamed at himself for letting Richard Sabol, a man made of pure evil, push him to the limits, where he would end up betraying his own father, a man he loved and wanted nothing more than to emulate. Now, for the second time in his young life, he thought he'd let down his father. The first was with his mother's death, which he blamed himself for. And now this. Not only had he humiliated himself, but he, ultimately, humiliated his father too. Vinny promised himself that he would make it up to his father no matter how long it might take. He would become a cop just like his dad. Only then would he be able to prove himself to his father and that he could improve society by putting criminals like Sabol behind bars, where they belong. Perhaps then, he prayed, his father would see that he was a worthy son and not a coward or fool who lied to save his own ass.

Coincidentally, the criminal Sabol was not seen or heard from again after that night. Another "case" seemed closed.

But it was not to be. Sabol returned to his violent life of crime but steered clear of Vinny and Debbie.

Word on the street was that he was busy committing armed robberies throughout Westchester County and on Long Island and was wanted for questioning by several police agencies. He had a violent fight with his brother at their mother's house. When she tried to break it up, he beat her and threw her against a wall. After that incident, he went into hiding somewhere in Yonkers.

April 17, the day of their blessed wedding, finally arrived. The service was beautiful, as was Debbie. She took his breath away every time he looked at her. At the altar, they kissed, completing the ceremony. He believed the love behind their kiss would last forever. They honeymooned in the Bahamas, spending their time as newlyweds do.

Then they returned to a lovely apartment and began their life together. Like most couples, they started off with plenty of friends, relatives, and bills. For the most part, they were living the American dream.

For two years, Debbie and Vinny kept their heads above water. The bills that seemed, at one point, insurmountable were gradually paid off. Life was good, they both had jobs, and they were in love, but time dragged for him as he waited and waited for word from the NYPD. The days were long, and the weeks longer.

Finally, he heard from them. His application was accepted. The wait was over.

Hallelujah!

As his January 1985 reporting date neared, so did his anxiousness. Like a runner waiting for the starter's gun, he couldn't wait to get sworn in, one of a total of 2,800 recruits, all with similar goals and dreams.

CHAPTER 3

The feeling Vinny had as he stepped off the train at Twenty-Third Street was the same exhilaration a child has when going to the circus or opening a Christmas present. He couldn't wait to get there after dealing with the disappointment of Friday, when he was sworn into what he believed to be the wrong police department.

On that Friday, a class of 2,800 recruits lined up waiting to take the oath. All had hopes of graduating in six months, after undergoing extensive training in law, police science, political science, and what would no doubt be agonizing physical training. This was the day Vinny had waited all his life, the day he would join the ranks of the New York City Police Department and begin to follow in his father's footsteps.

As he sat waiting, as instructed, he noticed that as the recruits' names were called out, they were being separated into three groups. When his name was finally called, he was told to report to the group on the left. He had no idea they would be divided into groups by plan. In descending order, those with the highest written scores on the entrance exam were assigned to the Transit Authority Police Department (TAPD), followed by the Housing Authority Police Department, and lastly, the NYPD itself. Vinny received a near-perfect score on the entrance exam and now found himself standing among over five hundred candidates assigned to the TAPD. Compared to the NYPD, he thought it was second-class. He couldn't believe it. What fucking bad luck! Since his father's promotion to sergeant, his patrolman's shield had been set aside for him at One

Police Plaza. Now he'd never be able to wear it proudly. The same went for his father's sergeant's shield. His father had told him there was a possibility this would happen.

Still! Damn the system. It wasn't fair.

He'd taken the entrance exam to become an NYPD police officer, not a transit cop. But his fate was sealed. If he turned down the assignment, he'd have to start the entire process again, from the beginning. Even then, there was no guarantee he'd get what he wanted. Initially, he thought it was a difficult decision to take, but upon reflection, he realized he had no choice. With a list of over fifty thousand applicants, he might have to wait another three or four years before he could stand again where he was that day. Reluctantly, and with reservations, he joined the ranks of the TAPD. By the disappointed looks on the faces of most of the recruits, he saw he was far from alone. Not many wanted that lousy job, stuck in the subway. It smelled like the bowels of a rotting corpse. They knew what awaited them: constantly dealing with the homeless and giving out summonses for turnstile-jumping or for smoking. No, there was no glamour there.

He looked around the packed auditorium and wondered how many of them had fathers, mothers, sisters, brothers, or some relatives who were on the NYPD. How many of them had come with the hopes of keeping a family tradition alive, only to leave in disappointment?

After getting over his initial disappointment, he decided that he would do a lateral transfer to the NYPD as soon as possible. He knew all the recruits attended the same academy and were treated equally there. He reasoned it would be wise to study hard and achieve good grades so the NYPD would have no reason to deny his transfer request afterward. And if they refused, he had other options. Graduating with good grades might also secure an appointment to a police department other than the NYPD. He could become a cop almost anywhere in the United States. But that was in the future. For now, he was determined to stay in New York, follow in his father's footsteps, and become a member of the largest police department in the world.

As Vinny walked down Lexington Avenue toward Twentieth Street to begin his first day at the police academy, he knew he'd made the correct decision. It was a long walk. It was cold, but he was sky-high. He felt the urge to stop people hurrying along the pavement and tell them, but he resisted it. They'd think he was just another of the many kooks they encountered daily. Thankfully, that feeling lasted but a short time. He had the urge to run, but the cold soon brought his adrenaline back down to normal levels.

The first day's excitement wore off quickly as training began. Enthusiasm gave way to perseverance. Putting on his uniform and badge was only the easy part of it.

There was a little paperwork, then more paperwork, and then a lot of paperwork. Day by day, it mounted. By the time Vinny reached home, he was exhausted. Debbie would ask what he'd done that day. At first, it was easy to relate the day's events, but as time passed, the question should have been rephrased to, "What didn't you do today?"

There were numerous dropouts from disenchantment, from physical or academic failure, or from the random drug tests to which everyone was subjected.

Vinny almost became a dropout statistic himself, but not for any shortcomings. Three months into the academy, he was doing well in all his subjects, but a family tragedy struck the Davis family once again. Vinny returned home after an exhausting day and was greeted by Debbie, who was home early from work and waiting at the door. She had a look of anguish on her face as she said in a frightened and barely audible voice, "Your mother called me at work and told me your brother Michael had an accident at work. He's in Jacobi Hospital!" She cried.

"What happened?" Vinny asked impatiently.

"Your mother said all she knew was that it happened at work."

Vinny and Debbie quickly got in his car and raced to the nearby hospital. Vinny was in a panic. *Please, God, not my brother too. Hasn't this family been through enough?*

Mike was his "Irish twin." He was born nine months and three weeks after Vinny. Raymond, their youngest brother, was born almost a year to the day after Mike. Vinny didn't know of any three brothers who were closer. Growing up, they were known as the Three Musketeers. Where there was one Davis boy, the other two were sure to be close by. After their mother died, that bond tightened. Vinny didn't know what he would do if he would lose a brother the way he lost his mother. Vinny remembered how happy Mike was for him on the day he got sworn into the academy. Mike, in anticipation of his appointment to the academy in July, after Vinny's graduation, asked him to save all his notebooks and academy uniform. Even before entering the academy, he was scheming to ease his way through. By having Vinny's notes, he thought he'd have a leg up on the other recruits. If there was a shortcut, Mike would take it.

As he and Debbie sped toward the hospital, he remembered when he and Mike got their first tattoos at Big Joe's in Mount Vernon. Vinny got a devil with "Vinny" written under it. Mike chose the same devil, lying on a cloud with his feet up, but under his devil was "Born Lazy," in bold letters. *Lazy* was, in fact, an understatement.

Growing up, he'd ask Mike to help him with the household chores. If he didn't see the importance in what Vinny asked him to do, he wouldn't do it, or he would say, "I'll do it later." *Later* never came, and Vinny ended up doing it for him. Mike's childhood dream was the same as Vinny's: to become a cop. He just didn't want to work at it. Vinny recalled the Saturday morning they were to take the written exam at Roosevelt High School, on Fordham Road, in the Bronx. Mike didn't want to get out of bed. The night before, Vinny made sure his two number 2 pencils were sharpened. He placed them, along with his admission card and keys, on his nightstand next to his bed so he'd have everything he needed. That morning, he was well rested, had showered, and had eaten breakfast while Mike was still in bed. They arrived with no time to spare before the bell rang to signal the start of the exam. The proctor asked to see his brother's admission card, which, of course, he didn't have. Fortunately for Mike, Vinny had the foresight to bring it and the required pencils for him.

His reverie was interrupted when they arrived at the hospital and quickly made their way to the emergency room, where they were met by Vinny's parents and an attending physician. Vinny rushed toward his father, who quickly exclaimed, "He's alive, and he's going to be all right!"

Vinny sighed with relief. *Thank God.* "What happened?"

His father began in the same manner a police officer would describe an arrest to a superior.

"While at a construction site he was working at, your brother and his work crew were completing the assembly of an 1,800-pound prefabricated wall when a machine used to hold the wall in place malfunctioned, making it impossible to complete the job without it. Your brother, along with six of his fellow workers, were instructed by the foreman to use a two-by-six as leverage and hoist the 1,800-pound wall into place. While they were attempting to do this, the weight of the wall became too much for the two-by-six, causing it to break. As the prefabricated wall began to collapse, your brother managed to push two of his coworkers out of danger before the wall fell on top of him, pinning him underneath."

"My God! How is he?"

Vinny's father, now visibly shaken, was unable to continue.

The doctor finished saying what his father couldn't. "The weight of the wall broke his back."

Those words left him speechless and unable to move.

The doctor concluded, "He's in surgery now, and they are placing two steel rods in his back and fusing the vertebrae. It's still too soon to tell about any permanent paralysis."

Vinny spent the night by his brother's bedside and never once worried about the consequences of being absent from the academy. His brother was far more important. His father told him he'd arranged an emergency day off for him. "But you must return to the academy at 0730 hours tomorrow, and that's an order. There's nothing you can do here, and your brother would want you to fulfill your dream," he said in a voice of authority.

Vinny looked at him and knew he was right. It suddenly struck him that Mike could never fulfill his dream of becoming a cop, too; therefore, he must.

When the six months of academy training finally came to an end, the transformation of Vinny Davis, civilian, to Vinny Davis, policeman, was apparent from the spit shine on his shoes and his immaculate uniform to the way he talked with and listened to people. He knew the procedures, the protocols, the chain of command, and the law. The training wheels were coming off. True grit was at hand.

The day all recruits strived for had arrived: Graduation Day!

Vinny arrived at Madison Square Garden at 0800 hours. He wasn't sure if he slept well the night before or just imagined he did. He was more awake than he ever had been in his entire life.

For an hour, the recruits went through the rehearsal, then they sat patiently and looked about as hundreds of families, and friends, began entering the garden. To this day, he still gets chills down his spine when he recalls the barked order, "A-TEN-HUT," when a sea of blue 2,500 rookie police officers snapped to attention and 2,500 white gloves saluted in unison as the opening of the graduation ceremony began. Then the introductory announcement: "The class of January 21, 1985." It caused such applause from jam-packed Madison Square Garden that it could be heard across the Hudson River in New Jersey. Vinny had never seen or felt anything like it.

After a congratulatory speech by His Honor, Mayor Ed Koch, saying how proud he was of this graduating class came another short speech from Police Commissioner Ben Ward about what was expected from the proud, new officers.

Then it was time for Vinny's moment in the sun. He mounted the stage and received his award for academic excellence from the mayor. Of his 2,500 classmates, there were but a handful that received the same honor. This was his first step, of many, to rehabilitate himself in his father's eyes. He'd just proved he was worthy to wear this badge of honor. The other twenty-nine members of Vinny's company did not earn the privilege of going onstage to receive an award. When Vinny received his, he couldn't remember if he walked or floated down from the stage.

Back on the floor, he said farewell to the people who had become his friends during the past six months. He didn't know if he'd ever see them again. In an attempt to locate his family, Vinny worked his way through the crowd.

People patted him on the back, shook his hand, and congratulated him. Other recruits introduced him to their families and thanked him for helping them with all the ordeals they went through during their training. Vinny wouldn't let anyone flunk out academically. After all, teamwork was stressed in the academy.

After the ceremony was over and the speculators departed, Vinny's company stood in formation one last time. It was time for the company sergeants to hand out their diplomas. Vinny received the same way the others did, but he didn't care. He already had his moment of honor when he was on stage.

As the event came to a close, another piece of Vinny's destiny was complete. He had a lovely wife, and now he was a cop.

Vinny finally reached his family at their prearranged meeting place in front of Madison Square Garden. His mother, father, grandparents, wife, Maria, and Raymond were there. And hiding behind his loving family was Mike, sporting a body cast, from the bottom of his armpits to his waist. He needed a cane to balance himself. Face-to-face, the brothers exuded brotherly love. Missing was any trace of envy, jealousy, or distress at the cruel fate that Mike could never become a police officer and that he faced the prospect of wearing the body cast for the better part of a year. And would he eventually defy the odds and walk and lead a fruitful life? With kisses, hugs, and congratulations out of the way, it was time to celebrate.

After a quick car ride up the west side, leading to Yonkers, the family arrived at Luigi's Restaurant on Central Avenue. As Vinny entered, all his friends and family were there to help him celebrate. Drinks and food flowed in abundance.

With the celebration in full swing, Vinny's father took him aside, away from the crowd.

"I am very proud of you," he said enthusiastically, but as he continued, his voice turned stern. "I know you have packed in enough information to last a lifetime, but like very good wine, there is a downside too. Times have changed since I first went on the force. Nowadays, you have more than just the Civilian Complaint Review Board keeping an eye on you. There are plenty of civilian agitators who want to make names for themselves just waiting for an opportunity to pounce on you. The police department is fair game, because it has a bad name and is an easy target. Everyone is afraid to back you up, even if you are right. Even after you're found innocent of any charges brought against you, you still have to worry about the federal government finding a loophole and charging you with violating someone's civil rights."

Sipping his cocktail, he continued, "The Transit Police have more contact with people than you would if in a patrol car or on foot patrol. Like I said, there's a downside, too. There will always be something happening in the subway, and Transit cops patrol alone. They have no backup and a radio system that doesn't work for shit. Transit cops are also on a different radio frequency than NYPD and Housing Police. Subway crime has been on the rise for years, and there's been no stopping it. Not only do you have to worry about robberies and chain snatches, but you have to worry about making an arrest by yourself as well. You must always consider the consequences of your actions. Don't be put into a position where you might be thrown onto the tracks and get hit by a train, or get fried by the six hundred volts on the third rail. If you see a suspect, wait for backup, and while you are waiting, remember everything you can about his description. If he gets away, you can catch him another day. What I am trying to say is, there are more crazies in the subway than on the streets and housing projects combined. Don't be a hero!"

They were interrupted by people calling them, so he thanked his father for the advice.

He embraced his father and said confidently, "I'll be careful, Dad, I promise."

When Vinny found out he was being assigned to the Transit Police, he thought of D-D, distraction equals death.

Speaking of distractions, Debbie walked over and began pulling gently on his arm, to lead him back toward the party.

"You two guys will have the next twenty years to talk shop," she said excitedly. "Now it's time to celebrate!"

Vinny's father tapped him on the shoulder and smiled, acknowledging that his bride was right.

When Vinny drove home from the party, he noticed a difference in his attitude. He now had a keen sense of awareness of his surroundings. He was no longer just looking out the window as he drove; he was observing. Somebody at the party mentioned to him that he'd changed. He now understood.

Vinny arose the next morning at 05:00 and made his way to Brooklyn, where the NYTP Academy was located, for what was termed intense training. But that day was different: he was a cop, wearing a full uniform, badge, and gun. It took an hour by train to get to Brooklyn's Jay Street station, and another ten minutes by foot to reach Gold Street, his destination. What made him feel good the first time he walked to the Transit Police Academy was the fact that when he got off the train and walked to the exit, he was joined by other police officer "probies." With each street he passed, others joined him. By the time he turned off Jay Street to Myrtle Avenue, it resembled the opening number of *West Side Story*. But instead of Jets, they were cops.

After his six months of training at the NYPD Academy, Vinny thought he'd seen the worst that could be thrown at him. He was wrong.

The first instructor to address the class of five hundred told them, in no uncertain terms, to forget what they had learned in the NYPD Academy.

"Starting today, you will learn how to survive on patrol alone. You are Transit cops. You will not have the luxury of a car, a partner, or even a radio that works. In three weeks, you will be riding subway trains from 8:00 p.m. to 6:00 a.m. six days a week. You will be alone at night, without backup, and we will teach you how to survive, so you can return safely home to your family at the end of your tour. You will listen to each instructor more attentively than you would a loved one or clergy. Officers have died in the line of duty, and we have learned from their mistakes. Our job is to teach you to stay alive. All of you will be in the gym for three hours a day. You will become experts in speed-cuffing techniques. Both male and female officers will participate in full-contact role-playing. There are no exceptions. A lot of you will be injured and grow to hate my fellow instructors and me. It is better that you hate us and are injured in the safety of this building than to become a statistic in the subway. I am not here to be liked. I am here to save your life and teach you to save one another's lives. Are there any questions?"

One could hear a pin drop.

CHAPTER 4

Hair combed and clean-shaven, Vinny Davis wore blue jeans and sweatshirt to help conceal his gun. There was excitement coursing through his veins that couldn't be explained to the average person. Unless, of course, that average person had waited their entire life to go on patrol as a cop in the South Bronx.

He'd received his orders assigning him to District 11, located at Yankee Stadium, 161st and River Avenue, the busiest Transit Police district in the Bronx. It encompassed the Fortieth, Forty-Fourth, Forty-Sixth, and Fifty-Second Precincts. The four NYPD precincts he would be patrolling by train were called A-Houses, meaning they were rated by the high command of the NYPD as being the highest crime area in the borough. It was where the action was, and that was exactly where he wanted to be.

"So today's your big day," Debbie said, wrapping her arms around him as he looked in the bathroom mirror.

He turned around and took her in his arms, looking at her beautiful, tanned face. "I can't wait!" he said excitedly, kissing her on the lips.

"Do you like this bikini?" she asked, pushing him away to arm's length, batting her eyes at him.

As he looked at her, all thoughts of work abruptly ended. Standing before him in a bikini, she looked stunning. To his mind, her body was perfect—rock-solid thighs on account of daily aerobic workouts, flat and firm stomach, and just-right breasts.

"You don't happen to have your handcuffs handy, do you, Officer?" she teased as she untied the top to her bikini, revealing her untanned breasts. She pressed up against him. "Well, do you?"

"No, I'm afraid I don't," he said, playing at being unimpressed.

"Why not?" she asked, narrowing her eyes as she pulled the bottom of her bikini down and kicked it across the floor.

"I don't need them for you. Now, come here," he said as he reached for her, unable to control his excitement a moment longer.

"No!" She ran defiantly from the bathroom, with Vinny behind her. When he tackled her onto the bed, she curled up beside him.

"I love you," he said, kissing her lips passionately.

"I love you too," she said, tearing at his jeans. "Now, make love to me like I'm a bad girl."

"You have the right to remain silent, if you can," he said as he ran his tongue over her stomach.

"I confess, Officer!" she sighed and spread her legs for him.

It was a beautiful July day as he exited their two-family house on Strang Avenue, in the Wakefield section of the Bronx. The sky glowed like a display of fireworks, red, gold, and orange, as the sun sparkled through the puffy white clouds. He'd decided to take advantage of the weather and walk to the Dyre Avenue subway station and take the train to work. He wasn't sure about the police parking situation by the stadium and couldn't chance arriving late to work for his first day on patrol. Besides, if he was going to be a Transit cop, he'd better get used to riding the iron horse, something he hadn't done since he was a kid, when he and his two brothers would ride the train from Woodlawn Road in the Bronx to Bay Ridge Avenue in Brooklyn to visit their grandparents. It was an extremely dangerous thing for three kids under the age of fourteen to do, but danger was something the Davis boys gave little thought to. They used to play war in a section of Owl's Head Park called Dead Man's Hill and had seen their first dead body, a young kid with a knife sticking out of his chest, by the time Vinny was eight. After two cargo ships collided under the Verrazzano Bridge, the three of them had found the head of one of the crew members washed up on the rocks under the pier on Sixty-Ninth Street. Even at that age, none of the boys feared any danger.

"Excuse me," Vinny said politely, displaying his shield to the railroad clerk busy counting tokens.

She looked up, unimpressed. "Well, go ahead through the gate," she said in a tense voice. "Nobody else pays their fare at this station."

Vinny produced a ready smile. "Could you tell me how to get to District 11?" he asked evenly.

The railroad clerk stared at him in disbelief. "You a Transit cop?" she asked, faintly amused.

He shrugged. "First day."

"First thing you better do is get yourself a subway map," she said, glaring at him sternly. "Take the 5 Train upstairs to 149th Street and change there for the uptown 4 Train, one stop to 161st Street," she said, sounding weary and impatient.

"Thank you," he said with a smile more like a grimace.

She smiled, as if she'd done him a favor, as he turned to walk through the exit gate. "Oooh, child, you best be careful in these subways. A good-looking white boy like you be eaten alive by the punks that ride these trains!" she shrieked over the crackled PA system.

He turned and smiled at her in a conciliatory fashion, then walked up the stairs to the platform. As the train pulled out of the station, he walked from one car to the next, looking for a suitable place to sit down. The subway cars were just as he'd remembered them. Graffiti covered the walls and windows that had not already been kicked out or smashed. Some cars had homeless people, reeking of body odor, booze, and stale urine, sprawled out on the seats, while other cars were filled with young partygoers playing their boom boxes at full blast, smoking weed and cigarettes, and drinking beer.

As he walked to the conductor's cab, the safest place to sit, because he was equipped with a radio to call for help if needed, some people took notice of his uniforms draped over his shoulder and smiled. Others looked at him like he was their prey, almost daring him to question whatever it was they were doing.

"This is going to be a long twenty years," he mumbled to himself as he sat across from a homeless woman with two shopping carts filled with empty cans. The train barreled along the elevated subway tracks. He stared out the window and watched as the neighborhood deteriorated the farther south he traveled into the Bronx. Before the train submerged into the bowels of the underground system at 149th Street, there was nothing left to look at but burnt-out tenements and newly erected city housing projects that looked as if they had already been through a war.

"One Hundred Forty-Ninth Street," the conductor's voice crackled over the train's intercom.

Exiting the train, he was immediately overcome by the intense heat and the foul smell of human feces that invaded the entire station. He quickly looked left, and then right, for a sign indicating a transfer point for the uptown Number 4 Train. Seeing none, he immediately walked toward the middle of the platform in hopes of finding the token booth. Vinny walked right by a couple smoking crack on a bench like it was legal.

This place was like a scene from a movie about hell. He walked through the exit gate toward the token booth.

"Where do I get the Number 4 Train?" he asked impatiently, skipping the formalities after his experience with the clerk at Dyre Avenue.

"You're on the wrong station, sweetheart," the young black clerk said with a bright smile. "You got to go one more stop to 149th and Grand Concourse for the 4 Train."

Vinny laughed crookedly. "That figures," he said, waving at her.

Suddenly, Vinny heard a scream behind him. He wheeled around. "Help! Police!" the voice shrieked again.

The clerk in the booth, clueless, was talking on the phone.

He banged on the window. "Get help. Take my uniforms," he said. The puzzled clerk stared at him. "Now!" he said. His voice reverberated throughout the station.

She simultaneously opened the booth door and hung up the phone.

"Take these," he said, handing her his new $550 uniforms, "and call for help." Not knowing exactly what the call for help was for, he drew his weapon, displayed his shield on his chest, and started toward the stairs to the street. He heard a thud and saw a man hit the floor at the bottom of the stairs. Looking up the stairs, he saw two youths fleeing, one of them carrying a briefcase. He took the steps two at a time, not wanting to lose sight of the suspects, who were standing nonchalantly on the corner of 149th Street and Third Avenue. Looking back quickly, he observed the victim at the bottom of the stairs was conscious, and heard voices asking him if he was all right.

Abruptly, one of the teens turned around and noticed Vinny standing with a gun in his hand. He felt his heart jump, and the foot pursuit began. Within half a block, the two teens ducked into an alley and disappeared. For several seconds, he heard nothing. Then there was a sound that came from a huge green garbage dumpster. He turned, aiming his gun in the direction of the sound. A moment later, there were people talking excitedly in Spanish from their apartment windows, laughing at some joke he couldn't understand. Then, for a few moments, it turned quiet, and he wondered if the thieves were still there.

They had to be. Where else could they have gone?

It occurred to him that he was alone in an alley without backup.

Remember your training: cover and concealment.

He moved slowly, moving behind a parked car.

How long do I lie here before I make some effort to call them out?

His mind desperately searching through seven months of stored information and training.

Suddenly, he heard footsteps rapidly approaching him from behind, the jingling of keys and the clanking of handcuffs a distinctive sound.

"Police, don't move!" a voice demanded.

Vinny's heart suddenly dropped from his chest into his stomach.

Remember your training. Don't turn toward them with a gun in your hands. Identify yourself, but don't move.

"I'm on the job!" Vinny exclaimed. "There are two suspects hiding in the dumpster!"

"You two, in the dumpster, stand up with your hands up!" the voice behind Vinny yelled.

Almost immediately, the dumpster top flew off and two black youths stood there with their hands pointed straight up to heaven.

"Don't shoot us, please!" they yelled in harmony.

Two plainclothes officers approached the suspects briskly, with their weapons pointed at their faces. Within seconds of approaching them, one officer had both suspects handcuffed and removed them from the dumpster to the roaring laughter and accolades in Spanish of the onlookers ceremoniously perched on their windows.

"Nice robbery collar, kid," the young plainclothes officer said with a victorious look in his eyes.

"Thanks," Vinny said, smiling sheepishly.

"Where exactly did it happen?" the officer asked Vinny curiously.

"The 149th Street station," Vinny replied, fidgeting uncomfortably, still amazed at what had happened.

The cop indulged him. "The reason I'm asking is that if it happened in the subway at 149th Street, we have to process the arrest at District 12, but if it happened in the street, you can go to either District 11 or the Forty-Second Precinct."

"The subway." He sounded tentative.

"Okay, fine. We'll help you bring these mutts to District 12," the cop said, trying to help and appear empathetic.

For the first two hours, it seemed as though nobody in the booking area at District 12 gave a damn about a totally lost and confused rookie cop.

"Could I get some help here as a matter of professional courtesy?" Vinny asked gamely of an old-time lieutenant standing behind the desk, wearing a golfer's hat with a white pom-pom on it.

"Wait a minute." He didn't look up from the golf ball he was about to putt into a plastic cup about ten feet away. He tapped the ball. It rolled in with a pop. Finally, the lieutenant looked up, puzzled. "Do I know you?"

"No, sir." He half-smiled.

"Who are you and why are you here?" the stone-faced lieutenant asked.

Vinny looked bemused. "I, ah, arrested two for robbery on my way to work," Vinny stammered.

The lieutenant shook his head vigorously without looking up as he placed another ball on the floor. *Pop.* Another ball in the cup. "Your name's not Davis, is it?" he asked suspiciously, making eye contact with Vinny.

"Yes, sir, it is," he said nervously.

"Do you know that District 11 has you marked AWOL for not showing up at roll call?" the lieutenant asked in a deep, froggy voice.

Vinny's eyes widened in horror. In all the excitement, he forgot to call his command. He'd just assumed they would have been notified where he was. "Oh my God! You get fired for being AWOL on probation!" Vinny shrieked.

The lieutenant smiled coldly. "Relax, kid, I took care of it. But you really fucked things up around here tonight. We wanted to keep the cell empty because we've got a retirement celebration going on. It's the midnight lieutenant's last night, and we told our cops not to make a collar unless someone got killed."

Vinny gave one of his condescending smiles. *Is this guy kidding, or is this nothing more than ironic banter? Better play it safe.*

"I'm sorry, boss, I had no idea." Vinny grinned.

The lieutenant returned a self-satisfied smile.

"No problem, kid. Go use the phone to call your wife and tell her you'll see her tomorrow night, then call those kids' parents and tell them their darling sons are spending the night in Spofford and will be arraigned in family court in the morning. When you're done doing that, go in the back and help yourself to some food and a beer, but don't get fucked up, because the duty captain will be by later, and he hates to see anyone drunker than him."

Vinny stared at him in shocked disbelief.

"My name's Mack," the lieutenant said, holding out his hand, which Vinny shook. "Welcome to the Transit Police."

Vinny walked to the booking area, then, with some trepidation, dialed home. "Hi, baby, it's me," Vinny said cheerfully.

"How's my hero husband? You do anything heroic your first day on patrol?" she asked drowsily.

"Nah, I just arrested two guys for robbery on the way to work," he said casually.

"You're kidding!"

"Dead serious, baby. That's why I'm calling. It looks like I'll be spending the night, then heading to court first thing in the morning."

"You're not kidding! Are you all right? You didn't get hurt, did you?"

"No, baby, I'm fine. I just didn't want you to worry about me not making it home."

"Well, I'm glad you called me. You can tell me all about it when I see you. I love you, Vinny."

He smiled to himself. "I love you too, Debbie. Now, get some sleep," he said lovingly.

"Good night."

Vinny then picked up the phone to dial Tweedledee's and Tweedledum's parents. After a brief conversation, in which both their mothers had wished their kids were dead, he proceeded to the locker room to have something to eat and to unwind.

By 6:00 a.m., the youths had been transported to Spofford Juvenile Correctional Facility. The arrest reports had been completed with the help of a slightly intoxicated veteran officer from the midnight tour, and Vinny finally arrived at District 11. A black lieutenant, whose shiny, bald head reminded him of an eight ball, was seated at the front desk and greeted him.

"Are you the asshole who made the off-duty robbery arrest?" he asked austerely.

Asshole? What the fuck's this? I arrest two assholes, and he's calling me one? Cocksucker.

Vinny lowered his eyes and stared at the floor.

"Fill out this special report explaining the arrest!" he barked, throwing the form at Vinny.

"Yes, sir," he said dutifully, too exhausted to explain. His uniform draped over his shoulder, he turned to walk away.

"Davis!" the lieutenant growled.

Prick.

Vinny turned to meet his glare.

"When you're done with that report, put one of those uniforms on and have your pathetic ass at family court by 0900 hours."

"Yes, sir," he said in a deadpan voice. He walked away counting his blessings that he hadn't taken Lieutenant Mack up on his gracious offer to indulge in a beer while on duty.

At 8:45 a.m., Vinny stood at a window on the seventh floor of the Bronx District Attorney's Office. Still wound up with the excitement of making a robbery arrest before even making it to work for his first day of patrol, he watched the morning sun shine over the South Bronx. Behind him, through closed doors to an outer office, he could hear the secretaries and assistants fielding unrelenting phone calls.

"TC!" he heard a female's voice call out from behind him.

He turned away from the window; he hadn't heard anyone called by those initials in years. He couldn't believe his eyes. There, standing in front of him, resplendent in formal dress, was his oldest friend, Tommy Cascione, the infamous TC, formerly of the Central Avenue Cruisers.

They both stood silently, staring at each other in surprise and disbelief. Finally, they both heartily embraced. Tommy leaned back and studied Vinny. As he did, he shook his head incredulously. "What the hell are you doing in that uniform?" Tommy asked sarcastically.

Vinny looked at him as if he were crazy. "Much easier to get on the subway this way," he said of his uniform, with a broad smile. "What are you doing here? Don't tell me you got arrested?" Vinny asked jokingly.

Tommy stared a moment longer. "Very funny, Vinny," he said quietly. With that, he opened his hand in a gesture to follow him into an office. "I'm now an assistant district attorney," Tommy said as they entered a rather-small office. He sat behind his desk and smiled.

Pulling up a chair, Vinny sat next to him. "You're an ADA," he said with a smirk on his face, staring at his friend.

"And you're a cop," Tommy retaliated with the same tone of disbelief.

"What's this world coming to?" they both asked simultaneously, unable to control their laughter.

"So how are you, Tommy? How's life treating you?"

For the next forty-five minutes or so, they carried on about old times, recalling their days growing up, best friends from the same neighborhood, the girls they'd dated, and then they updated each other on the women they'd finally married. They loudly laughed at their vivid memories of childhood pranks and how Tommy and his father forbade Vinny from ever going near Corinne, Tommy's sister, whom he'd loved since he was a boy. Tommy's smile was broad, and he laughed recalling the day he had physically thrown Vinny off his family's front porch when he caught him merely talking to his sister.

"How is Corinne'?" Vinny asked, the tears still running down his face from laughing.

"You're too late," he said flatly. "She's married."

"I never stood a chance, anyway," Vinny said in a defeated voice.

"You're right!" Tommy said, still laughing.

"My pal!" Vinny said as he stood. "On that note, I must find a bathroom and attempt to find the DA assigned to my case before I get my rookie ass in trouble." Gathering his hat and nightstick, he started toward the door. "I'll stop by on my way out to see you before I leave."

"If I'm not here, stop by anytime. We'll get together for drinks one night after work," Tommy said by way of a goodbye.

"Real soon." He made his exit.

The *black cloud* is a term commonly used by NYPD cops for those who always seem to find themselves in the wrong place at the wrong time. But good cops don't believe in coincidence. They just sometimes find themselves victims of spectacular bad luck, and when you're an active cop, you're bound to get hurt.

In September, Vinny had found himself on a monthlong paid vacation with torn ligaments in his right knee. He was injured while assisting another cop who'd been mistaken for a punching bag by a suspect whacked out of his mind on angel dust.

The morning after being treated at the hospital, and still in a significant amount of pain, he was ordered to report to Clinic 4 at Transit Authority Headquarters at 370 Jay Street in Brooklyn, to be examined by a department doctor.

Having a father assigned to the NYPD Health Services Division, he was completely aware of the need for the NYPD to document any injuries their officers sustained in the line of duty. As his dad had explained to him on numerous occasions, there were an awful lot of cops who abused the unlimited, paid sick day policy by faking injuries to avoid work. Cops called it dial-a-day. Wake up in the morning, decide not to go to work, and dial in sick. It was that simple. He could see the logic behind the department's natural suspicions, but after he had spent the night in the hospital, being diagnosed by a doctor, in his circumstance, it seemed like stupid overkill.

Visibly in pain, he sat on a chair in the hallway with Transit Authority motormen, conductors, bus drivers, and other cops. They were all waiting to be seen by doctors who had been described as veterinarians. Unlike the NYPD, who had three Health Services locations throughout the city manned by highly trained police surgeons to attend to the medical needs of its members, the Transit Authority had only one location in downtown Brooklyn, manned by workmen's compensation doctors, who attended to the medical needs of all Transit Authority employees. The TA cops were entitled to no preferential treatment for getting their heads caved in with a bottle while protecting subway passengers. He waited in pain, like a schmuck, for nearly six hours, only to have a five-minute examination that consisted of "Does that hurt?"

Vinny was told to report back in one month for further examination and placed on "no work" status. After handing over his paperwork to the sergeant, who sat in a small cramped office, as though socially ostracized from the rest of the TA, he was assigned a green dot, which meant he was permitted to leave his house without permission from the "sick desk" supervisor but had to be home for official department notifications every night, between the hours of 7:00 and 8:00 p.m. He was also not permitted to leave the borough in which he resided without obtaining permission prior to doing so. That rule was instituted after one ingenious cop decided to fly to Hawaii for vacation while he was "out, injured." He had his home phone calls forwarded to the hotel he was staying at. The plan worked perfectly until he received a department court notification to appear to testify at nine o'clock the next morning before a Manhattan grand jury.

Vinny hadn't seen Benny, Donny, and Joe, his three closest friends from the police academy, since graduation. So when Benny

DeStafano called him on a Saturday night and said the boys were getting together for "choir practice," cop slang for a night of drinking and exchanging war stories, he was good to go. Benny and Joe were assigned to the Forty-Sixth Precinct in the Bronx, Donny was assigned to the Thirty-Fourth Precinct in Harlem, and Vinny was the unfortunate Transit cop.

It was nearly 10:00 p.m. by the time Benny, Joe, and Donny showed up at Vinny's house. Debbie had since returned from a girl-friend's bridal shower. After greeting the three guys she'd grown quite fond of over the last nine months, she tossed Vinny the keys to the new Ford Thunderbird he'd bought her and told them all to have a good time.

All agreed they wanted to spend their night out in Lower Manhattan, barhopping in SoHo and Greenwich Village. It turned into a night filled with drinking, jokes, and uncontrollable laughter at the huge numbers and variety of weirdoes they saw in the bars and on the streets. It was nothing personal—they kept their jokes, about the lifestyles, the residents, or the eccentric way they expressed their individualism, among themselves. This was New York City, the greatest city in the world, where people dress and express themselves in any way they see fit. People with shaved heads dressed in Nazi uniforms; others with spiked purple-and-orange hair, wearing earrings through their lips and tongues; men holding hands; women kissing each other openly all added to the ambience and excitement of the city. Sitting in a bar in the village was like watching a huge television where the actors are just everyday people—reality TV at its best. But by 2:30 a.m., they'd decided the show was over. It was time to head home to the reality of their wives and families.

Vinny was driving slowly northbound on the West Side Drive, approaching Forty-Second Street.

"Let's go to that gyro place at Four-Two and Eighth," Donny said eagerly from the back seat.

"Yeah, I'm starving," Joe pleaded, sitting in the back next to Donny.

Vinny looked over at Benny seated next to him with a huge smile on his face. He and Donny had become extremely close during their time in the same company in the academy. Benny was not the type to pass on a meal.

"All right," Vinny agreed and turned eastbound on Forty-Second Street. "Wonderful," Vinny mumbled as they approached the traffic that was caused by the four lanes of traffic merging into one due to ongoing late-night construction.

"Ah, don't look so pissed," Benny said flippantly. "They can't close Forty-Second Street during the day to fix the road."

He's right. There's no sense getting mad.

Vinny smiled and relaxed.

"Hey, beautiful!" Joe yelled from the back seat at a couple of hookers dressed in some beat-up-looking lingerie.

"Those are fucking guys, you asshole," Donny said in a frazzled voice.

"You're fucking crazy. Look at the legs on her," Joe said defensively, twisting his neck to get a view at the hookers out the back window.

"Hey, guys, look at this!" Vinny said urgently, pointing to a Lincoln town car stopped directly in front of them, with a hooker's legs and ass hanging out of the driver's-side window. Her upper torso was in the driver's face.

"Does she have her tit in his mouth?" Joe asked in amazement while trying to wedge himself between Vinny and Benny for a better look.

"Here comes her partner in crime," Vinny said suspiciously as a second prostitute got into the passenger seat of the Lincoln.

"What are they going to do, blow him in traffic in the middle of Forty-Second Street?" Donny asked with fascination in his voice.

"No, they're going to steal his wallet and cash," Vinny said piteously. All three stared at Vinny in disbelief.

"How do you know that?" Donny asked.

A self-satisfied smile crossed Vinny's face. "The girl with her tits in the guy's face is also grabbing the driver's prick. While he's preoccupied with what's going on, the second girl's hands are busy going through his pockets, looking for cash and his wallet," Vinny said confidently.

"Now, how do you know that, Mr. Transit Cop?" Donny asked smugly, shaking his head in disbelief.

"Watch this," Vinny said indignantly as he lowered his window. "Hey, buddy!" Vinny screamed. "You might want to see if you still have your wallet!"

Almost immediately, the driver slugged the hooker on his side in the face and pushed her back from the window with such force that she fell to the ground. He then dragged the hooker inside the car, out of the driver's-side door, by her hair.

Vinny smiled smugly at his friends.

"I told you so," he said, trying to control his laughter.

"Hey, she's got a knife!" Donny said urgently, pointing to the hooker getting off the ground, ready to attack the owner of the Lincoln, who was still fighting with the second hooker, trying to retrieve his wallet.

"Police!" Vinny shrieked, exiting the car with his gun drawn. "Drop the knife!"

The hooker with the knife was astonished. She froze in the position of the Statue of Liberty, with a knife in her hand instead of a torch.

"Drop it, I said!" Vinny demanded.

As the knife dropped to the ground, the owner of the Lincoln grabbed his wallet from the ground, where the other hooker had dropped it before running down Forty-Second Street like she was on fire.

Benny was already out of the car. He took a position crouched at the front of Vinny's car, with his gun aimed at the hooker. "I got her, Vinny. Go get her," he said anxiously.

Vinny approached the prostitute with his gun drawn. Using his left hand, he grabbed her by the hair and directed her onto the hood of his car. With his gun pointed at the base of her skull, he ordered her not to move as he did a quick patdown to ensure she didn't have another weapon.

Suddenly, there was a screeching of tires as the Lincoln kicked up dirt and debris from the road, as the driver made a U-turn barreling into the orange-sand-filled construction dividers.

"Wait, you can't leave!" Benny screamed to the driver as they watched the taillights fade in the distance.

"Now, what the fuck do we do?" Joe asked. He was agitated. "We have no complainant."

The hooker, still spread-eagled on the hood of the car, began to laugh nastily.

"Just let me go!" she begged. "I ain't gonna give ya no trouble."

Vinny looked at Benny and then at a few construction workers who'd stopped what they were doing to enjoy the show.

"Shit. What do we do now?" Vinny asked, totally confused.

"We have no complainant." Joe shrugged indifferently, picking up the knife the hooker had dropped.

"I say we let her go," Donny said disgustedly, still seated in the back seat.

"What bullshit charge are you going to bring her in for? We're off-duty," Joe said harshly, looking at the knife in his hand.

"You're right. Fuck this!" Vinny said vehemently. "Take a hike, sister," he added, pulling the hooker off the hood of his car.

She turned to face Joe, her face creased with concern. "Can I have my knife back, please?"

For a moment, he looked at her quizzically.

"If you can find it, you can have it," he said, throwing it about thirty yards into an abandoned lot.

She smiled derisively. "That's okay. My pimp's got plenty, anyway," she said, waving as she walked away.

"That was wild," Benny said as he got back into the T-bird.

Vinny hung a U-turn the same way the driver of the Lincoln had. Vinny shook his head and smiled. "Yeah, it was wild, all right."

The sound of a siren and flashing red lights forced Vinny to immediately pull over. The cruiser pulled up behind him.

"The keys to the car out of the window!" a voice said over the police car's PA.

"We're on the job!" Vinny exclaimed, throwing the keys out the window while holding his shield in his hand.

Simultaneously, numerous officers, weapons drawn, surrounded his car. One officer grabbed the shield and ID card from his hand.

"He's a cop!" he yelled to the other officers, who immediately holstered their weapons.

"We got a call of four white males, armed with guns, who robbed and beat up a woman on Forty-Second Street. They took off in a black T-bird with your license plate number. Care to explain that?" the officer asked in a stern voice.

Vinny and his three friends began to laugh out loud at the outrageousness of the complaint, until Vinny looked up and saw the officer was wearing a lieutenant's shield.

"You boys have some explaining to do," he said with a dry smile. "Now, follow me back to the Midtown North Precinct."

CHAPTER 5

Vinny spent the next three months assigned to desk duty at the Communications Unit while Internal Affairs conducted a thorough investigation into the events with the hookers on Forty-Second Street. Meanwhile, rumors spread like wildfire throughout the Transit Police.

"Did you hear Davis was getting a blow job from a hooker in Hunt's Point and didn't want to pay, so he pulled his gun on her?"

"No, I heard it was a beautiful blond decoy sergeant working on Park Avenue and he'd tried to proposition her."

"Nah, I heard after he got his rocks off, he'd robbed her at gunpoint."

Fortunately, Internal Affairs located the hooker in less than a month and she told them the truth of that night's events. The construction workers who'd observed the incident also corroborated the story all four officers gave. However, that didn't curtail the jokes he was forced to face at the hands of his peers at District 11, or the loss of thirty days' pay he received as punishment for violating the department's sick procedures and for bringing adverse criticism to the Transit Police Department. It wasn't a lesson taught at the police academy. Vinny changed his ways. No longer would he be compassionate or rely too heavily on common sense when making a decision. It would be "by the book." If he had to take action, someone was going to jail, unless directed by a superior to do otherwise, and even then, he'd make sure he documented it.

Then it was springtime 1986, and romance was in the air as Vinny and Debbie approached their third wedding anniversary.

Family and friends had finally realized that they'd been mistaken, saying they were too young to get married. Now everyone remarked how they were surely a couple who belonged together. Even her parents, who wanted a purebred Italian in their family unit, realized that their had daughter married a strong-minded man with an admirable cause, who would do anything to make their daughter happy.

"Honey, I have to tell you something that's been bothering me," Debbie said cautiously while lying in Vinny's arms in their bedroom.

After they had been together in a relationship for almost six years, he knew by the tone in her voice that something was troubling her deeply. He lifted himself up onto one elbow so he could look at her face.

"What's the matter?" he asked gently.

"I wanted you to hear this from me before you heard it from anyone else," she said, warming up.

He looked at her quizzically.

"Sabol has stopped by to see me at my office a few times."

Vinny never took his eyes off her. "When?" he asked, trying to control his anger.

"June of last year, and about a year before that," she said, her face creased with concern.

"And you wait until now to tell me. Why?" he asked in disbelief.

"I told my mother about it, and she told me not to tell you about it. She said that you'd get upset."

He immediately became angry and feral.

"Why would I get upset? Did he threaten you in any way?" he asked, shaking his head in disgust.

"Well, ah, he said he would break us up and that he'd get even with you for stealing me away from him," she said with a sheepish smile.

Vinny was glaring at her sternly, yet puzzled. *Why is she telling me this now?*

Vinny had heard that Sabol had gotten arrested in December 1983 in Manhattan for beating and robbing a homosexual he'd picked up in the village. He'd also heard some information from his friend Ronny Howard, a Yonkers cop, that Sabol had attempted to kill a guy he held responsible for letting his friend die of an overdose at Rye Playland in April of 1984. Sabol's own brother had told the police that he'd blown out the front door to the guy's house with a shotgun blast. Ronny also said that, in June of 1984, Sabol had been arrested for beating up and pointing a shotgun at his mother's boyfriend, and in a separate incident, he punched his girlfriend in the throat before pushing her down a flight of stairs.

Vinny had deliberately kept this information from Debbie so as not to frighten her.

"Some federal agent called me and asked if he'd contacted me or threatened me in any way since his release," she said in a warm, calming voice.

Vinny nodded absently, unimpressed. "What'd you tell him?" he asked agitatedly.

"I told him what I just told you, and he said he might contact you. I told him you were a cop," she said hesitantly.

Vinny couldn't help but smile. "Did he leave a name and number?" he asked solicitously.

Her eyes were speculating. She hesitated.

"Well, did he?"

"No, he didn't, but he said Sabol is going to be sentenced in federal court in White Plains on April 10."

"The feds nailed his ass," he said, giving her one of his condescending smiles.

"Yeah, they got him," she said excitedly, "and he's going to be out of our lives for a long time."

A huge satisfied smile appeared on Vinny's face. "Come here," he said, grabbing her into his arms.

"You're not mad at me for not telling you about this sooner, are you?" she asked, nestled into his chest.

"I'm just happy that the feds got him and sent him away for a long time."

"Me too," she said in a voice like a whisper. "Me too."

Vinny felt a strange sense of freedom as he sat in the rear of the courtroom in the federal courthouse on Post Road in White Plains, ironically, less than half a block from the dentist office where Debbie worked. He was filled with excitement that not only would he actually see Sabol up close but also that, hopefully, it would be the last time he'd see him for a long time.

He sat back and reflected on the time Sabol abducted Debbie with a shotgun, threatening to kill her if she married Vinny. *"I'll throw acid on your face and make you so ugly no man will want you."*

"Excuse me," a voice said, snatching him from his reverie.

Vinny looked up to see a rather tall man in a Brooks Brothers suit smiling at him. Vinny returned the smile. "What can I do for you?" he asked politely.

"My name is James Stamp from the FBI. I was wondering if, and how, you are involved with this case."

"As a matter of fact, I'd love to tell you about that," Vinny said with a wry smile, producing his shield and ID card. "My name is Vinny Davis," he said, standing up and presenting his hand to Agent Stamp. "Maybe we can talk out in the hall," he added, firmly shaking hands with the agent.

"I've spoken to your wife, Debbie," Stamp said eagerly. "She seems like a nice girl."

Vinny smiled proudly. "She's the best."

"I can't picture her getting hooked up with an animal like Sabol," Stamp said earnestly.

"I'm sure she had no idea what kind of guy she was dating. She was just a kid then," Vinny said, trying to sound reasonable.

Stamp looked at Vinny with wistful indulgence. "So what brings you here?" he asked curiously.

"Pure curiosity," Vinny replied. "I want to get a good look at him, and I want to see the judge throw not only the book at him but also the entire fucking library!"

"I guess you've read that presentencing memo you have in your hands about what a fine citizen Sabol is," Stamp said sarcastically.

"Oh, yeah. I especially like the part where he beats up and robs elderly couples in Greenburgh or shoots a guy in the head and smiles about it. But the part I truly enjoy is that he is never prosecuted because he intimidates and threatens to kill the witnesses against him."

He shook his head in disgust, then looked up and met Agent Stamp's eyes, the eyes of a cop who had seen it all over the years. All the memories were still right there in his eyes.

"Are you one of the FBI agents this scumbag threatened to kill on the record in court?" Vinny asked gloomily.

Stamp met his stare. "Yes, I am."

"I guess you have no love lost for this guy," Vinny said in a tense voice.

"Not at all," Stamp said factually. "As a matter of fact, we almost didn't nail him on this case. He threatened to kill his ex-girlfriend, who testified in this trial. We had to sponsor her, and Sabol's brother, for the Witness Protection Program."

"Well, I can't speak for anyone else, but your perseverance in this case has made my wife and me extremely happy. Hopefully, after today, I'll sleep a lot better for a good many years."

Stamp smiled maliciously. "Well, I don't know about the judge throwing the whole library at him, but I know it will be at least a couple of rows."

Vinny smiled back with equal malicious satisfaction. "Let's go inside and see, shall we?" Vinny said as he opened the door to the courtroom.

The criminal Sabol entered the courtroom shackled and escorted by United States marshals. He wore a smug smile, as if he were there to receive an Oscar for Best Actor.

Instantaneously, Vinny had to control the urge to walk over to the defense table and smack that smug look right off his face.

An air of anticipation radiated throughout the courtroom, making it seemingly obvious that others in attendance shared in his feelings of anger and hostility toward this malevolent psychopath.

Judge Bryant smiled indulgently as he listened to Sabol's attorney, who sounded weary and impatient, describe what a rough life Sabol had had. But judging by the look on His Honor's face, he wasn't buying one word that was being spoken on Sabol's behalf. The criminal sat fidgeting uncomfortably in his seat.

When the defense attorney and prosecutor finished pontificating, it was the judge's turn to be heard.

"Mr. Sabol," he said, shaking his head vigorously from side to side without looking up from a report he was reading. "November 1, 1978: Armed robbery. After your arrest, you threatened to kill the two arresting officers," the judge said disgustedly, reciting what was written in the report. "January 25, 1979: While on bail on the armed robbery case, you were arrested by the Secret Service for possession of counterfeit currency. On June 27, 1979, while on bail on both those cases, you were arrested in Hempstead, Long Island, for burglary. You then jumped bail on all three cases and fled to Florida, where you attempted to avoid arrest by jumping into the Intracoastal Waterway."

A pause.

"According to this report," the judge said, trying to modulate his voice, "you were ultimately convicted of attempted armed robbery on November 1, 1978. Arrest, possession of counterfeit currency on January 25. Arrest, possession of stolen property on June 19, 1979. Arrest and was in state prison between September 19, 1979, and May 27, 1982. However, while you were incarcerated, you were arrested on April 2, 1980, for attempted murder in connection with an incident that occurred on August 8, 1979, in Baldwin, Long Island, and this court doesn't even have the particulars or a disposition of that case."

The judge looked up, puzzled, as Sabol smiled behind a hand covering his mouth. The judge then lowered his eyes, his face turning white with fury. "Mr. Sabol," he roared, "I have to agree with the sentencing judge on your state case, where he says, and I quote, 'As far as I am concerned, Sabol has an antisocial personality and is definitely a threat to the community.' I don't think you've shown any remorse of any kind. In the case before me, you not only threatened to kill two federal witnesses, one of which is your own brother, if they testified against you, but you also threatened to kill four FBI agents, in open court, in front of a United States federal magistrate, which is something that I can't believe anyone could have the utter audacity to do. Therefore, I find you to be a danger to society, with a long history of violent behavior, and in order to protect society from you, I am hereby sentencing you to twelve years in federal prison."

A hushed silence hung over the courtroom. Sabol continued to smile. He arrogantly put a huge unlit cigar in his mouth as he was escorted out of the courtroom by the US marshals.

Vinny sat in utter amazement as he watched his contemptuous display.

Agent Stamp approached Vinny with a victorious look in his eyes. "Well, it wasn't the entire library, but that animal will be off the streets for a long time."

Vinny never took his eyes off Stamp. "I knew he was bad, but I had no idea he was pure evil. I could swear I was looking into the eyes of the devil himself."

Stamp shook his head and smiled brightly. "Go home and tell your wife she can rest easy for a while."

Vinny grinned. "Thank you very much, Agent Stamp," he said. They firmly shook hands, and Vinny left for home to tell Debbie the great news.

Driving home, he had the opportunity to reflect on his career. After almost a year and a half on patrol, he'd concluded that he had no idea what he would be forced to face each day. The dangers of police work were drummed into his head since he was a boy. But after attending his first inspector's funeral, for a friend of his killed in the line of duty, he realized it might just as easily have been him. It could happen to any cop on any day, at any time. A cop who made it home in one piece at the end of each tour was lucky. And that was how they took it, one day at a time. He was already wondering if he'd make it through twenty years so he could get his pension, retire, and enjoy a long life with Debbie. He tried not to think of all the other cops still out there, the ones who wouldn't be so lucky. But this was the life he chose. It was what he'd wanted all his life, and he would make a difference. He was sure of it.

It was June 15, 1986, a little over two months since the beast had been put away for twelve years.

He was assigned to the Tactical Patrol Force (TPF). He rode the trains from 8:00 p.m. to 6:00 a.m. There was zero tolerance for any violations of Transit Authority rules within the unit. In fact, the TPF were so hell-bent on issuing summonses they created the Field

Internal Affairs Unit, commonly called shooflies, which was out, in force, during the hours the officers were on patrol to make sure they were doing their jobs correctly. They were merciless souls who would write a cop up for any infraction—from not issuing a summons to violators, to not having one's hat on one's head on a hundred-degree day.

Though the sun was setting on the streets above, the temperature in the subway was still near no degrees. Vinny was aboard a southbound Number 2 train as it barreled into the 125th Street and Lennox Avenue station. He placed his foot in the door's path to keep it open and stuck his head out of the subway car and looked both north and south to inspect the station platform. He noticed a couple entering the rear of the train. The female was smoking a cigarette.

Wonderful. Another friggin' smoking summons. Can't these dumb shits read the signs?

His legs were leaden as he approached the couple, who'd taken a seat in the third-to-last car. He sensed trouble in the air the farther he pushed, grim-faced, through the subway car. Something didn't feel right with this couple. He was a black male in his midtwenties, poorly dressed, and apparently a crackhead. She was an attractive white girl, about fifteen, neatly dressed.

What the heck's she doing with him? Something's not right here.

She had a look of panic on her face. The male had his right arm entwined with her left arm. His right hand in his pocket. She had the cigarette between her knees. Neither saw Vinny until it was too late.

"How are you two doing this evening?" Vinny asked politely, standing in front of them with his body bladed, turned sideways, to protect himself from a possible kick in the groin, while his hand was on his gun in its holster, turned away from the couple.

"Yo, Officer, she don't know no better. She's from New Jersey," he said, smacking the cigarette from her hands onto the floor of the subway car.

As he did that, Vinny glanced at the female's face. It was filled with fear and anxiety. Immediately he felt the chill of danger race up his spine.

"May I see some ID, miss?" Vinny asked, hoping his voice hadn't betrayed his suspicion.

"Yo, man, I told you she's from Jersey, man!"

Vinny looked at the girl again. Her hands were now trembling.

"Listen, asshole!" Vinny exclaimed, slowly removing his gun from his holster, but still out of view of the couple. "When I want to know something from you, I'll ask for it!"

The male lowered his eyes and stared at a spot on the floor.

"Do you have an ID on you, miss?" Vinny asked in a caring voice. She shook her head vigorously, without looking at him.

The train was pulling into the 110th Street and Lennox Avenue station. "Stand up, we're getting off here," Vinny said in a composed voice. "I'll verify your information by phone, issue you a summons, and you'll be free to go."

The male smiled thinly. "Me too?"

Why's this asshole so worried?

Vinny looked at him quizzically. "You mean you don't want to wait for your girlfriend?" he asked suspiciously.

"Yo, man, she ain't my girlfriend. I tolds da bitch not to smoke!"

Vinny smiled coldly. "Since you seem to be a perfect gentleman, you can stay on the train," he said sarcastically.

The doors opened as the conductor announced 110th Street and Lennox.

"Let's go," Vinny said, motioning the female to stand up and walk out the door with him. "Are you all right?" Vinny then asked wearily as they got onto the platform.

She looked at Vinny, then worriedly at the train, just as its doors were closing.

"He raped me! He has a knife!" she screamed as the train began to pull out of the station.

Instinctively, he grabbed his radio. "Eleven, TP One, Central. Southbound Number 2 train, car number 8112. Rapist armed with a knife on board. Hold train at Ninety-Sixth and Broadway."

"Eleven, TP One. Ten-five. Repeat."

No time for this.

He grabbed the girl by the hand, and they began to run up the steps leading up to the exit.

As they hit the top of the stairs, there were no police cars in sight. He could hear the dispatcher calling a 10-13.

"Officer needs assistance at Ninety-Sixth and Broadway. Eleven TP one, come in."

No time! I've gotta find a car to get to Ninety-Sixth Street, or I'll lose the train. He spotted a gypsy cab parked with the driver in it.

"Come on," he said, pulling her by the hand again. "I need your car," Vinny said as he opened the driver's door.

"Por que?" the driver said in Spanish. He looked confused.

"Rapido!" Vinny exclaimed and pulled the man from his car by the arm. "Get in!" He pushed the girl through the driver's side into the passenger's seat.

"I'll bring it back!" Vinny shouted as he stomped on the accelerator.

Within two blocks, traffic had stopped at a light. Vinny jumped the curb and rode on the sidewalk. When he reached the park entrance, he drove the cab down two flights of stairs into the park.

He grabbed the microphone on his radio.

"TP One! Southbound Number 2 train. Car number 8112. Male, black, twenties, blue jeans, dirty white T-shirt, armed with a knife."

"Ten-five. Repeat location, TP One."

"Nine-Six and Broadway Central," he repeated.

The cab had taken about all that it could when it hit the stairs exiting the park.

"Let's go!"

He grabbed her hand, abandoning the car on the stairs. The racing sounds of sirens were coming from all directions. Two cops were at the top of the subway stairs when Vinny arrived with the girl in tow.

"Watch her!" Vinny said to the officers as he began to run down the stairs.

There were about six cops running around the southbound Number 2 platform, where the train was being held with its doors shut.

"Over here!" Vinny yelled as he stood by car number 8112.

The officers ran in his direction as he yelled to the conductor to open the train doors. The instant the doors opened, the suspect was looking down the barrel of Vinny's gun. He stood totally astonished and speechless. Vinny smiled maliciously.

"Peekaboo."

"Don't shoot me, man!" he cried.

"Get on your face," Vinny said quickly.

"Okay, man," he said, getting down on the ground. "Just don't shoot me."

Vinny holstered his weapon and speed-cuffed the suspect while the other officers pointed their weapons at him. He searched the suspect while he was still on the ground and recovered the knife used in the rape.

Two officers arrived with the girl, who identified the suspect as the man who raped her. Vinny walked his prisoner upstairs to the street, where literally twenty radio cars were parked everywhere. Spotting a beat-up black-and-white Suburban Transit Police car, he walked his prisoner over and placed him in the back seat.

Suddenly, he heard a voice arguing vociferously. "Where's my car? The cop stole my fucking car!" As Vinny began to approach the commotion, the taxi driver recognized him. "That's him! That's the crazy cop that stole my car!" he cried, pointing an accusing finger.

Vinny smiled at the NYPD sergeant who'd taken the brunt of the cabbie's complaint.

"Did you borrow this man's cab?" the sergeant asked, faintly amused.

"Borrow? Borrow! That fucking nut stole it!" the cabbie protested.

"You learn English really fast," Vinny said sarcastically. "Maybe if you spoke to me in English, I wouldn't have had to commandeer your vehicle to get here. You could have driven me instead," Vinny said contemptuously, pointing his finger in his face.

The cabbie stared at him in disbelief, while the sergeant laughed nastily. "Where's this guy's cab?" he asked, trying to control his laughter.

Vinny grinned. "Follow me."

"My car! Look what you've done to my fucking car!"

The sergeant and numerous cops and passersby broke out into uncontrollable laughter as they stared at the car with two flat front tires and white smoke billowing out from under the hood.

"Who's going to pay for this?" he demanded.

Vinny met his stare head-on and smiled back condescendingly. "Yo no se, amigo!" Vinny said in his best Spanish, which means "I don't know."

He spent the next thirty-six hours processing the arrest at Manhattan Central Booking, then waited in the police complaint room of the Manhattan District Attorney's office at 100 Centre Street in the Manhattan Criminal Court Building. He slept on the floor in the hallway with dozens of other waiting cops.

After not seeing Debbie for two days, he arrived home exhausted. He had just enough time to take a shower before heading back to work.

"I don't understand why they won't give you tonight off," Debbie said in a low voice.

Vinny shrugged indifferently.

"Look at you. You've got bags under your eyes. You're exhausted," she said, her voice heavy with anger.

Vinny merely shook his head and smiled. "Come here, baby," he said lovingly, with his arms opened. Debbie walked over into his embrace. "I love you so much, Debbie. I won't be on TPF forever," he said in a warm, reassuring voice.

She raised her head and looked directly into his hazel eyes—the eyes she fell deeply in love with six years before at the beach in New Rochelle, the soft, caring eyes of a man who'd do almost anything to help another human being and never look for anything in return.

"I'm worried about you getting hurt or killed out there." She trembled and pulled close to him in an embrace that was as tight as a vise. She wanted to never let go of him.

He held her close in his arms. He knew she was right. The rape arrest was the second time in less than two weeks that he'd made a serious arrest and gotten no sleep.

The first was the night of the New Edition concert at Madison Square Garden. It was around 11:15 p.m. He was getting some fresh air after completing a train run to Grand Central Station when the call came over the radio.

"Ten-thirteen. Officer down at Thirty-Fourth Street and Eighth Avenue.

Vinny jumped into an NYPD radio car to respond to the location, but all the training in the world couldn't prepare him for the chaos he encountered when he arrived at the scene. He exited the back seat of the radio car smack in the middle of a full-scale riot. Cops were locked in a hand-to-hand battle with the rioters. The cops were swinging their nightsticks like ballplayers trying to hit a homer. Civilians trying to retrieve their stolen jewelry or pocketbooks were fighting with the rioters too. It was a free-for-all, where a cop could randomly choose who was going to get locked up and who'd be sent to the hospital.

He saw a uniform cop on the ground being stomped about his head by two youths. The cop was curled up like a ball, protecting his face as best as he could while holding on to his holstered weapon so he wouldn't lose it.

Vinny charged toward the downed cop like an actor on the set of *Spartacus*, with his nightstick coming down on the head of one of the suspects, whose leg was in midkick and aimed at the officer's head. The impact of the wooden stick with his skull made the sound like a fresh melon dropping on the floor in a supermarket. The suspect fell limply onto the downed officer as Vinny recoiled his stick, dropped low, and struck the second suspect with a full swing across his knees, immediately immobilizing him. He, too, toppled to the ground.

Motherfuckers.

Vinny quickly cuffed both suspects and looked at the officer, who was still on the ground.

"Don't leave me," the cop said despairingly as Vinny held him in his arms.

"I'm not going anywhere," he said with an encouraging smile. He removed his gun from his holster to protect himself and his fallen comrade from the surrounding chaos.

When the smoke cleared, Vinny had three rioters under arrest for robbery. They represented the only arrests made by the Transit Police. The NYPD made seventeen arrests on the same charges. Three cops were injured seriously, and over thirty robbery and assault complaints had been filed.

Afterward, Vinny was paraded on television with the three suspects. A press release was issued saying he performed an act of intelligence, evincing extraordinary loyalty and perseverance, and would be commended by the department.

What a night that was.

"Listen, honey," he said, still holding her close in his arms. "We'll be leaving for vacation in Acapulco in November."

Debbie pulled from his embrace, staring into his eyes, her face creased with concern. "Vincent, it's not even July yet, and you're talking about relaxing in November. Are you crazy?"

"November will be here before you know it," he said coolly, too tired to note the rising tension in her voice.

"Forget about it," she said in a frustrated tone and marched off like a petulant child into the bedroom, slamming the door behind her.

Shit. What'd I say wrong this time? There's no sense talking with her when she's like this. Best to leave her alone for a while till she calms down.

Since their wedding, they'd had their share of arguments like any other married couple, but they'd never gone to bed angry at each other. To his credit, he'd never left the house to go to work without kissing her goodbye and telling her how much he loved her. It was a rule they'd sworn to live by, for they never knew if the day might come when he would leave for work and never return.

He knocked on the bedroom door and poked his head in carefully.

"Can I come in?" he asked in the voice of a little boy who'd come to apologize to his mother for doing something wrong.

Their eyes met, and she smiled brightly. She was sitting with her legs draped over the side of their bed.

He immediately got on his knees between her legs and held her in his arms. "I love you," she said softly, running her fingers through his hair.

"Oh God, I love you too," he said, holding her tightly.

A few moments passed before he broke the embrace.

"I have to go to work," he said soothingly. He looked into her gentle eyes.

"I know you do," she said in a weary voice. "Just be careful out there, please."

"I will, baby, I promise," he said and kissed her softly on the lips.

What a wife, but no time for some loving. I gotta get to work.

When roll call was over, he accepted accolades from his peers as they filed out of the muster room.

"Davis," Lieutenant Parker said brusquely, "I want to see you in my office."

It's high time I get some praise from Lieutenant Hard-Ass. But why's he acting so gruffly? Hmm. I wonder what the fuck's wrong with this guy.

He entered the office, which was cluttered with coffee cups and old newspapers scattered about. Parker, a twenty-five-year veteran of the old-school TPF, sat stone-faced behind his desk. The TPF didn't have a captain assigned to each district to act as a commanding officer, so Lieutenant Hard-Ass was, in fact, the CO.

"Sit down, Davis," Parker said, seemingly without moving his lips.

He immediately took a seat, prepared to get a that-a-boy from his boss, who'd never uttered a positive syllable since he met him.

Lieutenant Parker was breezing through report after report he held in his hands. As he read them, he kept shaking his head from side to side in disbelief. Abruptly, he looked across and met Vinny's stare.

"You're to receive the TPF Cop of the Month award from the inspector for your rape arrest, and you've been approved for an Honorable Mention Citation. You've also been approved for a Meritorious Police Duty Medal for the three robbery suspects you grabbed at that concert fiasco."

Vinny smiled proudly.

So far, so good. Don't stop now, Lieutenant. I earned every bit of this.

"You're also looking at a few more awards for the other arrests you've made," he added decidedly.

"Thank you, sir," Vinny said appreciatively.

"Don't thank me!" Parker unexpectedly shrieked.

The temperature in the room suddenly dropped below freezing.

"When your final evaluation is due in six months at the end of your probation, I'm recommending that you be terminated from the department."

What the fuck! Terminated? What the fuck for? Maintain control…a thousand and one, a thousand and two…

"Why?" he asked, fighting to control his temper.

Parker smiled arrogantly. "Because the department doesn't need some wannabe-hero rookie cop bringing adverse criticism to the Transit Police! It's been over a year, and you still can't get it through your thick skull that you're not in the NYPD."

His eyes widened with horror. He couldn't believe what he was being told. "Why don't you roll over to the NYPD, if you want to run around making arrests in the street?"

"I tried! After I went through the medical, physical, and psychological exams all over again, my lottery number still came up for Transit!"

Parker emitted a nasty snigger. "Well, you better hope we merge with them before your probation is up, or you'll be out of a job."

Vinny's face turned white with fury.

This is ridiculous. My father's right about the Transit Police being a second-class department. I never wanted to be here in the first place, and now this shit of a lieutenant is going to fuck me.

All his hopes and dreams were being shattered.

"Listen to me!" Parker said with an exasperated look. "If you want a transfer out of here, maybe to Communications or someplace downtown, I'll endorse your request."

Where the fuck's he going with this?

"It might do you some good to work on a desk for a while—maybe you'll calm down."

Calm down? I thought arresting criminals is why we're cops. I can't win with this prick-head.

Vinny opened his hands and lowered his head in a clear gesture of submission.

"Good," Parker said as he rose, offering his hand.

Vinny stood and took it. It was cold, dry, and impersonal.

"Thanks for the warning, Lieutenant," Vinny said flatly. "I'll be gone before you know it."

Parker smiled thinly. "Good. You've made a wise choice."

Fuck you.

CHAPTER 6

After Lieutenant Parker's threat, Vinny was despondent for days. The pressure Parker applied on him to conform to the expectations of the Transit Police made him feel as though he wasn't wanted. The NYPD didn't care that he was a good cop. It seemed it didn't want such cops, only those who wouldn't upset its hidebound ways. But because he was unwilling to change his nature of trying to be the best cop he could be—fuck the system—he'd lost Parker's confidence. At this point in his career, Parker was the one who could abruptly terminate it.

Parker's Christmas deadline was looming. Vinny was boxed in. He had no intention of resigning, but if Vinny didn't get out from under Parker, the latter would end Vinny's career for him. He did what he had to do—lifted the phone, dialed Captain Flanagan at the Communications Unit, and asked for a job. Thankfully, he immediately put through Vinny's transfer.

For the moment, I'm safe.

Screw Parker. Screw the department. I don't care what they think. This job's too important to lose because of them. I didn't bust my ass to get this far only to have them ruin me. Screw going on patrol, too. They want to break me, but they have another thing coming. Once I get off probation, I can always return to patrolling. God, I miss it! Sitting behind this fucking desk, answering phones, dispatching cops to respond to calls sucks big-time. This is like riding the bench in the World Series—my team's playing, but I'm not. I should be out there! It's so disheartening and frustrating hearing them calling for help over the radio and not being able to be there too. But! Think of the bright side. This does have its benefits, too. Aside from the obvious, I don't have to worry about getting hurt or killed, the hours are steady. And things have stabilized with Debbie. She knows how much I love being on the streets, helping people, but at least now she's stopped complaining about me not being home for dinner or missing from our bed at night. Heh. That's the best benefit of all.

Vinny and Debbie went off to enjoy a much-needed vacation on Aruba. They spent the days Jet Skiing, parasailing, snorkeling, and lying on the white-sand beach. Nights were filled with romantic dinners, dancing, and lovemaking. There was nothing in the world they wanted more than to have a baby. In more practical moments, they decided to enjoy their time together and wait until Vinny passed the next sergeant's test in February. The extra ten grand a year in salary would certainly come in handy. They were but twenty-four years old, and there would be plenty of time to start their family.

In January 1987, Vinny's probation period was drawing to an end. Despite giving his word, Lieutenant Parker double-crossed Vinny by recommending that he be terminated. He was stunned. A man of his word, Vinny couldn't conceive that Parker would lie to him and try to stab him in the back this way after Vinny had kept his side of the bargain by transferring out of the Tactical Patrol Force. It was even more inconceivable that Parker requested Flannigan to endorse his recommendation. To his credit, and fortunately for Vinny, Captain Flannigan didn't share Lieutenant Parker's belief that Transit cops are highly paid security guards whose main job is to protect the Transit Authority's revenue and to generate even more by issuing summons. In his day, Captain Flannigan was a highly decorated cop. He didn't make his rank by staying indoors, studying for the next promotional exam. In fact, he was highly impressed that Vinny had made over thirty arrests, had won the TPF Cop of the Month award, and received six commendations in under a year. He wrote on Vinny's evaluation that he was a credit to the Transit Police Department. He also encouraged him to study hard for the sergeant's exam.

Vinny did exactly that. He studied long and hard. Part of the exam consisted of New York State penal law, which was his favorite subject at the police academy. It wouldn't be a problem. However, memorizing Transit Police procedures was more difficult. Comparing the two sets of procedures was like comparing apples and oranges. But when the exam was over, he left extremely confident that he'd passed and would be on the list when it would be certified and published that summer.

In March 1987, he was again in the department spotlight when, by sheer coincidence, he unexpectedly intruded on an armed robbery in Mount Vernon. As a favor to one of his colleagues, he'd swapped his regular day tour for a four-to-twelve shift so his friend would be free to close on the new house he and his wife were buying in Rockland County.

Not wanting to make a mess of the kitchen before leaving for work, Vinny decided to grab a bite at a diner down the street from his house. He took a seat at a booth facing the register, which is something cops do. It's a habit instilled in them at the academy: back to a wall with a full view of the entrance and the cash register. It becomes a survival instinct, so they are never caught off guard in the event of trouble.

"I've just been robbed. Call the police!" a hysterical woman screamed as she ran into the restaurant through its front door.

In that instant, the simple clarity of his new life vanished and everything changed.

Screw Lieutenant Parker and the Transit Police Department's way of thinking! I'm a cop first and foremost. I don't give a shit whether they like it or not.

He quickly moved to where the woman was standing.

"I'm a cop," he said calmly. "Where are they?"

"There are three of them. One has a big gun," she said nervously, her entire body trembling in fear.

He turned quickly to the cashier. "Miss, call 911," he said authoritatively, then turned back to the frightened woman. "Are they on foot or in a car?" he asked urgently.

"On foot! They ran toward the bridge leading into the Caldor Shopping Center."

"What'd they look like? Color, age, clothes," he asked in rapid succession.

The cashier was on the phone with the Mount Vernon Police, giving their location.

"Black kids, wearing black hoods over their heads," she said, closing her eyes, as though seeing them more clearly in her mind's eye. "The biggest one had the gun."

Experience had taught him that he should not approach three suspects alone unless it was absolutely necessary. If one had a gun, the other two might also be armed.

Vinny turned to the cashier, who was still on the phone with the police. "Tell them that an off-duty New York City cop is going after them and to notify Pelham Manor Police the suspects are headed toward the Caldor Shopping Center. Wait here for the police," he demanded as he ran out the door.

Jumping in his car, he drove slowly across the bridge into Pelham Manor, paying close attention to the large Caldor Shopping Center parking lot.

There they are. Stupid bastards, fucking up my dinner. How am I going to play this?

He removed his gun from his holster and placed it between his legs. Thinking that they would be too startled to move, he accelerated toward them, but they spotted him and took off running. One ran toward the rear, while the other two ran toward the front of the shopping center.

Two is better than one.

He turned left behind them.

Realizing they couldn't outrun his car, they ran in to the Modell's Sporting Goods store.

Vinny drove onto the sidewalk, stopped, and got out without turning off the ignition. With gun drawn and shield displayed on his chest, he entered the store and jumped over the counter, where he pulled the lone female cashier to the floor.

"I'm a cop, stay down," he ordered the petrified young cashier.

The two suspects had concealed themselves behind a round coatrack loaded with goose-down jackets.

Using the counter for cover, Vinny aimed his gun in the direction of the coats and yelled at the customers in the store to get on the floor.

"You two, behind the coats! Throw out your weapons and let me see your hands."

He could hear them talking, but they made no move to comply with his command.

He glanced at the cashier on the floor by his feet. "Pick up that phone," he said quietly, nodding to the one under the register, "and get me some help."

She immediately dialed 911.

Within moments, they heard approaching sirens. As they grew louder, Vinny yelled at the suspects, "You hear that? In about thirty seconds, there's going to be an army of cops shooting into that coatrack. Throw your guns out and you won't be hurt."

Desperate people can be exceedingly clever and sometimes extremely lucky, but with nowhere to run and a goose-down jacket to protect you from a hail of bullets, common sense should prevail.

"We only got one gun!" a voice from behind the coats cried out.

"Toss it out where I can see it. Now!" Vinny ordered without hesitation.

"Here it goes," the voice said as the pistol was tossed onto the floor.

Behind Vinny, the door crashed open as several cops entered, yelling, "Police, don't move!"

Without turning to take his eyes off the coat rack, Vinny called out, "I'm on the job. In the city. Two black male suspects behind the coatrack. They threw out the gun on the floor. I don't know if they have more." Vinny could hear the cops moving to find cover, one of them jumping over the counter to join him. With his gun pointed in the same direction as Vinny's, they exchanged glances.

"Place your hands over your heads and then stand up," Vinny's new friend ordered the suspects.

"Don't shoot!" they said as a pair of hands emerged above the coats.

"Stand up and face away from us," Vinny ordered.

Again, a plea as they complied, "Don't shoot."

Two officers moved in and quickly cuffed the suspects, while a third retrieved the gun off the floor.

"Oh my God," Vinny said. The hairs on the back of his neck were standing straight out.

"You all right?" the officer next to him asked in a worried voice.

"Yeah." Vinny nodded.

The third suspect, who'd fled into Caldor, was apprehended and identified by Vinny a short time later.

It was nearly 11:30 p.m. when he returned home to find Debbie patiently waiting on the couch in the living room, watching television.

"Hi, baby," he said, walking over to sit down beside her.

Leaning over, she threw her arms around him. "I was so worried about you after I heard about it on the radio."

He looked into her warm, loving eyes and kissed her on the lips. "Well, I'm home now. That's all that matters," he said drowsily.

Suddenly, Debbie's eyes peered off at the television set.

Vinny turned to see what she was looking at. It was a news report of a cop that was shot. They were not releasing the name until his next of kin had been notified. He got up to turn off the television. As he did, he realized how hard it must be for his wife to have to live her life this way.

"Come on, baby, let's go to bed," he said, standing in front of her with his hands held out.

Debbie looked up, a deep thought on her face. "Promise me that'll never happen to you."

Vinny didn't reply. He couldn't. Instead, he dropped to his knees before her and held her in his arms. It was something they'd never really discussed before. He'd hoped she'd never ask, but now she had. It was a promise he'd hoped he would never have to make.

Never is such an absolute. It stretches out to eternity, to the unknown future. I don't know how I can make such a promise and live to keep it.

Thomas DiCaprio was a good-looking, curly-haired blonde. He was also an assistant district attorney in the Westchester County DA's office at Mount Vernon and was assigned to the arraignment of the three robbery suspects Vinny arrested. DiCaprio sat behind his desk, reading a newspaper, when he appeared behind him at his doorway. DiCaprio looked over his shoulder and signaled him to enter.

"Nice arrest," DiCaprio said as he dropped his newspaper onto his desk before rising to meet him. "Tom DiCaprio," he said, extending a hand that Vinny shook firmly.

"Thank you," Vinny said. "I was just lucky."

"The newspapers love it." He picked up the newspaper and looked at the headline: TRANSIT COP MAKES OFF-DUTY ARREST. "That's admirable."

Vinny shrugged. "Like I said, just lucky."

"Have a seat."

For several minutes, the two discussed the difference between crime in the subways of New York and the growing crime in suburban Westchester. While they talked, he expected to be chastised again for getting involved off-duty, just as the duty captain who had to respond to Mount Vernon on the Friday night of the incident had done. His rebuke still rung in his ears.

"You'll never learn, will you, Davis? Why don't you join the NYPD, Davis? Better yet, why don't you see if they're hiring up here? I'm sure that they can use a hero like you in the suburbs."

Even when Vinny had to call the court desk that morning to report that he was on duty in Mount Vernon Court, the cop on the other end of the line had laughed raucously at him, saying it was the funniest thing he'd ever heard, a Transit cop in court outside the City of New York for making a robbery arrest. Vinny didn't see the humor of it.

But as he and DiCaprio continued talking, the more convivial he became.

Vinny began to feel like a cop rather than a fool.

"Wait here for me. I've got to head down to the courtroom. Make yourself at home," DiCaprio said in a nice tone of voice before departing.

Vinny looked out the window. The morning sun was working its way higher, rising above a cluster of white clouds into a brilliant blue sky.

I'm confused. Everything that's happened to me since I joined the TP is confusing and disheartening. I just don't get why the officers frown on us cops doing our jobs. On one hand, I'm fucked in the TA. I hate it. Yet on the other hand, I must have been put here for a reason. It's like some unknown force—maybe it's God, yes, it's God, of course it's God—has guided me here and He's protecting me. Whatever's ahead, however obscure or dangerous it is, comes along for a reason. I must be ready to deal with it. Everything happens for a reason, right? Right. Innocent women and children die in accidents that are unexplainable, for seemingly no reason. But there has to be a reason. Yes, it's all part of God's plan. We are here on earth to do His will, not to question it.

It was almost noon when DiCaprio returned and disrupted his thoughts. "Sorry that took so long," he said with an indulgent smile.

Vinny looked at him quizzically, then laughed.

"What's so funny?"

"I'm not laughing at you, Counselor. I'm laughing because, on occasion, I've slept on the floor of the Manhattan District Attorney's office for two nights, waiting to see an ADA. Never once has one apologized for taking so long!"

DiCaprio returned the smile. "Well, now, hopefully, I'll really shock you," he said, reaching into a pocket of his suit pants and retrieving a Jackson. "You like pizza?"

"With a name like Vinny, isn't that a silly question?"

"Touché. Well, I'm buying, you're flying, paisan," he said, handing him the note. "And since I'm buying and you're Italian, I want extra cheese and pepperoni. Capisce?"

"That's the only way to eat a pizza," Vinny replied enthusiastically. "I'll be back as soon as I can."

"Take your time. I've got plenty of work to finish up before I can enjoy my lunch."

"See ya," Vinny said as he walked out.

A harsh glare came in through the large front window of the pizzeria. Outside, a midafternoon sun was beating down on the lunchtime crowd, who hurried along the sidewalk to pick up their lunch or cash their checks at the bank across the street before scurrying back to their jobs.

I wonder how many of them are actually happy at their jobs. How many of them do the same boring routine, day in and day out, to earn their paycheck? How many of them dream they had a job they'd looked forward to going to every day? I may not be very happy now, stuck in the Communications Unit, but that's only a minor setback. Soon I'll be back on patrol, doing what I love to do, being a cop.

Abruptly, and for a brief moment, he observed what looked like a male striking a woman in front of the bank. A truck stopped at a traffic light obscured his view. A warning alarm went off in his head as he quickly walked outside to get a better look. Moving quickly, he walked between two parked cars and observed a woman fighting desperately to hold on to a large bank bag. It was inconceivable this could be happening in broad daylight, in the middle of a busy street, at lunchtime, but it was.

Dressed in a suit for court and not prepared to do battle, Vinny bent over to retrieve his .38-caliber snub nose from his ankle holster and simultaneously pinned his shield to his jacket. As he made his way across the intersection, the female lost her grip on the bag as the robber pounded her head. Only a few feet away, Vinny took aim and shouted, "Police! Don't move!"

He might as well have shouted, "Ready, set, go!" because the youth with the bag turned and fled like a jackrabbit. Vinny chased him through the lunch-hour crowded, dodging around people, his heart pounding. The suspect was half a block ahead when he darted through a hole in the fence that led down onto the Metro North railroad tracks. Vinny sped up, then scaled the fence—the hole wasn't big enough for him to squeeze through. His suit jacket ripped on the wire on top of the fence. Falling to the ground, bleeding from the arm, the suspect was only fifty yards away, but Vinny wasn't about to lose him. Twenty-five yards and closing. The suspect looked back. When he did, Vinny raised his gun.

"Stop or I'll shoot!"

For a moment, the criminal froze, then took off again. Fueled by adrenaline, Vinny resumed the chase. A train roared past from the opposite direction. Looking back, he saw there were no trains approaching on the track behind him. The suspect made an abrupt right turn behind a concrete pillar and stopped. Vinny ran the few remaining feet to the opposite side of it, then stopped, too. Cautiously peeking round the pillar, Vinny saw him, chest heaving and out of gas, there, sitting on the ground.

"Put your hands on top of your head," Vinny said angrily as he aimed his gun at the suspect's face.

Another one bites the dust.

"Where'd you go for the pizza? Italy?" DiCaprio snapped, then smiled to show he was joking.

Vinny stared at him for a moment, then let his eyes fall to the ground. As he did, DiCaprio noticed his torn suit jacket and the blood seeping through the hole.

"You're bleeding! What happened?" DiCaprio asked with concern in his voice.

Vinny looked up, bemused. He was agitated and nervous about having to notify the Transit Police he'd made another off-duty arrest, and what the duty captain would say when he arrived.

"I made a robbery-assault arrest outside the pizza place," he said despairingly.

DiCaprio looked incredulous. He stepped slowly out from behind his desk toward Vinny. "Are you all right?" he asked in a concerned voice.

Vinny's eyes came back to him. "They're going to have my ass for sure," he said, his voice frightened and barely audible.

"Who?" DiCaprio asked urgently.

"My department," Vinny said in a low, worried voice. "They don't take too kindly to their cops getting involved on duty, unless it's in the subway. But off duty? Not in the city of New York. Twice in three days—they'll have my head."

DiCaprio stared at him for a moment in silence, then backed slowly away to answer the phone that'd been ringing on his desk.

Vinny turned his head to the right, staring out the window, his heart still pounding.

"I'll call you back, thank you." DiCaprio hung up the phone and looked at Vinny. "Correct me if I'm wrong," he said factually, "but from everything I've just been told, it would be extremely difficult for your department to do anything but pin a medal to your chest for arresting a man who beat and robbed our chief of police's secretary."

Vinny glanced quickly at DiCaprio, who was smiling from ear to ear. "Holy shit!" Vinny swore under his breath.

The article in the newspapers read thus: ON-DUTY COPS GET SOME OFF-DUTY HELP.

Not only was Vinny recommended for two department medals for both incidents, but also the chief of the Mount Vernon PD sent a letter of commendation to the chief of the TPD for his "acts of bravery above and beyond the call of duty."

Soon afterward, Vinny was offered an assignment that he accepted, detachment to the NYPD Court Division, where he would transport prisoners for arraignment in Manhattan. Two of his new duties were checking prisoners for fugitive warrants and liaising with police agencies throughout the United States. He'd hoped to be promoted from this unit to detective in the Warrant Squad and finally return to some real police work, tracking down wanted suspects, apprehending them, and bringing them to justice.

A bright predawn September moon illuminated their bedroom. Not wanting to awaken Debbie, Vinny quietly searched for his white dress uniform gloves.

It was Valor Day 1988, the day the TPD honored members of the department with medals for extreme acts of bravery. Eighteen months had passed since he'd made the two off-duty arrests in Mount Vernon. The Commendation Review Board had long since endorsed the reports awarding Vinny an Honorable Mention Commendation for the robbery arrest of the chief of police's secretary and a Distinguished Duty Medal, the third highest in the department, excluding the Medal of Honor, which is almost always awarded posthumously, for the pizza parlor incident arrest.

For a long moment, Vinny stood staring into the closet. He wasn't certain how he felt or what to think. For nearly sixteen years, he'd been tormented by nightmares of his mother's death. It played over and over in his mind. He was filled with a gnawing guilt that somehow her death had been his fault, that it might have been prevented if he'd been a better son. He felt God had taken her from him as punishment. He remembered being afraid of real love because of the terrifying thought that someday it might be snatched from him again. For those reasons, and many more, he'd vowed to live his life helping other people whenever possible.

To atone, he'd become a lifeguard and saved many lives. He felt an indescribable joy reviving drowning victims, filling their lungs with his air, keeping them alive. He took an emergency medical course at Montefiore Hospital also to be licensed to work on an ambulance, and he delivered his first baby into the world after climbing into an overturned car where the mother lay pinned, unable to move. One April, he dived in to the frigid waters of the East River to save a drowning woman, almost drowning himself in the process because of the wicked currents and near-freezing water temperature. Being a cop and arresting people were only part of it. Saving lives and helping people were even more important to him. All the commendations and medals in the world couldn't replace the feelings he got from the look on a mother's face when she was handed back her child who was just saved from a burning building, or the look on someone's face when a loved one had just been given CPR and magically regained consciousness. To Vinny, that was what his job was about.

"What are you looking for, baby?" Debbie asked drowsily. She turned on the nightstand light, snatching him from his reverie.

"I'm sorry, baby," he said quietly. "I didn't mean to wake you." He turned around and looked in to her eyes, then smiled.

My God, how I love her. I've never felt more complete with anyone as I do with her.

"Did you find your hat and gloves? I left them out for you on the dining room table?" she asked, smiling.

He returned it.

"I'm glad you reminded me about the hat. I haven't worn one for over two years. There's no way the chief would let me approach the mayor without it. White gloves and no hat equal no medal."

"I would have made sure the hat got there. I'm positive one of your brothers would hunt you down and put it on your head."

He walked over to the bed, sat down beside her, and gently kissed her lips. "I'd be so lost without you in my life."

She sat up in bed, revealing her small firm breasts, and placed her arms around him. "No, baby, it's me who'd be lost without you."

A few moments passed. They held each other tightly. Breaking their embrace, she smiled seductively at him. Looking at her naked body, he immediately became aroused.

"Make love to me, hero," she said, running her fingers through his hair. Sneaking a quick peek at the clock on the nightstand, he kissed her and fell into her embrace.

A thunderous applause reverberated off the walls of the auditorium and shook the ceiling as the New York City Transit Police Irish Warpipe Band began their march through the aisles, marking the opening of the Valor Day ceremonies.

The family members of the honorees, resplendent in their dress uniforms, were filled with excitement and anticipation as they waited for Mayor Edward Koch to present the officers with their medals. It was the proudest day of many of these officers' lives. They'd cheated the angel of death. Perhaps the next time they might not be so lucky.

As quickly as the excitement and the applause had come, it evaporated when an account of a fine young officer was read to those in attendance. The officer was in the middle of transporting prisoners when a concerned citizen alerted him to a man with a gun. The officer could have radioed and had another unit respond to the call, but he didn't. Instead, he and a sergeant got out of their car and proceeded to investigate. Awaiting backup, the officer stood in front of a doorway to an apartment. Without warning, the door flew open and a gunman shot him in the face at point-blank range, killing him instantly.

As the narrator finished, there wasn't a dry eye in the house. Tears flowed down everyone's faces as they watched the slain officer's eight-year-old daughter salute the mayor as he put the gold Medal of Honor around her little neck. The glistening medal reflected the background of her white dress. Vinny remembered the frantic call coming over the radio, then responding to the hospital with dozens of cops to donate blood if it was needed. He vividly remembered the look on the slain officer's wife's face as their eyes met in the hallway. Now as he sat there, so many months later, his sense of achievement evaporated too. A dread swept over Vinny.

This medal means nothing now. What we are, why we're here, means nothing at all compared to the loss of that orphaned girl and her widowed mother. We're alive, but others who should have been here aren't. I'll never be able to explain this to Debbie or my family, except my father. He knows, too. It's a spiritual thing no one can possibly understand unless they've stood at death's door and been spared the invite.

CHAPTER 7

It wasn't long after they'd returned home from a trip, spending their sixth wedding anniversary in Acapulco, Mexico, that Vinny received an unexpected transfer back to uniform patrol in District 11. Due to the ever-rising crime rate in the subways, the Transit cops that were detached to work with the NYPD were forced back to Transit duties in seniority order. Since Vinny had but four years' service, he was one of the first to go.

He had mixed emotions. Part of him was disheartened about ending his assignment with the NYPD. There was strong talk of merging both departments. If that would happen, he would be a shoo-in for a permanent assignment with the Warrant Squad. With his excellent performance evaluations, his procedural knowledge, and his arrest record, he was almost guaranteed the position. But the rumor had been around since he was in the academy. Thinking it was about to become true, the Transit cops didn't sew the patches on their uniforms until just before graduation. The other side of him was excited with the prospect of going back on patrol in the Bronx. As crazy as it seemed, there were times when he'd truly missed it, in spite of the TPD's absurd outlook on subway crime as opposed to street crime. Since his transfer to the NYPD Court Division, he'd started taking the Metro North railroad to work. He rode the Hudson Line into Grand Central Terminal and then transferred to the IRT Number 4 train. The first year he took the train, he'd made two robbery and one grand larceny—a chain snatch—arrests. So in his heart he knew all along where he belonged, back riding the iron horse.

The roll call room in District 11 was exactly how he remembered it—dingy yellow floors, ceiling, and walls. It was the same decor as half the TP districts in the city. The air vents, which were designed to pump in fresh air from the streets, were still filled with thick black steel dust, caused by the steel wheels and brakes of the trains that roared by twenty-four hours a day, seven days a week. Rats, as though it were their natural right, still roamed the locker room, searching for fallen scraps from cops' lunches. Besides the filth, its other distinguishing characteristic was that it was a firetrap. The emergency exits at the rear and side of the command were cluttered with files and boxes filled with paper supplies. In the event of fire, it would be nearly impossible to get out—assuming you could find your way in a fire.

Vinny sat alone in the roll call room on a gray wooden bench that had been painted more than once. There were no tables, no chairs, only the bench. He'd arrived dutifully an hour early and had already changed into his uniform, which was all spit and polished, breast bars proudly displayed above his shield. In uniform, he looked handsome, but also tired and nervous, though eager to go out on patrol.

For a few moments, a short, pudgy sergeant stood in the doorway, staring at him suspiciously.

"Are you Davis?"

What's up with this fat fuck?

"Yes, sir, I am."

"The captain wants you in his office," he said sharply.

Shit. Some things never change. What the fuck is it now?

He paused a moment outside the door to the captain's office, took a deep breath, then knocked.

"Come in!"

Entering, he stood to attention before the captain, who was seated at his desk. His face was buried in what appeared to be Vinny's personnel folder. He looked up at him curiously. His face was that of a man who'd seen and heard it all. Slim build, with a full head of curly hair, he appeared younger than his age and seemed to possess far more vitality than many of the other captains he'd met the past four years.

"So you're Davis."

Vinny swallowed hard. "Yes, sir, I am." He inclined his head gravely.

"Have a seat," the captain said, his face lit with a sly smile.

"Thank you, sir," he said. He quickly sat before his legs buckled from fear.

"My name is Captain Shore. As you know, I am your new commanding officer," he said calmly, his smile still in place.

Vinny returned it. "Nice to meet you, Skipper," Vinny said cheerfully, using an acceptable term of endearment for a police captain.

Shore smothered his smile. "I've been going over your personnel file," he said, tapping his hand on the closed folder. "Let's see," he said haltingly, scratching his head. "How do I say this…ah, screw it. Diplomacy's never been my forte. Are you somehow related to, say, the police commissioner or the mayor?"

Vinny frowned for just an instant, then asked jokingly, "Who told you that?"

Shore studied him, then his face suddenly lit up with mischief. "That's what I thought," he responded, his deep voice laced with sarcasm. "Because only someone with a major hook—no, make that an anchor—could keep his job after some of the crazy stunts you've pulled in such a short time on the force. You are a duty captain's fucking nightmare! Do you know there are some who show up for work hoping you're on vacation in Guam?" He paused for a moment. "And even then, they're not sure they're safe from having to respond to some off-duty arrest you've made!"

Vinny usually had no problem asserting himself, but this man's persistence was overwhelming and quite comical. "It's a black cloud I have over my head," Vinny said, trying to suppress a smile.

Shore's eyes widened. "Black cloud? Black fucking cloud? I've heard you're independent, brusque, energetic, and even eccentric, but this is the first I'm hearing of a black cloud. Who told you about this fucking cloud? Some insane gypsy woman?"

Vinny could no longer control the smile that creased his lips. He was almost about to burst into laughter, but he caught himself.

"Listen to me, Davis! There's nothing wrong with being a good cop. Christ, you've got the medals to prove it. But I don't need a one-man army up here in the armpit of society—I need team players."

Vinny's eyebrow showed his skepticism. Shore's face was an odd combination of strength and vulnerability: a large mouth with a square jaw and wide-set blue eyes that managed to look sensitive.

"How does that work, Captain?"

Shore reopened his personnel folder, then looked at him.

"Your most recent evaluations have been excellent," he said lightly. "You have a good sick record, and you're presently on the sergeants list. If you stay out of trouble, I'll leave you in your present squad, assigned to steady days, with the holidays off. If you mess up your sick record, you'll go on rotating shifts and lose your holiday squad. If you get any ridiculous civilian complaints or cause me to write a fifty-page report to the chief explaining how you got into a blazing gun battle ten miles off post, I'll have your ass transferred to Coney Island." He hesitated, then resumed. "But if you manage to produce for me, bring me some robbery and grand larceny arrests, maybe a couple of guns, too, I'll put you into anticrime, plainclothes, with weekends off, as long as I'm not getting a lot of crime reported on them."

Vinny glanced around the small cozy office, at the comfortable green leather sofa, the old wooden desk, upon which Shore had propped his feet a thousand times. He looked at him with curiosity. The one thing he had to admire about this man was his directness.

"All right." Vinny smiled.

"So I take it we understand each other?"

"So far. I just hope I can lose the black cloud."

Shore's smile faded. "Just make sure you and your cloud stay in the subway."

Vinny shook his head. There was a thread of desperation in his voice as he rose and said, "I'll do that, sir."

Captain Shore grinned. "You'd better."

Within two months of his transfer to District 11, Vinny and Debbie moved in to a two-bedroom apartment on North Broadway in Yonkers. It was spacious, with a twenty-by-twenty-five-foot living room, dining room, and a terrace that had a spectacular view of the Hudson River and New York's skyline. The building was going co-op within two years, so moving in would give them the option to buy at the insider's price. It was a quick walk to Sacred Heart Church and Catholic School, where, when the time came, they could send their children. Until they saved up enough to buy their dream house in Rockland County, the apartment would do. They knew they'd have the money long before they'd be sending a child they hadn't conceived yet to school. But as Vinny's father had always said, "Have a nest egg in the bank for a rainy day and always have a backup plan."

Although they'd had no success in conceiving a child, they knew they had plenty of time. Until then, they were enjoying remodeling their new place. With the help of his father-in-law, they put in a new kitchen and bathroom. Vinny also insisted the management renew the old balcony. By summer, they were enjoying barbecues while watching the sun set behind the cliffs on the New Jersey bank of the Hudson River. Their life together was extremely happy and full of promise. Everything was going as planned. Then, like a biblical plague that always revisits sinners, the beast returned.

"What do you mean he called you at the office?" Vinny asked incredulously.

"What can I say? He's called a few times." Debbie was talking fast, avoiding his eyes.

"A few times? Why didn't you tell me? And what'd he say?" he asked quickly.

"He says he wants me back." Debbie turned to face him and added boldly, "He says he'll do anything to win me back. But I told him to just leave me alone."

Fuck, Sabol's back. A few times? And she's only telling me now? Why do I feel so betrayed? The man's living in the bowels of a federal prison in a ten-by-twelve concrete box, exactly where the evil and diabolical belong. Yet he's calling my wife? Repeatedly calling her, yet this is the first she's mentioned it. Thank God he'll be inside for eight more years.

"So if he's called you before, why are you telling me about this call?"

"Because this time he got pissed at me and told me if he can't have me, nobody will." She paused for a moment, her eyes glazed. "He said he's going to kill you."

Vinny bowed his head in disgust.

No, this isn't betrayal. It's plain, old-fashioned frustration. The same shit again.

"He can't hurt me, baby, he's in prison," he said nonchalantly as he poured wine for both of them.

He knew Sabol's brain was capable of cool, incisive thought, accurate and assertive, and uncluttered by emotion. *He's no amateur purse-snatcher like I arrest in the Bronx. He'll carefully plan his attack long before his release from prison. He'll make arrangements. The streets are crawling with scum who'll help him get the information he needs— where they live, their home phone number. Christ, he already has her work number and address. I wonder if she's holding anything else back.*

"What else did he say?"

She looked up with a grin. "Just that he's going to kill you," she said lightly.

His smile faded.

Just? What the fuck is this, and why the fuck's she grinning and being flippant?

"Very funny! Maybe someday he will. Then you won't be smiling," he said, shaking his head reproachfully.

"You just said he's going to be in prison! That's why I'm smiling. How can he hurt us?"

She's right. I've no right to be upset with her.

His face lit with laughter as he transformed into the young, stronger, and fearless man she'd married. Her smile brightened.

"That gives us at least eight more happy years before we have to worry about him and his threats."

She's absolutely right, again. He'll be out in more, like, five years, if he's granted parole. But for now, he's as harmless as an animal in a cage at the zoo. That same arrogance and inborn evil is still in him, I'm sure, but he's definitely harmless for now.

"He ever mention his wife and kid he has in Florida?" he probed.

She shrugged philosophically. "All the more reason he should leave us alone."

He glanced away from her. "Do you think he's going to continue bothering you at work?"

"Maybe. I'm not sure. I told him to leave me alone."

He stiffened and turned to look at her. "You say that as if you're not sure. What else did you tell him?" The tension rose in his voice.

"I told him he's a fool and that he should get on with his life. That you and I are very happy together and that he should leave me alone." Her hands clenched into little fists at her side. "He just doesn't listen. It's like he's possessed or something!"

She realized she should have kept her mouth shut about the phone calls, but they'd always insisted on having no secrets.

She's been keeping this a secret until now.

"Listen, baby," he said softly, realizing he was upsetting her. "There's probably nothing that can be done about him calling you at work, but I have to tell you, I'm worried about what's going to happen when he does get out."

Why the sly smile? What's going on in her head?

"By the time he gets out, we'll have our house in Rockland and I'll be home with our children."

"You really want to have a baby, huh?" he asked casually.

"Yes."

Great. Thank God she's not changed her mind.

"But I thought you wanted—"

"Shut up and make love to me!"

He reached out and gently caressed her face. "Come on, let's make a baby."

He awoke a couple of hours later after a restless, dream-ridden sleep, most of it just below consciousness. She was asleep. He could hear the soft sound of her breathing. He rolled over and got out of bed.

Fucking Sabol. Something's not right.

He walked across the living room and stepped through the open sliding glass door on to the balcony. The cool wind felt good against his naked body. He stared out at the Hudson below. Images of Sabol flickered in his mind's eye. The thought returned of him waiting for her after work and abducting her at gunpoint; his threats to rape her and maim her for life by throwing acid on her face sent a shudder up his spine.

Oh God, if he puts so much as a finger on her, I'll kill him.

His heart began pounding, his mouth was dry, and he had trouble catching his breath. The knowledge of Sabol's criminal insanity was horrifying.

How do you protect your wife and family from a man who has no reason?

Debbie was awake again. He felt her standing behind him. He smiled as he turned and moved toward her as she stood naked in the living room. For a long moment, she stared at him. He must have had a bemused expression on his face. She knew how much he loved her and would die before he'd let any harm come to her. When he tried to speak, she covered his mouth with her hand and locked her eyes on his. The intensity of her gaze held him. There was no need to speak. He knew what she wanted, so he picked her up and carried her back to the bedroom.

Forget Sabol. He can't harm us now.

At work, Captain Shore remained true to his word. Within two months, he assigned Vinny to the plainclothes anticrime patrol. Vinny had also stayed true to his word by keeping his black cloud in the subways. Within days of their first interview, Vinny made his first robbery arrest at 149th Street and the Grand Concourse. In the month that followed that arrest, he'd made six more arrests for robbery and grand larceny and made two gun arrests, all in the subways. The only time he'd come close to finding himself in trouble with a supervisor was when he pursued a purse-snatch suspect onto the tracks at 174th Street and the Grand Concourse.

It was an extremely hot and humid day as he patrolled the station in uniform. Wearing a twenty-pound gun belt had caused him to sweat so profusely that his bulletproof vest was saturated.

He was standing on the northbound platform as a D Train came roaring into the station. As the train doors opened, he looked north and then south for signs of trouble. Suddenly, he heard a woman scream for help. He felt his heart jump as he saw a male, black, take off running with a pocketbook in his hand.

Instinctively, he grabbed his radio. "Ah, 174th Street, in foot pursuit."

He heard Central acknowledge his location and knew backup would come quickly to his location.

He was right on the purse-snatcher's heels when they reached the end of the platform. The thief's eyes went to the staircase to the street, then to the darkness of the tunnel before him. Vinny felt his heart pounding even harder when the suspect leapt onto the tracks and began running into the darkness.

It wasn't fear of being electrocuted by the six hundred volts of the third rail or the possibility of being struck by a train that made him not follow in pursuit. It was the fear of the repercussion he'd face from his bosses if he did.

The Transit Police Patrol Guide strictly prohibits members of the department from entering the track area without positive confirmation that power has been shut off. The decision to shut off power and interrupt train service is at the discretion of the communications supervisor. The time of day will decide whether or not to interrupt service. At the height of rush hour, the Transit Authority will not stop the system to apprehend robbery suspects. Instead, the trains will proceed through the area with caution, and they usually get away.

Somewhere off in the distance, he heard the sound of approaching sirens.

Vinny hesitated, then pulled out his radio.

"Slow 'em down, Central. The suspect's fled onto the tracks northbound toward Tremont Avenue. Have units cover the emergency exits K."

"Eleven, operations lieutenant to Central K. No officers are to go onto the tracks. Have them acknowledge."

"Ten-four, K," Vinny responded after hearing the message loud and clear. Seconds later, Vinny eased out from the dimly lit catwalk onto the platform.

He was angry. He hated having to let a suspect get away. But what he hated more was that the NYPD could chase a suspect from the street into the subway, then proceed after him onto the tracks. Power would immediately be cut off for them, even at the height of rush hour. Vinny shook his head wearily. *Transit cops, who are trained in track safety, aren't allowed on the tracks, but NYPD cops, who have no training whatsoever, are? Just one more reason the two should be merged.*

"Vinny!" a voice echoed throughout the station.

"North end of the northbound plat!" Vinny responded.

Suddenly, Popi Rodriguez appeared from the shadows, with the elderly woman whose bag was snatched. Vinny felt a sudden urge of uneasiness that surpassed his anger. Staring at her, he knew this was not the first time she'd been the victim of a crime. That wouldn't make telling her he'd gotten away any easier, but at least she was used to dealing with vermin. He walked over and stood before her.

"I'm sorry I couldn't catch him," he said softly.

She took his hands and held them tightly. "It's okay. At least you're safe."

Vinny could feel the chill run down his spine, as if someone had dropped an ice cube down his back. He wanted to pull this woman into his arms and cradle her as if he'd known her all his life. She'd never seen him before, yet she was concerned for his safety. Happiness flooded him, warming him. The woman he'd thought would be upset with him had magically taken away his shame.

Popi glanced at him. "She said she got a real good look at him."

Vinny nodded approvingly. "Good. Maybe if she has the time now, you can bring her back to the district to look at some photos."

Vinny turned to the woman, awaiting her approval.

She nodded jerkily. "He got my entire paycheck. I just cashed it at the bank."

Vinny turned back to Popi. "Take her back to the district. I'll do a ride-through with the other guys to see if we spot him in the tunnel, then I'll meet you back at the district to take the complaint."

A *ride-through* is when the cops ride in the motorman's car at a slow rate of speed in search of the suspect.

Popi stared at Vinny. Popi had known Vinny since 1985 and called him El Gato, the cat. He was positive that should Vinny spot the suspect on the tracks, there'd be no stopping him. That woman's entire paycheck was in her handbag. She probably worked sixty hours a week to support her family. If he saw him, he was going to get it back.

"Don't go on the tracks, El Gato. The lieutenant will have your ass!"

Vinny thought for a moment, then smiled. "Me? Would I do anything as unorthodox as that?"

"Just be careful, El Gato." He turned, took the old woman by the arm, and led her away.

"El Gato," Vinny mumbled to himself as Popi escorted the woman down the platform. It was his newest nickname the Hispanic cops had given him. "The cat that has nine lives," they said.

If I keep it up like this, I'll need more than nine lives to make it through my twenty.

After completing two ride-throughs with negative results, he returned to District 11 to take the complaint report.

The old woman was in with some detectives when he arrived. "You can't catch 'em all, Davis," a sarcastic voice said.

Vinny turned to see Lieutenant Jordan Raymond, a lean, light-haired man with a lazy left eye, sitting behind the desk.

Vinny leaned over the desk so he could speak to the man who used to be his sergeant in Communications. "Maybe not all of them, but I've caught more in five years than you've had in twenty," he whispered.

Jordan hesitated and then said haltingly, "That may be, but I still make more money than you."

"Big deal," he said cheerfully. "I get all the excitement."

Jordan laughed raucously.

"My complainant pick anybody out of the photos yet?"

"Not yet."

Vinny shook his head. He could still hear her scream. It'd pierced him. He desperately hoped she could pick out her attacker's photo from the mug books.

Suddenly, the silence in the Command was broken by the screech of the radio dispatcher.

"All units, 10-10, man under the train, Tremont Avenue on the D Line. The call is coming from the train crew."

Vinny wavered, as though disoriented. "No way!" He met Jordan's gaze.

Vinny turned and walked a few feet to the detectives' office. "Keep her here until I call you. I got a strange feeling about this one."

He arrived at Tremont Avenue within five minutes.

The entire Grand Concourse was covered with emergency vehicles that had already responded. The precinct radio cars always respond to a Transit "man under" call.

It's a spectacle for cops and EMS workers to see what a person struck by a train looks like. Vinny had seen quite a few since he'd been on the job, and most of them were not pretty. The worst seem to be the kids who go "surfing," riding on top of a train. One minute they're on a fifty-mile-per-hour joyride, and the next minute, a steel beam smashes their heads off. Instant death.

Vinny walked up to an EMS crew and offered to carry some of their equipment into the subway. Walking behind him, they squatted under the yellow crime scene tape and jumped down onto the tracks. Walking carefully, they followed the beams of lights from the officers already with the victim.

The first silhouette he recognized in the illuminations of flashlights was Popi's.

"El Gato, I want you to see something!" he said.

Following close behind, Vinny trailed him to the side of the train. Squatting down, he brought his eyes level with the thief who stole the woman's purse. He was still clutching it to his chest.

"That's your boy, right?" Popi said shortly.

Vinny nodded somberly, looking at the shocked face of the thief. "It's my mother's purse," he said indignantly.

Vinny stared at him in disgust as the EMS workers handed the purse to one of the other cops.

"Hey, El Gato, look at this," Popi said, seemingly fascinated.

Vinny's eyes followed Popi's flashlight beam. It was aimed at the shiny steel wheels of the train.

Then he saw them, lying in the shadow on the tracks. Moving over, he picked them up, the criminal's legs, cut off with the precision of a surgeon's blade. The heat of the wheels had seared the veins and arteries. There was no blood. The mere sight of them was bewildering and terrifying.

Vinny shook his head. "Incredible."

Popi smiled indulgently. "What's incredible is that he doesn't have a leg to stand on in court."

Vinny returned a half-smile. "I guess he doesn't, amigo," he said as he handed the legs to an EMS worker. Vinny pointed at the purse the rookie officer was holding. "I gotta bring that back to the district."

The officer quickly handed it over. Vinny opened it to inspect its contents. Removing a bank envelope, he counted out the money in front of Popi and the rookie. He looked up at Popi's face with a look of exasperation. "Five hundred and sixty-four dollars. That man lost his legs for five hundred and sixty-four dollars," he repeated disbelievingly.

Popi lowered his eyes and stared at the money. "Well, he won't be snatching any more purses."

"Nah, I guess he won't."

By the end of that summer, Debbie became convinced that her miscarriage and, more recently, her inability to conceive were more than coincidences. She began to experience anxiety attacks and was soon placed on prescription drugs by her doctor to help alleviate them.

She'd been under tremendous pressure from her mother and eldest sister to seek the help of a fertility specialist. Vinny was totally against it but yielded to her wishes. He believed if they took their time and lessened the stress and pressure of trying to conceive, then she'd become pregnant. He just knew she'd conceive and deliver a beautiful child full of love and spirit, as loving as its mother. It was just a matter of time.

CHAPTER 8

D ebbie and Vinny appeared to be having a perfectly marvelous life. When people saw them together, they saw a couple in love. But what people didn't see, and it was always so, was a beautiful young woman slowly on the way to becoming clinically depressed.

Her eldest brother had had a baby girl, and her sister had just become pregnant again. Each time Debbie was around other people's children, she would later fall to pieces. One minute she'd be fine, but the next minute she'd become overwhelmed with emotion.

She'd undergone eighteen months of probing and testing by doctors. Along with eighteen months' worth of doctor bills and prescription fertility drugs, the total bill went about $1,200 a month. Fortunately, the overtime was plentiful due to increasing crime in the Bronx. But something gnawed at his mind and wouldn't stop. He wasn't sure working so many hours was healthy for their relationship. He lived responsibly and paid all their bills, but he was also reasonable and knew when to say enough is enough. She was distraught, and he yearned only to console her, to kiss her, and to make her distress go away.

"Okay, so this is what we'll do," he said cheerfully one night. "We forget all about these doctors and pills, and next month, we'll take a seven-day cruise to the Bahamas at Valentine's Day."

She wore a rueful look. "We can't afford it." She sounded weary. *This'll cheer her up.*

"If we couldn't afford it, how did I get these?" He produced two plane tickets to Miami and the cruise tickets from his pocket. "Happy Valentine's Day, and happy eight-year wedding anniversary!"

She was astonished.

"But how—"

"Shhh," he said softly, placing his index finger over her lips. "No more doctors, no more pressure, no more talk of babies. If we can't get pregnant, then we'll adopt. But I'm not going to have the woman I adore be torn apart by this."

She never took her eyes off his.

"Okay?" he asked with a bright smile.

She rose from the table and went to him. "Okay." She hugged him and whispered in his ear, "I have the most wonderful husband in the world, the most handsome man anywhere."

"You don't have to go that far! The tickets are paid for, and they're nonrefundable."

"You're nonrefundable!"

They sailed on the *Norway*, at that time the largest cruise ship in the world. It took them to Saint Maarten, Saint Thomas, and a private island.

The fantastic time they had was better than any prescription a doctor could write. They talked and laughed and spent each night making love slowly and gently, as though they were both innocents, as though it was the first time for both of them, and they had the rest of their lives to spend together. When they looked into each other's eyes, all they saw was love. When they returned to Miami, he extended their holiday a week and checked in to the Fontainebleau Hilton.

He fervently hoped she would stop drinking for a while and stop taking her antidepressants. But it was not to be. His love was clouding his objectivity.

On their return, they told her mother that they'd decided to give up on the fertility specialists. It was a huge drain on their budget, and nothing had come of it. Her response was surprising. She neither raged or berated, which was what Debbie expected, with something closely related to terror. Instead, her mother had smiled her little nonsmile, folded her arms across her chest, and said simply, "If you don't want to have children, that's fine with me." Her mother was hard to figure out.

When they moved to North Broadway, Debbie thought her mother would be happy that they had a bigger place with a second bedroom for the baby. Instead, the first time she came over, she settled back on their living room sofa and complained about having to walk up three short flights of stairs to reach their apartment. Debbie specifically wanted an apartment on the top floor so no one would be living above them. Another motive was so she could enjoy sunbathing in private on the terrace.

Vinny always had a vague perception that something was off-key. But he couldn't quite figure it out. He'd tried desperately to keep her happy for Debbie's sake. On a cop's salary, it wasn't easy. Debbie felt she was always in competition with her brothers and sisters. Her eldest brother had an extremely well-paying job in the family oil business. He provided his wife with nothing but the best. Her eldest sister had married a man who was also in his family's painting business. They'd bought a $300,000 home in Rockland County. She and her kids had whatever they wanted. Her other brother also married well and bought a big house, also in Rockland County. Lastly, her younger sister was engaged to a man who was extremely successful in advertising, had a luxurious penthouse on the eastside of Manhattan, and was pure Italian. From the moment he'd begun dating Debbie, that was something Vinny had been reminded he wasn't. Her mother played games, very contrived, power games. She was a control freak who had to have her say. Vinny wished Debbie would make a choice between him and her mother. Take a stand. Tell her to butt out so she could do what she wanted. But no matter the circumstances, he always ended up the loser. Well, to hell with her mother and her cold, imperious manner. He would demand respect from her even if Debbie wouldn't.

As the weeks since their return passed, Debbie's tendency to be willful resurfaced. They were back to square one with the fertility specialists and the bills. They tried artificial insemination and in vitro fertilization in addition to her daily fertility drugs. Each time she got her period, she would not talk for two days, despite all his efforts to cheer her up. All she would do was lie in bed, sipping wine and downing pills.

"All for nothing," she would say repeatedly. "I'll never have a baby." Bitter, angry tears ran from her eyes.

At work, Vinny's performance began to suffer. Captain Shore had retired and was replaced by one of the few black captains on the TP. No doubt he would soon be promoted to deputy inspector.

Vinny's sometimes-unorthodox ways of doing things didn't sit well with his new captain, nor with Timmy Dunston, his anti-crime sergeant. Dunston was a reformed alcoholic and born-again Christian. Before getting promoted, he'd been a clerical cop, working inside desk duty—a "house mouse." How he managed to become an anticrime sergeant was one of life's mysteries. He knew nothing about undercover police work and couldn't find a Jew in Tel Aviv, but there you have it, he was the new boss.

Fortunately, it wasn't long before an opportunity presented itself and Vinny could return to patrol. One day, he'd asked an officer on the desk to sign him off duty after driving a sick cop home. Cops are supposed to sign off duty in person at the front desk, but circumstances arise when that rule can be bent. A cop calling in off duty from court or a hospital to save him a trip back to the Command is done frequently. But when Vinny did it, Sergeant Dunston used it as an excuse to send him back to uniform as punishment, a punishment he'd gladly accepted. Being assigned to steady day tours would allow him the opportunity to be home at night with his wife, where he was desperately needed and wanted to be.

She was delighted to have him home for supper. Financially, they had almost no savings. They'd spent nearly everything on their last vacation and doctor bills, but money no longer mattered. They were together and extremely happy. And once again, they had abolished any future plans on visiting fertility doctors. To his delight, she also cut down her consumption of alcohol and rarely showed any outward signs of depression when her periods came. He explained to her that everything happens for a reason and someday the sun finally will shine on them.

It was the end of March when Vinny's father's terrible call came. Mike Flanagan, his father's best friend, had passed away. "An unexpected heart attack," his father had said. Vinny thought the world of Mike. For if it were not for Mike, Vinny's father not only would have never met his stepmother but he might also not have lived past that eventful day.

Vinny vividly remembered the day it happened. It was near the end of the same summer his mother had died in 1972. It was a hot, sunny day. He and his brothers were playing in the backyard pool of their Bay Ridge home. Their grandmother had taken his baby sister with her food shopping. The phone, off-limits to the kids unless it was an emergency, had been ringing relentlessly. He'd entered the house through the rear patio door and immediately heard a song blasting out on the stereo in the basement.

"What now, my love, now that you're gone? I'd be a fool to go on and on." The voice was Elvis Presley's.

"Dad, the phone's ringing!" he yelled loudly, hoping his father would answer it.

After getting no response, he answered the phone, thinking it might be an emergency.

"Hello?"

"Vincent, is that you?" Mike's voice asked frantically.

"Uncle Mike?" he asked hesitantly.

"Yes, Vincent, it's me, Uncle Mike. Where's your father?" he asked nervously.

Vinny paused for a moment. "He's in the basement, I think. The stereo's on real loud."

"Listen to me carefully, son. I want you to go down in the basement and stay with your dad until I get there."

Vinny instinctively tensed. Mike's tone was soft, but there was something alarming about it.

"Is everything all right, Uncle Mike?"

"Everything is fine, son. Just please do as I say like a good lad," Mike said in a calming voice.

"Okay, Uncle Mike, I'll do it!"

"Good lad. I'm on my way!"

Vinny hung up the phone and walked to the basement door. When he opened it, he could hear the song again being played at full blast. The words grew louder as he descended the steps.

"I felt the world closing in on me. Here come the stars, tumbling around me. And there's the sky, where the sea should be."

He reached the bottom of the stairs but still hadn't seen his father.

"No one would care, no one would cry, if I should live or die! What now, my love, now that there's nothing? Only my last goodbye! Only my last goodbye!"

The music stopped. It was then that he saw his father standing in the darkness, rewinding his old reel-to-reel tape player.

"Dad?" he asked worriedly.

His father spun around quickly, startled to see his son standing there in a dripping bathing suit.

"What are you doing down here?" he asked, sounding weary and impatient.

Vinny looked around nervously, then his eyes came to rest on a gun on his father's workbench. "I want you to come upstairs with me," he said in a low, wounded voice.

"In a little while," his father said tensely, tossing a rag over the gun and the cleaning materials.

"No, Dad, now," he said defiantly.

"Why does it have to be now, son?" he asked, putting up a semblance of a fight.

Even as a ten-year-old child, he'd had the instinct for danger and was smart enough to see through his father's composed expression.

"Because I don't want to be alone right now."

His father's eyes narrowed, not sure where his son was going with this. At ten years old, could he have figured out what he'd planned to do?

"Please, Dad!" he said, glaring at his father sternly.

"All right," he sighed with disappointment. "But only for a little while. I have to finish cleaning my gun." He picked it up and placed it on top of a tall cabinet.

"Thanks, Dad."

For what seemed like an eternity but was more like twenty minutes, he sat on the living room couch, staring at his father, who wasn't even aware he was there. He kept humming the words of the song over and over. With each verse, his eyes would glaze even more.

The doorbell rang. It pulled his father from his reverie.

"I'll get it, Dad," he said excitedly. He jumped off the couch and ran to the door.

Immediately he opened the door, and Mike asked hopefully, "Is he with you, son?"

"On the couch."

"Good boy." Mike smiled. "Now, go play in the pool with your brothers while I talk to your dad."

Vinny gave him a deferential look.

"Your dad's okay. He just misses your mom a lot. Let me talk to him awhile, then we'll share a beer. Just me and you," Mike said gamely.

"You got a deal, Mike," he said as he ran through the living room, yelling, "See ya in a little while, Dad!"

It was also Mike who introduced Vinny's dad to his stepmother and, two years later, was best man at their wedding.

His stepmother was a very attractive woman, with a voice that made angels sing. She was the spitting image of Julie Andrews but could sing the soundtrack of *The Sound of Music* better than Julie on her best day. This woman was not only striking, but she was also deeply blessed with an inner beauty. Not only could she sing, but she also, if there were truly a pot of gold at the end of a rainbow, then the end of the rainbow would end at her heart. Unlike the wicked stepmothers portrayed in movies, the Davis children were blessed with an angel handpicked by their mother in heaven to take care of them. She gave her love to them as if they were her own unconditionally. And in return, she was loved and respected by them as their mom.

It wasn't until Vinny was fifteen years old, when his father brought him to the police academy range at Rodman's Neck in the Bronx, that he'd learned what his father had planned to do that hot summer afternoon. For it was that day at the range that Vinny learned of a cop who'd shot himself with his own gun. He overheard the cops talking about how the dead officer had his gun-cleaning kit out and how the department couldn't decide if his death was a suicide or an accidental discharge. Being distracted while cleaning your gun, accidentally shooting yourself, your family is entitled to insurance money and department benefits. But intentionally falling victim to your own bullet leaves your family with nothing. Although Vinny and his father never discussed it, he knew what his father intended to do that day.

Yes, Mike Flanagan, the Davis family is forever in your debt for what you did. And now you are gone to heaven too. You and Mom will have many long talks and plenty of laughs. Be sure to ask her to sing for you. Remember how lovely her voice is? Don't forget. But no need to rush. You have forever.

It was almost 6:00 p.m. by the time the Davis boys had helped their father clear out Mike's apartment in Queens. It had been an exhausting day loading and unloading the truck, and Vinny was dying to get home to have dinner with Debbie. He'd agreed to drop his brother Michael off at the Davis house in Yonkers so his father could drive straight home to New Jersey from Queens.

He and Michael were stopped at a traffic light on Central Avenue. Vinny looked toward his brother in the passenger seat to answer a question when his eyes almost shot out of their sockets.

"What's the matter?" Michael asked despairingly, meeting his brother's glare.

"That's Richard Sabol!" he exploded, pointing to the driver of a Silver BMW stopped right next to them.

Michael spun around in his seat to look out his window. Almost simultaneously, Sabol glanced out his window in their direction.

Vinny's eyes widened as adrenaline shot through his body. Sabol smiled arrogantly as Vinny blinked uncomprehendingly. "I don't believe this shit."

Michael was completely thrown off.

"Are you sure that's him?" he asked, never taking his eyes off him.

As the light changed, Sabol gave a sadistic grin before throwing a huge cigar in his mouth, then took off.

Vinny was hesitant.

"Let's go after him!" Michael's voice was heavy with anger.

Vinny stared at the car in disbelief as it drove off, making a mental note of the Connecticut tags.

Michael looked at Vinny quizzically. "Aren't you going to go after him?"

Vinny laughed nastily. "I'm a cop. I can't do that."

Michael looked faintly amused. "Well, I'm not! Go after him and I'll throw him the beating of his fucking life!"

Vinny smiled maliciously. "That's just what he wants us to do," he said calmly.

Michael smiled back with equal malicious satisfaction. "That smile on your face tells me you have a plan."

"The guy he was in the car with was his codefendant on his last case. I think I'll have a chat with his parole officer first thing in the morning," Vinny said, trying to sound reasonable about it.

Michael's face creased with concern. "I thought he was doing twelve years? What's he doing out, anyway?"

Vinny gazed over at Michael. "I haven't got a clue, but I know for sure he's up to no good."

"Just be careful, big brother. That bastard's psycho!"

"Don't worry, I will. I'd better drop you off. I've gotta get home."

Vinny entered his house and poured himself a glass of wine. Debbie was tending to the barbecue.

"Did you know that your lunatic ex-boyfriend is out of prison?"

Her eyes widened in amazement. "How do you know that?"

"Because I just saw him in a car on Central Avenue about twenty minutes ago."

Debbie turned a steak on the barbecue.

"When did he get sentenced, 1986? This is 1991. That's only five years. You told me he'd be gone for twelve years," she said scornfully. "How the hell did he get out in less than half his time?"

"I'm clueless."

Her hands were clenched around the barbecue tongs so tightly her knuckles turned white. "Are you sure it was him?"

"Listen, honey, I don't know what the hell happened, but I plan on finding out first thing in the morning. Now, will you give me those things before your hand starts to bleed?" he said playfully, taking the tongs from her. "Here. Have a glass of wine to calm your nerves. There's no use worrying about it tonight."

She smiled and relaxed as she took it.

"I love you," he said in a warm, calming voice.

"I love you too." She hugged him tightly.

"Everything will be all right. Don't worry."

His abrupt intrusion on Sabol and his codefendant had been sheer coincidence. But since good cops don't believe in coincidence, he chalked it all up to God's way of maintaining his anonymity.

Sabol was too smart to be caught on purpose associating with a convicted felon, a parole violation that would send him back to prison. No, he must have turned informant and decided to work for the government in return for his early release.

Vinny had agonized for hours before finally coming to the conclusion that the most realistic thing he could do would be to call the United States Probation Office, explain who he was, and ask for help. In essence, going cap in hand to them in the hopes that they'd be able to protect him and his family. With luck, they would offer protection for his family and perhaps, in the best of all cases, consider the circumstances, revoke Sabol's parole, and send him back to prison to finish his sentence. After all, he not only threatened to kill just Debbie, but he'd also threatened to kill four FBI agents in open court.

His first phone call was made to the Manhattan office of US Probation. After speaking to a supervisor, explaining who he was and the past threats of violence by Sabol, he was referred to a parole officer by the name of Joe Mangeletti in White Plains. After several attempts to contact him by phone during the day, he finally managed to catch him before going off duty.

"Officer Mangeletti, my name is Vincent Davis with the Transit Police in New York."

"What can I do for you, Officer?" he asked politely.

"Well, I spoke to a supervisor of Probation earlier in Manhattan. He gave me your name and phone number. He said you're assigned for a Richard Sabol."

"What's he done already?" he asked disgustedly.

Vinny laughed shortly. "Well, that's just it. I don't know if he's done anything," he said hesitantly.

"You mean you don't have that prick in handcuffs for something right now?"

"I wish I did, but I don't."

"Too bad. What can I do for you, then?"

Vinny took a deep breath, then explained the story that started almost eleven years ago. When he finished, he could hear a sigh of frustration on the other end of the line.

"I tell you what, you come in here and make a federal complaint and I'll gladly revoke his probation. But I've got to warn you, this guy Sabol's a crazy son of a bitch. He threatened to kill one probation officer already. If you swear out a complaint and violate him, I can't promise you he won't be back out in a little over a year."

"A year?"

"That's right, Officer, a year. Eighteen months tops. And with this guy's tendency toward violence, you can bet your ass he'll make good his threats then."

"What? Are you trying to tell me I should let him get away with violating his parole in fear of what he will do when he gets out? That's insane."

"I'm just telling you the facts of life regarding his probation," he said defensively. "Now, if he is to get arrested again on another charge, then he'll be looking at a lot more time."

Vinny pondered for a moment, trying to control his temper.

It's not this guy's fault that the federal justice system's all fucked up.

"How about you set up a meeting with Sabol at the probation office so I can talk to him?" Vinny asked curiously.

"For what?" he asked suspiciously.

"I just want to have a man-to-man talk with him to make sure he doesn't go near my wife's job," Vinny said coolly.

"You know as well as I do, Officer, that we're dealing with a very dangerous individual. I don't think it's a good idea you meet him."

You're right. It's probably not a good idea. Fuck. What am I gonna do? "Well, I'll tell you what, Officer? Forget that I called. I appreciate your insight into the federal justice system, but I'll wait until Mr. Sabol decides to catch another charge. I'm sure he's working on some elaborate criminal enterprise as we speak."

"I wouldn't doubt it for a minute. If there's anything else I can help you with, feel free to call."

"I'll do that, and thanks again, Officer. I really appreciate it."

"Anytime, Davis, and be careful."

Within two days of Vinny's phone call to Officer Mangeletti, Sabol was on the defensive. He'd called and stopped by Debbie's office to inform her that if Vinny interfered with him in any way or dared call his probation officer again, she'd be the one to pay the price.

Vinny went ballistic and stormed into his captain's office to complain. "I'm dead serious, Captain, this is nothing to joke about!"

Captain Stevens was medium-built, almost completely gray-haired, with a fine, humble-looking face.

Vinny's gaze searched his expression.

"Captain, please. I know I've had my impulsive moments, but this isn't one of them."

"Maybe, but it's not like you to run scared just because some punk hoodlum decided to threaten your wife."

"This isn't just some punk chain-snatcher I arrested in the sub-way. This guy is a murderer who's been in and out of prison for the last ten years. He knows where my wife works!"

Stevens looked up, puzzled. There was a knock on the door. It was Sergeant Houston.

"Come in," Stevens said curtly. "Sergeant Houston, maybe you can be of some assistance in this mess, since you've worked as an FBI clerk."

Vinny turned his gaze to Sergeant Houston, the District 11 administrative sergeant assigned to clerical duties.

After Stevens explained the story, Houston looked bemused.

"Do you have any evidence or a number of someone we can call to verify what you're saying is true?" he asked, seemingly fascinated.

As Stevens handed Houston a copy of the presentencing memo he'd gotten at Sabol's sentencing, Vinny brusquely pushed a piece of paper under his nose with the name and phone number of the federal probation officer.

Sergeant Houston read the presentencing memo voraciously, then turned to Stevens.

"I know the agent from New Rochelle that arrested this guy back in 1987. I can call him and find out what he knows."

"Good. In the meantime, your request for weekends off is denied. If you want weekends off to be with your wife, put a request in to use your vacation time, but they'll only be granted on individual manpower basis. I'm also going to issue you a radio to keep in your house and care in case you need help. That's all I can do for now."

"Thank you, sir," Vinny said, with a look of exasperation.

Captain Stevens grinned. "You bet."

Vinny walked out of the office, with Houston on his heels. "Hey, Vinny, come with me to my office. I want to talk to you." They entered the office, and Vinny immediately took a seat.

"I'll make you a deal, Vinny. You keep up the good work on patrol and I'll put you to work for me in anticrime."

Vinny frowned. "Very funny, Sarge, but you're not the anti-crime sergeant. No-Balls Dunston is."

Houston grinned widely.

"No-Balls is getting promoted to lieutenant next month, and Captain Stevens asked me if I want the job."

For only an instant, Vinny's eyes widened with excitement.

"What would Captain Stevens say about that?" he asked suspiciously.

Houston smiled smugly. "I already asked him about you, and he thinks you should be in anticrime. Shit, you've got the best felony arrest record of any cop who works here. You're a little overzealous, but that's all right. There's nothing wrong with being ambitious and aggressive. That's what makes you a good cop. You've only had one civilian complaint in the past five years: for rearing up that kid's bus pass after he cursed you out and spit in your face. That's a vast improvement from 1985. If that kid spit in my face, I would have torn up more than his bus pass."

Vinny's brow immediately furrowed. "Listen, Sarge, right now my main concern is my wife's safety, not getting my ass blown off in anticrime."

Houston backed off. It was clearly not the right time to approach him. "I was only asking," he said, fidgeting uncomfortably behind his desk.

Vinny nodded miserably. "I don't mean to sound ungrateful, I really don't, but you can understand that my wife's safety means more to me than this job ever could."

Houston grimaced.

"Listen, Vinny. I'm going to call my friend Agent Stamp over at the FBI and find out what I can about this nut Sabol. In the meantime, if you could, maybe find out some information from your sources on the streets. Maybe you can bag this guy yourself or help the feds bag him and get a gold shield in the process."

"What makes you think so?"

"You think a guy like this," he said disgustedly, holding up Sabol's presentencing memo, "goes to federal prison and finds God? Maybe God gave him the money for that BMW you saw him driving, huh?"

Houston's right. If Sabol's hanging around Yonkers and his codefendant, he is up to something illegal. "I'll see what I can find out, Sarge." He then stood up to go and added, "But make sure you call your FBI friend today."

Houston nodded. "I'll call him right now," he said, picking up the phone as Vinny left the office.

Later that day, at home, Vinny told Debbie that they had to take certain precautions until additional action could be taken to end Sabol's renewed threat.

"Why do I have to stay at my parent's house if there's nothing to worry about?" Debbie asked wearily as she packed a suitcase in their bedroom.

"It's just a precaution," Vinny said simply. "Come on, baby, it's just for a couple of weeks until Probation has a talk with Sabol."

She sensed the bitterness layered beneath the lightness of his last utterance. "I just want you to know I don't think it's fair that I'm forced out of my own home because of this."

He smiled mischievously. "Think of all the fun we'll have making love in your old bedroom like we used to when your parents were out."

That sexy thought stayed with her as she continued to pack, smiling quietly to herself. She felt so comfortable and safe with him. He wasn't always the tough cop whose work amazed her, or the relentlessly determined man who'd do anything to protect her. He was a generous gentleman, vulnerable. He was the man she'd instantly fallen in love with, who made her feel she was the most important person in the world.

By the summer, Houston had made good on his promise to reassign him to the anticrime unit. Houston spent his time well when he'd go on patrol with Vinny. He'd not only filled him with admiration and enthusiasm but also primed him to do the job he loved. Houston hadn't been out from behind a desk in a long time and was thoroughly enjoying his days on patrol. But Vinny was convinced not to act compulsively and, thereby, compromise Houston's safety. He still had to relearn to trust his own judgment. Being a cop isn't like riding a bike. Sometimes it takes time to adjust to being back in the jungle.

It was a hot summer, and subway crime was skyrocketing. The anticrime unit's tours of duty were adjusted to meet the captain's needs. Some weeks they would work 6:00 a.m. to 2:00 p.m.; others would be 6:00 p.m. to 2:00 a.m. On Friday nights, which had become prime time for robbery and shooting sprees, they worked from 8:00 p.m. to 8:00 a.m.

Vinny didn't mind. He loved the excitement, and the overtime pay he was making helped tremendously with Debbie's mounting medical bills. She didn't seem to mind either. She was handling her depression much better, spending more time going out with her girlfriends at night, something that never bothered him, because he trusted her implicitly. He was convinced their marriage was rock-solid. She might be extremely overworked and under tremendous pressure about having a child, but she had more guts than any woman he'd ever met. He understood why her temper erupted on occasion. He expelled and accepted it. After almost nine years of marriage, they'd still never gone to bed mad at each other. They were as comfortable together as they were when they'd first met.

Vinny ordered two cups of coffee at the counter and took them over to a small booth and sat down with Allan, his partner for the day. Allan had gone through the academy with him and was extremely intelligent. He was thirty-three years old, with shocking red hair, bright-blue eyes, and pale Irish skin that burned in the shade. As an anticrime cop, he stood out like a sore thumb. Every criminal in the Bronx made him out as a cop. But Vinny didn't mind working with him, for he was also blessed with the black cloud that continued to bring trouble his way.

"Thank you," Allan said politely as Vinny placed the cup of coffee in front of him.

Allan gazed at him curiously.

"Why are you giving me that look, Allan?"

"It's too quiet."

"Do you think that means something?"

"Yeah, sure," he said, giving him a skeptical glance as he sipped his coffee. Vinny knew from experience that out of quiet times traumatic events often erupted.

"It means the Big Guy upstairs thinks I'm too busy today to be chasing bad guys," he said sarcastically.

Allan shook his head. "It means the shit's going to hit the fan real soon."

Vinny looked at him reassuringly. "You can' t always get what you want, Allan."

Allan was probably right. The excitement was growing every minute of every day on the streets of the Bronx.

Vinny was close to collapsing from exhaustion from the amount of overtime he was put in.

Vinny glanced away from Allan and deliberately reined in any sign of confirmation to his suspicions.

"Do you want to hit Bedford Park Station next?" Allan asked eagerly. Vinny took a sip of coffee and put it down on the counter.

Mr. Enthusiastic. He hasn't paid attention to a word I said.

"Whatever you want, Allan."

Suddenly, they heard an officer's shout over the other routine chatter on their radio.

"Ten-thirteen, Central. Shots fired. Bedford on the 4 Line!"

"Holy shit!" Allan shouted in amazement at the coincidence.

"It's what you wanted, isn't it? Come on!"

They ran out of the diner and into the street. Allan scanned traffic for a car to commandeer. Vinny saw a city bus and ordered it to stop.

"What are you doing?"

"I'm borrowing a bus. Now get in!"

"Are you out of your mind?"

"Get in, or I'll leave you here!"

Allan was tempted to argue with him but instead found himself acquiescing. He knew Vinny was taking the bus and there'd be no changing his mind.

Allan stepped on the bus and stood beside Vinny and asked curiously, "You do know this is bad, right?"

Vinny grinned mischievously. "I know. Straight ahead, driver, and don't stop till Bedford Park."

The driver's lips thinned. "You're the boss!" he said, bewildered by the sudden interruption of his boring routine of driving the bus.

They heard the frantic officer on their radio. "Male, Hispanic, eighteen, white T-shirt with blues. He's running south on Jerome Avenue, Central!"

"Slow down, driver, he's headed right for us." Vinny pointed out the windshield. He turned to Allan. "Go to the rear door! When we stop, jump out of the door when I tell you to." Then to the passengers, "You people, put your head's down!"

Everyone ducked.

The bus driver's ebony skin had turned ash white. Anger ebbed as anxiety flooded him.

"That kid's got a gun!" the driver cried out as they got closer.

"Amazing! Absolutely amazing."

The driver glared scornfully at Vinny. "Are you crazy?"

"Some people say that. Allan, are you ready?"

"As ready as I'll ever be!"

The suspect on the pavement was now but a few yards away.

"Stop the bus and open the doors!" From his place at the door, Vinny shouted, "Police, don't move!"

Allan was off first.

"Don't even think about it!" Vinny shouted as the suspect turned toward him, looking directly down the barrel of his gun.

The shots rang out simultaneously as the suspect raised his weapon and turned on Allan. Instantly, the suspect crumbled to the sidewalk. Vinny instinctively grabbed his radio.

"Shots fired, 196th Street and Jerome. Send EMS!" he said. "Allan, are you all right?"

"I don't know." He seemed bewildered.

"Are you hit?" Vinny asked impatiently, unable to mask the tension in his voice.

Anger suddenly jarred Allan out of his bewilderment. He whirled on Vinny. "Why did he turn on me?" he asked in disbelief.

Radio cars with screaming sirens were pulling up at the curb. The bus driver had hightailed it the second they'd jumped off.

"Are you guys all right?" a police sergeant asked, his voice heavy with concern.

His face was lean and tanned as his body, with a wide mouth and blue-green eyes.

"We're okay, boss," Vinny said somberly.

"What unit you guys with?" he asked quickly.

"Transit anticrime," Vinny said calmly, running his fingers through his hair.

"Five-two sergeant to Central K," he said into his radio.

"Two sergeant, K," the dispatcher replied.

"Two sergeant. Have Transit supervisor respond to my location for an MOS shooting, K," he said simply. *MOS* meaning a "member of the service"" involved in a shooting.

The sergeant looked at the suspect on the sidewalk.

"This is the guy who just shot those two schoolkids from the Bronx School of Science. He let a couple of rounds go at one of your Transit cars at Bedford Park."

Vinny went rigid. "Any of our cops shot?"

"No, thank God, and the two kids this piece of shit shot look like they'll make it." He paused for a moment while the EMS workers gathered around the fallen suspect. He looked at Vinny. "Nice shooting."

"Yeah, thanks."

A week after the bus incident, Vinny was back in Captain Stevens's office. "A city bus?" Captain Stevens asked incredulously as he rifled through a report on his desk.

Vinny shrugged indifferently. "It's not like I made the driver go off his route or something. He was headed in that direction, anyway." He tried to sound reasonable about it.

Stevens looked up quizzically. "But a city bus filled with passengers? You were on Kingsbridge Road. You couldn't find any other way to get to the call?"

"Well, there was on armored car in front of Chemical Bank, but I didn't think the guards would take too kindly to two guys with guns out asking them for a ride."

Stevens struggled to smother a smile.

"The bus driver went out on stress, you know."

"For what? He's a bus driver in the Bronx, for Christ's sake. What's he saying, that that's the first time he's seen a kid with a gun?" Vinny started to laugh.

"It isn't funny," Stevens said gloomily. "He may even sue you!"

"I doubt it. I don't have anything worth suing for."

"I'm trying to tell you, we've got a situation here. The Transit Authority not looking at this in the best light."

"Well, tell the TA to give us some unmarked cars and we won't have to inconvenience gypsy cabdrivers, private citizens, or city bus drivers to get to an emergency call."

Captain Stevens glanced away quickly. Vinny had struck a nerve. He knew Transit anticrime cops needed to be mobile, to be able to respond quickly to emergency calls.

"Well, at least you didn't steal the bus like you did with that cabdriver in Manhattan."

"You know 'bout that caper?"

"Come on! The entire division knows about that little incident."

"It was a good arrest, Captain."

"I know it was a good arrest. They don't give out Cop of the Month awards for bad ones. Listen, Vinny. You're disgustingly dedicated, extremely loyal, and an excellent cop. I like you, but sometimes you do things that are so close to crossing the line that you become a proverbial pain in the ass."

This is amusing. This guy's even better than Captain Shore. I wonder how he'll handle it if I "Yes, sir" him to death.

"I'll take that as a compliment, Captain."

A curious and thoughtful look crossed Stevens's face. "You guys were using your own cars for patrol over the summer, weren't you?"

"Yes, sir," he said cautiously.

"Good." Stevens grinned and leaned forward on his desk. "I'm going to tell Houston that from now on, I want at least two teams out there on patrol in their private vehicles, and I think you should be one of them. I might be crazy doing this, but I think it's the right thing to do. God knows, next time you might commandeer a station wagon full of nuns to bring you to your next gun battle."

It's about time. This guy's all right.

"I wish only to accommodate the needs of the department, sir."

"Get out!"

"Ten-four, sir!" he said, snapping to attention, and saluted.

"Be careful out there, Davis."

"I will, sir, I certainly will."

In November, Vinny received fantastic news from the Yonkers rumor mill. The beast had been arrested by the DEA in Georgia for attempting to sell two kilos of cocaine to an undercover DEA agent. It was also rumored Sabol planned on ratting on—testifying against—his nine drug-smuggling buddies who were arrested with him, in return for a lighter sentence. But not if Vinny could help it. A two-kilo sale should earn Sabol a life sentence, and if Vinny got his way, that was exactly what he'd get, no deals.

"I'm telling you, Sarge, the DEA got Sabol with two kilos in Georgia. All I'm asking you to do is call your friend Agent Stamp and ask him to call the DEA and confirm what I heard."

"I still think you have an obsession with this Sabol character," he said, his tone full of skepticism.

"Are you kidding? If it were you dealing with this bullshit for eleven fucking years, you'd think differently."

"All right, I'll call him," Houston said, trying to accommodate him and appear empathetic. "But how come you didn't tell me Sabol was running drugs from Florida to New York when you found out?"

Vinny laughed bitterly. "Why? So you can tell me again that you think I'm obsessed with the guy?"

Houston frowned but knew Vinny was right. "Touché. I'll make the call." He hesitated, then said, "But if you're wrong about this, it's your ass."

"I'm not wrong. Trust me."

Houston met his gaze. "For your sake, I hope you're right." He was simultaneously joking and serious.

"You believe in coincidence, Sarge?"

Houston's eyes narrowed, not sure where he was going with it. "Sometimes. Why?"

"You shouldn't, boss. A good cop knows there's no such thing as coincidence."

"I'll try to keep that one in mind," he replied in a superior, know-it-all manner.

"You do that. It might save your life one day," he said, then turned and left.

What an asshole. He never believes me, always doubts me, and always gives me a fucking hard time. God, how I love to bust his chops. It's the only way I can get even with the fuck.

Two weeks later, Bubba Parker and Vinny sat in his car on a robbery stakeout at 170th Street and Jerome Avenue, under the subway el.

"One more hour, El Cato, and we're home free," Bubba said enthusiastically. Since Vinny had spoken with Houston, FBI Agent Stamp had confirmed Sabol indeed had been arrested on the cocaine charge. Houston apologized to Vinny, who accepted it with grace.

No sense rubbing his face in shit, and there's no such thing as coincidence. Christ, the scuttlebutt in Yonkers was true.

"Do you think there'll be any food left when we get there?" Bubba asked nervously.

Harry Hernandez's wedding reception had already started at 7:00 p.m. The guys in the anticrime team had drawn straws to see who would be on the stakeout. It was scheduled to end at 8:00 p.m. They lost and would be late.

"I'm sure the girls will save us some food, Bubba."

Bubba raised an eyebrow. "Maybe your beautiful wife might, but mine…" He paused and shook his head vigorously.

"No way!"

Vinny held in a laugh. He'd met Bubba's wife at a few District 11 parties and barbecues. He was right—he didn't stand an Eskimo's chance in hell that she'd save him any food. Not that she was overweight—they didn't get along very well.

"Speaking of beautiful women," Bubba said quickly, "have you seen that DA since you and Allan were in court last week?"

Vinny looked at Bubba, puzzled.

"Don't give me that what-are-you-talking-about look, El Gato. You know the one I'm talking about. She was the one interviewing you on that Bedford Park shooting. The one that was looking at you like you were the last piece of white meat on Thanksgiving Day!"

Vinny smiled innocently. "You mean Christina Fusco?"

"You mean Christina Fusco?" Bubba mocked. "You know damn well I'm talking about her."

He hadn't thought the way Christina was acting that day was obvious to anyone else. There was a strong physical attraction, but

Vinny wouldn't be drawn into a marital misstep by sex. He remained cool and analytical.

He did, however, felt a warm rush when he thought about her. She was unbelievably sexy.

"In case you haven't noticed, I'm married."

Bubba laughed. "Oh, excuse me! If it were me and that woman looked at me like that, I'd do it right there on her desk and wouldn't care if my wife were watching. That bitch is F-I-N-E, fine!"

"Give it a break, will you, Bubba?"

He sensed Vinny's frustration. A few months ago, he was happy-go-lucky. Now he seemed annoyed and impatient. "That the hell's wrong with you?" Vinny took in a deep breath of the cool night air.

"Nothing, Bubba. I'm just tired, that's all." He was upset, but he wouldn't talk about it.

For some time, something had been wrong with Debbie. It wasn't constant, and he couldn't put his finger on it, whatever it really was. It was as though all the frustration and tumult she'd experienced since her miscarriage was festering inside her. She went from lethargy to spending more and more time out with her friends, drinking, then back again. On her nights out with the girls, she started coming home at erratic hours. At first, he'd thought it was due to her trouble conceiving, combined with worries about Sabol's threats. Then, oddly, when he'd told her Sabol was locked up in Georgia, she became even more introverted. She seemed truly upset by this good news. She didn't react the way he expected. Instead, she came across as actually hoping he'd reform himself and make a better life for himself in Florida. Their sex life evaporated too. Vinny couldn't remember the last time they'd made love. Now, tonight, Bubba had reminded him of a stunning woman who had an animalistic sexual attraction to him, and that made him feel vulnerable. That was a feeling he wanted to avoid at all costs. What he wanted was for everything to return to normal with his wife, a more tranquil life, with no more complications.

Boom!

"What the fuck was—"

Crash!

A crutch landed on the hood of Vinny's car. It could only have fallen off the subway El above them.

"Holy shit, Vinny. They shot a fucking cripple!" Bubba exploded.

Vinny calmly picked up his radio off the front seat. "Eleven, Crime One. Ten-Eighty-Five. Shots fired, 176th Street on the Number 4 line."

"All units! Ten-eight-five, from the officers."

"Let's go, Bubba."

"That was a big gun."

No time for fear.

They got out of the car, drew their guns, and scanned the area.

"Stay close to me, Bubba," he whispered as they climbed the stairs to the mezzanine.

Never separate from your partner. Never.

At the top of the stairs, they heard voices. "That was great fuckin' shot, bro!"

Vinny signaled Bubba. *I go high, you go low, while down on one knee aiming at the suspects.* Bubba was positioned directly above him. "Police, don't move!" Vinny snapped.

The taller suspect had a murderous gleam in his eyes and raised his weapon at them.

The second suspect's eyes widened in horror as he desperately attempted to yank his gun from his waistband.

It was as if God pushed a slow-motion button on life as the shots rang out. Then, almost instantly, it was over.

"Cover me, cover me, cover me," Bubba repeated frantically as he cautiously approached the two suspects on the ground.

Vinny inched slowly with his weapon aimed at his head as Bubba quickly cuffed them.

They could hear the sirens rapidly approaching and the railroad clerk talking rapidly into the phone.

"Twice in two months." Vinny laughed warily. "This black cloud has got to go."

The sirens began to grow steadier, louder. Bubba looked up with a face of exasperation.

"What location did you have it over the radio?" he asked accusingly.

Vinny stared back at him in bewilderment. "Ah, 176th Street. Why?"

Bubba raised a brow. "Because we're at 170th Street."

"Oh, shit," Vinny mumbled.

They'd been on a stakeout at 176th Street all day. He'd forgotten they'd moved.

Bubba quickly pulled out his radio, which was tucked into his bulletproof vest.

He remembered Vinny tossing his on the front seat of the car before they exited it.

"Eleven, Crime One. Ten-thirteen 170th Street on the 4 Line. Don't worry, El Gato, I have my moments of madness too."

Vinny half-smiled.

Bubba did have some doubtful charms.

"I guess we're going to miss the wedding," Vinny said philosophically.

Bubba laughed derisively. "You are one crazy son of a bitch, Davis."

Lieutenant Murphy was the first to arrive. "You guys all right?"

"Upstairs, Lou. You got a guy shot on the train."

He grabbed his radio as he ran through the exit gate. "Eleven, Lieutenant. Send three buses to 170th Street on the 4 Line, forthwith!"

The phone at the reception hall rang for ten minutes before anyone picked up.

"¡Hola!" a friendly female Hispanic voice answered.

"Se habla Englese?" Vinny asked in his best Spanish.

"Un poqm to, senor."

Wonderful.

"Senor Hernandez, el groom, rapido, pro vor for," he sputtered out in garbled Spanish.

"Un minuto."

A few minutes passed.

"Hello?"

"Harry, it's Vinny."

"You and that meathead partner of yours are late!"

"Listen, Harry, tell my wife and Bubba's wife we'll be there as soon as we can."

"Are you guys okay?"

Vinny glanced over at Bubba as the blood pressure gauge was about to explode.

"We're fine. It just wasn't a good night for the bad guys," Vinny said flippantly.

"On my wedding night you gotta get involved?" There were traces of a challenge and some disappointment in his voice.

"Couldn't be avoided."

Harry understood. He didn't lack the basic cynicism that makes for a good cop.

"Well, hurry up," he said sharply, "before your wife runs off with one of my cousins."

"What?" Vinny asked, surprised. "Keep those hot-blooded Latino cousins of yours away from my wife!"

He better be joking. I've got enough worry with her as it is.

"Then hurry up!" He laughed, then added, "Gotta go. The bride wants me!"

"Tell my wife to save me a dance," Vinny said enviously, then hung up. "This sucks," he mumbled, looking at Bubba.

"To protect and serve, El Gato," Bubba said shakily.

"To protect and serve."

CHAPTER 9

Vinny hoped 1992 would be a better year than the one that just ended. He'd given up hope Debbie would get pregnant. He hoped she would feel the same but doubted it. There was a constant feeling of uneasiness between them, as though they were from different worlds. He talked with her frequently about their problems, but he could not reach her. Something deep inside of her was near death, and Vinny was clueless as to how to effect a cure. That she'd been scared shitless by Sabol was understandable. As far as Vinny was concerned, with Sabol back in prison in distant Georgia for a long stretch, his shadow was fading to white.

So it has to be something else, but what is it? Maybe all she needs is time. But how much? Just be there for her when she needs me. But what if she doesn't need me anymore? What if she doesn't need me because she doesn't want me? And if she doesn't want me, am I to conclude she no longer loves me? These ifs are getting to me. I hate ifs.

By February, Sergeant Houston had managed to acquire the phone numbers of the DEA agents who arrested Sabol and the probation officers in North Carolina and Georgia who were in charge of his case. Vinny couldn't dial the phone fast enough after getting the numbers from Houston.

"DEA, Agent Gray," the voice answered correctly.

"Agent Gray, my name is Police Officer Davis. I'm with the Transit Police in New York City, and I'm calling to speak to you about an arrest of yours, a Richard Sabol."

"Really? You're the third agency that's called about that slimy little bastard."

Vinny was silent a moment. He hoped he wasn't too late to ask them not to make any deals with the beast.

"He hasn't made a deal, has he?"

Agent Gray chuckled. "No, but he's singing like a canary about everything and everybody in the hopes that someone's listening."

A canary? Fuck. I pray to God no one's listening. "I take it nobody's interested?" Vinny probed.

Another laugh. "We here at the DEA aren't going to use him, that's for sure. The guy's as slippery as a wet snake. He'd sell his own mother to get out of that cage."

This is easier than I thought it was going to be.

"Why are you guys from New York so interested in this parrot?" Gray asked suspiciously.

Us guys from New York? Who the fuck else is up here asking about him? "Well, I've got a long history with him. He's been my nightmare, my nemesis, for the past twelve years." Vinny explained the entire story as Agent Gray listened without interrupting.

"I'm sorry," Gray said earnestly when Vinny finished. "I can tell you one thing for sure: he won't be getting any deals from the DEA. I promise you that."

Easy to say. We'll see.

"Well, whom else might he make a deal with?"

His tone hardened. "I spoke to an Agent Stamp from the FBI. Not only do they not want anything to do with him, but also they're interested in the disposition of his case. Stamp said Sabol threatened to kill four FBI agents."

Okay. The FBI are the other guys up here sniffing this out.

"I'm sorry. I didn't mean to come off so harsh. It's just that I have trouble sleeping when it comes to this guy. I was beginning to think he could never be stopped. He would just go on and on until—"

"Officer, consider him stopped for at least the next twenty years. With the FBI and the DEA against him, there's really no one left he can turn to for help. If he tries to make a deal with ATF, I will personally make them aware of your situation as well as the FBI's position. There's no way anybody is going to let him work for them as a confidential informant."

"Thank God."

"Listen, officer, I have to call Agent Stamp when we have a disposition on this case. Give me a number I can reach you at, and I'll call you as well."

"That would be great." Vinny rattled off both his home phone number and District 11's.

"Okay. Take care of yourself, Officer." Then Gray hung up. He was smiling as he replaced the receiver in its cradle.

Houston looked up from his desk. "Good news?"

"Twenty years at least, Sarge! Twenty years!"

A month later, Vinny and Debbie had just returned home from New York City's Little Italy, where they'd enjoyed a romantic gourmet and candlelight dinner. The bottle of wine and soft music in the background drew them closer than they'd been in a while. Afterward, they'd taken a slow walk through Chinatown. Holding hands seemed a momentary cure for her lasting depression. He had hopes of continuing the romance in their bedroom, but their phone interrupted them.

"Don't think you're saved by the bell." He grinned mischievously as he moved toward the phone.

"Don't think it's you that's saved," she said, smiling seductively.

"Give me one minute." He smiled. "Hello," he said, annoyed. "Who the hell is this?"

She looked at him inquiringly.

His brow narrowed. "Son of a bitch!"

She watched him slam the phone down. "Who was that?" she asked nervously.

"Sabol!"

Her eyes widened in shock. "Where the hell's he calling from? And how did he get this number?" Her voice was a terrified monotone.

Vinny gave her an exasperated look.

"Is he out of jail?" Her voice went shrill with panic.

How the hell could he be out? He can't be.

"No, baby, he's not out."

Panic continued to soar through her.

"Does he know where we live?"

An eerie silence fell between them.

"Well? What did he say?"

"He said his name was Rocco and that you're dead," he said flatly.

"Oh my God!"

Vinny closed his eyes as he sat on the couch. In his mind's eye, he saw the look on Sabol's face that day in the Westchester court-room, then again in that BMW. He had never seen a colder, more savage face. He imagined Sabol raping his wife, hearing her screams of agony as he snipped off one of her fingers. It was all too much. He flinched from the thought, instead suppressing it as he always did. He'd become an expert, after twelve years, at blocking out those thoughts. He had to, or he'd surely go mad. He felt nauseous and filled with rage.

Goddamn that sneaky prick for making me feel weak and ineffec-tual. But no, I'm making myself feel that way. I've got to overcome him.

Vinny's gaze found hers. Tears streamed down her cheeks.

"Oh, baby," he sighed, dropping to his knees beside her. He gathered her tightly in his arms. He began to rock back and forth, as though she were a little girl. "It'll be all right, baby."

"He's going to kill us," she whispered. "He said when he took my virginity that nobody else would ever have me. He'd kill any man who'd touch me. He's crazy. He kills everybody and gets away with it. You, the FBI, or the DEA can't stop him. Nobody can stop him. He'll get out and he'll kill us all!" Her voice was shaky, her eyes filled with tears.

His arms tightened around her, and he pressed her head to his chest. He held her for a few minutes, his face turning white with fury.

"Listen, baby. You can't fall apart on me. I promise you, he'll never bother you again."

She muttered something under her breath.

"If he ever comes near you again, so help me God, on my moth-er's grave, I'll kill him."

"I know you would, but he's sneaky, and he'll do it when we're not expecting it. Shit! What did I ever see in that animal?"

"You're being too hard on yourself. You had no idea a guy who looks like the male version of Farrah Fawcett was a malevolent psychopath."

She hugged him tightly. It was hard for most people to see beyond his tough-guy persona to the loving, caring, generous man who lay beneath. But after spending twelve years with him, she could very easily.

"I love you so much," she whispered.

His grip tightened around her. "My God, baby, I'd be lost without you."

Suddenly, she pushed away from him. "What do we do now?"

He smiled to reassure her and lift the despair she felt. He reached for the phone. "First, I'll make a proper notification to the department. With Internal Affairs involved, they can make the proper federal notifications and get official answers."

The next day, he reported to Captain Stevens. "What the hell is going on?" He frowned at Vinny.

"Shit happens, Captain. I guess I have a monopoly on bad luck."

Stevens's expression softened. "How's your wife handling this?" His voice warmed slightly.

Vinny stiffened. "Not well. She cried herself to sleep last night. I think the only way to comfort her is to take away her feelings of helplessness. I don't think I'm doing a very good job at it. Right now, she feels helpless and is worried as hell."

Stevens nodded. "I spoke to Internal Affairs first thing this morning. After your phone call last night, they weren't quite sure how to handle it. They don't handle many death threats against Transit cops."

"Of course not," Vinny said sarcastically.

Stevens ignored his attitude. "Listen, Vinny," he said. "They've notified the DEA, the FBI, and the US Probation Department. They've all assured IA that Sabol is in a federal prison in Georgia and there is no way in hell he'll be getting out anytime soon. Even if he takes a plea, which they think he will, he's still looking at twenty years instead of life."

"Do you really think so? I doubt it."

Stevens smiled. "The feds have promised to notify IA with the disposition of the case. You and Debbie will be living off your pension on a beach somewhere by the time this guy gets out," Stevens said earnestly.

The ten-ton gorilla named Sabol was off his back. Stevens smiled as he watched Vinny's reaction.

"I've got some more good news I can tell you now, if you want to hear it."

Vinny gave him a suspicious glance. Too often, someone's good news had been nothing but bad news to him. He remained silent but nodded.

"You were named PBA Cop of the Month for November's arrest with Bubba."

Vinny brightened even more.

"The awards dinner will be held at Terrace on the Park in May. On behalf of myself and my wife, I'd like to congratulate you and thank you." He pushed back his chair to stand and offered his hand. Vinny took it.

"Why is your wife thanking me?" he asked curiously.

Stevens smiled and picked up a fax off his desk. "It says here that, as your commanding officer, I must attend this gala affair, and of course, my wife will be with me." He paused. "Obviously, you've had this honor before, so what does one wear to this affair?" he asked innocently.

Vinny smiled mischievously. "You got a tux?"

Compared to the last PBA Cop of the Month dinner they'd attended, which was unorganized and boisterous, the dinner at Terrace on the Park in Queens, the location of the 1964 World Fair, was professionally done with style.

The guests took up about thirty round tables around a large dance floor, where a band played the same festive music normally played at weddings. From the moment they'd arrived, they agreed it was extraordinary. Seated next to Vinny, who was wearing a black

Armani suit and crisp white shirt and tie, was Debbie. She looked stunning in a gown she'd altered after wearing it as a bridesmaid in the wedding of her younger sister, Linda, the previous year. Next to her was Captain Stevens and his wife, a very elegant woman in her fifties. From Vinny's conversations with Stevens, he'd learned she was a nurse in a hospital in Rockland County. Looking at him, Vinny was glad to see he wasn't wearing a tux. Although some of the dignitaries were, Stevens decided against it, as had the other captains. He'd have killed Vinny for embarrassing him if he'd been the only captain wearing one. Seated across from them were Bubba Baker and his wife, who sat impassively. When they'd first arrived, Bubba had mentioned to Debbie that he was still unsure why he was receiving this award. In reply, she'd smiled, threw her arms around Vinny, and said proudly, "This is why."

Bubba nodded in agreement.

Debbie made polite conversation with the other guests, while Vinny, looking relaxed and comfortable, smiled and acknowledged well-wishers and accepted their accolades. People stopped by to take his hand and offer praise for his acts of bravery. Everyone wants to shake a hero's hand. He kept an eagle eye on Debbie, but his fear that she might get drunk and reveal her split personality faded as the evening wore on.

She's being the perfect wife tonight. I wish she'd stay this beautiful and loving all the time. Who knows, perhaps she will. Her shrink changed the dosage of her prescription. Perhaps that's why. She seems dramatically better, almost like the old days. It's when she mixes alcohol with the pills that she becomes unreasonable and, at times, simply out of control. Please, God, don't let her Jekyll-and-Hyde on me here.

The only annoying conversation they had was with Bubba's wife. She insisted that in order for a marriage to be complete, it must produce children. Vinny took great pleasure interrupting her conversations with Debbie to engage her about how well they were living in comparison to her and Bubba: they lived in Co-Op City, one step up from a housing project. He could see it was beginning to annoy Debbie, and as the evening progressed, he considered telling Bubba's wife to knock it off. When he was on the dance floor with her, she insisted he not say a word. "A woman whose only conversation is about her kids is insecure and not really happy with her life," she said sharply.

Vinny could hardly control his laughter at her candor.

After the main course of prime rib, twice-baked potato, and string beans amandine, the awards presentation began. Rounds of applause shook the room after each of the accounts were read.

Debbie didn't know what to think, how to respond, or even how to react when the master of ceremonies read the narrative of that November night. As they sat listening, she would glance at him with an inquiring look. She'd never realized before that night that the stories he told her about his work were actually true. He'd tell her, but it never sank in.

"It's all creative writing," he whispered to her.

When Vinny and Bubba arose to accept their awards, Captain Stevens and his wife led the round of applause and standing ovation.

"You should be very proud of your husband," Stevens said with a smile that was kind-hearted and genuine. "He's a damn good cop, but don't tell him I told you so! He has enough confidence in his own omnipotence."

Debbie gave him a bright, reassuring smile. "Oh, don't worry. I won't tell him," she said sweetly. She threw her arms around him, kissing him passionately on the lips. "I'm so proud of you, Vinny."

"Do you know how much I love you?"

She nodded vigorously. "Almost as much as I love you." Her eyes were moist.

Coffee and after-dinner drinks were served along with mini Italian pastries. After dessert, it was on to the dance floor, where they danced with each other the rest of the night.

The US Justice Department notified the NYC TP Internal Affairs Division, they notified Captain Stevens, and he notified Vinny. DEA agent Gray notified FBI agent Stamp, who, in turn, notified Sergeant Houston, who also notified Vinny it had been confirmed and reconfirmed: Richard Sabol had pleaded guilty and was given a twenty-year sentence. The TP IAD were assured that if Sabol were to be released early for any reason, they would be notified.

Agent Stamp promised Sergeant Houston that if Sabol was so much as transferred, he himself would be notified and would immediately notify Houston.

Vinny was relieved. Their ordeal appeared to be at an end. There'd be no more scurrying about hiding Debbie or helplessly wondering if and when Sabol would seek his revenge. Vinny was sick and tired of that asshole, that beast, threatening his family and psychologically mind-fucking his wife. His frustration at not being able to do anything about it ended, too. He was no longer filled with rage and uncertainty. After twelve long years, the nightmare had finally ended. Debbie's reaction was spontaneous: emancipation, followed immediately by renewed hope of becoming pregnant. As traumatized as she had been, her main focus remained on what the doctors had said: when the stress was relieved, she should have no trouble conceiving.

That year Valor Day was held at the Fashion Institute of Technology due to the tremendous crowd invited to the ceremony. Vinny was surrounded by Debbie; his brothers, Michael and Raymond; his sister, Maria; and Tommy Cascione as they stood before the building, taking turns having their pictures taken with the man of the hour. Vinny's parents were heartbroken they couldn't attend—they were locked in on a prepaid trip to Ireland—to watch their son receive not one but two of the department's highest medals from Mayor Rudy Giuliani. It was an honor bestowed on few NYPD officers.

Reporters were swarming about.

Vinny fielded questions as he and his family watched the Transit Police Irish Warpipe Band practice. They put on a show for the spectators, who were patiently waiting outside for the ceremony to begin. Excitement was in the air. As they began to move toward the entrance, reporters bombarded him and Debbie, while photographers did their thing.

"How does it feel to be a hero?"

"I'm no hero. I was just extremely lucky."

"How proud are you of your husband?"

Debbie walked faster; her words were coming fast, vibrating with emotion. "I'm extremely proud of him. He's always been a hero. He's never turned away from anyone in trouble, and he loves his job." She walked purposefully, back straight, head held high, with a strong stride.

When they made it through the front doors, he turned to her. "Do you want to be my press agent?" he asked playfully.

She grinned. "Hopefully, after today, you won't need one." She hesitated and then placed her hand in his. "I can't imagine what your life is like, filled with death and violence. There're no advantages to living your life on the edge."

He reached out, took her other hand, and softly kissed it. "I love you, baby."

She pulled away. "Promise me, no more heroics, because, so help me God, if you ever get killed in the line of duty, I'm not marching on to some stage, the grieving widow, so some mayor can put a goddamn medal around my neck. And forget it, if you think for one minute that our son or daughter will do it either!"

Her outburst knocked him back on his heels. He looked at her, then at his family and Tommy. He shrugged wearily. "She gets very emotional at these things," he said defensively.

A slow smile lit her face. "Go and get your medal," she said sweetly, "but no more after today."

Shit. She just Jekyll-and-Hyde in front of everyone.

He quickly kissed her lips before turning on his heels to find his seat. He found himself smiling as he sat down.

Still, no woman could ever love me as much as she does. I'll do whatever it takes to make her happy. We'll fight her depression together and win. Okay. We've had our rough patches. Every couple does. But we're through it now and back on a smooth highway.

As the last recipient received his award and exited the stage, the room became silent once more. It was Vinny's turn. Every eye followed him as he walked to his assigned place at the center of the stage. He stood proudly at attention in his immaculate dress uniform, proud, practiced, and self-assured—the very picture of a police hero.

His brothers and sister proudly watched him as the master of ceremonies read the account of his bravery. Beside them, Debbie, unable to control herself, wept openly. When the master of ceremonies finished, the audience arose as one and applauded.

Vinny marched forward as their applause reached a crescendo. It seemed to rock the room, rising ever louder with each step that brought him closer to the mayor and the police commissioner. Vinny found his mark in front of the podium, stood to attention, and saluted in strict military fashion.

Mayor Giuliani placed his right hand over the medals on Vinny's uniform. "It looks like you don't have room for any more," he said admiringly.

Vinny looked proudly at them and said, as cavalier as ever, "I better make room, because I'm coming back up in a minute."

Vinny then removed his hat and bowed as Giuliani placed the red ribbon attached to the gold medal round his neck. He then shook his hand, snapped back to attention, and saluted again.

But the pinnacle was yet to come. Vinny turned, exited the stage, and marched before the boisterous crowd back to his place. He then about-faced and again climbed the stairs and stood to attention. The ovation grew even louder. The master of ceremonies read another account of his heroism. And once more, Vinny marched forward to receive his second award from Giuliani. Only this time, it was he who saluted Vinny first, which set off another round of applause that pounded the walls and shook the ceiling.

It was the proudest day of his life.

His baby sister, Maria, managed to get to him first after pushing feverishly through a crowd of well-wishers and reporters. "I'm so proud of you!" she cried, throwing her arms around him, brushing her lips across his cheek.

"A city bus?" Raymond asked with amazement on his face.

"Well, at least he didn't try to drive it," Michael chided, extending a congratulatory hand.

"Congratulations, Vincent," Tommy said excitedly. "But can we take this party somewhere else?"

"Lead the way, Tommy. We're all right behind you"

Vinny grabbed Debbie's hand, and they moved at best speed through the crowd.

Vinny took a deep breath of fresh air when they finally made it outside. He then turned to his family. "Does this mean we can go to Grandma's now?" he asked coaxingly.

"Let's go!"

"Then we're all going to Vincent's Restaurant on Sixty-Seventh Street like we did after the last Valor Day," Michael added quickly.

Vinny looked at Debbie with a victorious look in his eyes. "That okay with you?"

"Let's get out of here!" She pulled Vinny along by the hand.

His grandmother was shocked when she opened the door to her house to unexpected guests. The house was on Bay Ridge Avenue, where she'd lived happily married to his grandfather for the past fifty years.

"Vincent! We just saw you guys on television!" Hugs and kisses as they all bustled into the house.

"Hi, Grandma," Vinny said. He took her affectionately in his arms.

She pushed him back and studied him from head to foot. "Look at you in your uniform with all those medals. Your mother, God rest her soul, would be so proud of you!" Her eyes began to well up with tears. She stared at him for a long time before she reluctantly added, "She is proud of you, and she's watching over you from heaven."

"I know she is, Grandma."

If only his grandmother knew how he'd been haunted by the memory of that tragic day.

No, I mustn't ever tell anyone. It's my cross to bear. Nobody needs worry about me. I'm a man now, not a scared little boy screaming for God's help on a Brooklyn Street.

His grandfather broke the spell. "Sonny-boy!" He clutched Vinny in a bear hug. "Did you get a chance to tell off that pompous ass, the mayor?" he asked flippantly.

"I didn't think it'd be a wise career move."

His grandfather laughed. "The hell with him, anyway."

That was something he'd always admired about his grandfather. He worked hard all his life, was a self-made man whose joys in life revolved around his wife, kids, and grandchildren. He called a spade a spade and never kissed anyone's ass. He was strong, proud, and forever generous with people he loved.

While his grandmother passed out the hugs and kisses to Debbie and the rest of her grandchildren, his grandfather escorted Vinny and Tommy by the elbows into the living room.

"It's a little early, but I think some twelve-year-old scotch is in order for our hero."

His grandmother gazed at him warningly for a long moment. "Leo," she said, treading carefully, "don't you think it's a little early for that?"

His grandfather turned to Tommy and his grandsons. "Jean, they're grown men, for Christ's sakes."

She raised a skeptical eyebrow. "All right, Leo, but just one. They have a long drive back to Yonkers," she added protectively.

They all laughed simultaneously.

"Grandma, we're not going home for quite some time. We're going to Vincent's Restaurant for a double celebration. It's not only my day, but also it's Debbie's birthday, so we have lots to celebrate. We're hoping you two party animals will join us," he added.

His grandma turned toward Debbie and hugged her tightly. "Oh, congratulations, Debbie."

"Thanks, Grandma. So does this mean you'll join us at Vincent's?"

Grandma smiled at her. "No. You kids go and have fun. But first, come in and relax a while."

They all sat in the cozy living room, talked about the good old days when they were just babies. There was both affection and pride in Grandma's smile as she pontificated about how proud she was with Vincent. Grandpa wholeheartedly agreed with his beloved wife as he surreptitiously refilled the boys' glasses with scotch.

After about two hours of Debbie and Tommy graciously looking at pictures from when the Davis kids were babies, Vinny turned toward his brothers. "Ready to go, guys?" He was anxious to get going.

"Good idea," Michael said, taking the hint. He got up and kissed Grandma. "Are you sure you don't want to come with us?" he asked curiously.

"No, you kids go." She got up.

Vinny walked over and gave her a hug. "I'll be back down to see you in a few weeks."

She nodded happily. "I know you will, Vincent, but I want you to be careful," she said urgently as her arms tightened around him.

"I'll be fine." He kissed her forehead. Vinny turned to Grandpa, who looked depressed that his wife had turned down the dinner invitation. "Maybe next time, Grandpa. I love ya."

They shook hands. "You be careful out there, Sonny-boy." Tough, uncompromising, and a streak of humor, he was still an enigma whom he admired and loved with all his heart.

"I always am," he said confidently.

"Take good care of my grandson," Grandma said to take Debbie as they hugged.

"He'd better take care of me," she said sourly.

There she goes again with the negatives. That's twice so far today.

"Well, then, you two had better take care of each other," Grandma said evenly. She then rushed back to Vinny's side and slipped something into his pocket. She leaned to kiss him on the cheek.

"Buy your wife a drink on us," she whispered.

He gave Grandma a quick, tight hug. "Gran, I'm thirty years old. I think I can—"

"Shush! Don't answer back to your grandmother."

Vinny looked toward his grandfather, embarrassed.

"Don't look at me! You know your grandmother's the boss!"

"And don't you forget it, mister!" she half-joked.

After nearly four hours in Vincent's Restaurant, drinking and eating a fabulous meal, the owner surprised Debbie by bringing out a tremendous birthday cake for her. The customers in the restaurant all sang "Happy Birthday" and sent rounds of drinks to their table.

Vinny accepted accolades and well-wishes from people he'd never met before. They all said their prayers were with him and that the Lord would protect him. It was an overwhelming experience to have so many strangers congratulate him for what he'd done. The one thing he wouldn't accept was the gracious offer by the owner to comp the check.

After a brief argument over who between them would pay the check, Vinny accompanied Tommy to the bar.

"You had a good time today?" Tommy asked, smiling.

"Let's just say it's a day I'll remember for as long as I live."

"Thank you, my friend, for sharing it with me. I wouldn't have missed it for the world, paisan." He wrapped his arm around Vinny's shoulder. Tommy turned back toward the table, where Debbie sat with Vinny's family.

"What's going on with you and Debbie?" he asked suspiciously.

Vinny sat looking at Debbie, knowing how agonizing the past couple of years had been. He wondered if she'd ever again be the same loving woman he'd married. He felt that he could almost see her resilience and strength growing with each passing day. But he wasn't sure.

"It's all right, I guess," Vinny said haltingly. "I think she's feeling a lot better knowing Sabol won't be around for the next twenty years."

Tommy grimaced. "I don't mean to pry, but I've been hearing some things about Debbie that concerns me," Tommy said cautiously.

Vinny looked baffled.

What's he hinting at? What things?

"Well, actually, I've been hearing these things for about a year now, and I—"

Vinny cut him off. "What are you talking about?"

Tommy hesitated. "Maybe this isn't the time," he said evasively.

Now I'm really confused.

"Tommy, you've been my closest friend for almost twenty years. If there's something on your mind, spit it out."

Tommy drew a deep breath. "It's just that Debbie's been seen out at night with a lot of, how should I put it, unsavory characters."

Vinny sighed, rubbing the space between his eyebrows. She'd never failed to surprise him. Today, except for a couple of slips, she'd been smooth and self-effacing, letting him have his day in the spotlight, despite the fact that it was her birthday too. Yet she had been acting strangely for the past year, going out with her girlfriends, drinking and partying a bit too much. But he'd thought that was her way of dealing with everything that had happened.

"What does *unsavory characters* mean exactly?" Vinny asked curtly.

Tommy shook his head warily. "Drug dealers."

Jesus Christ, he means it!

He turned back to the table and gazed at Debbie. "No way!" he said defiantly, shaking his head vigorously.

Tommy shrugged absently. "I just thought you might like to keep a closer eye on her, that's all. I know she's been through a lot, and sometimes people do some strange things they wouldn't normally do when they're depressed."

Vinny nodded absently and glanced back at her. The lines of fear and strain were still present on her face. They'd been through too much together and had come too far for him to lose her to drugs. *His fault,* he thought wearily. He couldn't let this happen.

He turned back to Tommy. "I'll keep an eye on her. I've been so worried about everything else that's been going on. It's selfish of me to not pay closer attention to her and her needs."

Tommy cast him a look. "Vinny, you're far from selfish when it comes to Debbie. I've never met a man more devoted to a woman. Shit, if I knew when we were kids that you'd grow up and be able to settle down with one woman, I would have never thrown you off the porch that time I caught you asking my sister out." Tommy was smart. He had the sense to change the subject to something else. The mention of his sister Corinne's name struck a chord. Although Vinny was happily married, there still were times when he'd thought of what life would have been like if he had convinced her he was the serious type, not the lovable playboy he posed as.

"How's Corinne these days?" he asked innocently.

Tommy smiled back with malicious satisfaction. "She's getting divorced."

His smile faded. "Oh, I'm sorry to hear that. I was hoping she was happy." He meant it.

Tommy let out a sigh that was half-exasperation and half-relief. "It's for the best," he said flatly as he signed the check. "She's coming up to visit for the holidays. Maybe you can come by and cheer her up."

Vinny looked up at him, puzzled. "Does that mean you won't throw me off your front porch again?"

Tommy chuckled. "You're coming by to cheer her up, not try to take her to bed!"

Vinny burst out laughing. "See what I mean? You still wouldn't let me date her, even if I were single."

Tommy smiled brightly. "If you weren't married to Debbie, I'd let you marry her."

"Really?"

He put an arm around Vinny's shoulder. "I'd be proud to have you as my brother-in-law."

They were silent a moment before Vinny muttered, "Well, it's about time." They both laughed as Vinny glanced over at his wife. He was still sure nothing was really wrong, nothing so wrong they couldn't handle it together.

"I'm sorry, pal, but it's far too late for that to ever happen."

Tommy glanced over at Debbie when she suddenly began to walk toward them. "I know that, pal."

"You ready to go home?" he asked, taking her in his arms.

She kissed him gently on the lips. "Let's go." She looked at Tommy. "Thanks so much for the dinner. It was very nice of you."

Tommy's smile masked his concern. "It was my pleasure, Debbie."

CHAPTER 10

Vinny sat for a long time in silence on his terrace and watched as nighttime on the Hudson River cruised by.

I don't like this, but what can I do at, what, three in the morning and not a fuckin' word from her? I've been foolish, stupid even, to believe she'd change without getting professional help.

With the excitement of the Valor Day festivities behind him, he looked forward to enjoying the coming holidays. But this year, the only thing Debbie seemed to be thankful for was grape vineyards and the existence of pharmaceutical companies. The prescription medication for her mood disorder she'd been taking on and off for years didn't mix well with cheap Chablis. He'd waited another full hour in total darkness before he decided to retreat to the warmth of his bed.

Removing his clothes, he turned out the light and lay in the dark. Exhausted, he should have fallen asleep immediately, but too many worries were racing around in his mind.

The ringing intrusion of the phone on the nightstand startled him. Panic coursed through his veins. Like most cops—no, like most people—the worst immediately came to his mind when the phone would ring in the middle of the night.

Thoughts of an accident rushed through his head. How many times had he personally had to call people to notify them that a loved one had been injured or killed in an accident?

Too many. Way too many.

He grabbed the phone. "Hello?"

"Is this Vincent Davis of the New York Transit Police?" A woman's voice.

"Yeah, who's this? Is my wife okay?"

"This is Officer Cruz, Yonkers PD. There has been an accident involving your wife. She's okay," she added quickly to calm him. "But my lieutenant would like you to come to the First Precinct as soon as possible. Do you know where it is?"

"Yes, I do. I can be there in ten minutes."

"Sure thing, Officer. Thanks very much. I appreciate it."

He hung up, was dressed, was in his car, and was there in less time than that.

He approached the desk and was greeted by a very large, angry-looking uniformed lieutenant, who glared at him. "Please tell me you're Davis of the NYPD."

With trepidation, Vinny produced his shield and ID card and held them up for him to see, but unexpectedly, he snatched them from his hand, then smiled smugly.

"Did my officer explain to you on the phone that your drunken wife totaled the car she was driving by barreling it into a tree?"

Shit. This isn't good.

Vinny couldn't think of what to say, so he moved his head in an ambiguous way.

"Did my officer also inform you that your wife was rude and disrespectful to not only my officers but me as well?" He spoke in a hard, solid voice.

"I am very sorry for that, Lieutenant," Vinny said sincerely. "My wife's been extremely depressed since her miscarriage and has been on prescription medication. She's not supposed to be drinking while she's taking her pills."

The lieutenant shook his head and smiled. "Davis, you're a lucky fellow. If you'd come in here with the same attitude your wife had, I would lock her up. Luckily for you, I can see you're a gentleman, so I am going to let her go. But let me tell you something," he growled. "If she ever sets foot in my stationhouse again, there's a cell just waiting for her. Do I make myself clear?"

"Yes, sir. Crystal clear."

He gave Vinny a few minutes to relax, then brought Debbie from an office at the rear of the stationhouse. He could hear her yelling obscenities before he saw her. When he did, it was as clear that describing her as drunk was an understatement. She was toasted. Her speech was slurred so badly he could barely understand a word she was saying. If not for the assistance of the two officers who were holding her up by the elbows, she'd have fallen as she approached Vinny.

"What took you so long?" she said in a long, drunken, slurry shriek.

He ignored her and turned to the two officers propping her up. "Are you the two who picked her up?"

The younger of the two, who looked like he just graduated high school, responded with a smile, "Yeah, we picked up the job at about 0330 hours. When we got there, we found her sitting behind the wheel, trying to start the car. When we approached, she started laughing, telling us she'd move the car as soon as it started!"

"I'm surprised she's not dead," the older officer abruptly added. He looked serious. "The car's totaled!"

"I take it nobody was injured?" He knew if someone were, he wouldn't be hauling her home. He'd be arranging bail instead.

"Just the tree, but I don't think it's complaining."

As they balanced the semiconscious Debbie between them, Vinny held out his hand and shook theirs. "I can't thank you enough."

"Maybe someday you will," the older officer said. "Maybe someday you will," he repeated somberly. He looked at her piteously.

Vinny took Debbie from them, placing an arm around her, and hooked one of hers over his shoulder. He walked her to the door the younger officer was holding open. While they negotiated the stairs, the younger officer came after them. "Here. You're going to need this form to retrieve your car from the pound or for your insurance company."

"Thanks" He nodded to the officer to slip it into his right jacket pocket. "Take care of yourself."

"You bet."

The ride home was uneventful. Debbie fell into a near-catatonic sleep. He parked behind their apartment and carefully got her out without waking her. From past episodes, he felt it best.

As he carried her up three flights of stairs to their front door, she remained semiconscious. He laid her in bed fully dressed, afraid that he might awaken her by undressing her. If she woke up, there'd be a rumble, and he wasn't in the mood. He pulled the covers over her, then with the back of his hand, softly stroked her face. She looked so peaceful, almost angelic, the way she looked when he'd first met her.

What the hell went wrong?

A tear slid down his face.

Moments passed before he noticed the time on the alarm clock on the nightstand. He exited, quietly closing the door behind him. He went to the phone on the kitchen wall and dialed District 2. It rang several times before a groggy voice answered.

"Eleven, Sergeant O'Brien."

"Hey, Sarge, it's Davis."

"Top o' the morning to ya," he said with his best Irish brogue. Vinny and O'Brien had been friends since the academy. Sean got promoted to sergeant off the same list Vinny was on. If Vinny had scored one point higher on the exam, as Sean had, he'd be a sergeant too.

"What do you need, Vinny?"

"I need an E-day." The term used within the TP for an emergency day off.

"Are you all right?" he asked, concerned.

"I'm fine. It's Debbie's car that's on its way to the great scrapyard in the sky."

"Is she all right?" Now he sounded worried. He and Julie, his wife, had attended quite a few cop parties with Vinny and Debbie. Their wives had hit it off and always looked forward to seeing each other at their husbands' parties.

"She's fine, Sean, but I'll have to rent a car and deal with the insurance company today. On top of which, I haven't even slept yet."

"You got the day, pal. But do me one favor—pick up a receipt or something from a tow truck or gas station. I've got to cover my ass with the captain when giving E-days."

"No problem. Thanks again, boss," Vinny said, giving his friend the respect of rank he'd earned.

At 8:15 a.m., Vinny stood on his terrace, sipping coffee, as the sun worked its way across a brilliant blue November sky. The consummation of all that happened over the preceding months was disturbing. The idea of what was yet to come was more so. He felt as though he'd been swept into a raging sea. He had no control. Yet at the same time, he felt a calming sense that whatever lay ahead, no matter how bad it might get, he trusted in their love to see it through. He wondered if it was true for other couples. Would their love be strong enough to endure what was happening? Letting his mind drift, he turned his gaze toward the Hudson River and the cliffs on the New Jersey side.

Abruptly realizing the time, he dashed into the living room and picked up the phone. Frantically, he dialed Debbie's boss.

Dr. Lawrence Silverstein had done well for himself, and he treated her like a daughter. Larry, divorced, in his fifties, and the father of two, was a fanatic exercise enthusiast. Lucy, his live-in girl-friend, was an attractive forty-year-old ultraliberal. Each summer, Larry and Lucy would invite his employees to spend the weekend at their summer house in Massachusetts. The drive was always enjoy-able, with them watching the magnificent views of the countryside and touring the small towns. It was so nice just to get away from the madness of the city. The weekend would be spent sipping fine wines, lounging by the pool, and as usual, Vinny would be in charge of the cooking, something he loved to do. After dinner, they would drive to nearby Tanglewood State Park. On the grass, they would sit by the light of the candelabra, sipping wine and tasting cheeses while enjoying the music of an outdoor symphony.

So many happy times.

"Doctor's office. This is Maria. How can I help you?"

"Hi, Maria, it's Vinny."

"Hey, Vinny." Her accent was heavy Bronx. She was a twenty-three-year-old Puerto Rican recently hired as a receptionist. "Your wife's not in yet," she offered.

"I know. That's why I'm calling. We had a car accident last night. We're okay, but the car didn't make it, so she won't he in."

"Well, thank God you guys didn't get hurt."

"Yeah, thank God. Do me a favor and let Larry know that I have to take Debbie to rent a car and that she'll call him later."

"I'll do that."

Vinny hung up.

Damn. It's one after another. I hate this. Sooner or later, her boss'll figure out something's wrong.

Unexpectedly, Debbie appeared out of the darkness of their bedroom, looking lost.

God, what's happened to her? She was so beautiful Look at her now. She's falling apart before my eyes.

Debbie noticed him on the couch. She looked puzzled but smiled anyway. "I thought you had to go to work today." She was still slightly inebriated.

"I had nothing better to do today, so I decided to take the day off. How's your head?" He needed to stay calm.

"It's fine," she said defensively.

"Debbie, we need to talk. Come sit down over here." He patted a spot next to him.

"I have to call work."

Oh, shit. Now she's turned belligerent. Careful!

"I already called for you. I told Maria that we had an accident last night and that you'd call Larry later after we rented a car."

Debbie smiled and sat beside him, then leaned over, kissed him on the cheek, and whispered, "Thank you."

Now she's in her young-girl voice. She's playing me. Again!

"This has got to end!"

Instead of recoiling, she moved closer, put her leg over his, her head in the crook of his shoulder. He felt her warmth and her unsteady breathing.

"What the hell is going on with you? You have me taking off days from work because you don't come home at night. I'm up all night long, worrying whether you have been raped or killed or in an accident like last night. Are you unhappy with me? Is there someone else? Do you want a divorce?" He heard the anger in his own voice.

Damn, I'm not handling this as well as I thought I could, but she's pissed me off.

She looked astonished. "No, I don't want a divorce," she said blearily. "I love you. It's just that I've been so depressed lately. I blame myself all the time for what's happening to me!" she wailed in despair. Tears flowed.

Vinny felt his heart sink. He sat beside her, taking her into his arms reassuringly. "That's it with the fertility doctors," he said soothingly. "It was your mother's and sister's idea anyway. If trying to have a baby is doing this to you, we should forget about it. I don't need a baby if it means losing you."

Debbie looked at him, tears in her eyes. "You love me that much?"

He smiled. "Of course I do! Are you crazy? Do the words 'For richer or poorer, through sickness and in health' ring a bell?" The words he had softly spoken opened a flood of tears.

"I'm so sorry, baby! Please don't leave me."

He held her rightly. "Everything will be all right. We'll get through this together."

A few weeks passed. Thanksgiving came and went. Debbie was showing major improvement after another visit to her doctor, who changed her prescription.

Vinny approached Sergeant Houston, his anticrime boss, and complained of his problems at home. Sympathetically, he agreed to switch Vinny's tour of duty from 2:00 p.m. to 10:00 p.m., to 6:00 a.m. to 2:00 p.m. Getting off so early allowed him help with housework and prepare dinner each night.

Their relationship seemed normal again. He hadn't noticed her drinking at all, and she wasn't going out with her friends as often. When she did, she was home relatively early. He decided a vacation was in order. After clearing it with Dr. Silverstein, he hooked a two-week trip to Maui starting the first week in January. Despite his police training, he was not one who could keep a surprise to himself for very long. Christmas, when he planned to tell her about the trip, seemed so far away. Instead of waiting—he just couldn't—he planned a romantic way to spring his surprise on his wife.

After planning every detail, he called her at work and told her he was going to cook them a romantic dinner. He then went from store to store, gathering the necessities; to a florist, for a dozen roses for the dinner table; to a butcher, where he purchased two filets mignons; to a fish store, for two one-pound lobster tails; and finally, a stop at a specialty shop, for an assortment of candles and a few floating ones for the bathtub. He hoped they'd set the mood. While there, he bought two gold-foil-wrapped chocolates for the pillows on their bed. He felt they'd be a perfect end to their evening. He put the plane tickets under her pillow and both chocolates on it. When they retired to bed, she'd see them, lift the pillow, and find the tickets.

Vinny rushed home. At six o'clock, he began cooking their feast. A salad was placed in the refrigerator. Potatoes were baking in the oven, and he was prepping the hollandaise sauce for the steamed asparagus when the phone rang. Disturbed by the interruption, he picked up the phone abruptly while continuing to stir the sauce so it wouldn't thicken. "Hello," he said in a flat voice.

"Hi, honey, it's me," Debbie responded affectionately.

"Where are you?"

"Nancy called me at the office to ask if I'd give her a ride home from work. Her car broke down, and she's stuck." Nancy had been her best friend since high school. She never married but was a single mother with a son. She was also an alcoholic and not on his list of friends with whom his wife should be associating at this time.

"Do me a favor. Just drop her off in front of her house and say goodbye. Please don't go inside and start talking to her mother or playing with her kid."

"Don't worry, I'll be home shortly," she said defiantly, then hung up without saying goodbye.

Fuck. She challenged me. Damn it. I hope this doesn't set her off again.

Vinny sat in his living room, growing more furious as the hours passed. At first, when she hadn't called back, he thought there was a problem with the phone lines. That thought was laid to rest when he called Nancy's house, only to have her mother say she hadn't seen or heard from Nancy or Debbie. As the hours passed, he knew something was going on behind his back. What that might be, he refused to consider. Lethargically, he spent the rest of the evening, and most of the night, watching television, the whole time observing the wax melt off the candles onto the dining room table until they finally burned out. Fear and anxiety are impossible bedfellows, and this night had been filled with both.

By daybreak, when he still had no word, he decided to call and talk to Nancy. He frantically dialed her number. After several rings, a voice answered in a low monotone. "Hello?"

"Nancy, it's Vinny," he said brusquely. "Is Debbie there?"

"I haven't seen Debbie in three weeks."

Why's she acting cold?

He went rigid for a moment, unable to put words to his thoughts.

"Are you still?" Nancy asked, for some reason sounding irritated.

"Sorry to bother you." He hung up.

Looking at the clock, Vinny saw he was already forty-five minutes late for work. Again, picking up the phone, he quickly dialed District 11. It was answered on the first ring. "Eleven, Lieutenant Rodriguez."

Bobby Rodriguez was the midnight lieutenant, newly transferred from District 3 in Harlem. Together, Vinny and Bobby had spent quite a few tours of duty on barstools over the past few months. He was on the captain's list, and as boss, he was as strict as they come. But if you were an arrive cop, made your arrests without causing him paperwork or grief, he'd go to bat for you. It was a quality Vinny had deeply admired about him.

"Hey, Lieu, it's Vinny Davis."

"Nice of you to call, Vinny. What's it this time? Your wife run someone over?"

"I'm not sure yet," Vinny responded cynically.

"She's still not home yet?" Bobby asked worriedly.

"No boss, she's not," Vinny said nervously.

"Well, try not to worry, Vinny. She's probably sleeping it off at a friend's house. You know how women are," Bobby added semijokingly. "I'll let Houston know I gave you the day off yesterday. I'll tell him I forgot to mark it on the roll call."

"Thanks a million, Bobby. I owe you. Appreciate it."

"You're damn right you do! Next time we're out, the drinks are on you."

"Anytime, Lieutenant."

"Call me Captain." He said it in a barely audible voice. "I want to get used to it."

"Sure thing, Captain!"

He could hear Bobby laughing as he hung up the phone.

Later, Vinny lay, fully dressed, in their darkened bedroom. At 8:00 a.m. sharp, he was awakened by someone banging on the front door. He groaned and looked at the ceiling. Realizing where he was, he got out of bed and stumbled to the door.

Expecting to see Debbie when he opened the door, he was shocked to see two uniformed Yonkers cops. One was Jimmy Palumbo, with whom he'd attended high school. Vinny took a deep breath and closed his eyes. "Is she dead?"

"Is who dead, Vinny?" Palumbo asked, curious.

"My wife!"

"Calm down, buddy! We just came to ask you to move your rent-a-car from your neighbor's driveway. We were going to tow it, but I ran the plate and it came back to you, so I decided to come and get you."

Vinny looked at him blankly. Just as he was about to speak, he saw Debbie, passed out on the living room floor, between the soda and the coffee table. On the floor, near her lifeless body, was her pocketbook. Instinctively he began to rifle through it. In the hopes of finding the keys to the rental. After a few moments, unable to control his anger and impatience any longer, he dumped the contents onto the floor. Bending over to pick up the keys, he noticed a clear plastic bag containing white powder.

Fuck! Oh, shit! Fuck.

The cops both sucked in their breaths, then walked over and looked down at him.

"That looks like felony weight," Jimmy said incredulously.

Vinny looked up at them but was unable to speak. A few moments passed.

"Well, are you going to move that car or what?" Jimmy asked, making it clear to him that the plastic bag on the floor was "invisible."

Vinny quickly picked up the keys and stuffed the plastic bag back into her pocketbook. He then left with the officers to move the car. With the car parked in its assigned spot, Vinny turned to thank the officers.

"I trust you'll take care of that problem."

"You want to come up and watch?"

"No, thanks. Just take care of yourself," he added as they drove off.

Jesus fucking Christ! Coke! Bitch! Thank God I know him, or we'd be in deep shit right now. That could have been my job, my career! Bitch!

In a rage, he picked his wife off the floor and tossed her onto the love seat. "What the fuck have you been doing at night?" he screamed. The veins in his temple protruded, as if they were about to burst.

"Nothing!" she replied indignantly. Her eyes tried desperately to focus on her enraged husband.

"Nothing? Nothing?" He removed the coke bag from her pocketbook and waved it in her face. "You call this nothing?" he shouted.

"Give that to me! It's not mine!" She tried to grab it from his hand but failed.

"Whose is it?" he demanded furiously.

"None of your business!" She dashed into the bedroom, slammed the door, and locked it.

He walked to the bathroom door, which was opposite their bedroom door. "Open the door now or I will flush this shit down the toilet!"

A few tense moments passed.

"I'm not kidding, Debbie. Open the fucking door and talk to me, or I'm flushing this shit right now."

The bedroom door burst open, and Vinny was looking down the barrel of his off-duty revolver. His eyes went to the hand holding the gun, then back to her face. What he saw was no longer the innocent face of the woman he loved, but the face of a crazed and desperate junkie who would kill for a fix. He instantly knew not to underestimate her.

Think like a cop. Remember your training.

Vinny looked off, then back. "Calm down, Debbie."

She held him in her stare. "Throw the coke on the floor in front of me!" Her eyes were filled with hate.

Vinny stared at her for a moment, then did as she instructed. The baggie landed directly at her feet. When she bent over to pick it up, the barrel of the gun momentarily pointed away from him. He dove frantically for it. His right hand, grabbing the cylinder of the revolver, stopped it from discharging. Pulling the gun free from her grasp with his right hand, he simultaneously flung her, sailing backward with his left arm. She bounced off the mattress and landed on the floor. Without thinking, he picked her up and pinned her against their huge bedroom window. "I should throw you out this fucking window!" he screamed, shaking her vigorously. "I worry about getting shot every day at work, and now my own wife's trying to kill me!" He was out of control; his entire body was trembling with fear and rage.

"Go ahead, throw me out the window!" she screamed. "I don't love you anymore!"

Suddenly, as quickly as the rage had come, it subsided. Her words cut like a knife, straight to his soul. He put her down on the floor, staring blankly into her eyes. Frightened, angry, and emotionally drained, Vinny had the presence of mind to turn and walk away.

"Pack your bags," he said flatly as he exited the bedroom.

"All right," she said, waiting for him to leave before closing the door behind him and locking it.

Ten minutes later, she appeared carrying a suitcase and a large shopping bag with her jewelry box peeking out of the top. Silently, she opened the hallway closet and removed from it the full-length silver fox coat he had bought for her the previous Christmas. She then walked out the door as Vinny sat and watched speechless. She reappeared five minutes later and stood in the foyer by the front door. "Where's the coke?" She asked nonchalantly. He looked at her as if she were insane.

"I flushed it down the toilet."

Her eyes turned into tiny slits. "You'll pay for that! I'm going to file charges that you hit me. I'm going to tell your job about it, and I'm going to get you fired!" she shrieked.

He sat unfazed as her storm raged about him. All he wanted to do was help, but it didn't lift the feelings of guilt and helplessness that were tearing him up. "Get out," he said flatly, without looking at her.

"You just wait," she said ominously. She slammed the door on her way out.

Late in the afternoon, it started to rain heavily. A damp chill woke him. Sitting up, he realized his head hurt, his muscles ached, and his left shoulder was badly bruised from when he'd hit the wall. Getting up, he walked to the kitchen to brew some coffee.

There's no way I can find out what she's been up to. I just can't, or I'll run the risk of getting hurt. All I can do is wait and hope she comes to her senses before she ends up in life's gutter. I feel terrible, helpless, but I can't do any more for her. I gave it my best shot, but it wasn't good enough.

He poured a cup of coffee.

Glen Island Beach—how absolutely beautiful she was then, her bright smile and fantastic tan and the sparkle in her eyes when she looked at me. That was when she became everything to me. She was what love is, or should be, but she is no more, so our love is no more. Better get used to it and move on.

A knock on the door brought Vinny back from his reverie. He produced a self-satisfied smile and opened it. To his shock and disbelief, before him yet again stood two uniformed Yonkers cops. The male officer was the older of the two, a veteran, no-nonsense type. The female was much younger, in her early twenties, with a cynical look on her face.

"Are you Mr. Davis?" the male asked officially.

"Don't tell me she crashed the car or got locked up, because I'm not in the mood."

"No, nothing like that," the female said suspiciously. "May we come in?" she added politely.

"Sure, why not?" Vinny said casually, opening the door wide enough for both of them to enter. In the foyer, both officers stopped simultaneously and stared at the wall above Vinny's desk. The entire wall was covered with his TP/NYPD commendations and awards, along with several photos of him beside Mayors Koch and Dinkins.

"Are you on the job?" the male cop asked.

"I certainly am. What can I do for you?"

Surprisingly, the female officer took charge. "Your wife filed an assault complaint earlier today," she said accusingly. "She's got black-and-blues on her arms where she said you picked her up and tossed her around like a rag doll."

Ahhhhh, that's why they sent a female officer, and that's why she's taking the lead.

He looked bewildered. "What's your name?"

"Officer Gray." She didn't return his smile.

"Let me tell you a story, Officer Gray."

At the end of the story, he handed Officer Gray the empty plastic bag with cocaine residue in it. He then removed his shirt to show them his battle wounds. "Show her the bag with her prints on it," Vinny said indignantly. "If she insists on going through with the complaint, speak to the officers who responded here this morning. Then tell her she's going to be the one wearing silver bracelets."

"I think we've wasted enough of your time," the older officer said quietly. "We'll make sure she gets the message and instruct her that if she wants to proceed further with this, she should go to family court."

"Thank you. Appreciated," he responded as he showed them to the door. "Have a nice night," he added. He then closed the door and locked it behind them.

They're right, the line between love and hate is very fine indeed. Look what my sweet, sexy, loving wife's become: a wild-eyed cokehead. Our love's dead, and now it looks like war.

CHAPTER 11

In the weeks that followed, Vinny was hit with a few surprises. The first came in the form of a summons for him to appear in family court. He appeared without the presence of legal counsel.

Debbie, however, appeared accompanied by a high-powered attorney from White Plains. Her lawyer was an attractive female in her early forties, a devoted female rights activist. TC and several other friends in Westchester told him she was also a lesbian, once caught in the act of performing a deviate sexual act in a judge's chambers.

Appearing in Yonkers Family Court that day, Vinny thought he would end up skinned alive, but after explaining the mitigating circumstances to the judge and agreeing to a joint order of protection, he walked out of the proceedings relatively unscathed.

The second surprise came a few days later, when he was awakened by loud banging on his front door. Having been rudely awakened at such an early hour of the morning, he stormed out of the warmth of his bed, answering the pounding on his door in his boxer shorts. A short red-faced man with a full head of white hair greeted him.

"Vincent Davis?"

"That's me," he replied angrily.

"You've been served!" the man said as he dropped a white envelope at Vinny's feet.

Still half-asleep, Vinny stared at it. Finally, he picked it up and opened it. What he saw inside made him inhale sharply: a divorce decree with his name on it. It confirmed Debbie wanted their marriage dissolved, and there was no turning back. Their point of no return had passed.

He needed a lawyer. If he needed help, who better to call than TC? He always rose to the occasion.

TC had left the Bronx District Attorney's Office in search of greener pastures in private practice. He established a thriving private practice in Yonkers on Central Park Avenue. Every perp in the Bronx wanted him to defend him. After all, if he was the best in the Bronx at putting criminals behind bars, he would certainly know every legal loophole to keeping them out of jail.

Determined to make a stand, Vinny dressed quickly and without his usual attention to detail. Without calling to make an appointment, he drove to TC's office, hoping he would have a few spare minutes for him. He arrived at his office shortly after opening time and was immediately greeted by Champagne, TC's paralegal. Over the years, she'd become a close personal friend of the Cascione and Davis families. Single, in her midtwenties, she had red hair and the deepest blue eyes Vinny had ever seen. Like TC, Champagne was always available at a moment's notice to friends and family. Be it a sympathetic ear or a shoulder to cry on. They knew they could always count on her support.

"Hi, Vinny." Champagne sighed and warmly embraced him. Their eyes locked for a long moment. "I already know," she said soothingly. She looked into his eyes and saw his pain. Feeling uncomfortable, he looked away.

"Tell me what you know, my friend."

"Well…" She hesitated, not wanting to hurt him. "The rumor mill has it that Debbie has fallen off the deep end. She spends her nights at numerous lowlife bars in Yonkers, drinking, doing coke, and engaging in sex with a variety of lascivious men. She also filed a ridiculous petition in family court against you, which you, in typical Vinny fashion, handled masterfully. And finally, she's filed for a divorce, papers for which you should be receiving soon, if not already."

Vinny looked at her with amazement in his eyes as he produced the envelope from his inside jacket pocket. "I thought it was the wife who was the last to know?" Vinny asked philosophically while managing to produce a smile.

"Wait here." She went in to TC's back office. A moment later, she was leading Vinny by the hand to meet him.

Entering the plush office, the walls of which were filled with diplomas and awards TC had received from the District Attorney's Office and the Florida and the New York Bar Associations, he was greeted by Tommy and Angela, his beautiful wife.

"Greetings and salutations!" They bear-hugged. "You remember Angela, my wife?" he said, gesturing toward her.

"How could I forget her?"

"I hear you have a small problem." Tommy sat behind his desk as he began describing the situation. Angela politely listened for a few moments, shook her head, then left. Sometimes she thought her husband cared for his friends and family too much. If they asked, he'd do anything, no matter how busy he was or how much it took out of him. But that was his way, and there was no changing him.

Tommy sat patiently as Vinny explained in detail the pertinent events in his marriage as it disintegrated. Tommy jotted notes on a yellow legal pad, stopping him to ask a question or make the occasional comment. Tommy already knew most of the details but wanted to hear them afresh in case he was unaware of any vital facts. They'd attended numerous social gatherings together since they were reunited as friends back in 1985. As such, they didn't keep many secrets from each other. When Vinny was finished, he crossed his hands on the desk in front of him and shrugged.

"I know how much you love her, but she would have eventually ruined your life, and possibly your career. Based on what you've told me, and the word is on the street, I'd say her mind is pretty much made up."

He's realistic and giving it to me straight. No sense candy-coating the situation. I can dream and pray till my last breath, and it won't restore my marriage.

TC reached into a drawer and handed Vinny a stack of forms. "Fill these out at your leisure and drop them off with Champagne when you get a chance. Try not to worry. I'll take care of everything."

I'm glad he's so confident! I feel much better now. "Thanks, TC." He rose, and they shook hands.

"There are plenty of fish in the sea. Don't forget it! I'll be in touch."

He felt a strange sense of liberation while Debbie was out destroying her life. He also felt a terrible loneliness that couldn't be filled no matter how many people he was around with.

For the first time in nearly ten years, he had some time on his hands and was clueless as to what to do with it. So rather than waste his time lying about, he decided to throw himself back into what he loved most—being a cop. He spent most of his on-duty time making numerous arrests. Vinny's newest partner was Danny Johnson, a blond-haired, blue-eyed Irish American. He sported a goatee he thought made him look like an undercover cop. They quickly earned a reputation in District 11. Danny was younger than he expected, not yet thirty. That didn't surprise Vinny, who saw a large number of people younger than he was rising through the ranks of the department. Danny was in love with a twenty-eight-year-old Bronx ADA named Karen Jones. She had curly dark-brown hair, big brown eyes, a friendly smile, and a knockout figure. Unlike some of her peers, she never looked down her nose at cops.

Yes, he had his whole life ahead of him and a bright future as a detective.

It was three days after the loneliest Christmas of Vinny's life when he and Danny arrested Pinhead, who had committed fourteen robberies in the Fordham Road area over the span of three weeks. Pinhead was notoriously known in the Forty-Sixth and Fifty-Second Precincts. Not only cunning and unpredictable, he was the fastest perp known to man. He was a twenty-three-year-old black male, six feet tall, five of which were legs. Vinny had arrested him two years earlier on robbery charges in the same area. Unlike the first bust, this time Vinny had to chase him. Pinhead had been picked out of several lineups already, and they were ordered to pick him up on sight. Vinny and Danny were assigned to give special attention to the Fordham Road area due to the rising number of holiday shoppers being robbed.

Vinny was enjoying a slice of pizza, surreptitiously watching the subway entrance stairs, when Pinhead popped out while still holding a gold chain.

The foot chase ended six blocks away, when Vinny used the hood of a car to springboard into the air, land on Pinhead's back, and send him barreling headfirst into the grill of a parked truck. Although Pinhead received a nasty head wound, which caused blood to pour freely down his face, he refused medical attention. He was a professional who knew the price, if caught, for fleeing from them was a good beating. For him, his injury from his abrupt contact with a ten-ton truck was a welcome end to the chase. Moments later, Danny arrived with an elderly Hispanic female. She identified Pinhead as her attacker and the gold chain and crucifix as hers. Screaming something in Spanish, she proceeded to get in a few good shots on Pinhead with her umbrella before a Spanish-speaking officer calmed her down.

With Danny's Karen working the night shift at the Central Booking Complaint Room, it was obvious who was going to process Pinhead's arrest.

Stopping at a traffic light at 161st Street and Gerard Avenue, with Pinhead and Danny in the back seat, Vinny noticed Christina Fusco crossing the street. It was raining lightly, and she was carrying an umbrella in one hand and a pizza box in the other. She was young and incredibly sexy—too sexy for an ADA. At twenty-seven, she was single, had a house on Long Island, and was the newest, and probably brightest, ADA in the Bronx. She was also Karen's best friend.

Vinny rolled down the driver's-side window and hit the siren for a second. She immediately turned to see Vinny waving her over. As she walked toward him, her beauty momentarily stunned him. She met his stare head-on, then smiled coquettishly. "I can't believe it's you." She never took her eyes off his.

"Why's that?"

Hmm. This is interesting.

"Because I haven't seen you much, and I was asking about you just last week. Hey, Danny," she said, leaning into the car.

"How're you doing?" He glanced over to check Pinhead, who acted disinterested.

"Who's your friend, Danny?"

"This is Pinhead, wanted for several robberies in this garden spot of the Bronx."

"Say hello to ADA Fusco, Pinhead. If you're polite to her, maybe she'll go easy on you at your trial."

"I ain't be going to no trial, Davis," he said defiantly. "Only a fool go to trial. I take a plea!"

Vinny and Danny couldn't help but laugh. "Do you see what a good job I do, Counselor? Not only do I arrest them, but they're willing to arrange their own pleas as well!"

"I'm impressed. If you keep this up, I may have to find a new job."

"Well, we have to go. Duty calls. I just wanted to stop you and say hello."

"Danny," she asked unexpectedly, "are you taking this collar?" She smiled mischievously.

"I must." He smiled back.

"If you two are trying to talk in code, I'll have you know I know exactly why my young partner is so anxious to process this arrest at Central Booking."

"Good! Then while Danny Boy is busy with Mr. Pinhead, you can stop by my office. I want to talk to you about something."

Now she's being mysterious. She's never asked me up before. I don't know what to make of what she just said.

"I'll see you in a little while," she said eagerly as she turned and walked away.

"What do you make of that, Danny?"

"Shit, even I knows what to make a that," Pinhead interjected. "She's on fire and wants it big-time!"

They laughed so hard that by the time they led Pinhead from the back seat, tears were rolling down their faces. Even the sergeant on the desk wanted to know what was so funny. "Nothing, Sarge. Just a private joke."

Vinny was more than a little curious as he rode the elevator to the sixth floor of the Bronx Supreme Court Building. He knew Christina's wedding was to take place in three days, so Pinhead's theory had to be wrong.

It was 7:30 p.m. as he exited the elevator and headed for Trial Bureau 80. The building seemed deserted—not even the night cleaners were around. He paused in the doorway of her office and watched her review some notes. She sat with her legs up on her desk, shoes off, the slit of her skirt displaying her long sexy legs. She hadn't noticed him or felt his presence.

Christ, she's gorgeous. I could fuck her right there. Too bad she's getting married. Lucky bastard. Imagine getting to fuck that a few times every day.

"You look incredibly sexy sitting there like that."

"Oh my God, Vinny!" Her hands jerked protectively across her chest for a moment before she caught herself. "You nearly scared me to death."

"We, anticrime cops, are trained at being surreptitious. So what's this secret you have to talk to me about?"

"Come in and close the door," she said provocatively. Vinny entered and did as she instructed.

Not bothering to put on her shoes, she came around from behind her desk. She boosted herself up onto it and sat facing him. She smiled slyly. "Do you remember a couple of weeks ago, at your District Christmas party, you got a phone call shortly after receiving your Cop of the Month Award?"

Vinny thought about that night. He'd received two Cop of the Month Awards, for September and November, and was the only person without a date. Despite the honors, it was one of the loneliest nights of his life. He remembered Danny telling him he had a phone call in the lobby. When he answered, he only heard the sound of a few giggling females and loud background music. Vinny thought it might have been his wife, drunk at some bar, calling to annoy him. "That was you calling me?"

A mischievous smile creased her lips. "That was I."

"Then why didn't you say something to me?"

"Let me explain. It was my bachelorette party, and I was feeling a little tipsy. The girls and I were talking about who we thought was the sexiest guy around the office and what that guy would be like in bed. There were a few names mentioned, until your name came up. Let's just say you have a few admirers in the DA's office who wouldn't mind seeing what you'd be like in the sack."

Vinny was speechless and more than a little embarrassed by her story. "That was when one of the girls said you were getting divorced and would soon be available. I hadn't heard about your separation, but when I did, I got excited."

Her eyes were now filled with excitement, and she began to blush as she continued. "You see, Vinny," she said, moving closer to him, gently touching his face, "I've thought about you an awful lot since we first met, and that night, I wanted you so bad."

Vinny felt his heart racing as the sexual excitement rushed through him. "I take it that this is my chance to kiss the bride?" He ran his hand gently through her hair until it rested on the back of her neck.

"You bet it is," she said as she gave him a long, passionate kiss.

The sexual chemistry was unbelievable as their bodies became entangled. He boosted her back onto the desk and moved in between her legs.

"You'd better put something against that door," she said, her hands around his waist, looking up at him.

He went to the door, opened it, and looked out into the hallway. "The coast is clear," he said anxiously and placed a chair under the doorknob.

"It's late. Everyone has gone home," she said confidently as she brought her feet to the floor, slipping off her silk panties, then lifted herself back onto the edge of her desk.

"This is crazy," Vinny said, staring at her open, inviting legs. "I'm still on duty. What if I get a call?"

"Danny knows you're here," she informed him, undoing his belt, his jeans dropping to the floor, bringing his full erection deep inside of her. They had fast, erotic, and passionate sex right on her desk.

Vinny had to place his hand over her mouth as she had a tremendous orgasm, in fear of someone hearing them.

"You are an unbelievable lover," she said affectionately as he fell into her arms.

"You're not so bad yourself," he said in a whisper in her ear.

"No, baby, it's you," she said defiantly. "No man has ever brought out the sexual desire in me the way you just did."

"I guess that's all this was, just sex? One last fling before you get married?" Vinny asked with a quizzical look on his face.

"Of course not," she said defensively. "I've been crazy about you for a long time, but I'm getting married in three days. I just can't call off the wedding now. His parents are arriving from Florida tomorrow."

"Do you love him?" Vinny asked with a hint of sarcasm in his voice.

She lowered her head as if she were ashamed. "I guess I don't after just making love to you. Why couldn't you have gotten separated from your wife a couple of months ago?" she asked angrily.

"At this very moment, I wish I had," he said, pulling her close, kissing her full on the lips. "Will I see you again?" he asked half-heartedly. She couldn't read his expression, but it seemed as though the warmth had left his face.

"Don't be upset, baby. We'll just have to see what happens," she said in a sultry voice, kissing him once again, this time a longer, more passionate, lingering kiss.

"You got a deal," Vinny said, looking at his watch. "I have to pick up Danny at Central Booking."

"I'm sure Karen is keeping him happy at Central Booking, maybe not as happy as I kept you, but happy all the same," she said mischievously.

Fixing his clothes, he hurried toward the door. He turned around and whispered, "Call me."

"Don't worry, I will," he heard as he turned to walk away.

Christina sat in her office trembling. She'd never imagined sex could be like that. How good she could feel and still be feeling. Vinny had been gone for over an hour, but the smell of him, his cologne, his scent of perspiration was still on her, and she didn't want to lose it, not ever. She sat replaying it in her mind, how it happened, how one thing had led to another, how she'd reached for him, pulling him deep inside of her. She didn't want him to leave, not even for a moment. She just wanted him to be inside her forever. She had never met anyone as genuinely sincere, loving, and kind. His kiss was sweet, gentle, and at the same time, forceful. As she thought of his beautiful smile and muscular body, she could feel her own wetness beginning again. She hadn't meant for it to happen, but she couldn't control it. She suddenly threw her head back and laughed aloud. She was alone in her office and didn't care if anyone in the other offices might hear. She was getting married in less than seventy-two hours, and she was in love with another man.

With Vinny at thirty-two and going through a painful divorce, it was only natural that he fall for a twenty-seven-year-old beautiful, poised, and brilliant woman on her way to making a name for herself as a talented attorney. What he couldn't understand was what she saw in him. Although he considered himself an attractive man, finding it relatively easy to talk to women, he never considered himself the well-educated, sophisticated type a woman like Christina Fusco would be attracted to. That was why he was shocked when he received her phone call the morning after their hot and steamy lovemaking in her office, inviting him to lunch. It was his day off, and she explained to her bureau chief that she would like to leave for the day after lunch to meet her future in-laws, who were due to arrive from Florida later that day. Only meeting her future in-laws was the furthest thing from her mind.

Vinny picked her up in the rear of the courthouse and proceeded to drive directly to the Bronx's Little Italy, on Arthur Avenue. There they enjoyed fine wine, a gourmet Italian meal, and talked as if they had been lovers for years, neither one of them mentioning the rapidly approaching wedding day. It was raining when they finally decided to leave the restaurant, in which they had held hands and kissed, seemingly for hours. Neither one of them wanting their day together to end, they decidedly jumped into Vinny's car and proceeded to drive to the Botanical Gardens, where they parked as the rain fell lightly onto the car.

"Do you want to make love to me?" Christina teased, running her hand through Vinny's hair, a mischievous twinkle in her eye.

"Right here?" he replied, perfectly serious. "What if we get caught, a cop and a DA, making love in the middle of the day at the Botanical Gardens? Not to mention the fact that you're getting married in two days."

Christina shot him a look. "I didn't think you were afraid of anything," she said, leaning back, removing her lacy black panties.

Vinny smiled. "Are you sure?" he asked curiously, already beginning to feel his arousal.

She held his gaze, then pulled him toward her, kissing him passionately. Before either of them could stop, they were pulling each other's clothes off. They made love wildly in the bliss of mutual passion. She kept pulling him closer and closer, wrapping her legs around him, grinding until she had an orgasm with a series of loud screams.

When they were finished, they collapsed into each other's embrace. "That was unbelievable," she said, feeling totally satisfied.

"You're insatiable," he replied, catching his breath.

They held each other closely for what seemed like an eternity before she said, "I have to get going."

His eyes narrowed. "Why?"

Christina was unperturbed. "I have to go and spend time with my trailer-park-trash future in-laws," she said disgustedly.

Vinny shook his head. "I think you're making a huge mistake marrying this guy."

Christina crossed her impressive legs, withdrew a cigarette, and lit it. She drew deeply on her cigarette, stared at Vinny with a look of dismay, and said, "I couldn't agree more."

When Christina Fusco, now Christina Griffin, arrived back in New York from her honeymoon, she was delighted to learn that Vinny and Danny were testifying in a robbery trial and Karen was the prosecutor.

Vinny and Danny were in Karen's office the morning Christina arrived at work. When she unexpectedly arrived at Karen's office, Vinny was mesmerized. She looked particularly beautiful, with her hair let loose and wild. Her tanned body and her big brown eyes blazing with excitement. She wore a beige dress slit up the side, which accentuated her shapely legs, high heels, and a large diamond wedding ring on her finger. She was stylish and extremely sexy.

Closing the door to the office, she rushed into Vinny's arms, giving him a long, passionate kiss. "I missed you so much," she said affectionately, drawing him closer into her embrace. Karen and Danny stood dumbfounded. They both undoubtedly knew the two of them had had sex together, but the expressions on their faces showed they had thought it to be just a prewedding fling. Karen had told Vinny, casually, over lunch, while Christina was on her honeymoon, that he should accept what happened as a prewedding fling, a girl's way of living out her last fantasy before settling down. Karen had been the maid of honor at the wedding and was clueless that Christina had fallen so deeply for Vinny.

Within a month or so later, the two of them had become inseparable. Karen had a magnificent apartment on the Upper East Side, which was used as a place for Christina to rendezvous with Vinny whenever she could sneak away from the home she now shared with her husband in Bellville, Long Island.

It wasn't easy for Christina to sneak away as much as she would have liked, but they made the most of the time they spent together.

The assistant district attorneys in Trial Bureau 80 alternated homicide duty among one another at least once or twice a month.

Most of the ADAs hated doing homicide duty, because it was done in twenty-four-hour shifts and you had to stay within the city limits to respond to homicides in the middle of the night. Among her girlfriends in the DA's office, Christina would volunteer to do their homicide duty for them, which they would gladly accept as a kind offer. She would then tell her husband she was staying at Karen's apartment and would take the subway to work in the morning. Christina would then meet Vinny, Karen, and Danny there, and they either went out and painted the town or they stayed in and Vinny would prepare a gourmet meal for the four of them.

At the end of their evenings, Vinny and Christina would retire to the spare room in Karen's apartment and make mad, passionate love, hoping her beeper wouldn't go off in the middle of the night, calling them out to deal with some stiff. The few times it did happen, Vinny would drive her to the scene and stay with her until the investigation was completed. At the crime scene, the cops' suspicions were never aroused by an ADA showing up at a homicide with a police escort. They assumed Vinny was her driver assigned to the DA Squad.

He was not happy about her marriage. He hated the lying, cheating, and deception.

But when she would promise she was going to leave him, while kissing Vinny, pulling him close to her body, saying in the sultriest voice, "We have the rest of our lives together to make love," he would give in to her loveliness.

I can't help it! I'm falling in love with her.

CHAPTER 12

By early spring, word in the neighborhood was that Debbie's condition continued to deteriorate at an alarming rate. She had already lost the job she had held for over ten years to pursue her new party lifestyle. Living at home with her parents, she had applied for public assistance, claiming she was indigent. An obvious ploy in which her lawyer had put her up to in an attempt to help strengthen her claim for alimony in their pending divorce proceeding. Her lawyer also advised her to get maximum use out of the family court order of protection. The only time Vinny would hear from Debbie was when he would receive a phone call from her advising him what time she would be coming over to retrieve her property. She would then arrive as scheduled with a police escort and legally loot their apartment of whatever she wanted. Vinny had agreed to an amicable, quick, uncontested divorce, but her lawyer had convinced her to turn their divorce into the Wars of the Roses.

Vinny had been invited to Tommy's house to enjoy a Sunday dinner and iron out some of the details for the divorce proceedings. Tommy had bought a beautiful three-bedroom home in Colonial Heights in Yonkers, two blocks from the house in which Vinny grew up. Tommy's wife, Angela, had to run to her office in Manhattan to polish up a corporate deal that was to take place first thing Monday morning. So with Tommy playing dad to his son, Vinny had gladly accepted his friend's invitation to have dinner and assist at playing babysitter. Tommy was the proudest father Vinny ever met. He envied and admired his friend and his life with his loving, supportive wife and newborn son.

"What do you mean she wants me to pay for her lawyer's fees?" Vinny asked incredulously, holding little Anthony in his arms as Tommy continued frying the meatballs he was preparing for the sauce.

"I said she's asking for it." Tommy shot Vinny a mischievous look, dropping another meatball into the simmering tomato sauce. "There's no way in hell we can agree to that," Tommy said emphatically. "That dike is borderline criminal with what she charges her clients," Tommy said, smiling maliciously, dropping another meatball into the frying pan of hot garlic and oil. "Besides," Tommy continued, his voice becoming softer, yet more passionate, "I've reviewed your net worth statement. You should have filled it out in red ink." He was joking, of course. "Twenty-five grand worth of bills for fertility doctors, another twelve grand in credit card bills, no savings account or investments to speak of. I'd say you are definitely in the red." He was amused. "What do those doctors do for twenty-five grand?" Tommy asked, seemingly fascinated.

"I'm not exactly sure," Vinny said with a quizzical look on his face. "All I do know is that if you want one of these bundles of joy," he added, holding up Tommy's son, looking at him admiringly, "you pay the doctors whatever they want."

Tommy looked at his friend, who adored children. He could see the envy in Vinny's eyes as he held little Anthony lovingly in his arms, and he could also feel his pain. "Touché, my friend," Tommy said, holding up a glass of Chianti. "Touché."

"So tell me," Tommy said, changing the subject, "how are things going with the lovely Christina Fusco?" Tommy had a childish smirk.

Vinny's face immediately broke into an enormously bright smile. "Things are going along quite well," Vinny answered coolly.

"Quite well?" Tommy said rhetorically. "Let me tell you something, my friend. You are now the envy of many men. One of which happens to be me. Christina worked in the DA office while I was there. Men used to trip over their tongues when she walked by. Many men have gone to great lengths attempting to gain her affection, only to crash and burn in a blaze of humiliation. So do tell, how did you do it?" Tommy asked with amazement in his eyes.

Vinny thought for a moment as he put the baby in his high chair. "She picked me," Vinny said dispassionately, turning to meet Tommy's stare head-on.

"She picked you?" Tommy asked in disbelief, running his fingers through his thick black hair. Tommy refilled their glasses with Chianti, then sat at the dining room table. "Sit," he instructed Vinny, pointing to the chair next to him. "I want to hear, in detail, how she picked you," he said earnestly. "Spare no detail!" He was indignant, producing a ready smile.

By the end of dinner and their second bottle of Chianti, Vinny had finished explaining the story of their romance, from its inception to the present.

"That's the wildest story I have ever heard," Tommy said, bewildered. "You should write that stuff down and send it to one of those trashy romance novelist. They could turn that story into a best seller and make you a millionaire. So what's going to happen now? Is she going to leave her husband?" Tommy asked in wonder.

Vinny reflected on a conversation he'd had with Christina on Friday night as she lay nestled in his arms in the bed in Karen's spare bedroom. "I love you," she had said passionately. "It's just going to take some time to get a divorce. I just can't pick up and leave. I've only been married for a few months." The word *married* cut Vinny like a knife. Although he was not friendly with her husband, he saw him all the time at the courthouse, or at Boss Tweeds, a local bar around the corner from the courthouse—a bar whose primary customers were cops, court personnel, and lawyers. Seeing Christina in the bar with her husband, "charading" around as the happy newlyweds, was destroying Vinny inside. "We both knew what we were getting into when we began this affair," she had said irritably. "I promise you I am going to leave him. Just give me a little time to work this out. I love you," she had added, pulling him close, kissing him on the lips.

"She says she is going to leave him soon," Vinny answered, coming out of his reverie. "She just doesn't want to embarrass him by doing it so soon," he added thoughtfully.

Tommy stared at him. "Listen, Vinny," he said with a touch of concern in his voice. "We've known each other for twenty years.

You're like the little brother I never had. That's why I feel I can say this to you and feel comfortable in doing so."

Confused, Vinny looked at Tommy, waiting for him to say what was on his mind.

"Be careful, my friend," he said earnestly. "You're at a very vulnerable point in your life right now, and I don't want to see you get hurt. In case you haven't noticed, what she is doing is incongruous. She may appear to be sophisticated, loving, and caring, but if she could do this to him, she could as easily do it to you."

Vinny looked perplexed. Christina had told him the wedding was a mistake that never should have happened. She had been hopelessly in love with him for two years but stayed away, respecting the fact that he was happily married. She had said that if he had only separated sooner from his wife, she would have called off the wedding, but with only two days before her wedding, it had been too late. She had married the poor bastard anyway and was now unable to give Vinny up. Nor was he willing to give her up.

"I just don't want to see you get hurt," Tommy said, interrupting Vinny's thoughts.

"Don't worry," Vinny said reassuringly. "There's no way she would hurt me. You'll see, in a couple of years from now, she'll be sitting right here, having dinner with us and your wife, and it will be me changing diapers," Vinny added proudly.

Tommy shook his head in disbelief, knowing what he had tried to tell his friend went in one ear and out the other. "You're probably right," Tommy said amicably, not wanting to pursue the conversation.

At home, he suddenly felt disoriented and terribly confused. Tommy's words continued to play over and over in his mind, like a song you hear on the radio, only to find yourself constantly singing it for no known reason. What had been so decisive and purposeful such a short time ago seemed foggy, even vague, as if it were in the distant past.

Looking around his apartment, he tried to settle on the reality that Debbie was indeed gone. He felt terrible coming home to this empty place where so many happy memories had been made, locked forever within these walls. Pouring himself a scotch and water, to help ease the pain of his loneliness, he proceeded to play back the messages left on his answering machine. "God, I miss you so much." Christina's voice echoed throughout the room. "I can't wait to be with you Friday night. I love you."

"I love you too," Vinny said affectionately, as if she were really there.

Christina's message was followed by two collection agencies looking for late due payments. Without Debbie's second income, it was next to impossible for Vinny to pay all the bills they had acquired over the last year. He worked as much overtime as was humanly possible, yet he still found himself living from paycheck to paycheck. The thought of claiming bankruptcy was starting to look like his only option. Vinny had tried to call Debbie to discuss the situation like mature adults, but he was informed by his mother-in-law that Debbie was vacationing in Germany with her new boyfriend.

Wonderful, Vinny had thought. *She moves in with her parents, gets fired from her job, is getting public assistance, and is enjoying herself in Europe while I work my ass off so I don't end up in the poor house. Whoever said life is fair?* Vinny had to stop his mind from thinking, even if for just a little while. He had to not think.

Disturbed and frustrated, he had gone into the living room and turned on the TV when the phone rang. In the hopes that it was Christina, he answered it before his machine picked up.

"Hello?" he said anxiously.

"Mr. Davis?" a male voice asked suspiciously.

"Yes. Who's this?" Vinny said, disappointed.

"This is Mr. Hudson of MCI Credit Corporation. We represent a Dr. Stang—"

"Hold on a minute! I paid the good doctor 150 dollars last month."

"Yes, sir, you did, but that still leaves you several months behind on your payments."

"That's it!" Vinny shouted into the phone. "You tell the good doctor he's not going into the hat next month!" Vinny said indignantly.

"The hat?" the voice said questionably. "I'm afraid I don't understand what hat you are referring to."

Vinny took out a cigarette, lit it, and took a long drag. Feeling the effects of the wine he had drunk with Tommy, mixing with the scotch in his hand, he decided to have some fun with the annoying bill collector. "The hat," Vinny said brusquely, "is my new way of bookkeeping since my untimely separation from my wife, who left me with this astronomical amount of bills." Vinny took another drag of his cigarette, then continued, "So each month I take all the bills and place them into a hat. I then close my eyes and withdraw five of them, and those are the ones I pay that month. Pretty good system, wouldn't you say?" Vinny asked, holding back his laughter.

There was no response on the line, so Vinny continued to antagonize.

"You see," Vinny said decisively, "by placing all the bills in the hat, closing my eyes, and picking some, everyone has a fair chance that they might get paid that month. But since you have called me on a Sunday night, explaining the good doctor is not happy that I made an effort to pay him, this month he will not be put into the hat," Vinny said irritably. "Do you understand my method of madness when it comes to dealing with collection agencies?" Vinny asked simply.

"I believe I do, sir," the man said disgustedly.

"Good," Vinny said enthusiastically. "Then you have a good night." As Vinny hung up the phone, he broke out in an abrupt laughter, picturing the bill collector's face as he explained the facts of life to him.

Putting out his cigarette in the ashtray on the coffee table, he decided to go to bed. He'd had enough fun for one night. No matter how unaffected Vinny tried to feel, his affair with Christina was weighing heavily on his conscience. Yet he felt powerless to stop himself from seeing her. They had been together for five months, and his devotion was unquestioning, but her decision to leave her husband had not been forthcoming.

As previously arranged, Christina and Karen would meet Vinny and his brother Michael after work, at a bar down the street from

Vinny's apartment. His partner, Danny, had an unexpected family emergency at home that he had to attend to, leaving Karen alone for a Friday night. It was Christina's last-minute idea to invite Michael to keep Karen company. Karen had met Michael after spending Easter Sunday trapped in Yonkers, after Christina left her sleeping in Vinny's spare bedroom. Christina and Karen had spent that Saturday night at Vinny's apartment.

When Christina awoke late on Easter Sunday morning in Vinny's bed, she inadvertently left Karen behind in her rush to get home to her husband. Vinny remembered when Christina called later that morning Karen grabbing the phone out of his hand mid-sentence. "I'm trapped in Yonkers, Christina." But Karen didn't seem to mind. She and Vinny had become close friends, and she freely accepted his invitation to spend Easter with the Davis family. That was when she met Michael, and the two of them became friendly. Neither one being the other's type, but as platonic friends, they had a lot of laughs together.

Olde Tymes Pub is a quiet neighborhood bar whose patrons were mostly blue-collar, working-class men. Vinny liked it because it was close to home and there was rarely any type of trouble in there. It was not the type of bar that had seen the likes of two classy and beautiful women in it before. So when Christina and Karen entered, there was an eerie silence.

Vinny rose from his barstool to greet them. He kissed Karen on the cheek before he took Christina in his arms and kissed her passionately.

"That's enough of that," Karen said, using both of her hands to separate their embrace. "There will be none of that in front of me while my man's not around," she said jokingly.

"Okay, you win! But all bets are off when we get back to my apartment."

"Fine," Karen said, giving one of her famous condescending smiles.

"Hey," Christina said playfully, pulling on Vinny's hair, "don't I have a say in this?"

"Of course you do, baby," he said.

"What kind of beer do you have, bartender?" Karen asked, pulling up a barstool while lighting a cigarette.

"That's George," Vinny said, making the introduction. "This is Karen," he added, gesturing toward her. "And this beautiful young woman is my girlfriend, Christina," he said while placing his arm around her.

"Nice to meet you, ladies," George replied. "How's Rolling Rock?" George offered in way of beer.

"That will be fine," the girls replied.

After a few beers and some shots of peach schnapps, the uneasiness of being in a seedy bar seemed to dissipate. By the time Michael arrived, the trio was feeling pretty good, singing along to the songs on the jukebox.

"Hey, Michael!" Christina yelled, rushing to his side to embrace him. Michael returned her embrace, kissing her on the cheek.

Turning his gaze toward Karen, who was playing pool with Vinny, he yelled, "Hey, Street Meat!" A nickname Vinny had no idea where it had come from but she had responded to since Easter Sunday.

Karen smiled, giving a friendly wave before sinking the eight ball in the corner pocket. "You owe me a beer," she said winningly to Vinny.

"I think you're a hustler," Vinny said petulantly.

"Sore loser," she said, grabbing him by the arm to join Michael and Christina, seated at the bar. "How are you doing, Michael?" Karen asked, kissing him on the cheek.

"Better than my brother, by the looks of things," Michael responded with a grin. "How many beers did you take him for?" he asked curiously.

"Only two," Karen responded proudly.

"You should know you can't beat Street Meat here," Michael said, placing his arm around her while she smiled triumphantly.

"Hey, George, give Minnesota Fats and my little brother a beer," Vinny said pleadingly. Calling his brother Michael *little* was by no means meant literally. Ever since the accident that almost left him paralyzed from the waist down, he had begun a vigorous weight lifting program and had managed to keep himself in excellent shape. Although Vinny was no slouch, he admired his brother's determination to maintain his muscle size.

Within the next hour, the four were feeling relatively no pain, thanks to the free-flowing shots that George was not only pouring but also drinking.

"What do you say to a barbecue on your terrace?" Christina asked excitedly, looking at Vinny with her big brown eyes.

"That sounds like a great idea," Karen added.

"Ask and you shall receive," Vinny said eagerly, placing his arm around Christina and Karen.

It was an unseasonably warm day for the first week in May, a perfect night for a barbecue. While Vinny and Michael went into the supermarket to pick up the necessary food, the girls went into the liquor store to pick up some wine. Unsure of what the girls wanted to eat, Vinny picked up a little of everything. Steaks, hamburger meat, hot dogs, buns, potato and macaroni salad, corn on the cob, and all the necessary ingredients for a fresh-tossed salad. Before leaving the meat department, he grabbed a whole cut-up chicken and a rack of spare ribs, just to be on the safe side.

"You think you have enough food?" Michael asked sarcastically.

"What we don't eat, I'll freeze," Vinny said casually, smiling at his brother. "You're really in love with this girl, aren't you?" Michael asked hesitantly.

"Is it that obvious?" Vinny asked shyly, as if he were a child caught doing something wrong.

Michael smiled at his brother. "Let's put it this way," he said coolly. "Only a fool could miss the look in your eyes when you look at her."

"You see," Vinny said with a self-satisfied smile, "you just answered your own question."

The warm May sun was still shining brightly in a crystal blue sky when they arrived back at Vinny's apartment. The view of the Hudson from his terrace was breathtaking, as everything had already begun to blossom.

Christina joined Vinny on the terrace, while Michael and Karen blasted the Eagles *Hotel California* CD on the stereo.

As Christina sat on a lounge chair, sipping a glass of chardonnay, Vinny couldn't help but stare at her, amazed. She was the most exciting woman in the world—unbelievably gorgeous, strong, determined, and very independent. Sometimes it all seemed like a fantasy the way they had met and fell in love. When Debbie left, he never dreamt he would find such happiness. It was unfortunate that he wasn't able to save Debbie from her self-destructive excesses, but he now had Christina, and life was getting better all the time.

Christina smiled at him. "What are you thinking about?"

Suddenly he got up, went over to the terrace railing, and stared out at the Hudson. "I'm a real dirtbag," he said, shaking his head in self-loathing. "Making love to you in your husband's house."

"It's my house too," she offered defensively. There was a moment of silence.

"We can't keep going on like this. Ever since you introduced him to me at Boss Tweeds that night, I haven't felt right about this. He's invited me to go to Atlantic City with the court officers next month, for Christ's sake!"

She shrugged, looking at him hopelessly. She wanted to say something funny and amusing to help clear the air, but she couldn't think of anything. She got up from her chair.

"You can't leave me. I love you." She stood behind him, slipped her arms around him, hugging him close. "I need you. I don't want anyone else," she whispered in his ear.

Vinny threw his arms around her. Facing her, he noticed her eyes were filled with tears. "What are we going to do?" he asked gloomily, gently wiping away her tears with the back of his hand.

She considered, shrugged her thin shoulders, and said, "I'm leaving him."

"That's great. I'm not even going to ask how soon. I just needed to know in my heart that you would do it, and now I know."

Christina sighed with relief as she saw the pleasure on his face. "I love you," she said emphatically, kissing him slowly on the lips, running her tongue across his teeth.

"I was so scared you didn't love me enough to leave him."

"I do, baby. I honestly do."

"What's going on out here?" Karen interrupted. "I said we'll have none of that," she said disingenuously. "Not until after you feed me, anyway," she added playfully.

"All right, I can take a hint," Vinny said, breaking their embrace, heading to the barbecue.

"Come and do the dance with me and Michael," Karen demanded, pulling Christina through sliding glass doors into the apartment.

Vinny smiled to himself as he lit the barbecue, watching the three of them dance to the soundtrack from *Reservoir Dogs*.

While Michael taught the girls the dance from a scene in the movie *Reservoir Dogs*, they agreed on having a hot dog each to hold them over until the main course was cooked. Vinny was glad he had decided on buying out the meat department at the supermarket, because each of them was in the mood for something different. Karen wanted the chicken, Christina cheeseburgers with blue cheese dressing, and Michael opted for a steak. While the hot dogs were cooking on the grill, Vinny boiled water for the corn on the cob and began slicing tomatoes, cucumbers, and green peppers for the salad. He also washed the chicken and rubbed fresh garlic into the porterhouse steaks. Cooking was one of the passions he shared with Tommy, who could also whip up a gourmet meal in no time at all. When the hot dogs were cooked, Vinny brought them nonchalantly toward the bathroom, where Christina was standing.

"Vinny, you have a fire in the bathroom!" Michael said.

Moving quickly, Vinny went into the apartment to check the bathroom. He stood incredulous in the doorway to the bathroom as bright-orange and yellow flames were coming right through the walls. "Everyone get out!" he exclaimed. Anxiety shot through his body. Flames had broken out into the hallway and were climbing up the walls. He knew the fire must have already consumed the apartments below, and feared the floor might give way, sending them all to a fiery death.

Within seconds, all four of them were safely on the outer stairs to the complex, heading down to the courtyard.

While the girls rushed ahead, Vinny instinctively began banging on his neighbors' doors. On the second floor landing, he realized he had a young kid in his early twenties who worked midnight to eight as a security officer at Saint Joseph's Hospital. Fearful his neighbor might have been sleeping before the fire started, he felt the door for heat. It was extremely hot, which meant he would have to quickly get out of the way when the door opened. He positioned himself in front of the door. Lifting his right leg, he kicked his foot forward in one forceful motion and the door crashed open inward. Simultaneously, he dived to his right, bracing himself to the wall as the flames roared out of the door. The thundering of the flames was like a raging surf, as the ceiling ignited into a rolling fireball that went from one end of the room to the other.

Vinny got down on all fours in the doorway and began to yell, "Jack, it's Vinny! Get out of there!"

No response.

He then looked to his right and saw his brother Michael.

"You're not going in there!" Michael shrieked, meeting his brother's gaze.

Reflectively, Vinny remembered the last time he went into an apartment building fire at 170th and Grand Concourse three years earlier. He remembered the frantic screams of a young Dominican woman. "My babies are in there!" After climbing six flights of stairs, he kicked in the door and crawled on his hands and knees through thick black smoke and intense heat. He had almost given up his search, thinking the kids had already been rescued, when he heard the faint cry of a child coming from the closet. It was there he found two little girls too frightened to move. He cradled both of them in his arms as he ran out of the apartment into the arms of two firemen who were about to enter. He will never forget the feeling of not being able to catch his breath after being helped outside by the firemen. Nor will he ever forget throwing up uncontrollably as EMS administered oxygen to him.

"You wait by the door," he said, fixing his brother with a stare. "I'll be able to hear your voice from inside and find my way back out."

The apartment was identical to his own, so although he couldn't see through the thick black smoke, he crawled through the two bedrooms with relative ease in under a minute. The heat was so unbearable. Any breath he took seemed to sear his lungs.

Finding no one, he headed back toward his brother's voice. Halfway to the door, he bumped into Michael, who was on all fours, holding a dog. "Let's get out of here," Michael said, dragging the dog along the floor.

Outside the doorway of the burning apartment, Michael held the dog's mouth close with his hands. He then placed his mouth over the dog's snout and blew a few short breaths. Amazingly, the dog immediately responded and began barking.

Coughing profusely, trying desperately to catch his breath, Vinny passed out while listening to the arriving sounds of sirens. He was only out for less than a minute, but EMS insisted on taking him to Saint Joseph's Hospital to have a blood gases test. The medics quickly latched him to a stretcher.

He could have easily disobeyed the persistent emergency workers, but when Christina demanded he go, he agreed. Michael and Karen stood by the rear door of the ambulance as he, Christina by his side, was being loaded into it.

"We'll wait here for you guys," Karen said cheerfully.

"Yeah," Michael said. "As soon as the fire is out, we're going to salvage the food and wine," he added with a grin.

Treated and released within two hours for smoke inhalation, they returned back to the scene of the fire. The doctors wanted to keep him overnight for observation, but Vinny was insistent he had to get back before whatever could be salvaged from his apartment was looted. An argument with merit that not even Christina could disagree with.

The courtyard that led to the rear of the building was in total darkness. A few neighbors from the adjoining apartment buildings stood around, commiserating among themselves.

As Vinny and Christina walked down the darkened pathway, they could hear voices filtering from the rear of the apartment. "Here, Street Meat, catch this," Michael said eagerly.

"I got it," Karen replied excitedly.

Christina looked up to the spot where Vinny's living room window was and saw Michael leaning out of it with a bottle of beer in his hand. "Here comes another one," he said, dropping it into Karen's awaiting hands.

"Got it," she said, laughing aloud.

"What are you two maniacs doing?" Christina asked disbelievingly.

"Thank God you two are back," Michael said joyfully. "Now we can start the party!"

Christina looked at Vinny, who merely shook his head.

The entire scene was as mystifying now as when the fire started.

"Did the firemen say it was safe to be in there?" Vinny asked protectively.

"Yeah," Michael said reassuringly. "The living room area and master bedroom are under a couple of inches of water. It's the rest of the place that's trashed," Michael added innocently.

"Might as well go up," Vinny said abruptly, looking for Christina's approval.

"After you. Hey, Street Meat, are you coming?" Christina asked playfully.

"Don't you start calling me that now," Karen said flippantly.

Looking around at what was left of his apartment, he felt unbearably close to being sick to his stomach. The color was gone from his face, and sweat had beaded up on his forehead and upper lip. He held out his hand, and it was trembling. As he stood there, it became unequivocally clear that he had lost everything. Suddenly, his entire body began to tremble, and he was certain he was going to be sick, then the feeling passed. As it did, he became aware of something stirring inside of him, and at almost the same time, he heard the sound of his own voice telling him that this was no accident.

It's got Sabol's name all over it.

"It will be all right." Christina could see the tenseness in Vinny's neck muscles. "We still have my furniture," she said with a reassuring smile.

Vinny immediately felt all the tension dissipate. "You're right, baby," he said with a beaming smile. "What do you say we eat and have some more wine?"

"Now that sounds like a plan," Michael said encouragingly.

"Uh, Christina," Karen said haltingly, with a look of concern. "There happens to be a slight problem with your Volvo," she added reluctantly.

"Oh my God," she breathed. "I forgot all about my car."

"It's not that bad," Michael interrupted gently, "except for the entire front bumper and part of the hood that melted from the heat of the fire. The fire truck pushed it out of the way before it burned too bad," he added anxiously.

"Where is it?" she asked worriedly.

"I parked it down the street," Karen said soothingly. "It's drivable. It just looks like hell."

"Well, I guess it's a good thing I decided I'm going to leave Bob," Christina said nonchalantly. "Will someone pass me a beer, please?"

After a few hours of drinking and eating, it was decided that Vinny had to spend the night at the apartment, and Christina insisted on staying with him. Michael and Karen would go back to the Davis house in Christina's car and they would meet sometime in the morning.

Shortly after Michael left with Karen, Vinny and Christina crawled into his wet bed, fully clothed. For reasons she couldn't explain or begin to understand, she felt more sexually aroused than she had ever felt her entire life. An insatiable hunger had uncontrollably swept over her so powerfully that she could not control her need to make love to him.

Lying in his arms, Christina whispered in his ear, "I thought you were going to spank me?"

He gave her a perplexed look. "Do you think I'm some insatiable stud?" he asked mischievously.

"I know you are," she said, kissing him slowly and passionately on the lips.

He couldn't stop himself from grinning as his hands began to explore under her dress. "You asked for it," he said, slowly stroking her soft legs.

She grinned back at him. "That's right, I did," she said as she surrendered into his embrace.

CHAPTER 13

In the months that passed, Vinny had moved in to the Davis home in Colonial Heights in northeast Yonkers, an area known as the richest section in the city. Grandview Boulevard was a street lined with expensive, stately homes and ancient oak trees. A neighborhood in which a couple of any age could take an after-dinner stroll without fear of being attacked and children could play in the schoolyard free of gun-wielding drug dealers.

Immediately following Vinny's father's retirement from the NYPD, he began working full-time at the New York Times Plant in New Jersey. A job he had worked part-time for the past twenty-five years to help supplement his income as a cop. With his children fully grown, Vincent married and out of the house, and his youngest son, Raymond, soon to also be married, Mr. Davis moved with his wife into a lovely three-bedroom Tudor in Tenafly, New Jersey, leaving the Yonkers home with his mother and two remaining children, Michael and Maria.

As the years passed, so did their grandmother, who helped raise the children after their mother had died in 1972. Soon after their grandmother's passing, Maria, the baby of the family, married and moved out to start a life with her new husband, leaving the family home in the not-so-capable hands of Michael, a devoted bachelor. Michael worked for the Westchester County Department of Corrections by day and a bouncer at a local topless bar by night. It was while working his job as a bouncer that he implemented an ingenious plan to help alleviate some of the household bills and cure the loneliness he felt living alone in a six-bedroom house. While working in the bar, he became friendly with the dancers who happened to tour the East Coast working each bar for one or two weeks at a time. It was then that Michael decided to start renting out space at the house. Instead of the dancers paying fifty dollars a night to stay in a cheap hotel arranged for by the bars' management, Michael would charge them twenty-five dollars a night to stay with him. And as a bonus, he would drive the girls to and from work, saving them on the cab fares they would have had to pay if they stayed at a hotel. His plan worked fabulously. With six bedrooms and the den converted into an extra bedroom, Michael was turning a nice profit, along with the many fringe benefits he received sharing a house with up to seven beautiful naked women at a time.

When looked at from the outside, the Davis home had the appearance of a well-kept, old colonial home. With the exception of the landscaping, which had been left unattended over the years, the house looked the same as it had when Vinny was growing up. It wasn't until the morning after the fire, when Vinny arrived with Christina, still wearing the smoke-filled clothes from the night before, that he saw the devastation that had virtually destroyed the inside of their family home. Reflectively, Vinny remembered the first words out of Karen's mouth the minute he and Christina exited his car. "He calls me Street Meat!" Karen said musingly. "Wait until you get a load of what's inside," she added while sitting on the side porch, sipping a cup of coffee.

"Is there any coffee left?" Christina asked eagerly, meeting Karen's stare. "You'll have to ask one of Michael's servants about that," Karen replied disingenuously, her eyes never leaving Christina's.

Entering the kitchen through the side door, Vinny was immediately overcome by shock and disbelief. Not by the presence of a beautiful young woman wearing nothing but a G-string offering him a cup of coffee, but by the sheer destruction of the kitchen. Aside from the sink overflowing with filthy, unwashed dishes, the entire kitchen was filled with bags of garbage and a mountain of beer bottles and cans. The floor under the sink was literally buckled upward and the floor tiles removed, due to excessive water damage, leaving the rotted plywood foundation exposed. The stove and countertops bore the remnants of what appeared to be a year's worth of spilled or discarded food.

Vinny and Christina stood speechless, unable to speak. "Where's Michael?" Vinny asked the topless, big-breasted female standing before them.

"In his bedroom," she replied cheerfully. "Are you sure you wouldn't care for a cup of coffee? It's fresh."

"No, thank you," Vinny said nervously, unable to take his eyes off the naked woman standing before him. "Come on, honey," he said, pulling Christina by the arm toward the doorway leading to the hallway.

As they proceeded up the stairs to the second floor, where the master bedroom was located, two buxom females, one a blonde, the other a redhead, who were also naked from the waist up, approached them.

"Good morning," the blonde said nonchalantly with a bright smile. "Is there any coffee made?" she asked politely.

Vinny stammered. "I don't know. Yes. Maybe. I'm not sure." Pointing down the stairs in the direction of the kitchen.

"We'll check it out," the blonde said flatly while the redhead stared at Vinny.

"You're cute," she said, running her index finger down the side of his face.

"Thanks," Vinny said with a smile as Christina yanked him by the arm up the stairs.

"My God! There's no way I'm going to let you live here," she said, trying to control her temper.

Vinny nodded absently and continued up the stairs, smiling pleasantly at the girls at the bottom of the stairs. "*Hot* is a better word for him," the blonde was overheard saying as they rounded the stairs. Christina was glowering at them, but she kept her mouth shut.

Michael was lying supine in his bed, wearing a pair of gym shorts, watching MTV on his television, when they entered his bedroom.

"What have you done to this house?" Vinny roared in disbelief.

"Is something wrong?" Michael asked in wonder. He smiled at Christina. "Good morning, sis," he said affectionately, intentionally attempting to avoid the subject.

Christina smiled back. "Nice harem you have living here," she said sarcastically.

"I had to improvise after grandma died and everyone moved out," Michael said calmly.

"Improvise?" Vinny said, his face red with anger. "Michael, it's not so much that you have turned this house into a brothel, as much as it is the amount of damage that's been done. There's a crutch and a chair holding up the dining room ceiling, for Christ's sake!" Vinny rumbled.

"The bathtub overflowed," Michael said defensively. "I'll get around to fixing it."

"Has Dad seen this house lately?"

"Ever since Grandma died and Maria got married, he's never here. But now that you're moving in, you can help me fix up the place."

"He's not moving in here with those naked girls running around!" Christina interrupted.

"Fine. With you living here, I don't need the extra income for the upkeep of the house, but you're the one who has to evict them."

"I have no problem with that."

Christina was true to her word. Within two weeks after explaining to her husband how her car was burned during an unexpected party with Karen at Vinny's house, she left him and moved in with her mother, with the stipulation that as soon as he found a place of his own, she would return to her home, which she would buy him out of in their divorce. Her mother, a widower, lived alone in a house around the corner from the home Christina had bought with her husband, where he was now staying. You could literally throw a stone from one house and hit the other. Ironically, while Christina was redecorating the bedroom she had had growing up, so was Vinny. She was actually happy to be living with her mother, the woman who adopted her as a child and raised her along with her own children as if she were her own. Christina's adoptive father, whom she loved dearly, had passed away a couple of years earlier. His unexpected death devastated Christina so badly that she sought the help of a therapist for over a year. By moving back in with her mother, she now felt she could enjoy spending time with her before she, too, left this world to spend eternal peace with her father in heaven. Christina spent the weekends over the summer at the Davis home, meeting with Vinny's family for barbecues, or leisurely days spent on the Long Island Sound on his father's boat. Vinny's parents felt Christina was a pleasant change they welcomed in their son's life. There was an excitement in their son's life that had been missing for some time.

Vinny certainly had his work cut out for him. A thorough cleaning of the entire Davis home was first. After the cleaning, whatever restoration he could do, with little help from Michael, with his limited ability and financial means, he decided he no longer needed his new car and sold it.

He then purchased a used Ford Crown Victoria, a retired State Police car, from an auction dealer on Jerome Avenue in the Bronx. After he had spent a minimal amount of money on the car restoring it to look like a gypsy cab, it was the perfect car for work. He and Danny, and whoever else was assigned to work with them, could drive around the streets of the Bronx, responding to calls virtually unnoticed. Instead of commandeering a car to drive them to an emergency call, they would drive themselves. By responding quickly, they were afforded the opportunity to put a complainant in the car with them and canvass the area surreptitiously, usually apprehending the suspect. The routes they searched were left to their own ingenuity at the time of the crime. Its charm was its simplicity and their mobility, and because of that, it worked, time and again. Even the NYPD's anticrime units, who were afforded the luxury of driving department unmarked cars, were arriving too late to make the arrest. The second advantage to selling his new car and replacing it with a beat-up Crown Victoria was the money he saved each month. No more car payments, which left him more money each month to replace some of the things he lost in the fire.

During the summer months, as Vinny's love for Christina grew, so did crime in the subways of the Bronx. William Bratton, the newest chief of the New York City Transit Police, who vowed to make his department second to none, wanted action. Before he had taken on the job as chief of the ninth largest police department in the nation, morale was low. The morale in the Transit Police had always been low, its officers treated like second class in comparison to the prestigious NYPD officers. Almost all the Transit Police chiefs had been high-ranking members of the NYPD before being promoted chief of the Transit Police. Needless to say, after they had spent over twenty years as high-ranking members of the NYPD, looking down their proverbial noses at the Transit and Housing Police Departments as sewer rats and security guards, their attitudes carried over with them when they became chief.

For years, the Transit Police had a defective radio system. It was a piece of shit.

Not only didn't it work underground, but it didn't work above ground too. That left a Transit cop pursuing a suspect aboveground unable to obtain assistance. If it weren't for the NYPD, who installed aboveground repeaters after the tragic murder of a Transit cop while in the street, Transit cops still might not have aboveground communications. The Transit Police were also assigned a total of four beat-up and antiquated Chevy Suburban that could barely run to cover the entire Bronx. While other police departments in the state of New York moved with the times in upgrading its equipment, the New York City Transit Police was still in the Stone Age.

Unlike his predecessors, William Bratton came from Boston, not from the ranks of the NYPD. Amazingly, he saw the Transit Police as a forty-five-hundred-member crime-fighting machine. Vowing to the men and women under his command that he would personally make whatever changes were necessary to make them proud to be Transit cops.

First, he started by asking the high-ranking officers under his command what they needed to bring the department into the nineties and motivate its officers. He then personally visited each command throughout the city, attending roll calls to ask his officers what they needed to boost their morale. Almost immediately, changes were made. Transit cops no longer had to do special reports for arrests made in the streets. Reports that were closely scrutinized by the brass as to the reason a Transit cop made an arrest in the street and wasn't in the subway, where they belonged.

The chief was quoted as saying, "I don't care if you're in the street, the subway, or a housing project. If you see a crime being committed, you will make the arrest, on or off duty." Aside from eliminating the bureaucratic paperwork, he began holding the commanding officers of each command personally responsible for crime within his district.

Within months, a fleet of new white-and-blue police cars were patrolling the streets, five cars per district. He also authorized Transit cops to carry 9mm Glock automatics and outfitted his troops with new uniforms. Each officer was issued his own brand-new personal Motorola radio, and he began an extensive overhaul of the communications system citywide. Before long, the officers of the NYPD wanted to know when they would get 9-millimeters, new radios, and cars. It was then that the New York City Transit became second to none.

"Get these, guys!" Captain Stevens roared through the small roll call room. Turning angrily, he saw Sergeant Houston staring at him. When their eyes met, Houston abruptly lowered his head. "I want results, or you'll all be back in uniform, giving out fare-beating summons!" he added before he stormed out of the room.

Houston glanced around the small room at his men. "Dammit, guys!" He was angry and confused. "Why the hell can't you get these guys?" he asked disbelievingly.

There was nothing but dead silence. With their sergeant angry and emotionally drained, all twelve men had the presence of mind not to press it. Suddenly, there was a sharp rap at the door. It opened immediately, and Juan Lopez, a twenty-five-year-old uniformed cop, entered. "Sir, 174th and the Grand Concourse just got hit. A robbery. The Gentleman Bandit," he recited quickly. Simultaneously, every officer in the room took off out the door.

Vinny and Danny were the third unit to arrive at the scene, but this time, there would be no searching for the suspect with the complainant in the back seat of the car. This time, the complainant, a sixty-three-year-old Hispanic housekeeper, was going to the hospital after being thrown onto the subway tracks by the so-called Gentleman Bandit. He was now wanted for seventeen armed robberies at stations from 167th Street to Tremont Avenue on the D Line, which ran under the Grand Concourse. He was described as a light-skinned black or Dominican in his early to midtwenties. He was six feet tall, slim build, and wore a white do-rag on his head. His modus operandi was to approach elderly females while they waited for the train. He would sit or stand next to them and engage them in friendly conversation, then he would produce a large-caliber automatic from a white plastic shopping bag and politely request their money, and jewelry. After the victim complies, he waits with her until the train arrives, walks her to the doors, and waves goodbye to her as the train leaves the station. He then casually walks out of the subway to parts unknown. Last week, he performed this routine at the 167th Street station in front of a four man plain clothes team from Citywide Task Force, who had been sent by the brass to help catch him. When interviewed by the Captain, that team said the suspect was so smooth they thought he knew his victim and was making sure she got on her train safely.

Vinny and Danny had been parked surreptitiously, about fifty yards south of the subway entrance, for about two hours. They listened attentively to, not only the Transit Police radio, but to the N.Y.P.D radio they had signed out of the Forty Fourth Precinct. Their job was not to catch the suspect in the act, that was the job of the plain clothes teams assigned to ride on the trains or wait patiently on the platforms, but to be able to respond in search of him if he did attack. The NYPD radio was an excellent tool for them to have as they wait, in case the City Police received the first call over 911 at any of the other locations he may decide to strike at. "So, how are things going with you and Christina?" Danny asked lightly. Vinny produced a bright smile. "You ever find yourself thinking about a woman all the time. I can close my eyes and see her face." Danny's eyes never left Vinny's. "No, I haven't," Danny said indignantly. "Not even with Karen?" Vinny stared in disbelief. "I thought you two were real hot for one another." Danny smiled deviously. "Real hot, absolutely. But close my eyes and see her face? No way," he said defiantly. "As soon as a man feels like that, his life is over," Danny added sarcastically. Vinney could only smile, thinking about how lucky he is to have found a woman like Christina. Staring off, he sat reflecting about how much his life had changed. His past, nothing more than a vague memory. It all happened so quickly. After everything with Debbie was said and done, he tried to find the answers as to what went wrong. There were none. And it seemed to be the end of the line for him until he met Christina. He knew then that for the rest of his life he would never love anyone else.

Vinny was snatched from his reverie by the crackling of the City Police radio. "Units in the Forty Sixth Precinct, report of a ten-ten, man with a gun, Tremont and the Concourse by the subway entrance. Light skin male, black, six feet, blue jeans, white T-shirt. Gun is concealed in a shopping bag." "Six King responding." "Six Ida on the back Central." Simultaneously, Danny's and Vinny's eyes locked in shocked disbelief. Moving quickly, Vinny started the car and pulled away from the curb as Danny picked up the Transit Police radio to notify, not only Central, but to alert any Transit Officers in the area of the possibility of confronting an armed suspect, and that plain clothes cops are responding to the area. Confronting an armed suspect is one thing, but being confronted by a fellow police officer who doesn't know you're a cop? That's extremely dangerous and gets cops killed.

"If you fuck this up and someone gets robbed on this station while we're responding to a call in the street, there won't be any dispensation. The captain likes you, but he's due to retire next year," Danny said despairingly as Vinny drove quickly without a red light on the roof or siren wailing.

"I'll keep that in mind," Vinny said half-heartedly as they were stopped at a traffic light at the intersection of Tremont Avenue and the Grand Concourse.

Like most good street cops, Vinny had a sixth sense, a gut reaction to alert them to danger or a crime about to be committed. A clairvoyance that would never hold up in court as a standard of proof, but it would keep one alive, which was all that mattered.

As they waited for the light to change, they observed the first NYPD radio car arrive with roof lights flashing. The uniformed officers exited their car with weapons drawn and ordered a man fitting the suspect's description up against the wall of an apartment building. Almost instantly, a second car arrived to back them up, with the officers also exiting their car with guns drawn.

Vinny and Danny observed what was going on as the light changed, and they proceeded slowly through the intersection. It was then that they observed a male fitting the description of the gunman crossing the Concourse directly in front of them, surreptitiously looking over his shoulder at the uniformed officers searching the male they'd stopped. The hair on the back of Vinny's neck was standing up.

"That's him," he said, feeling his adrenaline pumping.

Danny stared at him in amazement.

"Keep an eye on him, Danny," Vinny ordered as they passed the suspect, awaiting the opportunity to make an inconspicuous return in the heavy Concourse traffic.

"He's standing by the subway stairs," Danny said confidently as Vinny made a U-turn, almost being sideswiped by a livery cab. Danny had one hand on his Glock and the other on the door handle as their car barreled onto the sidewalk directly in front of the suspect.

"Police, don't move!" Danny yelled, pointing his weapon directly at the suspect, who immediately bolted into the subway, with Danny on his heels.

Vinny instinctively grabbed the closest radio to him and said quickly, "Foot pursuit. Tremont. In the hole." Signifying their location as the Tremont Avenue subway station.

Without waiting for an acknowledgment, he was out of the car with gun in hand, directly behind Danny.

Reaching the bottom of the subway stairs, Danny screamed at the suspect, "Stop, or I'll shoot!"

The suspect, seeing the uniformed officers approaching from the opposite end of the passageway, thereby preventing his escape, threw the plastic bag he was carrying to the ground, simultaneously throwing his hands up. "There's a gun in the bag, don't shoot!" he yelled fearfully.

"Turn around and face the wall," Danny ordered while aiming his weapon at the suspect's chest.

Vinny also had his weapon trained on the suspect as the uniforms rapidly approached with their guns drawn, yelling, "Police. Drop your guns!"

"Transit Anticrime!" Vinny yelled authoritatively to the officers, never taking his eyes or gun off the suspect and his partner.

As the uniforms approached cautiously, Danny speed-cuffed the suspect in textbook fashion. As Vinny and Danny holstered their weapons, so did the uniformed responding officers. "I'm glad you heard us," Vinny said thoughtfully in the direction of the uniformed officers as he bent down and opened the plastic shopping bag the suspect was carrying, removing a fully loaded military-style Colt .45 caliber and a white do-rag. "Bingo!" Vinny said joyfully, smiling at Danny, and their suspect, who, up until then, had lived an exceptionally charmed life.

With the suspect in handcuffs, they exited the subway to the wailing sounds of the sirens of the responding radio cars. After they had called for assistance before running into the subway, the radio operator had lost contact with them because of dead spots in which they could not receive or transmit by radio. She therefore made it a 10-13, an "officer needs assistance" call, in which every officer, no matter what he is doing, stops immediately to assist his fellow officer. "Eleven Crime Three, Central. Call it off!" Vinny said urgently.

Immediately, the dispatcher hit the Alarm button on her console, which signaled a five-second beeping sound, followed by her encouraging. "No further units at Tremont and the Concourse. Are there any injuries, Eleven Crime Three?" the dispatcher asked worriedly.

"Negative, Central. We have one under arrest, armed with a gun," Vinny said proudly.

"Ten-Four, Eleven Crime Three. One under at your location," she said affirmatively. "Transit Task Force Sergeant to Central K," the radio roared.

Vinny could hear the anger and resentment in his voice. "Go, Task Force Sarge."

"Have Eleven Crime Three stand by. I'm one minute out," he interrupted heatedly.

"Ten-Four, K," Vinny responded quickly to the sergeant's order to stand by. "This is going to get good," Vinny said mischievously, smiling at Danny's concerned face.

Rude and obnoxious, Sergeant Gallo was forty-seven, a twenty-year veteran newly assigned to the prestigious task force unit after serving three years as a patrol sergeant in District 11. Vinny knew him well, and they never saw eye to eye.

"How's it going, Sarge?" Vinny asked politely.

Cold would be an understated description of Gallo's demeanor. He was furious, frigid, and totally insolent. "Thanks for the collar," Gallo said belligerently.

Vinny took a step toward him, his eyes glistening with emotion.

"What?" Vinny was outraged.

"You can't take this collar. How do you think it will look to the brass downtown when they sent up all these task force officers and the district anticrime team makes the arrest? It won't look too good for us," he added with a self-satisfied smile.

Vinny met his stare head-on and smiled back smugly. He then picked up his radio and said calmly, "Eleven Crime Three, Central."

"Go, Eleven Crime Three."

"Do you have the time of arrest and shield number handling the details?" he asked politely.

"Fifteen forty-four hours for the arrest. I need a shield for the officer handling details," she said dutifully.

Gallo smiled maliciously as he brought his radio up to respond.

"Make that number fifty-fourteen," Vinny said proudly into his radio.

"Ten-four, K," she responded, repeating the information back. Vinny could see the rage and resentment in Gallo's face.

"You're going to regret you just did that," Gallo said through clenched teeth.

Vinny stared at Gallo for a moment, then turned to Danny and said, "Take that piece of shit to District 11 in Eleven, boy," pointing to the marked Transit Police car. "I'll meet you there in a little while."

Danny nodded vigorously as he led the prisoner to the rear door of the radio car.

"Whose car is this?" Gallo asked petulantly, pointing an accusatory finger at Vinny's car still parked on the sidewalk.

"It's my personal vehicle," Vinny responded impatiently, opening the driver-side door.

"Do you have permission to use your own vehicle?" Gallo asked with raised eyebrows.

"Yes, I do," Vinny said as he got behind the wheel.

"Let me see your memo book, Officer," Gallo demanded.

Vinny reached across the front seat to retrieve his memo book, which had the post he was to be covering, what time he arrived on post, and an entry made that he was using his private vehicle for patrol.

Sergeant Gallo snatched the memo book from Vinny's hand and inspected it. "Your post is 174th and the Grand Concourse. What are you doing here?" Gallo asked scornfully.

"Responding to a 'man with a gun' call, sir," Vinny responded officially.

"You're off post," Gallo said emphatically, tossing Vinny's memo book on to the front seat next to him.

"Take it up with Captain Stevens," Vinny replied respectfully. "With the mood he was in when I left, shortly after your task force team let this guy get away with another robbery, I'm sure he will be more than gracious to you," Vinny added mockingly as he started his car.

"I'll see you back at the district!" Gallo barked, his voice resonant with anger.

By the time Vinny had parked his car outside District 11 and secured his and Danny's equipment, Sergeant Gallo was already in Captain Stevens's Office. When Vinny entered the district, he was greeted by the desk lieutenant and Danny, who were busy processing the prisoner's personal effects.

"Davis, get in here!" Captain Stevens's voice thundered.

"Uh-oh," Vinny grunted, smiling at Danny. "Sounds like the skipper has a hair up his ass," he added musingly as he headed toward his office.

Standing at attention in the doorway to the captain's office, Vinny asked courteously, "Did you need to speak to me, Skipper?"

"Get in here and close the door! What was your assigned post today?" Stevens asked austerely as Vinny closed the door behind him.

Vinny's eyes locked on the captain's. "Sir, 174th Street on the D Line."

"How did you happen to be at Tremont Avenue on the D Line to make this arrest?"

"We responded to a 911 call of a 'man with a gun' that came over the NYPD radio."

"Where did you get the NYPD radio?"

"I signed it out of the Forty-Fourth Precinct radio room," Vinny said nonchalantly.

Sergeant Gallo looked perplexed.

"They let you do that?" Stevens asked disbelievingly.

"Ever since Bratton became chief, they have. In fact, the NYPD seem to bend over backward to help us."

"I don't see the problem here, Sergeant," Stevens said judiciously. "Davis responded to a radio call in his personal vehicle, which he was authorized to use by the lieutenant on the desk."

"My men were assigned to Tremont Avenue on the D Line," Gallo said accusingly.

"Then where were they?" Stevens roared in disbelief.

Gallo's face turned white. "Oh, ah...," he stammered, running his fingers through his hair. "They were on their assigned meal," he said defensively.

Stevens stared at Gallo in disbelief. "What kind of shit are you shoveling? You come in here making it sound as if you caught my officers off post, driving around in their own car, while your officers, who are assigned that post, are off enjoying their lunch God knows where, while a robbery goes down."

Vinny smiled. He was thoroughly enjoying watching the blood race back into Gallo's face.

"Who do you think you're dealing with?" Stevens was outraged. Picking up a report on his desk, he glanced at it, then threw it in the trash basket. "Get out of my office, Sergeant!" he exclaimed. Gallo turned to leave, and he exchanged surprised glances at Vinny.

"Have a nice day now," Vinny said coldly as Gallo stormed out of the office.

"Another one of your clairvoyant arrest, eh, Davis?" Stevens raised an eyebrow in admiration.

"Plain, old-fashioned luck," Vinny said, smiling brightly.

"Real nice work, nonetheless. Have a seat," he said politely, directing Vinny to a chair in front of his desk.

"Thank you, sir," Vinny said, taking a seat.

"Do you know what this is?" Stevens asked as he brusquely shoved a typed report under Vinny's nose. "It's your endorsement for your promotion sometime in the beginning of the year, and your transfer to the Special Operations Squad."

Glancing at it, Vinny immediately returned the captain's smile.

"Don't thank me," Stevens insisted before Vinny had a chance to speak. "It was the only way I could come up with to get rid of you," he added with a cynical smile.

Vinny was speechless.

"Besides, you may not thank me when you have to answer to a putz like the one who just left my office," Stevens added sarcastically.

Vinny was unsure what to say. A few moments of silence passed.

"Well, get out of here," Stevens said in a deadpan voice.

Vinny got up and headed for the door.

"Davis! Try to stay out of trouble until your transfer comes through."

"I'll try," he said innocently. "I'll try."

CHAPTER 14

It had been almost a year, incredible as it seemed, since Debbie had gone. Over the summer, her parents finally became aware of her alcohol and drug abuse.

Vinny had received a frantic phone call from his father-in-law in the middle of the night requesting his help after Debbie physically attacked her mother and youngest sister, Danielle, after they had found cocaine in her pocketbook. With the assistance of the Transit Police Department's Employees Assistance Unit, a psychology unit designed to help members of the department and their families with psychological problems, dealing with the stress of being a cop, or alcohol problems, they were able to bring her to a detox center, commonly referred to as the Farm, in Carmel, New York. Vinny and Debbie's family believed it was a positive step on the road to her recovery. Only, Debbie decided, after three weeks in the program, that she was cured, and within a week of her being out on the streets, her addiction was worse than before.

An unexpected surprise came in the last week of August, when Vinny's youngest brother, Raymond, got separated from his wife and moved in to the Davis family home. Raymond had been married for a little under two years to a sweet young girl who worked in the same office as he did. Despite Raymond's dire observations regarding her, Vinny found her vastly entertaining, high-spirited, and enthusiastic and seemed to have the same frame of reference as Raymond. They liked the same movies, listened to the same music, and always seemed to think the same things were funny. They always seemed to understand where the other was coming from. She wasn't what

Vinny would call a real beauty, but she was petite, trim, and stylish. So when Raymond announced he was getting separated and moving in with Vinny and Michael, the entire family was surprised.

Vinny was delighted to have Raymond living with him. Unlike Michael, Raymond very much wanted to cook and help clean the house. They were three brothers three years apart, yet each of them unique, nothing like the other. And for those reasons, they all got along fabulously. The three of them proceeded to furnish their home, went to work every day, and at night, would go their separate ways with their respective girlfriends.

Meanwhile, Vinny and Christina's relationship had soared to new heights. Her soon-to-be ex-husband had found a place to live in Brooklyn and had since moved out, leaving her the house, as promised. Vinny spent weekends and a few nights a week at her house, or she spent the weekends at his house. It was as if they'd been lovers for a very long time and shared in the thrill of not knowing what they would do next. Yet as long as they were together, nothing else mattered. Christina also brought about dramatic changes in Vinny that was noticeable and welcomed. She knew that beneath the rough, tough cop exterior, a softer, gentler, intelligent man lay dormant within. It wasn't too long after the fire that Christina took him shopping for clothes, which presented him as a self-confident Eastern preppy with sophistication, rather than the "tight jeans, black leather jacket, tough guy" look from the streets of Brooklyn. Along with his new style of dress came his yearning to be better educated, well read, and properly voiced with English. One of his favorite sayings, "Not for nothing," which made him sound like an Italian street hood, was soon struck from his vocabulary, replaced by the words "Excuse me." In the hours that followed their sessions of lovemaking, he'd decided to read in bed rather than watch television. He wanted her to be proud of her diamond in the rough.

Christina had proved to be a girl who cared deeply about what other people thought. She was strong, smart as a whip, and went after what she wanted. Men were crazy about her. Still, despite the incongruous relationship that developed between them right from the start, Vinny knew he wanted to eventually marry her. And to do that, he would have to be prepared to socialize with her friends, who were the biggest collection of boring intellectual types, without sounding like a functional retard.

It was a bitterly cold night for the beginning of November. Vinny had been on a stakeout for fourteen hours and was happy to finally be home.

Finding no one home, he had proceeded to search the refrigerator for something to eat when the phone rang abruptly. Hesitant to answer, he decided he should. His sister, Maria, was due to give birth to her first child any day, and he thought it could be his family calling from the hospital.

"Hello?" he said, picking up the phone on the kitchen wall.

"Hi, honey, how are you?" Christina sounded light and cheery.

"I'm fine, baby." Vinny smiled at the warmth in her voice.

"I thought you might be someone calling from the hospital with word about the baby."

"Did Maria go into labor?" she asked, concerned.

"Not that I know of. It's just that no one's home, and I thought maybe…" Vinny was stammering.

"You're so cute. You sound more like a nervous, expectant father-to-be rather than an uncle," she said affectionately.

"I'm just a little nervous about her, that's all. Is the jury still out on your case?"

"Yeah, and I am stuck here in my office, all alone. I tried paging you all day. How come you didn't call me back? Were you with another woman?"

"Never happen. My pager doesn't work in the subway. I was on a stakeout at 167th Street for fourteen hours. Danny and I were cramped into a small stuffy porter's room, taking turns by the hour looking out a small hole in the wall. The only thing that kept us awake was the stench of stale urine."

"Ahhh, the glorious life of an undercover Transit cop. I guess you had no luck."

"No, we didn't, which means that tomorrow I'll spend another intimate day trapped in a room with Danny," he said half-heartedly.

"Maybe you should do as we discussed, go back to school and become a lawyer."

"Are you kidding? And give up this glamorous life I lead making the world a better place to live?"

"Doesn't it ever depress you, the work you do? You never struck me as the image of a typical cop."

"I'm not. As a matter of fact, I am far from a typical cop," he responded, cavalier as ever. "I happen to care and think I make a difference in what I do. You're not unhappy with what I do for a living, are you?"

"Okay, you've convinced me, I'm happy. Jubilant, in fact. Do you know what I'm in the mood for right now?"

"Does it have anything to do with the fact that it's late and you're all alone in your office?"

"Oh, yes. I want to make love to you right now, but first, I'd love some Kentucky Fried Chicken. Will you bring me some, baby?"

"Honey, I just got home from the Bronx."

"Please. I'll make your trip worthwhile."

I can't resist her. It's hopeless.

"All right, I'll be there in a half-hour."

"You see," she said, halting. "That's why I love you so much. I don't think there is anything in the world you wouldn't do to make me happy," she added implicitly.

"You're absolutely right, baby. There isn't anything I wouldn't do to make you happy. That's how much I love you," he said, his voice filled with emotion.

"I'm a very lucky girl to have found a man who makes me as happy as you do. I love you so much, Vinny," she said in a low whisper. Vinny paused a moment, letting her sweet words register in his mind.

"I'm leaving this second," he said with finality. "I love you." Then he placed the receiver in its cradle.

Thirty-five minutes later, Vinny parked his car in the rear of the Bronx Supreme Court Building. Producing his shield to the court officer assigned to the security detail, he proceeded to the elevators. While riding to the sixth floor, he thought about how well he and

Christina had grown to know each other so well. He never even felt it necessary to ask her what she wanted from Kentucky Fried Chicken. He already knew. They would share a rotisserie chicken, mashed potatoes and gravy, a large macaroni and cheese, and two cans of Lipton ice teas. They both knew each other's likes and dislikes, as well as every intimate location to touch on each other's bodies.

"And what kind of an incredible, exciting evening do you have planned for us tonight?" Vinny asked with a bright smile, standing in the doorway to Christina's office.

Christina grinned as she paraded barefoot around her desk. "God," she said, holding him in her arms, "how come I've missed you so much?"

"Because there is an unbelievable sexual chemistry between us," Vinny said affectionately as their bodies became entangled.

Christina melted into his embrace. She appreciated every sexy inch of his body. In bed, she felt as if the sex they had together couldn't get any better, except that each time it had. "What's in the bag?" she asked with a sly grin.

"All your favorites," he said obligingly, placing the bag of food on her desk, removing the contents.

"I'm starving," she said desperately, looking at the roasted chicken.

"Have a seat," he commanded as he began to fix her a plate.

"Did Danny tell you he broke up with Karen?" she asked solicitously, after devouring half her plate of food.

Vinny looked up from his plate and met her stare head-on. "No. When did that happen?" he asked disbelievingly, taken totally by surprise.

"You really didn't know, did you?" she asked primly.

"No, baby, I didn't," he reiterated affectionately. "I was trapped in a tiny room with him for damn near fourteen hours, and he never said a word."

"Well, that's just like him to be a coward," she said angrily. "He knows how close you and Karen are and figured you would give him hell for what he did."

Vinny looked perplexed. "What did he do?" Vinny asked lamely.

"Last night after they had made love, he turned to her, completely out of the blue, and said, 'I'm going back to my ex-girlfriend.'"

Vinny sat speechless.

"Needless to say, Karen got real upset. She called me at two in the morning, hysterically crying. She asked me, 'What kind of a man makes love to you, only to break up with you immediately afterward?' Do you know what I told her?" Christina asked with a cynical smile.

Vinny had an unnerving feeling he knew what she was going to say before the words left her mouth.

"A cop," she said disgustedly.

Vinny felt his heart sink. "That's right, Christina," Vinny said defensively. "We cops are notorious for being self-righteous, egotistical maniacs who cheat on our wives and are pathological liars. Did I leave anything out?" he asked with a condescending smile.

Christina laughed loudly as she got up from her chair, walked around her desk, and sat on Vinny's lap.

"Let's not get too pessimistic," she warned, kissing him slowly on the neck. "I know one cop who is the sexiest, is generous, caring…" Her tongue was slowly running up next to his ear.

As his hands began to explore under her blouse, she responded.

"Have I left anything out?" she asked, whispering into his ear, her hot, steamy breath driving him crazy.

"Tell me more," he said anxiously as her hand slid between his legs. "Shit!" he exclaimed. His pager was going off.

"Turn that thing off," she demanded as her hand worked vigorously on the zipper of his jeans.

"It's an 911," Vinny said excitedly, fully aroused, as Christina took him into her soft hand. "Baby, stop a minute. It could be the hospital," he said pleadingly.

"I forgot all about that," Christina said thoughtfully, getting off his lap. "Here, honey," she said, handing him the phone.

Vinny frantically dialed the number that appeared on his pager as Christina sat anxiously waiting on her desk. The phone was answered on the second ring.

"Vinny, is that you?" It was his brother Raymond.

"Yeah, it's me," Vinny said nervously.

"You're an uncle!" Raymond shrieked through the phone line.

"I'm an uncle!" Vinny said excitedly, locking his eyes with Christina's. "A baby girl!" he said triumphantly. Christina never took her eyes off him.

"I'll be right there," he said, hanging up the phone.

"Congratulations!" she said, throwing her arms around him, kissing him gently on the lips. "Seeing how excited you are about your sister having a baby, I can only imagine how excited you will be when we have one of our own," she said softly.

Vinny felt himself smile. "That will be the happiest day of my life," he said enthusiastically, holding her tightly in his arms. "I have to go and see my sister *and* my new niece," he said with resignation, hoping she would understand.

"Of course you do," she said, kissing him on the lips, showing her understanding.

Vinny hesitated, and for a moment, Christina thought he was going to change his mind, then he relented. "I'll call you later," he said with a beaming smile as he raced toward her office door.

"Don't forget," she said, smiling at the thought of how deeply her man cared for the well-being of his family.

"I won't forget," he said earnestly before dashing out the door.

Within ten minutes, Vinny arrived at the hospital, parking in a "no parking" zone by the front entrance. His first inclination was to find a legitimate parking space in the street, but when that didn't pan out, he decided to take advantage of a professional courtesy.

"You can't park that car there!" a heavyset uniformed security guard erupted.

Vinny quickly withdrew his shield attached to a shoelace from under his shirt. "I'm on the job," Vinny said authoritatively, throwing the keys to the car to the officer. "Move it if you have to," Vinny said impatiently, heading toward the hospital entrance.

"No problem, Detective," the security officer said admiringly as Vinny disappeared into the lobby.

"Maternity?" Vinny asked at the front desk.

"Down the hall and make a left, Detective," the smiling, gray-haired woman behind the desk said, looking at his badge.

"Thank you," he replied, walking quickly in the direction she indicated. "Mom," Vinny said affectionately as he approached her in the hallway.

"Well, all the proud uncles are present and accounted for," she said appreciatively as Vinny kissed her on the cheek.

"How's Maria? Is she okay? How's the baby? Where is she? Can I see her?"

"Calm down, Vincent," his mother said soothingly. "Your sister is fine, and so is the baby. There are already too many people in the room at the moment. As soon as someone comes out, you can go."

"Through there?" Vinny asked with a wry smile, pointing to the double swinging doors in front of him.

"They're going to throw you out," she said, smiling, as Vinny pushed open the doors and entered, ignoring his mother's warnings.

Within a few minutes, he found his family behind a curtain, surrounding his sister and her newborn baby.

"There you are," he said softly, walking toward the bed Maria was lying in, holding the baby in her arms.

"This is Nicole," Maria said quietly, looking at the baby. "Nicole, meet your eldest uncle, Vinny, the cop," she said, touching his shield that was dangling from his chest.

"Hello, Nicole," Vinny said, touching the baby's tiny hand with his index finger, which the baby immediately grabbed onto in a firm grip. "She looks just like you when Mommy brought you home," Vinny said, his voice filled with emotion, staring at his sister. Vinny looked over at his brother-in-law, Michael, and extended a hand. "You made a beautiful baby, Mike," he said earnestly, shaking his hand.

"Did you find a parking space?" Vinny's father asked curiously with raised eyebrows.

"Of course I did," Vinny responded nonchalantly, winking at his two brothers sitting in chairs at the foot of the bed.

"I bet it's parked on the curb by the front door," Raymond said with a self-satisfied smile.

Their father turned and stared at his son. "Don't tell me that's where it is," his father said disbelievingly.

"No, Sarge, it's not," Vinny said defensively, with one of his condescending smiles. "You see what you started, Raymond?" Vinny said accusingly.

"I'll bet money that's where your car is parked," Raymond said defiantly with a devious smile.

"All right, enough about the damn car already," Vinny said harshly. "How are you feeling?" he asked, turning toward Maria. "Do you need anything?"

"Just some rest," she replied softly.

"Well, I can take a hint," he said, kissing Maria on the cheek. "I'll stop by tomorrow and see if you need anything," he added, shaking Mike's hand once more.

"Goodbye, Grandpa," Maria said, using the baby's hand to wave after everyone made their goodbyes.

"Grandpa," Vinny said with a childish smirk, looking at his father.

"That's right, Grandpa!" his father said proudly.

In the weeks that followed, the Davis family had been operating on excitement-charged electricity. The entire family was ecstatic over the birth of the baby. Amid a great flurry of presents Maria received from every living relative on the Davis and Lanteri sides of the families, Christina insisted that Vinny accompany her to Bloomingdale's to help relieve the store of their entire stock of baby clothes.

Maria was a wonderful mother, completely devoted. That was why she felt terrible having to go back to work, leaving the baby so much of the time. Her husband, Michael, had opened up an Italian restaurant in Rockland County and was working fourteen hours a day, but he needed the help of Maria. Finding a babysitter was no problem. There were volunteers at the ready on both sides of the family. Vinny and Christina didn't mind taking care of the baby. They would talk and laugh late into the night, long after the baby went to bed, and when they left to go home, they found themselves wishing they had a baby of their own.

Christina knew Vinny intended to ask her hand before Christmas, and would probably expect to be wed an appropriate six months after that. But neither of them had gotten their divorce as yet, so she thought of his engagement plans as a whimsical inspiration.

She laughed mirthlessly. "We can't get married yet," she insisted. "The ink's not even dry on my divorce paper yet, and you're still married."

"Tell you what?" Vinny said in his most persuasive voice. "Christmas is in less than three weeks. We can get engaged for Christmas and get married when you think the time is right. I personally don't care how it looks, but I will respect your wishes for your ex-husband's sake," Vinny added thoughtfully.

She laughed as she lay naked on top of the covers of his bed. "What are you laughing at? I'm serious."

She laughed again, her naked breasts bouncing. "I've heard of shotgun weddings before, but I'm not even pregnant!" she howled.

Undaunted, he climbed on top of her naked body. Her legs were bent under her, her body arched, and her head was thrown back. She looked incredibly sexy. "Now, will you marry me?" he asked, pinning her hand down to the bed, running his tongue across her nipple.

"This isn't fair," she sighed, opening her legs.

"Too bad," Vinny replied gruffly, positioning himself, ready to enter her.

"Oh, don't stop, baby," she said with another sigh.

"I'm not putting myself inside of you until you say yes," he said flatly, leaving her feeling rejected as he pulled his hips back.

"Yes!" she exploded, pulling his body on top of her, forcing him inside of her. "I love you, Vinny," she panted. "I'll marry you, just don't stop!"

After they made love for hours, she snuggled beside him and closed her eyes. She was asleep almost instantly. As she slept in his arms, he thought of how truly lucky he was.

Forget the past, by which so much of life is marked. Painful things happen, and we take a little of it with us.

He should have simply drifted off, but he didn't. Maybe he was overtired. Maybe the adrenaline rush kept him pumped up.

Whatever it was, he was wide awake. He could visualize how beautiful Christina would look on their wedding day. He could see her holding their newborn daughter in her arms at the hospital. At first, she said no, that marriage was too impulsive, but after making love to her, he told her nothing was more important to him than spending the rest of their lives together and having a family. He was serious. She could see it in his eyes when she pulled back to look at him, and could feel it in his touch as he ran his hand gently down the side of her sweet face. "Yes, I'll marry you," she had said with a smile.

Within two days of their deciding to get engaged at Christmas, their first major argument erupted. Vinny and Danny were to receive Cop of the Month awards at the District 11 Christmas party. After spending the evening alone at last year's Christmas party, Vinny was not looking for a repeat performance. He took it for granted that, since Christina had gotten her divorce, she would be proud to be with him when he received his award. But not only did she have no intention of attending, she was also adamant that he not accompany her to the Bronx District Attorneys' party at the Marina Del Ray.

"Are you embarrassed of me?" he said, steaming. His stare was fierce, determined. She returned his stare.

"It's…" She hesitated. "Too soon."

"Too soon, my ass!" he retaliated. "You don't think that I'm good enough to be seen with you at your Christmas party. After all, what would those stuck-up pricks in the DA's office have to say with their seven years of higher education? 'How come a woman as beautiful and intelligent as Christina Fusco is dating a lowlife, no-class cop?'"

"You're being an asshole," she said scornfully. "Cops are assholes, and I don't want to be around them socializing," she said defiantly. "I'm not making a judgment, merely giving you a fact, in the light of the things I've seen with my own eyes."

Vinny could feel the anger and resentment rising within him as she continued.

"They are loud, obnoxious, and uneducated. They drink too much, are pathological liars, and fuck any woman they can get their hands on."

For a moment, the room was deathly silent. They just sat there on the couch and didn't move. They barely breathed.

"How dare you take it upon yourself to make such a general-ization, stereotyping cops as you did! Am I to assume that you are referring to me as well in your comments?" She never took her eyes off his. "Tell me, Christina," he said lightly.

He'd hit a nerve and caught her off guard. "It's an unfair question."

"I know," he said quietly, "but I'm asking anyway because I need to know if that's how you feel about me."

"Come on, baby, you know how I feel about you." Her voice was calm, almost sympathetic.

The time they'd spent together had been like no other. She had touched him in a way no one else ever had, but maybe everything he felt was his alone. Maybe he misread whatever they had between them and it had been all fleeting and one-sided.

"No, I don't think I do know how you feel about me," he said blearily.

For a moment, she sat stunned. "Listen to me, please," she said, smiling, patting a place on the couch next to her.

Vinny looked at her without smiling, then sat down beside her.

"You are the love of my life," she said passionately, looking into his eyes. "It's unfortunate you're a cop, yet I am very fortunate that you're far from a typical one, besides being the sexiest man I've ever met. You're loyal, honest, trustworthy, and the most dedicated cop I know. You care about people, a quality I don't often see in cops. And your love and devotion to your family and me is something I've never known to exist in a man. So when I said *cops* before, I, in no way, was referring to you. I was referring to the countless number of these egotistical maniacs I deal with every day at the office. The ones who are wearing a wedding ring, trying to pick me up or stare at me like I'm a piece of meat. The ones who are exactly like your partner, Danny, who broke Karen's heart. So please forgive me if I don't jump at the opportunity to spend a drunken evening with him and the rest of his idiotic friends while he talks about what a great lay Karen was."

He sat expressionless. "Now that you put it that way," Vinny said understandingly, "I guess the idea of you coming with me to the party is quite outrageous. I had no idea that you were so upset about Karen."

She smiled and relaxed. Vinny was no longer angry or confused. For him to think that Christina thought of him as part of her cop analogy was crazy. It wasn't possible. He believed every word she'd just told him. They loved each other too much for him not to. Her love meant everything to him.

"This time of year is a very tense time for me, Christina. Please forgive me for acting the way I did."

She remained seated, her eyes locked onto his. "In my entire life, no one has ever made me feel the love I feel for you," she said, pulling him to her.

He kissed her slowly, gently on the lips and felt her respond. Whatever fleeting thoughts he had about her loyalty and devotion to him were gone, as if they never existed.

As agreed, Vinny went alone to his Christmas party for the second year in a row and received his award without anyone to share in his excitement. Amicably, they agreed that Christina would attend the PBA Cop of the Month awards dinner at Leonard's of Great Neck in May, when Vinny was to receive an award from Mario Cuomo, the governor of New York. Christina had said it was an affair that would be attended by the high-ranking, politically correct members of law enforcement, who would conduct themselves as professionals.

It was raining and snowing the night of the Bronx District Attorneys' Christmas party. Vinny lay in bed beneath the covers.

Tommy's wife, Angela, had taken ill and was unable to accompany Tommy to the party. A party he attended every year to keep in touch with his old colleagues. Tommy had called to ask if he wanted to join him in Angela's absence. Vinny had become friendly with some of Tommy's friends from the DA's office and figured the boys would make a night out of it after the party.

But he respectfully declined Tommy's gracious offer, explaining to him that he didn't want Christina to think that he was checking up on her. Tommy understood the circumstances and exonerated his friend for passing up his generous offer. Since the party was being held at the Marina del Rey in the Bronx, Christina had told him she would call him before she left the party. She had said that, depending on the weather, the hour, and how much she had to drink, it might be more prudent to spend the night at Vinny's house rather than drive home to hers, an hour away on Long Island.

Vinny appreciated her kindness when she said she'd call him before coming over, but he quickly reminded her that she had her own key to his house and was welcome to come by at any time. He had nothing to hide from her.

It was nearly one thirty in the morning when the phone rang abruptly, waking Vinny from a deep sleep. Behind him, in the dark, he could see the bluish-lighted numbers displayed on his alarm clock as he reached for the phone. "Hello?" he said groggily.

"Oh, baby, I'm sorry I woke you," Christina said innocently.

"Where are you?" he asked.

"I'm in Manhattan, dropping off Karen at her apartment. This song came on the radio."

In the background he could hear, "It's a lonely old night…"

"Can you hear it?" she asked, turning the radio volume up.

"I can hear it," he said as she sang along with the song.

"It's a lonely old night, and I'm going to put my arms and legs around you," she said enthusiastically. "I'm on my way," she added, then hung up.

A short while later, the doorbell rang as Vinny lay awake in his bed. "What the hell is she ringing the doorbell for?" he said to himself out loud.

Vinny greeted her at the side door of his house, wearing only jeans. Christina studied him for a moment.

"May I come in?" she asked, breaking an awkward silence.

"I'm sorry, come in," he said, smiling, opening the door wide for her.

Immediately, she moved closer to him so she was standing directly in front of him. Everything about her, the wetness of her lips, the movement of her body as she drew closer to him, was totally sexual.

"I want to make love to you," she said provocatively, her hand sliding over his crotch. "Come upstairs," she whispered. "I'm so wet." Forcefully he drew her closer to him, kissing her wildly on the lips.

Abruptly he stopped and pushed her gently away from him. He felt a terrible chill down his spine. It was something about the way she kissed him. "You've been seeing someone else," he said nervously.

She turned her back and stared out the window. She was thrown back, taken by surprise.

"Answer me," he demanded as he twisted her around to face him.

She met his stare. "It was just sex," she replied recklessly.

His face turned red, incredulous.

"Vinny, I know how you feel, but it just happened." She was calm, almost nonchalant.

"It just happened? How the hell does it just happen?" he growled.

"It was just one time!" she said indignantly. "Besides, you know I have condoms in my house."

Vinny became enraged. "I didn't think the condoms were there to be dispensed like a vending machine to any dick that came your way!" he sneered.

"I can see you're not going to be a mature adult about this," she suddenly lashed out.

Rage shot through Vinny as he stared at her. Suddenly, his eyes receded to little slits and the vein on the side of his head protruded with each beat of his heart. Vinny knew she was still talking to him, but he didn't want to hear any of it. He could only envision her in bed with another man.

"Get out!" he roared, his voice loud enough to stop a speeding freight train. She gasped for breath and pulled away. Never in her life had she seen anyone filled with such rage or as dangerous-looking as he was now. With a sigh, she turned and bumped into Michael, who had appeared from nowhere, half-asleep.

"What's going on?" he asked irritably.

"Ask her," Vinny said disgustedly, his face ridden with anxiety, as he walked out of the kitchen.

Michael entered the living room to find his brother downing a glass of Scotch. "She wants to know if she should pack her stuff now or wait until another time," Michael asked cautiously.

Vinny stood in a daze. It was inconceivable to him that she would do this to him. Vinny stammered, "I don't know. I'm not sure." Turning angrily, he saw Michael staring at him.

"How about I take her to the diner while you calm down?" Michael said thoughtfully. "I'll call you from there in a little while to see if you've cooled down."

"I'll pack her stuff." Vinny was trying to be civil while trying to make sense of what was so overwhelming to him. "It will be on the porch by the time you get back."

Michael met his brother's glance. "About an hour," he said flatly.

"Michael, do me one more favor?" he asked, pleading. "Get back the key to the house."

As Vinny heard the door to the house close, he poured himself another glass of scotch. Moving quickly, he went into the adjacent dining room to see Christina getting into her car with Michael. Watching the car pull away, he downed the full glass of scotch and hurled the empty glass at the wall. "You whore!" he shrieked as the glass smashed into a thousand tiny pieces. Face bleeding from the shattered glass, he walked into the living room and retrieved his half-empty bottle of scotch. Picking it up, he stared at it blankly. Then he raised it to his lips and drained it in several gulps. Dropping the empty bottle, he proceeded to his bedroom to pack her things.

CHAPTER 15

Vinny sat listlessly in his living room, which had been beautifully decorated, along with the rest of the house, for the baby's first Christmas. He no longer craved a woman to love, a family, or even his promotion. His only craving was a bottle of scotch and the screaming desire to forget Christina and the pain she'd caused him. The only emotion he was capable of feeling was betrayal. He was heartbroken. He felt as though a part of him had died; his mother had died all over again, and nothing could make it right. He'd not seen Christina since the night of the District Attorneys' Christmas party, when she broke his heart as he never thought possible. He wished he had the strength to make sure that she would never, ever, come near him again.

Vinny wasn't the only distraught cop in District 11. Julia Rivera, a thirty-year-old, fairly attractive female with the mendacity of a whore, was overheard commiserating in the female locker room about Vinny's up-and-coming promotion and transfer to the Special Operations Squad. She was also heard saying that she was going to place an anonymous phone call to Internal Affairs informing them that he and the officers in anticrime were filling up their private vehicles with gas at the police precincts and Transit Authority's bus depots. Although acquiring gas in that fashion was a violation of the Patrol Guide, it had become quite commonplace since the Transit Police abolished its practice of reimbursing its anticrime officers sixteen cents a mile while using their personal vehicles on patrol. It was bad enough having to destroy your personal vehicle daily responding to emergency calls, sometimes getting into an accident, but to pay for your own gas on a cop's salary to do it was ludicrous. So unwritten concessions were made, the rules were bent, but the result justified the means—the anticrime team's arrest record proved it.

Julia Rivera's motives for breaking the blue wall of silence, a term used by cops never to rat on another cop, was revenge. Vinny was reassigned from anticrime back to uniform patrol as an administrative punishment for an argument he had had with a sergeant a few years previously, when Julia Rivera was forced to transfer from District 3 in Harlem after a falling-out she had had with her sergeant, who was also said to be her lover.

While she was assigned to District 3, she did as she wanted, with virtual impunity, because of whom she was sleeping with. A nice job indoors, working steady days, with weekends and holidays off, suited her just fine. After all, why deal with the elements of the weather and the dangers of being on patrol when you could be a forty-six-thousand-dollar-a-year secretary? And to obtain and keep such a job, by giving up some ass to a boss, was not such a big deal, until she set her sights on a job in Headquarters and a chance for promotion by graciously withdrawing her sexual favors from the mere sergeant, swapping him for a captain. Her downfall was when the captain got bored with her whining and dumped her. She found herself assigned to uniform patrol on the worst posts in Harlem.

Shortly after her undistinguished transfer under the black cloud of her indiscretions to District 11, she became particularly charitable to a sergeant who was going through a tough divorce. Within no time, she was assigned to steady day tours, with a steady seat in a radio car. Shortly after that, without making so much as an arrest, she was mysteriously assigned to the district's anticrime team. She was highly unqualified, and no one wanted to work with her. She was inadequate, inexperienced, unmotivated, and dangerous to work with. Despite all her faults, she was assigned as a rotating partner, as a third member of each team, thereby allowing the two-man teams to perform their job, in the hopes that she might learn something from their experience. It was inevitable that one day her inability to perform her job would get one of her partners injured or killed.

Vinny was at the end of his administrative punishment and was due to be reassigned to anticrime in a few days as he sat inconspicuously in a marked radio car two blocks away from a stakeout. Eleven Anticrime was on at 174th Street and the Grand Concourse. The suspects Eleven Anticrime were looking for were both armed with guns. One of the suspects was armed with a TEC-9 machine pistol, capable of firing thirty 9mm rounds in less than ten seconds. The three-man anticrime team assigned to the stakeout was composed of Bobby Hanley, a twelve-year veteran, with oodles of experience; Joe Allegra, his partner of over two years, who learned everything he knew about undercover work from Bobby; and lastly, Julia Rivera, who was absolutely clueless.

Vinny was enjoying a ham-and-cheese sandwich with his partner, Jonathan Phelps, a twelve-year, no-nonsense street cop who wanted to put in his twenty and retire as just that, a cop. He wanted nothing to do with promotions or advancement in a bureaucratic department that was politically operated by the Transit Authority. It was Jonathan's personal belief that the TP were used as highly paid security guards to protect the Transit Authority's precious revenue. He felt, as most Transit cops did, that placing uniformed cops in front of token booths during peak hours to ensure that the passengers paid, while people were falling victim to robberies on the platforms and trains, was preposterous. The NYPD had the TNT (tactical narcotics team) unit. Jonathan used to joke that the Transit Police had a TNT unit of its own: tokens-n-turnstiles. Cops couldn't help but laugh at that, because they knew it was the truth.

"Ten-thirteen, 174th and the Grand Concourse. Southbound, on foot," Joe's voice crackled over the radio. "Man with a gun. Male, black. All in black."

Vinny's foot was to the floorboard with the gas pedal as Jonathan monitored the radio.

"There they are!" Jonathan exclaimed, pointing to the opposite side of the six-lane Grand Concourse.

"I see them," Vinny said as he barreled the radio car over two concrete dividers. Bobby and Joe were wrestling the suspect on the ground, trying to cuff his hands, as Julia stood astonished. Jonathan dived onto the melee with his six foot, three-inch, 250-pound frame, with enough force to knock the wind out of any professional football linebacker.

Scan the crowd, Vinny thought as he exited the radio car with his gun in his right hand. *There's supposed to be two of them.*

"Police, don't move!" he screamed, aiming his weapon at a black male wearing a long black leather coat that was bulging on one side. In one incredible instant, Joe Allegra jumped off the suspect on the ground toward the suspect Vinny was aiming at, who stood motionless, never taking his eyes off Vinny's. In one sweeping motion, Joe had tackled the unsuspecting male to the ground.

Vinny moved quickly, placing his knee into the neck of the male as he forcefully placed the barrel of his gun on the man's skull. "If you so much as blink, I'll blow your fucking head off!" Vinny said vociferously to the oblivious male now flat on his stomach. "Give me your cuffs, Joe," Vinny said decisively, not having a free hand to get to his own.

"They're on the other guy," Joe replied, while forcing the male's hand behind his back.

Looking up, Vinny saw Julia.

"Give me your cuffs!"

Julia stared blankly at him. "I don't have any," she said evasively.

"What? Take my cuffs off my gun belt," he demanded furiously.

She hesitated, then did as she was told. Joe immediately took the cuffs from her hand and got one cuff on as Jonathan, who came over to assist, pried the suspect's other hand from underneath him.

After they had secured the second cuff, the suspect was lifted to his feet. And on the ground where he was tackled was a TEC-9 machine pistol.

"Holy shit!" Joe exclaimed, bending over to pick it up. "How did you know?"

Vinny grinned. "It's almost eighty-five degrees, and this guy's got on a full-length leather coat that's being weighed down on one side."

Suddenly, Joe realized what had happened. Julia could have gotten them all killed. "What the hell were you doing while Bobby and I were trying to cuff that guy?" he asked her, his voice angry.

She remained reticent, afraid, and desperate, yet she was still silent.

Literally frantic, Joe tried one last and, in retrospect, perhaps the most obvious question. "Where are your handcuffs?"

"I forgot them," she said, smiling arrogantly.

Vinny and Joe both stared at her in disbelief. The sad, tragic thing was that she saw absolutely nothing wrong with what she had let happen.

"Forget it, Joe," Vinny said, turning to walk the prisoner to the radio car.

"Thanks for the backup," Bobby was saying to the numerous City and Transit cops that responded to their call for help, as he got into the back seat of a radio car with the other prisoner.

Back at the district, Julia insisted that it was her arrest because she was next in rotation for that team.

Then Vinny heard her pleading with the desk officer. He was unable to control his temper. "If you even think about putting your name down on an assist on that arrest, I'll bring you up on malfeasance charges!" Vinny said vehemently, rage coursing through his veins.

The entire command stopped what they were doing and stared toward the front desk.

"You may have some magical female persuasiveness that works on some cops, but not this one," he said sharply, pointing his index finger at himself. "I'll take that arrest myself if I feel like it!" he added ominously.

Julia Rivera stood speechless, in shock and disbelief that anyone would have the audacity to humiliate her in front of the entire command. The sergeant on the desk was perplexed, having no idea what had happened on the street.

"Let him have the fucking collar," she retaliated as she walked away in a fury.

Within a week of the highly controversial and talked-about incident, Officer Rivera found herself back in uniform and had not only held Vinny personally responsible but had also vowed to seek revenge. So when word of Julia's intentions to notify Internal Affairs about the gas reached him, Vinny precariously requested Sergeant Houston to have him reassigned to uniform patrol as punishment, in an attempt to pacify his vengeful adversary. After explaining Officer Rivera's intentions to Sergeant Houston and vowing not to implicate any of the officers he worked with, or the sergeant himself, he was assigned to uniform as a steady driver of a radio car.

CHAPTER 16

"**A**re you going to sit in this living room all day, or are you going to help me in the kitchen to prepare this food?" Raymond asked accusingly, snapping Vinny from his reverie.

"Yeah, I'll help."

"Good."

As Vinny got up, Raymond's face was filled with concern.

"What's the matter?"

"I know that you are not in the most festive of moods," Raymond said cautiously, "but everyone is coming over here for Christmas dinner. And if you keep drinking scotch, you'll be passed out before anyone gets here."

"I am impervious to this stuff, but you are right, little brother," he continued, putting his arm around Raymond. "Just because I'm miserable doesn't mean I have to make everyone else miserable," he said sincerely, handing Raymond his glass of scotch. "Now, let's go in there and cook up a meal that's a king's delight!" he said enthusiastically, his arm still around his brother's shoulder, leading him toward the kitchen.

Looking at the clock on the kitchen wall, which read eleven in the morning, Vinny knew he had plenty of time to have everything set before their guests were set to arrive at two o'clock. Raymond had gotten up at seven in the morning to throw the turkey, which was stuffed and prepared the night before, in the oven. While the rest of the Davis family spent Christmas Eve celebrating at the Lanteris' house, feasting on the traditional Italian spread of different kinds of seafood, Raymond and Vinny feverishly prepared the food to be served on Christmas Day. Tommy had stopped by with some holiday cheer, while Vinny and Raymond prepared the lasagna and the hot and cold antipasto salads. Tommy, who never passed up the opportunity to put his culinary expertise to work, began preparing the stuffed mushrooms and artichokes before departing to take his family to midnight Mass.

Christina. He was thinking of her as he remembered her. Time and again she would come into his thoughts, and time and again, he'd force her out. What she had done was unforgivable, but what's done is done. You can't turn back the hands of time and erase a mistake. When the time came and he finally had to face her, that was when he would deal with it, but for now, it was Christmas Day with his family that had to stay centered in his mind.

"Raymond, get the phone," Vinny said flippantly, his hands busy rolling meatballs.

"Merry Christmas!" Raymond answered festively. "I'm fine. How are you?" he asked casually, looking at Vinny worriedly. "Yeah, hold on. He's right here," Raymond said, slipping the phone into the crook of Vinny's neck.

"Hello," he said in wonder, wiping his greasy hands on a dishtowel.

"Merry Christmas." Christina's voice was frightened and barely audible.

Vinny closed his eyes in disbelief. The sound of her voice pierced his heart like a sharp blade. "Yeah, sort of merry," he said vacantly.

"I know you hate me, but I wanted to call anyway to wish you and your family a merry Christmas."

Vinny was thrown back, not sure what to say. "Well, that's very nice of you to call," he said lamely.

"I was hoping to see you in court this week," she said quickly. "I have a Christmas present in my office for Nicole."

Vinny was taken aback further by the sincerity in her voice.

"Well," he said hesitantly, "I thought it best for me not to see you."

There was an eerie silence on the line.

"I am so sorry I hurt you, Vinny," she said, her voice filled with emotion.

"So am I," he said, fighting back the tears that began to form in his eyes.

"I love you," she said pleadingly, her voice cracking, on the verge of tears.

"Merry Christmas, Christina," he said gloomily, hanging up the phone. "Goddamn it, Christina!" He turned back away from the phone. He was angry and hurt and confused. "Why the hell did she have to call?" he asked, looking into Raymond's eyes.

"Because the women of the nineties are more fucked up in the head than men are," Raymond said contemptuously, with a wry smile.

Once again, he felt the awful loneliness and unending fear that went along with it. In less than one year, he had lost the only two women he had ever loved so deeply and completely. They were gone, vanished into thin air, forever. The whole situation was a blur, and he was having a lot of trouble with reality. Sweat ran down his face as he remembered the fierceness in Debbie's eyes before turning to ice, as her finger tightened around the trigger of his gun. How his body shook uncontrollably, trying to find and form the right words to stop her from shooting. His fleeting thoughts ended as quickly as they had started. His thoughts then turned to Christina as they had lunch in Little Italy. Sitting at a table, holding hands. Her eyes were filled with love and affection. Kissing her gently, passionately making love to her.

Suddenly, the kitchen door was pushed open. Vinny turned around and saw his parents coming through the doorway. His mother watched his eyes find their way to hers, and she knew they'd startled him from out of a dream. "Merry Christmas!" she said cheerfully.

Vinny's face was red, and his breathing was heavy, as if he'd been hyperventilating.

"Vincent, you look like you're getting sick," she said worriedly, placing her hand on his forehead.

Raymond interjected. "He just got off the phone with Christina, and he's a little peeved."

"He's burning up," she said excitedly, looking at her husband.

"I'm fine," Vinny said, cavalier as ever, reaching for his glass of scotch.

"You might want to lay off that stuff," his father said harshly with contempt in his eyes. "Your brothers tell us you haven't had a sober night since you had that argument with Christina."

Vinny stared blankly at his parents. Had it really been every night?

Maria and her husband, Michael, arrived with the baby shortly after two in the afternoon. Vinny immediately took the baby in his arms. In that one incredible moment, his anger and confusion about the realization of the events that had drastically changed his life over the past year were magically gone. In that moment, all doubts about what life had in store for him disappeared—they no longer mattered. For the life he held in his arms was more precious than his own.

The festivities began with the opening of some wine with the hot and cold antipasto, followed by the opening of presents in the living room, where holly and colored lights were strung to decorate the mantel. The tree was decorated with over three thousand white lights that twinkled brightly, along with the flickering flames of a roaring fire. The opening of the presents took hours, since the proud uncles and grandparents insisted on having an enormous number of gifts for Maria and the baby piled under the tree, each one intricately wrapped, and only one present at a time was permitted to be opened, so Grandpa could take photos, immortalizing his granddaughter's first Christmas. By the time they were through with all the unwrapping, the "Oohs" and "Aahs," the kissing, and the hugging, it was time for dinner.

Vinny and Raymond had prepared the very special Christmas dinner that was brought to the table by their sister and mother. After grace was said by Michael, the family enjoyed their dinner, a dinner in honor of a very special little girl. The day had turned out perfectly, despite all of life's travesties, until the dinner conversation turned to an infuriating subject.

"Did you hear your buddy Sabol is out of prison?" Michael asked curiously, looking at Vinny seated next to him.

"What?" Vinny asked haltingly with raised eyebrows.

"Yeah. I saw him in a car last week with Gerry," Mike said quickly.

Closing his eyes, Vinny bowed his head over his plate, with his hands clasped forcefully together. He then chuckled at their ironical remarks. "That's impossible," he said confidently, raising his head out of his plate. "Sabol's doing at least twenty years this time on a federally sponsored vacation. If he were out, I would have been notified," Vinny added defiantly.

"Gerry said he's out on a work release program," Mike insisted innocently.

"After serving two years on a twenty-year sentence?" Vinny asked incredulously, trying to control his temper.

"Didn't you have something to do with him getting arrested?" Maria asked solicitously, with a hint of concern in her voice.

Vinny turned to look at his sister with amazement in his eyes. His mind furiously trying to decipher the information it abruptly received.

"No, I didn't," Vinny said vaguely, his thoughts ending abruptly.

Vinny's father took one look at his nervous face and said reassuringly, "It's probably all a mistake. I'm sure he's still in prison."

"I don't think so," Mike said flatly, I'm positive about this.

The air that filled the room with impending doom was contagious. Vinny's face was filled with panic. "You're not worried that guy will come after you, are you?" His mother's voice was a soft reproach.

Vinny was forced to accept the fact that it was highly probable that Sabol would attempt to make good on his promise to someday kill him and his family. The criminal Sabol, Vinny knew, was not the kind to suffer easily having anything he owned taken away from him, whether he valued it or not. Losing Debbie to Vinny was bad enough, but to lose his freedom because of Vinny was unforgivable.

"Son of a bitch," Vinny said under his breath so that his mother wouldn't hear him. Unfortunately, his father did, and he looked at Vinny with a worried glint in his eye.

"No one is going to go after anyone," his father said emphatically.

Suddenly, Vinny jumped up from the table, glaring at Mike. "You tell your friend Gerry that Sabol is a rat bastard and should be doing twenty years!" Vinny exploded. "I don't know who he ratted on or who he sold to get out, but he's going back to prison if I have to take him there personally this time." Vinny was livid as he turned and walked out of the dining room.

Their father's mouth was a straight line. They all knew that expression. It was always there when he was angry or disapproving. Michael attempted to excuse himself from the table, only to be motioned by his father to sit back down.

"Leave him alone so he can calm down," his father said wisely. "He'll be all right in a little while."

Vinny sat alone on the couch in the living room, commiserating, with a glass of scotch in one hand and a cigarette burning in the other. Suddenly, his heart began to palpitate violently, and he broke into a cold sweat. As the palpitations increased, he felt as though someone were sitting on his chest. He was terrified, struggling to breathe, his mind filled with thoughts of Sabol and how he would seek his revenge. Sabol was like an entity that appeared at different times—pure evil, reappearing each time, more powerful than before, preying on the innocent.

Will he go after Debbie for betraying him and marrying me, or will he eventually find out through Mike's friend Gerry that Maria is my sister and go after her and the baby?

Breathing deeply, he began to come around. Pulling himself from the depths of his own emotion, he suddenly felt more alone than at any time in his life. He wasn't quite sure why his entire life had been turned upside down, most of which he knew there wasn't anything he could do about. Debbie and Christina were both gone, along with his apartment and most of his possessions. A vindictive female cop wanted to even an old score by destroying his chance for promotion, and he was back in uniform on patrol. That left only one piece of his bizarre life that he could do something about, Sabol. His first inclination was to inform Sergeant Houston the first day he returned to work, but Houston would never believe it. He would think that his obsession with Sabol was now out of control. After all, the feds promised the Transit Police Internal Affairs Division that if Sabol was released for any reason, they would be notified.

"I'll need proof that Sabol is out," he said quietly to himself, "but that will take some time."

"Are you all right?" Mike asked in a barely audible monotone.

Vinny was snatched from his thoughts by his brother-in-law, who stood smiling next to the Christmas tree, holding the baby in his arms. "I thought I heard you talking to yourself."

Vinny glanced at him without smiling, then poured himself another glass of scotch.

"Mike," he said hesitantly, "you will make sure you warn your friend about Sabol."

Mike looked at him quizzically.

"Don't tell him I told you," Vinny said cautiously, "because I don't want him to tell Sabol it was I who warned him. If Sabol finds out, I don't know what he'll do."

"What exactly do you want me to tell Gerry?" Mike asked suspiciously with raised eyebrows.

"Just tell him that you heard somewhere that Sabol is supposed to be doing twenty years on a drug charge in Georgia and that rumor has it that he ratted on some of his codefendants so he could get out."

Mike stared at him. "Do you think that's how he got out?" he asked, seemingly fascinated.

"It's the only explanation I can come up with," Vinny said earnestly, taking a long sip of his scotch.

"Then why didn't your job get notified that he's been released?" Mike asked scornfully.

"A technicality," Vinny said philosophically. "If Sabol's out on a work release program, then he is not officially released from custody. He is supposed to go to work during the day and return to his little cubbyhole at night. Granted, he's not allowed to be driving around Yonkers while he's supposed to be at work, but knowing how crafty Sabol is, he found a way around that little obstacle."

"How the hell do you know that?" Mike was astonished.

"Because it's the only logical scenario I can come up with that makes any sense," Vinny said decisively, a victorious look in his eyes.

"Listen, Mike," he added reluctantly. "From what I saw in the bathroom at your engagement party and the stories I heard on the streets about your friend Gerry, he's no altar boy either. It's none of my business who he is or what he does, but if he's anywhere near Sabol when I go after him, he's going to wind up sharing a cell with him. So make sure he receives your warning to stay far away from him. Capisce?"

Mike never took his eyes off Vinny. "I'll make sure," he said appreciatively. "Believe me, I'll make damn sure!"

The front doorbell rang. Maria went to answer it.

"Merry Christmas to all," TC said cheerfully as he entered into the foyer with a wrapped Christmas present under his arm.

"I'm glad to see you, TC," Vinny's mom said, kissed him on the cheek, then escorted him into the dining room.

"Happy to see you all well and joyful this holiday season," Tommy said merrily, extending his hand in greeting to all that were present. "Where's Vincent?" he asked curiously.

Vinny's dad threw a glance over his shoulder in the direction of the living room. "He's not so good," his dad said with a wink at Tommy. There was no need to keep Tommy in the dark about what was going on. If anyone could help, his father knew Tommy could. The entire family had been walking on eggshells and knew it, their father included. For all intents and purposes, Vinny had been in a bad way all day, but the news of Sabol being out pushed him over the edge.

"Merry Christmas," Tommy said with a bright smile, extending his hands, which held a beautifully wrapped present.

Vinny shot Tommy a warning glare. "What's so merry about it?"

Tommy sat down beside his friend, placing the unaccepted gift on the coffee table. Gesturing toward the box, Tommy said, "I was going to buy you a bottle of Chivas Regal for Christmas, but Angela insisted on a crystal decanter with matching glasses instead. She remembered the set you had in your apartment before the fire and thought it would be nice to replace it."

Vinny rubbed his hand together and sat back on the couch, then looked at Tommy, who was staring at him with concern in his eyes.

Expressionless, Vinny got up and walked over to the Christmas tree, then he picked up three wrapped gifts and handed them to Tommy. "These are for little Anthony," he said gloomily. "Tell Angela I said thank you for her thoughtfulness." He then sat back down on the couch.

Tommy looked dismayed. He'd never seen his friend in such a state of depression. "You'll have to deliver those presents to Angela and Anthony yourself," Tommy said defiantly. "Angela will have my head if I walk in the door on Christmas Day with gifts without Uncle Vinny," he said sarcastically.

Suddenly, a knot tightened in Vinny's stomach. He didn't give a damn about anyone's personal feelings. His mind was consumed with thoughts of Sabol and no one else.

"What?" Vinny said harshly, catching Tommy staring at him. "What are you thinking about?"

"Sabol's out on a work release program!" Vinny erupted.

Tommy glared at him incredulously and started to reply, but Vinny held up a hand to stop him.

"He's running around with Gerry Camp-Something-or-Other, my brother-in-law's best friend."

"Holy shit!" Tommy said furiously, picking up a cigarette from a pack on the coffee table and lighting it.

Increasingly irritable remarks by Tommy, underscored by long periods of silence, the collective frustrations of two men trying to piece together how this could be.

"He must have ratted on his codefendants in that cocaine bust in Georgia," Vinny said convincingly.

"But I thought that if he was to ever get out of prison, the feds were going to notify Internal Affairs so you could be warned?" Tommy asked irritably.

"Maybe the feds don't consider being allowed to run around during the day on a work release program out of prison," Vinny said disingenuously.

Tommy sat pondering the imponderables for a few moments. "So what do you do now?" Tommy asked innocently.

"I told Michael to warn his friend that Sabol's supposed to be doing twenty years and must have ratted on some people to be out on work release."

"Do you think Gerry will listen to Mike?" Tommy asked.

"It better work," Vinny said emphatically. "Mike knows how much I hate Sabol, and will do whatever is necessary to keep him in jail, where he belongs. If he's smart, Gerry will have nothing to do with Sabol anymore, then I'll find out what new illegal activities Sabol is up to and pass it on like the last time."

"Do you think Sabol's going to go after Debbie?" Tommy asked, running his finger through his hair.

"He'd be crazy if he did," Vinny said curtly. "I hear she's now dating an FBI agent. Ironically, his name's Richie also."

"I don't like the feds not notifying you about his early release." Tommy's voice became softer, yet more passionate. "Are you going to notify your job about Sabol being out?" Tommy asked cautiously.

"They'll never believe me without proof," Vinny said contemptuously. "Sergeant Houston already thinks that I'm eccentric or neurotic about Sabol. If I go to him with this story without any evidence, he'll have me sent to see the department shrink for sure," Vinny added flatly.

"Talk about being kicked when you're down," Tommy said sympathetically. "First, the mess with Debbie, then your apartment burns down, Christina turns out to be a flake, and now this. No wonder you're such a mess," Tommy said grimly.

"One hell of a year," Vinny said blearily, his eyes glistening as tears began to form.

"What about Suzanne?" Tommy asked, trying to change the subject. "She was all over you at my office Christmas party last week."

Vinny's expression went blank, as if he'd suddenly forgotten his train of thought. Suzanne had been Angela's closest friend since high school. She was at Tommy's office Christmas party, dressed in a sexy red dress and black silk stockings. She looked stunning as she made her advances toward Vinny, but he was too busy drowning himself in self-pity to be bothered.

"It was too soon," Vinny said, mustering up the dignity to defend his actions.

"You're kidding," Tommy hissed. "She could surely help you forget your problems faster than that drink in your hands," he added genuinely.

Vinny couldn't help but smile. "You really think so?" he asked half-heartedly.

"The way she looks, she could make a blind man see," Tommy said, looking at Vinny enviously.

Vinny shook his head and smiled.

Tommy gave him a few minutes to relax before standing up. "Let's go to my house to give my son his gifts," Tommy said decidedly, with a bright smile.

Vinny returned the smile. Standing up, he placed his empty glass on the coffee table. Together they walked to the foyer to get their coats.

As they did, Vinny's father glanced in Tommy's direction and nodded. "Don't let him drive anywhere, Tommy," he said austerely.

"I'm doing the driving, Mr. Davis," Tommy responded. Then they immediately headed out the front door to the street.

Three hours later, at 9:45 p.m., Vinny returned to the solitude of his living room and poured himself another glass of scotch. As usual, on Christmas Night, his family would drive to Staten Island to visit their grandparents, aunts, uncles, and cousins. Vinny had deliberately stayed late at Tommy's house so no one would try to persuade him to go. He wasn't feeling festive and wasn't in the mood to pretend like he was. He also didn't want to ruin his family's Christmas by having them worry about him. He just wanted to be alone in his misery.

Later, as he lay in the dark, he tried to blank the vision of Sabol from his mind, but it would not go away. It revived a deep, almost primal fear that no matter what he did, one day Sabol would have his revenge.

CHAPTER 17

For old acquaintance be forgot, except Richard Sabol, Vinny pondered while sitting on his living room couch partially inebriated, waiting for a houseful of guests to arrive for a New Year's Eve celebration. In less than one week since the news of Sabol's triumphant return to society, liquor became Vinny's life, and he was quickly becoming clinically depressed.

I'd better go see Houston. I know he's going to give me shit again just like he always does, the prick. I just don't see that I have any other choice.

Against his better judgment, Vinny approached Sergeant Houston with the information he had obtained from his brother-in-law on Christmas Day.

"You are obsessed with this guy to the point that I think you need psychological help," Houston said scornfully as Vinny sat quietly in the small anticrime office. "How long ago was it?" Houston asked hesitantly, rubbing a nervous hand across his face. Vinny stared blankly. "I'll tell you how long ago it was that the feds informed Internal Affairs that Sabol was going away for twenty years. Less than two years ago!" Vinny sat motionless and said nothing. "What do you want me to do?" Houston stared at Vinny in disbelief.

Vinny was filled with doubts and fears. "Have your friend Agent Stamp from the FBI look into it for you?"

"And tell him what?" Houston retaliated disgustedly. "That your brother-in-law's best friend is driving around Yonkers with a guy the Justice Department swears was put away for twenty years?"

That does sound stupid, but it's the fucking truth. Why the fuck do you always fight me on this? What is it? Unless you see it with your own eyes, you refuse to believe?

"Why don't we get Internal Affairs involved, too?" Houston added patronizingly. "I'm positive that's just what we need in the midst of this gas caper Julia Rivera has started. Internal Affairs will come here to investigate your bullshit complaint about a phantom federal prisoner driving around your neighborhood, get pissed off when the feds tell them Sabol is still in prison, doing twenty years, and retaliate by ramming a complaint up your ass for misappropriation of NYPD gas, your partner's ass for being with you, and my ass for failing to supervise you! Is that what you want?" Houston shrieked.

You're a fucking asshole. It's not bullshit. I've never bullshitted you, but you never want to believe me. What's your fucking problem? Okay, stay calm. Fight it.

"What am I supposed to do? Wait for the prick to blow my head off as I park my car at night?"

Houston smiled coldly. "The feds do not let a scumbag like Sabol out. I don't care whom he ratted on in Georgia. Not only did Sabol threaten to kill you and your family, but he also threatened to kill four FBI agents in front of a federal judge. The feds are very protective of their own, so there's no way in hell they let him out," Houston said in a low, confident voice.

Vinny ignored his reticence. "He's out there, Sarge. Maybe it's because of a technicality that we weren't notified, because as long as he's on a work release program, he's still in custody. But as positive as I am that God made little green apples, that's how sure I am that Sabol's out during the day."

"Then do what you do best and bring me proof. If you want to waste your off-duty time chasing ghosts, by all means, knock yourself out, but I'm not notifying anyone until you do."

Bastard. Fuck-head.

"It'll take time, but you'll have your proof!"

"You bring me proof and I'll eat my hat."

Proof? My word's never good enough for him. Eat shit and die, asshole. Vinny shook his head and smiled. "I hope you're hungry that day."

On New Year's Eve, Vinny was kicking back on his couch with a drink, reliving his last encounter with Houston. His guests were in the kitchen when Tommy joined him.

"What! Do you live on that couch?"

"Hey, TC, how's it going?" He rose to embrace his friend.

"Can I get one of those, or are you hording all the scotch for yourself?"

"Come on, the good stuff is hidden in a cabinet in the kitchen." Walking to the kitchen, they were greeted by their friends dressed in New Year's Eve party hats, blowing horns.

"Looks like this will be one hell of a party," Tommy said.

"Yeah, wonderful," Vinny replied sarcastically.

I'm not in the mood for this, I'm really not, but fuck, it's New Year's Eve.

"So what's new and exciting?" He poured a large scotch on the rocks.

"My sergeant thinks I need to see a shrink."

"You decided to tell him about Sabol, didn't you?"

"Don't ask me why. It was against my better judgment."

"What was the outcome of this obviously one-sided conversation?"

"He basically said that he is not going to look like a fool for me or for all the tea in China. He also suggested that I bring him proof, and if I did, he would eat his hat."

"Well, that sounds like a reason to motivate you. How long do you think it will take before he dines on his hat?"

"I don't know. A month, maybe two. It'll all depend on how many of his enemies get word that he's out and find out what he's up to. Once word gets around, information on him flows like Niagara Falls."

"Is your brother-in-law's friend—what's his name, Gerry?—still hanging out with him?"

Tommy grabbed a chair at the table and sat. "Mike says he gave Gerry the warning about Sabol and that he wants nothing to do with him anymore."

"Well, that's good. At least you don't have to worry about Sabol finding out that Maria is your sister. God only knows what that sick bastard is capable of."

Vinny stared off, then got up and walked across the kitchen. "I don't know if I'll be able to get the goods on him this time and maintain my anonymity. As it is, most of his friends have already labeled me as the reason for his drug arrest."

"Let's not get too pessimistic. Wait and see what you find out before you start worrying."

"You're right. Let's see what I can find out."

The Davis boys didn't customarily throw fancy parties. The dining room table was filled with trays of baked ziti, meatballs, sausage and pepper, eggplant parmigiana, and two six-foot heroes, along with plastic plates, knives, forks, and spoons. There were two kegs of beer on the porch. They felt no need to impress their friends with opulence they didn't have or seduce them with champagne and elegance. Their friends came to party because they were friends. It was in full swing. Some were dancing, others enjoyed the food and conversation, and lovers sneaked off into any obscure place to enjoy the pleasures of each others flesh one last time for 1993.

Vinny was visibly intoxicated, highly agitated, and disgusted with his life.

He looked out the window; the snowflakes were large, and the wind grew angrier by the minute. The drifts in front of the house grew. Radio weather forecasters announced the brunt of the storm had passed but would continue throughout the night.

Suddenly, without warning, he felt a tear slide down his face as he reflected on the desolation he felt on the night his mother lay dead in the street. The complete feeling of helplessness, of not being able to save his mother's life, and the deeply hidden guilt, knowing that if he never challenged her to that foot race, she would have still been alive today. When someone you love dies, you don't lose them all at once; you lose them in pieces, little by little, over time. Now, almost twenty-two years later, not a day had passed that he hadn't relived the horrible memory of that night.

He closed his eyes and visualized exactly what happened. It was burned into his memory, how he and his mother and his friend George watched the last episode of *Ironsides* on television; the fragrance of Ivory soap on her body as he lay nestled on his mother's lap while she ran her fingers through his hair while watching the show; the smell of the ocean brine emanating from the waters of the Verrazzano-Narrows as the three of them exited the front door to walk George home, a short block away; the smile that creased his mother's lips when she accepted the challenge of the race by her son; and how she gave the boys a head start out of her sense of fair play. How could he forget her long legs leaping by on the narrow sidewalk, the vision of a gazelle, passing George as Vinny ran full speed in the street past parked cars along the way, finally reaching the corner behind her, watching her body fall almost in slow motion to the ground with an abrupt thump as her head hit the cast iron base of the streetlight? "Nooo!" he'd screamed in anguish, as he cradled her in his arms while screaming for help.

He blinked a few times, as if he were dragging his mind back to the present. His thoughts quickly returned to the beast Sabol, who'd always fed on other people's pain and suffering like a colossal tumor forever growing that needs to be destroyed.

Sabol was the epitome of why Vinny became a cop, to lock evil away and make this world a safer place to live. But Vinny was now losing his fight against evil, and Sabol would use his grief, the pain he was feeling, for his own selfish reasons. When the time was right, Sabol would seek revenge on Vinny, killing everyone in his path without remorse.

"Do you want to dance?"

Vinny turned to see a very attractive blonde he had never seen before. He grinned in pleasure, happy to be snatched from his dwelling on the past. "Not just now," he said evasively.

"Aren't you Raymond's brother Vinny, the cop?" she asked solicitously with a gleaming smile.

"Yeah, that would be me," he said, looking faintly amused.

"My name's Tracy," she said, still smiling, extending her hand, which Vinny graciously accepted. "I just love cops. A man in uniform is so sexy and really turns me on," she added, still holding his hand.

"Can I ask you a personal question?"

"I don't see why not."

"It's New Year's Eve, you're a stunning-looking woman dressed to kill, so where is your boyfriend, husband, or significant other?"

"He's in California on business and won't be back for another week," she said, wrapping her arms around his shoulders. She was wearing a strapless black dress that barely covered her breasts and was made of see-through fabric at the midriff.

"So he wouldn't mind you spending New Year's Eve wrapped in the arms of another man," he mumbled, brushing back some hair that was hanging in his eyes.

"What he doesn't know won't hurt him," she said provocatively, moving her hand down to his groin.

"The truth is," he said hesitantly, "I'm involved with someone. She, too, is away on business."

"That's perfect," she said, pressing her body closer to him.

"As a matter of fact, it is perfect between her and myself. That's why I would never consider cheating on her."

"You're kidding, right?" she asked in disbelief.

"About what?" he asked sheepishly. "The fact that I have a girl-friend or that we love and trust each other enough not to cheat on each other?"

"Well, it's obvious by looking at you that you have a girl-friend, but I have yet to meet a man who wouldn't cheat," she said incredulously.

Vinny smiled winningly. "You have now. Will you excuse me, please?" he said, brushing past her firm body. "My brother's waving me to come to the kitchen."

"Sure," she said vaguely as he walked away.

These are the women of the nineties, he thought to himself, reaching for the half-empty bottle of scotch he had hidden in the kitchen cabinet. Not so long ago, it was the homely women who were pro-miscuous. Now it seemed the more beautiful and educated women were insecure about themselves and needed to get laid by different men in order to feel special.

So this is the modern-day women of the nineties. Marvelous.

Disgusted with the party, and his life in general, he opted to retreat to the solitude of his bedroom, accompanied by his newest and most trusted friend, a bottle of Johnnie Walker Black. Vinny sat on his bed alone in his room and stared at the scene on television at Times Square.

Reflectively, he thought of how almost ten years of marriage went down the drain and how Christina had managed to let him down. Suddenly, he felt a terrible loneliness deep inside of him that couldn't get filled no matter how many people he was around. Debbie was gone, Christina was gone, and nobody could tell him why. Hesitating, thinking it through once more, he reached for his Glock. Holding it in his hand, pointing it toward him, looking into the small hole, where death comes out.

Looks easy, he thought, taking a long sip of his scotch, the simplest and quickest way to end all his pain. No more Debbie, Christina, or Sabol. They would all vanish with his pain in a milli-second. His mother had gone to a better place at about the same age. So why not be with her? Why stay in a world filled with human evil and perversity? A world where no matter how hard a person fought human injustice, evil prevailed. All he ever wanted in life was a loving wife and children and a job where he could help people. He suddenly found comfort in his conviction that it was he who was to blame for losing the women in his life. As he thought of Christina, picturing her safe in his arms in their new home on Long Island, living the life they once dreamed of, a longing fell over him that was unbearably painful. On the walls of his bedroom, he saw the faces of their chil-dren and could hear their laughter. He saw Christina's face and felt the warmth of her embrace. He was smiling, about to kiss her, three minutes left of 1993.

"What are you doing?"

Vinny looked up abruptly and saw his brother Michael stand-ing in the doorway, staring at the gun in Vinny's hand.

"I'm sorry, Michael, but I can't."

Michael moved quickly, snatching the gun from his hands. "Are you crazy?" he asked incredulously, his eyes filled with emotion.

"I can't take the pain anymore," Vinny sighed, meeting his stare.

Michael looked at him with commiseration for a moment. "You're ridiculous!" he sneered. "You're a good-looking guy who can get any woman he wants, and you have a job you love. To this day, I have never met anyone who actually enjoys going to work every day besides you."

"You don't understand," Vinny said softly, sadly. "I'm not happy with my life anymore. I want to get married and raise a family."

"So by putting a bullet in your brain, it's going to help you achieve these goals?" Michael asked sarcastically, examining the gun in his hand.

Vinny could only stare blankly at his brother.

"Listen, Vinny, we were all shocked about what Christina had done. She had us all fooled with her class and sophistication. I was shocked and sickened to think she could do that to you. But it's better that you found out now that she's not playing with a full deck than ten years from now, like Debbie," Michael said, sounding uncharacteristically philosophical.

A tear suddenly escaped Vinny's eye and rolled down his face.

Michael understood his brother's pain and automatically put a comforting arm around him.

"I can't take being hurt like this…not after that. You can see that, can't you?" Vinny asked, taking a large gulp of scotch, draining the glass empty.

"First of all," Michael said forcefully, looking directly into his brother's eyes, "you have had enough of this stuff for tonight." Taking the empty glass from his hand. "Your drinking is turning your brain to Jell-O." Michael turned his gaze toward the television, which was on in the room, with the sound muted. "Hey, look," Michael said cheerfully, pointing to the TV as the party downstairs erupted into a thunderous roar. "Happy New Year."

Vinny smiled at Michael and hugged him tightly. "Nineteen ninety-four will be a much better year for all three Davis boys," Vinny said excitedly.

"Yes, it will be," Michael said and nodded. "Now, let's go downstairs and enjoy the party."

Almost four weeks had passed since Vinny's cowardly act of desperation, and he still found himself living his life like a man walking on a high wire, doing a balancing act, with no net below him, with seemingly no one to turn to for support. Although Vinny had known and worked closely with Sergeant Houston for almost three years, and he knew that Vinny had never gotten bad information on Sabol before, he was treating him as if he were a paranoid rookie. Vinny was driven by the pursuit of the truth, at any and all costs, while Houston was acting selfish, ruthless, and even cruel toward his own officer by ignoring the truth and notifying the day-tour sergeants that Vinny had become unstable, even delusional.

Vinny sat alone at the bar, sipping a scotch and water, for the third straight week in a row, waiting for his chance to arrive to find out what Sabol had been up to. He knew in order to convince Houston to contact his friend in the FBI, in the midst of the gas investigation that could cause him grief with the department, he had to have proof positive that Sabol was not only violating the terms of his work release but also dealing in some sort of crime. Vinny knew that Houston needed an ace in the hole, and Vinny was determined to give it to him.

A cold, wet snow had been falling for the second night, and the people in the bar were already complaining about it. Vinny saw the door to the bar swing open, and a man wearing a hood to protect himself from the wet snow sat at the bar directly across from him. The vision of the man became infinitely clearer as he removed his hood. It was Martel, a fierce archenemy of Sabol's.

He saw Vinny almost immediately, and his face turned white and taut with fear. Then straightening up, smiling his nonsmile, he waved at Vinny, who sat casually blowing smoke rings.

Vinny smiled back at him with only a slight trace of bitterness and waved him over to have a seat next to him. Hastily, Martel walked over in sort of a distorted, slow motion, smiling reassuringly as he took a seat.

"How are things, Martel?" Vinny asked in a friendly voice.

"Not too bad, Officer, or should I say Detective now?" Martel asked with a wry grin.

"Why not keep this informal and call me Vinny? What are you drinking, Martel? They're on me tonight."

"Call me Vinny, and drinks being on a first name basis means to want something from me?" Martel said suspiciously with raised eyebrows.

"Bartender, I'll have a shot of Johnnie Walker Black and a beer, and get my friend here whatever he wants," Vinny said politely.

The bartender, a stocky Irishman from Mayo, walked over with two beers and two shot glasses he then filled with scotch.

"Cheers!" Vinny said as he belted down the shot, chasing it with a mouthful of beer. "Play it again, Sam," Vinny instructed the bartender, who stood at the ready with the bottle in hand.

"You better slow down, young Vince," the bartender said with his Irish brogue. "That's your seventh shot since ye came in the door."

"You're a good man, ye are, Sean," Vinny said in his best Irish brogue. "But a wee bit a this don't affect me much," Vinny added, downing the second shot. "Drink up, Martel, they're free."

Martel studied him idly, wondering what Vinny's rush was to get drunk.

Within the hour of free-flowing shots and their polite conversation about nothing of importance, the alcohol had the effect on Martel he had hoped it would.

"I guess you've heard your old pal is on the streets again and up to his old tricks," Martel said vindictively.

"What pal might that be?" Vinny asked dispassionately.

Martel smiled arrogantly. "I was just trying to give you a warning, but if you want to be an asshole about it, forget it," Martel said, standing up to leave in a hurry.

A murderous gleam appeared in each of Vinny's eyes. "Sit down and tell me a story about my pal Sabol," Vinny growled, never taking his eyes off him.

Martel looked faintly amused as he took his seat. "Your pal Sabol is on a work release program out of New Jersey. The word on the street is that he has some sort of arrangement to pay his boss to lie for him and pretend he's at work during the day."

Vinny produced a self-satisfied smile. "So he's not working, yet he has the money to pay his boss to cover for him," Vinny said mischievously, taking a sip of beer. "Does the word on the street happen to know how he manages to do that?" Vinny asked flippantly.

Martel smiled coldly. "Word is, he's been palling around with a guy named Gerry, who's a good earner for one of the crime families. I heard that just today, the guy Gerry gave Sabol ten large to put down on a warehouse in New Jersey for a legit business, but you know Sabol as well as I do, and he has never done anything legit in his life."

Vinny sat completely thrown back. He couldn't believe what he'd just heard. For whatever reasons, Gerry hadn't listened to Michael. It now made no difference to Vinny. Sabol was free from prison and up to his old tricks—that was now a fact. And now Vinny would have to get Gerry out of the way before he could get at Sabol. But how?

"Do you have any word on what Sabol is up to?" Vinny asked in wonder.

"If there's big money involved, that's where you can find Sabol, but exactly what it is, I have no idea," Martel said implicitly, shaking his head from side to side.

"Why did you decide to tell me this wealth of information?" Vinny asked, seemingly fascinated.

Martel laughed derisively. "Because you hate that asshole more than I do, and I know that by telling you what I told you, you'll be like a dog who found a bone. I also know for a fact that you are going to bury that bone real deep."

Vinny gave one of his condescending smiles. "What makes you so sure that I can manage that if the feds let him out?" Vinny asked innocently.

"Everybody knows you had something to do with his last arrest, and Sabol has vowed to get even with you," Martel said despairingly. "If that's not enough motivation for you to nail his ass, I don't know what is."

Vinny sat impassive, a perplexed look on his face.

"You're a good cop," he added decidedly. "If anybody can nail that slimy piece of shit, you can."

"Thanks for the vote of confidence," Vinny said courteously.

"Listen, Vinny, if it's any consolation, I think Debbie's a great girl. I always thought you two were a great couple who'd never split up. But now that you have, don't put it past Sabol not to go after her. He's a demented fuck who doesn't like to lose what he considers his property, and he considered Debbie one of those properties," Martel said cautiously.

Vinny was trying to control his temper. "If he so much as touches one hair on her head, Jesus Christ himself won't be able to help him," Vinny said, his voice heavy with anger.

Martel smiled confidently. "I thought you'd say that."

Vinny grinned broadly. "I've got to go, Martel. Thanks for the heads-up on this. I owe you one."

"Put that prick away for life and we'll call it even," Martel said sharply as Vinny walked into the snow outside.

As Vinny drove slowly, easing his way along the icy, slick hills of Yonkers, his thoughts turned inward. In a way, he was angry, yet at the same time, he was filled with relief. Getting the information on Sabol had been easier than he'd imagined. What he didn't like was that Gerry hadn't listened to Mike, and it bothered him a great deal that he might be involved with Sabol in some illegal deals in New Jersey. The problem was that if he was involved, then Vinny would be responsible for putting his brother-in-law's best friend in prison along with Sabol, and that bothered him a great deal more than he would like to admit. But the fact is, as he reminded himself, he might have little choice in the matter. It also worried him again to think what would happen if things went wrong; he'd now have two enemies who knew him and his family personally. He was now clearly bewildered.

Arriving home, he marched straight into the living room and poured himself a large glass of scotch on the rocks. His mind was so confused he didn't know what to think or even feel. After two more glasses, his anger at Gerry for not listening to Mike began to grow.

Finally, he decided that to make sure nothing went wrong, to make sure that his family would be protected, he had to warn Gerry himself. Hesitating, thinking it through once more, he dialed his sister's house. Mike answered abruptly on the second ring.

"Hello, Mike, it's Vinny."

"Hey, what's up?"

"I'll tell you what's up. Your asshole friend didn't listen to a fucking word you told him. That's what's up," Vinny said with no attempt to hide his anger.

Mike paused, and for a moment, he was afraid he'd hung up. "So what do you want me to do?" Mike asked wearily.

"I want you to call him right now and get his ass over here. Tell him it's important and can't wait, and tell him you can't talk on the phone. That ought to rattle him," Vinny added confidently.

"I'll call him right now," Mike said hurriedly, hanging up without saying goodbye. The few minutes that passed seemed like hours as Vinny waited for the phone to ring. Aggravated, he hit the redial button on the phone.

"Maria, it's Vinny."

"What's going on?" she asked defensively.

"Nothing for you to worry about. Just do me a favor and make sure your husband gets Gerry over here. It's important I talk to him," Vinny insisted.

"I'll call him back right now," she said eagerly.

"Thanks sis," he said, hanging up the phone.

Forty-five minutes passed before Vinny heard the doorbell ring. He was drunk, burning up with heat, and running on pure adrenaline when he answered the door with no shirt on.

"You want a drink?" Vinny asked politely, holding up the scotch in his hands.

"No, thanks," Gerry said agitatedly, entering the kitchen, with Mike behind him. Maybe it was the booze, but Gerry seemed a lot bigger than the last time Vinny had seen him at Mike and Maria's wedding.

"What's so important that you make Mike drag my ass over here?" Gerry asked anxiously.

Vinny met his stare head-on, his eyes black and dangerous-looking. "Why didn't you listen to the warning Mike gave you?" Vinny asked, refusing to be rattled.

Gerry shook his head and smiled. "Because I don't believe Sabol's a rat, that's why," Gerry said defiantly.

Vinny was completely taken aback; he didn't expect that answer. He knew he would have to come up with something quickly to make Gerry nervous enough to trust him. Vinny nodded vigorously while forcing his drunken brain to think of something.

"I was probably wrong about Sabol ratting on the people in Georgia," Vinny blurted out. "It's you he plans on ratting on," he added forcefully.

Gerry stared in shock and disbelief. The look on Gerry's face said it all. Vinny had struck a nerve. "If that's true, I'll kill that son of a bitch!" Gerry exploded, his entire body trembling in rage.

Watching Gerry yell vociferously, Vinny broke out into a derisive laughter. "Kill him," Vinny said agreeably. "There's nothing in this world that would make me happier. You'd be saving me a lot of time and energy, and the taxpayers a lot of money."

Gerry was astonished. He had doubts mixed with fears as he watched Vinny laughing. The laughter stopped as abruptly as it started. Vinny looked at Gerry and produced a wry smile. "Just remember one thing," Vinny said cautiously. "If what I heard is true and he is working for the feds, if you harm Sabol, you will be killed or spend the rest of your life behind bars, because he will have federal agents a heartbeat away from him at all times."

Gerry stared at Vinny, perplexed, as the reality of what he'd just heard sank in. Vinny's persuasiveness seemed to have worked, as Gerry bowed his head, shaking it vigorously from side to side, commiserating.

Vinny had no idea what illegal activities Gerry had gotten involved in with Sabol, but Gerry was scared, and that was exactly what Vinny wanted to do, scare him away from Sabol.

"So what do I do?" Gerry asked despairingly.

"Stay away from him," Vinny said without resignation.

Gerry looked at Vinny quizzically. "I got a problem with that," Gerry said curtly. "I gave him ten grand to open a legitimate business out in Jersey. I'm not staying away from him until I get my money back," he finished angrily.

"Problem, that's no problem," Vinny said piteously. "Tell me where to find him and I'll take care of that problem for you. If the only thing you've done is give him ten thousand dollars to open up a business, then he should give it back. So what's the problem?" Vinny asked solicitously, hoping Gerry would give him some useful information, the proof he needed to show Houston.

But Gerry wasn't stupid—he wasn't going to tell a cop about anything illegal he'd done. "How do I know you're telling me the truth about Sabol?" Gerry asked suspiciously, his dour expression never changing.

Vinny thought for a moment. The scotch was clouding his mind. "Come sit down inside," Vinny said politely. "I have something I want to show you."

The three of them walked casually into the den. "You two have a seat. I'll be right back," Vinny said graciously, walking into his living room.

Within a minute, Vinny had found what he was looking for in his desk and returned to Gerry and Mike.

"I shouldn't be showing this to you," Vinny said despairingly, handing Gerry two small pieces of paper. "On that paper are the names and phone numbers of the federal agents involved with Sabol's arrest in Georgia. It even has the prosecutor's name and phone number on them." Vinny hoped that by showing Gerry what he would think to be confidential police information, he would trust Vinny implicitly and inadvertently give him the desperately needed information into Sabol's present criminal activities. In actuality, all Vinny was showing Gerry was of public record and perfectly legal for him to do. "If you don't believe me that Sabol's supposed to be in prison for twenty years, why don't you call the people listed on those pages and ask them?" Vinny asked confidently.

Gerry read voraciously, then threw the papers onto the coffee table, rubbing his hands on his face.

"How do I know you're not going to turn me in?" Gerry asked disbelievingly.

"For what? I don't know of anything illegal that you've done," Vinny said nonchalantly. "However, if you have done anything illegal with Sabol, the feds probably have you on both audio and videotape by now, anyway. So they wouldn't need any help from me." Vinny's voice resonated with confidence.

Gerry looked at Vinny incredulously, as if he'd never heard of such technology before. "Do you really think they have tapes?" Gerry asked urgently, with fear in his voice.

"Oh, that's gospel," Vinny said indignantly. "The feds are very high-tech. They have listening devices that can pick up the sound of a snake farting in Cairo," Vinny added amusingly.

"That fuck gave me this cell phone," Gerry said sharply, inspecting it curiously.

Vinny couldn't pass up the golden opportunity that Gerry had just presented to him. "Well, that clinches it," Vinny said, in a deadpan voice. "Whatever you've talked about on that phone is now on tape."

Gerry immediately banged the phone down on the coffee table, as if he were trying to break it open. Stopping abruptly, he looked at Vinny, then at Michael, then back at Vinny with amazement in his eyes. Moments passed as the three sat impassively without speaking a word. Then straightening up, smiling his nonsmile, Gerry stood up while pointing a casual finger at Vinny. "I hope you're wrong about this," he said without malice.

Vinny rose to his feet, giving one of his condescending smiles. "For your sake, Gerry, so do I," he said empathetically.

Vinny and Mike began to walk through the living room with Gerry in tow. Vinny opened the door to let the two out. Mike smiled winningly at Vinny and said, "Thanks a million, pal."

Vinny returned the smile. "No problem. But, Gerry," Vinny said haltingly, "if you mention my name to Sabol as the person who tipped you off, or if you take too much time getting your money back, all bets are off!" Vinny's glare was enough. The edge in his voice only added to it.

Gerry nodded and turned for the door.

As Vinny closed and locked it behind them, there was a sudden gleam of humor in his eyes. "Jesus," he said under his breath. "As soon as Gerry gets his money back, I'll have Sabol just where I want him, and I'll get my gold shield."

CHAPTER 18

O ver the next few weeks, Vinny spent his days at work patrolling the streets of the South Bronx in a radio car, and his nights in dark, shady bars, on fishing expeditions, hoping to hit pay dirt on Sabol. After all, he had got nothing left to lose except his job, which was the only thing stopping him from falling into the abyss. Everything else he felt was important in the world was gone.

His past few days at work had been spent concentrating on trying to track down an armed suspect wanted by the TP and NYPD for a rash of robberies. Although he was no longer assigned to the anticrime unit, he habitually reviewed the district's recap sheets and crime reports, in search of crime pattern similarities. After finding what he was looking for and devising a plan to catch the suspect, he vacillated over whom to approach to obtain permission to put his plan into effect. Finding a tour commander to take him seriously would be no easy task, amid the insinuations Houston had decided erroneously, that he was suffering from delusions and should be heavily supervised for his own safety.

"I'd like to help you out, Vinny," Lieutenant Bobby Rodriguez, the midnight tour commander said empathetically, "but for one thing, you're no longer in anticrime, and number two is, no way in hell the Transit Authority station supervisor is going to let you pose as a railroad clerk."

A smirk creased Vinny's lips as he stared at the lieutenant. "What if I told you that not only did I already obtain permission from the TA brass but that they also already gave me a clerk's uniform to wear?"

The lieutenant raised his eyes slowly, nodding with glee. He picked up a stack of roll call sheets off a clipboard, looking for something. He flipped through the pages and found what he needed. "Tomorrow morning at 0500 hours. What do you think?" he asked worriedly.

"Sir, 183rd Street on the D Line at 0500 hours is when I'd have to be there," Vinny said confidently.

"Who do you want for a partner?"

"Why, Danny-Boy, of course," Vinny said coolly.

"I don't know if Sergeant Houston will go for this," he said wearily.

Vinny sneered. "The last time I looked, a lieutenant, who is soon to be a captain, outranks a mere anticrime sergeant."

"It'll look bad for his unit if you make this collar," he said mischievously, staring at Vinny.

"Do you think he cares how bad you look right now with all these robberies going down on your tour? Besides, I owe him one for spreading all these vicious rumors about me."

"But if you mess this up, do you know how bad I'll look?" he asked, struggling to keep an even voice.

"I won't let that happen, Bobby," Vinny answered implicitly, his confidence showing in the sparkle of his eyes.

Bobby picked up the roll call and began to scrawl in red ink. "Be here at 0500 hours tomorrow in your clerk's getup, and I'll borrow Danny from anticrime, but if I smell booze on your breath or you mess this up, you'll be riding trains northbound and southbound until the day you retire."

"Don't worry, Bobby. You know how much I hate trains."

The next day, Vinny arrived at work at 0445 hours, well rested, dressed impeccably in his railroad clerk uniform consisting of a light-blue shirt with a white-and-blue-striped tie, navy pants, and matching blazer with the Transit Authority patch embroidered on the left breast pocket. "Should I ask to smell your breath?" Bobby asked cynically.

"Very funny, boss. Is Danny here yet?"

"He's in the locker room, putting on an extra-bulletproof vest," Bobby said, laughing out loud at his own wit.

"You ready to go to work?" Vinny asked Danny, who appeared out of the radio room with two radios in his hand.

"Ready as I'll ever be, getting up at three in the morning to drive to work," Danny said contemptuously.

"Let's go," Vinny said enthusiastically, walking out the door to the district at the 183rd Street Station. Ms. Sanchez, the railroad clerk on duty that knew Vinny since he was a rookie on the job, admitted Vinny into the booth.

"Hey, Davis, I see they sent you to catch that son of a bitch."

Vinny smiled brightly. "Someone's got to do it. Anita, you got a good look at him last time, didn't you?"

"I sure did," she replied, frightened and barely audible, as if she might be overheard.

"Do me a favor, then. If he shows up, just pretend that you don't recognize him. We don't want to scare him off or get an innocent passenger hurt," he said, giving her an assuring look. "You and I will just wait until he moves to make his escape. Danny will be watching from the hole in the wall in the porter room, and I will signal him by radio when to come out."

Anita was smiling as if she were enjoying the thrill of the chase.

"Now, there are two things I need you to make sure you do for me," Vinny said soothingly. "When I leave this booth to chase this guy, you must immediately lock the booth door behind me. As soon as you've done that, use your emergency phone to call for help."

Anita smiled and relaxed. "I can do that," she said, smiling at Vinny winningly.

"Good girl," he said, placing his hand softly on her shoulder.

From the booth windows, Vinny had a clear view of the entire mezzanine area. On the left, some twenty feet away, a homeless man—a *skell* is the term more commonly used by cops—was picking through a dumpster, looking for food and empty bottles and cans. At the opposite side of the station, another homeless man trundled along, pulling two shopping carts full of cans and possibly everything he owned.

A few minutes passed.

Vinny noticed a tall black man with dreadlocks arguing meekly with his girlfriend.

"What's that?" Vinny heard Danny's voice coming over the radio.

"Just a lover's spat," Vinny reassured him, keeping the radio out of sight.

"How come I have to freeze my ass off in this foul-smelling room while you are nice and warm in that booth with Anita?"

"Next time, you come up with a plan and I'll freeze my ass off. Now, stay off the air," Vinny said curtly.

Police work is 90 percent boring wait, wait, wait, and 10 percent excitement or sheer terror. One such incident would be more than enough excitement for most civilians, but patrol cops go out day after day responding to emergencies. It's their job and their duty. Their work permeates their every cell.

"I think that's him," Anita said casually, looking toward a male Hispanic wearing a purple jumpsuit positioned in the darkness of the street stairway.

"Just act natural," Vinny said reassuringly to Anita. "Oh, Danny-Boy, we have a possible. Male Hispanic in his twenties, wearing a purple jumpsuit," Vinny sang in a low monotone into the radio he had kept out of sight on the counter.

"That's not the words to the song," Danny said. "And that voice, you definitely don't sing like your mother does."

"Oh, shut up and get ready," Vinny retaliated.

Anita looked at Vinny with wistful indulgence, as if he were a child doing something wrong and needed to be set straight. "Aren't you going to grab him?"

"Not yet, we're not," he said, flashing a bright, eager smile while his eyes were scanning the mezzanine area for a possible victim. His eyes locked onto an emaciated older Hispanic woman with her handbag securely strapped around her neck and shoulder, which should deter an armed suspect.

As she approached the booth, she reached into her handbag, and simultaneously, the suspect rapidly approached from behind. He was upon her in an instant, with his left arm around her neck and a gun to her head.

"What do you want?" she yelled over her shoulder in broken English.

"The money. Give me the money!"

"Help me!" she cried out, her eyes wide with horror. She looked desperately into the booth at Vinny.

"Shut up and give me the money!" he screamed at her.

Vinny pleaded with the woman and clenched his fist. "Please, lady, give him the money."

The criminal jerked her forward, pounding her frail body against the token booth, and shook her roughly. She tried to resist, but he held her tightly.

"Help me!" Her cries and protests could be heard throughout the desolate station. It took tremendous restraint and years of training for Vinny not to react hastily. If Vinny left the booth, he would not only put Anita's life at risk but also the Transit Authority's precious revenue. As hard as it was to bear witness to this violent act, Vinny and Danny held their ground.

Suddenly, the woman's eyes rolled back in their sockets, the color drained from her face, and she sank slowly to the floor.

The suspect grabbed her purse from around her neck and took off toward the stairs leading to the street.

"Lock this door!" Vinny shouted, pulling his gun from his waistband while flying out of the booth.

Danny and Vinny were side by side, running at lightning speed on pure adrenaline. As they hit the top of the stairs, the suspect had vanished into thin air. Danny ran ten feet to the corner of 183rd Street. Looking westbound, he threw up his arms in frustration.

"This way!" Vinny yelled, hearing the sound of a buzzer used at the front entrance of an apartment building. Danny was directly behind Vinny as the suspect entered the first of two secured glass doors. Danny frantically pushed numerous doorbells in the hopes to get buzzed in. Vinny grabbed the barrel of his gun and forcefully swung it, shattering the glass.

Danny forced his gun hand through the shattered glass.

"Police. Don't move, you motherfucker!"

The criminal froze. The threat in Danny's voice made that perfectly clear.

While Danny's gun was trained on the suspect, Vinny punched his bare hand through to undo the lock. Vinny was filled with uncontrollable rage as he raced into the lobby.

"Face the wall!" Danny yelled as Vinny raced forward, grabbing the suspect by the back of his hair, ramming him face-first into the wall. They could hear the popping sound of the bones in his face as the blood drooled down the white tiles of the hallway wall.

With fire in his eyes, Vinny snapped. "You like to beat on old women?" Vinny had thrown caution to the wind by not recovering the suspect's weapon. "Pick on me, you fucking scumbag!" he screamed, hoisting the suspect off his feet, sailing him headfirst into the opposite wall.

"Vinny!" Danny's voice dropped to a pleading, guttural sound. "You're gonna kill him!"

Vinny grabbed the criminal's gun from inside his waistband before dropping him to the floor like a rag doll. Danny placed his gun in his holster and quickly speed-cuffed his hands behind his back.

"Holy shit, Vinny," Danny said, trying to modulate his voice.

Vinny lowered his eyes to the floor somberly. He heard the rapidly approaching sirens as he reached for his radio.

"Eleven Crime One, Central."

"What's your location, Eleven Crime One?"

"No further units. Inside 2810 Grand Concourse. We have one under. Notify EMS to respond for a cardiac victim of a crime at 183rd Street by the booth."

"Ten-four, Eleven Crime One."

"Eleven, Operations Lieutenant to Central K."

"Eleven Ops, go."

"Notify Eleven Crime One the victim merely fainted. We're en route for a show up of the suspect."

Looking at the suspect sprawled out face-first on the floor, in a puddle of his own blood, Danny shook his head vigorously. "Well, that prick won't be robbing any little old ladies for a while."

Vinny blinked his eyes uncomprehendingly. "I lost it, Danny. I really wanted to kill that guy. That woman's face changed a thousand times in a few seconds. From my mother's, to my grandmother's, to a nun from the Catholic school I went to. It was crazy."

Danny sighed, rubbing the space between his eyebrows. "Fuck him. I would have done the same thing if I had a front-row seat," he said as he picked the suspect off the floor.

"Amazing," Lieutenant Rodriguez said as he entered through the broken glass at the entrance to the apartment building. "Absolutely amazing," he said, looking at the bloodied suspect "I take one look at that perp and I see resisting arrest written all over his face." Rodriguez smiled sardonically.

Vinny half-smiled shyly, showing the suspect's automatic weapon.

Rodriguez nodded absently, unimpressed. "The token booth clerk told me how it went down. It must have been traumatic having to watch something like that and not be able to react."

"I thought he killed her," Vinny said somberly.

"Nice job, Vinny," Rodriguez said, smiling behind his hand covering his mouth.

Danny laughed.

"Let's take flocko here outside so the victim can properly ID him," Rodriguez chided, amid the laughter.

As Danny marched the suspect out the door and into the street filled with police cars, Rodriguez turned and smiled at Vinny. "Would you consider working midnights, Davis?"

"No thanks, boss. I'm afraid of the dark."

That was yesterday.

He sat alone and confused, celebrating his birthday at Charlie Brown's Restaurant down the street from his house. Sometimes he thought what was happening to him was just a temporary setback.

That everything happens for a reason. Yet at other times, he wondered if God was punishing him for some unknown reason. At thirty-two years old, he was closer to obtaining his life's dreams a decade ago than he was at this very moment. He was still not certain how his life fell apart so quickly. Debbie's self-destruction, the fire, Christina's betrayal, the indefinite hold on his promotion, and the return of a malevolent psychopath into his life.

As he sipped his wine, his thoughts turned to Christina.

She's all I can think about. I wonder how she's doing with her new boyfriend. Is she happy? If not, does she miss me at all? Or does she still love me and want me back? Did she ever really love me at all? Christ, I don't know. And I hate not knowing.

Vinny had spoken with Karen shortly after seeing Christina parading down 161st Street arm in arm with another man. While stopped at a traffic light in a radio car, he saw the two of them walk directly in front of him. Vinny felt as if he had been stabbed in the heart with a rusty, dull blade. It hurt so badly. Studying the man she was with, he saw the personification of money and prestige.

Mr. Wonderful, a rich and successful Long Island yuppie. *There isn't one iota of toughness in him. He's a fucking weak, spineless man who couldn't fight his way out of a wet paper bag. He'd have to pay his butler to cut him out.*

"It won't last long," Karen said.

"What makes you say that? He's got more money than I'll ever have."

"Because she doesn't love him, she loves you."

He shook his head no vigorously without looking at her. "She's got a strange way of showing it."

"You don't understand women very well," Karen said, running her fingers through her dark hair. He shrugged indifferently.

"First of all, you steal her away from her husband two days before her wedding. Then you two have a magical, romantic love affair, vowing your eternal love for each other. Everything is the *Days of Wine and Roses* until you, my friend, make one fatal mistake."

Vinny looked up, puzzled.

"You ask her to marry you and talk about starting a family."

Before Vinny could utter a word, Karen silenced him with her hand like a cop in Midtown halting traffic.

"A woman just coming out of a troubled relationship is in no rush to commit to another one, no matter how good it is. She needs time for her to make sure that she's not going to make the same mistake twice. Every woman knows that men are on their best behavior in the beginning of a relationship, constantly wanting to impress by being attentive and caring, but as time goes by, the real man emerges from deep within, and presto, your prince is now a prick."

Vinny stared bemusedly.

"Listen, Vinny, I know you're a great guy and you've been badly hurt by what happened, but I talk to Christina all the time and all she talks about is how much she misses and loves you. She doesn't give a shit about this rich asshole. He's there because you're not. She thinks you'll never find it in your heart to forgive her, that you're this rough, tough cop that sees things only in black-and-white. I'm not saying call her right now and try to work things out. Give yourself some time to heal and maybe understand her side."

Vinny looked doubtful.

"She was scared and she made the biggest mistake in her life," Karen insisted stubbornly. "You two were great together and still can be if you find it in your heart to forgive her."

"How do you forgive someone for doing something like that?"

His glass was empty.

"Bartender, another Chianti Classico, please." The bartender poured him another glass as his pager went off. He pushed the button to display the phone number and saw it was his in-laws. He dialed the number.

I wonder what trouble Debbie's fuckin' gotten herself into now.

"Hello?" Debbie answered cheerily.

"Well, it doesn't sound like you're in any trouble," he said sarcastically.

"Happy birthday, soon-to-be ex-husband."

"Thanks," he said unenthusiastically.

"What's the matter with you? You didn't get laid for your birthday?" she asked flatly.

"No, I can't say I have."

"Do you want to?" she asked invitingly.

"Are you drunk?" he asked curiously.

"Why? Do I have to be drunk to want to fuck my ex-husband on his birthday? Just because we're getting a divorce doesn't mean you're still not the best fuck of my life."

"Thanks for the rave review, and my birthday wish, but I have to pass on your offer," he said thoughtfully.

"Well, that's too bad about that. We could have had some fun. But anyway, I still have to see you. It's important that we talk," she said urgently.

"Can't you tell me now while you have me on the phone?" he asked.

"Where are you?" she asked.

"I'm at Charlie Brown's," he said.

"I'll be there in ten minutes," she said, then hung up.

Happy birthday. Here are your divorce papers and a pen to sign them with. Wonderful.

"So where are they?" he asked accusingly as Debbie took a seat next to him at the bar.

She looked perplexed. "Where are what?" she asked suspiciously, with raised eyebrows.

"The finalized divorce papers," he said indignantly.

"Next month, baby," she said confidently. "Whatever happened to hello first or 'You look great'?" she asked, looking at herself admiringly.

Vinny took a moment to look over his beautiful ex-wife. He had to admit, despite all she'd been through, she was as sexy as ever. "You look beautiful," he concluded, kissing her gently on the cheek.

"You're as handsome as ever," she said with a seductive smile, running her tongue across her front teeth.

Vinny returned the smile, shyly. He knew she still had her insatiable sexual appetite. "So what's so important that you had to come and see me right away?" Vinny asked, clueless.

Immediately, the warmth left her face as it metamorphosed into despair. "It's gotten back to me that Sabol is going to kill you," she said, her voice resonant with fear.

"What? Who told you that?"

"It got back to some of my friends that Richie's pissed off about some vicious rumors you said about him," Debbie said. She paused and took a deep breath before she continued. "You called him a rat, and the guy you told wants his money back. Richie's telling people that not only are you destroying his chances to make some big money before he is released, but you're also fucking up his chances of finishing his work release program and getting out early."

"Early! Early!" Vinny was incredulous. His eyes were the fire of two burning coals. "That maggot ex-boyfriend of yours is out on the streets after spending only two years in prison on a twenty-year sentence, and he's complaining! Excuse me," he said apologetically, turning to the elderly couple seated next to him at the bar, enjoying their Rob Roys on the rocks.

"Why can't you just leave him alone?" Debbie asked innocently.

"Because he threatened to kill you, your family, my family, and quite a few other innocent people."

"Not if you leave him alone!" she said, shaking her head violently, her eyes wide with horror.

Vinny looked desperately into her eyes. "Listen to me," he said forcefully. "I'm a cop. He is a no-good, murdering scumbag who breaks the law with virtual impunity and belongs behind bars in a cage for the rest of his life. You now want me to believe that if I leave him alone, after all these years, he's just going to forget. Look at me in the eyes and tell me you truly believe in your heart that he will do that.

Debbie stared at him, knowing what she'd just heard was the truth. "So what are you going to do?" she asked nervously.

Vinny looked at her, puzzled. "I have to think about it."

"There's one more thing I heard. He thinks you had something to do with his drug arrest in Georgia. That's why we got that threatening phone call a couple of years ago." She paused. "You didn't have anything to do with that, did you?" she asked accusingly.

"How the hell would—"

"Listen to me, Vincent Davis," she said disgustedly. "I know you much too well to fall for that line of shit. I know how long you can keep a hard-on, how that mind of yours works. If someone pissed you off enough, you'd catch them dirty in fucking Siberia and somehow make the arrest. So don't talk to me like I'm some perp you arrested for a robbery."

Vinny nodded absently as her eyes locked onto his.

Looking to his right, he saw the older woman raising her glass at Debbie, grinning from ear to ear. "What's got your curiosity up, lady?" Vinny asked with a bright smile. "My persistency at catching bad guys or how long I can keep a hard-on?"

The woman laughed loudly. "Honey, I wouldn't give two shits about you catching bad guys. I want to know how big it is."

Debbie leaned across Vinny and motioned for the woman to come closer.

The woman moved closer as Vinny sat wedged between her and Debbie. "He's hung like a horse, knows how to use it, and it never goes down," Debbie said almost in a whisper.

"Oh my," the woman mumbled. "Then what are you doing here?" she asked Debbie with a bright smile.

"Ask him," Debbie said, breaking the huddle.

"Excuse me," he said, turning his back on the woman. "Sabol hasn't threatened you, has he?"

"No, he hasn't," she said hesitantly, "but my sister got a phone call from a guy named Mike, who said he's a friend of Richie's. He left his phone number in New Jersey and said to call him."

"Wonderful."

"Don't worry, I'm not going to call him back. I want him to stay far away from me."

"Can I have the number?"

"Forget it! You can forget about trying to use those eyes on me, because it's not going to work."

"Please?"

"No way, forget it! I want you to leave him alone. If he's doing something illegal, then let someone else catch him!"

Vinny knew too well that his persistence would be a waste of time with Debbie, when her mind was made up; good, bad, or indifferent, her mind was made up.

"So how are things with your boyfriend, the FBI agent?"

"Pretty boring," she said. She lit a cigarette.

"Well, at least you're well protected in case Sabol tries to come after you."

"Sabol has no desire to come after me. What's done is done with him. It's you who has to worry about him, not me."

"Well, I appreciate the warning, but if he comes near me or my family, I'll kill him."

"Oh, I know you will, but can we stop talking about him and maybe move on to a more interesting subject?" she said provocatively, running her fingernails down the length of Vinny's thigh until they rested on his crotch. "What do you say we go back to your house? I'll let you do whatever you want, for as long as you want."

"Ah, what the hell! It is my birthday."

After three and a half hours of what could only be called wild, almost-primal sex with Debbie, he got in his car and drove to his sister's apartment on the chance that Mike would be home alone. Vinny knew his entire family had met at their parents' home in New Jersey to celebrate his birthday and that Mike stayed behind to babysit Nicole. Vinny hated the fact that he'd lied to his family by saying he had to cancel at the last minute because he'd made an arrest, but he was in no mood to celebrate that he was a year older and no closer to achieving his goals in life.

Driving to Mike's apartment, he continued to vacillate about the Gerry-Sabol situation. Debbie had now confirmed that Gerry told Sabol that it was Vinny who labeled him a rat. Gerry had been warned twice to disassociate himself from Sabol, yet he hadn't heeded the warnings. He was also warned not to tell Sabol where he heard the information. Again, he didn't listen, and now Sabol was on to Vinny, vowing to kill him. It was now abundantly clear that in order to protect himself and his family, he had no choice but to take matters into his own hands before he lost all he had left in this world.

Vinny had decided that Sabol would go down in flames, and he would take Gerry with him.

"Come on in," Mike said, holding the door to the apartment open while talking on the phone. "No, it's Vinny," Mike said impatiently to whomever he was speaking with.

Vinny walked briskly to the kitchen and began to uncork a bottle of Chianti he brought with him to celebrate his birthday, while Mike continued his phone conversation. Pouring only himself a glass, knowing Mike didn't drink, he proceeded to take a seat on the living room sofa. He gazed around the room; it was as clean and immaculate as always, with each of the baby's toys meticulously arranged in their proper place. With the amount of time he had spent in their apartment babysitting for his pride and joy, he felt very comfortable turning on the television while he waited for Mike to finish with his phone conversation.

"Aren't you supposed to be with your family in Jersey, celebrating your birthday?" Mike asked suspiciously, shaking Vinny's hand.

"Got stuck at work," he lied.

"So you have nothing better to do than come here with a bottle on your birthday?" he asked pathetically, dropping himself onto a love seat.

"Believe me, I wouldn't be here if it weren't important," Vinny said cynically.

Mike looked bemused.

"What's wrong? Your pal Gerry let Sabol know that it was I who called him a rat."

Mike was astonished. "How do you know that?"

"I just do. I also know that Sabol now has plans to kill me."

Mike lowered his eyes and stared at a photo of Nicole on the coffee table. "I'm not worried about being able to protect myself, as I am about you, Maria, and the baby."

"You think he'll do that?"

"You know as well as I do that he's a sick fuck and is capable of just about anything."

"So what are you going to do?"

"I'm going to find out all I can about what Sabol is up to, and if your pal Gerry is involved, he's going down with him."

"Let me talk to him again!"

"And tell him what?" Vinny asked with no attempt to hide his anger. "You going to tell him something better than the lie I came up with to convince him to stay away from that piece of shit? When you first told me about your friend being involved with Sabol, I was sympathetic and willing to help you convince him to stay away from trouble, but now he's made a fool out of you and has me doing a perpetual look over my shoulder. I know he's been your friend since you were kids, but you're not kids anymore. This is a grown-up world, and this type of people play for keeps. You've got a wife and a little girl to be thinking about now, and if anything happens to either one of them because of your friend's stupidity, so help me God, I'll kill him." Vinny's entire body was trembling.

"Listen, Vinny! Gerry just wants his ten grand back. Let me talk to him, give him one week to get the money back. If he doesn't get it back and he continues to run with this kid, you do what you gotta do."

Vinny pondered for a few moments while sipping his wine. He really didn't want to have any part of Mike's friend ending up in jail. Vinny's relationship with Mike, his sister, and the baby had become very close over the last three months, and he didn't want to destroy that. "Mike, you're not involved in anything illegal with Gerry, are you?"

"No way!"

Vinny breathed a sigh of relief. "Thank God," he said, running his fingers through his hair. "He's got one week, but if I have to, I'll get in contact with the feds and get a wire."

"One week, Vinny, that's all," Mike said reassuringly, holding up the index finger of his right hand.

CHAPTER 19

It was ten days later when Vinny received the frantic call from Debbie insisting that they meet at Charlie Brown's. He'd hoped that the conversation he'd had with Mike was effective at scaring Gerry away from Sabol once and for all. Not even Gerry would be stupid or crazy enough to go near Sabol, knowing that Vinny was going to call in the feds to nail him. But that was something he had no intention of doing just yet. He was still clueless as to what Sabol was up to, but as soon as he did, he'd watch Houston chew on his hat as he dialed his friend Agent Stamp of the FBI with his intelligence.

For two and a half hours, Vinny sat drinking double shots of Absolut on the rocks, waiting for Debbie. He'd switched from his regular Johnnie Walker scotch because a few of the cops at work complained to him that he reeked of alcohol from spending his nights boozing in some shithole while attempting to get the desperately needed information on Sabol's illegal activities. Exhausted and quite drunk, he concluded Debbie wasn't going to show up. He paid his bill.

Outside, all he saw was snow, relentless snow. In his drunken state, the flakes seemed the size of snowballs and covered everything in a thick blanket. Driving in the snow petrified Debbie.

That was why she didn't show. Thank God it was only three blocks home.

He slowly maneuvered his car up the slick hills of Colonial Heights.

Ten minutes later, he was safely home in his kitchen, dusting the snow off.

The phone rang.

"Where have you been? I've been calling you and paging you for two hours!" Debbie shrieked, talking three times her normal speed. He'd had nothing to eat since breakfast, he was plastered, and his mind wasn't registering what she was saying fast enough. "Do you hear me?" she asked harshly.

He fumbled with his pager to see if the battery had gone dead. "I was waiting for you at the bar."

"You're loaded!"

"Whaddaya want?" he asked belligerently.

"Sabol called me." Her voice was aggressive. "He says you fucked up his deal and now he's going to kill you and your whole family!"

Her words hit him like a speeding Mack truck. Instantly he was sober.

"Did he threaten you?"

"No, not at all. Just very pissed off and insistent on killing you." She hesitated. "Actually, he asked me out."

"Debbie, listen to me very carefully! I don't care how nice he talks to you or how you may feel about him, but whatever you do, under no circumstances are you to meet with him. There are things going on that you know nothing about, and he may try to hurt you in some way to get at me."

"Are you crazy? I told him I never want to see him and that, if I were him, I'd stay as far away from you as possible. I told him that you hate him with a passion and plan on seeing him spend the rest of his life behind bars."

"What else did he say?"

"That was it, except that he was sort of warning me he'd be around."

"Do you have that phone number your sister got?"

"I'll have to look for it."

"Okay, great! When you find it, call me back?"

"I hope you know what you're doing, Vinny. He's really crazed."

"That's exactly how I want him. Call me back," he said and hung up.

Vinny stared out the kitchen window and took in the heavy snowfall.

Look at it piling up. Jesus! So it worked. Gerry must have gotten his ten grand back from that little scumbag, and now he's pissed. Pissed is good, because angry people are all on emotion and make stupid mistakes. I've got him right where I want him, away from Gerry and isolated, with no one to interfere with my plans to nail him to the wall. The only problem now is his threats to kill my family and me. Maria! It's six forty-three. She should be home.

It took four rings for her to answer. "Hello?"

Her baby had been running a slight fever.

"How's the baby?" Vinny asked casually.

"She's getting better. How're you doing?" she asked suspiciously.

His slurred speech and the concern in his voice gave him away.

"Not too bad. I just got off the phone with Debbie, and I'm going to go snappy any minute," he said, using uncharacteristic street slang.

"Why?"

"Sabol called her up!"

"Get out of here! What the hell did he say to her?"

"About me and about me fucking rattin' him out and the feds and all the rest of the shit," Vinny said. He was jumbling parts of the last conversation he had with Debbie on his birthday with the one he'd just had.

"Get the hell out of here!"

"Yeah, he wanted to know what the fuck I have against him. He says I'm fucking crazy, I'm giving up my job, and that they're going to take care of me and this and that."

"Wonderful."

"Debbie played dumb, pretended not to know what he was talking about. Then he asked, 'What the fuck does he have against me? Why is he trying to stop my early release?' So Debbie told him, 'My husband can't stand you, and he'll do everything in his power to make sure you spend the rest of your fucking life behind bars.'"

"Yeah. Well, that wasn't too smart of Debbie either."

"Nah, that's okay. Let her tell him," Vinny said lamely. "Then he asked her to go to dinner with him. Of course, she asked him if he was fucking crazy. He then told her he was going to be around, and this and that. I asked her if she took that as a threat, but she said no. I tell you, I'm going to kill him."

"Shhh," she sighed. "This is just wonderful!"

"I tell you, Maria, I'm going after him with a vengeance."

"But you can't do that!"

"Oh, yes, I can!" he said belligerently, unable to control his anger at the fall.

Sabol had threatened to kill his family. But there was one part of his conversation with Debbie he didn't tell his sister.

"She's going to call me back with the number he's been staying at. I'm going to run it, get the address, and then I'm going to wait and have a little talk with him."

"And then you'll lose your job," she interjected.

"I don't care anymore, Maria! I don't care! This is it!"

"And I don't know what to tell you," she said despairingly, not wanting to argue with him. She knew her brother's temper and thought it was more drunken talk than anything else.

"Has anyone seen you-know-who?" he asked, referring to Gerry.

There was an eerie silence before she replied, "Yeah," nonchalantly.

"Yeah? And?"

Another strange silence and whispers in the background.

Gerry's there now. I know it. His cop intuition kicked into overdrive.

"Where's your husband? Is he there?" he asked quickly.

"Huh? Yeah, um, can I have him call you right back?" she asked nervously.

"Yeah, I'm home."

"Okay. Bye," she said and hung up.

Gerry's there. I fuckin' knew it!

He snatched his car keys from the kitchen counter and headed out the door. With the amount of vodka he'd consumed on an empty stomach and the snowy road conditions with near-zero visibility, the short drive to his sister's apartment seemed to take an eternity. As he slowly drove on, his mind was racing with thoughts of what he would say if he was lucky enough to catch Gerry still there.

I wonder if he'd be so grateful to me that he'd give some insight into what criminal activities Sabol might be up to. Maybe he'll be so pissed at Sabol that he'd help set him up to get even. Shit, what if this plan backfires? What if Gerry doesn't believe my tall tale about Sabol? What if Gerry now thinks of me as his enemy? Shit, then I'm stuck between two vicious psychopaths instead of one. Fuck. Don't be an idiot. Think positive. I have to play this out. It's too fucking late to turn back. I can pull this off and be the hero. Sabol will end up back in his cage—for life. Think positive.

Mike answered the door, standing nervously in the doorway. He glanced over his shoulder at Gerry, who was sitting on the living room floor, playing with his baby.

I was fucking right.

"Are you going to let me in?" Vinny asked bluntly, glaring at Mike's worried eyes.

"Sure! Come on in," he said, stepping aside to let Vinny pass.

"Hi, sis." He waved at her in the kitchen, washing dishes.

"I'll be done in a few minutes," she replied.

"Hey, Gerry," Vinny said, turning to look at him still sitting on the floor.

"I don't want any arguments with you two," Mike hurriedly interjected, pointing an accusatory finger from Vinny to Gerry, who, from the look on his face, was clearly hoping Vinny wouldn't start one. A silence fell over the room. Gerry continued to roll a ball at the baby without looking up.

"I'm not looking to start an argument, but in light of the phone call I just got from my hysterical soon-to-be ex-wife, I'd like to know if Gerry here has taken care of the problem we discussed."

"I think we need to have a little talk about *my* problem," Gerry said testily, locking eyes with Vinny.

"Why don't we go down the street to Jesters Pub?" Mike added helpfully. He quickly picked up his daughter just in case.

"Sure. Why not? I could go for a few more cocktails."

"Let's go," Gerry said, rising to his feet.

"Honey, the three of us are going to Jesters. We won't be long," Mike said.

"Good! The roads are getting worse out there," she said as she closed the door after them.

The three sat in silence as Vinny drove the half-block to the pub. Inside, the bar was filled with locals eating and drinking, talking about the storm and how long it would last. They took a booth toward the rear to ensure their privacy. After the waitress brought a double Absolut on the rocks for Vinny and a Coke for Mike, Gerry broke the ice with his first question.

"Why did you lie to me about Sabol?" he asked without malice, staring at Vinny across the table.

Vinny returned his stare. "I never lied to you about Sabol." The eye contact continued.

"Do you know who my father is?" Gerry asked ominously. Vinny gave him a puzzled look. "I'll tell you who he is," Gerry said proudly. "He's a capo in the Lucchese crime family! That's who he is. That ten large I gave that little scumbag Sabol is Mob money. We were supposed to use it to open a legitimate magazine company in New Jersey. That was until your little lie fucked everything up." Gerry stuck his chin out, trying to look like an arrogant Mafia wannabe who had muscled people around all his life.

But Vinny didn't waver. He sat nodding, unimpressed.

"I looked into what you told me, and do you know what I've found out? I found out that you and Sabol have a long history together, that he used to date your wife before he went to prison, that he threatened to kill her, you, and your families. I know you tipped off the feds when he was moving two keys a week into New York from Florida and that you're pissed that he's getting out of prison early. Now, I know for a fact that he's no rat, because I used to make five grand a week with him. I've also been dealing with him in some swag, machine guns with silencers, and small amounts of heroin for the last three months, on the side, without my father's knowledge, and nothing's happened so far. That means you lied to me in hopes that I do your dirty work for you!"

Vinny sat for a few moments, so stunned he couldn't think of anything to say.

Thoughts of Sabol machine-gunning his family turned his face red with rage.

"You know what, Gerry? I don't give a fuck if you believe me anymore. The gloves are off now since he told Debbie he's going to kill my family and me. I'll kill him if I have to. I don't give a shit! In fact, now that you told me he's got machine guns with silencers, why don't you give me one? I'll kill him right now."

Gerry laughed loudly, like a maniac. "Oh God, you're a funny guy. I like you. You know that? You got big balls."

Vinny rubbed both his hands through his hair with a look of disgust, then held up his empty glass. "Waitress! Get me another, please."

"I'll get it for you," Mike insisted. He realized their plan had fallen apart and used the offer to get new drinks as an excuse to get away from the table.

"That prick Sabol won't give back the ten grand," Gerry said as Mike walked to the bar.

Vinny laughed. "So what if your father's who you say he is? He pisses away ten grand in a weekend in Atlantic City."

"It's the principle of him not giving the money back, not the amount involved. By not doing as he's told, he shows a lack of respect to the family, and that can't be tolerated."

Vinny stared blankly at Gerry. The words he spoke sounded like a line from *The Godfather*.

Is this guy living his life trapped in some Mafia movie reruns? Is he on drugs? Or is he simply psychotic? Incredible!

"My advice to you, Gerry, is to forget about the ten grand and stay far away from Sabol. He ratted on those guys from Georgia, and he'll do the same to you. Now that my past with him is all out in the open, I can tell you honestly that I am going after him before he comes after me," Vinny said coolly.

Mike returned to the table and put down Vinny's drink. "I'm going home to my wife now. It doesn't look like you two are going to kill each other, so my job is done," Mike said lightly, shaking Gerry's hand first. "You two have fun," he said, then shook Vinny's hand before departing.

Vinny looked at Gerry. "You know, I would never have gotten involved with this mess if I weren't worried about Sabol going after my sister and the baby to get even with me."

"So now you want a gun to even the score?" Gerry asked mischievously.

"Nah, forget that idea. I'll handle this alone, without any help."

"I gotta use the head," Gerry said, getting up from the table.

"You want another drink?"

"Yeah, sure. Why not?"

While Gerry was in the bathroom, Vinny sat trembling at the table.

I can't believe he's been so forthcoming by divulging Mob information. It was too damn easy. What's he trying to pull? Is he trying to set me up for something? Does he think I'll kill Sabol? Is Gerry going to kill me now? What the fuck have I gotten myself into this time? This thing has become a clusterfuck supreme.

Gerry returned with another drink for Vinny and sat down.

Looking at Gerry, he noticed white powder under his nostrils. "You might want to wipe that off," Vinny said, nonchalantly pinching his nose with his index finger and thumb.

"I don't give a shit who sees that!" He wiped the back of his hand under his nose. "Whaddaya say we take a little trip down to the Bronx? We hit a topless bar, pick up some coke, get laid?"

Fucking shithead.

"I don't do that shit, Gerry," Vinny said contemptuously.

"Yeah, sure you don't! Then let's go check out the girls."

"Not tonight, pal," Vinny said evasively. He downed the drink. "In fact, it's getting late, and I have to get going."

"Can you drop me off at my girlfriend's up the street?" Gerry asked politely.

"Sure, let's go."

Outside, the storm had turned into a full-scale blizzard. As he pulled out of the parking lot, his car almost spun around.

"Whoa, detective! This cop car you're driving has too much power for you to hit the gas like that!"

Heh heh heh, he's shitting bricks, the asshole. Some tough guy.

"This drive home's going to suck for me. I'm never gonna make it up the hill by my house."

"Just take your time. So tell me, what kind of gun do you carry?"

"Glock, 9 millimeter."

"Do you have it on you? I want to take a look at it."

Oh no, this is it. He gets me to park my car somewhere and shoots me with my own gun, makes it look like a suicide. Distraught cop going through a bad divorce, lost everything he owns in a fire, gets drunk and eats a bullet. I may be bombed, but I'm not fuckin' stupid.

"I left it at home tonight," Vinny said calmly, hoping his voice wouldn't betray him.

"That's too bad. I would have like to let a few rounds go out the window, see how it fires."

"Sorry. I can't help you out."

"Pull in to this building on the left."

Vinny turned the wheel quickly, causing the car to spin out of control before slamming against the curb.

"Sorry about that," Gerry said, opening the car door. "I'll walk the rest of the way. It's much safer that way," he said with a laugh.

Vinny hesitated. "Gerry, do yourself a favor and stay clear of Sabol. He's going down, if it's the last thing I do!"

Gerry smiled from ear to ear. "My breath is bated. Drive carefully." He slammed the door close and slapped the roof of the car with his palm.

As he drove off, he watched Gerry through the rearview mirror enter an apartment building on Midland Avenue.

What's really going on?

A few minutes later, the phone rang at Mike's.

"Hello?"

"Blue?" It was Gerry, calling Mike by the nickname he got from the Blue Devils football team they played on together as kids.

"Yeah, what's up?"

"I just got home. That kid's out of his mind!"

"Yeah. Why? What happened?"

"He's out of his mind. You better tell Maria to call and make sure he got home all right, 'cause he's all over the road."

"Really?"

"Yeah. Doing ninety, all over the road."

"What? In the snow?"

"Yeah. He dropped me off at my girl's house. He's out of his mind."

"What happened with the other thing? Nothing, right? You're just gonna let it go, right?"

"Yeah. He's out of his mind. Why do I feel like I'm a cop talking to a criminal?"

"I'm a good guy, not a cop. I'm talking to you as a friend. He is a good guy. He's a nice guy, and he's a good person," Mike said earnestly.

"You're right. I took a liking to him, man, but he's got to stop showing off like that. He's gonna hurt himself if he drives like that. I couldn't take him anymore, between his chain-smoking and the double Absolut. God, he won't stop. He's like, 'Come on, let's go down the Bronx,' you know?"

Mike laughed. He knew Vinny well enough to know that Gerry was bullshitting him. "Yeah, right."

"He's out of it, Mike. His gun, the Glock, he's pulling it out. He says, 'Here, take a few rounds out of it.'"

"No, he didn't! I don't believe you."

"Yeah, he did. He says, 'Just do it, go ahead, I'm a cop.' So I blew six rounds out the window. He's fucking insane."

"Yeah, he's a sick guy," Mike said, humoring Gerry's fantasy. "He's a real wild man. Listen, Gerry, I gotta go, okay?" He still had to finish the menus for next night's dinner specials at his restaurant.

"Okay, bye."

Increasingly, Vinny distrusted his judgment.

Gerry had lied to Mike about breaking all ties with Sabol. What else had he lied about? Was he lying about his illegal dealings with Sabol and the Mob? I don't like this. I don't know for sure what's going on. Maybe nothing's going on, but if something is, the last thing I want is to end up in the middle of some fucking federal investigation. I hate all this behind-the-back shit. Maybe I was fooling concocting that story about Sabol being a rat. Fuck, I was drunk up out of my mind. I don't even have an idea why I said that to Gerry. Let's face it, I was clutching at straws, anything to get that beast out of our lives once and for all. Perhaps I should have called the FBI, but no. Trying to fucking explain this bizarre story to the FBI isn't like trying to have a parking ticket taken care of. They'd ask questions I'm not sure I can answer. It could become awkward. An untrusting agent might even call Headquarters to report it. There might be other ways to maintain my anonymity, but finding them, as I had done in the past, would take time, and time is now my enemy. Houston doesn't believe me. He thinks I'm obsessed with Sabol and imagining shit that ain't there. Fuck him! There is no way he'll be able to ignore the information I just got from Gerry.

On Vinny's first day back to work, two days after his second meeting with Gerry, he was still vacillating as he sat in the District 11 anticrime office, while Sergeant Houston conducted roll call. When the boss completed handing out the plainclothes officers' assignments and the officers were instructed to hit the streets, Vinny stayed behind.

"We need to talk, Sarge."

Sitting behind his desk, Houston looked up hard. "What's the problem?"

Hesitating, thinking it through once more, he began to explain as best as he could remember exactly what he'd learned. Through it all, Houston said little: a question here or asking him to repeat a detail there. He didn't take notes. He simply listened.

When Vinny finished, Houston sat as baffled as he had ever been. "Are you sure about this?" Houston asked. His voice was little more than a whisper.

"What the hell does that mean?" Vinny asked insubordinately. "We're talking about Sabol running around with an Uzi machine gun with a silencer, a 9-millimeter machine gun with a thirty-round magazine. A real people pleaser. And you're asking me if I'm sure about this?"

He studied Vinny carefully and had a strong sense of whom he was dealing with. What he had seen and done in his ten-year career as a cop was in his eyes, and Houston knew instantly that Vinny knew exactly what he was talking about. He also knew instinctively that once Vinny got ahold of something, he would never let it go. Houston let out a sigh and picked up the phone. "You know what this means." His smile was thin, almost devilish, as if in some crazy way he was enjoying this.

"I don't want my brother-in-law involved," Vinny insisted as Houston dialed the phone.

"Don't worry, he won't be."

When they say "Don't worry," that's the time to start worrying.

"FBI Agent Stamp."

Transferred to Maine, Stamp was the agent who had arrested Sabol in 1985, and he probably hated Sabol as much as Vinny did.

"How's it going, Jimmy?"

"Barry! How the hell are you?"

Houston sat back in his chair. "You're not going to believe what I am going to tell you." After a brief explanation, Houston said, "He's right here. I'll put him on."

Vinny got on the phone with Stamp as Houston sat and listened to the conversation in shocked disbelief.

"So what do you make of this?"

"Well, I can tell you one thing for sure. There's no way he's working for any federal agency, because each time he attempted to cooperate, I was notified, and every time a federal agency called to ask me for my opinion on Sabol, I informed them that he is a danger to society and cannot be trusted. Also, if Sabol is to ever be released, I'm to be notified immediately."

There was a moment of silence on the line as they both pondered what might have happened.

"Well, James, I'm no FBI agent, but let me tell you what I think," Vinny said enthusiastically. "Three years ago, when I called up Agent Gray and explained to him about Sabol's threats to my family, I begged him not to let Sabol make any deals. He assured me that although he was trying to make a deal to rat on some drug dealers in

Ohio and Georgia, the DEA had no intentions of using him as an informant, and he was looking at a twenty-year sentence. But what if he worked out a deal with the prosecutor Martha Stevenson directly? That in return for his testimony against these guys, he would receive a huge sentence reduction if they got convicted. Then, after the convictions came down, they transferred him from Georgia to New Jersey for his protection. He then qualified to finish his sentence in a halfway house, allowed to go out to work during the day and must be back inside at night. Technically, if he's in a halfway house, he's not officially released, and that's why you or my job weren't notified as promised."

"Wow, that's got to be what happened."

"Not bad for a Transit cop, huh?"

"Not bad at all, Vinny. Listen to me. See what else you can find out on the streets about Sabol. Chances are, this guy Gerry is not being totally honest with you. So use your contacts in Yonkers and find out what you can. But don't get too close on this one, or you might find yourself having to testify in court. And I know you want to stay out of this for obvious reasons. In the meantime, I'll make some calls to the US Attorney's Office in Georgia and ascertain from Martha Stevenson what deal he made. Oh, and, Vinny, if this pans out and we nail Sabol for the third time, he gets a mandatory life sentence."

"Thank God, 'cause after almost fourteen years of Sabol's shit, I'm getting tired of it."

"So am I, Vinny, so am I. Be careful. I don't want you to end up hurt by these guys. Just keep your ears and eyes open, and I'll call you back as soon as I have some news for you."

"Okay, James. Thanks for your help."

"No, Vinny, thank you for yours," he said, then hung up.

CHAPTER 20

The phone started to ring and woke him. For a few moments, he had no idea where he was. Bright sunlight came in through the blinds of his bedroom window. Still half-asleep and hungover, after spending another night in bars relentlessly searching for information on Sabol, he rose on one elbow and grabbed the phone.

"Hello?" he said in a deep, froggy voice.

"It's Christina. Sorry. I didn't mean to wake you."

"That's all right. What time is it?"

"It's almost one o'clock."

"Hmmm." He reached for a cigarette and lit it.

"Vinny, I need to talk to you. I have the rest of the day off, and I was wondering if I could come over and speak with you."

He let out a long sigh as he stretched out his aims. "What would Mr. Wonderful have to say about that?"

"I dumped him. He wasn't what I was looking for," she said. "Is anyone home now? I'd really love to see you."

"I'm all alone," he said, taking a long drag. "Come on over. I'd love to see you too."

"I'll be there in half an hour." She rang off.

Getting out of bed, he looked around his bedroom. Clothes were thrown everywhere. He walked into the bathroom, where more clothes and towels lay strewn on the floor. To his left, one of his cowboy boots was perched unceremoniously on the sink.

Shit. If she sees this, she'll know I've fallen off the deep end.

He saw his reflection in the mirror above the sink. His mind drifted to thoughts of her.

There's something about her that puts my mind at ease, no matter what's going wrong. God, how I want to be with her, and make love to her, and hold her in my arms always and forever. Nothing could be more important to him. *The trouble is, I don't think she feels the same way. Hell, she'll be here any minute. I gotta get cleaned up.*

He turned on the shower. His entire body ached, and what didn't was numbed by the effects of the alcohol he had consumed, and the hurt wouldn't go quickly. He felt as though he'd lost a fight. He wasn't sure he hadn't. The hot water felt excellent, but there was no escaping the pain.

The doorbell rang. Provoked by the intrusion, he reached for a towel and wrapped himself in it. Still wet, he went downstairs to the kitchen door. Moving the white lace curtains aside, he saw Christina standing on the porch, wearing a London Fog coat. She was shaking from the cold.

"It's freezing out there," she said as she brushed off a light dusting of snow.

He couldn't help staring at her, and when she caught him, she kissed him on the lips.

"What was that for?" he asked shyly, looking down at himself.

"I missed you so much. You sure you didn't overdress for me?" she asked provocatively, running her perfectly manicured nails down his chest, stopping at the towel wrapped around his waist.

Oh, no!

"Can I take your coat?"

"I'd better hold on to it until after we talk."

"Do you want to talk in the living room?"

"Sure, why not?"

"Do you want me to put some clothes on for this talk, or is it come-as-you-are?"

"I'm a big girl. Come-as-you-are is fine," she said as she sat on the couch. He noticed her silk stockings and heels.

"I'm glad to hear that, because I don't feel like getting dressed yet." His tone was more kindly.

When he sat down beside her, she threw her arm around him. He lowered his eyes and stared at her legs.

Nice. What's on her mind?

"The first day I saw you, I fell in love with you," she said. Her voice was soft and loving. He nodded somberly but let her go on. "What I did to you was terrible, and unforgivable. But I want you to know that not a day goes by that I don't think of you and all the good times we've shared together. You're the sexiest, most exciting, and most passionate man I have ever met. I was a fool to give you up, but I was afraid things were moving too fast. I was afraid I was rushing into things."

He shrugged indifferently. His expression didn't change, yet he was weakening, and she knew it.

"I'll spend the rest of my life trying to make up for what I did."

He looked at her with a sad smile. She lunged forward and kissed him passionately on the lips, her teeth biting his lower lip, and then she sighed, "I love you."

"I love you too."

Dammit! I submitted too easily.

Abruptly she pushed away from him and stood up. He looked puzzled. "What's the matter?"

"You can take my coat now," she said, half-smiling, shyly. She undid it while standing in front of him. To his surprise, she was wearing only a black lace teddy underneath. "You like?" she asked in a sultry voice.

"You allowed me to think I had a choice in this. That's the height of deception," he said as he slid a hand up her bare arm to her neck.

"Yes," she said, smiling.

She knows how turned on I am staring at her perfect body.

He pulled her onto the couch, pulling on the teddy, exposing her firm, round breasts.

I can't resist her. I can't. I forgive you, and from now on, I'll love you unconditionally.

At 0730 hours on March 16, 1994, Davis stood at District 11's Second Platoon roll call.

Twelve days had passed since he'd officially notified FBI agent Stamp of Sabol's alleged dealings with the Mob. Vinny was still uncertain as to why Internal Affairs and Agent Stamp weren't notified of Sabol's release, but after much thought, he concluded that, theoretically, Sabol was not "officially" considered released from custody while in the work release program and, therefore, no one was notified of this change in his status.

It's out of my hands, and life's on the upswing. Christina's back in my life, and I don't have to waste any more off-duty time in bars, searching for information on Sabol. She's the most important thing now. Besides, with Stamp now investigating the allegations, I'm out of it. Thank God!

"Davis!" Sergeant Flannigan, the midnight desk officer, shouted. "You have a phone call on line 06. Take it in the lieutenant's office."

Vinny walked briskly to his unoccupied office.

"District 11, Davis."

"Vinny Davis? This is James Stamp with the FBI."

"Well, it's about time."

"Hey, how're you doing?"

"I'm fine. How're you?"

"Good."

"I haven't been able to get the phone number of the place in North Bergin that Sabol's staying at with that guy Mike yet. I'm still working on it."

"Oh, yeah," Stamp said. It took him a second to figure out what he was talking about.

"When do you think you can get the number for us?"

"I hung out all night last Thursday trying to get it, then I had to take the next day off because I was so hungover."

"Okay. Do you know how to spell Gerry's last name?"

"Sorry, I don't, but I know he uses two different ones and that he's around twenty-five or twenty-six and was an inmate in Valhalla last month. He also has a Yonkers address," Vinny added, attempting to be helpful.

"Have you ever met his father? Do you know his name or how old he is?" Stamp asked anxiously.

"I don't know. I've never met his father. In all, I only met Gerry a couple of times." He pulled a cigarette from his pack and lit it.

"Okay. Have you seen Sabol yet?"

"I haven't seen him, no, but Gerry's been with him numerous times…" He paused to exhale the smoke through his nostrils. "Whenever he travels, as far as this work release thing goes. Mike, whose house is in North Bergin, is the guy whom Sabol stays with."

"Now, did you say a house or a warehouse?" Stamp asked, confused.

"No, it's a house that Sabol's staying at. But Sabol and Gerry are hooking up to get a warehouse, and Sabol took ten grand from Gerry and won't give it back." He took another drag and blew smoke across the office.

"What about this ten grand they want back?"

"They want the ten grand back because I leaked to them that Sabol is a rat and that's how he got out of jail. You follow me?" He wasn't sure if Stamp remembered the details of the ruse he'd played on Gerry.

"Okay. Now, see, this is what I found confusing the last time I talked to you. You mentioned something about you telling Gerry that Sabol's working for whom?"

Is he asleep? He's not paid attention to a word I've said.

He took a long drag on his cigarette and crushed it in the ashtray on his lieutenant's desk.

"I just told him that," Vinny said indignantly. "I made it up! I said, 'Sabol's a rat. He must have ratted on some guys. That's how he got out of prison. So you better watch yourself, or you'll end up in prison next.' I was just saying that so he would get in touch with Sabol, so I could find out where I could find him, and find out what he's up to. Then I could let you know, so that you can send him back to prison again, and so, two years from now, we won't have go through this all over again!" He made no attempt to hide the anger in his voice or his dissatisfaction that Sabol, after making a deal, was free on the streets again. Vinny had no doubt Sabol would attempt to regain his freedom in a few years by making another deal.

Vinny was as sure as shit that if Sabol got out again and returned to Yonkers, he'd find out what Sabol was up to and send him straight back to where he belonged—behind bars. The FBI might not give a rat's ass that Sabol threatened to kill four of their agents, they might not care that Sabol might be able to buy his way out of prison with information, but the biggest mistake Sabol ever made in his life was threatening Vinny and his family. Cops have long memories, and if Sabol's own brother had to be placed in the Witness Protection Program because he was going to kill him, Vinny would stop at nothing to see that Sabol was behind bars and his family was safe.

"All right, now." Stamp seemed oblivious to the rising tension in Vinny's voice. "I spoke with the assistant US attorney down in Georgia, Martha Stevenson. She's keeping her cards close to her vest, but she did tell me that Sabol's got some sort of work release program."

He must have ratted on someone important down in Georgia to get such a sweet deal. That's why she's keeping her fucking mouth shut.

"I'd like to call our Newark Office of the FBI and let them know, because Sabol's out there."

"Well, Sabol's in New Jersey, but he rarely crosses the bridge. Now he won't come to New York, because he thinks Gerry is going to kill him. Sabol also made some threats to Gerry, but he just takes them with a grain of salt. Gerry's a mental case. He just doesn't give a shit."

"Who's worse, Gerry or Sabol, as far as crazy goes?"

He knew full well what Sabol was capable of, but Gerry was an unknown.

"Gerry's the type of guy that would take a machine gun and shoot up an entire place. Sabol's more calculated. He would think about it, plan it out, and kill you silently. Which, in my book, makes Sabol far more dangerous," Vinny said, despair in his voice. He thought of the beast hiding in the bushes with a silenced machine gun, killing his entire family without anyone hearing a sound.

"Now, you said there were four silencers?"

"Yeah. Gerry gave Sabol the silencers for the machine guns," Vinny insisted. He wanted there to be no doubt in Stamp's mind about Sabol being armed, so he could warn the agents in Newark. Vinny knew that if they went after Sabol and they didn't know what kind of firepower he had, they could all end up dead. If they caught him, this time he would shoot it out rather than go to prison for life.

"Now, you mentioned something about them making five grand a week?"

"Before Sabol went to jail on the Georgia bust, he and Gerry were making five grand a week. I just found out about that." He was proud of that piece of information he'd uncovered.

"I'm fascinated. How'd you find out about that?"

"I keep my ears to the ground when it comes to this guy Sabol."

If Stamp only knew how many nights I've spent in bars, how many drinks I've downed, and how many hangovers I've nursed obtaining information on him, then he'd understand how important it is for me to keep my family safe from that psycho.

"Well, you know, you've got your wife over there, Debbie, right?"

His heart sank at the mention of her name. Fifteen years and that lunatic still wouldn't leave her alone.

"Yeah, Debbie. That prick called her up, and she's really upset about this whole mess."

"Would there be any problem with you meeting with agents from Newark?"

"No. That'd be no problem, as long as I'm kept out of it, because I've got not only my wife to worry about, but there's my sister, my brothers, and the rest of my family too. Because if he gets caught and makes another deal, that prick will be out walking the streets again."

"Yeah, I hear ya. Wouldn't that be a pisser?" Stamp said, amused, followed by a short laugh.

Vinny didn't see the humor. "Yeah, well, let me tell you something. I've nothing against the feds, but the way this seems to be working is that this guy is untouchable, and it's starting to really piss me off!"

"Yeah, I hear you."

But Vinny was not about to be pacified. He was pissed off and wanted to be crystal clear. "You know, if he got caught selling two kilos of coke to an undercover Georgia State Police officer, his ass would be in jail for the rest of his fucking life!"

"Yeah, well, this guy should be in for the rest of his life," Stamp said with equal vehemence. "Is there anything else you can remember?"

"No. I just want my name kept out of this! I don't want him planting any bombs in my car, and he'll do it."

"I know he's crazy, and if this Gerry's crazier—"

"Crazier without thinking. The only reason Gerry hasn't killed Sabol already is that Gerry thinks the feds are following him to set him and his father up."

"Well, I know a couple of agents in Newark who'll be glad to hear about this."

"Oh, that'd be great. If they play Sabol, they'll catch him. If he was stupid enough to sell two keys to an undercover, he's not as smart as he thinks and will do something else dumb."

"All right. Let me make a couple of phone calls, and hopefully, one of these agents will get back to you."

"Okay. Thanks very much, and please make sure they keep me out of this. God forbid. If anything happens to me, you'll hear from Houston. He and I are tight, and he knows about this whole thing better than anyone."

"Yeah, and you do the same for me." He tried to make Vinny feel important. "That will be the day the FBI seek help from a Transit cop if something would happen to one of their agents. They'd be selling snow cones in hell when that happens. All right, take care now!"

Staring at the wall, he became angered that he couldn't get some definitive grasp on what was really going on.

Is Sabol working for some federal agency or not? And if he is, which one? And why won't they let Stamp know, so he doesn't end up in the middle of some interagency bureaucratic shit-storm. Fuck it! The problem's no longer mine.

He got up and left the smoky office, closing the door behind him.

I only hope Michael understands that what I did was to protect our family. I had no choice. No one will ever hurt my family!

CHAPTER 21

T he morning sky, as predicted, was overcast, and a light, cold rain was falling. Vinny sat alone in a booth by the front door of the Red Oak Diner, in Fort Lee, New Jersey, and ordered a coffee. The diner was filled with people on their lunch hour stretching the hour before heading back to the grindstone. They sipped coffee, played with the food on their plates, smoked cigarettes, or looked over newspapers. A booth away, a couple dressed in business suits was having a heated argument. Next to them, a fat woman in a floral tent, with shocking red hair, leaned forward in her chair, exposing her equally fat tits while reading a newspaper. Looking up from his coffee, he observed two men by the cash register dressed in matching Brooks Brothers suits, giving the patrons the once-over.

They may as well be wearing flashing neon signs that say FEDERAL AGENTS *across their chests. Frick and Frack.*

He gave them a short wave, rose from his seat, and introduced himself. The taller of the two, with blondish hair and round apple-pie face, introduced himself as Special Agent Morley and the shorter one, with the preppy, I'm-a-Yale-graduate look, as Agent Stone.

"It's a pleasure to meet you, gentlemen." He shook their hands. They exchanged brief pleasantries, talked about the job, ordered coffee, then got down to the purpose of their meeting.

They seemed fascinated as Vinny explained in detail the events that began nearly fourteen years before, and the steps he had taken to ensure the safety of his family. He wound up describing the latest chain of events as factually as he could remember from his two drunken meetings with Gerry, plus what he'd managed to find out on the streets.

"Wow," Morley said. He shook his head in disbelief. "Do you think, if we get into this thing, we're gonna stumble over anybody?"

He's suspicious and cautious. He's asking me? How the fuck should I know?

"You mean another federal agency? I doubt it. Let me tell you something. This guy Sabol must have ratted on somebody big-time to get out of a twenty-year sentence, because when Stamp asked Martha Stevenson, the AUSA in Georgia, about it, she wouldn't tell him shit!"

"Well, I can tell you for sure, Sabol's not working for the FBI," Morley said. "Agent Stamps a serious guy, and Sabol threatened to kill him. He takes that shit very seriously. So before we do anything, we'd check around first."

"That's what I'd do," Vinny said.

They're the experts. They'd better be, because my life may depend on these guys.

"So Gerry clued you in that Sabol was out of prison, after you heard rumors he was out?" Morley asked.

He's asked me this already. Why don't they take some notes so I don't have to answer the same questions over and over? This is getting to be a pain in the ass.

"It's like I told you before, the rumor I heard, on Christmas Day, from my brother-in-law, was that Sabol was out and hanging around with his best friend, Gerry. Then, I played around the field a little, to see what I could find out. On January 25, I met with Gerry and tried to scare the shit out of him so he would, hopefully, turn on Sabol, which was exactly what he did."

"Is your brother-in-law involved in this shit?" Morley asked with raised eyebrows.

"No. No, not at all! He and I have never seen eye to eye on a lot of things, but he knows I would kill him if he ever got involved with anything illegal. No, he would never be into anything illegal. He's a hard worker and opened his own restaurant. He just had a baby girl.

My sister would kill him. Mike's not involved in this thing. The man doesn't even drink."

"So they just know each other because they live near each other?" Stone asked.

"They've been friends since they were kids. They grew up together, played ball together. They're into bodybuilding at the gym all the time."

"Now, Gerry and his father are into racketeering and all that shit?" Stone asked.

"It's like I said, it seems to be common knowledge throughout Yonkers, but Gerry said to me, 'If they have me on tape, I won't give up my father. He's a big shot.'"

"Are you speculating on that, Vinny? That Sabol's got him on tape?" Morley asked nonchalantly.

"Yeah," Vinny said, laughing. "I made up the thing about the phones being bugged, the whole nine yards, to scare him away from Sabol, in the hopes he would turn him. It worked like a charm!"

Why the fuck did they just smile at me like I'm an amateur?

"You think your wife still has Sabol's phone number?" Morley asked.

"Knowing her, she's probably thrown it out, but I'll be able to get it from Mike somehow."

"But he's not in with these guys, right?" Stone asked.

Vinny shook his head in frustration at their repeated probing about Mike.

These fucking guys still don't believe me about him. They don't get it.

"Mike's friends with Gerry. That's it! He's not involved with this mess, but I might be able to convince him to get me the number from Gerry. He knows I'll do everything in my power to put Sabol away, and he doesn't want to see his friend caught up in it."

"Why did Gerry tell you what he and Sabol are up to?" Morley asked.

Now he's back to an innocent question. But is any question an FBI agent asks innocent?

"Because he obviously thinks I'm a crooked cop for telling him the feds are on to him. He doesn't know I was lying to him to get at Sabol."

Hey! What's this with them exchanging devious smiles?

"We're very interested in this whole case," Stone said. "The difficult part is that we're gonna be in New Jersey, and we're interested in this warehouse with the swag. It would be great if the father was involved. He'd be a great target."

Oh, no! I know exactly where this is going. They want to plant an already-established, crooked cop into the middle of a Mob investigation.

"Yeah, when you're saying your brother-in-law, Mike," Morley said, "I'm sitting here, going—"

"Nah, no, no! My brother-in-law's not getting involved at all!"

"Hmmm," Stone sighed.

"Trust me, fellas. You follow Sabol and you'll come up with a good case. That's the whole thing. Put him in jail."

Morley smiled and relaxed.

"Look, here're all the phone numbers I have of the federal agencies I've spoken to about Sabol over the years." He reached into his leather jacket and handed his PBA calendar book to Morley. "Maybe one of them can give you more information about Sabol than I can. All I know is what I've told you. I don't want it to come out that I was involved."

Morley scanned through and copied down the names and phone numbers. Included among the federal agencies' info was the Yonkers Police complaint number and the Internal Affairs control number for the threatening phone call he'd received at home in March of 1992. Vinny explained to them that if anything would happen to him, Sergeant Houston, Internal Affairs, and the Yonkers Police were all well aware of Sabol's past threats and would immediately make him the prime suspect.

"Hmm. Hmm," Morley mumbled. "This is what makes me nervous. I don't want to stumble into another agency's investigation and get into a gunfight. Do you think Sabol's working for Agent Cray and the DEA?"

Vinny shook his head. "I don't think so. I really don't. The person you've got to get in touch with is Martha Stevenson down in Georgia. She wouldn't say shit to Agent Stamp, but maybe your supervisor can find out more."

"I gathered that from Jimmy Stamp," Morley said, rubbing his forehead.

"Well, if he's in our territory, dealing with heroin and machine guns, she should tell us something," Stone said.

"You think Probation knows something?" Morley asked.

He's as baffled by this as I am.

"Probably not, but his probation officer's name and number are on that paper I gave you. In '91, I tinned my way in to the federal building in Manhattan and spoke to his probation officer. I explained the past problems I had with Sabol, and he showed me Sabol's file. There was nothing of interest in there, but I asked him to make a copy of the file anyway. That was when he saw my NYPD ID and threw me out of the office."

"Did that file you saw have any of the stuff regarding his arrest with the two kilos? Or was it old stuff?"

What's with these fucking guys? For two trained FBI agents, they sure don't pay attention. Sabol didn't get arrested with the two kilos until November 1992, so how the fuck could Sabol's probation officer have information about something that didn't happen yet?

"Old stuff! Presentencing stuff, court records from his old cases. Anyone can get that stuff. It's public record."

"It's different from police stuff, though. The stuff you have is all mixed together," Stone said.

I'll wipe that smug look off his face!

"I have a regular folder on Sabol. I have everything on him. Would you like to see my notes?" He pulled out more notes he had on Sabol's past criminal activities and the notifications he'd made to the federal probation officers. "The last time I spoke to anyone about Sabol was a couple of years ago, when I was told he was going down for twenty years. I breathed a lot easier back then, knowing he couldn't harm my family. And now comes Christmas, and he's out on a work release program. I don't fucking get this at all!"

"Does your boss, Barry, know all about the problems you had with this guy?" Stone asked with concern in his voice.

"Yeah, Barry knows. I told him, if anything would happen to me, to notify James Stamp."

"Absolutely," Morley said reassuringly. "I tell you, there's no love lost between Sabol and Agent Stamp. You know, when you threaten an agent in New York, you threaten all of us. It's like threatening a cop. You threaten law enforcement, you're drawing the line. I mean, obviously, you don't want him threatening anybody—"

"You know he killed somebody," Vinny interrupted.

"Yes, we know. Agent Stamp told us," Morley said. "But he can't have a gun as a convicted felon. How the hell did he justify—"

"I don't know!"

"It's bizarre. It really is bizarre, you know that?" Morley asked.

"Tell me about it," Vinny said. "Think of how I've been for the past fourteen—"

"To end up here," Morley interrupted. "This is bizarre. Well, apparently, we'll have to give Agent Gray a jingle and see what the scoop is down in Georgia."

"Let him know you spoke to me. He'll remember I called him about Sabol threatening my family. Then tell him I got the new information on Sabol about the machine guns and heroin." Vinny hesitated a moment, thinking about what he'd just said. "Or if you don't want to leak that information to him, I don't know how you can."

"I think we'll hold on to that," Morley interrupted. "We'll say we think he's actively involved in crime of some kind."

"So it is true. You feds are glory boys who don't share information about what you're working on."

That reminds me of a joke I heard years ago. Three federal agents were at an airport with their K-9 specialist dogs. One agent was from the DEA, another from the Secret Service, and the last one was from the FBI.

The DEA agent says, "Watch what my dog can do." He lets the dog off his leash.

Moments later, he returns with a suitcase full of drugs.

The Secret Service agent says, "Watch my dog," as he lets him go. Moments later, his dog returns with two suitcases full of counterfeit money.

The FBI agent is unimpressed and says, "Watch this." He unleashes his dog, which then rapes the other two dogs, steals the money and the drugs, and proceeds to call a press conference.

"It would be nice if we could get Sabol, Gerry, and his dad," Morley said, snatching Vinny from his reverie.

"Make sure you leave me out of it!" Vinny said.

There's no way I want to be held responsible for Mike's friend and his father ending up behind bars. I don't want them. I want Sabol."

"I have no problem with you letting Sabol know it was me this time," Vinny said. "I have no problem with that. But as far as Gerry and his family, I don't want any part of it!"

"That might not sit too well with your brother-in-law, who, you say, is not involved with this, right?" Stone's voice had an accusing tone to it.

Asshole. I wish I could club some sense into his head. How the fuck did he get to be an FBI agent?

"It won't sit too well with him. It won't sit too well with my sister. And it sure as shit won't sit too well with me!"

"But they're just friends, best friends. But they don't do anything criminal together?" Stone probed again, in a mocking tone of voice.

Smart-ass motherfucker!

"Mike's not involved! My sister would never tolerate it. Never! I mean, Christ, he busted his balls doing menial jobs until he made enough money to open his restaurant. They both work their asses off, and they're still living in a one-bedroom apartment. There's no money there! There's no philandering going on. He's not involved!"

Stone met his angry stare head-on and smiled slyly.

The conversation then shifted to Vinny. When did he learn Sabol was out of prison? When did he first meet Gerry? And when did his sister marry Michael?

I don't like how this interview is going. For some reason, these ass-holes don't believe I'm telling them the entire story. They're desperately looking for something that's not there. Why? What do they want?

"Way back when you first met Gerry at the engagement party, did you know he was with Sabol then?" Morley asked.

"No. I didn't find out until Christmas," Vinny said.

"And then you told him he picked a bad guy?" Morley asked.

He's confused, and his confusion is aggravating the shit out of me, and confusing me too. Are these guys really so stupid? This is ridiculous. I gotta end this Spanish inquisition soon.

He nodded to the waiter to bring the check.

"I told him the story I made up! So listen! If this works out, I want to go to the FBI Academy in Quantico. They send one sergeant a year from my job to the thirteen-week program."

"It's difficult to get in," Stone interjected. "There's a long, long waiting list."

He's putting me off. Let's try some sugar on this sourpuss.

"Well, it would be nice if you could help me."

"Everything they do now is on a board to preclude any unfairness," Morley said.

"Yeah, but you can tell the board that this city cop helped you out on a big case."

"Those kinds of things we can put in. They'll definitely consider it, yes," Morley said amicably.

That's better.

"Well, let's talk about it after you make your big bust. In the meantime, give me an application and I'll fill it out. Just remember to keep my name out of this, until it's all over. I don't need Sabol showing up at my house with a silenced machine gun," Vinny said.

The waiter dropped the check on the table.

"Don't worry," Stone said, "we'll keep you out of it."

They'd better!

"Very nice meeting you guys," Vinny said as he extended a hand across the table.

"Just give us a call with any information you can get," Morley said. He handed Vinny his card.

"You bet."

He left the interview and headed to Christina's house on Long Island.

What a pair of condescending and self-righteous fucks Morley and Stone are. I hate their haughty, superior attitudes. I heard about federal agents from the day I got on the force, but to experience it is surreal. They're obviously looking for something they think Mike's involved in, but I've no idea what it is. It was supposed to be an interview of cops exchanging information, but it seemed every answer I gave them, they took to be a calculated avoidance, when in fact, I told them the truth. Cop or not, I shouldn't be surprised. You're either one of them or you're not. If you want to be on their team, you have to be invited. That takes trust. And that's something Morley and Stone don't have in me—because I'm not one of them. They're enigmas hidden behind masks of unmitigated arrogance. So for the most part, they treated me cordially, with professional courtesy, but I bet they'll keep me in the dark—I'll be the last guy to know what's happening with the case. But perhaps that's for the best. Perhaps that's the way I want it. Perhaps I'm a chicken, but I'll enjoy living life free from having to constantly glance over my shoulder. I told them to keep me the fuck out of it. I hope they do. Pricks. Fuck them.

"So how did your meeting go with the FBI? Did you boys play nice together?" Christina asked as she washed the dinner dishes and Vinny wiped down the kitchen table.

"There was no reading those guys. Their entire persona is like a deliberate flaunting of their colossal egos."

"Did they believe you about Sabol being out?"

"I think so, but I think they're more interested in Mike's friend Gerry, and his father, than they are in Sabol."

"You're dealing with the big boys, honey. Arresting Mob figures makes headlines and leads to promotions. Sabol's a little fish compared to them."

"Well, they'll never get to the Mob guys if I didn't give them Sabol."

"My hero," she said and kissed his lips.

"They think Mike's involved somehow."

"That's because he's best friends with that guy. So naturally, they're going to think he is, but you and I both know he's not, and soon, so will the FBI."

She's more optimistic than I am.

"What I'm worried about is your ex-wife's psychotic ex-boyfriend coming after you with a machine gun before they nail his ass."

He smiled and took her in his arms. "I guarantee you, the second Agents Frick and Frack get back to their office, they'll set up surveillance on Sabol at his halfway house."

"I'm still nervous about Sabol."

"That's why I think I should spend more time out here with you." He started undoing the buttons on her silk blouse.

"Maybe you should stay with me," she said and reached for the zipper on his pants.

"Much safer for the both of us, I'm thinking," he said. He slid her blouse off her shoulders. It fluttered to the floor.

"Much, much safer." She tugged at his pants until they dropped around his ankles. "God, I feel safer already."

Police work, dealing with human evil and perversity every day, can get the best of any man. As a cop, Vinny understood that he had suffered a massive psychological trauma not just during the past year but also from childhood, although he could arguably point to the bizarre circumstances of the last year as the most tumultuous of all. His dignified, honest, and honorable life helped him survive with his head held high. But what had happened to him was too mysterious and implausible to try to make sense of. And it was his inability to make sense of what was happening that continuously weighed on his mind. He just couldn't escape from it, no matter what he did.

The day after Christmas was especially disturbing. It continued to haunt him because his brain was so clouded by booze he couldn't say for certain exactly what had happened. But on April 2, two days after meeting with the FBI, where he washed his hands of Sabol and found the courage to let them handle it, the consequences of his prolonged alcohol abuse finally caught up with him.

Second Platoon roll call was conducted, and the uniform assignments were already handed out to the officers.

"Davis, see me after roll call," Sergeant Breslin ordered.

"Yes, sir," he responded dutifully.

Just great. I'm going to get stuck driving the duty captain around to Community Board meetings all day.

As the officers exited, Breslin approached Vinny with a somber look on his face. "Let's go to the lieutenant's office."

"Sure thing, Sarge."

Sergeant Breslin was a cop in District 3 before getting promoted and transferred to District 11. He had less time on the job than Vinny and was not considered an aggressive cop. Prior to joining the TP, he was a schoolteacher with oodles of education, combined with good test-taking abilities, and there was a young man who could ace the scores on promotional exam through the rank of captain. Being an active cop who made a lot of arrest and who learned the job on the streets was no guarantee to promotion. Knowing the Patrol Guide and how to take tests was a faster route. The only problem with bosses with book smarts instead of street smarts was that they became spineless, they became company men, administrators, instead of what they were supposed to be—cops.

As they walked into the administrative lieutenant's office, an eerie feeling rushed over Vinny the instant he saw Lieutenant O'Malley's cynical face. "Davis, come in. Sergeant, close the door behind you."

Vinny entered and stood passively before his desk, while Breslin closed the door and sat down.

"It has come to my attention on numerous occasions, since before Christmas, that you have been acting irrational and coming to work reeking of alcohol so badly that it smells like you came straight to work from a bar," O'Malley said matter-of-factly.

Vinny lowered his eyes and focused on a spot on the floor.

What can I say? It's an extremely accurate account of my last few months.

"I know you've been through some extremely tough times, what with Debbie leaving and the fire that destroyed your home, but the department has the Employees Assistance Unit to help you. We were all hoping that you would seek some help on your own, but it's obvious to your supervisors that your condition has not improved. Therefore, I am left with no choice but to ask you for your gun and shield. The duty captain is responding by relieving you of duty."

Vinny looked up in shock and disbelief. "I'm not unfit for duty now!" He made no attempt to hide his anger.

"That's for the captain to decide. Sergeants Breslin and Davis both confirm they smelled alcohol on your breath at roll call."

Vinny quickly turned toward Breslin, his face turning white with fury. "You what?"

I stayed at Christina's last night and had one glass of chardonnay with dinner.

"Why is he lying?"

"Just give him your gun," Breslin said cautiously. He gave a furtive glance at O'Malley, who sat impassively behind his desk.

Vinny removed his Glock 9mm from the holster on his gun belt and passed it to O'Malley, who inspected it as though he thought it had recently been fired.

"And the .38 snub nose you have strapped to your ankle also," Breslin continued.

He pointed to the bulge on Vinny's left ankle.

"I don't know why you two are doing this to me. I'm as sober as a judge."

"We'll let the duty captain decide that too," O'Malley said sternly. He inspected his .38 in the same manner as his Glock. Vinny then took his shield off his duty jacket, held it in his hand a moment, then tossed it onto O'Malley's desk.

"Go cool off in the locker room until the duty captain arrives!" O'Malley ordered.

"Well, I would like to thank you two fine men for trying to destroy my career," he said belligerently as he turned and walked out of the office.

Vinny sat alone and confused in the locker room before his locker and awaited the duty captain.

This doesn't make sense. I haven't come into work hungover since Christina came back. My guns! Why did he smell my guns? To see if they have been fired lately? There's got to be something going on they're not telling me. But what? What?

He was staring at his hands, angry and confused, when a voice interrupted him. "I was somewhat surprised to hear it was you they were calling me about, Vinny," Captain Rosenberg said earnestly. He stood in the aisle of the locker room crisscrossed with asbestos-wrapped pipes. Black steel dust clung to everything like a second skin.

Vinny looked up at the kind and gentle face of a man he'd known and respected for years. Captain Saul Rosenberg was in his early fifties, with a full head of curly salt-and-pepper hair, with soft, gentle eyes and a kind smile. He became a cop to piss his Jewish family off, by not becoming a doctor or lawyer. He was extremely intelligent, studied hard for promotional exams, and rose up the ranks as a result. He gave many rookie cops his wise investment plans for their money so they'd be able to retire in comfort instead of trying to get by on just their pensions.

"How are you, Captain?" Vinny asked in a composed voice.

"I think I'm supposed to be asking you that question," Rosenberg replied. He sat beside Vinny.

"Oh, I'm just wonderful, Saul."

"Vinny," he said slowly, "for some unknown reason, it would seem your bosses have a hair up their asses."

Vinny met his stare head-on with a broadening smile.

"Now, Vinny, before you say a word, let me tell you, I know all about your divorce and the fire. I also know exactly what you're going through. Last year, as you probably already know, I went through a rough divorce. My wife of twenty years took me to the cleaners. She got the house, the kids, half our money, and half of my pension. Fortunately for me, I can't stand the taste of alcohol, so I didn't go that route. But I became so depressed I felt like I was losing my mind. My attitude about everything at work changed, and I began to display apathy toward everybody and everything. I was soon placed on modified assignment, desk duty, and sent to the Psychological Services Unit."

"Yeah, but you're a captain, Saul, and I'm just a cop. Besides, no one was accusing you of being unfit for duty because you were drunk at work."

Captain Rosenberg studied the photos proudly displayed in Vinny's locker, seemingly oblivious to the rising tension in Vinny's voice. "I don't think you're drunk right now," Rosenberg said. He leaned back against a locker, making himself comfortable. "I can't smell any alcohol on your breath, and you seem perfectly sober to me."

"So what are you going to do?"

"First of all, I'm giving you the day off. Then I'm going to spend the morning having your lieutenant send your sergeant out for coffee for me while I write a report on how I arrived here to find a perfectly sober and coherent officer. I am then going to interview the two of them as to how they came to their conclusions. After that, I'm going to order your lieutenant to type up this excruciatingly boring report, about ten times, until it is perfect."

Vinny smiled. "What happens to me?"

Straightening up, he placed a hand on Vinny's shoulder. "At 0730 hours tomorrow, you will report to the Employee Assistance Unit at 300 Gold Street. There's a cop who's a counselor I want you to speak to. His name is Donny Hoyle. He's the cop I spoke to about my problems, and I think he can help you. I'll fax him a copy of my report today so he'll have it before he meets you."

"So then I'm not in trouble?"

Rosenberg smiled brightly. "As far as I'm concerned, I have found you to be fit for duty, but I am sending you downtown to cover my ass. If Hoyle says you're okay to resume patrol, after he interviews you, then you'll be back here in a couple of days."

Vinny couldn't help but smile too.

"Listen to me, Vinny." His voice instantaneously turned serious. "You're an excellent cop with a brilliant future. Every time I turn around, your name's on some report for commendations for bravery. I worry that you're oblivious to danger, or maybe you're romanticizing it. Which is it?"

Vinny looked into his blue eyes. He was asking a question that Vinny himself had strictly avoided for years. The question was too personal. But after what Rosenberg had just demonstrated, he felt he deserved an explanation.

"I guess I've been cheating the grim reaper for some time now."

"Why do you think you do that?"

"I guess I never worried about dying before. I never feared it, because I feel that when you die, you go to a better place. In fact, on New Year's Eve, I felt like dying would be a relief. I was fighting a losing battle with depression, drowning my sorrows in booze every night, and I suppose, with everything that had gone wrong in my life, I thought it was the only way to stop the pain. But all that's changed over the last month, and I'm back on track."

His admission brought a watery glaze to Rosenberg's eyes. He understood exactly what Vinny was going through.

"Take the rest of the day off," Rosenberg said, slapping a friendly hand on Vinny's thigh as he stood up. "Make sure you're downtown at 0730 sharp, and don't worry about this. I'm a nice Jewish boy who writes fabulous reports," Rosenberg said jokingly in a Yiddish accent.

"Thank you, Captain!"

"My pleasure, Vinny. Just be careful out there. You have a lot of good years ahead of you before we meet in that better place you speak so highly of," Rosenberg said in a warm, calming voice as he turned and walked away.

Vinny sat a few moments, reflecting on the scary truth, since his supervisors had made their sentiments known that his own self-destructive habits had to end immediately. If he fucked up again, he might not have another chance. And as difficult as it was, the only way forward was to forget the past, not think of the future, and find the courage to trust the FBI to do their jobs.

CHAPTER 22

Two days later, Vinny had his guns and shield back, was back on patrol, and found himself deep in the enemy territory of Internal Affairs.

"Davis, get in here." Captain Stevens's voice cracked like thunder as Vinny walked in the door to the district. He had just had a miserable first day back on patrol. He and Jonathan Phelps had responded to a suicide at Fordham Road on the D Line earlier that afternoon.

"Tag 'em 'n bag 'em" is the term TA cops use for subway jumpers.

Vinny could never understand why a person who wanted to take their own life would jump in front of a speeding train. Getting splattered by ten tons of speeding steel had to be as painful as it was messy. Vinny, Jonathan, and the Emergency Service cops had picked up thirty-seven pieces of that day's suicide. He'd jumped at the northbound end of an incoming southbound train. Eight of the ten cars had run over the body before it came to a complete stop. Vinny held the man's head by the hair like a bowling ball, while halfway along the station, Jonathan was picking up the man's genitals and placing them in an evidence bag. The rest of his body was scattered between where he was hit by the train and beyond where it halted.

Like most cops, Vinny had a strange sense of humor. It was their built-in defense mechanism. Without it, they'd go crazy or become clinically depressed, which, nonetheless, happened all too often. The suicide rate among cops was high. So six cops crawled under a train with their flashlights on and laughed back and forth about what body part they found. Cruel and insensitive? Yes, but it was just their way of fighting to keep their sanity.

Vinny entered the captain's office and immediately observed two suits with sunken faces seated before him. They needed no introduction. Their perpetual dour expressions gave them away. They were Internal Affairs.

"This is Sergeant Taylor, and this is Detective Black," Stevens said, pointing at each of the two as he introduced them. "They want to interview you, Vinny. Do you want me to call in a PBA delegate for you?" he asked protectively.

Vinny just smiled, and Stevens knew he could handle himself without the PBA there to babysit him.

"Nah, Captain, let's see what it is these two fine gentlemen have on their minds." His smile never left his face.

"You heard him, gentlemen. He waives his right to PBA representation, but as his commanding officer, I'm staying," he added forcefully.

Taylor looked at Black. Black looked at Taylor, who shrugged. Vinny took a seat beside Stevens and lit a cigarette.

"I don't smoke," Black said scornfully. Vinny took a long drag from his cigarette and blew the smoke in his direction.

"Too bad. Maybe it might help you relax. Maybe improve your disposition," he said cheerfully. "Now, what do you want?"

Both IAD investigators turned to Stevens with the faces of petulant schoolchildren waiting for the teacher to scold the class clown. Stevens sat impassively. It quickly became obvious that he would permit Vinny to smoke if he wanted.

"We have received a complaint that you have been stealing gas from the NYPD and using it in your own personal vehicle," Taylor said irritably, using his hands to fan away the smoke in the room.

"*Stealing* is a very powerful word. Now, if the question is, Officer, do you put gas in your car at city police precincts after being authorized to use your car for patrol? the answer would be an emphatic yes."

Taylor shot Vinny a look as if he'd just won the lottery. "You admit it?"

Vinny did his best to blow a smoke ring. "Absolutely. You don't expect me to pay for the gas to patrol the streets of the garden spot of the world out of my pocket, do you?"

Taylor looked at Black in shock and disbelief. It was as though they had an entire "good cop, bad cop" routine all rehearsed and were disappointed they weren't getting a chance to try it out.

"You've committed a crime by doing what you did," Taylor said harshly.

Vinny studied him and idly wondered how and why this pompous ass ever became a cop. "Tell me, Sergeant, what crime is that?"

Taylor's eyes widened in confusion as he looked at Black. He was desperate for an answer.

I know full well I bent the fucking rules, but I'll never break the law.

"Listen, Sergeant, I'll save you the trouble of running to the New York State Penal Law to look it up. There is no criminal charge. I was authorized by the captain to use my car for patrol. The desk officer would make a blotter entry with my name, make and model of my car, and my assignment. I was then issued an official police vehicle placard, which made my car an official city vehicle. I would then go to the Forty-Second Precinct, identify myself to the desk officer, and ask for the key to the gas pump and the gas logbook. I would pump the gas, fill out the book, and return it—signed—back to the desk officer when I was finished. So let me ask you again, What crime have I committed?"

Taylor's expression suddenly changed from confident and self-righteous to angry and feral. "You know what I hate about hero cops? They think they can break the rules!" He shook his head violently.

God, I'm enjoying playing with these jerks. They're assholes. Fuck them! Pussies.

"What about your partners? Were they aware of what you were doing?" Black asked curiously.

"Nope. I always went by myself."

Black produced numerous sheets of copied memo books, while Taylor pulled out the Forty-Second Precinct's gas logs. "Your memo book shows you working with Sergeant Houston, Officer Johnson, Officer Carter, and Officer Hanley on several occasions when you received gas at the precincts. Can you explain that?"

"Well, Houston's a sergeant, so he basically does a lot of paperwork in here. You have to check with him. As for my partners, they must have been on meal, or had an arrest, when I did it. But I can tell you one thing for sure: they were never with me when I got gas."

"Guess what?" Taylor chided. "If you give up your sergeant and partners, maybe tell us who else is doing this, I'm sure we can get you a deal."

The thoughts of a prosaic, petty little mind. Now he wants me to rat on my partners. What a fucking moron. Prick.

"You know as well as I do that this has been going on since Bratton became chief. But now that he's gone, the TA has a puppet for a chief at Jay Street. A real TA man likes the Transit Authority Police just the way it was—run by the TA. It's really a shame, because Transit cops were really beginning to take pride in their jobs. What a shame it is to go back to the Stone Age when we'd come so far."

There was a somber moment of silence. The words Vinny had spoken were true. They all knew it but didn't have the balls to say so.

"So you're gonna take the heat from this alone?" Taylor asked sharply.

"That's right there, tough guy," Vinny said in his best Jerky Boys imitation, attempting, in his true characteristic style, to be comical in the middle of what could be a serious career problem.

"Captain, is he being insubordinate to me calling me a tough guy?" Taylor asked seriously.

"That was my best Jerky Boys imitation. Why, didn't you like it?"

"Are you now calling me a Jerky Boy?" Taylor asked furiously.

"Ah, forget it," Vinny said, dismissing Taylor with a sweeping hand motion. "Listen guys, this has been fun, but I have this DOA's brain all over my uniform, and I'd really like to change and go home. Maybe get a good night's sleep tonight and dream that I was on a police department that provided cars for their cops and gas to go in them. Can I go, Captain?" he asked dutifully.

Stevens glanced at the two IAD investigators, who said nothing. "That will be all, Officer," Stevens said officially, attempting to hide his smile.

Vinny exited the office quickly, closing the door behind him.

"Captain, is their something wrong with that guy, or is he drunk?" Taylor asked.

"No," he said matter-of-factly. "He gave up drinking. That's just the way he is normally."

Taylor looked perplexed.

"No, he's sober. A little crazy, and a bit immature, but he's a damn good cop," Stevens added proudly.

"He may not be for long," Taylor said contemptuously.

Not long afterward, in the District 11 parking area on Babe Ruth Plaza, at Yankee Stadium, Taylor and Black, who were standing by his car, greeted Vinny. As he approached, Black handed him two parking summons.

"Parking tickets!" Vinny roared with laughter. "Oh, that's precious," he said, keeled over at the waist. "So this is what you've become, meter maids! It must be a new department directive for you IAD guys: if you can't give the chief a cop's head, you nitpick him to death."

"Laugh all you want, Davis, because when we're done with the district attorney, you'll be in cuffs!" Taylor retaliated.

"If Bobby Johnson decided to prosecute me for stealing gas, I'll let you use my handcuffs on me," Vinny said, still laughing. "Let me ask you something, Taylor. How does it taste?"

"How does what taste?" Taylor asked, thrown off guard by the question.

"Ass!" He gave them one of his famous condescending smiles.

Taylor went rigid. His face turned red.

"I figure a man who has kissed as much ass as you have should be a connoisseur on how it tastes."

Taylor exploded. His face rapidly changed colors as he lunged at Vinny, only to be restrained by his partner.

"Let him go!" Vinny demanded. "I'm off duty and would love nothing more than to kick his mangy ass all over this parking lot."

The rest of the Second Platoon officers who were headed to their cars stopped to watch the commotion. They'd have loved nothing more than to see an IA sergeant strike an officer first. It would give Vinny the green light to beat the shit out of him and the IA prick couldn't.

Taylor was trembling with anger as his partner held him in a bear hug.

"Let him go!" the officers on the sidelines chanted.

"Don't worry, fellas, I won't file a complaint if you hit me. I don't rat on cops, even if they are a pair of Headquarters punks with badges who'd lock up their own mother for a promotion," he taunted them, hoping they'd fall for the bait.

"Let him go! Let him go!" The chanting was growing louder, faster.

"Come on, Sarge, he's not worth it," Black said, still holding his boss.

"I'll have your badge!" Taylor wailed, pointing an accusatory finger at Vinny.

"Not for this gas bullshit, you won't." Vinny got into his car and started it. He rolled down his window and stuck his head out. "Come on, get in your car. I'll let you write me a speeding ticket!" He laughed, floored his car, and left them choking in a trail smoke.

He arrived home to find Christina busy cooking and Tommy sitting at the kitchen table, enjoying a glass of Chianti.

"Hi, baby, how was your day?" she asked as Vinny kissed her cheek.

"Simply wonderful." He looked into a pot of white clam sauce.

"Vincent, how goes it?" Tommy rose to embrace him.

Vinny smiled. "I had a guy who decided he wanted to fight with an oncoming D Train at Fordham Road. He lost. Then I got back to the command with fucking blood all over me. Internal Affairs wanted to arrest me for stealing gas from the Four-Two. Other than that, nothing exciting happened."

"What?" Tommy and Christina asked almost simultaneously. "Two days ago, they take your gun and shield and accuse you of being drunk, and today they want to lock you up. What the hell did you do? Sleep with the chief's wife?" Tommy asked. Christina shot Vinny a curious glare.

"Thanks, TC. Just what I need to end my perfect day."

"Christina knows I'm only joking, don't you?" Tommy asked defensively.

"I've seen the chief's wife," she said as she threw her arms around Vinny. "She's no competition for me." She kissed Vinny's lips.

"Why do you think they're harassing you?" Tommy asked, handing him a glass of Chianti.

"I have no idea, pal, but none of this makes any sense. If a cop shows up really drunk for work, the bosses cover for him, let him sleep it off in the locker room. They don't call the duty captain. And now this gas thing—all the anticrime cops are doing it, yet they singled me out." He shook his head without looking at them.

"Don't worry about it, baby," Christina said with a bright smile. "Bob Johnson will laugh them out of the DA's office if they bring this to him. If you're authorized to use your car and you signed for the gas, there's nothing they can do. Besides, if they arrest you, I'll defend you for free."

"Very funny! With the luck I've been having, they'll assign you to prosecute me."

"I doubt that. I gave my notice today. I got the job with Snider and Webster in Hicksville, Long Island, twenty minutes from my house!"

"Congratulations, baby!" He gathered her to him.

"I couldn't convince her to come and work for me," Tommy said briskly. "She wanted too much money."

"This is great news, baby. I'm so proud of you," Vinny said earnestly, holding her tight in his arms. "Friday night, we'll celebrate. I'll take you to that restaurant in the city you always talk about."

"You'll even try the black ravioli for me?" she asked suspiciously.

Vinny looked at Tommy for help. "Don't look at me! You wouldn't catch me dead eating black pasta."

"Please," she enticed, then whispered in his ear, "I'll make you happy you did."

"You win, baby. I'll try the black ravioli."

She winked at him. "That's why I love you so much. You're so willing to try new things."

Vinny looked at Tommy. "I know that look in your eyes. Don't say a word!"

"My lips are sealed, paisan!"

The next few months saw Christina change. She acquired lofty principles and ideals and became the image of a patrician defense attorney: friendly, polite, and earnest with her clients. Suddenly, world peace, civil rights, and about our country's involvement in the affairs of other countries—the mantra of left-wing politics—became her concerns, too. She talked about joining Amnesty International and traveled to London to meet with them. It touched Vinny that she desired to make a difference in the world, and he thought it miraculous how well they managed to get along, despite the widening political chasm between them. It was as though their renewed love had magically erased the past hurt and pain her past indiscretion had caused him. His love for her bordered on idolatry. She was the glamorous personification of what he'd always dreamed the perfect woman should be. But he'd found himself once again worried that he didn't possess the qualifications she considered essential in a husband. He was a cop who loved his job. He was neither rich nor socially acceptable within her clique. Trying to improve himself in her eyes, he changed for the better what things he could. She knew his faults and was frequently upset with him, but he loved her like no other. He felt she loved him, selfish as she was at times.

They had lengthy discussions about her accompanying him to the PBA Cop of the Month ceremonial dinner, held annually to honor those deserving policemen who allied with extreme bravery. It was an honor he'd received twice before. The venue was Leonard's of Great Neck. Governor Mario Cuomo would present Vinny his award, an honor he knew would only be bestowed on him once in his career. Yet each time he mentioned he wanted her to attend the ceremony with him, she replied with a vigorous "No!" Her position was that it wouldn't be politically correct for her, a defense attorney, to attend a ceremony that honored heroic cops.

So a saddened Vinny attended the dinner alone.

It was a night where deals for promotions would be made and asses would be kissed, in the grandest of NYPD traditions.

Because the governor would attend, the department spared no expense. A cocktail hour of top-shelf liquor and the finest hors d'oeuvres—oysters Rockefeller, cracked king crab legs, baked scallops wrapped in bacon, clams, mussels, and caviar was laid on. Following the cocktail hour, a photo shoot, polite conversation, and accolades from the governor.

To his embarrassment, he was the only one without a date. He picked at a few shrimp cocktails and drank some expensive French wine, but he was so consumed by anxiety over being alone that he hardly enjoyed the meal. To ease his low spirits, he tried to deceive himself that the night was a learning experience. He tried to justify it as "You have to learn to be accustomed to enjoy the good things in life without someone to share them. It builds character."

Yeah, right!

His attempt at self-deception failed. After receiving his award, he still felt completely inadequate when he returned to his place at the table—she wasn't there to throw her arms round him, to congratulate him, and to say "I love you." He felt socially ostracized. He felt like shit and soon left.

Fuck political correctness. Since when does political correctness trump love? She says she loves me, yet she wouldn't attend one of the biggest events of my *career because of political correctness?*

He'd just learned a home truth: to a leftist, ideology is supreme. It comes first, before God, country, and to Vinny that night, love.

His friends and family considered Christina selfish, egotistical, and an outright bitch, in every sense of the word. He couldn't deny any of the charges they leveled against her, but denial and defense are different things, and he defended her to the hilt. Perhaps he was the only person who saw her good qualities: interesting, fascinating, amusing, and extremely loving. She had a way of lighting up his life with just a smile.

His previous five months at work had been static. He continued to patrol the streets of the Bronx, assigned to drive a radio car. The threats Internal Affairs had made to proceed against him never materialized. He knew there would be some form of disciplinary action in the future, but there was no chance of them filing criminal charges or terminating him for what he'd done.

Then all his good fortune and happiness came to a screeching halt when he saw an article in a local newspaper.

Mob Link Arrested

> *Twelve members of the Lucchese crime family, a section of the New York Mob, were arrested and brought to Newark, New Jersey, to be arraigned on racketeering and conspiracy charges.*

The name Gerry Vittorio jumped off the pages at Vinny.
Holy shit!
The federal investigation was assisted by a confidential informant who had managed to infiltrate the Mob family and their plans to open a warehouse in New Jersey, where they would store stolen property. Although twelve were indicted in the case, the investigation had to be terminated early when the identity of the confidential informant was leaked to the Mob by an unidentified New York City cop.

"Oh my God!" he said out loud and dropped the paper.
This is not good. I'd better get my ass to Tommy's, pronto! If this is what I think it is, I'm fucked. But if anyone can sort it out, TC can.

It had been almost seven years since Tommy left the Bronx District Attorney's Office and opened a private practice in Yonkers. Since then, he had opened a second office on Vesey Street in Lower Manhattan, which soon flourished more than his Yonkers office did. His clients ranged from rich bank executives with awkward divorces, hotheaded bodyguards who punched out Hollywood actors, to the not-so-wealthy personal-injury victims who needed a good lawyer. When you had a criminal case and you wanted to win, you called Tommy. He was a thinker, a pontificator, who'd win a case you'd have thought impossible. For those reasons and many more, Vinny thanked God TC was his best friend.

Just as Vinny thought, TC arranged a meeting with the federal authorities in New Jersey.

"So this meeting we're going to is called a Queen for a Day," Vinny said, looking out the window of Tommy's Lincoln Town Car as they drove across the George Washington Bridge, heading to the federal building in downtown Newark, New Jersey.

Tommy laughed and nodded. "That's what they call it. Anything we discuss at this meeting can't be used at any criminal proceedings against you."

Vinny looked nervously at him.

"Don't even say that." Vinny paused for a moment. "As a matter of fact, don't even think that," he added despairingly.

Tommy gave him one of his infamous reassuring smiles. "All you have to do is explain this story to the assistant US attorney, Juan Gonzalez. When I spoke to him on the phone, I explained that this entire situation is too bizarre to sound legitimate, but it is. You'll explain your past fourteen years of dealing with Sabol's threats. Debbie and your family can corroborate the story, and that should be the end of it. The government didn't do their homework when they decided to use Sabol as an informant in Yonkers—not when half the city held a parade in honor of him getting sentenced for twenty years. It's not your fault, it's theirs."

"Do you think he's happy with the twelve Sabol gave him?" Vinny asked curiously.

"He should be," Tommy said emphatically. "Someone from the twelve will rat in turn for a lighter sentence, giving him twelve more to play with. It's the revolving door of justice the feds have. If you have someone to give up, to take your place in a cell, they're happy. The more you have to trade, the more time you get off."

"That's the most ridiculous thing I've ever heard of," Vinny said disgustedly. "Fucking cops get killed trying to put these guys away, and the feds play 'let's make a deal' with them! That's what they call justice?"

"It's not my sense of justice," Tommy said defensively. "It's just how the feds deal with justice."

"So let me ask you this," Vinny said curtly. "Is Sabol going to be set free again because of his cooperation in this case? Are they going to set him free from a twenty-year sentence, living somewhere in reasonable comfort, on my taxpaying dollars, for the rest of his life?"

Tommy stared straight ahead at the traffic on the New Jersey Turnpike. He then nodded somberly.

"Son of a fucking bitch!" Vinny shouted, punching the dashboard on Tommy's Lincoln with his fist. He was livid. "Please tell me the United States government is not going to set this murderous scumbag free!" Vinny glared at Tommy, who had known his friend long enough to understand that he had to let him vent his rage.

It took ten fucking years for the government to get an airtight case on him and put him away for twenty years, a man who has plagued society since he reached puberty and, without remorse, committed every crime known to man. He has threatened to kill God knows how many people, including four FBI agents, and he is going to be set free! Vinny began to calm down as he sat silently, shaking his head in disgust.

"Are you finished kicking the shit out of my car?" Tommy asked, a humorous smile creasing his lips.

"I'm sorry, Tommy, I didn't mean to lose it like that," Vinny said, bowing his head in shame.

"Listen, don't worry about the car," Tommy said briskly. "I'm glad you got it out of your system now, before we go into the meeting."

Vinny's jaw dropped, as if it were going to detach itself from the rest of his face. His eyes were cloudy and indifferent.

"Tommy, I've spent my entire life dedicated to helping people. I've put my life on the line more times than I like to remember so that justice can be served. The law is the only thing I know, and being a cop is all I've ever wanted to be my whole life. Now you're telling me that it's been all for nothing, that the law and our justice system are nothing more than a monstrous lie we ram down the public's throat. The state system doesn't work like that, and you know it."

"Sure, the State has a plea bargain system to alleviate the cost of going to trial, but the feds work things differently. You don't work for the feds, so you don't have to deal with risking your life for nothing," Tommy said, trying to sound reasonable about it.

"If they have it their way, I won't be working for anybody," Vinny said with a smile that looked more like a grimace.

Tommy smiled at him in a conciliatory fashion. "This has just been a misunderstanding. You're not going to lose your job over this."

They reached the federal building and entered.

Assistant United States attorney Juan Gonzalez introduced himself as they came through the glass double doors leading to a waiting room filled with comfortable-looking leather couches and chairs. He was a short, in his late twenties, wearing an off-the-rack JCPenney suit, crisp white shirt, and standard, government-issued dark tie. His face was filled with tension, and he wore a mustache and goatee to give the appearance that he was a regular guy. They exchanged pleasantries, shaking hands, then were buzzed into a corridor by the receptionist seated behind what appeared to be bulletproof glass.

"Nice office building you have here." Tommy was trying to sound friendly.

"It's not bad." Gonzalez glanced at him, smiling arrogantly, then led them through a ganglia of corridors filled with the faces of malcontented federal employees. At the end of a hallway, Gonzalez pushed through a door into a room filled with unfamiliar faces and an air of antipathy so thick one could cut it with a knife.

Quickly scanning the room, Vinny's eyes came to rest on Agents Morley and Stone, who sat grim-faced at the end of a rectangular conference table. Instantly, he was struck by panic and fear. He had no idea what Gonzalez had in mind, but whatever it was, Vinny knew it wasn't conducive to exonerating him in any way.

"Why am I here?" Vinny asked nervously.

Gonzalez walked to the end of the long conference table and sat down. "Have a seat, gentlemen," he said, motioning with his hand to two vacant chairs. They sat down simultaneously, Tommy never taking his eyes off Gonzalez. "Before we begin, some forms need to be signed as a matter of formality," Gonzalez said, trying to look friendly while pulling on the hair of his goatee.

Tommy inspected the immunity forms in a judicial manner, then slid them in front of Vinny to sign, which he did dutifully without looking at them. He sat lethargically as he waited for Gonzalez to begin his questioning.

Gonzalez looked up from the forms that were handed to him. "Okay," he said anxiously. "You already know Agents Morley and Stone from the FBI. These two gentlemen to my right are Agents Conti and Lopez of the United States Customs, whose investigation you managed to destroy."

Vinny bowed his head into his hands in disgust.

So Sabol couldn't get any help from the FBI or the DEA for his cooperation, so he turned to Customs, as a last-ditch effort to buy back his freedom. Who the hell would ever believe the same guys searching bags at the airport would be conducting a fucking sting into organized crime? No wonder the FBI and DEA had no idea fucking Sabol had been placed in a work release program. Fucking Customs!

"You seem confused about the Customs agents," Gonzalez said eagerly.

"I think my client is a little thrown off by Customs being involved. They'd never entered either of our minds as a federal agency that would be investigating organized crime," Tommy said cautiously.

Vinny stared at Gonzalez. There was no mirth in his deep-set dark eyes.

"They are a federal law enforcement agency," Gonzalez said in a composed voice.

"They check bags at airports," Vinny said contemptuously. "How could I possibly think they were involved in this case?"

"Well, they were involved in the case, and you obstructed it," Gonzalez said flippantly, pointing an accusatory finger at Vinny. The charge of obstruction reads, "Knowingly and willingly impedes an investigation."

"How can I knowingly obstruct an investigation I knew nothing about? Let alone a Customs investigation?" Vinny asked animatedly, waving both hands in the air.

Gonzalez's eyes creased into little slits, as if he'd not given much thought to that possibility.

"I think we're getting ahead of ourselves here," Tommy intervened, putting a stop to Vinny's rising temperament.

"Yes, we are," Gonzalez said amicably. "Why don't you explain your story to me about how you got involved in this case?"

Vinny looked at Tommy as if he were asking for permission. After receiving an affirmative nod, he began to explain the entire story from the very beginning, back in the summer of 1980, when he first met and fell in love with Debbie. After a few moments of awkwardness, they settled down on their expensive chairs and began writing numerous notes as Vinny talked nonstop for thirty-five minutes.

When he finished, Gonzalez dropped his pen onto his legal pad and rubbed his eyes and face with both hands.

"Why don't you just tell us what really happened?" Morley said. "Because if a guy like Sabol had threatened my family for the past fourteen years, I'd want to hurt him real bad."

Motherfucker! Sure! "Come meet us at the diner. We'll get together, have a few laughs, and put the bad guys away. You can trust me, I'm a cop like you." Yeah, right. Fool me once, shame on you. Fool me twice, shame on me.

"I've already told you all I know for the second time, Morley. There's nothing more to tell," Vinny said, trying to control the temper in his voice.

Morley looked perplexed, as if he expected his "trust me" line to work a second time.

"How did you know we had Gerry on audio and videotape?" Gonzalez asked with a wry smile.

"I made it up. It was a lie!" Vinny insisted.

Gonzalez laughed bitterly. "And you want us to believe that?" he asked with a crooked smile.

"Well, it's obvious to me that you don't believe me, so what can I say?" Vinny asked. His voice was heavy with anger.

Gonzalez ignored his comment. "When did you find out Sabol was a rat?"

Vinny smiled coldly. "As I have stated before, I thought he'd ratted on some other case and that was how he got into a work release program. I had no idea he was an informant working on a current case with Customs!" Vinny held on to the word *customs* as though it were stuck to his tongue.

Gonzalez shook his head and smiled. "I don't believe you."

"Well, there's a news flash!" Vinny said sarcastically.

"Are you planning on charging my client in this case?" Tommy asked in disbelief.

Gonzalez smiled arrogantly. "Not yet, we're not."

Giving Gonzalez one of his condescending smiles, Tommy grabbed Vinny by the elbow. "Let's go," he said innocently.

"My client knew of no ongoing Customs or federal investigation into organized crime. He had absolutely no idea whatsoever that Sabol was involved as a confidential informant, and whatever he told Mr. Gerry in regard to his past criminal activities, including his twenty-year sentence for drug trafficking, was of public record. It is, however, unfortunate that a lie he conjured up and told Gerry was accurate and caused your investigation to draw to an early conclusion, but no crime has been committed by my client."

"We'll see about that," Gonzalez said, trying to sound cool and professional, but he was clearly thrown off guard by the turn in the interview.

"I only ask one thing," Tommy said, sounding surly. "If you plan on arresting my client on these charges, would you notify me so I can have him surrender like a gentleman? I'm sure you have compassion enough not to embarrass him at work, by parading him out in handcuffs."

Gonzalez smiled sardonically. "We'll let you know first."

CHAPTER 23

Internal Affairs completed their investigation into the "L'affaire gasoline" and submitted administrative charges to the Transit Authority. It then offered him the option of either resigning or being hauled before a hearing, at which the TA would strongly recommend termination. He opted for the hearing. It was held at the Office of Administrative Trials and Hearings, at 20 Vesey Street in Manhattan, coincidentally the same building in which Tommy's law firm had offices.

Sergeant Houston and Vinny's partners all took the stand and swore they had no knowledge of what he was doing. As Vinny had promised earlier, he'd never ratted on his partners to IA. Instead, he made the TA look like fools for having their officers pay for the gas needed to run their own vehicles used on patrol.

In April 1995, the administrative law judge took pity on Vinny by sentencing him to forty-four days' loss of pay. In his opinion, he also wrote that the Transit Authority should take a serious look at their policy regarding gas reimbursement.

Considering the alternative, Vinny could live with his decision, thank you very much.

Also, in the first week in April came the day for which Vinny had waited ten long years, the day he could wear his father's NYPD shield.

Rudolph Giuliani, the newly elected mayor of the city of New York, and William Bratton, his first police commissioner and one-time chief of the TP, had managed what was thought to be impossible—the merger of the TP into the NYPD.

For my own future and sanity, I must put my past history of the TP behind me forever. Still, it's amazing I'm going to be forced out of work for forty-four days without pay for doing something that's now permitted by the new department. Screw it! What's done is done. I now have a bright career ahead of me—once those forty-four days are behind me.

The entire month of April was spent in a transition phase in which he was right in the middle. Having been the only TA cop to work with the NYPD in their court division, he knew all their procedures and paperwork. He became the unofficial District 11 NYPD training officer. He taught supervisors how to fill out the new department's sick forms and advised them on how to call in sick. He was the resident expert on UF-49 reports, required in special instances. The radio cars had to be repainted, so the department had him drive them out to Queens. If someone needed to know something about NYPD's procedures, they were directed to him, and when an emergency arose in which the duty captain had respond, it was Vinny who drove him to the scene and informed him what the procedure was.

And slowly, time began to heal his deeper wounds. The truth about Christina and her promiscuous ways, the realization that she never loved him but rather loved having him love and adore her hit him hard. He didn't like it, but he accepted it. He realized all those nights she would leave him at home, on the pretense of going to the gym, wearing tight spandex shorts and StairMaster. He found it easy to despise her. He thought back, when over two years before, Tommy had called her incongruous. Vinny wondered if *Webster* had changed the meaning of that word to "unscrupulous bitch."

That May, when he began to serve his forty-four-day suspension, he was grateful and relieved. He knew there were golden opportunities ahead for a bright young active cop under Police Commissioner Bratton's command and newly appointed leadership.

He spent his days off remodeling his home or babysitting Nicole while his sister was a work. He paraded her around in a stroller as though he were the proud father instead of her uncle. They went everywhere together. His entire outlook on life changed dramatically; he'd never been happier.

But on Sunday, June 25, 1995, the last day of his unpaid punishment, his life was thrown into turmoil once again. He received a phone call from the desk officer at District 11. He advised Vinny that he was being placed on modified assignment pending a new Internal Affairs investigation. They suspected he was associating with organized crime, and a sergeant would be dispatched to his house to confiscate his gun and shield. The past two and a half years had already been brutalizing enough. Now this.

Why the fuck is this happening again? Have I offended God in some way that I must be punished even more than I already have been? And why is the NYPD now looking to destroy me? They must think they have a strong case, but why? I only met with Gerry twice, and the information I learned, I passed on the proper authorities. So why do they think I'm associating with organized crime? AUSA Gonzalez! He's the only one I can think of. Is he seriously considering going after my job, in truth, in revenge for unknowingly obstructing his investigation? If it's him, he's fucking nuts!

As ordered, the following day, he arrived at One Police Plaza to get his new ID card that identified him as an NYPD officer. On the back were the words *no firearms*, stamped on it to designate his status as modified assignment. Every police officer in the state of New York must carry an ID card to be able to identify himself to other law enforcement officers. Whether you were on modified assignment or not, you were still a police officer and must take appropriate police action if a crime occurred. When Vinny was informed that not only was he not to receive a modified ID card but also that he was not a member of the NYPD, he was astonished. He notified the NYPD PBA, who stated that his name was on the memorandum of understanding between the TA, the City of New York, and the NYPD and that, as of April, he had become a member of the NYPD. He explained he was well aware of that and had been working since that date after being issued his father's NYPD shield and ID card.

Vinny was commanded to report to District 11 and await further orders.

Months passed. The powers that be at One Police Plaza and the civilians in the Ivory Tower at 370 Jay Street in Brooklyn—the

TA and MTA headquarters—were at war. The TA's position was that Vinny wasn't their problem—he was merged with the rest of the TAPD. The NYPD held fast that although Davis's name was on the memorandum of understanding and he did possess an NYPD shield and ID card for eighty-four days, he was under a pending TA investigation, technically making him ineligible to be merged. The legal battle raged with Tommy and the lawyers for the NYPD's PBA leading the charge. The TP Union was dissolved when the merger took effect. All his union benefits were transferred to the NYPD PBA at that time. The NYPD's union held strong on the position that he was a dues-paying member of that union, thus making him a member of the NYPD. It was a legal bureaucratic shit-storm, and Vinny was smack in the middle of it. He was a cop without a police department.

At District 11, Captain Stevens, Vinny's rabbi, a term used in the police department as protector and mentor, had retired. He was now faced with a new commanding officer, a thirty-eight-year-old shining star of the NYPD who'd already made up his mind that Vinny was a crooked cop. He didn't like the fact that Vinny was assigned to work at District 11, but what he truly hated was Vinny's newly acquired and uncharacteristic insubordinate attitude.

Captain Rosenberg had approached Vinny and inquired as to why he was wearing an NYPD uniform while performing clerical duties. Vinny's answer was strictly professional, informing him that it was procedure to wear the uniform while on duty. It was then that the captain informed him that he was not a member of the NYPD and to take it off immediately and put on a Transit Police shirt. Instantaneously, Vinny transformed from the order-obeying soldier he'd always been to a rebel without a cause. He told the captain that since he'd just clearly pointed out that he was not a member of the NYPD, then he would not take orders from superior officers. He'd further stated that being a member of a police department that no longer existed, he was promoting himself to chief. Not only would he not wear a uniform but would also not comply with any department procedures until he was merged. The captain became infuriated, complaining to the brass at police headquarters. They told him to refer his complaints to the Transit Authority, who would handle it.

But each time the Transit Authority, a civilian administration, which had no police powers, tried to intervene, Tommy and the NYPD PBA threatened to sue. The City and the Transit Authority's hands were literally tied.

By September, Gerry and his father's crew had been convicted and sentenced to terms of imprisonment ranging from 18 to 156 months, with Gerry as one of the members sentenced to the max.

Tommy hoped the convictions would put an end to the obstruction fiasco against Vinny and he would finally be merged into the NYPD, but the Transit Authority insisted they would obtain the necessary evidence to bring Vinny to an administrative trial and have him terminated. Yet the TA, as civilian administration, had no authority to investigate a police officer, so they requested the Internal Affairs Division of the NYPD to step in and assist in the investigation that began a legal nightmare.

A *GO15* is an interview that is conducted by a ranking officer of the police department in which the member of the department must answer questions truthfully put to him by a superior officer. Under the rules and guidelines, nothing the officer testifies to may be used against him in a criminal proceeding. This brought forth two very serious legal issues for Tommy and the attorneys for the NYPD PBA to contend with. First, the questions that were put to Vinny were done so by a Transit Authority civilian who could testify against Vinny at a criminal proceeding, because he was not governed by the rules of the agreement under the GO15. Secondly, having a lieutenant from the NYPD IAD present during the questioning who could also testify as to the proceedings in criminal court further invalidated was evasive and, at times, outright lied to protect himself from possible self-incrimination.

Vinny was neither disillusioned or optimistic about his future as a police officer. He was emotionally divided by what had happened to him. One side of him just wanted it to end, while the other was more angry and defiant.

The past ten years of his life had been the study and investigation of a seemingly endless succession of violent crimes, mostly robberies. It bred in him a profound hatred of violence and the suspects who committed such acts. It was a tough job and far from rewarding. If you wanted to solve your cases, you pushed people. You never asked for permission; you just kicked from behind a desk. Vinny knew exactly what to look for in crime patterns and would still be able to make a difference. It just wasn't going to be fun anymore doing it. Vinny despised the fact that Gonzalez was building a case against him, which would not allow that he might, in fact, be innocent. He was uncomfortable being the victim of a witch hunt, and that was what interrogation reeked of. Now the powers that be at One Police Plaza decided that Vincent Davis was the quintessential dirty cop, bought and paid for by the Mob, and that feeding him to the feds was the best solution to some very complicated problems he presented.

Vinny felt it made no sense for Gonzalez to inflame the situation, but no one seemed willing to try to stop him. None of it made sense. After all the trouble the DEA went through finding Sabol, arresting and booking him, then accepting his twenty-year plea seemed little more than precipitous. But who was Vinny to second-guess the Justice Department? He was only a street cop, a protector of the innocent, the man who made the arrests. All his training and experience were in enforcing them.

Vinny had always wanted to do some honest good, to help people, to make a difference and be an active part of making society a better place. He wasn't a cynic. He truly wanted these things. He thought he had come a long way toward achieving those goals. It wasn't for his ego or self-aggrandizement that he had gone out on a limb so many times, putting himself in dangerous situations. He never wanted people to suffer, but such sensible thoughts weren't doing his mood any good. He would make no apologies for his priorities—this was who he had become, and it was worthwhile. Vinny's father had always told him that on the police department, you can go from hero to zero in a heartbeat, but when you're down, the thing to do is always look ahead. He tried to do his best at work but felt empty and broken inside. He'd become the laughing stock of the police department, the only cop in the state of New York who walked around with a letter in his pocket from his captain identifying him as a police officer.

TO WHOM IT MAY CONCERN:

The man who presents you with this letter is a police officer. If you need to verify that information, please contact me at District 11.

Vinny felt utterly alone and confused. A kind of pressure built up inside of him and threatened to overwhelm him. He was left utterly bereft in the mess that had been made of his life as he waited for his career to come to an end. For it was just a matter of time until he lost what was once considered to be the most important thing in his life—being a cop.

By the summer of 1996, the Transit Authority became unnerved in the wake of the lawsuits that were planned against them. In desperation, hoping to force Vinny to resign, they decided to suspend him pending the outcome of their investigation. Again, another battle ensued with reseizing the moral high ground and defending it against the NYPD. However, the day he tore up the letter he'd carried for sixteen months identifying himself as a police officer and received his NYPD ID card, he was suspended for thirty days under the rules and regulations of the NYPD. It was a moment so surreal and disorienting that all he could do was shake his head in disgust and wonder if and when this horrific nightmare would ever end.

When his thirty-day suspension ended and he returned to work in November, he was handed the official charges and specifications the NYPD had levied against him. They read like a Chinese menu. Select five from column A, and six from column B, all of which might as well have been written in Chinese.

How can they bring these extensive charges in fucking violation of the NYPD patrol guide from two years ago, when I was a Transit cop and not governed by the rules of the NYPD? I know how the system works. They can do whatever they want in order to get rid of me. No one can say I'm setting myself up so I can return vengeful and righteous later.

In his mind's eye, he saw himself receiving his medals for bravery, a heroic cop with a bright future. Yesterday seemed like a fantastic dream, but somehow he knew it couldn't last. He knew he was never meant to be that happy. There were days when he thanked God for protecting him on Patrol, and other times he'd cursed Him for not letting him die so he could be with his mother.

But she was an angel, a living angel taken too early from this earth. *She's protected me from evil and helps me make sense of this senseless life. But now, why is everything going so wrong?*

Christmas—a season of giving and goodwill to men—had always been his favorite time of the year. He still carried the same excitement he'd had when he was a child. He loved to go see the tree all lit up at Rockefeller Center and see the excitement on children's faces as they stared in awe at the window displays along Fifth Avenue. Family gatherings and how beautiful the church would be decorated at midnight Mass. But Christmas 1996 would be as miserable this year as it had been for the past five years, because the NYPD scheduled his department trial four days before. A trial that Vinny knew wholeheartedly would be the end of an eleven-year career. He knew the department would misjudge him. That it was not the powerful and benevolent police department who'd stand behind one of its officers in the wake of a federal scandal. The department brass were shrewd businessmen who understood when a cop had lost his usefulness and must be removed to minimize bad press for the department.

In the wake of the most recent scandals that plagued the NYPD, the Morgue Boys, a group of cops from Brooklyn who'd meet at an abandoned funeral casket warehouse to divide up the proceeds they had stolen from drug dealers, and the Ditty Thirty, where up to thirty cops from Harlem were arrested for being involved in selling guns and drugs, Vinny didn't stand a chance. Besides, the outrageous rumors that had traveled throughout the thirty-eight-thousand-member department over the past two years, which ranged from Vinny being a made member of the Mafia, to being the highest-paid hit man on the Mob payroll, were enough to tarnish his career for life.

The trial was but a formality for the department to get Vinny's badge. Very few officers make it through the trial room at One Police

Plaza and keep their jobs. Rather than his resigning, he and the PBA attorneys decided to give it the old college try. But any chance they had at winning was blown to kingdom come when FBI agent Stone took the stand and testified that they had FBI wiretaps that could prove that not only did Vinny associate with known members of organized crime but that also one of the Lucchese crime family soldiers had fired his weapon out of the window of his car in March of 1994. The testimony not only shocked Vinny and his lawyers, but also, the trial judge was appalled.

Vinny never bothered to take the stand in his own defense. It would have been useless.

Gonzalez had won and proved himself meticulously efficient at getting his revenge for Vinny unknowingly interfering in his precious federal investigation.

It wasn't long after he'd been terminated that he and TC were once again summoned to return to Newark for a meeting with AUSA Gonzalez.

Vinny glanced out through the glass passenger-side window as Tommy drove. Suddenly, he realized he wasn't listening, not even thinking, but instead just staring, reacting to his own fear and the numbness he felt. Rage and anger surged through him like a massive wave. Turning angrily, he saw TC staring at him. When their eyes met, TC saw the pain and abruptly looked away.

"What the hell is going on?" Vinny asked, no longer able to control anger and confusion. It was as though his life was slowly being taken away, reducing any feelings he'd had left to sadness and pity, slipping away into a dark corner, beaten like a dog, alienated from everything and everybody he ever loved or cared about. "Why can't you tell me what they want? Are they going to arrest me?"

Tommy could hear the uncharacteristic fear in Vinny's voice and was unsure of anything comforting to say. "We have to wait and see. It's been three years. Maybe there's been a flagrant breach of Mob etiquette and Gerry's now made a deal with Gonzalez."

"A deal for what?" Vinny snapped.

Tommy lowered his head in disgust. "For you, my friend. Maybe he made a deal for you."

Vinny ran his hand through his hair. Then, brutally and with a rush, he realized what Tommy had laid. "That's insane! Gonzalez can't hate me enough for messing up his investigation to let Gerry go, could he?"

"Vinny, listen to me, please." There was urgency in Tommy's voice, but he also was upset and confused. "They may want you to work for them."

"What do you mean?" Vinny's eyes narrowed, as he was not sure where he was going with this.

He stared at Tommy, wavering as to what to say, angered and outraged at what had been so ruthlessly done to him already by the feds.

Tommy hesitated. For a moment, he thought about not telling Vinny what his gut instinct was telling him. Then he relented. "Listen, Vinny, if they offer you a deal to work for them, don't go ballistic."

Vinny was astonished and amazed. "You want me to consider working for them? After what they just fucking did to me?"

Tommy's voice became filled with deep concern. "The feds must know that we filed in state supreme court to get you reinstated to the police department and that, in all probability, you will get your job back. As you know, we are dealing with ruthless people who get what they want. And if that means dropping a federal indictment on you and smearing your name in the media to stop you from getting your job back, they will. This thing has become very ugly, and I'm reluctant to say it, but we have no choice." Tommy had hit a nerve. They'd never discussed it before, but Tommy had thought about it and probably hadn't stopped thinking about it for quite some time.

"Maybe I don't want to be a cop anymore," Vinny said, shaking his head gravely. "I became a cop to put the guilty in jail and make them pay for their crimes. I don't want any part of this 'let's make a deal' system of bullshit justice where the guilty go free. You know what, paisan?"

"What?" Tommy pantomimed casually.

"I, just this moment, realized why the lady who holds the scales of justice in hands is wearing a blindfold."

"Why's that, pal?" Tommy asked, trying to sound reasonable enough to listen.

"It's because she can't bear to see the kinds of deals these people make to let the guilty go free. As far as I'm concerned, this country has gone to shit. They may as well rewrite the Pledge of Allegiance to read from 'And liberty and justice for all' to 'And liberty and justice for some.'"

Tommy smiled thinly. "I never thought I would say this about the law, because I love it as passionately as you do, but I think you're absolutely right."

At Gonzalez's office, Vinny stared at him, wondering if he would be as cantankerous and sly as he was at their last meeting.

"The information we are about to discuss remains in the confines of this room," Gonzalez said belligerently, looking directly at Vinny. "You made a mistake by interfering in my last investigation, and look what it got you," he said, his voice dripping with acid sarcasm. "That, too, will remain in this room, unless you decided not to cooperate, then you will force me to take you to trial and you will go to prison. Do I make myself perfectly clear, Mr. Davis?" Gonzalez asked contemptuously.

"Crystal," Vinny responded harshly, his posture becoming more tense and resentful. "But considering the mistakes I have made in the past, what makes you think I'm qualified for whatever it is you have in mind here today?" Vinny asked in a low, worried voice.

Gonzalez smiled, as if he were doing Vinny a favor.

"Oh, you are more than qualified! With your recent unexpected demise from your department, you are now the perfect candidate. The lowlifes of society will trust a washed-up and disgraced, crooked cop. Especially since they think you tried to help the Mob, thereby causing your demise. There couldn't be a more ideal situation. They will feel they can own you in some way and that you can be trusted. For you have proven to be as greedy and ruthless as they are." Gonzalez smiled wryly. He was getting perverse pleasure from insulting Vinny. "They will also think that you need money and will be out for revenge against a system and society that cost you the job you loved so dearly and your precious pension. It's perfect!" Gonzalez said, smiling enthusiastically.

Vinny sat closemouthed and defiant, thinking of the enormity of what was just sprung on him. He now hated him. Now it was so perfectly clear what was happening and what Gonzalez had done to make it all possible. After a three-year investigation, Internal Affairs had come up empty-handed regarding any wrong they thought he'd committed. And why should they? He wasn't a dirty cop. Gonzalez, finally realizing that IAD couldn't do the job for him, sent a nice, neat little package to One Police Plaza filled with enough circumstantial evidence to cause alarm.

When it came to the members of the department, the NYPD hated all negative publicity. Gonzalez then put a big bow on the package by sending an FBI agent to testify against Vinny at his department trial. The final nail in Vinny's coffin was when the agent testified at Vinny's trial as to the authenticity of a phone tap, a conversation in which Gerry informed Vinny's brother-in-law, Michael, that Vinny let him shoot his Glock 9mm out of the window of his car. It was an outright lie! But if there's one thing any police department will not tolerate, it is an officer's failure to safeguard his weapon. It is an unforgivable sin and calls for immediate termination. The administrative law judge who presided over Vinny's department trial might have sided with him, given the mitigating circumstances and Vinny's outstanding commendation records, until he heard an FBI agent testify, which meant it had to be gospel, as to the unauthorized use of a firearm by one of its members.

The party was over, and so was Vinny's career. *What an elaborate plan,* Vinny thought as he burned inside with horror and frustration. He had spent his life helping people. Show Vinny someone in trouble and he was there. He had always been that way. He had put his life on the line more times than he cared to remember. And for all the good that he had done in his life, this was the way he was to be repaid. It was now all a blur of hate, confusion, and despair. He now waited to wake up from this horrific nightmare, for he was sure this could not be reality. Vinny sat patiently as the agent explained about the case they were working on. He then described, right down to the smallest detail, how Vinny would infiltrate and obtain the necessary evidence to build a rock-solid case for them.

When the presentation was concluded, Gonzalez glared over at Tommy and asked sarcastically, "Would you like a minute to discuss your client's options with him?"

"Yes, please," Tommy responded grimly.

Vinny and Tommy exited the conference room into the adjoining hallway. Vinny was furious. Tommy sensed it yet remained cool, calm, and collected. Vinny spoke first, breaking the momentary silence, and exploded. "Do you believe this shit?"

"Calm down, Vincent," Tommy said in his most emphatic voice. "And let me talk." Tommy began a slow, methodical interpretation of what had transpired. "What they have done to you is blatantly obvious, and the most appalling act I have witnessed in my entire career. But what's done is done, and the game they plan to play is going to be played by their rules. Worse than that, they are playing with the deck stacked in their favor. We now have to decide if you want to play the game or force their hand." Vinny listened to Tommy carefully. He trusted his friend implicitly. Vinny remained speechless as Tommy vacillated. "If you go to work for them, it will take time to build a case. In the federal system, the wheels of justice turn very slowly. In the meantime, I've already filed and Article 78 in Supreme Court. There's an extremely good chance a judge there will reinstate you to the department. When that happens, the department will be notified by the feds that you are involved, working deep cover on a case for them. The NYPD will be forced to assign you to the Joint Terrorist Task Force, which will provide you with not only the feds' protection but the NYPD's as well. When the case is over, you can put in your papers and retire a hero. Plus, you will have all your back pay to fall back on."

Vinny jumped in and said sarcastically, "I've played the hero before, and look what it's gotten me. No job, no pension, the humiliation of being stereotyped a dirty cop. And an ex-wife that, when she's not fucked up on alcohol or drugs, suffers from personality disorders so bad that she has no idea who the fuck she is! If that's the life of a hero, you can keep it. And what about the danger involved?" Vinny asked curiously.

That question caused Tommy to let out a laugh as he said, "Are you kidding me? Vinny, I've seen you at numerous awards dinners in your dress uniform. You have more medals than George-fucking-Patton! And we both know they don't give those out for issuing parking tickets."

Vinny couldn't help but grin and asked, "What's our other option? Or don't I have one?"

"Of course, we do," Tommy said. "We can watch Gonzalez pull a rabbit out of his ass, indict you, and go to trial. That, my friend, will cost time, money, and energy that neither of us can afford. And if it goes as far as a trial before Judge Schwartz and we lose, he will order you shot by a firing squad right in his courtroom. Vinny, the ball's in your court. But remember, no matter what you decide to do, I am going to be beside you every step of the way."

"Thanks, pal," Vinny said jokingly, placing his arm around the shoulders of his friend. "I always did want to play James Bond!"

They entered the conference room to find all five agents laughing and joking with Gonzalez. Vinny was no doubt the brunt of their joke, because the laughter ceased the moment they looked at Vinny's red face.

"So?" Gonzalez said. "Have you reached a decision?"

Vinny nodded affirmatively, unable to speak due to his built-up rage and his rising blood temperature, which was now nearing its boiling point.

"Good. Wise choice," Gonzalez said ominously. "Now we can discuss the logistics of how we will make this thing happen." He explained slowly and meticulously each well-thought-out detail of his plan.

Vinny sat silently, intrigued by each syllable that spurted out of Gonzalez's mouth. "Marvelous idea," Vinny said, trying to keep the sarcasm out of his voice. "And just how are you going to accomplish a cover for me?"

Gonzalez paused, as though he didn't want to give away any state secrets. "We already have," he said condescendingly. After his cover was explained, he thought the plan ludicrous and doomed. Yet he was fascinated by the tremendous possibilities it presented. It would indeed be a challenge. But if it worked out as Tommy planned, Vinny would have his career and his life back. For that, no challenge was too great!

On the drive home from New Jersey, Vinny sat silently, deep in thought, while Tommy drove.

I don't like what I'm now being forced to do by my own government. No. Not by the government, but by Gonzalez. But in effect, he is the government. Shit. I especially didn't like the way they went about it. They humiliated me in front of the entire department, the men and women I've worked with and would have, if necessary, given my life for. No matter the outcome of this case, I've got to fucking work for that bastard. I'll never be able to tell anyone of my involvement, not even the cops I worked with. Since I can't tell them, I'll always be looked upon with suspicion for the rest of my life! That's truly disheartening, but Gonzalez's solution is as clear as it's concise: either join their highly fucking selective and restricted organization—and I no longer fucking trust it—or force Gonzalez to make the entire story public, a story based on theory and assumptions that could be misconstrued, that I, Vincent Davis, a highly decorated NYPD cop, may be a member of a Mafia crime family! They'll fuck me with the lies and selective details—they can paint me any way they want! To get their way, they'll call disrepute on me, an honorable man. But more importantly, the media attention will make it impossible for me to get a fair trial if it comes down to that. So in reality, I have no fucking choice. Bastards!

CHAPTER 24

May 21, 1997, was a beautiful, sunny spring day. As Vinny got out of his Nissan 300ZX, he felt the wonderful, warm sun on his face. Vinny was happy to be alive. To think that three short months ago, he was fired from the job he had loved for thirteen years. He lost his pension, annuities, variable supplement, deferred compensation, along with his medical, dental, and prescription drug plan. He would have been retired at the age of forty-two, with half-pay and all those benefits. He could not believe how proud he was of himself and the way he was handling his misfortune. He had just gotten home from Rio de Janeiro, after spending two weeks with his brothers and Mike Ignozzi. He sorted his mail, and there it was. A letter addressed to him from the New York City Police Department. He opened the letter, dated February 27, 1997.

> *After being found guilty of administrative charges filed against you by the New York City Police Department, it has been the recommendation of the administrative judge that you be terminated as of the date of this notice.*
>
> *Signed, Commissioner Safir*
> *New York City Police Department*

Vinny was proud of himself. He didn't try to drown his sorrows in a bottle of Johnnie Walker. From experience, he'd learned that didn't work. He pulled himself up by the bootstraps, called TC, and told him to file an immediate appeal. He then drove straight to the airport with his brother Michael and got on a plane to Jamaica's Hedonism II, where they spent the next ten days soaking up the sun, watching beautiful women parade around all day, wearing nothing but a smile on their beautifully tanned faces. He couldn't afford it, but he didn't care. He wasn't going to wind up a drunken fool, feeling sorry for himself, drowning in his own self-pity. He'd spent two very long years on administrative desk duty while the department decided what to do with him. So instead of worrying about what fate had in store for him, something he had no control over, he began preparing himself psychologically and financially for the possibility that he'd be fired. He prepared his résumé in case he couldn't get his own business started and began planting seeds through contacts of people he had met over the years socially and professionally. Within two weeks of his return from Jamaica, he had started up his own private investigations business and was also director of sales for a California-based company, which, although was in its infancy with only two locations in New York, had great potential and plans to establish twelve more locations over the next year.

Within three short months of carrying a beeper and a cell phone instead of a gun and badge, Vinny was well on his way to becoming very successful. He had an office on Central Avenue in Yonkers, a short ten-minute drive from his house. With five salesmen and eight telemarketers and his first commission check totaling over $12,000 for one month, he clearly saw that he could definitely get used to that line of work.

His father had always told him, dating back to when he was a manager for Jack LaLanne Health Spas, that he had a future in sales. It was a high-pressure job. He began as an instructor, which had nothing to do with sales, but he was young, nineteen, and loved to work out. Having a job to show people how to work out and getting paid for doing it was his kind of job. But it didn't take long before he saw how much more money there was to be made in sales. He'd only been working there for about a month when he happened to sneak a peek at the assistant manager's paycheck. He then decided to pay close attention to the sales techniques of all the salespeople. He quickly came to the conclusion that he should ingratiate himself to Joe Temple, the manager. One week later, he was in sales. Six months later, he was an assistant manager of Jack LaLanne's largest superspa and was making over $40,000 a year. In 1981, that was an excellent salary, especially for a nineteen-year-old. His father said it was more money than the average person earned, especially an NYPD officer, whose annual starting salary, at that time, was $21,811. Vinny still had another year and change before his twenty-first birthday, when he would be eligible to become an NYPD cop, and not even a $20,000-a-year pay cut was going to stop him from fulfilling his goal of becoming one. His father said he needed to get his head examined. On reflection, he saw his father, as usual, was right.

Central Square Café, on Central Avenue in Greenburg, was a perfect choice for the Davis family to gather for their mother's birthday. Although Vinny's parents had never eaten there, he and his brothers were regulars because of its excellent food and great atmosphere. It proudly stood where the old Ground Round stood. Two brothers who owned the Eastchester Diner bought the property, tore down the Ground Round, and built an oasis. They spared no expense on the building. The exterior was strong and demanded attention. The inside was elegant and included its own shop, where you could buy, among other things, fresh pasta, cheeses, and cakes. The bar area was art deco, with a sitting area that had high-back wicker chairs, palm trees, and its own espresso coffee bar. With soft music and low lights, it became quite the place for the upscale over-twenty-five crowd who liked to kick back and relax in the bar area or meet friends and have a quiet, romantic dinner. For bachelors like Vinny and his two brothers, it was a great place where they could have dinner at the bar without feeling like outcast. Vinny knew his mom was going to enjoy herself.

Vinny looked at his watch as he was parking just after 5:00 p.m. For a change, he was early.

Good. I'll grab a drink and check things out.

He entered and made his way to the bar, where he was struck by lightning.

Vinny had heard the old tales about how some fortunate men saw the women of their dreams for the very first time and were so captivated by their beauty that they felt as though they'd been hit by a lightning bolt out of the blue.

Seated at the bar was the most magnificent woman he'd ever seen. Not only did his heart skip a beat, but he also felt as though all the air was permanently sucked from his lungs, leaving him hopelessly breathless. He wondered from where his next breath would come. Finally, slowly, he got his lungs working again and took a seat directly behind her at the bar. He now fully understood the truth behind the tales.

While he desperately tried to find the right words to say, Gary, the bartender, greeted him. Vinny managed to order a glass of merlot, which seemed to be what was in her glass. Taking a sip, he became aware of how dry his mouth was, brought on, obviously, by his nerves.

She turned forward in her chair, no longer looking at the front door.

She must be waiting for someone. I wonder whom. I hope it ain't some asshole.

He now had a perfect view of her fantastic profile. He tried to speak, but nothing happened. He stared at her face and noticed she had exquisite skin: flawless, soft, and velvety smooth. She was wearing a navy-blue outfit, which much resembled the sailor suits young children used to wear to church. But when she crossed her legs, all thoughts of church vanished—doing so revealed legs so long and sexy they could make a blind man see.

Vinny found her totally irresistible and forced himself to speak.

"I am sure you hear this all the time, but you are very beautiful," he said nervously.

A gleam of happiness came over her face, along with a brilliant white smile. "No, I don't, but it's very nice to hear. Thank you!"

Vinny asked curiously, "How long have you been in real estate?"

"How did you know that?" That beaming smile remained on her face.

"Lucky guess," he replied confidently. "I used to be a cop in New York. After a while, you get good at guessing people's ages, nationalities, and professions."

"What do you do now?"

"I do some private investigation work, and I have a small business on Central Avenue, in Yonkers." He introduced himself as Vinny as he extended his hand with the hope she'd shake his.

"My name's Judy," she said as she shook his hand.

"It's very nice to meet you."

So far, so good.

He continued the conversation by explaining his reason for being there and told her how glad he was to have arrived early. She felt it necessary at that point to explain to him that she had a boyfriend of two and a half years, but she added, "I am waiting for my two very attractive and single girlfriends to arrive. I am sure they would love for me to introduce you to them."

Vinny wasn't sure if the muscles in his face betrayed his disappointment, but he managed to respond. "My two brothers are also due to arrive, and they're also single."

They continued talking as though they were two old friends who hadn't seen each other in a while yet missed each other so much that they were dying to catch up on what'd been going on in each other's lives. Neither was nervous anymore, and as they talked, they found themselves hopelessly gazing into each other's eyes. She was magnificent, and Vinny had never seen eyes so alluring.

His two brothers arrived, and a few minutes later, so did his parents, followed by his sister and her husband. As they arrived, Vinny made the obligatory introductions. He noticed his father giving him a look. He knew his father quite well, and before he could ask a question, Vinny said impatiently, "The table is ready. I'll be with you in a few minutes. I don't want to leave Judy alone at the bar as the prey of unscrupulous men. Go have a seat and I will join you as soon as her friends arrive."

Hesitantly, Judy said she'd be fine, but always the gentleman, he insisted on keeping her company.

The longer they talked, the more he realized that not only was she the most beautiful woman he had ever seen but that she also had a strong, warm, and generous personality, making her all the more beautiful and desirable, more beautiful than any model he'd seen on the cover of a magazine or leading actress on a movie screen. He was completely captivated by her.

Her first girlfriend, Cathy, soon arrived and was quickly introduced. She was around thirty, about five feet, five inches tall, with a slim build and a very pretty face. Although Judy had told him that Cathy held an executive position with IBM, it was obvious that she had gone home to change her clothes. She was wearing tight blue jeans torn on one knee, a white T-shirt rolled up at the sleeves, and a pair of black Justin cowboy boots. Michael, Vinny's younger brother, preferred younger girls with darker hair and complexions. But Vinny, looking at the way she dressed, knew they'd have a lot in common— regarding social activities, that is. For Michael, the mere thought of a stuffy woman in a business suit made him break out in hives, and it was a very rare occasion when one would find Michael in a suit. His word association would be a suit equaled work, and work was something as foreign to him as understanding the intricacies of a Harley-Davidson motor was to Vinny.

They exchanged pleasantries, and immediately Vinny had the impression that she was as interested in him as he was in her. This made him very happy. Normally, such a disinterest by an attractive young woman would have raised his curiosity as to why. But right then, he couldn't care less. A song was playing on the radio. Vinny could not believe the words "You're just too good to be true," from "Can't Take My Eyes Off You" by Frankie Valli and the Four Seasons. As Judy and Cathy chatted, Vinny sat smoking a cigarette, listening to the lyrics. He couldn't take his eyes off Judy.

Michael then leaned over to them, said a quick goodbye to the girls, and asked casually, "Would you like to have dinner with us? It's Mom's birthday!"

"Holy shit!" Vinny shouted. "I forgot all about that. I'm sorry, ladies. I have to go sit down."

Judy smiled at Vinny and said coolly, "Go enjoy your dinner. We'll be here for a while."

As Vinny and Michael walked away from the bar, Michael said vaguely, "Forget about her. Do yourself a favor, big brother, and forget about her!" But all during dinner, Vinny couldn't stop thinking about her. It was extremely obvious to his family that he couldn't wait to get back to her. When the others were ordering appetizers, Vinny was ordering dessert; they were enjoying their entrées as Vinny was asking for the check.

Finally, his mother said, "Vinny, she's very beautiful. Go snatch her up before you lose her."

"Thanks, Mom," he said enthusiastically, kissed her cheek, and turned toward the bar.

"We'll see you on the way out. One more thing," his mother said cautiously. "If she's as beautiful on the inside as the outside, hold on to her. If not, remember, looks can be deceiving."

Vinny turned back and said anxiously, "I'll see you on the way out."

As he walked away, he couldn't help but wonder how lucky he was to have a family that loved him that much and a mother who couldn't stand the thought of her son being hurt again. In light of everything that'd happened over the past three years, they'd all been there for him, one way or another, but that last cross to bear happened in February, when he lost his job, a devastating blow his family thought would surely be the end of him. While he was down, he didn't stay down and give up, and he had his parents to thank for that. How could he when they hadn't? In February, he'd begun to think clearly as he looked back at the people. It was the farthest thing from the truth.

Judy and Cathy greeted Vinny, and she was closer to Vinny's age, maybe a little older. She kept herself in fine physical shape, standing bust and a thin waist. She was dressed well and her complexion was dark, as Michael liked. Vinny could see how things would progress with his two brothers from the vibes. Vinny thought Kim might be flowing as freely as they were, and neither Judy nor Vinny went anywhere near the subject of her boyfriend. They were too busy laughing and having a good time to concern themselves with him.

Vinny's brothers made it over to the bar, and he decided to be frivolous. He ordered a bottle of champagne with strawberries. The others converged at the bar and sang "Happy Birthday" to their proud, embarrassed mom and forced her to have a glass of champagne.

Michael and Cathy were talking about God-knows-what. Raymond and Kim were talking about banking, and Vinny was talking with Judy about what she looked for in a man. The more she talked about it, the closer she came to the realization that the man she had been with for the past two and a half years was nothing like the man she wanted to spend the rest of her life with.

"I want to feel mad passion," she said affectionately. "I want to be passionately in love with a man who makes me feel like no man has ever made me feel before. Someone who is strong and fearless, so I can feel safe lying in his arms. A man who likes the same things I do and is not afraid to take risks. A man who, when I am apart from him, I can't wait to see or at least hear the sound of his voice on the phone. He should be in charge of his own life, not living at home with his parents, trying to mold a woman to emulate his mother, so as to take care of him like his mother." She was looking into his eyes. Hers were brilliant with excitement when she said, demandingly, "And he must be the sexiest man I've ever met!"

Vinny didn't know whose hand hit what, but he was now wearing about a half-glass of merlot all over the front of his suit, shirt, and tie. Judy tried to wipe it off with a napkin, but Vinny said nonchalantly, "It will be all right. I'll go wash off in the men's room."

While cleaning up, he couldn't stop thinking of the things Judy had said to him and the look in her eyes. He felt intense sexual excitement. He just wanted to grab her in his arms and kiss her soft, luscious lips. He threw some cold water on his face, dried himself off, and exited. As he walked down the narrow hallway past the ladies' room, he saw her walking toward him.

She grabbed his hand and spun him round, back in the direction of the narrow hallway. Mischievously, she said, "Come with me. I have to talk to you!"

They didn't make it five steps down the hallway before Vinny grabbed her and ran his fingers through her hair at the back of the neck. He pushed her against the wall and used his hand to position her face perfectly in front of his. With her eyes burning with passion, he kissed her already-wet, waiting lips. Their tongues were entwined in each other's mouths, then he gently bit her lower lip. His free hand caressed, ever so slightly, her face as they continued to kiss, bringing them both to a state of ecstasy. She energetically swung Vinny around toward the wall opposite. The force of her action sent them crashing through the ladies' room door and right into the first stall. Still entwined with him in a passionate embrace, she kicked the stall door closed. He pinned her against the door as he ran his tongue up from the bottom of her neck to her ear, while his breathing drove her frantically wild.

My God, I have never felt such mad passion like this before. I want to ravage her right here and now on the floor.

He ground against her and felt her excitement. As sweat began to form and glisten on her neck and breasts, they heard Cathy's voice. "Judy, are you in here?"

Quickly, silently, and instinctively, he sat on the toilet and raised his feet to give the appearance of only one person in the stall, should Cathy take a peek under the enclosure.

"Are you all right?" Cathy called out.

"I'm fine. I'll be out in a minute," Judy said as they both held each other and laughed silently.

They heard Cathy retreat and the door close.

Vinny told her to make sure the coast was clear and he would slip out first. That would give her time to fix her makeup. She opened the stall door and gave a quick look. On her signal, he bolted out the door and returned to the bar, where he asked Gary for a glass of ice water. Judy returned about five minutes later. He handed her the same and said sarcastically, "I think you can use this."

"Thanks, baby," she said and asked if anyone had said anything.

"No, not a word," he replied.

Michael looked to be having a good time with Kim, but Vinny noticed his brother Raymond was gone, and so was Cathy. Judy asked Vinny if he had seen Cathy when he came out of the bathroom. She explained that it was her voice they heard in the bathroom and she must have gone home.

Vinny suggested he pay the check so that the two of them could get some "You must be a mind-reader," she said, smiling provocatively. They told Kim and Michael they were going outside to get some air.

"Have fun," Kim said disingenuously. "Is that what they call it nowadays?"

It was refreshingly cool outside. The moon was full, and every star was crisp. Vinny motioned to them and said how romantic they were. She agreed it was a special night and proceeded to prove to him how knowledgeable she was in astronomy by pointing out different constellations: Big Dipper, Little Dipper, the Sickle and Taurus, and so on. Between enjoying the night air and the stars, they kissed and held each other close. It felt great, and it was good to know that even embracing and kissing at this nice, slow pace was arousing as much passion and excitement as they had inside the bathroom.

"I don't want this night to end," Vinny said lovingly. "I want to hold on to you as tight as I can and never let you go, but I know I will have to."

"I know how you feel," she said grimly. She would have to make a very difficult decision real soon. *Do I give up the safety and security of an old shoe, or do I risk it all on a man I hardly know? Although he excites me like no other man has ever done before, he may not be what I really want.*

They continued to kiss and hug like two teenagers in love, until they were rudely interrupted by a couple of voices in the dark yelling, "How's the air out there?"

Abruptly, Judy said she had to go. She jotted her work number on the back of a business card, then said emphatically, "No promises," as a frown crossed her face. "Where were you two and a half years ago?" she yelled at him as she walked toward her car.

Vinny walked after her, caught up, grabbed her in his arms, and in as reassuring a voice as he could muster, said, "I'm here now, and I'm going to be here for as long as you want me to stay. I'm not telling you to go call your boyfriend right now, break up with him, and run off with me! That would be a cold and insensitive thing for you to do. Give yourself some time to decide what you truly want in life. If this guy is what you have always dreamed about, your white knight in shining armor, then stay with him. I have already made a wrong decision once in my life, and I want the woman I fall in love with and marry to be sure that it's me she truly wants. Someone she's waited her whole life for and will love me unconditionally. When we were in the restaurant, you told me a long list of things you were looking for in a man. I admire you for telling me, and luckily for me, I am all those things."

That brought a huge smile to her face.

Vinny continued, "I am all for a woman who knows what she is looking for and won't settle for less. That's the way it should be. You will never be happy if you settle for less. The rest of your life, you will wonder if you would have been happier if you waited to be sure. I've been divorced for four years. I've dated a bit. My friends and family ask me when I am going to find the right woman to settle down with and have children. I've given the same answer so many times that no one will ask anymore. It's a simple answer. When I find her, I'll know. Do you want to know what I'm looking for in a woman?" Vinny asked earnestly.

Again, with her brilliant smile, she said, "Tell me!"

"I'm looking for a woman who is sophisticated, beautiful, a fantastic lover who is uninhabited in bed, and most importantly, someone to be my best friend, who can be popular and well-liked by my family and friends, affectionate toward me and will love me as much as I love her. My friends tell me I will never find what I'm looking for. I think someday I will, but one thing I will not do is settle. People can call me selfish, and selfish I may be, but this is my life, and this time I am going to live it my way, and to hell with what other people say. It's better to live in truth, no matter how terrible, than to destroy yourself by living a lie."

She looked at Vinny with what appeared to be a gleam of happiness, and with the moonlight shining off her face, she was more beautiful than before. Then she said, "You really are a romantic."

"Helpless," he replied, "simply helpless."

"So what do I do now?" she asked curiously.

"About what?" Vinny replied.

"About my boyfriend!" she responded defensively.

"I can't tell you what to do," he said somberly. "You have to listen to what's in your heart and what you want. Not what I want or what he wants. The one thing I can tell you is that you will never change him. You might scare him by telling him you're unhappy and want to date other people, forcing a change to occur in him, but trust me, as soon as he feels that potential threat is gone, he'll return to his old ways. If you told him you've been unfaithful and he begged and cried for you to take him back, would you want him?" Vinny asked suspiciously.

She looked as if she didn't quite know how to answer, then said, "I don't know!"

"Well, if he did that, wouldn't it prove to you that he really does love you and that he loves you so much he's willing to put the whole matter behind him? What if I told you that you could be dealing with the male ego and that it has nothing to do with how much he loves you? He may candy-coat it and make it sound like love, but it really was his male ego whining. He would then be marrying you for all the wrong reasons. Out of pride, or because he has invested so much time and emotional energy he feels he can't change his mind in fear of looking like a fool, thereby suffering a fatal loss of self-respect. My advice to you is to take some time for you, Judy, to find out what it is you want."

Vinny handed her his business card with his home phone number on the back and kissed her slowly, again caressing her face with his hands. She started her car and waited for him to start his. They drove down Central Avenue together, stopping at every light to talk. When they got to his block to turn, she stopped at the light and he asked her to come up for a nightcap.

She smiled and said, "No! I'll take a rain check and I'll call you."

He watched as her taillights faded away down Central Avenue and hoped to God that she felt the same way about him as he did about her.

Until that night, Vinny had exhausted every possibility of ever experiencing the kind of passion he'd just experienced with Judy. According to Shakespeare, comedy and tragedy often go hand in hand. As he lay in bed, he couldn't stop thinking about how unbelievably romantic the entire scene was and the tragedy that would, no doubt, result from it for her soon-to-be ex-boyfriend. He was thinking like a schoolboy with his first crush on the cutest girl in class. He also realized a need to feel safe and secure with a woman he could trust, someone loyal that wouldn't let him down, as he had been let down previously. He knew he couldn't withstand having his heart broken again. It'd taken him four long, painful years to erase the past and the hurt caused by it. It took four years to forget Debbie, yet he was still haunted by all the lies and the cheating—cheating he could never quite prove but believed to be so. Four years to forget his nights filled with rage and misery over the destruction of a disillusioned love. He would now allow himself to once again be a helpless romantic and someday marry Judy, the woman of his dreams. But for now, he must try to be passive and not yet wear his heart on his sleeve, where it could easily become damaged yet again. He thought he could let his feelings be known, but he had to be prepared for the possibility of disappointment, for fear of the unknown, of love, can be frightening.

The next morning, as he dressed for work, he noticed two cards with phone numbers on them. He only remembered Judy giving him her card. Taking a second look, he saw the other one belonged to Kim, Judy's girlfriend. He'd forgotten she'd given it to him early on in the evening while Judy was in the ladies' room.

Now I remember. It was right after we all got a complete demonstration of how her black lace Wonderbra works. Michael despises fake silicone tits and the fact that so many women have been getting them. I loved it when he insinuated to Kim that her tits might be fakes, because hers are so firm-looking and don't sag.

A quick examination of her breasts, combined with a brief explanation of the working of the Wonderbra, had them thoroughly convinced that au naturel far surpasses silicone implants.

As Vinny stood in front of the mirror, mulling over the previous night's events, he thought the entire "breast conversation" and Kim's tits meant absolutely nothing to him.

No. Judy's the one. In one night, she's made me feel more sexual excitement than I've ever felt with any woman in my life. I wonder if she wants me as badly as I want her.

Vinny walked by Michael's room to see if he was awake yet.

I don't know why I bother. He's under the mistaken idea that getting up at the crack of dawn is getting his head off his pillow before noon.

Vinny left him a note on the door telling him to take something out of the freezer for dinner and if he was not going to be home for dinner, to call him at the office to let him know.

Vinny poured a cup of coffee and went out to the patio and planted himself at the table next to the hot tub. The beautiful spring morning was so peaceful. The sun was shining, birds were chirping, and the air smelled of freshly cut grass. He sat and admired all the work he had done renovating the old house since he retired his barstool and, instead, put his time, energy, and money to good use. He was very proud of the results.

Vinny hadn't given up drinking altogether, nor did he intend to, but the plan of action he put into effect three short years before seemed to have worked out fairly well. Although he'd lost his job, in small part because of his drinking, things still had worked out quite nicely—so far. He didn't think anyone, including himself, knew why he was taking on so many home repair projects around the house. Add to that new hobbies that consisted of cooking, vegetable gardening, and exterior landscaping and design. What he did realize was he always liked to reap the rewards of things he'd done. He'd never gotten the recognition he thought he deserved from the projects he had done, and truth be known, he didn't care. He knew the amount of work, money, and determination it took to restore the house. He recalled how much his father loved it. His father worked very hard when he wasn't exhausted from working two jobs to pay the bills to keep his family living in this house.

Growing up, Vinny used to dream of owning a house, a little smaller, but exactly like it. With two additions: a pool with white gravel around it and low-voltage lighting with beautiful, colorful landscaping, and a hot tub, for him to relax in with the woman he loved as they watched their adorable two children play with their beautiful golden retriever puppy he had surprised his wife with. He never thought he was asking for too much, and he was willing to work hard to afford these things and achieve his goals.

So what went wrong?' Why am I thirty-five and have yet to reach one of these goals? Mistakes, mixed with more bad choices, compounded with yet more mistakes. I remember TC telling me once—yes, we were sitting in my hot tub, smoking cigars, sipping cognac, and admiring the finishing touches I'd put on the house— that I see the world through romantic eyes, that I want things to be the way they are in storybook love stories, although they fucking usually aren't. Yes, people make mistakes. That's why I will never judge people too harshly, because although people make some terrible mistakes, they can still be very nice people. Making mistakes doesn't make someone evil. They're just human. We all make mistakes, all of us. It's our nature. I can't always ride in on the white horse and save the princess, because they're not all princesses, and many of them don't wait to be saved. I've got to stop myself doing that.

Sipping his coffee, Vinny heard a car horn and got out of his chair to see who it was. "Tommy!" Vinny yelled.

Tommy sat in his Lincoln Town Car. "Greetings and saluta- tions, Brother Vincent," Tommy replied. "I saw the kitchen door open and a puff of cigarette smoke rising from the patio and knew it had to be you. God only knows your brother Michael would never be awake at this ungodly hour. How goes it?" Tommy asked casually.

"I met a girl," Vinny replied excitedly.

"Vinny, you meet more women than Carter has little liver pills. Many a man should have your problem."

"No, Tommy, I mean I *met* a girl!" Vinny said seriously.

"Oh, no!" Tommy replied. "When you say it like that, I know we are in trouble!"

"Tommy," Vinny explained, "she is an absolute princess. The most beautiful woman I have ever seen in my life. Wait until you meet her. You're going to love her!"

"All right, Sir Lancelot," Tommy said sarcastically, "before you jump on your white horse and ride off into the sunset with this princess, I must go to court, and you, no doubt, must go to work. What are you doing this weekend?" Tommy asked.

"No plans yet!" Vinny responded.

"Good, I'll call you later. We need to go over the final plans for Pig Roast '97," Tommy said as he drove away.

As Vinny drove to work, he couldn't think of the last time he had felt so good. For some reason, everything seemed new. He'd removed the T-top, and with the wind blowing through his hair and the warmth of the sun on his face, he felt great.

He parked his car and went up the stairs to his office on Central Avenue, in Yonkers, above a real estate agency. He asked Rose, his secretary, if he had any messages. She said no, so he went to his office.

As he poured a cup of coffee, he skimmed through the mail. He noticed none of his sales representatives were in, and rather than bother Rose, who was busy doing payroll, he decided to check the assignment board, a method of keeping track of where his employees were. If it was good enough for NYPD to monitor its detectives' assignments, then it was good enough for him to monitor his salesmen. One look told him all his sales reps were on appointments, each in different parts of the city. If a customer called in an order, Rose would beep the sales rep in that area. When he called back, he'd get the location from her and go on the call. When the sales rep met the customer, who had decided what they wanted, the sales rep would call Rose back to see about availability. While the sales rep was on hold, Rose would call our main warehouse, where the office manager would check availability and confirm a less-than-twenty-four-hour delivery. Rose would then inform the sales rep and wait for a confirmation of the order, either by credit card, cash, or certified check. Vinny's job was to keep his employees motivated, make sure they got referrals and follow-ups. If they were not on a lead or an appointment, they should be at their desk, on the phone with potential customers. Vinny ran his office in the same manner his bosses supervised him. As long as the numbers were up, he didn't care what they were doing. Just keep doing it. By looking at the assignment board, he could see everyone was busy. For the month of May, the figures were up, and he was happy.

This afforded Vinny the time to run his private investigations business, which consisted of one additional business line, which Rose answered, Expo Investigation, *expo* standing for "ex-police"—i.e., himself. Business was by referrals and networking. With the number of cops, district attorneys, lawyers, judges, and professional people Vinny knew over the years, it practically ran itself. Clients would call Vinny's office if they were friends. He'd then refer them to a trusted private investigator he knew who wouldn't rob them blind. In return, that agency paid him a 10 percent referral fee. If a prospective client called from an ad he ran in the phone book, he would do the paperwork for the investigation conducted by a reputable investigator, thus making him the consultant, because he was so inundated with work. Vinny would then tack on 20 percent for a job well done. On a rare occasion, as the client he took on last month, he would conduct the complete investigation himself, which meant he'd be absolutely positive he'd recover lost property or damages and receive his 33.3 percent, just as a lawyer received on a case he signed on consignment. The case Vinny was presently working on should be cleared up in a couple of months and see him a $30,000 (before taxes) recovery fee from the insurance carrier. Vinny's sales company alone was a well-paying job, but nothing was as gratifying to him as police work and having this private-cop business. He still felt like he'd done his share at righting some wrong the legal system had failed to do. Besides, it paid well.

Vinny went into his office and locked the door so Rose would know not to disturb him.

He took out Judy's card and decided on a new approach. He dialed the number.

A woman's voice answered the phone. "ABC Contracting, how may I help you?"

"How are you, miss? My name is Bob," Vinny lied. "I own the Cascade Florist down the road from you, and I have an order here for a dozen long-stem yellow roses, but my son left your address off the order. May I have it, please?"

The voice gave him an address on Saw Mill River Road, in Elmsford. "Thank you, ma'am. One more question before you hang up, if you don't mind? Do you have a Judy—I can't make out the last name—working there?"

"That must be Godfrey," the voice said. "Yes, she works here."

"Thank you," Vinny said and hung up.

He quickly looked up the florist's number, then dialed it.

"Yes, sir. I'd like a dozen long-stem yellow roses to be delivered, please."

The voice on the phone took all his details and then asked innocently, "What would you like written on the card?"

He hadn't thought of that. Then it came to him. "Write, 'I need you, I want you, I have to have you!' but leave the name blank."

Twenty minutes later, Rose knocked on his door.

Shit, I forgot to unlock it. "Come in," Vinny said.

"There's a Judy on line 2," Rose said. "Are you in or do you want me to take a message?" she asked sarcastically, knowing full well by the look on his face he'd take the call.

"I'll take it," he said. He bolted upright in his chair, picked up the receiver, and asked politely, "And how are you this morning?"

"I'm okay," she said, sounding exhausted, "but I was up kind of late after I left you last night. I was feeling really guilty about what happened, so I drove to my boyfriend's house, woke him up, and told him what happened."

"You did what?" Vinny was shocked. "Why did you do that?" He was hoping to himself that she did it to break up with him.

"I yelled at him," she said reluctantly. "I explained to him that I have been warning him for months that he'd better stop taking me for granted, but he never listened. I told him that he forced me into cheating on him and that I needed to feel loved."

Vinny said the only thing he could think of. "How much detail did you give him?"

"I just told him that I kissed you and that it felt great."

Vinny's next question, of course, was, "While you were relieving yourself of this enormous guilt you were feeling, by confessing your sins to him, did you feel it absolutely necessary, in order to be completely absolved of your sins, to tell him the man that made you feel great last night just signed a lease to rent office space in the same building directly above him?" After a short pause, Vinny knew the answer before she said, "Yes."

"Good mother of God!" Vinny cried in disbelief. "It's one thing to be upset enough to tell him what you did. Honesty can be an honorable quality and is very rare in today's society. But it's another thing to be so pissed off at him that you would want to hurt him by telling him that what you did felt great. But it is totally inconceivable to me that you could possibly be deranged enough with contemptible hatred toward this man you say you love that you would crucify him by waking him up in the middle of the night, telling him you cheated on him and that it felt great. But to top it all off with 'By the way, you will probably see him every day, because he rents the office space upstairs from you'? This is ludicrous! Did I leave anything out?" Vinny asked, with more than a bit of sarcasm in his voice.

"Listen, Vinny!" she said, sounding irritated with him. "I've never cheated on him before, and I felt terrible. This was the man who, until you came around last night, I had every intention of marrying. Last night, I felt something with you I never felt before in my life. Now that I know I can feel that way, I am not so sure I want to marry him anymore. I lay in bed last night crying, and I couldn't stop thinking of how good you made me feel and how something that feels so right, so good, could be so wrong. As far as the melodramatic play-by-play you just gave, let me remind you that, besides my head spinning in confusion of how I felt about you, I also had to deal with the amount of wine and champagne we consumed last night!"

What can I say? She made a valid point.

"I'm sorry," he said innocently. "I had no right being judgmental of you. How are you doing this morning? What was the outcome of your discussion last night?" he asked, hoping they had broken up.

"First, he got really upset," she said, "and I had to throw a glass of cold water I was drinking at him to calm him down. Then he started to cry, saying, 'I can't believe I'm going to lose you! I love you so much.' He was so loud his mother yelled downstairs to ask if he was all right."

"Judy, how old is this guy?" Vinny asked calmly, laughing to himself about the inquisitive mother.

"He's thirty-three. Why?" she asked.

"Is he Italian?" he asked.

"Yes. How did you know?" she asked.

Vinny couldn't say what he was thinking without sounding insensitive. *He's thirty-three years old, crying like a baby, and lives downstairs from his mommy.* So he simply said cautiously, "I was just curious, that's all. So finish telling me the story."

"I held him in my arms and told him that I've been warning him for months. It's not like this came without warning! I finally got him to stop crying. It was a really bad scene. I never saw a man cry like that. Then he started with the promises. 'I'll change. I'll pay more attention to you. Please, I can't lose you. I'll die without you!'"

"Judy," Vinny interrupted, "before I break out in tears, tell me what the result was!" As if Vinny didn't know.

"I told him he's not going to lose me but that we can't go on like this. He's going to have to change. 'I'm your girlfriend,' I told him, 'not your mother. I come over here and your mother starts on me. "Do his laundry, iron his shirts for work, cook for him!" I'm fed up, and if you don't change and get your mother off my back, there won't be any more chances!'"

"Well, I am glad I could help you out," Vinny said sharply.

"Vinny," she said despairingly, "don't be like that. I love him, and we have been together for two and a half years. I owe him a second chance, and if it doesn't work out, at least I can say I tried my best. I just can't walk away from him and leave him like that. What kind of a person would that make me? Would you even want to be with a woman like that?"

"Judy," Vinny said sincerely, "I am not mad at you about your decision. I think you are doing the right thing by giving him a second chance, but I've been on this ride before, and I've learned how not to kid myself into believing people can change. The truth is, they can't! But you will have to find that out for yourself. People can have the best of intentions and say they'll change, and do change, but it's only a quick fix to a problem that will never be permanent. Mark my words: we are coming up on Memorial Day Weekend. By today, or tomorrow, at the absolute latest, he will send you flowers and come up with some last-minute romantic getaway weekend for the two of you. He will be Mr. Wonderful for the three-day weekend. Maybe for a little time when you come back, he will continue to try to be what you want. Not what he is, but what you want him to be! Then, eventually, he will go right back to his old self."

"How can you be so sure he's the same as any other man?" she asked impatiently.

"Not just men," Vinny said. "Don't get me wrong, I am talking about women as well as men. This lesson I am talking about, which I learned, I can assure you, was not taught to me by any man." That brought a chuckle of laughter on her end of the line.

"You are really something else, Vinny Davis. The girl that is lucky enough to catch you better hold on tight and never let you go. Not only are you the sexiest man I've ever seen, but you also bring out a passion in a woman like you would not believe."

Vinny laughed and said, "Thanks for the compliments, but I don't bring that passion out in all women, just one. Listen…" He hesitated. "If you need someone to talk to, feel free to call me, and don't worry, you will never hear 'I told you so' come out of my mouth. Do you have a pen and paper?" Vinny asked.

"Yes," she said.

"Write this down, because it's too late to stop it and I am not sure that I would even if I could."

"What are you talking about?" she asked suspiciously.

"Are you ready?" he said.

"Yes. Go ahead."

"Write down, 'I need you, I want you, I have to have you.'"

"What does that mean? It's beautiful," she said.

"You'll find out soon enough," Vinny said confidently. "I just didn't want you to make another mistake and get you into any more trouble than I already have."

"You didn't get me into trouble," she said. "I managed to do that all by myself."

"Let me know how your romantic weekend goes," Vinny said.

"Thanks again, Vinny," she said.

"Anytime at all, princess," he said, "anytime."

It was around 3:00 p.m. when Rose, his secretary, told him Judy was on line 2.

"Thanks, Rose," he said. He picked up the receiver and said, "Please tell me you did not call him to tell him I sent you roses."

"They are the most beautiful roses I have ever seen. How did you know yellow is my favorite?" she asked.

"Good guess," he said, "because red roses are a sign of love, white symbolizes purity, and yellow signifies friendship."

"You are amazing," she said. "And by the way, you were right. He called about twenty minutes after your flowers were delivered and told me to pack a bag because we are going away for a three-day weekend at Memorial Day."

"Well, miracles never cease," Vinny said. "Where is he taking you, if you don't mind my asking?"

"Philadelphia," she said. Vinny had to laugh at that. Philadelphia, home of the cheesesteak sandwich and everyone's favorite Italian, Rocky.

"How romantic," he said, still laughing.

"It's not funny," she said defensively. "At least he's trying!"

"I'm sorry," he said half-heartedly, still laughing to himself. "I know it was last minute and every place must be booked solid, but you are right, he's trying."

"So does your crystal ball on your desk tell you anything else about my future?"

"I can't tell you any more of my predictions," he said, "because if I do, you might not tell me if I was right or not. So when you get back, if you want, give me a call next week and I'll tell you how your weekend went."

"You got a deal," she said, sounding very anxious by the fact that Vinny gave her a reason to call him next week.

"Have a great time," Vinny said sadly.

"You too," she said.

Vinny hung up.

I hope she calls next week.

CHAPTER 25

Tommy taught scuba certification at the Boy Scout Camp at Durland, in Rye, New York. After years of diving without being qualified, Vinny took the course the year before so he could finally go diving completely educated in all the very good reasons one shouldn't go diving.

Vinny amazed himself at times. He did dangerous things over and over with absolutely no fear, but when he did the "mature thing" and boned up on what he was doing, it brought on instant panic. Ignorance is, indeed, bliss. Learning under TC, his best friend of twenty-five years, made it doubly nerve-racking. When TC told him, "Don't worry about the practical part of the exam, I'll help you," Vinny knew it was time to worry. He also knew he'd be the brunt of some sort of "boobery."

A week before he was to take the officially certification exam to be a diver, TC and Vinny took a trip to Weatherall, Rhode Island, to do a test run, so to speak, on what he'd learned during the past twenty weeks of classroom studies. They stowed all their gear and set off.

The water temperature in the Atlantic Ocean off the coast of Rhode Island, in the middle of May, was in the forties. Even with neoprene diving suits, booties, and gloves to ward off hypothermia, it would still be cold.

TC and Vinny did a beach entry, which simply means walking into the water and putting everything on while in the water. Even with the protection, it still felt near freezing. They submerged, and at about twenty feet, Vinny noticed he was having a hard time staying down. He tugged on TC's arm. He quickly knew what Vinny meant. TC hadn't put enough weight on Vinny's belt to compensate for the suit he was wearing. They both knew it would take forever to surface, take off all their equipment, walk back to the car, and start again. That option was totally unacceptable, so TC grabbed Vinny by the arm and pulled him back down to the seabed. Visibility was about two feet.

This is no fucking fun at all. I'm freezing and can't see much of anything. What in the hell am I doing here? I could be home in a warm bed. Damn!

TC decided to solve part of the problem. It began with Vinny carrying a few rocks he found on the ocean floor. After all, they'd been Boy Scouts—TC an Eagle Scout, Vinny but a second class. Scouting better prepared one for the curveballs the game of life threw from time to time. TC was on the right track, but they needed to weigh Vinny down even. Next, TC unzipped Vinny's semiwarm suit and began to ram rocks in if Vinny rapidly began to freeze. The rocks did the trick.

Shit. If something would go wrong now, in eighty feet of water, I'll be a permanent fixture on the ocean's floor, until such time as some poor bastard snags me on his fishing line and reels me in, thinking he's hooked a prize tuna. Vinny the Tuna. Visibility sucks, I'm nearly frozen solid, and now I'm so weighed down I'm barely able to drag myself along the seabed. Fuck, it's cold!

It's all coming back home. Now I remember why I only dive in warm, tropical places: beautiful, colorful fish and coral to look at, and the water's warm! At a depth of one hundred feet, you can look up and see the bottom of the dive boat. Not like here. Not much to see down here. A few lobsters, that's about it. We've been down about twenty minutes, and we still have not found that old VW Bug TC talked about on the drive here.

Vinny suddenly lost sight of him because his fins were kicking up an incredible amount of sand in front of Vinny. Vinny stopped to look for him, but with only two feet of visibility, TC could be right above him and Vinny wouldn't have known it. Vinny felt blindly in front of him and found what appeared to be some sort of cave. If

Vinny had learned anything in scuba school, it was two very important things: never to dive alone and never go in to caves or wrecked ships. Even experienced divers have run out of air before they have found their way out of them.

So here I am. I've been diving for years without any formal training or certification. I'm alone, in almost thirty feet of water, and I am about to break the second major safety rule of diving, in search of my best friend, who, if I didn't know any better, is trying to kill me.

Vinny had proceeded cautiously into the mouth of the small cave when, suddenly, he was scared shitless by what appeared to be some sea creature. His regulator popped out of his mouth. He panicked but remembered to retrieve his regulator and pop it back in before he did anything else. Still in a state of panic, but at least breathing with his regulator back in his mouth, he began to swim away from the rocks. As he was swimming for his life, he felt hands grabbing him, and he saw Tommy's face. Vinny calmed down when TC signaled to surface with him. Anxious to lighten his load, Vinny started jettisoning the rocks crammed in his BC and wet suit. Still, they rose to the surface slowly. At last, heads above water, Vinny yelled, "What the hell was that?" still unsure of what he'd seen.

"An upside-down horseshoe crab I held up in front of your mask!"

"You son of a bitch! Are you trying to kill me?"

"No, but you did pass the 'retrieving your regulator' part of the practical exam!"

"Very funny!" They both laughed as they swam to the shore.

The Memorial Day weekend came and went. The weather was beautiful for boating, which was where Vinny and his family had spent most of the weekend. To relax. His father owned a twenty-seven-foot Sea Ray. It was equipped with a galley, bathroom with shower, and enough room to sleep six. Using the Sea Ray as often as possible helped keep the Davises close. But Vinny knew his dad didn't get all that much relaxation from it because of the constant repairs, maintenance, and basic upkeep—the downside of boat ownership. His dad spent a lot of time, energy, and his hard-earned money maintaining it. It wasn't so much for himself as for his family.

It took all of Vinny and TC's persuasiveness to convince Angela, his wife, that it was safe to take their kids out on the boat. Angela was the ever-nervous and overprotective mother of Anthony, their five-year-old, and Marie Claire, their three-year-old, also known as Beaner. Tommy and Vinny took Anthony out for a day on the Long Island Sound the previous summer, but Angela and the very boisterous Marie Claire referred to it as Scuba School for Men Only. That, of course, was a clever way to keep the fearless Marie Claire from tagging along.

It was a hot day. Everyone was having a great time on board, including Tommy's wife and kids. They even dragged Maria, Vinny's sister, and Nicole, his niece, out for the day. They didn't venture too far from New Rochelle Marina, only to what boaters called the backyard, a quiet cove located on a peninsula near the New York Athletic Club, which Tommy and his family belonged to. It was perfect weather for Vinny to regain the slowly fading tan he got in April, on his last trip to Jamaica. He loved sitting back, enjoying a beer, taking the sun, watching the kids at play, their mothers watching them like hawks.

TC and Vinny were discussing the final plans for Pig Roast '97. The yearly pig roast was a tradition begun more than twenty-four years before, when TC and Vinny were still juvenile delinquents. Back then, the annual gathering was held at Tommy's parents' house while they were away, and quite without their knowledge. How they never found out was one of God's great mysteries. The first year, about fifty people gathered to drink beer and eat hamburgers, hot dogs, and of course, the pig they roasted in a pit in the ground. One year, everyone got so smashed they forgot where the beast was buried.

Now, some twenty years later, the cast of characters who attended exceeded three hundred. They were the oddest group one could ever imagine gathering to party. A beautiful Academy Award-winning actress, city councilmen, judges, and district attorneys represented the upper classes. At the other end of society were members of the Hells Angels and the Blue Knights, a group of motorcycle-riding policemen. Between the extremes were senior NYPD officers, local cops, and the New York Shields, including the department chaplain, court officers, reporters, and clerks from Manhattan, Bronx, and Westchester. A host of relatives, friends, neighbors, and of course, we can't forget, clients. The gathering grew too large to be held at Tommy's house. So for the third year running, it would be held at the Davis estate, and this year, they were expecting the largest turnout yet. In anticipation of this crowd, they increased the amount of beer, liquor, and food they laid on: 2,009 hot dogs, 1,500 hamburgers, 300 pounds of hot and sweet Italian sausage, and four 100-pound pigs, 1,200 pounds of assorted salads, ranging from shrimp, chicken, potato and egg, pepper, marinated mushrooms, and antipasto, to your basic potatoes, macaroni, coleslaw, three-bean, cucumbers, and pickles.

"Everything else is all set," Vinny told Tommy. "I spoke to Champagne. Bottoms Up, the official pig band, is confirmed, and Champagne will be performing with them again!"

"Vinny," Tommy whispered.

"What's the matter?" He noticed TC was looking around to make sure nobody could hear them.

"Do you remember talking about the pig roast being on the same night as the Tyson fight?" TC asked.

"Yes, I remember."

"And do you remember No-No from my office saying it would be a great idea if we could rent a big-screen TV to show the fight?"

"Yes, I remember," Vinny said, anxious for TC to get to the point. Then he asked, "Are you trying to tell me you rented a big-screen TV for the party?"

"No," Tommy said, his voice almost at a whisper, "I bought one, and it's being delivered to your house. Can you keep it until I can find a way to break the news to Angela?"

"Of course I can, but aren't you worried about it being destroyed at the party?"

"No, it will be all right," Tommy said confidently. "I always wanted a big TV."

"No problem. You know I'd let you bury a body in my yard if you asked me to."

"Thanks, Vinny." Tommy laughed. "Enough about the pig roast. Tell me about the girl of your dreams you met, before the wife comes back."

"Oh my God, Tommy! She's the most beautiful woman I have ever seen in my life. She puts any model in this year's *Sports Illustrated* swimsuit issue to shame."

"Are you trying to tell me she's better-looking than Miss Colorado you were dating for a while last year?" Tommy asked, disbelief in his voice.

"This girl—Judy's her name—puts that girl to shame! She's about five foot eight, with an unbelievable body. You gotta to see it to believe it—a perfect 36-24-36, with long straight dark-brown hair and the most alluring hazel eyes. They can put you in a trance. Exquisite skin, flawless, velvet smooth to the touch. She has a brilliant smile that can light up any room, lips that taste like candy, and harbor enough unbridled passion to jump-start a human heart. Long shapely, firm legs that should be insured by Lloyd's of London for at least a cool million. And get this, TC, all that beauty, with brains and intelligence as well, and a strong, compassionate, loving, and caring personality. She's going to be thirty in November. She has a great job in employee relations in Hawthorne. She was a model for Pepsi Cola. Never married, lives alone in Hastings on the Hudson. I think that covers it! TC, let me ask you a question."

"Sure, Vinny, go ahead." He was amazed by his friend's enthusiasm.

"Have you ever met a girl and felt like you were hit in the chest with a sledgehammer so hard you couldn't breathe, you can't catch your breath?"

Tommy put his hand on his shoulder, looked him in the eyes, and said, "If that's how you feel and she feels the same way, be prepared!"

"What's that supposed to mean?" Vinny said challengingly.

Not breaking eye contact, Tommy said, "I felt the same exact way you just described, once!"

"Really? What happened?"

Tommy's eyes left Vinny's, and he looked directly at his wife and kids. He followed Tommy's glance. "Angela?"

"That's right! Angela!"

On a quiet Friday afternoon three weeks before the pig roast, Vinny was at work. The clock was ticking toward five o'clock. Poor Rose, Vinny's secretary, had been handling RSVPs for it all day. The phone rang, and Rose answered, then yelled to him, "Vinny, phone call on line 1. It's Judy!" She knew by then not to ask if he'd take a call from her.

He picked up. "Hi! How was your romantic weekend in glorious Pennsylvania?" He was trying to be nice.

"It was terrible! You were right about everything." She was upset.

"I'm sorry to hear that. I was hoping, for your sake, at least, that it would turn out the way you wanted it to."

"I think it did."

"What do you mean?"

"I broke up with him, and I've been thinking about you like crazy."

"Well, I'm glad, because I haven't stopped thinking about you either. Do you have plans tonight?" He sounded like an anxious schoolboy.

"No, I don't."

"Good! How about I meet you after work for drinks and we will take it from there?"

"Great! Do you know where the Tarrytown Marriott is?"

"Yes! I know it well."

"Good," she said. "I'll meet you at around 5:15 p.m. at the bar on the right of where the club is. Do you know it?"

"I'll be there at five fifteen!"

"I'll see you then," she said, then rang off.

"Rose! You lock up the office for me. I've got a date and can't be late. I have my beeper on if anyone needs me. Thanks, Rose. Bye."

He heard her say, "Have a good time," as he dashed out.

Shit. I've barely time to drive home, clean up a bit, remove the T-tops, and head out on the highway. She broke up with him. She's been

thinking of me just as much as I've been thinking of her. Fuckin' fantas-
tic! Man, I've missed her. She's free-for me!

At the speed Vinny drove, the Tarrytown Marriott was but a twenty-minute drive from his home.

The bar inside that he was meeting her at was quiet—the perfect place to meet to have a few cocktails, talk, and get to know someone better. Its lighting was deliberately kept low in the lounge area to give you just enough light for the right amount of privacy. If you desire to hold hands or kiss, you can do so with little or no worry of your privacy being invaded. At least not by anyone except the cocktail waitress, who was quick to come and take his drink order. The jukebox in the corner left a lot to be desired. Vinny scanned through the title selections in hopes of putting on some mood music, but that was a complete waste of time unless your idea of mood music was Ricky Nelson or John Denver, even if you started out in a good mood. After a few bars of that music, you'd want to go out, get drunk, and shoot somebody. Or yourself. The music reminded Vinny of a bumper sticker he read when he was stuck in traffic. Vinny laughed so hard he had to remember it: "If you love something, set it free. If it comes back to you, it was meant to be. If it doesn't, hunt it down and kill it!"

He looked up from beside the small pool table—there she was, beautiful as ever.

"Hi," she said as she walked toward him and kissed him on the cheek. "I'm sorry I'm a little late."

"You're not late," Vinny said innocently. "I'm early, and that is the way it's supposed to be, because a woman will always show up a little late. That's in order to give a man extra time to get there before her. Women hate to sit and wait, especially for a man. If a man's smart, he'll always be considerate and be on time. Then she won't be upset for having to wait alone."

She smiled and shifted the subject. "How old are you?"

"I was thirty-six in February. Why?"

She smiled. "You know an awful lot about how to please a woman for being only thirty-six."

He returned her smile. "You should only know!"

"Oh, boy! I need a drink! What are you drinking, pinot gri-gio?" she asked. "It's Santa Margarita, but I believe they also have Torresella, if you'd prefer a less-fruity wine."

"You also know your wines. I am very impressed!" She ordered the same, then they sat down in the corner booth, hidden from the bar area, but right in front of a pathetic jukebox that he hoped to God nobody'd decide to play.

Though they were still feeling each other out, they conversed like a couple who had known each other for a long time, the same way they had talked the first night they met at Central Square Café. It was startling how many likes and dislikes they had in common. They talked about their families, having to deal with being uprooted from their childhood friends at an early age by moving—she from Plainfield, New Jersey, to Hastings on the Hudson, New York; Vinny from Bay Ridge, Brooklyn, to Yonkers. Both of their mothers' lives were taken by tragedies at such very young ages. Both still carried the emotional scars from their otherwise-normal childhoods. Her father never remarried, and lived alone in Poughkeepsie, New York. Judy, at that time, was twenty-nine years old, the youngest of four girls. Her sisters, Jane and Jill, were married with children. Janet, her other sister, was single and lived not far from her dad. Judy had already met Vinny's entire family when they first met and said how nice it was they all got on so well. He assured her it wasn't like that all the time.

She laughed, saying she knew exactly what he meant.

As he looked into her most alluring eyes, he leaned forward and kissed her ever so gently on her soft, moist lips. As they separated, he hesitated, then asked, "Is it just me, or do you feel it too?"

"It's not just you. I feel it too." She kissed him again.

I've never felt this way before. What is this I'm feeling? Passion? Lust? I've never felt such intense sexual excitement with a woman. Or could it be I'm falling in love? So soon? Whatever it is, I love the way I feel, and I never want to lose this girl. Maybe this is that once-in-a-life-time feeling you hear so much about, the kind of love people wait their entire life to find. I feel so good because she says she feels it also. He could now take down the shield he had had up to protect his heart from being broken. He could now regain a trust that had been lost for some time now.

She smiled and said, "I have to make a phone call! I'll be back in a minute." She took off in a slow trot like a little girl who just got money to go to the candy store. She was back within five minutes with a huge smile on her face, like the cat that ate the canary, and said enthusiastically, "Let's go!"

"May I ask where?" he asked.

"Yes. I want you to take a ride with me to meet my friend Marie. Her husband's working, and she's home with the kids. You don't mind, do you? I want to show you off."

"No. Of course, I don't mind. I want to meet your friends."

"That's three so far. You're doing very well," she said mischievously.

"Doing very well at what? And three what?"

"That was just the third bonus point you've earned tonight. One was being on time and knowing why you should be. Two was knowing your wines and letting me make my own selection. And three was saying you don't mind and want to meet my friends. Number three is a big one, because my friends are very important to me."

"Do you want to take my car or yours?" Vinny asked as they walked to the parking lot hand in hand.

"Let's take yours."

"This way," Vinny directed as he gently pulled on her hand. They got to the passenger's door of his car. He unlocked and opened it for her. As he walked around the rear of his car to get in, he noticed her lean over to unlock his door for him. She then stuck her head through the open T-top, smiled, and said, "That was number four."

"You mean by me opening your door for you?"

"Yes."

"For you, that was number…I don't know, because I've lost count already." He motioned toward his door.

Her smile was now more brilliant than ever. "You lost count?"

"You've done way too many things right since I've met you. It's impossible for me to keep count." He smiled.

She pulled him to her, kissed him gently, and whispered, "So have you, babe, so have you."

En route, they had to make a pit stop at a gas station near the I-287 East on-ramp. "I love this car," Judy said. "People who buy a sports car like this and don't have a five-speed manual are wimps."

"I agree with you 100 percent."

"I used to have an Acura Integra before my Legend," she said as Vinny got out.

"I'll be right back! Do you need cigarettes?"

"Marlboro Lights."

He paid for the smokes and gas. When he returned to the car, she was in the driver's seat, looking at him, not sure what to say or what he might do.

She's testing the waters, so to speak. God, she looks great behind the wheel. Sexy. I wonder how she drives. There's only one way to find out.

He got in the passenger's seat and said, "Let's go!"

"Just like that? You're going to let me drive your car?"

"I trust you!"

I can't believe I just said that. I haven't said those words to a woman in ages.

She made a U-turn to get to the highway, changing gears like Mario Andretti as she got used to the car. Vinny sat back and relaxed.

I love trust. She has the most intense smile on her face. God, her hair looks gorgeous as wind blows through it. If she's as happy as she looks, I'm a lucky man. She drives this car like it's as natural as breathing.

She shifted into fifth and said, "This car shifts like butter!" He nonchalantly glanced at the speedometer.

110 MPH. Not bad. She changes lanes with the same ease as a beautiful woman wearing nothing but a thong would through the crowds at the Super Bowl. Talk about graceful.

Vinny lit and handed her a cigarette.

"What kind of music do you like?" she asked.

"Anything but I-want-to-kill-myself country music."

"I hate country too."

Thank God! I fucking hate that shit.

They high-fived. "What tape is that in the cassette player?"

"The best of TKA."

"Oh my God! There's a perfect song for you on that tape."

Vinny pulled the tape out and looked at the song titles. "What's the name of it?"

"I don't know. Put it on for me."

He shoved it in and cranked up the volume.

Loud. That's the only way to listen to this group. By the look on her face, she agrees. Good.

They listened and sang along with the tape. Then the song she wanted him to hear started. "This is it! This song is for you. Listen to the words and I'll sing to you."

The song started. The first word was *girl*, which she sang as *boy*.

"I can't get you out of my mind. Just one look, I knew you were one of a kind. Your love is hot, so give me all you've got. I need your love, too much is not enough!"

The song was still blasting, and she was still singing when they arrived in a tire-screeching stop in her girlfriend's driveway.

Judy ran up and hugged her friend as though she hadn't seen her in the longest time. He caught her whispering something in Marie's ear. "Hey, no secrets until after you introduce me!"

Marie extended her hand. "Nice to meet you, Vinny. I've heard a lot about you, and that's no secret."

"Isn't he gorgeous?"

"Absolutely!" Marie said. "He's much better-looking than Bobby!"

"Marie! I thought you were my friend!"

"But you know I never liked him."

"Oh, so that's his name," Vinny said innocently.

"Baby, it doesn't matter what his name is," Judy said. "His name was going to come up sooner or later, so let's just forget about it."

Both girls just laughed, and Marie jokingly asked Judy, "Are there any more where he came from?"

Judy laughed. "No! And he's all mine!"

"Well, excuse me," Marie said as she escorted Judy inside. "So tell me how all this happened. I'm so happy!"

It was a nice house undergoing major renovations. Marie apologized for the mess, but it was unnecessary—he understood and was enjoying looking over the work her husband, John, had done as the girls slid off, just out of earshot, and engaged in an intense conversation.

That's women for you. They're probably going on about Bobby and his recent demise. Let 'em talk. It's their nature. John's doing a really good job. He's a fine craftsman.

After a while, they apologized and insisted he join them in the kitchen for a glass of wine.

As he sat there sipping his wine, he couldn't help but wonder if he were a lamb being led to slaughter. He knew Marie was dying to find out if his intentions were honorable. They talked about his job, his marriage, his divorce, children, and his plans for the future. It was fun, and he enjoyed the "good cop, bad cop" routine to which they were subjecting him. The more they drank, the funnier it got, especially when Marie would ask a personal question and Judy would lightly slap Marie's arm and say, "Marie!" But she would then turn to Vinny to hear his answer.

After about three hours of what felt like the Spanish Inquisition to him, they said their goodbyes.

As Vinny drove through town, Judy said, "Thank you."

"For what?"

"For being you—so nice and understanding. Can I ask you a question?" she asked seriously.

"Sure."

"Are you going to hurt me?"

Vinny pulled the car over and parked. He looked at her, gently turned her face to him, looked right into her eyes, and said, "Never! The question is, Are you going to hurt me?"

"Never, Vinny. I am crazy about you."

CHAPTER 26

The fear of the unknown, of love, can often be frightening. To be deeply in love for Vinny was an unknown experience. Forget Debbie, all the lies and the thoughts of her cheating adulteries, of his nights filled with rage and misery over the destroying awfulness of a disillusioned love. He drew Judy closer and wondered if there was any feeling in the world that could compare to the feeling of waking up for the first time beside the woman he had unknowingly desired all his life. She provoked his fascination. Before meeting her, Vinny had absolutely exhausted the possibilities of extreme passion.

He knew how much she loved him. She was too honest to be deceitful. That made him feel blessed, secure in the knowledge that for the first time in as long as he could remember, someone loved him. He had learned to listen to his heart and not be afraid to trust again. They made love not like strangers but as if they had known each other for years.

It had been almost four years since Debbie. Although he dated quite a bit, he couldn't find what he was looking for in a woman to spend life with and start a family—a smart, sophisticated, beautiful, intelligent woman, a fantastic lover, uninhabited in bed, and most importantly, someone to be his friend. He found all that and more in her. She was popular and well liked by his family and friends. Affectionate toward him and loved him as much as he adored her without having to work at it. He didn't know how he was lucky enough to find a woman who was not only the most beautiful woman he had ever seen but was also equally beautiful on the inside. It was extremely rare in today's society to find a woman who possesses both inner and outer beauty. Maybe God had finally taken pity on him. And after Vinny had made penance for sins he had made in the past, God had decided to send him an angel. All he knew was finally, his life was back on track, and he couldn't be happier. He had paid dearly for his life's past mistakes. And if losing his life's dreams was the price tag he had to pay for the happiness he had now found, he would do it all over again.

He watched as she got dressed. She was so beautiful. She came over to the bed to kiss him and said, "Stay in bed. I'll let myself out."

"I wouldn't dream of it," he said as he rose and put on a robe. He walked her out to her car. She got in, started it, then let her window down. He leaned in to kiss her one more time.

When their lips separated, she looked at him, her eyes brilliant with love, and said, "You are the sexiest man I have ever met, and I am hopelessly in love with you."

"I love you too, princess. Now, drive carefully. Tell your dad I am looking forward to meeting him as soon as he feels better."

"I will, and I'll be home early!"

He watched as her car faded away in the distance. He already missed her.

Saturday, June 28, 1997

After Vinny had spent the entire night last night initiating Judy to the preparations involved in setting up for Pig Roast '97 festivities, the pig roast committee, consisting of about a dozen of Tommy and Vinny's closest friends, worked feverishly until about 2:00 a.m. in preparation for the once-a-year party that began approximately twenty-three years before with a small gathering of about 25 friends drinking, getting drunk, and attempting to roast a pig. Over the years, it had grown to outrageous proportions. At last year's count, they had over 350 people in attendance during the course of the day and night. With this year's anticipated number to reach 500 people, the committee had its work cut out for them. The night's activities consisted of clearing Vinny's basement to make room for the video games for the kids, the sides of the house and the backyard had to be transformed into a huge illumination, tents had to be erected for the bands and the dance floor, two bars and three beer and soda stations had to be stocked, porta-potties were delivered and set in place, a barbecue rotisserie to display one of the pigs and a microwave were set up, and tables and chairs were delivered, set up, and decorated.

Aside from the liquor and beer deliveries, there was a seemingly never-ending string of food deliveries—five one-hundred-pound marinated and ready-to-cook pigs, two thousand hot dogs, twelve hundred hamburgers, three hundred pounds of Italian sausage, chickens, and close to one thousand pounds of assorted salads. Coleslaw, potato, macaroni, shrimp, chicken, antipasto—you name the salad, they had it. Judy had never witnessed a group of friends, or anyone else, for that matter, plan a party so huge. The experience amazed her. After a good night's rest, there were only minor preparations left to do the next morning. Now they were ready to enjoy the fruits of their labor.

The afternoon was mainly for the little kids. Beside the video arcade in the basement, they had a thirty-by-thirty-foot air castle, and Zooky the Clown entertained the kids with magic tricks, face painting, and games. But as the invitation stated, as soon as the sun went down, the kids went home. Then the party really began.

Everybody who was anybody made it to the pig roast. Judges, lawyers, politicians, cops, district attorneys, court officers and clerks. Throw in some of Tommy's clients, a few Hells Angels, and mutually insane childhood friends and you have the makings of a great party. Which, believe it or not, no matter how drunk this mixed hunch got, no one ever caused an ounce of trouble.

Vinny and Tommy being the hosts of a party that big meant they spent a lot of time greeting guests and ensuring things ran smoothly. Unfortunately, this dragged Vinny away from Judy more than he would have liked, but she was more than understanding. Every time he turned around, he would find her mingling with his sister and her babies, talking to his friends, or taking time to sit and talk with his mother. She also had her best friend, Kathy, to keep her company. When the bands were playing, you could find the two of them, drink in hand, out on the dance floor. Champagne got up to do a few songs, accompanied by the official pig roast band Bottoms Up. For the third year in a row, she brought the house down.

As for Vinny, he had never been happier in his entire life, and it showed. Everyone wanted to finally meet the woman who had obviously removed him from the single life permanently. Everyone who met Judy concurred that she was a great catch, and made every effort to let his or her feelings known to Vinny how lucky he was to find her. His response was the same every time. "I don't know what I did to get so lucky to find her, but I will do everything in my power to keep her."

Vinny's mother, a very skeptical woman, pulled him aside, not only to give him a two thumbs up of approvals, but also to suggest it might be time to consider settling down again—only this time with the right woman. He told her she'd get no argument from him about Judy. He knew he was totally in love with her as he had never been in love before.

Cops he hadn't seen since his termination told him they were worried how he would be doing in light of all the bad luck he had had the previous three years, but once they saw the look on his face, they could see happiness they hadn't seen for as long as they had known him. One of his ex-partners said he didn't know Vinny was capable of smiling. His comment surprised Vinny, who hadn't realized his misery was so obvious to so many people. He now owed this beautiful woman more than he could ever possibly repay. She had transformed him from a life of loneliness and unhappiness into a new life filled with promise and, more importantly, love. Judy had given him a new reason to live, to love, and to have the best time of his life. And that was exactly what he was going to do.

The weeks and months that followed seemed to fly by. Extreme passion and irresistible chemistry of sexual attraction. The happy couple agreed on everything. Compared with having found a best friend, Vinny was in ecstasy. They had even agreed on religion. She loved the fact that he would give up his Roman Catholic upbringing to become a Lutheran, as she wanted to someday raise their children as Lutherans. She told him it reinforced her love for him. Once again proving to her how much he truly loved her. By agreeing to do something no man she had ever dated before would even consider doing. Vinny never believed two people could be as close as they were. They shared all the same interests, goals, ideas, and dreams. Weekdays, they spent time together preparing gourmet romantic dinners for each other.

Weekends were their escape from the reality of work and the real world into adventures. Vinny would call her up at work on a Friday, tell her to pack a bag for the weekend, and off they would go. It didn't matter to either one of them where they were going or where they would wind up. All that mattered was that they were together. They spent time in Atlantic City, the Jersey Shore, and the Catskill Mountains. The simple fact that they didn't know where they were going only added to the excitement of their adventures.

Labor Day weekend, the mark of the end of the most fantastic summer of Vinny's life, they checked in to the Hilton in Summerset, New Jersey, a little hideaway for a romantic weekend his uncle had told him about. They lingered three days without a care in the world. Surprisingly, Judy just so happened to love horseback riding more than Vinny did. They had found a stable not far from the hotel. At least it wasn't far once they found it. They somehow managed to get lost and almost ended up back in New York. They both laughed when they saw the signs for New York and realized they had been so engulfed in conversations that they didn't realize Vinny had been driving for two hours in the wrong direction! When they finally arrived at the stables and mounted their horses, Vinny paused to take her picture. There was just something overwhelming to him, seeing the most beautiful woman he had ever seen high atop a horse. As she took off like a professional jockey, Vinny tried his best to keep up, but she was much too good. She was determined to show him up. This didn't bother him at all, because as long as his princess was in front of him on a horse, he'd follow her to the ends of the earth no matter how painful it might be.

Back at the hotel, they tore each other's dirty clothes off without missing a beat. The sexual excitement was intense and uncontrollable. Vinny had never made love continuously so much in his life.

Exhausted, they came together again for the seventh time and lay still in each other's arms. They fit perfectly together, either while making love or while holding the other close in each other's arms. As she lay peacefully in his arms, she rolled over and looked into his eyes.

"You make me feel the way I had always dreamed it would be when I met the perfect man for me. The man I would want to spend every waking moment for the rest of my life with. You, Vinny Davis, are that man. I love you as I have never known was possible. I have waited twenty-nine years to find you, and I want to spend the rest of my life with you."

Vinny looked at her as a tear began to roll down his cheek. "Princess," he said, "it has been me who's waited all my life to find you. I don't know what I have done to deserve you. But I promise you this: I will spend the rest of my life cherishing every moment I spend with you for the rest of my life."

As he cradled her in his arms, he thought of how he had always wanted to feel safe and secure with a woman he trusted, someone loyal who wouldn't let him down, again. In exhausted relief, he had surrendered all his fears, all his anxieties, and all his bared emotions to this angel who lay in his arms. He intended to marry her, and nothing was going to stand in his way.

Judy was the youngest of four girls, born in Ridgefield, New Jersey. Her family moved to Upstate New York when she was young. Judy and her sisters were very close, but as they got older, her sisters married and went their separate ways. This left Judy living at home with her father and mother, both of whom she adored. Judy and her mother were especially close, which is often the case with the youngest daughter living in the nest while the elders have left. She had a special bond with her mom that couldn't be broken. That was until her mother was stricken with cancer, which quickly took her life. Her father decided to sell his house, and Judy was forced to make a life on her own.

Unlike her sisters, who had husbands to console them, Judy had no one. Her father helped her get started financially. She bought a co-op in Hastings, New York, and furnished it beautifully. There were times when she had to work two jobs to pay her bills, but working never bothered her. Judy wasn't the type of person to wish for something to happen. She was much too strong for that. If she wanted something, she worked hard for it and got it. That was one of the main reasons Vinny had planned a huge surprise thirtieth birthday party for her. It would be a party she would remember for the rest of her life. The biggest problem would be keeping the party a secret. Vinny recruited the assistance of Judy's sister Jill, who lived with her husband, Tim, and their beautiful daughter, Andrea.

Judy and Vinny had been to their home in South Jersey a few times since they began their romance. Vinny hit it off very well, and he felt quite comfortable with both Jill and Tim. Jill had let Vinny know in their last visit that she had never seen her sister so happy and hoped Vinny would ask her to marry Judy. Jill and Tim also knew of the story that cost Vinny his job but were never judgmental toward him. Judy had explained to them that she didn't want Vinny to win his appeal and get his job back on the force. She felt the job was too dangerous, and she didn't want to spend her nights wondering if Vinny would come home or not. And to be perfectly honest, Vinny no longer felt the slightest desire to return to that life. In fact, his business was doing exceptionally well, and plans were in the making to open up twelve new locations in the New York area over the next year. Jill loved the idea of a surprise party for her sister and was more than willing to help. She helped compose a list consisting of all her friends from her childhood and all her jobs. With a list consisting of approximately sixty people, they should have a really nice party. Vinny also recruited the services of his friend Donny, who was one of the owners of the Breezeway Bar, the place of choice for the party. Donny not only supplied the location but also put together a package for Vinny. It consisted of a full open bar, caterers, and a cake. He also arranged for a DJ, with karaoke, so they could enjoy singing to one another and with their friends. The party was set for Saturday, October 31, a week before her birthday. The RSVPs had been coming in, and it looked as though everyone invited would attend.

This gave Vinny the opportunity to prepare some of his own special dishes. Even though the food was being catered, he could not pass up this opportunity to show off his fine culinary skills to Judy's friends and family. He spent two weeks preparing trays of eggplant rollatini, baked ziti with meatballs, and sausage and peppers. The day of the party arrived as quickly as the summer had past. Jill and Vinny had already had it preplanned. She and Tim would come to work and spend the weekend as guests at Vinny's house.

Little did Vinny know the cat had been let out of the bag almost as soon as the plan had started. Women seem to have a secret code of honor among one another, never to let one another get caught not looking their best, especially as it was a surprise. Judy had no problem with looking beautiful. It came as natural as breathing. Being that she already knew about the party, he left her alone to spend time with her sister. Vinny borrowed Tim to help with the final decorations at Breezeway.

When she walked through the front door, it was obvious that she had been tipped off, but the look of surprise when she saw all the people in attendance was enough to throw her a little. Although there was a storm, the strength of which was equivalent to that of a typhoon, brewing outside, no one seemed to care. Everyone drank, ate, danced, and sang along with the laser karaoke. It was a night filled with memories Judy could cherish for many years to come. They sang songs from the *Grease* soundtrack together. There wasn't a dry eye in the house when he sang "The Wonder of You" by Elvis to the woman he'd grown to adore.

Everyone could see the love in Vinny's eyes as he sang each note.

One of Judy's girlfriends put her arm around him and said to Judy, "He cooks, he sings, he throws you a party for your birthday. What doesn't he do?"

Without hesitation, Judy said, "He does it all." She then put her arms around him and kissed him passionately while pushing her girlfriend away from him.

That was one thing Vinny noticed about her. Although she knew he loved her with all his heart and soul and would never stray from her love, she had a zero tolerance for any woman, friend or not, innocently or not, attempting to move in on her man. It had nothing to do with insecurity; it had to do with showing respect. That made Vinny feel more self-confident than ever before. She had a magical way of making him feel special. He adored her for that. Throughout the evening, the burning question was, When are you going to propose to this woman?

Vinny had decided to wait until Christmas. He wasn't sure whether he would ask her at the Rainbow Room, a very elegant restaurant located in the NBC building at Rockefeller Center overlooking the Christmas tree. She had never gone to see the Christmas tree at Rockefeller Center before, so he thought that would be a romantic way to do it, following the proposal in the restaurant with a horse-and-carriage ride with a bottle of champagne through Central Park. He had all the ingredients for a truly romantic evening. His other thought was to hold off until Valentine's week.

As part of his birthday gift, he had booked the two of them on a trip to Paradise Island in the Bahamas for nine days. That would be another truly romantic alternative. But he knew there was no way he could wait that long to ask her. With the exception of Tommy and his wife, nobody knew Vinny had already purchased the ring she had fallen in love with while they were shopping one day over the summer.

It was slowly burning a hole in Vinny's pocket. The way he felt at this very moment, he could throw himself at the feet of this beautiful woman and beg her to marry him immediately.

CHAPTER 27

It was a week before Christmas, and the day of Vinny's long-awaited proposal to Judy had finally come. He was the happiest man in the world. As he drove to work, it was both raining and snowing. With half his mind concentrating on driving, the other half thought of her.

Before I met her, my life had lost meaning and purpose. Women came and women went. Some lingered long enough to try to drag a commitment out of me, but they weren't right for me. I've always wanted children, but the price of being stuck with the wrong woman isn't worth it. Everything changed when I met Judy. Anything's possible now. God, she's insatiable, incredibly sexy, unbelievably beautiful, and has a sharp mind to go with it—beauty and brains. She's brought out bits of me I never knew existed, a talkative side, a trusting side. We always talk. God, how we talk! I love spending time on long walks or drive with her. There's never a dead space. When we smile, it's spontaneous. We laugh at the same things. We're best friends, too. Yes, that's so important, too. We share our days and nights because we want to. I'm damn lucky. It is almost ten o'clock. Good. I'm not late.

He was parking his car in front of his office on Central Avenue when, suddenly, he found himself surrounded by vehicles skidding to a stop beside his car.

What the fuck?

Men jumped out, guns drawn and pointed at him, and screamed at him not to move.

Holy shit! Mob hit! On me! Fuck! In seconds, they'll have my lifeless body laid out in the middle of Central Avenue for unsuspecting Christmas shoppers to view on their way to the mall.

"FBI! Don't move!" a voice yelled as he rapidly approached, his gun pointed at Vinny's panicked face.

FBI? What the fuck do they want with me?

As the FBI agent yanked him from his car and placed handcuffs on him, he said furiously, "I thought AUSA Gonzalez promised my attorney that if I would be arrested, he'd notify my attorney so he could surrender me to a federal magistrate? What's with the melodramatics and the SWAT team takedown?"

The agent glared at Vinny with prejudiced eyes. "We thought you were working for us. You should have done as you were told and made that trip. Does that answer your question?" the agent asked belligerently.

So that's what this is about. Bastards!

He stood in the middle of Central Avenue in handcuffs, snow and rain falling about them, as the agents took time to critique what an excellent job they had done arresting an unarmed, unresisting, passive suspect. With all the congratulations, high fives, and handshakes, you would have thought they'd just arrested a suspect on their "ten most wanted" list. He couldn't believe the elite FBI were acting like a high school football team that'd just scored the winning touchdown in a championship game.

"Excuse me, gentlemen. Could you maybe put me in a car out of this rain and snow and take me to jail?"

A sympathetic agent placed him in the back seat of an unmarked car, its red light still flashing conspicuously on the dashboard. He politely thanked the agent.

I can't believe how vindictive Gonzalez is. "You should have done as you were told." Huh? Fuck them!

The madness had started about two weeks before Judy's surprise party with a frightening, obtuse telephone call to Vinny at his office. The caller was the agent in charge of the investigation the feds had Vinny working on. "I suggest we meet as soon as possible," he'd said.

"My superiors are most anxious for me to brief you on a trip they want you to take immediately."

"What the hell are you talking about a trip? A trip where? And what do you mean immediately?" Vinny asked furiously.

"I will be at your office in less than an hour," the agent said harshly, "and I suggest you be there!"

Before Vinny could refuse, the line went dead. Within an hour, Special Agent Stone was standing in Vinny's office. He was a handsome young man, well educated, a graduate of Brooklyn Law School who decided to put his law degree to better use working for the feds instead of a prestigious law firm. Vinny had grown to like and admire Agent Stone, who treated him with the respect he thought was well deserved. He was extremely sympathetic toward Vinny, who he knew had gotten a bum rap with regards to the Gerry and Sabol situation. But he had a job to do and was therefore forced to make sure Vinny cooperated fully with the investigation he was placed in charge of. Fortunately for Vinny, Agent Stone knew the risks he was taking and did his best to minimize any potential danger Vinny might face. Until now, Vinny's assignments had consisted of nothing more than reconnaissance missions. Going from one meeting place to another, paying close attention to the potential targets of the investigation, Agent Stone made sure that no matter where Vinny went, backup would not be far behind. Vinny respected and admired him for taking a personal interest in him and his safety. "I want you to know this is not my idea," Agent Stone said sincerely. "The orders came straight from Washington, and my hands are tied."

Vinny looked at Agent Stone agitated and confused and said anxiously, "You've been on the level with me so far, which I appreciate, so just tell me the unvarnished version of what they want me to do!"

Agent Stone gave Vinny a despairing look and explained, "They want you on a plane as soon as possible to a destination that, for security reasons, is irrelevant for you to know at this time. You will spend as much time as necessary gathering information for us, with all expenses paid, compliments of Uncle Sam. While abroad, you will report all necessary intel back to me, here in the—"

Vinny interrupted involuntarily and asked curiously, "You? Here in the States? Who's going to be the agent in charge while I'm abroad?"

Agent Stone looked at Vinny and reluctantly said, "No one. The government you will be dealing with has no diplomatic relationship with the United States. Therefore, none of our agents are permitted in their country in an official capacity."

Vinny sat perfectly still, in shock and amazement, momentarily unable to breathe, let alone speak. For what seemed an endless succession of seconds, Vinny sat thinking of the enormity of what was just sprung up on him. When Vinny spoke, his voice was frightened and barely audible. "It's one thing for me to be a spook for you guys, going to places you can't go, gathering intel, and making introductions, with the hope that one of your agents can gain the confidence of the suspects you are investigating, which would hopefully eliminate me from this operation. But it's an entirely different story to ask me to go God knows where, with no backup from my own government. The entire idea is ludicrous!"

"I understand how you feel," Stone assured him. "I know this puts you in a rather precarious position, but I need an answer. Now!"

Vinny exploded. "I need to check with my family, my lawyer, and my soon-to-be fiancée. Not to mention the president of this company I now work for. How do I explain my picking up out of the blue and disappearing for an unknown amount of time?" Vinny asked furiously.

"We already have a cover story arranged for you if you decide to do it," Stone replied confidently.

"Marvelous!" Vinny said sarcastically. "That leads me to my next question. What if I decide this ludicrous plan is far too dangerous and choose not to go?"

Vinny knew the answer to that question as he sat handcuffed in the back seat of the unmarked car now entering a rear parking garage of the federal building in Newark. He was removed from the back seat of the car and brought to what could only be a very sophisticated booking area. This area far surpassed the booking area of the NYPD with its very expensive equipment.

A fat federal marshal greeted the FBI agents and their prisoner. He had the blackest eyes Vinny had ever seen. "You guys get bored and arrested one of your own?" the marshal asked disingenuously, referring to the fact that Vinny was dressed in a suit and had "law enforcement" written all over him.

"Very good guess," Agent Sable said emphatically, "except he's not a federal agent. He's an ex-NYPD cop."

"What's he charged with?" asked the marshal.

"Obstruction of justice and pissing off Judge Schwartz, which everyone knows is as serious as murder!" replied Agent Sable sarcastically.

"My name is Big Bob," the marshal said, extending his hand to shake Vinny's, which he accepted as he introduced himself. "Listen, Vinny," he said courteously. "I can tell by the look on your face that you're scared and confused. So let me put your mind at ease. I am going to do the booking procedures that you have probably done a hundred times yourself. When I'm finished, I'll put you in a holding cell, alone, until they call you before the magistrate for your bail hearing. Does your lawyer and your family know that you are here, and will you need bail money?" Big Bob asked sympathetically.

Vinny answered, "Yes," in a low, barely audible voice.

"Good," Big Bob said enthusiastically. "Then you will be out of here before you know it, and I don't have to worry about finding you safe accommodations in the Union County Jail overnight."

Vinny was happy that he had found a friend who didn't think of him as a common criminal. But what Vinny couldn't understand was the concept of bail. Would a magistrate place bail on a misdemeanor obstruction charge? And if so, how much? Would his father bring enough? Vinny's mind began to race with a million thoughts. He looked at his new friend, Big Bob, who had amusement in his eyes and a self-satisfied smile on his face. Yet Vinny knew enough not to ask any foolish questions. It would only slow the booking process, and that could possibly cause a delay in seeing the magistrate. Vinny was hypnotic throughout the entire arrest process. Big Bob performed his job systematically, professionally, as he had obviously done on thousands of previous occasions.

When they were finished, Vinny sat commiserating, hoping he would not have to be placed in a holding cell.

But as luck would have it, when dealing with a bureaucratic system, Big Bob was forced to place Vinny in a cell. "If it were up to me," Big Bob said sadly, "I'd let you sit and wait with me, but I have no choice in the matter."

Vinny smiled at his compassionate, new friend, who, if it were up to him, would have let Vinny keep his dignity, and said appreciatively, "I understand it's your job. Thank you for your help."

"You'll be okay," he said as he locked the cell door.

Inside the holding cell, Vinny paced rapidly back and forth, trembling from fear and anticipation, sweat rolling down his face. His eyes wide open, darting in different directions at nothing, betraying his obvious panic. He thought of the enormity of what was happening to him. He could not contemplate that one drunken, foolish indiscretion could put him behind bars. He could not understand the vindictiveness of AUSA Gonzalez to arrest him a week before Christmas in front of his place of business. It was incomprehensible. Vinny was filled with frustration and began acting strangely, like a caged young animal becoming increasingly annoyed by his confinement. He was acutely cognizant of where he was, of how he had gotten there, of the stupid, self-destructive acts of a drunken fool. And what he would now feel for the rest of his life: shame, humiliation, and regret. There had been times in the past that Vinny had felt that God almighty was testing him to the edge of his endurance, to see if he would put a bullet in his head to remove his pain. At this very moment, he wished he had a gun. The lonely hours that passed by seemed like days as Vinny patiently waited to hear his name called to see the magistrate.

When his name was called, it was not a minute to soon, for he felt he would soon lose his mind.

Shackled by his hands and feet, he was escorted by federal marshals through the rear door of a huge courtroom, where he saw Tommy standing anxiously at the defense table. In the first row was the pain-stricken face of his parents and sister. It was extremely obvious by the look on his parents' faces that they were appalled at seeing their son shackled and chained like some mass murderer. Vinny gave a confident nod to his family and was embraced by Tommy, who assured him everything would be all right. Vinny stood proudly next to Tommy at the defense table. He felt a heavy sadness come over him for putting his family through this. Vinny looked over at the prosecution table and watched as AUSA Gonzalez sat frozen in his chair, with the look of a mature, savvy, and experienced prosecutor. Not the look of a spiteful, manipulative, vindictive son of a bitch, which was surely a man Vinny now deeply hated.

"All rise," said a court clerk as the magistrate entered the courtroom. He was a tall man in his late forties, with a dignified look about him and a kind, earnest face. His eyes were pale blue, soft and compassionate. It was at that moment, as Vinny looked into his eyes, that he knew they were not dealing with the infamous Judge Schwartz, who would presumably preside over Vinny's eventual trial.

Gonzalez spoke in a soft monotone as he made his appearance for the record and proceeded with the reading of the charges. When the magistrate asked for his position on bail, Gonzalez responded by asking for $100,000, as though asking for chump change. Suddenly, furiously, Vinny whipped around in his seat toward his family, his eyes glaring, focused, and filled with horror.

Tommy responded to the bail request as a professional, an admixture of ignorance, innocence, and concern. As Tommy addressed the court, Vinny sat frozen in his chair, his face pale. His lips were parted slightly in breathless expectation. His eyes were glazed, and his heart was hammering so loud he knew his family could hear it. He wasn't conscious his right hand was clenched in a fist, a sure sign of his burning rage. Vinny knew Gonzalez wanted nothing more than to see him spend Christmas behind bars. Sure as shit, the magistrate set bail at $100,000.

Gonzalez got what he wanted.

But Tommy surprised him when he informed the court, "The $100,000 is available, and my client is prepared to make bail immediately."

That brought an immediate sigh of relief to Vinny, who had unknowingly forgotten to breathe. It also aroused an agitated and impatient look on the face of Gonzalez. Vinny looked at Tommy with admiration and said softly, "Thank you."

"You will be out of here within the hour," he replied.

Vinny looked back toward his parents again. His mother could barely hold back the tears that were quickly filling her swollen red eyes. "I love you," he whispered as the marshals escorted him back through the rear door of the courtroom to his cell, where he would wait patiently to be released from his living hell.

Within forty minutes, Vinny was released into the loving arms of his family. Vinny's father could not control his outrage as he vociferously let his feelings be known, as he exited with his son out of the courthouse.

As Vinny and his family stepped outside the courthouse into the cool December air, he stopped momentarily to take a few deep breaths of freedom. He was angry at himself for being afraid, even though the source of the fear was understandable. It was so unfair, so bitterly unjust, that he and his family should be humiliated this way.

Vinny became even more outraged at his inability to get any serious consideration from those hell-bent on destroying his life. Determined not to be ruled by fear, Vinny, his hands shaking, his brow damp with perspiration, turned to Tommy and said exuberantly, "No deals."

"I hear you," Tommy agreed. It was inconceivable he'd think Vinny would lose his nerve over anything at all, not even over something as bizarre and frightening as what was happening to him now. How could he lose nerve when all he had ever been was nerve, 185 pounds of solid nerve?

Vinny hugged his mother in a loving embrace, kissed his sister, and thanked his father before getting into Tommy's car. They had plenty to discuss on the trip home, although Vinny wasn't sure he was up to it.

"Did anyone call Judy?" Vinny asked.

"Champagne spoke to her earlier," Tommy said. "Champagne told her she'd call her back as soon as we'd sprung you."

"How did she take it?" Vinny asked.

"Champagne said she was pretty upset the first time she spoke to her, but when she called back to let her know you were free, she was really happy. She said to tell you she loves you and she'll be waiting at your house."

"Thanks a million, TC," Vinny said appreciatively. "I don't know what I would have done without your help."

"Don't worry about it," Tommy said sharply, handing Vinny his cell phone. "Just call her now and let her know we are on our way home."

Vinny dialed her office. When she answered, her voice calmed him. "Hi, baby, it's me," Vinny said proudly.

"Oh my God! I can't believe what those mangy bastards did to you! Are you all right?" she asked worriedly, on the verge of tears. Vinny needed every bit of his diplomacy and persuasiveness to convince her that he was all right.

"Listen, baby," Vinny said wearily. "We are on our way and should be home within the hour."

"I can't wait to see you," she said lovingly.

"I can't either, baby. I'll see you soon." Vinny handed the phone back to Tommy and said, "If I lose this girl, I'll surely die. Losing her would be worse than going to prison."

"You are not going to lose her. She loves you far too much. As for going to prison, I doubt that will ever happen even though we are dealing with lunatics." Tommy's tenacity and confidence brought an immediate smile to Vinny's stress ridden face. As Tommy pulled up to the front of Vinny's house, he noticed Judy's Acura Legend in his driveway.

"Well, I see Judy's arrived already, so I will leave you two to comfort each other," Tommy said mischievously.

"Are you sure you don't want to come in for a drink?"

"No, Vinny, that's okay. If I went through what you went through today, the only place I would want to be is anywhere alone with my wife. So just go and be with Judy and we'll talk tomorrow."

Vinny took his friend in a bear-hug embrace and thanked him again. "It'll be all right. Now go be with Judy."

Vinny watched Tommy drive away as he walked up the stairs to his door. Judy opened it immediately and threw herself into Vinny's awaiting embrace.

They held each other tightly, neither one wanting to let go of the other.

"I love you so much!" Judy exclaimed as tears rolled down her face.

Vinny kissed her over and over. All over her beautiful face. While he declared his never-ending love to her, they went inside the house. Judy got two glasses of wine, while Vinny observed her hands were trembling.

"Sit down, baby," Vinny said, removing the glasses of wine from her hands. They sat down together, staring into each other's eyes, basking in each other's affection.

"So what happens now? Do they have a case after all this time has gone by?"

Vinny laughed derisively. "What the hell do I know?" Vinny said. "We'll most likely go to trial."

Judy looked faintly amused. "You can't lose, can you?"

"I'm innocent! They don't put people in prison for lying unless it's under oath!"

She recoiled slightly at the vehemence in his voice.

"I'm sorry, baby," Vinny said as he took her in his arms. "I didn't mean to snap at you. It's just that I feel so goddamn helpless."

She kissed him and said, "Why don't you go upstairs and lie down? I'll be up in a little while to give you a massage." She drew the tension from him.

"Sounds great to me."

Feeling dirty and wanting to wash, he went up to the bathroom. The mirror confirmed his suspicions that he looked worse than he felt. He could hardly believe the grimy, bloodshot-eyed, depression-lined face reflecting back at him was his. He washed his face, but it didn't make him look any better or less distraught. He walked into his bedroom and, without turning on the light, stripped. He then lay in bed and thought about Judy. She was the absolute best, everything he'd ever wanted. He couldn't imagine being with anyone else.

She opened the door of the darkened bedroom. He was fast asleep, his body inviting. As she studied him, she thought of how this charming, kind, and handsome man, with his unbelievable bedroom performance, had stolen her heart. He was a man she'd never known existed. He was undeniably special. She'd been drawn to him as she had never been drawn to another. Suddenly, she heard and felt her own breathing. She touched her swollen nipples and was aware of the aching urgency between her legs. She walked to the foot of the bed and undressed.

"Vinny," she said gently, "wake up, baby."

He opened his eyes.

"I'm here for you, baby," she said quietly. She had never wanted him with such ravenous desire. "I'll never let you go!" she cried as she mounted him.

Later, after they collapsed into each other's arms, he looked into the beautiful, little-girl's eyes of this very special woman. Suddenly, they turned distant and sad. A slight smile creased her lips. Vinny didn't hazard to ask any questions, content to have his loving woman in his arms.

He fell asleep. She lay awake, deep in thought. *It's so terrible, so unnecessary, so painful. He dares not acknowledge it, yet by denying it, it increases his anguish. Debbie, his inconsequential ex-wife, who filled his life with treachery and deceit, is where this all began.* She fantasized an existence with him filled with love and happiness, wishing it were all so simple, so unencumbered. But it wasn't. She loved him, loved his mind, his body, even his suffering, for she understood him so completely.

CHAPTER 28

T hey entered to the sounds of soft music playing in the ballroom as they checked their coats. Judy was dressed to kill.
She was wearing a black evening dress tapered tight at the
waist and sleeveless, with three-inch black heels that had her almost
towering over Vinny. She was carrying a small black-sequined bag in
one hand, her other holding Vinny's. Her long black hair was shim-
mering from the lights of the glittering chandeliers in the ballroom.
Tonight they would celebrate New Year's Eve at Harbor House in
New Rochelle, overlooking Long Island Sound.

Although Christmas had been destroyed by the devastation of
the arrest, thereby postponing Vinny's proposal plans until after the
trial, Vinny would not put Judy in the peculiar, helpless position of
asking her to marry him before the outcome of the trial. He loved her
far too much to ask her to wait for him if he found himself convicted
and sentenced to serious prison time. But tonight they decided to
put all the misery behind them and bring in the New Year in style.

As they mingled through the cocktail hour, which was already
underway, Vinny couldn't help but notice the number of heads, male
and female, that turned to look. Judy was far beyond beautiful most
of the time, but tonight she was the ultimate of gorgeousness. She
could stop a speeding train. Vinny was all smiles as they approached
a group of people who were seated at their assigned table. After the
cordial introductions were made, the group was all smiles. What
Judy didn't realize was that they were all smiling at her.

Vinny glanced over at the dance floor. "Would you like to
dance?"

"I thought you would never ask!"

Vinny and Judy could cut up a rug. When the two of them had gone away for Labor Day weekend, Judy had found out firsthand that not only could her new love dance extremely well, but he could also lead, which was something she had never experienced with other men she had dated.

The two of them danced, drank, ate, and sang songs throughout the night as if tomorrow were the end of the world.

When the ball dropped, they held each other in a loving embrace and kissed passionately in the middle of the dance floor as if they were the only two people in the room. Judy grabbed two glasses of champagne from a passing waiter. Handing one to Vinny, she began a toast. "To 1998!" she exclaimed. "The year I marry the man of my dreams."

Vinny found himself full of love and benevolence as he grabbed Judy in his arms and exclaimed loud enough for all to hear, "I love you!" This brought a small round of applause from the people who were close enough to observe him kiss her passionately on the lips.

In the midst of all the excitement and fanfare, Judy noticed a crowd gathering at the opposite end of the dance floor. Her curiosity brought her there to see what was going on. Vinny had gone off to get them some drinks and had returned to their table. Judy returned to the table with a look of despair on her face.

"What's the matter?"

"Some woman had a heart attack over there." She pointed to where the crowd had gathered.

Vinny stood up calmly, grabbed Judy by the hand, and unobtrusively walked over to the scene of the commotion. Pushing his way through the crowd, Vinny came upon the scene of a man doing a terrible rendition of a CPR. Knowing CPR done improperly could kill someone, Vinny immediately got down on his knees to take charge.

"Sir, stop CPR," Vinny demanded.

The man, in his sixties, stopped what he was doing and looked at Vinny with fear in his eyes. "Help me," he said despairingly. "This is my wife. Please don't let her die."

Vinny immediately thought of the night his mother had died and the vow he had made never to stand helplessly by while someone died. "I won't let her die," Vinny said confidently. "Just let me do my job." He began assessing the victim. He took her pulse; it was weak, but there. He then checked her airway. The victim's dentures obstructed it. He put his fingers in her mouth and removed them, then tilted her head back, placed his mouth over hers, pinched her nose close, and administered three short, quick breaths. Judy and the entire crowd stood watching Vinny in complete silence and heard the woman gasp for air. She was now breathing on her own, and her pulse became stronger.

As Vinny knelt by his victim's side, holding her hand while checking her pulse, he was relieved to see the color return to her face.

A man in a tuxedo came rushing through the crowd and said hysterically, "I called an ambulance!"

"Good," Vinny said calmly. "Now, go back to the phone and tell them an off-duty New York City cop is performing CPR and needs assistance. A call to the Brother of Fellow Law Enforcement will get a faster response."

The man in the tux gave Vinny a quizzical look. "Just do it!" he commanded.

The man in the tux took off through the crowd like someone had shot a rocket up his ass.

As Vinny knelt next to the woman, who was still unconscious but doing fine, he looked into the eyes of the husband, who knelt next to his wife, holding her hand.

"Thank you," he said with tears in his eyes. "I'm a doctor, and I just panicked. My God, thank you for saving my wife's life," he repeated joyously.

"It's okay," Vinny said as if it were nothing. "She's going to be fine."

Within moments, the paramedics arrived and Vinny explained what had happened. His job was done.

As he rose to his feet, he caught Judy's admiring look. She grabbed him in a loving embrace. "I am so proud of you!"

He kissed her lips. "I love you."

"I love you too! Now, let's get a drink. I think you could use one."

"You are absolutely right," Vinny said as he placed an arm around his future bride, motioning her away from the crowd toward the bar. At the bar they stood in momentary silence, taking in the events of a near tragedy that just transpired.

"If only they knew the real you."

"Who?"

"Gonzalez, Judge Schwartz, the people who will be on your jury," she explained. "If they only knew the soft, gentle, compassionate, and loving person you are, they would never do what they are doing to you."

"All those qualities you just mentioned are qualities neither AUSA Gonzalez nor the Honorable Judge Schwartz possess. As for the jury ever hearing about any of my good qualities, I will bet you dollars to doughnuts Gonzalez and Schwartz will make sure they don't."

"That's not fair!"

"I know, baby, it's not. But it's the law. The prosecution will not make my case a character case. By their choosing not to, Tommy will not be able to bring out any of my acts of heroism or the thirty-plus commendations I received for bravery. It's like all the good I have done my entire life doesn't exist—unless the prosecution brings it up. They'll be selling ice water in the Arctic before Gonzalez does that," Vinny said jokingly, trying to make light of an awkward situation.

Tears began to form in her eyes. "They won't take you away from me, will they?"

Vinny held her close in his arms and said confidently, "It will be an even colder day in hell when that happens." The confidence in his voice brought an immediate radiant smile to hers. He kissed her as the band resumed. "Let's dance."

"After you." He led her to the dance floor.

Three weeks had passed since that wonderful night, as Tommy and Vinny schlepped their way through the traffic nightmare known as the New Jersey Turnpike, en route to the federal courthouse in Newark for Vinny's arraignment. Vinny couldn't help but think Judy was right—it was just not fair. But then again, life isn't fair: it's hard and often even cruel.

Sometimes Vinny could not remember why he ever became a cop. Looking back, it seemed more an act of madness than a career choice. Perhaps there is such a thing as destiny, a power that drove people through life, or act of fate that forces one to choose a profession.

Since that tragic night in July 1972, when Vinny's mother died, he had become independent-minded, wise beyond his years, finding himself unable to be a child. Vinny was forced to grow up that night. From that night on, he was an adult in a child's body. He had an atypical personality, with certain character traits he saw as strengths but others saw as attitude problems. As he matured, he became tough, yet he had an air about him of a man who had known great loss and was capable of enormous compassion. The type of compassion, reason, and understanding he hoped would inevitably prevail in the bodies and souls of the jurors selected for his trial. Certainly, the jury would see him as a human being capable of making a mistake, absence of malice. While he was drunk and going through a depressive state of mind, that could only be diagnosed as clinical depression. Hopefully, the jury would also see Gonzalez for what he was, an overzealous prosecutor who was congenitally incapable of compassion.

As Vinny and Tommy entered the courtroom, Vinny took a moment to look around and observe the surroundings, which was, he thought, far more intimidating than he remembered. It was so strange to think of himself coming to a house of justice as a defendant.

AUSA Gonzalez greeted Tommy with a menacing smile and a limp handshake. Vinny gave his adversary a hard stare.

Gonzalez wore a gray Brooks Brothers suit, crisp white shirt, and an unattractive-print tie—standard dress for federal employees.

While Tommy and Gonzalez were engaged in conversation, he removed his three-quarter-length black leather overcoat and placed it on the rail behind the defense table. He looked like he'd stepped off the cover of *GQ* magazine, impeccably dressed in a black Armani suit, white silk shirt, with a colorful silk tie and matching hankie. He was extremely handsome but looked like a mobster. As Tommy had explained to him on the drive to court, "You can never dress like this again for court. The jury will convict you on your looks alone!"

Tommy gazed over at his friend sitting alone at the defense table. Vinny's face bore an expression of deep melancholy, a resigned melancholy, not the bitter, rebellious look most cops wear today. It was obvious, at some point of his life, he'd suffered some inexpressible agony.

"All rise!" the court clerk announced as the Honorable Judge Alfred Schwartz entered.

The long-awaited meeting with the infamous Schwartz had arrived. He was a stocky man in his early fifties, with a really bad hairpiece, deep-set, evil black eyes, a pale complexion, and a cynical smile.

"Appearances for the record!" he barked before he was seated, anxious to get started.

"Juan Gonzalez, on behalf of the government. Good morning, Your Honor." He was kissing ass already.

"Tommy Cascione, on behalf of the defendant, Vincent Davis. Good morning as well, Your Honor." Tommy tried to sound as congenial as his foe.

"Let's hear your plea," Schwartz said impatiently.

"My client pleads not guilty, Your Honor," Tommy said, full of confidence.

"Fine. Let me hear motions for the court," Schwartz ordered with an air of arrogance.

Gonzalez then handed Tommy two boxes filled with approximately forty audio tapes and four folders of transcripts.

Tommy looked at Gonzalez quizzically as he responded to Schwartz's question. "Your Honor, as you can see, I have just received the necessary Brady material and respectfully ask for time to carefully review the evidence before I prepare any motions for the court's review."

Schwartz looked faintly irritated as he replied, "Maybe you didn't hear me. Do you have any motions to put before this court?"

Vinny sensed it was going to be a bad day the moment he'd awakened. Schwartz's attitude just confirmed it. Tommy, who always projected himself as supremely competent and cocksure, with a life-of-the-party, nothing-can-touch-me persona, was now at a loss before this judge, who was evil incarnate.

Having pondered the imponderables, Tommy decided to shoot from the hip. "Your Honor," he said in a commanding voice, "I move that the charges against my client be dropped on the grounds that they violate my client's First Amendment right to free speech."

As Schwartz heard this, whatever patience he had disappeared. "Let me see if I have this straight," Schwartz said contemptuously. "Your client was a police officer, a sworn public servant, who tipped off organized crime that they had an informant in their ranks. This, you're telling me, is constitutional?" It was obviously a rhetorical question that need not be answered. "Put it in a brief, Counselor. It should make for some interesting reading! Are there any other motions, Mr. Cascione?"

"No, Your Honor," Tommy replied disgustedly.

"Mr. Gonzalez, are you all right with the bail set at $100,000?" Schwartz asked disingenuously, that cynical smile beaming brightly.

Vinny looked stone-faced at Gonzalez. He knew if Gonzalez wanted a higher bail, the good judge would gladly oblige him.

"Yes, Your Honor," Gonzalez said half-heartedly. "The bail set is acceptable to the government."

Vinny began to breathe again, something he momentarily forgot to do.

"I want a speedy trial on this case," Schwartz said, obviously annoyed that Gonzalez would not ask for a higher bail, affording him the opportunity to jail Vinny immediately.

"Next month, February 18?" he asked innocently.

Gonzalez responded, "That's fine with me, Your Honor."

Tommy removed his black appointment book from his jacket pocket, but before he could scan it, Schwartz, with a face of exasperation, asked, "Is that date okay with the defense?"

Astonished by such a short trial date, Tommy looked up, and Schwartz took that as a yes.

"Fine," Schwartz said excitedly. "The trial date is set. Counselors, have your briefs ready and submitted to me by February 1. We are adjourned."

Vinny sat in shocked amazement. Tommy would only have but five weeks to prepare for a trial Gonzalez had been preparing for four years.

Outside the courtroom, Gonzalez asked Tommy flippantly, "Are you really going to take this to trial?"

Tommy looked faintly amused when he asked, "You want me to take a blind plea for my client before that madman?"

Gonzalez responded stubbornly, "Vinny broke the law and you know it. I can convince the judge that a three-year sentence will satisfy the government."

Vinny lost his patience and exploded. "Three years? Are you insane? I may have unknowingly and unintentionally broke the law, but three years? This isn't about justice, is it, Jose?" Vinny asked belligerently, not expecting an answer. "This is about vengeance. I messed up your investigation by accident, and when I wouldn't take a trip overseas to get my head blown off, you decided to have that psychopath in there do it for you!"

Gonzalez became agitated, but before he could speak, Tommy cut him off. "You heard my client. I'll see you in court." Tommy briskly removed Vinny from what could become a hostile situation. Knowing Vinny as well as he did, he knew it was a wise decision.

After the adrenaline had dissipated, Vinny sat in the passenger's seat of Tommy's Town Car, staring uncomprehendingly at the indictment, thinking of the inexplicable events of the day. The entire situation was too hilarious to contemplate. Yet he felt in greater danger than ever before in his life, infinitely more vulnerable than he had been when shots were being fired around him on the streets of the South Bronx.

Tommy looked over at his friend, shaking his head incredulously. He threw up his hands in exasperation. "This is the twilight zone!" Tommy said disgustedly. "But then again, that's what this country's coming to. This country no longer just lets the lunatics run around free, they actually put them in charge."

As Tommy continued to vent his frustration about the federal justice system run amuck, Vinny sat silently, troubled by fear, anger, frustration, and desperation so intense it made him nauseous. Despite all the human tragedies in which his job brought him into contact, Vinny continued to believe in the decency of men. It would sustain him through this trial.

CHAPTER 29

With Vinny's thirty-sixth birthday and trial rapidly approaching, the hunt was on to find Debbie, Vinny's ex-wife, who was to be subpoenaed to testify for the government. She had mysteriously disappeared off the face of the planet, as soon as word had spread of her having to appear to testify at the trial.

Tommy had read her grand jury testimony and was extremely interested in speaking to her prior to the trial. When Tommy read her testimony, for some unknown reason, he became suspicious. With Gonzalez issuing a subpoena for her to testify for the prosecution, Tommy's suspicions were raised to an alarmingly heightened awareness. Tommy knew something was amiss, and he needed to find out what it was. There could not be any surprises from her at this trial, for the results could be disastrous.

Over the years, Vinny came to understand his ex-wife in terms of her obsessive-compulsive personality—the emotional wreck she had turned into toward the end of their marriage. Yet she was a woman he still cared deeply about and was there to protect her in her most desperate hours of need. Before he'd been separated, he'd been a happy man, with seldom a worry, always the optimist. More than two years later, he still had difficulty believing she was gone. Scotch became his only indulgence. Well, scotch and a lot of self-pity were his ways of dealing with the loneliness that was destroying him faster than bullets from a perp's gun could have done. But all that changed when he met Judy. As crazy as the last four years had been, he needed a stabilizing influence. Vinny would enjoy being married again. It would give him security and balance in his life, for once. He certainly hadn't found it with Debbie. Thank God he found Judy. He felt secure in their mutual love and trust. She gave him more strength and support than he'd ever thought possible. He loved her for it.

Vinny was tired, and as he drove to Judy's apartment for a relaxing evening, his beeper went off. Checking the number, he recognized it as the Breezeway Bar's. He was close by and so decided to stop in rather than call. He figured it was Champagne calling to ask him to join her for a drink or to provide an update on the desperate search for Debbie, which was concentrated on every drug location in Yonkers and the Bronx.

Vinny entered the crowded, dimly lit, smoke-filled bar. Thursday nights were always a busy night in the Breezeway. The laser karaoke DJ and drink specials always drew a large crowd of locals.

As Vinny walked around, his eyes scanning for Champagne, numerous well-wishers greeted him. Everyone in Yonkers knew about his upcoming trial. He took a seat at the bar and was immediately approached by Donny, who asked anxiously, "Did you get my beep?"

"That was you? I thought it might be Champagne inviting me for a drink or a Debbie update."

"That's why I beeped you," Donny said, full of confidence. "Debbie's here! Full of piss and vinegar, bombed out of her mind, ranting and raving about having to testify in court." Vinny followed Donny's eyes as he spoke, to where Debbie was sitting.

"Thanks a million for calling me," Vinny said earnestly. "Can I borrow your phone?"

"Sure," Donny said, handing Vinny the cordless phone from behind the bar.

Vinny quickly dialed Tommy's answering service and left an urgent message. "Debbie is at the breezeway! I'm here now, come or call quickly!"

Vinny handed the phone back to Donny, thanking him once again. Vinny knew Tommy was at a meeting with the New York Shields, a police organization of cops for cops rallying support for Vinny's trial. Tommy should either call or stop by shortly after getting the message.

While Vinny waited, he sat vacillating whether or not he should talk to Debbie without his attorney present. He knew he was in enough trouble without Debbie telling tall tales to Gonzalez that he tampered with her. Vinny decided it would be more prudent to wait at the bar for Tommy to arrive. He couldn't chance talking to Debbie. She was too unstable.

As he sat sipping a glass of wine, watching Debbie as surreptitiously as possible, he thought about how quickly she'd deteriorate, in spite of all his and her family's efforts to help her. Shortly after their separation, she'd moved back home to live with her parents and Danielle, her youngest sister, who was still at college, studying to be a dentist. Debbie had told her family terrible lies about their marriage filled with mental and physical abuse, a story his father-in-law believed only half-heartedly. Still, in an Italian family, blood was thicker than water. The allegations turned her family against Vinny, causing him great anguish, for he loved her family as though it were his own. Despite all the lies, Vinny remained silent about her alcohol and drug abuse. He figured, since his marriage was over, there was no need to tarnish her name to her family. He knew eventually the truth would reveal itself to them.

Within four months of their separation, Vinny received a frantic phone call from his ex-father-in-law at three in the morning. "Would you please come to our house?" he asked desperately. "We need your help."

Without a moment's hesitation, Vinny dressed and sped off to his ex in-laws' home. He greeted Vinny at the front door, apologizing profusely for doubting him.

"What happened?"

He explained how Debbie had been acting strangely, drinking too much and experiencing terrible mood swings.

Welcome to the club.

"Apparently, Danielle had known, or had strong suspicions, that Debbie was involved in drugs. When she came home tonight, she was extremely loud and became so aggravated to find no wine in the house she began yelling, waking us all up. 'Where's the goddamn wine?' she screamed. While my wife tried to talk to her to calm her down, Danielle grabbed her pocketbook and dumped the contents on the kitchen table. A baggie of white powder fell out, and Debbie went berserk. In a fit of rage, she threw my wife into the china closet and began to beat her sister. I grabbed her, but she had superhuman strength and continued to hit her sister. I had no choice but to hit her," he said defensively, on the verge of tears. He looked at Vinny as tears filled his eyes.

"I had no idea what you were going through. I'm so sorry," Vinny said somberly. "It's all right," he added as he embraced his father-in-law, a man he admired and respected. Vinny spent the night cradling Debbie in his arms like a small child.

In the morning, he was on the phone with the police department's Employee Assistance Program. By early afternoon, Vinny and Debbie's family left her at an upstate drug rehabilitation center arranged for by the TAPD for thirty days. A strict program that would help her with her addiction, but only if she desired. Within three weeks, she had checked herself out of the one-thousand-dollar-a-day program, proclaiming she was cured. It was a tab Vinny would be pleased to pick up if the treatment had worked.

Within a month, the phone began ringing off the wall at all hours of the night. He would find himself at a bar, retrieving her and her car after she had been involved in some type of physical altercation where the police had been called. Or at a police station, using his professional courtesy, from one cop to another, to spring her from jail without charges being filed.

This went on for a little over a year before Debbie hit rock bottom and decided she needed help. Vinny turned to his close friend Frankie Shoes, who worked for the Catholic Archdiocese, and arranged for her to spend three months in Upstate New York at a halfway house, where she could regain control of her life, free from alcohol and drug abuse. Through Frankie's help, Vinny learned that Debbie had done extremely well, gotten a job, and continued to go to meetings at Daytop. At last, the frantic late-night phone calls had ceased.

Vinny must have lost track of time and place, as he sat deep in a hypnotic state, dwelling on the past. Before he realized where he was, Debbie had managed to nestle up next to him at the bar. "Hi, Vinny," she said grimly.

"Where the hell have you been?" Vinny asked accusingly.

"I don't answer to you," she replied heatedly.

"I'm sorry," Vinny said courteously, not wanting her to start a scene. "It's just that the FBI has been questioning everyone I know as to your whereabouts, as though I have been hiding you or something."

"I've been hiding," she said nonchalantly. "I don't want to testify at this trial."

"Why hide? You haven't done anything wrong. If anything, you're a victim of Sabol's. All you have to do is tell the truth about all his threats and how evil he is. No jury in the world will convict me for trying to protect you from that animal who hasn't left you alone in thirteen years."

Tears started rolling down her face, and she was trembling. He took her in his arms and, in a soft monotone, said reassuringly, "You don't have to worry about a thing. It'll be all right."

"No, it won't," she said despairingly. "I have something to tell you that will surely make you hate me. I had hoped I would never have to tell you. I wanted to spare you the pain and humiliation, because you have always been so good to me, but now my past has come back to haunt me."

Vinny's face was quizzical, because he had no idea what she was talking about. He thought it had to do with something she had done during their separation, while she was in an inebriated state. "The past is the past. You don't need to explain," Vinny said, as cavalier as ever.

Debbie looked at him as though outraged by his unconcern. However, it wasn't that at all. He was merely trying to spare himself from being hurt any more than he already was.

"I had an affair!" she exclaimed, loud enough to be heard over the music in the bar.

He was momentarily thrown back by her outburst and was speechless. He wasn't sure if he should ask any further questions, for fear of what her answer might be. "With whom?" he managed to ask suspiciously.

When she spoke the name Richard Sabol, Vinny thought he would explode.

"When? How long? Why?" he asked repetitiously, without waiting for an answer.

"Since the first time he got out of prison. Before we were married," she said in a terrified monotone.

Confronted with the knowledge that his entire relationship, and marriage, was nothing but a sham, he became disgusted, nauseous, and speechless. To think the woman he once loved was sleeping with an evil monster throughout their entire marriage was incomprehensible. He was the evil Vinny thought he'd been protecting her from for all those years, the evil ultimately responsible for costing him his job and might possibly land him in prison. Vinny suddenly nearly exploded with a rage so intense that he could barely contain it. It was like nothing he had ever felt. He wanted to scream at the top of his lungs until his throat ached, but he knew if he was to utter another word, he'd surely lose control and hit her.

Vinny loathed her, no longer able to comfort her as she stood frantically crying, trying to apologize.

Tommy entered the bar not a moment too soon. Seeing the look on Vinny's face, he knew it could turn ugly at any second. "Greetings and salutations, Vinny, Debbie," TC said in an exuberant voice. "Debbie, come with me. We need to talk," Tommy said without giving Vinny a chance to speak.

As Tommy ushered Debbie away, Vinny became sick with apprehension and furious for being made such a fool. They sat down two tables away from him.

What did I ever see in the woman? Look at her, withered and debilitated by her greedy appetites and self-indulgence in booze, cocaine, and sex with that fucking beast Sabol.

Disgusted, he stood up and walked away, leaving Tommy to continue his questioning. But he dared not stray too far. Tommy might need his help depending on how obstreperous Debbie might become. He knew from experience how incredibly vicious she could become if she didn't get her way.

"I still love you!" she screamed. "Do you hear me?"

"I hear you," Vinny said, trying to placate her.

"We still have a chance!" she insisted stubbornly. She glared at Vinny, now beside her, and saw a matching anger in his face and eyes. His teeth were clenched so tight his jaw muscles bulged and a vein protruded by his temple.

"Wait for me outside!" Tommy demanded, knowing full well his friend was about to lose it. Vinny stood stone-faced. "Now!"

Vinny retreated into the parking lot, thankful for his friend's presence of mind to make him leave before he exploded.

Within five minutes, Debbie stormed out of the bar, screaming vociferously at Tommy, who stopped and stood in the doorway.

TC greeted Vinny as he re-entered the bar. They both sat silently for a moment, somber. Despair crept back into Vinny's thoughts.

Tommy began to speak in a soft but authoritative voice. "I'm sorry, Vinny, but at least we found out the truth now instead of in court. If we found this information out in court, it would have been disastrous to us. Besides…" Tommy's voice now changing to enthusiasm. "You now have Judy in your life. We both know how lucky you are to have a girl who loves you as much as she does. She adores you!" Tommy proclaimed. "You'll never again have to worry about being lied to. Judy doesn't have a disingenuous bone in her body. Soon, this whole mess will be over and the two of you can get married and live the life most people can only dream about."

"You're absolutely right. To hell with Debbie and her lying, deceitful ways and her adulterous past. I am the luckiest man in the world to have found Judy. Now, all you have to do, my friend, is keep me out of prison," Vinny said sarcastically, a cynical smile on his face.

"Don't worry. I'm supposed to be the best man at the wedding. We can't have a wedding without a groom, now, can we?" he asked playfully, holding up his glass to a toast position.

Vinny raised his glass and tapped Tommy's gently. "To victory!"

"To victory and the happy couple. May you two be as happy for the rest of your lives as you have been up to now."

"Thanks, Tommy."

"Don't mention it. Now go to Judy, where you belong. We'll talk tomorrow."

Vinny got into his car and drove as fast as he could to her apartment. Using his key, he unlocked the door and let himself in so as not to awaken her. He undressed in the darkened bedroom and slipped naked under the sheets next to her. She always slept naked too. The feel of her body close to his brought out immediate passion within him.

"I love you," he whispered in her ear as he held her close in his arms in a warm embrace.

"And I love you," she replied, holding him tight, a captive to her strong desire.

"I never want to leave this bed," Vinny said happily. "We're together now, and we will be forever."

Taking her face in his hands, he kissed her slowly and passionately. To his delight, she responded immediately. They made mad, passionate love.

When they finished, she kissed him on the lips and snuggled into his loving embrace. "Good night, baby," she sighed contentedly.

"Good night, princess."

TC's right. I'm the luckiest man in the world. I have a woman so exquisitely perfect, a woman I hadn't even dared dream about, not even in my wildest fantasies.

CHAPTER 30

For Vincent Davis, the four years that had passed since this entire inconceivable tragedy of events started seemed like only yesterday. The fact that AUSA Juan Gonzalez had exerted his political muscle and influence as part of the US Organized Crime Task Force of the US Attorney's Office to indict and now prosecute him was incomprehensible. Not since 1986, when federal authorities in New Jersey, which had become synonymous with organized crime, launched an attack on the Mob, landing an indictment and subsequent trial that encompassed the entire leadership of the Lucchese crime family in New Jersey, a trial that was to be a major debilitating blow to the Mob, a trial that was to have been the government's shining moment in the war on the Mob, a trial that was hosted as the Mob that took on the feds! Not since the devastating loss of that trial for the government in 1988 had an opportunity arisen for an aggressive, headline-making crime fighter like Juan Gonzalez to even the score with the Mob.

Seven long years had passed before the government's prayers were answered. Answered in the name of Richard Sabol, the career criminal who promised to hand over not only the leadership of the Lucchese crime family but the entire New York section of the La Cosa Nostra as well. AUSA Gonzalez's zeal to do what couldn't be done in the courthouse across the street a decade ago by a prosecutor whose name ironically was Vinny was that he overlooked one very important problem, his star informant Richard Sabol's past history in the neighborhood they would send him to work as a confidential informant.

In Gonzalez's aggressiveness and dreams of fame as the prosecutor who took down the La Cosa Nostra, he never anticipated Vincent Davis, a New York City Transit cop, a man who loathed Richard Sabol and made it his life's ambition to see him spend his life behind bars, would foul his plans.

Although Gonzalez made a case against eleven members of the Lucchese crime family and successfully prosecuted them, it did not have the political recognition he so desperately sought. His aspirations of fame became nothing more than a small article on page 10 of a local newspaper.

But today, four years later, he would make the man he held personally responsible for destroying everything he worked for pay.

This trial would not be about justice. It would be about vengeance. Gonzalez would stop at nothing until he got it! Unlike the original trial that took place in 1986, presided over by US District Court judge Alfred Ackerman, a fair and honorable man, which was what a judge should be, this trial would be presided over by evil incarnate Judge Harold Schwartz.

In New Jersey federal courts, cases were assigned by a random wheel, which spun off each new case to the next judge in line. However, this time the system was bypassed. Judge Schwartz hand-picked this case. Judges feel a sense of excitement and are greatly pleased with them when they preside over a significant case they have prepared all their professional lives to do, preside over a case of major and lasting importance.

But Vinny destroyed Schwartz's one big chance to enjoy that pleasure.

Together, he and Gonzalez shared the same goals and ambitions here today. To make Vincent Davis pay dearly for his role in warning off the Mob to the biggest federal investigation New Jersey had seen in a decade. Judge Schwartz and AUSA Gonzalez both knew the stakes in this trial were high. If this case were to be lost, the results would be devastating to their careers. It would not only be a personal embarrassment to them, but it would assure that Vinny would be reinstated to the force, an outcome totally unacceptable to both men. Revenge is sweet, and they wanted it at all costs.

Although Vinny had spent more time than he wanted inside courtrooms and had testified in numerous felony cases, this would be the first time he'd see an entire trial from jury selection through to the very end, either acquittal or conviction.

Vinny was proud to be sitting next to TC, known as the best of all the district attorneys in the Bronx. Vinny was confidant justice would be served, and after four years of waiting for this day, he thought he would finally be vindicated. He'd be free at last and would never worry about this skeleton ever coming out of his closet. It would also clear the way for him to win his appeal and get back the job he dearly missed. Vinny was truly excited to take on two people he had grown to dislike more and more over the past four years: the Honorable Judge Harold Schwartz and Assistant US Attorney Juan Gonzalez, two men who, under different circumstances, he might have admired. It might appear to the average citizen that the two of them were willing do whatever it took to see justice done, but truth be known, they used the federal criminal justice system to their own advantage. They managed to turn a courtroom and the justice system into a revolving door. The most heinous criminals received a get-out-of-jail card if they had information to sell the government and it was in the market for what they were are selling. They would buy their freedom and even a new life at the taxpayers' expense, thanks to these two public officials who were supposed to prosecute and sentence human filth, thereby making our streets safe.

They'd helped turn our justice system into a barter system. They continued to set free criminals they considered little fish, in a never-ending attempt to catch what they, or the media, considered to be the big fish, thereby helping themselves in their ultimate goal of becoming famous, landing huge promotions or book and movie deals. These two men had godlike powers to decide which criminals they considered worthy of giving time-off sentences or to set them free, based on what information they had and if these deals helped their self-serving purpose of fame or promotion.

Till Vinny's involvement in this case, he was led to believe that, as a police officer, you arrested the perpetrator. The prosecutor presented the case, and the judge ensured justice was administered fairly and without prejudice. But as Vinny sat waiting for jury selection to begin, a jury that would ultimately decide his own guilt or innocence, he realized that everything he had ever thought of about our system of justice had been nothing but fiction. Reflectively, he couldn't help but think of how lucky he'd been over the past thirteen years as a police officer that he had not been killed or permanently injured while making an arrest, only to find out later that the person he arrested was set free because he had a bigger fish to sell a prosecutor in return for his own freedom, set free to possibly kill or injure a police officer while committing his next crime. How could society be assured of its safety when criminals knew they would not be punished to the full extent of the law for the crimes they committed?

Judge Schwartz entered the courtroom.

As Schwartz sat, Vinny caught him giving a dirty look, an imperious sneer, toward the defense table. He was legendary as a federal judge. He was known for his zero tolerance for bullshit, his bias from the bench, and his hypocrisy toward anyone who had had the displeasure of finding themselves seated before him. He was a man with a tremendous ego and terminal ambition. Aside from his eccentric personality, he had a face that seemed to be in a state of perpetual hostility. Vinny sat rigidly in his seat as he thought of what Tommy said was going to happen at this trial. *We're not dealing with a single psychopathic judge. We are dealing with an obsessed zealot for a prosecutor. A raging fanatic perfectly willing to do what ever it takes to send you to prison.*

Vinny had as little respect for AUSA Gonzalez as he did for Mad Bull Schwartz. His ferocious ambition at the arraignment showed itself as a desire to impress. Yes, if it were up to him, there would be no trial. There would be a gentlemanly discussion between himself and Tommy leading to a plea bargain and another case closed. Vinny glanced over at the prosecution table, where gathered around Gonzalez were his trusted assistants, all clutching capacious folders. Behind them, like moths to a flame, were the FBI and Customs agents assigned to the case. They were at the beck and call of Gonzalez's every whim to see Vinny get convicted. Staring at Gonzalez, Vinny knew he could be tenacious and ruthless when it came to prosecuting defendants, especially one he held personally responsible for destroying the case he thought would make him famous.

The potential jurors began to fill the courtroom. Vinny made eye contact with a few of them. As he did, they seemed to look away, looks of fear on their faces. It was at that moment he realized he was no longer the good guy; he was no longer the cop riding in on his white horse to take the stand, to put the bad guy away. He realized that he was now considered the bad guy, and now the look of fear must be on his face.

As the reality hit him, he began to recall statistics of what jurors thought of jury duty. The fact that federal prosecutors had a 95 percent conviction rate first came to mind, and second was an article he had read sometime ago about potential jurors. Statistics showed a full quarter of good citizens called for jury duty in this country showed up at the courthouse already harboring the belief that criminal defendants wouldn't be there unless they were guilty. With a cop as a defendant, the number probably tripled. Factors that made any single juror desirable on one level with regard to one aspect of his case could make him an enemy on another. These were the psychodynamics of human bias multiplied by twelve. The unforeseen twists that were common to many trials could, in one bad day, turn the best jury into a hanging mob. Armed with that knowledge and the fact that jurors arrived at court with one driving notion, that their job was to convict, that it was their civic duty. This was the sword that was now hanging over Vinny's head, and Tommy must lift it by the end of this trial. Vinny also couldn't help but think of what a fool he had been for all his years as a cop. To think about all the testimony he had given at trials was believable because he was good at his job and a credible witness. He now realized the jurors arrived at court with a predetermined notion that the defendant was guilty of the crime he was charged with and that his testimony had little to do with convincing them of a defendant's guilt.

Schwartz began the voir dire, a list of questions that would be put to potential jurors. The questions were used by the prosecutor, defense attorney, and judge to decide whether or not a prospective juror would serve in a fair and impartial manner. Unlike State

Supreme Court, where the prosecutor and the defense attorneys were allowed to ask questions of potential jurors, in his courtroom, the judge was the only one allowed to put questions to the jury pool. This, Vinny noted, was troublesome to TC. They had talked about this at length, and TC had explained that when he would pose certain questions to a potential juror, he could get a better feel for that person by paying attention to their body language.

But Schwartz took matters into his own hands. He was as cold as ice and had no personality at all. He was like a robot and ran the jurors through a barrage of questions in a strict, military fashion. You could hear fear in the voices of some of the potential jurors, obviously afraid that if they answered the judge incorrectly, they would be subject to some type of ridicule or punishment.

Vinny had not been witness to many jury selections over the years, but Tommy had, and Vinny could see a look of frustration on his face. It was plain to see that he had never seen a jury selected in this manner. It was like an automotive assembly line. Vinny had never heard of a jury being selected and seated for a trial in less than two hours. Most New York Supreme Court cases took, on average, two days to select a jury.

Vinny was amazed by how quickly Schwartz managed to seat twelve jurors and four alternates out of the first group of about sixty prospective jurors. Of the sixteen people seated to determine Vinny's fate, he only remembered the questions and answers asked of the last one, juror number 12. Two answers stuck in his head: he'd recently passed the New Jersey bar exam, and his father was a retired cop. Vinny saw this juror as a disaster waiting to happen, but Tommy saw it as a golden opportunity.

Tommy explained, "First, his father is a retired cop. No son of a cop could find a cop guilty. He would look at you and see his father sitting there, and there's no way he will put his own father in jail! Second, he just graduated from law school and knows the law. He will see that based on the evidence in this case, the prosecution has not met the burden of proof beyond a reasonable doubt. And hopefully, he will be strong enough to sway the other jurors of your innocence. Even if the jury turns against you, hopefully he will be of strong conviction and insist on his not-guilty verdict and will thereby hopelessly deadlock the jury. If that happens, there is no way the government will retry this case and this nightmare will be over. Either way, an acquittal or a hung jury, we stand victorious!" Tommy said enthusiastically.

For the first time this morning, Vinny felt confident. The jury consisted of eight females and four males, with four alternates consisting of three females and one male. The entire jury was a mosaic of all types of ethnicities, and by the look on Gonzalez's face, Vinny could tell he was pleased with what the good judge had selected for him.

Vinny looked at Tommy. He sensed his frustration at the selection process. But Vinny also sensed the "I can't wait to get at them" attitude. This attitude filled Vinny with confidence, as he saw his friend no longer as a lawyer but as a warrior who was determined to move to the sound of battle.

With the jury selected and seated before him, Schwartz took the opportunity to scold them like schoolchildren, instilling an instant fear in not only the jury but also to everyone in the courtroom. He proceeded to instruct the jury as to what was to be expected of them and made it perfectly clear that he would not accept anything from a juror that he would not do himself. Schwartz was a meticulous and punctual man. He would surely be critical of the jurors.

He continued. "I arrive at the courthouse promptly at 6:00 a.m. in order to be prepared, without interruptions, for the opening of court at 9:00 a.m. sharp, which is the time I expect all of you to be seated and ready to begin. I will not tolerate lateness!" he exclaimed. "We will take a fifteen-minute break in the morning, one hour for lunch, and another fifteen-minute break in the afternoon. Court will end a 4:00 p.m. each day. On Wednesdays, court will begin at 1:00 p.m. to allow the morning hours to preside over civil matters. I have been informed by the prosecution and defense that they will need approximately two weeks to present their case to the jury, at which time the jury will be charged and given the case for deliberations. The same court schedule will be kept during deliberations, unless I am notified otherwise. Mr. Cascione and Mr. Gonzalez, you will be in court by 8:30 a.m., and I will hear any motions or arguments at such time. Ladies and gentlemen, do you have any questions? Mr. Cascione, any questions?"

"No!"

"Very well. Mr. Gonzalez, we will take a brief recess. When we return, I will hear your opening arguments."

During the recess, Vinny sat vacillating over the events of a hearing held two days before, in which Schwartz ruled Debbie to be an incompetent witness, with no credibility. Vinny was unsure if her inability to take the stand was helpful to him or not. Without her testimony, Vinny would be compelled to take the stand in order to explain the past history of threats and intimidations by Sabol. On the other hand, if she testified, it could be disastrous, because there would be no telling what she might say about Vinny or her relationship with Sabol. After hearing her testify at the hearing, Tommy declared her a loose cannon who could cause irreprehensible damage to their case. The truth was, after all was said and done, looking back on his years with Debbie, Vinny was left with the conviction that he'd lived a good life, but it just didn't pan out. He felt he spent too much time at work, hadn't spent enough time at home, and accepted the blame. What had shocked him most when Debbie filed for divorce was that after thirteen years, he had felt only a mild regret that he'd spent so much time in their charade of a marriage.

Vinny gradually came to realize that he had just stopped caring. The job he once loved, working at putting away the most venal and lowlife scum, had shown him a profound cynicism about humanity in general. That was why he had turned to booze and why he had continued to do so for some time. He wanted to make himself numb. Then there was the law, which he had worshipped and served for all his life, which had now turned out to be a sham. Vinny was strong, willing to put all of it behind him and start a new life. Now, with the nature of Debbie's betrayal revealed, his faith was shaken to its foundation.

Hearing her testify in detail about her affair with Sabol was heart-wrenching. Never in his life had he been so humiliated. She told the court she had never done anything wrong until she met Richard

Sabol at the age of sixteen, and now, it seemed, everything she did turned out badly. With her parents in attendance, she explained to the court how she never wanted to make Sabol mad at her, accuse him of anything, or put him on the defensive. She couldn't believe it when he was arrested in 1979 for attempted robbery. She had no idea he was like that. Until now, at age thirty-six, she had experienced only one serious wrinkle in her otherwise-smooth life. That was Richard Sabol, who was not at all, yet quite a lot, what she tried not to be. Whatever his flaws, none of which she thought to be too serious, she could help him with them, and thereby ensure his appreciation and love. Plus, she had been very physically attracted to him. She had let him be the one to take her virginity, and eventually, he would marry her. When he went to prison, she said the hell with him! That had been her original reaction. But when he was released, she began an affair with him, an affair she saw absolutely nothing wrong with. She hadn't been able to keep the judgmental tone out of her voice. After all, it was only Richard Sabol, a man she was sleeping with for two years, a man she once loved and planned to marry, until Vinny came along.

Listening to her nonchalant attitude enraged Vinny. He gazed across the courtroom to where his in-laws were seated, listening to their daughter's adulterous confessions, anguished looks on their faces, hearing for the first time that their beloved daughter was a *puttana*, an amoral whore. As they listened to her attempts to justify her actions, they looked disgusted. For they knew if it weren't for their daughter's lies, the son-in-law they had had and loved as if their own wouldn't have lost his job and be sitting at the defense table a few feet away.

"All rise!" the court clerk ordered, snapping Vinny out of his trance.

Schwartz entered and took his seat. "I'll hear your opening, Mr. Gonzalez," he said impatiently.

"Thank you, Your Honor," Gonzalez said, rising to his feet to address his captive audience. He began his proclamation. "May it please the court, counsel, members of the jury, good morning. About four years ago, on a cold night in January, a young man named Gerry got a telephone call from a friend, a friend he had known since childhood. The call that Gerry got that night in January was unlike any other call he'd ever gotten from his friend. In fact, it was unlike any other call he'd ever gotten in his life. It would be unlike any other call he ever would get again. That phone call changed Gerry's life forever. You see, at the time he got this phone call from his friend, Gerry had been doing a lot of illegal things. By the age of twenty-six, Gerry was a hard-core criminal and he had spent some time in jail. Recently, he had been hanging out with a guy named Richie, doing illegal things. Richard was another man with a long criminal history. And in the months of November and December, preceding this telephone call, Gerry had provided Richie with drugs, he provided Richard with guns, he provided Richard with silencers for the guns, provided Richie with stolen property. In fact, on the day before he got this telephone call, he provided Richie with $10,000 to open up a business, a business that would be used, among other things, to conduct more illegal activity. So when Gerry got this telephone call from his friend, a man named Michael, he felt a knot grow in his stomach.

"Michael told Gerry that he was in trouble. Michael told Gerry that it was serious and he should come to his apartment right away. Michael said nothing else. About a minute later, Michael's wife called Gerry, and she, too, told Gerry to come to their apartment right away. After getting this telephone call, Gerry knew he had a problem. When he arrived at Michael's apartment, Michael said to Gerry, 'You're in trouble. You're being set up.'

"Gerry said he was stunned. 'By who? Who is setting me up?' he asked.

"Michael said, 'Richard is setting you up.'

"Naturally, Gerry didn't want to believe it. He wanted to know how Michael knew that Richard was setting him up. Michael said, 'Vinny told me. Vinny said that Richard is a rat.'

"Michael and Gerry then drove to meet with Vinny. Gerry wanted to hear it from Vinny himself. He now wanted to know how it was that Vinny knew that Richard was setting him up.

"A few minutes later, when Michael and Gerry arrived at Vinny's house, Vinny was upset. You see, Vinny didn't want anybody to know that he was meeting with Gerry. More importantly, he didn't want anybody to know that he was the one who was providing the information to Gerry that Richard was setting Gerry up. That's because Vinny was a cop. He was a police officer, and cops aren't supposed to associate with criminals, much less tip them off.

"Vinny followed Michael and Gerry to a neighborhood bar. There, Vinny sat at a table with Gerry alone, and Vinny told him everything. He told him that Richard was a government informant. He told him that Richard was setting him up. He told Gerry that all his illegal transactions with Richard had been recorded on tape. He told Gerry Vittorio that Richard was supposed to be in jail for twenty years and that the only reason Richard was on the street was to set Gerry up.

"Upon Gerry's hearing this, his blood began to boil. That's because he had introduced Richard to his entire circle of crime. 'How do you know all this?' Gerry asked.

"Vinny looked at him with the assurance that only a police officer could give and said, 'I just know.' And then Vinny said, 'Gerry, you only got one choice: You got to whack this kid. You got to kill Richard!'

"Ladies and gentlemen, if I can, at this time, reintroduce myself, my name is Juan Gonzalez, assistant US attorney, charged with presenting this case on behalf of the United States. This case is also about Gerry's friend Michael. His full name is Michael Lanteri. This case is also about the guy that Gerry was hanging out with. His name, full name, is Richard Sabol. But above all, this case is about Vinny, a cop, the cop, a one-time police officer with the New York City Transit Police. His full name is Vincent Davis, and he is the defendant, and he is seated right there."

Gonzalez paused and pointed an accusatory finger at Vinny for a dramatic effect.

"This case is about these men and the actions the defendant took that one cold night in January. For on that night, January 25, 1994, to be exact, the defendant, Vincent Davis, did quite accurately tell Gerry Vittorio that Richard Sabol was a government informant. You're also going to hear, as I said earlier, that the defendant told

Gerry Vittorio that he should kill Richard Sabol for setting him up. You're also going to hear from witnesses that he said something else I didn't mention to you earlier. You're going to hear the defendant told Gerry that if Gerry didn't want to kill Richard Sabol, Gerry should provide the defendant with a gun, that he would do it himself.

"Now, as the evidence you're going to hear in this case will show, the defendant's journey into this courtroom today did not begin on January 25, 1994. It actually began many years ago, when he met and later married a woman by the name of Debbie Manzo. Debra Manzo had a boyfriend in her life prior to meeting the defendant. That man's name was Richard Sabol. As you will hear, Richard Sabol was, on the night of January 25, 1994, a career criminal. He had spent about half of his thirty-four years in prison. On that date, as the defendant, you'll hear quite accurately, told Gerry Vittorio, Sabol was still in prison doing time on drug charges.

"In November 1991, Richard Sabol was arrested and ultimately convicted in Atlanta, Georgia. While he was on parole for having served six years in prison on credit cards, he was arrested and convicted for trying to buy two kilograms of cocaine from an undercover agent. Based on the latest conviction, you will hear that Sabol decided to cooperate with law enforcement authorities in Georgia and ultimately with the US Customs Service here in Newark, New Jersey. Based on a proposal from the US Customs Service, Customs agent John Conti obtained approval to utilize Sabol as a confidential informant in an undercover investigation. Under the terms of that approval, you're going to learn that Richard Sabol was permitted, under the supervision of Customs agents, to be taken out of jail during the day to meet with or to place telephone calls to the subjects of the Customs investigation. After the phone calls and the meetings with Customs, he was taken by the Customs agent back to jail.

"One of the subjects of the Customs investigation, as you will hear, was Gerry Vittorio, also known as Gerry Carbone. He got that name, Carbone, from his stepfather, Vito Carbone. As you will hear, during the course of this trial, in the fall of 1993, during the Customs investigation, Vito Carbone was a captain, or caporegime, in the Lucchese crime family, one of five crime families that are part of the Mafia, or La Cosa Nostra, headquartered in New York City and operating in the New York–Northern New Jersey area. Membership in the La Cosa Nostra, or the Mafia, you will hear, composed of two types of persons. There are made men and associates of made men. Captains or capos, such as Vito Carbone, are made men who are responsible for supervising a crew of made members, soldiers, and their associates. The captains, in turn, were subordinate to the family's upper echelon, the boss, the underboss, and the family consigliore or adviser. You're going to hear that in the fall of 1993, it was Gerry Vittorio's desire, his goal, his ambition in life to become a made man in his stepfather's crew of the Lucchese crime family. You're going to hear that from September 1993 to January 24, 1994, Richard Sabol, under the supervision of Customs agents, gained the confidence of Gerry Vittorio; his stepfather, Vito Carbone; and other members of the Carbone crew. You're going to learn that Sabol's success was due in part to a friendship he had forged with Gerry in 1991, prior to being arrested in Georgia. You'll see that his success was also due, in no small measure, to his personal skills. Now, you're going to hear…"

Gonzalez was garrulously explaining to the jury, in detail, every trivial aspect of the government's case, none of which had anything to do with Vinny's involvement, other than the admitted fact that Vinny had compromised, albeit unknowingly, a sensitive undercover investigation. His opening argument was redundant and extremely boring.

Vinny glanced over at the jury box. It was filled with sixteen extremely weary faces. Upon closer observation, Vinny noticed juror 2, the schoolteacher, was sound asleep, with her head tilted back and her mouth flopped open. Vinny tapped Tommy on the shoulder, leaned over, and whispered into his ear, "The drunken schoolteacher's asleep."

Schwartz glared at the defense table, his eyes saying, "How dare you talk in my courtroom!"

Vinny and Tommy casually looked over to the jury box simultaneously. So did Schwartz.

"Excuse me!" he erupted. "Members of the jury! I have to ask that you pay strict attention to what's going on. If you're tired and you need a break, let me know and we'll take a recess. This case is very important for the parties involved, the government and the defendant. It's absolutely crucial that you pay strict attention to what's going on. So if you need a recess, let me know. Go ahead!" he said to Gonzalez.

Gonzalez was thankful to the good judge and realized he must speed it up a bit before he put all the jurors to sleep.

"In January 1997, you're going to hear that it was Mr. Gerry who decided to cooperate with law enforcement authorities and to provide testimony in this case. You're going to hear Gerry Vittorio describe the meetings that he had with Sabol prior to January 25, 1994. You're going to hear him recount the meeting he had on the night of January 25, 1994, with Michael Lanteri and the defendant, and you're also going to hear Gerry Vittorio recount for you a second meeting he had with the defendant on the night of March 2, 1994. A meeting in which the defendant, as you will hear Mr. Gerry say, urged him to kill Richard Sabol.

"Now, as I mentioned to you earlier, Gerry, like Sabol, has a criminal history, which is an often-violent one. Like Sabol, you will hear him tell you that he decided to cooperate to earn a reduction in his sentence. He also decided to cooperate to earn a new start on life in the government's Witness Protection Program.

"After Gerry, you're going to hear from Michael Lanteri. You're going to learn that in addition to being Gerry Vittorio's friend, Michael Lanteri is also the defendant's brother-in-law. You're going to hear that Michael Lanteri provided testimony to the grand jury in this case in December of 1994, and you're going to learn that he was given immunity from prosecution by being compelled to testify by the grand jury.

"As Judge Schwartz stated, the indictment is not evidence. It is not evidence, and the defendant is presumed innocent. The burden of proving the defendant guilty on the charges in the indictment rests squarely on this table. That burden is one beyond all reasonable doubt. We welcome that burden.

"When the evidence is done at the end of the case, when I have a chance to talk to you again during closing argument, I'm going to come back, and I'm going to say that we believe we met that burden, that we have, in fact, proven the defendant guilty of the charges in the indictment. Until then, ladies and gentlemen, thank you very much for your patience and for the service you're about to render."

"Thank you," Schwartz said. "Mr. Cascione, you may proceed."

"Thank you, Your Honor," Tommy said, smiling, as he walked to the podium. "Honorable Judge Schwartz, Mr. Gonzalez, various well-wishers from the government, ladies and gentlemen, I wish you good day.

"I like to start off, although we have only just met, in thanking you for the time and attention you will spend on this case. I realize, everyone in this room realizes that you are taking time out of your lives for a civic duty, but it's an important civic duty. I think the judge impressed you with that, and from my part as a professional and part of this process, I personally appreciate what you do, which is to pay attention, listen, come here on time, and do your job. That is a very, very good thing, whatever your verdict. The fact: that you're here, attentive, and ready to do the job is all anybody can ask, and I thank you for that in advance.

"Now, an opening statement is something that is optional to the defense. It is the government's obligation because they have that burden of proof Mr. Gonzalez just talked about, but it's a privilege allowed me and it's a privilege I welcome. I appreciate the chance to get up and give you a preview of what I expect will be shown in this courtroom.

"Firstly, again, I introduce myself, Thomas Cascione. I'm a lawyer from Yonkers, New York, and I represent Vincent Davis, for many years a police officer in New York City and himself a resident of Yonkers, New York.

"So what's with this case?

"I didn't intend to get up and tell you a story, because as the judge has pointed out, this is about what's going to be proven, but inasmuch as Mr. Gonzalez says, yes, there is a history here, the history I do expect you to hear and see. You're going to hear that Richard Sabol, the confidential informant, was a very bad person, was a career criminal of frightening proportions, and was a teenage boyfriend of the woman that my client would eventually marry, Debbie Manzo, who became Debbie Davis.

"Throughout this case, you will hear references in many statements from my client, whether tape-recorded or wiretapped or whatever, and through testimony you'll hear that his overriding concern was a fear, a fear that Richard Sabol would come back into his life and do harm to him and to his family, and a well-founded fear. Because through the testimony, you will hear that Mr. Sabol had a history of violence, of threatening witnesses in cases, of threatening people he dealt with, including the women in his life, of harming the women in his life, of telling Mr. Davis's wife, then Sabol's sweetheart, that if she gave up on him, he would cut off her fingers and mail them back to her family and throw acid in her face so no one would ever want her again.

"You will hear that my client, while Mr. Sabol was away on one of his many government-sponsored vacations in a correctional facility, fell in love with and married this woman, then went on to become a police officer himself with New York City in the Transit Division.

"There came a time when Mr. Sabol got out of jail and made another appearance in the life of Mr. Davis and his wife. Then Sabol went back to jail on new charges. Mr. Davis, you will hear, again was greatly concerned about this man Sabol and his effect on himself and his family, a concern shared by federal agents who had dealt with Mr. Sabol, who themselves came to fear him as a dangerous man.

"So finally, and there is a lot here, so I'm not going to belabor it, Mr. Davis learns that Sabol got arrested down in Georgia. The arrest you heard about from Mr. Gonzalez now, and he's curious enough to make his own inquiry through his department, through his superiors. He reaches out to the people that arrested Sabol down in Georgia.

"Mr. Davis was informed that Sabol faced a long jail sentence and that he could rest assured that Sabol would not be back to bother him or his family for a good, long time. Mr. Davis spoke of this, documented this, knew of this.

"Now, ladies and gentlemen, I don't touch on what people felt and their emotions. I think that that's something you can infer through the evidence but I have no business getting into, but you can picture, if you would, the thoughts that went through Mr. Davis's mind when you hear through the evidence that he is informed around about Christmas of 1993 that although only two years earlier Sabol had been sent away for some twenty years or so, he was back, back on the scene, back on the loose, out of jail, up to his old tricks.

"Now, you're going to hear that this upset and concerned Vincent Davis to no end.

"You're going to hear through the testimony that he reached out again to his superiors with his concerns that this man, this monster, this man that was promised to go away for twenty years, is back on the scene in only two.

"And you'll hear that he was informed by his brother-in-law, Mike Lanteri, that Lanteri's childhood friend, Gerry Vittorio, was, in fact, spending time and doing business with Richie Sabol.

"So you'll learn that Mr. Davis went to confront Gerry, to tell him the man is no good, the man is a danger to his family, the man is a danger to him, to his brother-in-law, to his sister, to his sister's child, certainly to his soon-to-be ex-wife.

"As it turns out, Vinny and Debbie were going through a divorce at that point.

"What you will not hear from any source, other than Gerry, is that Mr. Davis made any threats upon the life of Richard Sabol.

"You will hear, and I will agree, this word will be bandied about, that Vincent Davis told Gerry Vittorio that Sabol was a rat. For very good reasons, because how does one turn a twenty-to-life sentence into freedom in two years if one did not give up your confederates in that charge?

"Ladies and gentlemen, you will again hear that that term did not mean that Sabol was a current government informant. In fact, the proof will show a lot of things.

"Let me get through the story first.

"Anyway, you're going to hear that conversation went on, and admittedly, you'll also hear that when this whole thing came up, my client had had way too much to drink and this was a barroom conversation, had over many a cocktail, but that after time, this was sup-

415

posed to end the whole situation, but Mr. Davis learned that Sabol was still around. In fact, he learned it because Sabol called his then wife, Debbie, out of the blue.

"Mr. Davis again went to ask Gerry, 'What's going on? Are you still hanging out with this guy, this no-good bum, this rat?'

"Now, in the course of these conversations, you're going to learn that Mr. Gerry did more than just absorb information from Vincent Davis. He paid that information back, quid pro quo, you tell me something, I tell you something. He told Mr. Davis about machine guns, silencers, drugs, stolen goods. He spilled his guts, to use the vernacular, and when he did that, Mr. Davis did his job as a police officer. He reported it.

"You will hear in the testimony that Vincent Davis voluntarily, of his own initiative, nobody calling him, nobody asking him, nobody making inquiry of him, all by himself, set up a meeting with the FBI to tell them what Gerry Vittorio and Richard Sabol were up to and offered to get more information to help them again with Sabol, to put Sabol back in jail.

"You'll hear tapes of the FBI responding to Mr. Davis, saying, 'Good, this is good stuff. Go get us more information. See what you can do here.' That is the conduct of Mr. Davis, which is brought before you.

"You will hear that within a day or two of his March 2 meeting, Mr. Davis was on the phone with the most recent FBI agent he could associate with the Sabol case, James Stamp, the man that put Sabol away back before the drug case in Georgia, that Davis reached out to Agent Stamp, telling him, 'This is what these people are up to.' You've already been asked to conclude that Mr. Davis was plotting a murder while he was giving this information to the FBI.

"Now, again, you're going to hear only one person suggest at any point that Vincent Davis ever had a thought about killing Richard Sabol.

"You will hear Davis's own words. He is quoted saying, 'I'll do anything I can to put him back in jail, but when it comes to the killing part, you have to rely on Gerry Vittorio.' A man sentenced to 156 months, who wants to be like his friend, Richard Sabol, who is now free as a bird in the Witness Protection Program, living in some community among people like us.

"Now, Mr. Gerry wants to join him.

"There are two ways of saying this. Defense attorneys, for years, always say, 'There is no evidence.' That's different from what I'm about to say to you. There is proof to the contrary of the following things: It's already been admitted now in the opening that Mr. Davis is not a member of the Lucchese crime family, nor was he associated with the crime family. You will hear that. You will also hear that whatever contraband is referred to in this case, whatever guns, whatever drugs, whatever counterfeit money, whatever stolen goods, that Vinny Davis never saw this stuff, touched this stuff, had any connection with this whatsoever.

"The only thing that you're going to hear about that relates this contraband to Vincent Davis is the tale that he told the FBI, 'This is what's going on,' and he named the things that he had heard. That's the only relation you'll hear about.

"You will also hear that he did not profit one penny, nor was he expected to profit a penny, nor was he offered a penny, that he was not bribed with anything at all in this case. Nor did he solicit, ask for it. Nor is anyone going to come in and say he expected it. No proof whatsoever. In fact, their own witness will say no, there was nothing offered him for this. He did not take a bribe.

"You're also going to learn that throughout the course of this, Vincent Davis did not speak to, write to, contact, or in any way, shape, or form, connect with this supposed witness Richard Sabol, the man he's accused of intimidating. No contact whatsoever. You will have that right out of the government witnesses' mouths.

"You will hear that after an exhaustive investigation, the agencies involved all precluded that nobody ever told Vincent Davis anything, that he had no special information, that he had no tip-off because he was a cop, that he had nothing. You only hear that he had the knowledge, the common sense of public knowledge that a man sentenced to more than twenty years in jail, or supposed to be sentenced to that, was walking around in two.

"That's where this all comes from.

"You're going to hear basically nothing more than I told you, and if you do your jobs in this case, if you listen attentively, if you follow the evidence, if you look past the big allegations at the proof, you will conclude that Mr. Davis has not violated any law, that the only violation here was a violation by the government of public trust by unleashing Richard Sabol back in the same community they took him out of and put him in jail for, to get a benefit, to build a new case.

"Knowing, I would assume full well, that Richard Sabol had done many crimes right in that community, the city of Yonkers, where Vincent Davis comes from, and that there were many people that knew what a bad man he was and had many bad things to say about him.

"That was a calculated risk they took when they put him back in his own hometown, and it blew up, and their case did not come out as good as it was supposed to.

"And now, four years later, we're here to punish the person they blame for blowing it up.

"Ladies and gentlemen, if you listen to all the evidence and the lack of evidence and the contrary evidence in this case, again, if you do the hard part, listen to all this, the last part is going to be easy. You're going to find my client not guilty.

"Again, I thank you for your time and attention. I'm a human being. I like to smile. I like to laugh once in a while. I have no particular ominousness against the other side in this case. You're not going to see me walking around here with a face like the world just ended, but this is a serious job, serious duty that you are entrusted with. Believe me, I do take it seriously. Again, I thank you."

"Thank you," Schwartz said as Tommy returned to his seat at the defense table, next to his very impressed client.

"Ladies and gentlemen, this might be a good time to take our luncheon recess now. We'll break for one hour, so please be back ready to go at one o'clock, and at that time, we'll start the taking of the testimony. I want to caution you again: you cannot talk about this case among yourselves or anybody else. I'll see you in one hour."

As the first witness for the prosecution, Agent Conti, US Customs Service, took the stand, Vinny was struck with the memories of days he pulled duty at Yankee Stadium, when an important game was about to begin. You could feel the tension in the air. The butterflies some of the players felt—the pitcher, the batter, and then the first pitch. This was the first batter. In this courtroom, an irresistible force rushed toward a helpless object. His hopes, his goals, and his life rode on the outcome of this trial.

Agent Conti took the stand and was sworn in.

As Vinny studied him for the first time, he came to realize how Richard Sabol manipulated him and sold him and Gonzalez a false bill of goods. Conti was a small man who obviously took the job with Customs to be an authority figure. Customs was the type of job that fitted this spineless little man perfectly. He got to wear a badge, carry a gun, and feel his own self-importance and never have to face the dangers that were all too commonplace for a real police agency.

Richard Sabol had manipulated his way through the ranks of every federal agency he could, and after being rejected, he came to Customs as a last-ditch effort to sell himself as a confidential informant, in an attempt to buy his freedom once again.

Agent Conti described to the jury that Sabol had made contact with Customs while he was incarcerated in Georgia on federal drug trafficking charges. Conti explained to the court that Sabol was willing to work as a confidential informant in return for a reduction in sentence and a new identity in the Witness Protection Program. A new identity he would surely need, because he was going to rat on the Mafia, which meant certain death if they should ever find him. For the rest of his life, Sabol would live each day looking over his shoulder, wondering if the day would ever come when he was recognized and subsequently killed for violating the sacred oath of silence he took when he was initiated into the Mob. By violating this oath, a man signed his own death warrant. It is said that there is no honor among thieves. That may be true, but the one exception is the label of a rat. If you rat, you die. It's as simple as that, and it is unquestionably understood by all criminals, not just the Mafia families. Some might say they would rather be in jail than to live their life in constant fear, waiting for the day they are killed, but as Conti continued his testimony, Vinny continued to think about the criminal Sabol and the reign of terror he had caused over the years. Information Vinny learned about him as early as 1986, when the FBI arrested him for credit card fraud and numerous other charges.

When Vinny attended his sentencing on those charges in 1986, he had the opportunity to read his presentencing memorandum. Vinny was disgusted to learn how many crimes that animal had committed and, by one way or another, managed to do minimal or no jail time. He would commit forcible home invasion robberies against the elderly throughout the richest sections of Westchester, tying up elderly victims and beating them until they revealed where they kept their valuables hidden. He did these push-in robberies without trying to hide his identity with a mask or stocking over his face. He had no fear of prosecution because he would do as he had in the past. Before the trial, he would return to his victims' homes and beat them, warning them that if they testified against him, he or his friends would return and kill everyone in the house. Of course, the terrified victims refused to testify.

In his early years, he also masterminded armed robberies of supermarkets. However, Sabol was a coward and could never actually commit the robberies himself. Instead, he enlisted the help of a young black kid who had more balls than brains. Sabol would wait in the getaway car, parked close by, with the motor running. After his partner committed the robbery, he would run to the getaway car and jump in the trunk. Sabol would conceal his partner by pulling a stretched-out piece of black felt over the entire trunk, thereby giving the appearance the trunk was empty. The responding police would be looking for a male, black, not a male, white.

One time the plan was put to the test as a radio car stopped the getaway car near the robbery location. The officers searched the entire vehicle, including the trunk, and never knew the suspect was there.

The kid's nickname was Swifty, because of his amazing speed running from authorities. Sabol and Swifty were very successful committing dozens of armed robberies throughout Westchester and the Bronx, until Swifty became greedy and began doing his act solo.

When Swifty got caught, as all criminals eventually are, he "ratted" on his partner. Sabol was arrested and charged for his role in the robberies, but the case never went to trial. Ironically, Swifty was found in the trunk of a car with a bullet in the back of his head. Dead men tell no tales, and again, Sabol escaped prosecution for his crimes.

Vinny looked over at Gonzalez as he asked Agent Conti questions about how Sabol managed to infiltrate made members of the Lucchese crime family. As Vinny listened to the way Gonzalez asked Conti the questions, he realized what this experienced and savvy prosecutor was doing. He was painting a picture for the jury that Conti, an overzealous Customs agent, was responsible for striking up a deal with this monster, which would eventually free him and give him a new identity. Once again, freeing this monster who would continue his criminal activities and, no doubt, one day take the life of an innocent person.

After a short recess, they returned to their places. Gonzalez resumed his direct of Agent Conti.

Vinny noticed that during the lunch break, someone had set up three televisions in the courtroom. Tommy knew Gonzalez would stage a show-and-tell for the jury. He also assured Vinny he wasn't on any of the videotapes. Tommy further explained that this dog-and-pony show Gonzalez was about to put on was to show the jury the magnitude of the Mafia enterprise and how much time and work was done by Sabol and the undercover agents, thereby leading the jury to believe Vinny single-handedly obstructed and destroyed a major federal investigation into the Lucchese crime family and various organized crime figures, that he compromised the safety of Sabol, a career criminal with lifelong ties to members and associates in not only the Lucchese crime family but the Genovese and Gambino crime families as well.

The audio and videotapes would also show that from October 1993 to January 1994, the government inserted Sabol as a confidential informant. He had gained the confidence of numerous members and associates of the Carbone crew, a crew that operated under the control of the Lucchese crime family. As a result, the Carbone crew sought to utilize Sabol to establish a drug distribution network in New Jersey, to set up an import-export company in New Jersey for the importation of narcotics and exportation of stolen vehicles. Fence shipments of stolen property acquired by the Carbone crew and established illegal gambling operations. The tapes would also show Sabol acquired a variety of illegal items from the Carbone crew, including heroin, $10,000 in cash to open the import-export business, a .38-caliber handgun with hollow-point bullets, a 9mm submachine gun equipped with a silencer, and a shipment of fur coats valued at $750,000, all of which Vinny had nothing to do with.

With Agent Conti still on the stand and having a short pause while the videotape was being changed, the judge looked at Gonzalez and asked, "Is this a good time to stop for the day?"

"Yes, Your Honor," Gonzalez replied without hesitation, observing the boredom on the faces of the jurors, who were fighting to stay awake. Tommy offered no objection, and the court was recessed until 9:00 a.m. tomorrow.

As they drove on the NJ Turnpike heading toward the George Washington Bridge, Tommy called the Yonkers office to retrieve any messages of importance.

While he was on the phone, he said, "Champagne wants to know how the home team did."

Vinny answered confidently, "We're alive, partner!"

Tommy added excitedly, "It's the Alamo, and there are a lot of dead Mexicans, but we're alive!"

CHAPTER 31

After three days of extremely boring testimony, Vinny and Tommy showed signs of fatigue. For three days, it was the same exhausting routine. They would wake up at 6:00 a.m., shower, shave, and dress for court. Vinny would drive over to Tommy's house by 6:30 a.m., load Tommy's car with boxes filled with transcripts and evidence for court, then take their coffee to go in an attempt to fight the rush-hour traffic on the George Washington Bridge and the NJ Turnpike, arriving at the courthouse in Newark by 8:30 a.m.

After a gruesome day in court hearing the same boring testimony, Vinny and Tommy would pack up the car and fight the rush-hour traffic back home to New York. Where they would again unload the car of the materials they would need to review for court the following day. After Tommy cooked dinner, the children were put to bed, and the two of them would retreat to the basement to review notes to ensure their readiness, in order to have that air of confidence that had served them so well in the trial. Whatever the boys from New Jersey were prepared to throw at them, the boys from New York were going to be well prepared to handle it.

Yesterday's testimony was given by Agent Velez, the second Customs agent to testify in this case. Agent Velez continued to authenticate audio and videotapes for the jury, explaining how Sabol infiltrated Gerry and the members of the Lucchese crime family. He described Sabol as the great link to the underworld of organized crime, whose undercover guise provided the open door they so desperately needed to fulfill their mission. That Sabol was the man who provided them with instant access to the inner sanctum of the Mob. He described numerous meeting between Sabol and the associates of the crime families whose trust he had managed to gain. That within a few months, in fact, Sabol had these mobsters moving right into his chicken coop, and like a happy fox, Sabol was welcoming them. The family's activities, Agent Velez said, comprised of a full menu of criminal operations. Which included narcotics, automatic machine guns with silencers, a ten-thousand-dollar loan of Mob money to be used to open a warehouse to import and export stolen vehicles and heroin, and to a lesser extent, stolen property consisting of a shipment of high-jacked furs valued at $750,000. Agent Velez puffed up Sabol to be the greatest single wealth of information about the Mob the government ever encountered. Yet the jury seemed unimpressed. In fact, as Vinny scanned the jurors, he observed juror 2's boredom had put her in a deep sleep, for the second time since the beginning of the trial. This infuriated Vinny.

How the fuck can this woman fall asleep? She's one of twelve people who'll decide my fate. I haven't liked her from the instant I laid eyes on her. She's Irish, in her early forties, yet she looks much older; divorced with no children, she probably doesn't like men much. She's been an elementary school teacher for the past seventeen years—probably a leftist who hates cops. Fucking Gonzalez has injected race into this case, an Italian Mafia case. I've never met many Irish who'd be all that sympathetic toward a man who's being portrayed as a no-good, crooked New York Italian cop, even if I am half-Irish.

Vinny had gotten a closer look at her during a court recess. She was standing in front of the courthouse, telling other members of the jury how bored she was. As she was taking long, hard drags from her cigarette, a vivid picture came to Vinny's mind of her standing in front of a firing squad, taking a drag of a cigarette for the very last time. Vinny also noticed her swollen red nose and blotches on her cheeks—two telltale signs of alcohol abuse. Chances were, she accepted jury duty as a means of a small vacation from the children she tried to teach. A few good nights of swilling shots at a local gin mill, showing up for jury duty pie-eyed and hungover, catching as much sleep as she could in the jury box was a vacation for her.

Schwartz noticed the rage and frustration on Vinny's face. Either that or her loud snoring finally got his attention. It forced him to stop Agent Velez's fascinating testimony. "Ladies and gentlemen!" Judge Schwartz shouted toward the jury box, immediately awakening Sleeping Beauty. "As I have told you before," he said, his eyes ablaze, piercing this woman like a stiletto, "if anyone needs a break, please ask for it." His statement was a mix of bile and sarcasm that provoked instant fear on the faces of the jurors.

How will this jury find me not guilty if they fear some form of retaliation from the judge? Shit.

Shortly after the judge yelled at them before, Gonzalez realized he was boring them to tears and hurriedly completed his direct questioning of Agent Velez.

It was now Tommy's turn to dismantle the government's charge of conspiracy to obstruct justice. Until the previous day, Vinny was never afforded the opportunity to watch his friend in action in a courtroom. Vinny was very impressed.

Tommy Cascione had the handsome features one would expect in a Hollywood actor playing the role of a high-powered attorney. His eyes were a soft brown, without a trace of hardness or indifference. His hair was jet-black and pushed back in a fifties hairstyle. He came across as friendly, unguarded, and beaming with self-confidence. He had a bright smile, and his humor was delivered casually, almost as an afterthought that seemed to sometimes surprise him. He was a big man, standing over six feet. To look at him, you would think he was a man who had been fighting a long battle with his waistline, yet he was rarely on a diet. He was a born idealist who enjoyed all sorts of people and was always ready to engage in conversation about a good book, politics, or culinary recipes. He was an extremely intelligent man with an effusive personality. He was also the warmest, most caring, and most compassionate person Vinny had ever met, and he was proud to be his friend. Vinny watched Tommy in amazement. His mere physical presence was electrifying, as he moved with such assurance. He exuded confidence. Aside from being well-read, Chapter and verse, on every question he asked Agent Velez, he was charismatic and outright charming as he strategically abstracted the answers he wanted from this inexperienced Customs agent.

Vinny could tell by the expressions on the jurors' faces that they were enjoying the verbal judo Tommy was performing on his unsuspecting victim. It was evident that this jury, up until now, had been bored to death for the past two days and were finally getting to see some action. "Agent Velez," Tommy said, pausing for effect. All eyes from the jury box fixed on Tommy as he was about to launch his next question like a guided missile. "At any time during the course of this extensive undercover operation, was it ever discovered that my client knew the government was conducting an ongoing investigation into the Mafia?"

"No time," Agent Velez responded, a look of exasperation on his face.

"Agent Velez, was it ever determined by any federal, state, or local police agency if and how my client knew of your investigation into the Mafia?"

"No, it was not," Agent Velez responded despairingly.

The jurors were looking at Agent Velez, who sat on the witness stand with perspiration pouring off his face, looking toward Gonzalez in desperation for the answers to these unexpected questions. Gonzalez had not done his homework in preparing his expert witness. He obviously thought the questions Tommy was asking would have been saved for the testimony of the FBI agents in charge of the compromised investigation. Not a Customs agent who now looked as though he had gone twelve rounds with Mike Tyson.

Vinny looked to his left at his New Jersey co-counsel, Gerry Salutti, who also seemed to be enjoying Tommy's performance. It had been previously agreed upon by Tommy, Gerry, and Anthony, of Iacullo and Salutti PC, New Jersey co-counsels, hired by Vinny, that Tommy was clearly to be the man in charge. He would be lead counsel on the defense team, handling the direct and cross-examinations of witnesses, while Gerry and Anthony would handle the legal briefs, take trial notes, and plan strategies in the likely event that an appeal would be necessary. The three of them established a consistency early on to ensure that they would be able to work well together as a team.

Tommy's first agenda was to have a spirit of camaraderie between the three of them. Which he did by arranging to meet for business dinners at a popular steak house in Englewood Cliffs, the adjoining town where Vinny's parents lived.

The first meeting in which Vinny was in attendance went well. The three barely knew one another, so the evening served as a get-acquainted time for them. Tommy had already worked out a preliminary battle plan and was interested in obtaining some feedback. Gerry and Anthony were a lot like Tommy. All three had worked as assistant district attorneys, getting their feet wet in the courtroom by prosecuting a multitude of criminal cases, developing and fine-tuning their courtroom expertise, and learning about criminals up close and personal. Tommy was extremely knowledgeable of the laws of New York State. As a prosecutor with the Bronx District Attorney's Office, he had a reputation as a pit bull who could take the weakest case and produce a victory. However, this was a federal case, and Tommy needed the assistance of lawyers with special skills, lawyers he could count on. Although Gerry and Anthony were relatively young and unknown, they were experts on the rules of federal procedures as well as rules of evidence. They were attorneys who were prepared to go into battle in the courtroom. But more importantly, they believed in Vinny's innocence and were determined to win. Vinny wanted to see Gerry get his crack at the enemy, but his was not to reason why. These two gentlemen with seven years of higher education, were experts in their field of law and the rules of battle associated with a jury trial.

Vinny's life was in their hands now, and he vowed not to interfere or question their courtroom tactics, but Vinny could see, even as a layman, that Gerry wanted to do battle. He was obviously not used to sitting around, watching a fight; he was used to fighting it.

As Tommy seemed to be winding down from the verbal assault on Special Agent Velez, Gerry surreptitiously slid a piece of paper across the table. He leaned on Vinny's left shoulder, drawing him close, and said, "Give this to Tommy."

Vinny got Tommy's attention while he was still questioning Agent Velez and handed him the note.

Tommy unfolded and carefully read the message. Simultaneously, he dropped the note, letting it float down onto the defense table as he turned toward the judge and said, in a most confident voice, "I have no further questions for this wit."

Schwartz looked at Tommy, faintly amused, then turned to Gonzalez and said, in a tone that hinted for him to do something, "Redirect, Mr. Gonzalez?"

"No, Your Honor," Gonzalez responded, deciding not to throw salt into Agent Velez's open wounds.

As Velez walked off the stand, visually shaken, a look of anger in his eyes, Vinny looked at the paper Tommy had dropped on the table. It read, "Say goodbye to the conspiracy charge, you're finished with him!"

In the rear of the courthouse, well out of sight of any jurors or witnesses, Vinny gave Tommy and Gerry a high five in a sign of humble jubilation. Conspiracy was one of the more serious charges against him. In order to have a conspiracy, you must have two or more people involved working for the same illegal goal. Vinny's sister, Maria, was never charged for calling Gerry on the phone, instructing him to come to her house. Nor did they charge her husband, Michael, for doing the same thing. And why should they? Neither of them knew why it was so important for Gerry to meet with Vinny. Therefore, there was no conspiracy, which was proven by the government's own witness's testimony.

Tommy was visibly proud of himself and the testimony given by the government's own witnesses over the last three days, as he said very coolly, "In a jury trial, it is a constant battle. There are no winners until the very end. We will have our good days and bad ones. One thing is for sure, they won't all be good."

Vinny looked at the clock by his nightstand: two thirty. He couldn't help but think of Tommy's words. It had been a half-hour since Vinny made it home to the comfort of his own bed, but he was unable to sleep. He lay awake, worried about what tomorrow would bring with Gerry's testimony. He also couldn't stop thinking about how much pain he was causing his family. As Vinny attempted to sleep by closing his eyes, he remembered making eye contact with his baby sister, Maria, as she sat in court, watching the trial. He could see the anguish on her face and the pain in her eyes. Maria held herself somewhat personally responsible for this little psychodrama. But Vinny never blamed his sister or Mike, her husband, for any of this. The circumstances involved were far too bizarre to place blame on anyone but Gonzalez: Vinny marrying Debbie, whose first love was Richard Sabol, in 1983; his sister marrying Mike Lanteri in 1990; and Mike's best man and childhood friend being Gerry Vittorio, the government's star witness. Then in 1993, his wife's first love and his brother-in-law's best friend joined forces in a criminal enterprise that landed him on trial for obstructing an investigation he knew nothing about. It was Murphy's law—whatever can go wrong will go wrong. His baby sister, pregnant with her second child, vowed to be in court every day to show support for him. He thought back to when his sister needed his support and he almost wasn't there for her.

Mike early on had a lot of hopes and dreams of get-rich-quick schemes. His idea of working was to have someone else do the work and he'd reap the profits. Vinny had to admit he talked a good game, but like the boy who cried wolf too many times, eventually, no one would come. With no education to speak of, no job, no security, and nothing to offer his sister, one could only imagine what the family thought when they learned of her engagement to him. Vinny knew what he went through getting married, and he was a man. He knew it was going to be an uphill battle for his sister. Unfortunately, he had no input when it came to his father. When he made up his mind that he didn't like someone, it would take more than an "act of God" to change it.

Ironically, the engagement party, held at a yacht club in New Rochelle, was just the type of party his father would refuse to go to, and true to form, he did not attend, but Vinny and his brothers did, and that was a party he now wished he hadn't. For it was that night he was formally introduced to Gerry Vittorio, now the government's star. Gerry snorted coke and displayed a 9mm handgun in the men's room.

When Vinny observed this behavior, he wasn't impressed. But what could he do? Arrest his brother-in-law's best friend, at his sister's engagement party? Besides, he was off duty and outside the city of New York. The local police would laugh at him for getting involved off duty. The duty captain, who would have to respond from New York, would get pissed; he would have him back in uniform, guarding turnstiles in the subway. And his sister would never speak to him again. No, it was best to look the other way.

Maria, a beautiful woman, on her wedding day was more beautiful than ever, and he was truly glad he attended. He remembered it as if it were yesterday. Vinny and his father had signed a pact not to attend, as a sign of disapproval, both for their own selfish reasons. It was snowing that day, and although Debbie and his mother had vowed to go, alone, if necessary, Vinny decided it was best to go to a local watering hole and get quietly drunk. Debbie knew exactly where he was and showed up dressed for the wedding. She proceeded to the pay phone in the rear of the bar, and within a minute, she called Vinny over and said, "The phone's for you."

When he heard his mother's voice on the other end, he knew he was in trouble. She, in no uncertain terms, told him to get home, shower, and be dressed within the half-hour, or he'd face the music.

When he asked to speak to his father, she said, "He's in the shower, where you should be."

He was glad his mother intervened.

The family became even closer with the arrival of Nicole, his father's first grandchild. The delivery of this beautiful little girl brought the Davis and Lanteri families together. Vinny "adopted" her as his own. She looked exactly as Maria did when she was a baby, and as he did with Maria when she was an infant, he was proud to once again change a diaper.

With his sister working full-time and Michael well on his way to being successful with their new Italian restaurant, Vinny was more than happy to kick in by babysitting in his free time.

Vinny lay tossing and turning in his bed, his mind racing with thoughts of Gerry, another animal, testifying against him the next day. He couldn't keep his blood from boiling, if not for anything else but the simple reason that that animal brought the real risk of danger so close to his beautiful, innocent little niece. That was enough to enrage him. In fact, it had enraged him four years ago—so much so that he might now to go prison, a price he might have to pay for protecting his beloved family.

The alarm clock awoke Vinny from a fitful sleep. It was time to get ready for what would prove to be the most important day of testimony.

CHAPTER 32

T his day the jury would hear from the prosecution's star witness, Gerry Vittorio, or Gerry Carbone, an alias he used while associating with other made members of the Lucchese organization. The day it became official, the day he would take the stand and turn informant—a rat, a transgression punishable by death, extracted by all five families of the New York Mafia.

Since the very beginning, the one thing that was never tolerated was a rat within their organization. It mattered not what crime was committed or how much prison time awaited the mobster. In that so-called honored society, members were expected to take whatever punishment judges handed down. They were expected to keep their mouths shut. In the early days, in order to receive their buttons, or become made members, the Mob would search their ancestry back to Italy. If their ancestry couldn't be proven, they would never become a made member. This was to ensure the families that they never broke the "blood of silence."

Although Gerry was not a made member of the Lucchese family, his stepfather, Vito Carbone Sr., was a caporegime, or captain, with them and had sponsored his stepson to become a made member. When Gerry took the stand, not only would he never become a made member of that exclusive criminal family, but also, he'd be signing his own death warrant. Today, he would disgrace his family and would never be able to see or hear from his family ever again. He would receive a new name, identity, and place to live, compliments of the US government's Witness Protection Program and the hardworking Americans' tax dollars.

As Vinny sat in the courtroom and scanned the spectators seated, waiting anxiously for the arrival of the government's star, he noticed some unfamiliar female faces in the last row and wondered who they were.

The court clerk announced the beginning of court. "All rise!"

The judge entered the court from his chambers, and upon taking his place at the bench, he shot Vinny a look of hatred and contempt. For he, too, had waited four years to hear the testimony that would hopefully seal Vinny's fate with a long prison term.

The buzz of anticipation, which had risen in intensity, subsided. The chatter in the courtroom dissipated.

All eyes were on Gerry as he entered the courtroom with an obvious air of arrogance, which had always been his trademark. It had been three long, anguished years since Vinny had last seen him, on that drunken, snowy night, a night Vinny now wished could be erased from time as though it had never happened, a night that was a recurring nightmare he couldn't stop.

Vinny watched in amazement as Gerry placed his hand on the Bible. His swearing to tell the truth, the whole truth, so help him God was ridiculous, a fucking joke—his testimony had been bought and paid for by the US government!

He studied Gerry and noticed that the government also bought him the clothes—a pair of loose-fitting Dockers and a short-sleeve polo shirt—he was wearing for his performance in court. Whoever on Gonzalez's team thought of that outfit was indeed a genius. Dressing him to look like an East Hampton yuppie in the summertime made him look somewhat credible, which would force the jury to pay closer attention to him, as opposed to putting him in a double-breasted suit and tie, which would obviously make him look like the mobster, hood, thug he really was. They also opted not to have him testify in his federal-issued prisoner orange jumpsuit. That would have revealed his tremendous size and the jailhouse tattoos all over his body, thus giving the jury the impression he was somehow paying for the crimes he committed and would do or say anything to get out of prison.

Gonzalez began his direct, questioning Gerry about his present incarceration at Lewisburg Federal Prison for the crimes he committed.

Gonzalez then asked, "Why did you decide to cooperate with the federal government on this case?"

"Because I felt that I was offered a Rule 35 motion, which would reduce my sentence according to the judge's decision," Gerry responded innocently.

"Now, did you ultimately enter into any kind of an agreement with the government?"

"Yes, I did," Gerry replied.

"Do you recall the terms of that agreement?" asked Gonzalez.

"In turn for my full cooperation and truthful testimony, I will receive a Rule 35 sentence reduction and be sponsored for the Witness Protection Program, which includes relocation, new name, new identity."

"Are you being protected now?" Gonzalez asked.

"Yes, I'm in the Witness Security Unit, because if I would be at Lewisburg, I would be dead for cooperating, because it's not what you do in the penitentiary. Any cooperating, with any kind of law enforcement, people find out about it and you're dead!"

"Why do you want to go into the Witness Protection Program?" Gonzalez asked.

"Because, basically, I'm blacklisted now in my neighborhood and I would be a target for any young Turk who would want to rise in the ranks of organized crime. Shooting me would be a big trophy, and I would never feel comfortable or safe again."

"Now, Mr. Gerry, do you know the defendant, Vincent Davis?"

"Yes, I do," he answered impatiently. "Do you see him in this courtroom?"

"Yes," he said confidently. He pointed at a somber Vinny, who refused to make eye contact with his adversary.

"Indicating my client, Your Honor," Tommy said involuntarily.

"Mr. Vittorio, how do you know the defendant?" Gonzalez asked.

"He's my best friend Michael's brother-in-law. Mike's been my best friend since 1982."

"Were you friends with or socialized with the defendant?" Gonzalez asked.

"Yes, on several occasions, such as the engagement party, the wedding, a Christmas Eve party. Vinny was more an acquaintance than anything else."

"You indicated a background in organized crime. Could you explain that background?" Gonzalez asked.

"Yes," Gerry said proudly. "I was an associate in the Lucchese crime family. By *associate*, I mean an aspiring member. Basically, they're on like a prospect list to become made members to the family. They conduct a whole array of criminal activities for their immediate superior, who is usually a made member or a soldier. A *made member*, or a *soldier*, is someone formerly inducted into the family through a ceremony attended by captains, soldiers, and the boss. A captain, or capo, is the immediate superior of a crew of soldiers."

"What other crime families are there, and where do they operate?"

"There are five families in the New York area. The Gambino, Genovese, Colombo, Bonano, and Lucchese. They operate mainly in the New York area, but also Jersey, Connecticut, and other parts of the country. They are all part of La Cosa Nostra, which is the larger organization that these crime families belong to."

"Now, did your stepfather have a position in the Lucchese crime family?" Gonzalez asked.

"Yes. He is a captain," Gerry answered nervously.

"Now, returning to the Lucchese crime family in particular. Are you familiar with the structure and who was in charge of that family in the 1990s?"

"Yes." Gerry then explained who the acting boss was, because the boss was on the run. How the acting boss cooperated with law enforcement and the family was left without an administration. The family was run by the five families, like a committee. He further explained that in 1992, his father and uncle were arrested for murdering the capo of their own crew, the same crew his father would eventually take over after his acquittal.

Gonzalez then began a series of questions that revealed Gerry's entire criminal past, starting when he was twelve years old, when he defrauded newspaper for which he delivered the daily paper. He explained how he would collect the money from his customers, then inform his boss he was "robbed by niggers."

Vinny glanced at the jury box for their reaction. Juror 1 rolled his eyes. The three black female jurors put their hands over their mouths in disbelief. A fifth sat quietly with a look of disgust on her face.

He stole his first car, a Maserati 7, when he was fifteen years old, but that was nothing compared to the crimes he went on to explain he'd committed. Robbery, assault, weapons charges, gambling offenses, and drug dealing. He recited these crimes as if from a résumé he was proud of. And he was proud! He bragged about how he and a friend broke into another friend's café on Gramatan Avenue, Mount Vernon. "We cracked open the doors of his gambling machines, Joker Poker machines, and robbed $10,000 out of them," he said enthusiastically.

He then explained how those machines were Mob-owned and could be found in bodegas throughout the city. He continued to explain how he and another friend were tipped off by an associate of theirs who owned a jewelry store about an Indian guy who carried jewels worth $70,000 to $100,000 in a big suitcase. The owner of the jewelry store wanted Gerry and his friend to rip the Indian guy off. "We attempted it, but the plan failed!" he exclaimed. Gerry's career moved on with him as a bouncer in Mob-owned topless bars in Queens and Rockland County, where he also collected protection money in the amount of $300 a week. As a bouncer, Gerry bragged about how he had assaulted fifty or more people. He recalled one night when he cornered a guy between two buildings outside a bar. "I proceeded to crack his head fifteen or twenty times with a metal rod!"

"What were you doing by hitting him fifteen times? Were you trying to kill him?"

"I don't know if I was consciously trying to kill him, but I wasn't really aware. I wanted to hurt him real bad. I wanted to disable him so we would never see him in the club, because he was making me look bad."

"Is this a good time for a break?" Schwartz interrupted, contempt in his voice.

It was obvious that he wanted to disrupt Gerry's damaging testimony. "Yes," Gonzalez responded thankfully.

"Let's take a ten-minute recess," Schwartz ordered.

While court was in recess, Vinny sat contemplating his testimony.

The more he talked, the more Vinny realized that the testimony Gerry was giving about himself was just the beginning of what the government had planned for poor Gerry.

He was a regular *Encyclopedia Britannica* of the fucking Mob. He testified about, in detail, every person he had dealings with in all five families, none of which had anything to do with this case. He not only gave their names but also gave dates, times, and places for each and every one of their criminal activities. He had incriminated everyone in his testimony, even the don and his son. But he was no Salvatore "Sammy the Bull" Gravano. The fucking asshole would now have to look over his shoulder for the rest of his life. Good.

The recess ended.

The jury was already seated when Gerry took his place of dishonor on the stand. Gonzalez resumed his line of questioning about his life of crime. Gonzalez was making damn sure Tommy would have no "bombs," or surprise questions, to throw at him in regards to his character.

"In May of 1992, you were arrested in Manhattan. Could you explain what that was for?"

"I shot a guy three times outside the China Club," Gerry explained sarcastically. "I got into an argument inside the club with a guy from Brooklyn. They thought they owned the VIP lounge. A fight broke out, and I got jumped. I told the guy, 'If you come outside, I'm going to kill you!' They followed me upstairs. At that point, I turned around and shot him three times—in the hand, the groin, and the chest. I ran, but an ex-cop and some street cops stopped me. I was outmanned and outgunned, so I dropped my pistol and got arrested."

"What ultimately happened on that charge?"

As if he doesn't know! Fucking bastard.

"My father sent somebody to talk to the guy who got shot and told him basically the deal, to keep his mouth shut! We weren't sure if he was going to testify or not, but it was arranged. He definitely wasn't going to testify now, because of the warning we gave him. I pleaded guilty to weapons possession and received five years' probation."

"Any other weapons charges that you recall?"

He was happy to see the jury had little reaction to the shooting arrest.

"Yeah," Gerry said abruptly. "About two months later, I was set up by the manager of a topless bar in Rockland County. The owner was aggravated because we used to hang out with a lot of the girls there, and he felt…I guess he felt he was losing authority when we were there, because he couldn't control the situation, he couldn't control us!" Gerry said belligerently.

"So you were arrested and charged with possession of a weapon?"

"I received five months and did three," he replied casually.

Several jurors now had disconcerted expressions.

After about two more hours of Gerry exposing every made and "unmade" man in the La Cosa Nostra, it came time for his introduction to Richard Sabol, the beast.

"What were the circumstances under which you met Richard Sabol?"

"He was with a friend of mine one night who's now dead. We had a dispute, and they wound up leaving. As they got in the car, I pulled my gun out and put it to the window, and they drove away. Then about a week later, I saw Sabol in another after-hours club on Eastchester Road, in the Bronx. We began talking. He explained to me that what I did to him was out of line. Sabol found out who my father was, and he was in with an associate of the Gambino crime family, both of whom are now incarcerated in the John Jr. case."

"What role did this Gambino associate play in your introduction to Richard Sabol?"

"Well, I knew him from the neighborhood, and Sabol also knew him. So the word was passed that Sabol was all right and could be trusted. Sabol then picked me up at the apartment I was staying at, and we went to a diner and discussed, you know, a few things with him. Business ventures and stuff."

"Now, did you begin any kind of, like, social relationship with Sabol?"

"Yes, soon after we almost got shot by some guys who jumped out of some bushes by his house. Sabol had ripped the guy off, and they were going to kill him. After we got away, we went to my house and I got my .380 automatic and went looking for the guy. We found the guy, threw him in our car, and the whole time in the car, I was pistol-whipping him! We drove to I-95 with the initial plan of shooting him, but I didn't feel comfortable with it because I wasn't familiar with Sabol. So I threw the guy out of the car on 1-95 and left him there."

Gerry's last statement caused a few of the jurors to look at him in horror and disbelief.

He continued to explain his relationship with Sabol, the man ultimately responsible for his and ten members of his crew ending up behind bars. Three short years ago, it was Sabol in the seat Gerry was now occupying, confessing his sins and associations with the Lucchese and the other crime families, in return for his freedom and safe passage into the Witness Protection Program. "Sabol and I discussed robbing some Columbians of a couple of kilos of coke, but that never transpired. The deal went sour," Gerry said somberly.

Gonzalez then carefully implicated Vinny's brother-in-law, Michael, in the hopes to discredit him as a possible witness for the defense.

"To what extent did your friend Mr. Lanteri know about what you did?" Gonzalez asked harshly.

"Well, he knew about my fights and stuff like that in clubs. And he knew I was involved in dealing with drugs."

"Did you do drugs in his presence?"

"Yeah, at clubs and social occasions."

So much for Michael being just an innocent in this mess! Fuck!

Gonzalez then changed his line of questions back to Sabol and the case that landed Gerry in jail. "When did you next speak to Sabol?"

"We got together in October of '93 and discussed moving some swag, stolen property, liquor, and stuff like that."

"Mr. Gerry, in front of you is an exhibit in evidence, government exhibit 29," Gonzalez interrupted. "For the benefit of the court, and the ladies and gentlemen of the jury, everyone should have a copy if they want to refer to it," Gonzalez suggested. "Let me direct your attention. First of all, Mr. Gerry, does this chart look familiar to you?"

"Yes, it does," Gerry said with a sarcastic smile on his lips. It was a chart used at Gerry's trial to convict him. A chart that consisted of names, dates, times, and places of every illegal transaction in which Sabol had set him up with for the government.

Time to bore the jury with a lot of useless information that has nothing to do with me. Maybe he thinks if he bores them to death and wastes enough of their time, they'll return a quick guilty verdict just to get home to their families as fast as possible. Either that or he's stupid as well as vicious.

After several hours of rehearing audio tapes and re-reading transcripts, the jury became obviously bored, as two of them fell asleep and the rest, relentlessly, sat checking their watches.

"Mr. Gonzalez, why don't we stop it here?" the judge said sharply. "Ladies and gentlemen, we will stop it here. Remember, you cannot discuss the case. I'll see you tomorrow morning. Have a good night."

Court adjourned for the day.

"Well, what did you think of Gerry's testimony?" Vinny asked anxiously as they entered Tommy's car parked behind the courthouse.

"Very well-rehearsed! But I don't think he scored any brownie points with the jury. Especially the three female black jurors, and juror 1, the construction worker, who looked at Gerry as if he would like to get him alone in a dark alley. Other than that, what else can I say? He's an evil, sadistic man who would do anything, including sell his own mother, to get out of jail!"

"Do you think the jury sees that, TC?"

"If they don't, they are deaf, dumb, and blind!" Tommy said. "But we still have a lot of work ahead of us again tonight. We have to be prepared for anything they throw at us. So let's go home."

After another relentless night spent at Tommy's house, reading and re-reading notes of Gerry's testimony until the wee hours of the morning, Tommy and Vinny were visibly exhausted as they sat patiently at the defense table, awaiting the beginning of today's proceedings.

"All rise!" the clerk announced authoritatively.

The courtroom became quiet as Schwartz, in his flowing black robe, entered and took his seat of honor. Vinny stared at the man he'd come to loathe. A man whose every move was measured precisely for political effect, a man whose eyes were starstruck on the political heavens. He was, without a doubt, relishing every moment of this trial. A cop facing jail was his idea of social justice.

Gerry entered the courtroom looking as clean-cut as yesterday. He had an exuberant look in his eyes, for he knew, if this charade of his paid off, he would be free from his chains of incarceration.

"I remind you that you are still under oath," Schwartz instructed cautiously to Gerry.

"Yes, sir," Gerry responded.

Gonzalez began, "At yesterday's break, we were playing government exhibit."

Vinny turned to look at the jury, several of whom let out quiet sighs of "Oh no."

"All right, folks, we're on page 49," Gonzalez said sympathetically as he began to play the first of several tapes.

The tapes were as boring as ever. The only interesting part of them was listening to these brain surgeons explain to one another how one of their partners dropped a loaded gun he was taking out of his trunk onto the ground. The gun discharged and shot one of the members in his family jewels. Vinny recognized the name of the man who accidentally shot himself. He'd known his wife for twenty years.

When Vinny was a manager for Jack LaLanne, on Tuckahoe Road, he would see and talk to her all the time. He always thought of her as such a sweet woman.

Gerry continued his testimony. "The reason this guy came to work on my crew was that he wasn't kicking back money to his immediate superior, which in this case was…"

When he said the name, Vinny almost choked.

This guy lives around the corner from me and Tommy. I went to school with his sons! Maybe the rumors about Yonkers are true. All I ever heard growing up was whose father was a mobster. Shit.

Gerry continued his testimony, talking about heroin from Pakistan, ripping off drug dealers, machine gun sales, and who was in charge of who from every Mafia member of all five families, none of which had anything to do with this case or what they were here for today. Gonzalez was now posturing.

He was filling the jury's head with so much useless information in an effort to confuse them to the point where it had become ridiculous. Presenting the jury with this testimony was prejudice. Gonzalez was giving the illusion that Vinny was somehow associated in some way with these people. Tommy's hands were tied. He was helpless to stop it. The judge would gladly overrule an objection, saying the government was building a foundation for the jury by describing the magnitude of the case in which his client obstructed. Tommy knew it. It was written all over his anxious and frustrated face.

After several hours of insignificant, albeit informative, testimony about the activities of the La Casa Nostra, the time had come to reveal the name of the person who had single-handedly had "saved" the Mob from certain destruction.

"Did something happen that prevented you from meeting with Sabol to sign a lease for a warehouse that was to be used for illegal activities by organized crime?" Gonzalez asked contemptuously.

"Yes!" Gerry said anxiously. "I received an urgent phone call from Mike Lanteri, Vincent Davis's brother-in-law. Blue, which is Mike's nickname, told me to meet him. It sounded urgent. I figured the only thing I was doing wrong were the things out in New Jersey at that time, so it had to be something out there. I met Blue at his house, and we drove to Vinny's house. On the drive over, Blue was telling me that on Christmas Day, he told Vinny about how I was going with Sabol out there in New Jersey, that we were making moves out there, and he said Vinny got real upset, saying there was no possible way Sabol could be out. Blue said Vinny helped put him away for twenty years down in Georgia. Blue told me Vinny had instructed him not to tell me his name, because he just didn't want anyone else to know where the information came from."

"What happened when you arrived at the defendant's house?" asked Gonzalez, who gazed over at Vinny with accusing eyes. A brilliant strategic move that forced the jury to do the same.

"Vinny was there. He had some jeans on with no shirt, and he seemed a little disheveled. He seemed paranoid."

Vinny grabbed a yellow legal pad and wrote the words "DRUNK OUT OF MY MIND," in big letters, and slid it across the table in front of Tommy, who just smiled.

"At that time, he told me I was being set up, Sabol was a rat, this and that."

Vinny noticed a few of the jurors look toward him and grimace.

"He showed me a piece of paper. I think it had a prosecutor's name on it, and an agent."

"What else did he tell you?" asked Gonzalez, with an almost-evil smile on his face.

"He told me Sabol got sentenced to twenty years in Georgia for drug conspiracy. He told me the prosecutor's name and the agent that arrested him. He also said the reason he knew this information was that he was somehow responsible for Sabol's arrest. He then went on to tell me the feds had me on video and audio tapes. He said, 'You have to do something about it. You got to take care of it.' One instance he told me, 'Get me a gun, I'll do it.'"

Vinny was ready to explode.

That lying son of a bitch!

"Did he tell you why he was telling you all this information?" Gonzalez prodded.

"Well, initially, he made like he was helping me, trying to help me out. But he also stated that he had a rocky past with Sabol, that he didn't like him because Sabol used to go out with his wife, and that federal law enforcement was supposed to notify him or his job if Sabol ever got out, because Sabol threatened him and his wife in the past."

"Then what happened?" Gonzalez asked mildly.

"Well, the meeting lasted about twenty minutes. I left and called my father and told him the story. My father got real mad and said they're trying for me again. The *they* meaning the feds. I told my father I would kill Sabol, and he looked at me like I had five heads. He said, 'You're crazy! There's probably twenty-five agents around him at all times. Forget about him.' My father told me to try to get back the $10,000 we gave Sabol for the lease on the warehouse, but other than that, to leave him alone."

"Did you engage in several conversations with Mr. Sabol over the next few days?" Gonzalez asked calmly.

"Yeah, I told Sabol the deal was off and that my father wanted his ten large back. Sabol became belligerent and came up with every excuse under the sun not to give back the money."

"Did there come a time when you informed Mr. Sabol about him possibly being a rat?"

"Yeah. At first, I told him I learned it from an FBI agent we had in our pocket. I made that up to see what Sabol would say. He totally went crazy! Begging me for the name of the agent."

"BINGO!" Vinny wrote on his legal pad.

The FBI got involved in this case, thinking they had a rogue agent. Washington must have sent a hundred agents to investigate this case. No wonder they're so pissed at me. The FBI must have spent hundreds of man-hours investigating this case to expose one of their own linked to the Mob. When the truth came out that it was just a lonely Transit cop from New York, Washington decided it was payback time. Now it is crystal clear why they're pursuing this case with such vengeance!

"At one point, you said to Sabol, 'I really don't think you're bad.' Was that true at this point?" Gonzalez asked.

"I wasn't 100 percent sure that he wasn't a rat, because I kept having in my mind that Vinny had bad feelings toward Sabol, and maybe he was motivated by something else. I eventually believed

Sabol, and I told him the true source was Vinny Davis. It put me in an awkward position, because I didn't want to expose Vinny, because of my relationship with Michael and Maria. I was friends with them for so long."

"Now, Mr. Gerry, during the course of these conversations with Richard Sabol, did you, at any point in time, mention or suggest the defendant wanted you to kill Sabol?"

"No, I did not," Gerry said.

Thank God, Vinny thought as he looked over at Tommy's smiling face. Tommy had already written on his legal pad in block letters: "GOODBYE WITNESS TAMPERING!" Both Vinny and Tommy knew if Gerry lied and said yes to the last question, Gonzalez would have had a solid witness-tampering case. But you can't tamper with a witness who never knew he was being tampered with. Sabol was not being called to testify by Tommy or Gonzalez. Gerry was the only person who could prove Sabol was ever threatened. And now the truth was told—he wasn't! Surely, the jury would see this. It was like trying to convict someone for assault without an injury or even a victim.

Gonzalez immediately began a new line of questioning about the second meeting, which took place between Vinny and Gerry, approximately a month after their initial contact.

"Do you recall that day?" Gonzalez asked angrily, still upset with Gerry for missing his cue on the witness-tampering question.

"Yes, I do."

"What happened on that day?"

Gonzalez's question was deliberately vague, leaving him as much room as he needed to get back to correct his mistake. But he didn't figure out what Gonzalez was trying to do. So he answered, "I met with Vinny Davis. Blue arranged it. We met at Blue's house, and the three of us went to a bar down the road from Blue's house. Vinny was very interested in what was going on with Sabol. You know, he asked me for a gun again. I kind of just took it in. I didn't blow him off right from the start. I said, 'Yeah, I'll see what I could do.' But I didn't have any intention of giving him a gun, because he was a cop."

"Was that the end of the meeting?" Gonzalez asked. "Vinny drove me to my girlfriend's house."

445

"Did you see the defendant, Vincent Davis, after that night?"

"No."

"What happened next?" Gonzalez prodded.

"A few months later, my father and the entire crew got arrested."

"Have you had any telephone conversations with your friend Blue since your decision to cooperate in this case?" Gonzalez asked somberly again, trying to imply that Vinny's brother-in-law was involved with the Mob.

"No, I haven't, because of my status right now as a witness. Basically, all my friends in the neighborhood are no longer there for me. I'm basically in exile as of my cooperation. It was kind of a self-imposed exile. I have no friends, and I have no relationship with my family. I'm finished in the New York area the rest of my life."

Vinny could swear he heard violins playing softly in the background. *Does he actually believe that the jury is going to feel sorry for him?* Mr. Gonzalez chimed in with the violins. "Your Honor, the government has no further questions for Mr. Gerry at this time."

Vittorio had done everything Gonzalez expected him to do. He had said everything they paid him to say. He had told a great story. He had described the Lucchese crime family in intimate detail. He identified all its members, along with all the members of the other four crime families. He described every detail of their operations from the perspective of one of their own. And lastly, he incriminated Vinny as a Mafia informant.

The judge nodded to Tommy. "You may proceed, Mr. Cascione."

Tommy straightened his notes and looked at the judge. "Thank you, Your Honor," he said solemnly.

Then he turned toward Gerry. Tommy had been waiting patiently to get a shot at him. He'd paid close attention, hanging on to every syllable, in anticipation of ramming it back down Gerry's throat.

"Good morning, Mr. Vittorio," Tommy said with a smile on his face. "My name is Tommy Cascione. I'm the attorney representing Vincent Davis. I have a number of questions to ask you. If anything I say is unclear, please don't hesitate to ask me to rephrase it. First question: Did the government buy you the clothes you are wearing in court today?"

"Excuse me?" responded Gerry hesitantly.

"Federal prisoners wear orange jumpsuits," Tommy remarked, then repeated his question.

"Yes, they did," he said reluctantly.

"Is, or was, Vincent Davis a member of your crew or any Mafia crew?"

"No."

"As far as your business or anything else, he was not an associate of yours?"

"No, he was not."

"Prior to these incidents, did you ever have a discussion with Vincent Davis where the issue of the Mafia or racketeering came up?"

"No." The questions hit Gerry like a barrage of artillery fire. Gonzalez sat at the prosecution table, nervously fiddling with his pen, as his star witness began perspiring profusely right through his shirt. He was nervous.

Tommy cast a look at the jury. They were enjoying it.

"You really are not having any problem in your heart and soul coming in here and testifying against my client, do you?"

"No," Gerry replied arrogantly.

"Now, it's been three years since these events took place, correct?" Tommy asked roughly.

"Yeah."

"When you first showed up in January 1997 to testify in the grand jury in regards to this case, you took the Fifth Amendment and declined to answer questions?"

"Yes, I did."

"About two weeks later, you came back and you told the grand jury a story that would implicate Vincent Davis to be guilty of something. What motivated you to change your original Fifth Amendment to testify in the grand jury?"

"My discussions with my attorney," Gerry replied suspiciously.

"And then you cut a deal with the government?"

"Yes," he answered impatiently.

"Your decision to testify was motivated solely by self-interests, is that correct?"

"Self-betterment, yeah. Self-interests, if you want to call it that," Gerry replied belligerently.

"Now, you testified in the grand jury that Vincent Davis showed you an official document with a DEA agent's and a prosecutor's name on it." Tommy approached the witness stand and handed Gerry a copy of his grand jury testimony.

After a brief look at it, Gerry said, "Yeah."

"Isn't it true that Mr. Davis showed you a handwritten piece of paper with some names and phone numbers on it? Not a report, not a typewritten official document, just a plain old piece of paper with names written on it? You never saw any typewritten documents with Mr. Sabol's name on it, did you?" Tommy asked, in a voice of authority that demanded an answer.

"Not that I remember, no!" Gerry replied angrily. He was becoming testy. Tommy had caught him in a big lie! Lying to a federal grand jury is a federal offense.

Vinny hoped the jury paid careful attention to what was just said. He knew Gonzalez caught it, as he quickly put his head down and furiously scribbled some notes on his legal pad.

"What was Vincent Davis's demeanor on the occasions in which you met with him?" Tommy asked.

"He seemed ticked off that Sabol was on the street," Gerry replied wearily.

"Was he also drunk?"

"No, he was not."

"Was he drinking?"

"No, not that I recall. I don't know what he did before, but he wasn't drinking in front of me!" Gerry replied harshly.

Tommy walked over and handed Gerry a tape transcript and instructed him to read it aloud to the court. Gerry only stared silently. If looks could kill, Tommy would be dead. "Read it," Tommy ordered.

Gerry read reluctantly did. "Then Vinny drove me home and he had a few drinks and he was all over the road. I was kind of concerned about him. I remember calling Blue, telling him that Vinny was really drunk and I was worried he might crash and kill himself."

"There's more!" Tommy said, not pausing for effect for the jury. Tommy took the page and read:

> *Question: Did you see how many drinks Mr. Davis had?*
> *Answer: He had more than one Stoli and lime.*
> *Question: Do you recall approximately what time the meeting began?*
> *Answer: Maybe around eight, in between eight and nine, but Vinny already had a few drinks in him before he met me.*
> *Question: Did he seem drunk to you when you first met him?*
> *Answer: He was staggering, because I know he drinks a lot!*

Look at the smoke coming out that prick Gerry's ears! Vinny thought. *There isn't a thing he could do. If the jury doesn't see him now for the liar he is, they're as blind as a bat!*

Establishing Vinny's intoxication was of paramount importance to his defense. Not even the evil Schwartz would be able to deny Tommy's motion for an intoxication defense. Now he would be forced, at the conclusion of the trial, to charge the jury with intoxication. Tommy had explained this defense in detail to Vinny on numerous occasions. It is when voluntary, or involuntary, intoxications are elements of the crime charged. There is no special plea that raises the defense of intoxication. The defendant simply pleads not guilty. Nevertheless, the defense of intoxication is an affirmative defense in the sense that the defense has the burden of going forward and must prove some evidence of intoxication, unless the prosecution's own proof shows the defendant's intoxication. Once the evidence of intoxication has been introduced, it negates the element of the crime and the jury must be instructed to find the defendant not guilty by means of intoxication.

Gonzalez was fuming, and Judge Schwartz was visibly irritated. They both knew this presented major problems for the prosecution. Gonzalez could continue to prosecute this case on rumors, innuendos, speculation, and on prejudice. He could twist it and attempt to make what Vinny did as evil, but the reality was, Vinny had been drunk.

There were amused smiles on the faces of several jurors as Tommy continued his cross-examination of Gerry.

"At your meeting with Mr. Davis on January 25, you became excited and upset, didn't you?" Tommy continued his questioning like a prizefighter who had his opponent against the ropes.

Gerry appeared almost surly. "Yeah," he said.

"Come March 2, you were much calmer, easier-going, meeting with Mr. Davis."

"Yes," Gerry said.

"And didn't you decide, going into the March 2 meeting, that you did not believe Mr. Davis?"

"I didn't 100 percent disbelieve him, but Sabol wasn't meeting me, and it was getting late, so I figured that I was had."

"Now, Mr. Davis explained to you that his problem, his main problem, was he didn't want Richard Sabol coming over to Yonkers. Is that correct?" Tommy asked cautiously.

"I don't think he wanted Sabol around, period!" replied Gerry sharply.

"I didn't ask you what you thought," Tommy responded matter-of-factly. "I asked you what you did hear. What did he tell you?" Tommy asked heatedly.

"I don't remember him saying that to me," he responded belligerently.

Tommy handed Gerry a copy of his grand jury minutes. "There are 128 questions," Tommy said. "Eighty times, eighty occasions. They're numbered. Mr. Gonzalez gave a narrative question: 'Isn't it true that this and that happened?' And you just said yes. Is that correct?"

"Same way you're doing now!" Gerry exclaimed, knowing full well Tommy was now making him out to be Gonzalez's puppet, who would answer the way he was told to do.

Schwartz saw what Tommy was trying to do and became enraged. "May I see you?" he said contemptuously.

Vinny could see clearly the expression on Schwartz's face. It was as red as a ripe tomato. He looked ready to explode. The jury box was filled with bulging eyes as Schwartz admonished Tommy while raising a pointed finger at him.

"Mr. Cascione, I cautioned you last week off the record, and now I'm cautioning you on the record. If you want to put questions to the witness, do so, but don't make a speech, look at the jury, and make facial expressions."

"I'm sorry. I wasn't aware I used facial expressions," Tommy remarked sarcastically.

Schwartz thundered, "Don't make a speech to the jury. Look at the witness when you're questioning. Now, let's go!"

"Mr. Vittorio, you didn't have to be prepared for the grand jury, because you were just asked questions by Mr. Gonzalez and you just said yes. Is that correct?" Tommy asked cautiously.

"Yes and no," Gerry replied.

"But all the facts of your case were developed, not through your mouth, but through the mouth of the US attorney!"

The objection was thunderous as Gonzalez sprung to his feet. "Mischaracterization!" roared Gonzalez. "I object to counsel's mischaracterization of the grand jury testimony," Gonzalez continued, crying like a spoiled child.

"Sustained," responded Schwartz angrily.

Tommy didn't miss a beat as he lobbed the next grenade at Gerry.

"You didn't tell the grand jury anything about Mr. Davis asking you for a gun on March 2. Isn't that correct?"

"I don't know?" he responded, now totally confused.

"Your Honor, I object to reading in something that's not in evidence," Gonzalez said, sounding more like a sore loser by the minute.

"He can look at it," Tommy interrupted. Then he said, "Fair enough. I'll withdraw the question. Is there any particular reason you left out that little cogent fact about the gun in your grand jury testimony?"

"Well, at that time, I was just pulled out of Lewisburg, and my frame of mind wasn't on too much of this case," Gerry said defensively.

"Now, of course, you're here for the purpose of your own, are you not?"

"Yes."

"Did you enter into any agreement with Vincent Davis to kill Sabol?"

"No," responded Gerry involuntarily, almost without thinking.

Tommy was a genius. He managed to piss off Schwartz, Gonzalez, and confuse the shit out of Gerry. Then, from out of nowhere, without warning, he threw a bomb at Gerry, and before anyone could stop it, it exploded right in their faces. There was never any agreement between Gerry and Vinny to harm Sabol! In order for the government to prove a conspiracy existed, they needed an agreement between two people working toward a common goal. The government's star witness, a man who sold his soul for his own freedom, who took the stand in an effort to destroy Vincent Davis's life, might have, unknowingly and unintentionally, just saved it.

Tommy was on a roll and didn't want to stop just yet.

"Mr. Vittorio, you told Vinny's brother-in-law that you shot Vinny's gun six times. Did you not?" Tommy asked curiously.

"Yes, I did."

"You made that up?"

"I was posturing."

"So you lied."

"Yes," Gerry responded, barely audible.

"How often were you in the habit of concocting tall tales like that?"

"I don't!" Gerry protested, not liking the fact that he was being made out to look like a fool and a liar.

Tommy decided he had already scored the points necessary to dismantle the charges against Vinny, so he rehashed the vital parts of Gerry's own testimony by Mr. Gonzalez's direct examination of him. Letting the jury hear once again what an evil demon he was, the vicious crimes he had committed against society, and how many times he had previously gotten away with it.

"Just a couple more questions, Mr. Vittorio," Tommy said innocently. "You became a cooperating witness about a year ago. Have you testified in any other case?"

"No," he said indignantly.

"Have you given information on any other matters?"

"Yes," he said through clenched teeth.

"Without asking you specifically, what kind of things?"

"Objection!" Gonzalez exploded.

"Sustained!" Schwartz responded instantly.

"I have no further questions, Your Honor," Tommy said, full of confidence.

Tommy's face was exuberant as he walked toward the defense table. He'd accomplished what he had set out to do, and he did it extremely well. The government's star witness had been reduced to nothing more than a degenerate criminal, a rat, who sold his testimony to the prosecution to get out of prison.

CHAPTER 33

Strange as it was, when Vinny was safely in his bed, free from the pressures of the courtroom, the jury, and Schwartz, he lay awake, too troubled to sleep. Although he ached with physical exhaustion, all his overactive mind could think about was his family and how supportive they had been. Over and over, he recalled his youngest brother Raymond's words, the tone in his voice when he said, "You have to fight for your innocence." Vinny's eyes refusing to close and let him forget the events of the day, he stared at the ceiling and saw the courtroom, the judge, and the faces of the jurors, as if they were all part of a stage and he were in a front-row seat. Vinny turned in his seat at the defense table, toward the audience. He made eye contact with his brother Raymond, seated in the front row, visibly in pain, a pillow kept tightly to his chest to ease the expansion on the sutures in his chest as he breathed. It was only two short weeks ago since his successful open-heart surgery, which saved his life from the same rare disease that had claimed their mother's life at thirty-one years old. If it were not for the two-week postponement of the trial, a postponement Schwartz reluctantly had to make due to his own scheduling error, Vinny would have never been able to be at the hospital for his brother when he needed him most. Luckily, through that quirk of faith, he was there and the operation was a complete success. Looking at his brave little brother in the front row, showing his support for him, Vinny couldn't help but think how lucky the Davis family was. If God granted only one miracle this year, he was glad his brother Raymond received it. For Vinny would gladly rot in a jail cell than see harm come to any member of his family. Losing his mother so young was more than he could bear.

Vinny had plunged suddenly into sleep as dawn tried to sneak through the blinds in his bedroom window, and lay oblivious to everything until the alarm sounded. He showered and began choosing his clothes for court. But his thoughts were on the courtroom battle that had turned into a spiritual thing, a constant battle, with no winner until the end, and he could not afford to lose his faith, not for a minute.

After Vinny and Tommy completed what had become their daily routine, they arrived at court. Maria and Mike greeted them in the hallway outside of the courtroom. Vinny immediately took notice of the look on Mike's face as he stood speechless, mouth gaping, eyes wide with fear, the personification of stage fright.

Vinny kissed his sister on the cheek, reassuring her that everything would be all right.

"They want me to testify," Mike said with noticeable irritation in his voice.

"I figured they would," Tommy said philosophically. "Gonzalez seems to be ruthless and unpredictable when he is pissed, and at this stage of the trial, he is totally pissed."

"What can I testify about?" Mike asked acidly.

Tommy shuddered. "I can't see you being able to hurt us by testifying," Tommy said soothingly.

"I think Gonzalez knew we were going to call you to testify for us, so he cut us off at the pass." Mike's initial fury quickly abated. He realized that Tommy was right. Slowly he took a seat.

"Okay, now, try to relax," Tommy said. "We'll be inside."

Gonzalez was becoming increasingly frustrated. The testimony that had been presented by Gerry was not as devastating as he'd expected. All the luridness of the Mafia was being presented to the jury. The problem was that it was Gerry's involvement, and it had nothing to do with Vinny as pertaining to this case. What was happening was a deliberate blurring of the evidence by Gonzalez. What little importance there was in Gerry's testimony was being buried under a mountain of speculation and irrelevancies. Tommy was also doing an excellent job, constantly reminding the jury it was Gonzalez that had made the deals to free Sabol and Gerry in return for their testimony. It would seem that Gonzalez's haste to buy Gerry's testimony might be a fatal flaw for the prosecution. So today, he reached into his prosecutorial bag of tricks and summoned Mike Lanteri to testify against his brother-in-law. Tommy had studied Mike's grand jury testimony voraciously and could not understand how Mike could possibly help the prosecution's case. There was a sudden air of expectancy in the courtroom as Michael Lanteri was called to the stand.

Mike took the stand and was sworn in.

He was also a man who thought he knew the true value of friendship. He and Gerry had been best friends since early childhood. Mike's mother took care of Gerry as if he were her own son. Now the reality that their friendship was only one-sided had left him jaded. His best friend had orchestrated this horrendous personal disaster that had caused such heartache for his wife and her family. The harsh reality that he could have been charged with conspiracy in this case, sitting in a chair next to his brother-in-law, was enough to permanently remove his humorous, nonchalant attitude about Mob life forever. The thought of going to prison for five years when all he did was call his friend on the phone, telling him to come to his house, was a frightening reality for him. The more he thought about it, the more despicable it all seemed. The absurdity of the whole thing hit him like a ton of bricks when he took the stand.

For several moments, there was silence. Mike straightened in his chair. It scraped loudly on the floor of the quiet courtroom.

Gonzalez began his questioning as a mere formality. "How are you employed, and how long have you worked there? Do you know the defendant and his family? When did you marry the defendant's sister, and do you have any children?"

Mike was calm and polite as he responded to the questions posed to him. Mike explained how he had been best friends with Gerry since he was six years old, growing up in the same neighborhood, attending the same schools, socializing together by going to sporting events and clubs as they reached their early twenties. Little by little, their relationship started to dwindle when Mike began dating Vinny's sister, Maria. Instead of their seeing each other every day, it might have been once or twice a month.

Gonzalez prodded with questions about whether Mike knew Gerry's stepfather, Vito Carbone, the capo of the Lucchese crime family, and Gerry's goal to become a made member of that family. Further questioning revealed that Gerry had been obtuse with Mike in regards to his illegal Mob activities, such as drug dealing, gunrunning, and a shipment of stolen women furs. Mike explained to the jury how he had seen Richard Sabol on a couple of occasions with Gerry but never really spoke to the guy other than to say hello or gesture a friendly wave.

"What, if anything, did Mr. Davis tell you about Mr. Sabol?" Gonzalez asked in wonder.

"Well, back through the years, Vinny had mentioned that he's a sick guy and he's capable of anything. Basically that Sabol is a nut. Vinny had a lot of fear of Sabol. He had threatened to throw acid on Vinny's wife, Debbie, and my wife if he got out of jail. My wife had always been very nervous and afraid of Richard Sabol."

"Now, did the defendant become emotional in describing Mr. Sabol to you?" Gonzalez asked solicitously.

"For the most part," Mike said earnestly. "Like I said, he feared the fact of Sabol getting out and possibly going to hurt his wife, my wife, or his family. During the time I have been with my wife, Sabol's name has come up a few times. Every time it comes up, it's the same thing. Vinny would say Sabol's crazy and if he gets out, he's capable of doing a lot of damage," Mike added decidedly.

Gonzalez, being a shrewd and savvy prosecutor, realized it was time to turn up the heat in his questioning. "Do you recall testifying voluntarily at the grand jury?"

"No, I didn't," Mike said harshly.

"Okay! Were you compelled to testify after you were given immunity from prosecution?" Gonzalez asked accusingly.

"Yes," Mike grudgingly agreed.

"Underneath you, to your left, you should find a copy of your grand jury testimony from December 1994."

Mike reached under his seat and retrieved a copy of his testimony as instructed by Gonzalez. "Do you recall telling me in the grand jury that Mr. Davis despised Mr. Sabol?" Gonzalez asked in an intimidating manner.

"Well, this is after everything came out at Christmas," Mike said defensively. "Vinny was real aggravated that Sabol was out of prison and neither he or his job was notified about it. He was real nervous and in fear for himself, his family, and us."

"Was the defendant jealous of Richard Sabol?"

"I don't know, per se, jealous. I really don't know of his jealousy or to what extent he was jealous, or if he was jealous at all. In my conversations with him, he was more nervous and fearful for his family."

At this point, it was evident Gonzalez was not getting the responses from his witness he wanted. You could feel the volatile chemistry between them. Gonzalez stared at the ceiling tiles of the courtroom for a moment, collecting his thoughts, then tried a new approach.

"Was there a family gathering with your wife's family on Christmas Day 1993 in which you and the defendant were present?"

"Yes."

"Could you explain how the subject of Richard Sabol came up on that day?" Gonzalez asked encouragingly.

"I believe his brother Michael had mentioned something first, that he had heard that Sabol was out. Vinny said, 'No way!' Then I said, 'Yeah, I saw Gerry and Sabol in a car together a couple of weeks ago.' Vinny got real upset. I think he had mentioned either a judge or some federal agent from Georgia should have notified him or his job if Sabol was transferred, or moved, or anything that was going on with him, for his family's safety. Vinny was shocked," Mike added hesitantly. "He said Sabol was supposed to be in prison for a long time on a drug charge. Sabol must have ratted on the people he got arrested with down in Georgia in order for him to have gotten out so soon. So Vinny told me, 'You better tell your friend Gerry to stay away from Sabol, that the guy's no good. He's nothing but trouble.' So I warned my friend shortly after Christmas of what Vinny had said."

"Now, you indicated there was some point in time later that the subject of Richard Sabol came up again with your brother-in-law. Could you explain that?" Gonzalez asked, seemingly fascinated.

"If I remember correctly, Vinny called my house about a month after Christmas. When he called that night, he was wrecked, drunk, cursing at me to the fact. 'Get your fucking friend down to your house now! I need to talk to him, it's important.' So I called Gerry and my wife called Gerry five minutes later to make sure he was coming to my house."

"Would this have been the first night that you or the defendant advised Gerry that Sabol was actually an informant?" Gonzalez asked with a derisive smile.

"He wasn't still an informant," Mike insisted. "He was an informant. The conversation at my house that night was basically that my brother-in-law came over drunk and he was screaming and yelling at Gerry to the fact, 'How stupid can you be? After Mike told you to stay away, Sabol's no good, you're going to get yourself in trouble, yet you're still running around with him. What are you, a moron?' That's basically the gist of the conversation at my house that first night. Vinny and Gerry going back and forth, cursing at each other."

"Now, did you have any conversations with the defendant after the first meeting in January 1994 in which the defendant related his conversation with Gerry to you?" Gonzalez asked superciliously.

"There was one time about a month or so later. I believe it was Vinny's birthday in February. He came by my apartment and had spoken to me and Maria. He told us if Gerry didn't stop playing around with Sabol, he was going to do whatever it took to put Sabol back in jail. And if Gerry had to be part of it, he would be part of it. That was when I got a little twisted with Vinny, because Gerry's been my friend since I was a kid, and I really didn't want to see him get in any trouble. That was why the whole time I kept telling Gerry," Mike continued pleadingly, "to stop hanging out with Sabol, get away from him. But he would just 'yes me,' that he wasn't with him anymore, but evidently he was."

"Well," Gonzalez said musingly, "did you relay that information to Gerry?"

"No," Mike said indignantly. "First of all, I didn't want to get involved in this any more than I already was, because I wanted nothing to do with either one of them. My job was done. I told Gerry numerous of times to stop what he was doing, but he ignored me. So at that point, if that was what it was going to be, that was what it was going to be. I wasn't going to get involved and risk any harm coming to my wife and child. I'm a legit guy, and I didn't want to get myself into this more than I already was."

"When you say he was going to get in trouble, do you mean he was going to get arrested?" Gonzalez asked.

"Yes. If he kept doing illegal things like that, reality is, you're going to get arrested. But that night when Vinny came to me and Maria, he said 'If I got to get both of them.' He even said, 'If I have to wear a wire, I'll do it. I'll do whatever it takes to put Sabol back in prison. And if your friend has to go, he's going to go.' I never relayed that to Gerry word for word, because I didn't want a confrontation. But Gerry knew Vinny was going to take Sabol down. I had warned him, but he didn't listen."

"Let's go to the second meeting involving all three of you. What happened?"

"I don't know who called who, but I know Gerry came to my house, and then Vinny showed up. I was there, my wife, and the baby. This meeting was totally different from the first meeting. There was no screaming or yelling. Gerry was playing with the baby. Vinny said he wanted to talk to him. My wife didn't want a repeat performance of the last meeting in the house, so we went down to Jesters Pub. When we got there, Vinny ordered a double Absolut on the rocks. He had had a few drinks before coming to my house, but he wasn't as drunk as the first meeting. Vinny asked Gerry if he was still hanging around with Sabol. Gerry said, 'I got to get my $10,000 back,' cursing Sabol. 'I want my money.' Gerry was well hungover on the ten large he had given Sabol, and he thought he was going to lose it. He had gotten crazy about the money."

"Mr. Lanteri, I'm going to ask you some questions off this transcript," Gonzalez said, handing him a copy. "Turn to page number 6."

Mike did as Gonzalez directed.

"Five lines from the top. Mr. Davis says, 'If you know who doesn't want to take care of the problem, I'll just need to get in touch with you-know-who to get a certain thing to take care of the problem, and then I'll do it myself.'

"What is your understanding of the *who* of the you-know-who?"

"He's saying if Gerry doesn't take care of the problem," Mike responded coolly.

"What's your understanding of what the problem is?"

"In other words, if Gerry hasn't stopped at this point dealing with Sabol, then Vinny's going to you guys to set him up."

"Now, do you see where he says a 'certain thing'? What is your understanding of what the 'certain thing' is?" Gonzalez asked, smiling maliciously.

Mike appeared confused. The question had come out of nowhere. He pondered the question for a moment, then proposed his answer. "A wire," Mike reiterated.

Gonzalez stood shell-shocked, contemplating the tremendous damage his own witness had inflicted on his case. There was an instant stunned silence throughout the courtroom. "He was going to wear a wire for Gerry?"

Gonzalez sighed, looking disdainfully at his own witness. "Do you know whether Gerry had any ability to wire people?" Gonzalez asked off-handedly.

"I'm talking about Vinny," Mike insisted. "Vinny would get the wire."

Tugging on an ear, Gonzalez turned away from the witness stand and looked at Schwartz, his illustrious leader, for help.

Predictably, Schwartz gave Mike one of his slow, evil glares. This was certain to have an insidious effect on the jury. Turning back, Gonzalez looked perplexed, then angry. He then persisted, annoyed. "I'll just get in touch with you-know-who to get a 'certain thing' to take care of the problem."

Mike didn't appear fazed. He remained calm. "I believe Vinny was talking about Gerry and going to somebody in law enforcement to do what he told me he was going to do months before because my friend was not listening."

Gonzalez stood back at the podium, his face grim and his eyes intent. "Did you have a conversation with Mr. Davis in which he specifically said he would get a wire?" Gonzalez asked disbelievingly.

Mike stared back at him with cold, undisguised contempt and said, "Yeah, he mentioned it at my house the night of his birthday."

Gonzalez became infuriated. His face was beet red. "And you're just remembering this now?" he asked in a voice of a petulant child.

Mike looked perplexed. "You just played the tape for me!" he answered in a loud voice.

"But you don't remember independently of this, an earlier conversation in which the wire came up?" Gonzalez asked with obvious condescension.

Mike remained firm. "Yes, I do."

"And in these earlier conversations, you're saying now, based on this tape, you now recall the defendant saying he would get a wire?" Gonzalez asked disingenuously.

"A wire, surveillance, something to the fact. He worked with the feds before, so I assumed that he was referring to that. That's what he threatened he would do the night he came to my house."

Gonzalez became more enraged and cried out, "Do you recall testifying anything about this in your grand jury testimony?"

"Objection!" Tommy shouted as he rose to his feet.

"Overruled!" Schwartz shrieked, not giving Tommy the chance to be heard.

"I don't recall," Mike answered earnestly.

Gonzalez looked at Mike with an expression of martyrdom. He knew that Mike would not change his answer, and there was nothing he or the judge could do about it without a recess. The taped phone conversation was innocuous in and of itself. The tape wasn't exactly the stuff convictions were made of, but it was all Gonzalez had. The actual hard evidence in this case was nonexistent. Now, what he thought was the one solid piece of evidence to support his theories was just smashed to pieces by his own witness.

"Could you look at your grand jury testimony and tell me if you testified about a wire? Take a few seconds, if you can," Gonzalez said politely.

"Take a fifteen-minute break!" Schwartz rumbled, his face flushed with anger. His evil little eyes, cold, empty, and spiteful, glared at Mike. He then threw his copy of the grand jury transcript at him in his patented, offensive style and demanded, "You read that grand jury testimony!"

Mike looked perplexed. "The whole thing?" he asked innocently.

"The whole thing!" Schwartz exploded in frustration, his eyes blazed in anger. There was a shocked silence in the courtroom.

Mike looked around the courtroom in surprise. Everyone shared his astonishment.

The court clerk, quickly realizing the potentially damaging display of open hostility toward the witness by Schwartz, immediately ordered, "All rise!" so the jury could be removed from the court.

As soon as the jury exited, Tommy asked politely, "May I be heard?"

"What?" Schwartz growled as he rubbed a nervous hand across his face.

Tommy began saying, "I believe that Mr. Gonzalez—"

"Wait until the witness leaves the courtroom," Schwartz said haltingly. "Step outside!" he ordered Mike with the sweep of his hand, motioning him out of the courtroom.

As soon as Mike exited, Tommy was again on the attack. "It would appear that Mr. Gonzalez is asking his witness a question regarding a grand jury proceeding run by Mr. Gonzalez, where he never asked the question directed to that area of inquiry—"

Schwartz interrupted heatedly, his dour expression never changed. "What's your objection?"

"My objection is this is not a fair question for his own witness—"

"Overruled!" Schwartz interrupted irritably, not having the decency to let Tommy finish his objection. "He can impeach his own witness! Fifteen minutes!" he ordered ominously, exiting the bench.

Outside the courtroom, the proverbial shit hit the fan. Mike was sitting on a bench in the hallway, surrounded by his family. As he voraciously read his grand jury transcripts, Gonzalez approached like a stampeding elephant. "Do you know what *perjury* is?" he demanded.

Mike was nervous; you could hear the tension in his voice. "Yes, I do."

"Well, let me tell you something!" Gonzalez said, his tone insistent.

At that moment, Vinny saw red; he wanted to smash Gonzalez's face in, but the moment passed quickly and his arrogant enthusiasm overcame his rage-filled depression.

"Juan doesn't like when things don't go his way," Vinny said antagonistically. "Do you, Juan?" Vinny persisted, hoping the prosecutor would lose his cool and do something stupid.

But Gonzalez only laughed. "God, I don't believe this," he said incredulously, running his fingers through his hair. He then turned back to Mike, who sat stunned with disbelief, and said with a touch of contemptuous pity, "You may be immune from prosecution on this case, but you are not immune from prosecution for perjury!"

The hallway fell into a shocked, amazed silence.

Then an anguished Tommy jumped in, his face flushed with anger. He couldn't believe a federal prosecutor was threatening his own witness. Tommy spoke in a hard, solid voice. "I hope to God I didn't hear you right, Counselor!"

Gonzalez stood there peering back at Tommy. "Tell me something, Tommy," Gonzalez said thickly. "Did you tell him how to answer that question?"

Tommy looked faintly amused, then asked piteously, "How can I tell him an answer to a question you're asking him on the stand? He's your witness!"

Gonzalez didn't move or answer. Several curious onlookers were observing the commotion as Gonzalez, realizing he had made a gaffe, smiled sheepishly and laughed heartily in an attempt to show he was only kidding. "Ah, what difference does it make?" Gonzalez said with finality as Vinny and his family watched impatiently, saying nothing.

Tommy took a step toward Gonzalez. "Look," Tommy snarled through clenched teeth, "you may be able to buy witnesses' testimony, but you can't threaten them!"

"All right," Gonzalez said, still annoyed. Without another word, he put his hands casually in the pockets of his pants, turned, and walked away.

Mike sat motionless on the bench, his deep-set eyes metallic and expressionless.

"You know," Tommy said musingly, trying to lighten up a tense situation, "I think Mr. Gonzalez is a sore loser."

Mike looked up at Tommy. He tilted his chin, looking thoughtful and sort of noble. "I guess he wasn't expecting the answer I gave," Mike said wearily.

"No," Tommy said confidently, "but it was an honest answer. The truth and honesty are two things Mr. Gonzalez is not interested in." Tommy looked at Mike, who was looking confused and besieged. "Are you going to be all right when we go back inside?"

Mike shook his head from side to side in a kind of ambiguous answer. "Truthfully, I won't be all right until I am the hell out of New Jersey."

"Me too," Tommy said, his face grimaced. "Me too!"

Mike, his indomitable stroll taking him back to the witness chair, was reminded before he sat down that he was still under oath. As Mike sat in the witness chair, the courtroom became filled with an air of anticipation, which radiated from the bench.

Mad Bull Schwartz's mouth widened with a predatory grin as he looked down at his prey.

Mike had made it undeniably clear in his testimony that the only thing he wanted was his friend to stay away from Sabol, a known criminal. Mike seemed completely comfortable on the witness stand, cool and decisive, as he explained the true story exactly the way it happened. He spoke in a low monotone as he explained how depressed and upset Vinny was about Sabol being out of prison and how afraid he was for his wife and family.

"The times you were together with Gerry and Vinny, did anybody turn the conversation to killing Sabol or anybody else?" Tommy asked dispassionately.

"No, not that I recall," Mike said earnestly.

"If somebody said, 'Let's kill somebody,' would that stick in your mind?"

"Yes, I think so," Mike said sharply.

"And if Vinny were to ask Gerry for a gun, would that stick in your mind?"

"Yes," Mike said firmly.

"Do you recall anything like that happening?"

"No."

"In fact, would that have made sense to you, your brother-in-law asking your friend for a gun?"

"I find it a little odd. Vinny has guns. He always had a gun on him, so why would he need a gun from Gerry?"

"No further questions, thank you."

CHAPTER 34

Another day dawned and found Vinny wide awake, eyes staring up at his bedroom ceiling. He'd promised himself some rest to help clear his fatigue, but a frantic and sleepless night had simply created more conflict in his mind. Eleven sleepless nights in a row had been creating havoc in his mind.

Whatever Tommy had accomplished has brought the simmering pot to its boiling point. The criminals have been let loose among us, whether they're into small-time thievery or murder—two extremes with basically the same ruthless intent. They are free to do what they want and have no sense of guilt. The government will find justification for anything they do, even for killing and maiming the innocent. The Russians have a great saying: "Spare a thief, a good man dies." I still can't believe this fucking shit!

His anger mounted with his frustration. Vinny spent the next hour making his own notes on his talk with Agent Morley, comparing them with earlier statements to Agent Stamp. No divergence, just more in-depth explanation. A simple clarification at that meeting could have changed the entire picture. Carefully, he went over the series of questions asked to him by Morley.

Why the hell hadn't I been more explicit in the first place? But when Morley met me to discuss the case, I was sure he'd fucking send Sabol away for life. I didn't think it necessary to go into precise details about how drunk I was the nights I met with Gerry. I had assumed, in typical cop fashion, that the agents knew I could never be guilty of anything. I believe in doing the right thing, and that's what's now gotten me into this shit. Everything I've done, all the moves I thought were right, it has turned out horribly wrong—a fucking disaster!

Knowing and willing intent to obstruct justice were the two elements of the crime Gonzalez must prove existed to obtain his precious conviction. Thus far, it had been major problem for the prosecution—they hadn't proved it. The government had not submitted one iota of evidence to suggest Vinny knew Sabol was working as a government informant. For Vinny to surmise that Sabol was a rat was extremely plausible. The truth was, that was exactly what Vinny did surmise. You don't have to be a cop to figure it out. Anyone who's convicted and sentenced to twenty years in prison but released after but two has to have ratted on someone. Vinny truly believed Sabol ratted on the people with whom he was involved in drug smuggling down in Georgia. That was how he got out of prison. Vinny was sure that was what happened.

It had been two days since Mike's devastating testimony rocked the prosecution's case to its foundations.

Immediately, Gonzalez sought damage control, calling Special Agent Gray of the Drug Enforcement Agency, Sabol's arresting officer in Georgia. Under questioning by Gonzalez, Agent Gray told a story to the jury that was straightforward. He repeated the story he had given at Vinny's department trial, in a voice that was forthright and earnest, not a glib, verbatim response, but sometimes with hesitation as he tried to recapture the sequence of events. It was an account of his involvement with Vinny—his phone conversations assuring Vinny and his boss that Sabol was not working for the government, and his dealings with Richie Sabol. What Agent Gray testified to was of no significance in helping the prosecution's case. However, he was adding to the mountain of evidence supporting the defense's claim that not only had Vinny pleaded with every federal agency not to make any deals with Sabol but also that each of those federal agencies had promised Vinny and the NYPD that Sabol was not being utilized as an informant and was still incarcerated.

The following morning was filled with inaccurate and confusing testimony given by Lieutenant Houston. At that time, he was Vinny's anticrime sergeant, who initiated the original joint investigation with the federal agencies involved with the Sabol situation. It was his initial belief that Vinny was overreacting to Sabol's threats against him and his family and that Vinny was obsessed about the threat Sabol posed. That was his thinking until he contacted his old friend FBI Agent Stamp, who assured him that any threat made by Sabol should be taken extremely seriously.

Vinny glanced at his nemesis Lieutenant Houston as he approached the stand. Tall and thin, with thick, sandy-colored hair, he wore a dark-gray suit he'd bought off the rack at Sears fifteen years ago. Houston's equally quick glance veered away in disinterest as he took the stand. As he testified, Vinny studied his expressions. It was indecisive, doubtful, even troubled. He was flustered and nervous, talking too much about details the jury didn't need to hear. He was so confused he began talking about postal inspectors, which even baffled Gonzalez.

When Tommy cross-examined him, he became thoroughly shaken.

Tommy played a taped conversation between Houston and an Internal Affairs lieutenant who headed the police department's investigation. On the tape, his voice was clearly heard throughout the courtroom stating that Officer Davis notified him shortly after Christmas 1993 that Sabol had been released from prison.

"Did the defendant notify you after Christmas 1993?" Tommy asked.

Houston smiled nastily. "I don't remember," he said, growing apprehensive and dismayed.

Vinny stared at Houston, both mystified and alarmed. His lips tightened, his jaw rigid. Everyone in District 11 knew he was a coward and an office boy, a term more commonly used by cops as a house mouse, who stayed within the safety of the walls of the command. But this was not his usual style.

Something's not right here. What's put him on the edge? Has Gonzalez and his pack of wolves at the FBI gotten something on him, threatening to indict him, as they did my brother-in-law and sister— unless he got amnesia on the stand? Or is he afraid that, since the merger of the Transit Police with the NYPD and his recent promotion to lieu-

tenant, if the department brass found out he failed to make proper noti-
fications, he, too, would lose his job?

Tommy rewound the tape and played it again for the witness.

"Having heard the tape a second time, does this help refresh your recollection as to when Officer Davis notified you about Richard Sabol's release?" Tommy asked petulantly.

"No," Houston insisted, his face faintly amused. Tommy's look was of shocked disbelief.

The jurors were now speculating.

Strange, Tommy decided. He might be answering out of pique, but the whole situation was definitely strange, unsettling—disturbing, in fact. Tommy played the tape one more time and asked Houston again if it helped refresh his recollection.

Houston stared blankly at Tommy. "No," he reiterated.

"Is that your voice we heard on that tape?" Tommy asked irritably, his anger beginning to break.

"Yes," Houston replied reluctantly.

For a moment, a heavy silence hung over the courtroom. "I have no further use for this witness," Tommy said with obvious condescension.

Vinny stared at Houston as he lumbered away from the witness stand. He then glanced at Gonzalez and detected a slight smile that infuriated him.

When Tommy returned to the defense table, Vinny snapped. "Why didn't you try to provoke him?" His tone made both of them uncomfortable, especially Tommy, as he knew Vinny's stormy temperament so well.

Tommy shook his head in frustration. "Look," he said calmly, "they got to him, and no matter what I do, he is not going to be swayed. Gonzalez must have something on him, because he is scared to death. Besides, the jury could clearly see he was hiding something."

"Do you really think they got something on him?"

Tommy nodded without emotion.

Vinny looked up at Schwartz, his formidable adversary, who thoroughly enjoyed hovering above the court like some Greek god watching the demigods and mere mortals battle it out. Today he was the picture of sophisticated tranquility and sardonic splendor. But neither Vinny nor Tommy would underestimate him or his encyclopedic grasp of the law and his uncanny ability to help the prosecution maintain their strategic goals in the face of daily tactical disasters.

Yes, the deck is stacked against me.

The day before, Gonzalez, realizing that his case was in dire straits, decided to change gears and attempt a character assassination of Vinny by calling two witnesses from NYPD Internal Affairs to testify. Both witnesses, a lieutenant and a sergeant, testified that Officer Davis was the subject of an intensive Internal Affairs investigation relating to his association with the Mafia. Twenty-four-hour surveillance was established on the subject officer, on and off, for over two years. Both investigators also testified that Officer Vincent Davis had been the subject of several complaints for blatant disregard of proper procedure in violating the Patrol Guide. He also received several disciplinary reprimands from the department. His latest charges, prior to his termination from the department, were for associating with known criminals without direct permission from the chief of the department. That charge brought an instant smile to Vinny's face, as he remembered the puny Hispanic sergeant who never spent a day out on patrol trying to explain that in a convincing manner to the jury. Her expression never changed from one of total indifference. She was likable enough, with a cynical wit, but she was an ignoramus on the subject of undercover work.

Throughout his career, Vinny had maintained relationships with any number of alleged criminals: drug dealers, burglars, car thieves, etc. They were essential in obtaining vital information on the streets. It was commonplace for most good cops to have a ready supply of snitches. Besides, he was an undercover Transit cop, and if these people didn't commit any crimes in the subways of New York City, it was not his goal in life to bust them. So long as they left him alone and stayed out of his personal life, something Sabol had managed not to do; it was not his job to save the world.

Vinny marveled at Tommy's patience as he waited for his turn at the investigators. When it came, they were like lambs being led to the slaughter. Gonzalez must have forgotten to warn his witnesses that Tommy was a former assistant district attorney in the Bronx and knew more about cops and the tricks they played than they did.

When Tommy was finished with them, it was revealed that after their extensive investigation was complete, there was not one piece of evidence that could suggest that Vinny was a dirty cop. In fact, the only thing they did find was that Vinny had received two parking tickets. One was for an expired registration on his car, the other for an expired inspection sticker, and that Internal Affairs detectives issued both summons.

This morning, FBI special agent John Morley was sworn in as the last witness for the prosecution. He appeared affable, with a ready smile, an effective disguise for a devious mind. He now looked more grim-faced than the previous occasions in which Vinny had the esteemed pleasure of meeting him. He cast a polite look at Tommy and a friendly nod at Gonzalez as he took his seat on the witness stand. Until now, Vinny had always had the utmost respect for the FBI. He thought of them as truthful, consummate professionals, not people who testified as to strong presumptive evidence that substantiated their own personal beliefs.

In movies, scenes of FBI agents testifying in court were often the climax. Agent witnesses were like gods to juries. All prosecutors had to do was ask them to recite their credentials, and when they were through, the defendant would be convicted. However, at this trial, the jury appeared to be unimpressed. The jurors, who appeared to have been paying attention at the beginning of the trial, were now yawning openly, while others put their heads back and slept. The jury had been forced to watch numerous videotapes of the Customs surveillance operation—relentless hours of members of organized crime coming and going, in and out of the government's undercover apartment. The most interesting part of the tapes was watching one of Carbone's crew. Every time he came to the apartment, he'd ask Sabol what he had to eat in the house. The government was portraying this poor bastard as a big-time gangster when he couldn't afford to put food on his own table. Ironically, the famished gangster was the same one who accidentally shot himself in the groin. It was almost comical watching the same routine with each new video he appeared in. The jury laughed openly at one point when the poor guy said to Sabol, with a mouthful of food, "Hey, times are tough."

Tommy and Vinny were waiting for the elevator after court that day when they were joined by some of the jurors on the case. One of them said, with a wry smile, "I hope they're feeding that guy better in prison." The comment brought about an abrupt outburst of laughter.

Agent Morley answered questions put to him by Gonzalez. He correlated the dates and times of the audio tapes previously introduced into evidence and heard earlier in the trial. He then described his meeting with Vinny, in March 1994, in detail. It was not a fascinating display of investigative work on behalf of the FBI. As Vinny continued to listen to Morley's testimony, he found himself mystified. Vinny had gone to them with the information about Sabol and Gerry, as Morley pointed out. Yet there were discrepancies. Morley was insinuating that Vinny knew the FBI was on to him, and by meeting with the FBI, he was attempting to do some type of self-serving damage control. But that seemed implausible, because what person, especially a cop, would meet with the FBI and explain exactly what he had done? Vinny's analytical mind tried to imagine what the probability of such an occurrence would be.

I'd say about zero, Vinny thought to himself as he listened attentively. *It seems the more Morley talks about his theory on the stand, the more he believes it.*

Morley testified that Vinny admitted deliberately leaking information to Gerry that Sabol was a rat and that the government had them on audio and videotape, and also that Sabol was supposed to be doing twenty years on drug charges in Georgia. Morley's testimony had little to no impact on the jury. They were visibly bored. They sat slouched and unmoving, eyes straight ahead and unseeing, keeping a stolid silence.

Morley's testimony was redundant. The defense never denied Vinny had made those comments. There was nothing illegal in what he had done. Calling someone a rat, relaying public information about another person, even if the person receiving the information was a criminal, was not against the law. It would be, however, if Vinny had divulged confidential police department information that

473

he obtained as a law enforcement officer. But thus far, the testimony presented by each and every witness for the government had proven beyond all doubt that Vinny hadn't obtained any confidential information involving this case. A three-year federal investigation proved the government's case was not only implausible but also preposterous.

Throughout Morley's testimony, Gonzalez was shrewd not to ask questions pertaining to the FBI soliciting information from Vinny about Gerry and Sabol's criminal activities or how the FBI manipulated him into believing he was, in fact, working for them. But as Gonzalez wound down his questioning of Morley, it would certainly be one of the main focus points of Tommy's cross-examination.

"Do you have volume 1 of the transcripts up there?" Tommy asked, putting niceties aside. Under Gonzalez's questioning, Agent Morley had been obtuse in his testimony, and Tommy was going right for the jugular.

"Yes, I do," Morley said nervously, somewhat confused by Tommy's directness.

"I believe it's your testimony that you ascertained that the source of the compromise was Vincent Davis on or about February 18, 1994?" Tommy asked in wonder.

"Yes," Morley said.

"Turn to page 18 of transcript 8 in volume 1," Tommy instructed.

Agent Morley did so.

"In that transcript, dated February 1, 1994, there is a statement that Sabol made that he was greatly disliked by Officer Davis, correct?"

"That's correct," Morley said coolly.

"Now, at this point, we're only one week into the compromised investigation. Is that fair to say?"

"That's correct."

"With that information disclosed to you on February 1, could you not have gone directly to Police Officer Vincent Davis to ascertain what was going on?" Tommy asked curiously.

"No," Morley responded defensively, realizing he had fallen into a trap. Morley had already testified that Vinny was not the subject of the investigation until February 18 and was not interviewed by the

FBI until March 31. If the FBI had gone to Vinny or the NYPD after learning that he could be fouling up a federal investigation as early as February 1, one week after Vinny's drunken meeting with Gerry, the compromised investigation could have been saved. Vinny would have never pursued Sabol or met with Gerry the second time if he knew this.

"Why not?" Tommy asked incredulously.

"For a number of reasons," Morley said urgently. "Once we ultimately determined there was somebody by the name of Vincent Davis, we didn't know who exactly he was at that point."

Tommy looked at Agent Morley quizzically. "With all your resources available to you, the FBI couldn't inquire if, in fact, James Stamp was the FBI agent who had arrested Sabol, or ask Richard Sabol himself, who was in government custody, and inquire about who Vincent Davis is?" Tommy asked indignantly.

"All those things were done," Morley replied agitatedly.

"But they weren't done for three weeks?" Tommy demanded furiously.

"I can't remember the exact time sequence of this," Morley offered in his defense. It was a potentially telling point that did not go unnoticed by the jury. They had to be wondering why the FBI did not just order Vinny to stay away from Sabol and Gerry instead of waiting until March, leading him to believe he could assist them in their investigation.

Tommy moved on to Gonzalez's next inference to the jury that Vinny acted criminally by tinning his way into a federal building.

"Now, you were asked a reference to Officer Davis tinning his way into the federal building. Is that correct?" Tommy asked full of confidence.

"Yes," Morley said.

"And is it possible to enter a federal courthouse wearing a gun, without showing your badge and ID?" Tommy asked innocently.

"No," Morley replied.

"So when a police officer tinned his way into the federal building, there was nothing improper about that?"

"Not that I'm aware of," Morley answered reluctantly.

Vinny turned toward the prosecution table, where Gonzalez sat rigid, a disgusted look on his face. It was obvious he was extremely agitated watching Tommy's performance.

"Agent Morley, the badge, or the shield, as it's called, carried by federal agents, does it resemble the one carried by police officers in the city of New York?" Tommy asked.

"I'm assuming it does not, but I'm not sure," Morley said gloomily.

"So there was no advantage that a police officer could gain by showing his badge at the door, other than to identify himself and the fact that he was armed?"

"In that context," Morley grudgingly agreed.

Tommy pressed on. "What was your stated purpose to Officer Davis for the March 31 meeting with him?"

"I believe we said to him we wanted to find out what was going on, what this was about."

"And in fact, he made the appointments with you. I think one earlier than March 31 that you actually couldn't keep, correct?"

"That's probably correct," Morley said reluctantly, knowing full well it was two meetings he had canceled.

"He was no way compelled by you to attend this meeting? Is that correct?"

"That is correct," Morley said.

"He was very much a willing participant in this meeting? Is that correct?"

"Yes, he was," Morley said.

"And the tone of the meeting was one of an informal discussion among people in law enforcement, am I correct?"

"Correct," Morley said, looking faintly amused.

"And of course, Officer Davis had no way of knowing that you were tape-recording the entire conversation?"

"That's correct," Morley responded, a self-satisfied smile on his face.

"During the course of this lengthy dinner conversation, there were several references to the possibility that there might be another agency involved in this case, either working Sabol from the inside or investigating the entire criminal conspiracy from the outside. Is that fair to say?"

"Yes," Morley agreed.

"And yet you assured him it was not the FBI?"

"That's correct," Morley said. Another excellent point brought out by Tommy for the jury to hear.

The FBI had led Vinny to believe that they were unaware of any ongoing investigation, and by their soliciting information from him, he was further led to believe he was assisting the FBI into Sabol's illegal activities, not the target of an investigation.

"Were you aware of the history of threats that Sabol had made to Police Officer Davis, who was the target of your investigation?" Tommy asked emphatically.

"I was made aware of them by the defendant," Morley said.

"Were you aware of threats Sabol had made to FBI agents, including Agent Stamp?"

"Yes, I was," Morley said.

"Do you recall asking Officer Davis on several occasions to gather further information for you? Things like phone numbers, an address, a license plate number?"

"Yes, I probably did," Morley said lamely.

"And did you have an expectation that he would act upon a request made by an FBI agent, a fellow law enforcement officer?"

"He possibly would," Morley said hesitantly, trying to figure out where Tommy's line of questioning was going.

"And by that point in your investigation, you were privy to the wiretap evidence that we've heard in this courtroom, where Richard Sabol, a career criminal who we know has shot at least one person in the head, had told Gerry Vittorio, another career criminal who has, by his own testimony, beaten people almost to death, throwing them out of moving cars on the highway, that Davis was lying to him and trying to set Gerry up?"

"Yes," Morley said. His voice was cold, contemptuous.

"Yes," Tommy repeated, his eyebrows raised. "Didn't you perceive that by informing Officer Davis that he had to do more work for the FBI, assist you in getting more information, you were indeed putting him at risk?" Tommy asked brusquely.

"No, I didn't have him doing more work for the FBI," Morley retaliated, not concealing his rising irritation. "The work he was doing was on his own, but I didn't believe that he was putting himself at risk for this," Morley added pleadingly.

"On his own," Tommy repeated accusingly, shaking his head vigorously from side to side. "You were here, in this courtroom, when the recorded phone conversation between Officer Davis and Special Agent Stamp was played, in which Special Agent Stamp, employed by the Federal Bureau of Investigation, asked Vincent Davis, a New York City Transit cop, to attempt to find out more information on Gerry Vittorio?"

"I'm not quite sure I perceived it that way," Morley responded lethargically.

Vinny studied Morley's face. It was tense, even if his voice seemed normal. "Perceived," Tommy said quietly. He looked faintly amused. "Are we discussing your perception of what Agent Stamp was telling the defendant, or you don't think it was actually said?" Tommy asked flippantly.

"Probably my perception," Morley said vaguely.

"Turn to page 15 in TR 140, at the bottom of the page."

As Morley did so, Tommy read his copy for him. "We hear Mr. Davis say, 'But I can get you the phone number.' Agent Stamp says, 'All right.' There are other references in here also as to address and things of that nature," Tommy said, holding up the transcript and pointing to it for Morley to see. "Do you recall them?" Tommy asked harshly.

"Yes," Morley said reluctantly, knowing he could not dispute taped evidence.

"So in the interim, it was certainly stated that Officer Davis was obtaining information at the request of the Federal Bureau of Investigation?" Tommy asked nonchalantly.

Morley mastered his anger. "Well," he said, giving Tommy one of his condescending smiles, "just the one line that you gave me...

have to re-read these things again." Morley was stammering while searching for a way out.

Vinny looked with disgust at this man who had the audacity to utter patently false platitudes. His testimony was nothing but exaggerations, half-truths, and superficial amenities. From Vinny's perspective, he sounded more like an unctuous used-car salesman than the experienced FBI agent that he was.

The point had been made to the jury, but Tommy was not letting Morley off the hook yet. "Would you agree that what Vincent Davis was told by Agent Stamp could be perceived as a consent, or a request, to go and get the information?" Tommy asked indignantly.

"I take it that Mr. Davis is already involved in this thing and he's advising Agent Stamp what he's doing," Morley said defiantly. "I don't know that Agent Stamp is really in a position to, you know, have Mr. Davis doing an investigation." Morley continued his mental masturbation. "If Mr. Davis is doing one, I don't know that we have the right to stop him or let him go or whatever, but in this particular case here, you know, Agent Stamp says, 'All right.'"

"You, personally, Agent Morley, definitely asked Officer Davis to get more information for you at the interview, correct?" Tommy asked, holding up the transcript in his right hand while pointing to it with the index finger of his left hand. There was a decided edge to Tommy's voice. He'd had enough of Morley's perceptions and now wanted facts, and he was staring at Morley, waiting for an answer.

Morley stared at Tommy, perplexed, and, after a few seconds, said, "I think he offered to do it, and we accepted."

"Would you consider it prudent under the investigation to have a New York City Transit cop walking around, trying to get license plate numbers, or phone numbers, while the investigation is still ongoing with Customs?"

There was a moment of silence while Morley considered Tommy's question, which, he had to admit, contained a modicum of validity. "I don't think I quite understand that," Morley blurted out. He momentarily lost control. "In some ways, you're putting it as if we're specifically asking him. He's already involved in whatever it is," Morley insisted. "He has his brother-in-law, he's friendly with Gerry.

He's saying, 'I think I can get this stuff from him' and stuff like that. Now, I don't quite understand!"

Vinny looked over at Gonzalez. He noted the tension on his face, his eyes rounded in astonishment. Using his position to carry out a personal vendetta was an egregious misuse of his official authority and power. Gonzalez understood the ramifications of what he had done. Yet his inability to pin any direct evidence to Vinny was progressively distressing to him. Vinny took much comfort at the notion of poetic justice being done.

"But by your statements," Tommy said, continuing his questions ravenously, "you created an intended impression that he was assisting the FBI in their investigation."

"I did leave the impression that he would be of assistance to us, yes," Morley reluctantly admitted.

"In fact, Officer Davis left off with you that he would like to take the FBI training course. You appeared to be in agreement with that thought, were you not?"

"He said that he would like to be considered for the FBI National Academy, and I told him the procedure," Morley said without malice.

Nice of him to admit that. Their undercover microphone must have been turned off when they told me when this case goes down, they will see to it that the NYPD send me to the FBI Training Academy. Cocksucker.

"Now, could you not, at that time, have simply just said, 'Look, you're a police officer, you're in over your head. We have this under investigation, and you may have compromised it. So we're directing you, as FBI to local police officer, that this is where it ends. We don't need your help. What we want you to do is keep your mouth shut and stay out of this.' You could have done that, could you not?" Tommy asked accusingly.

"Could I have said that to him? Yes," Morley admitted reluctantly.

"Do you agree, Agent Morley, that you had it within your power to stop this entire situation at an early date by simply intervening and speaking to Mr. Davis?"

"It's not my responsibility to terminate until we have all the facts that we can gather in this investigation!" Morley insisted indignantly.

"So to what you just described, you intentionally, throughout your conversations with him, left him in the air as to what was really going on?" Tommy asked despairingly.

"I did not give him the full scope of what was going on," Morley said evasively.

"I have nothing further for this witness," Tommy said piteously, shaking his head in disbelief that the FBI not only set up Vinny but also admittedly used him to incriminate himself by attempting to help them.

After a brief redirect of Agent Morley by Gonzalez, in an attempt to repair the damage that had been done to the prosecution's case, it was over.

In a black mood, as Agent Morley walked off the stand, Gonzalez felt disappointed and despondent. He had the disheartening sense that he just saw his last chance of nailing Vinny slip away.

CHAPTER 35

The government rested, and Tommy immediately requested a Rule 29 motion from Judge Schwartz. The motion was for Schwartz to order a judgment of acquittal if the evidence presented in the case by the prosecution was insufficient to sustain a conviction of one or all the charges against Vinny. The justification for the motion was simply logic. Each and every witness for the prosecution had testified that Vinny had no knowledge of any grand jury or wiretap proceedings involving Sabol as a confidential informant. Gerry was clearly heard saying that Vinny never entered into any agreement with him to harm Sabol, and by no means was Sabol ever threatened or intimidated in any way because of what Vinny had told him. In essence, the government had presented enough credible evidence to warrant an acquittal. But Tommy knew, wholeheartedly, that he would have a better chance attempting to extinguish a fire using gasoline than have Schwartz render a fair decision in favor of acquittal.

"I'll rule on that motion while the jury is deliberating," Schwartz said, with a cynical smile on his face. "Call your first witness," he ordered abruptly.

"The defense calls FBI special agent James Stamp," Tommy said. He hoped Agent Stamp's testimony would clearly have a dramatic effect on the jury. He believed whatever tactics Gonzalez had used to divert attention from the evidence, Agent Stamp would ultimately help the jury see right through it. After all, he was one of them.

Special Agent Stamp of the FBI was in his forties, trim, with an amiable face and soft, sermonizing style. He was not an imposing figure. Standing nearly six three, he weighed only 170 pounds soaking wet. He had curly light-brown hair and was wearing an impeccably tailored navy pinstriped suit with white shirt and dark maroon tie. He was an eighteen-year veteran of the bureau who could pass himself off as a school principal or accountant. As the bearer of ill tidings, he wouldn't be exactly popular in a room full of eminently important people. The fact that he was implicated by Gerry as the rogue agent who tipped off the Mob alarmed and angered him. Although he hid his emotions, displaying an air of professionalism, he found himself in the peculiarly helpless position of being called as a witness for the defense. Vinny wasn't sure how many times an FBI agent had been subpoenaed to testify for a defendant, but he was sure it was a first in this courtroom. As the clerk swore in Agent Stamp, Vinny studied the faces of the jurors. His presence had an effect—curiosity, if nothing else. Producing one of his ready smiles for Agent Stamp, Tommy exchanged the kind of meaningless pleasantries that might take place between a toll collector at the George Washington Bridge and a successful businessman. Tommy saw no need to suggest to the jury that they were on friendly terms. The truth was, the two had never met or discussed the case or what Agent Stamp intended to say on the stand before this very moment.

Agent Stamp began his testimony answering questions about how he came in contact with the criminal Sabol. He explained how he had arrested Sabol in September of 1985 on credit card fraud charges. He explained in detail the events that took place, which led to the arrest. That it was Sabol's own brother who turned him in and that, after a jury trial, Sabol was sentenced to twelve years in federal prison, a rather-lengthy sentence he received due to his violent past history. The judge in that case was quoted as saying, "Sabol is a menace to society."

"Now, in the course of that investigation, were there any threats made by Sabol?" Tommy asked him directly.

"After we arrested Sabol, I and three other agents brought him before a magistrate in Manhattan. Sabol was remanded to the custody of the US Marshals after meeting with the magistrate. He then turned to me and the other agents that were present and said, 'When

I get out, I'm going to get you, you, you, and you,' while pointing to each one of us as he said it."

"And was this a threat you took seriously?" Tommy asked curiously.

"Yes, it was."

"And was that threat based on your knowledge of Sabol's numerous acts of violence throughout his criminal history?" Tommy asked solicitously.

"Yes, numerous acts of violence," Stamp insisted.

"Was there an individual named Sheri Stone involved in your investigation?"

"Yes. She was a former girlfriend of Sabol's. He had threatened her prior to the investigation. But because she testified on my case against him, it activated the threat."

"Was there special concern about Sheri Stone? And what was the nature of that?"

"There was special concern for her safety," Stamp admitted. "She was very fearful of Richie Sabol. He had threatened to shoot her if she testified against him at the trial. He told her that he shot this kid and would do the same to her if she testified against him. When she testified at the trial against him, she stood up in front of the full court and said, 'Now he's going to kill me.' She began to cry and ran off the stand. Later, she decided she didn't want to go into the Witness Protection Program, which I was willing to sponsor her for, as I did Sabol's brother. She decided to have her identity changed," Stamp added firmly.

"Was it your appraisal that even though five or six years had passed between the trial and Sabol's release, Sabol still posed a threat to either yourself or Ms. Stone?" Tommy asked suspiciously.

"I stayed in contact with Sheri Stone and her mother. They would call me every three months and ask me where Sabol was. They wanted to know if Sabol was still in prison and how much longer he was going to be in."

"Now, did you have any special instructions or special attention that was being paid to Mr. Sabol on your own behalf?"

Up to this point, Agent Stamp had been direct, but for the most part, he had kept it friendly. But with this question, his tone changed. It was sharp, even ugly, and decidedly accusatory. "Well, since he had threatened me and my witness, I paid close attention to Sabol's whereabouts in prison. I made sure the prison personnel knew that Sabol had a long criminal history. I also sent them a letter detailing his criminal activity, so they would have a full understanding of what they were dealing with."

The expressions on the jurors' faces said it all. If an FBI agent could fear Sabol enough to pay that much attention to him, why shouldn't a New York cop?

"At Sabol's sentencing, in 1986, did you have any conversations with an individual who identified himself as Vincent Davis, a New York City Transit Police officer?"

"Yes, I did," Stamp answered solemnly. "He said his wife, Debbie, had previously dated Sabol before he married her and he wanted to see Sabol convicted. He said that Debbie was threatened by Sabol, something along the line that he had threatened to throw battery acid in her face."

Several of the female jurors winced at the thought of that happening to them.

"Was that threat consistent with other information you had about Richie Sabol?" Tommy asked disgustedly.

"Yes, it was," Stamp replied grimly.

"Did there come a time when you again had an occasion to speak to Police Officer Vincent Davis, and do you remember when that was?" Tommy asked.

"Sabol was released on my case in March of 1991. I got a call from Vincent Davis stating that he had seen Richie Sabol in a silver BMW with another known felon by the name of Robert Garran. This was of interest to me, because associating with other felons is a parole violation."

"Do you know if Mr. Davis related any information about what Sabol might be up to?" Tommy prodded.

"He was from Yonkers, and he knew a lot of people in Yonkers who knew Richard Sabol. Sometime in 1991, he called me and told me Sabol had been arrested on a drug charge in Atlanta, or North Carolina. I made some calls to probation, and they put me in touch with DEA agent Grey, who confirmed what Davis had told me. Soon after that, Sabol was contacting various federal agencies in an attempt to become a confidential informant. In turn, each agency would contact me regarding using Sabol as a confidential informant. Every couple of months, I would receive calls about him. Each time I basically tried to convince them not to use him because he is a danger to society."

"Did you ever use the words 'time bomb waiting to go off'?" Tommy asked innocently.

"I'm sure I did," Stamp responded with a malicious smile.

"At any time prior to 1994, were you the FBI agent who had special interest in Sabol, for your own safety, who informed that Richard Sabol was getting out of prison or was going to be used by any agency as an informant?"

"No!" Stamp responded curtly.

"Did there come a time when you heard that Sabol was out of prison?" Tommy asked sarcastically, knowing what the answer would be.

"I was contacted by Vincent Davis on March 4, 1994. He told me Richard Sabol was out of prison," Stamp said incredulously. "I had asked if he had seen him. He said no but he had solid information that Sabol was involved with machine guns, heroin, silencers, and that he was on the streets in New Jersey somewhere. I asked him if he could find out more about it, where he was staying, phone numbers, things like that."

"The reason you asked Officer Davis to obtain this information for you was for you to get an investigation undergoing into Sabol's new criminal activity. Is that fair to say?" Tommy asked accusingly.

"I wasn't sure he was out at that point," Stamp said defensively. "I mean, he hadn't seen Sabol, so I did some checking to see if it was, in fact, true."

"And did you take steps to do that?" Tommy asked coolly.

"Yes, I did. I contacted the AUSA in Atlanta. When I asked her if Richard Sabol was out of prison, she said, 'I'm sorry, I can't talk about it,'" Stamp said flippantly.

Vinny was thoroughly enjoying this. Here was Gonzalez, trying to convince a jury that he knew Sabol was released from prison to work as a confidential informant, while an FBI agent, whose life had been threatened, couldn't find out jack shit from his own people.

Tommy's eyes widened with excitement. In a low, monotone voice, he asked, "Did Vincent Davis comply with your requests for information?"

"Yes, he did," Stamp responded without reservation.

"One last question, Agent Stamp," Tommy said, full of confidence. "During the time and the contacts you had with Officer Davis over a number of years, stemming back to Sabol's 1986 conviction, did he convey to you that he was in fear of Richard Sabol?"

The answer, "Yes," bellowed throughout the quiet courtroom.

"I have no further questions, Your Honor," Tommy sneered as he casually walked to his seat.

Vinny was overjoyed with Tommy's performance and Agent Stamp's honesty. He felt his uneasiness finally dissipating.

As Agent Stamp's testimony drew to its conclusion, it was clear Gonzalez was becoming increasingly frazzled. He could see the jury box filled with exasperated faces, amazement in their eyes. It appeared crystal clear to the jury that his theory was utterly ridiculous. Sabol was a clear and present danger, not only to Vinny and his family, but also to society in general. Even if Vinny did say to Gerry, "I'll kill him," or "Give me a gun," it was a reasonable reaction, even for a cop, in dealing with the type of sadistic madman Agent Stamp just finished describing to the jury. People always say things like that in the throes of their anguish, especially when they're drunk. They were just angry words spoken in vain that didn't mean a thing. Listening to Agent Stamp explain to a jury of wondering eyes as to Sabol's brazen cruelty, senseless violence, obscene delight in his intimidation of witnesses, all not to be forgotten, never a thing of the past, made Vinny's blood boil. Repentance and forgiveness instead of hate and violence was not Sabol's way of life.

"Enter to learn, go forth to serve" is the slogan of the New York City Police Academy.

Vinny reflected back to his days patrolling the South Bronx. He had learned plenty over the years. But serve? What did that mean? Now, protecting the innocent was a horse of a different color. Something that was understood. If you cared, like Vinny did, and hurt because you screwed up, you hurt too, real bad. Your family never knew because you never brought the job home. You left it in your locker, and you never talked about it, except to yourself or maybe your reflection in the bottom of a bottle when you tried to forget. It wasn't your heart that broke the first time you recalled the inexpressible horror of seeing someone's head blown off, or an innocent child gutted like a pig and thrown in a dumpster like yesterday's trash. It was something else. It became a motivating force that brought you to work every day, why you ended up, after so many years, doing what you were doing. The people Richard Sabol killed, and the witnesses he threatened to do the same to, weren't some appliance you bought at Sears, covered under a warranty if they got broken. They were not pawns to be played with in some ludicrous game of bureaucratic chess, to be put in harm's way at the discretion of some overzealous prosecutor who had his eyes on the political heavens. They were people, living and breathing human beings. The sole reason law enforcement officers put their lives on the line every single day of their lives. How dare the federal government put peoples lives in danger by letting Richie Sabol loose in society, armed with a machine gun!

A sound on the far wall of the courtroom snatched Vinny from his reverie. He looked up and was back in court, watching Gonzalez take his crack at Agent Stamp. Vinny glanced around the courtroom. Everything was normal, and every juror was engrossed by the questions and answers that were calmly spoken.

"In March 1991, when you found out that Richard Sabol had been paroled, did you make contact with Sheri Stone and her family?" Gonzalez asked.

"Yes," Stamp stated.

"And between March 1991 and November 1991, when Sabol was arrested again, did Richard Sabol threaten Sheri Stone?" Gonzalez asked mischievously.

"Not directly," Stamp retaliated. "Sheri's sister received a telephone call about a week prior to Sabol's release by an unidentified male caller who stated he was a friend of Sabol's and was looking for Sheri. Then the caller said, 'Oh, that's right, she changed her name.' He then provided her sister with her new name and said Sabol was looking for her."

Gonzalez was astonished by the answer. "Okay," he said hesitantly. "Beyond that, was there anything else conveyed to your recollection?"

Stamp shook his head and smiled. "That was it," he said scornfully, as if to say she had to have a toe tag on her foot before Sabol's threats would be taken seriously.

The caller knew a federal witness's new identity. That should be enough, Vinny thought to himself.

Disheartened, Gonzalez decided to play a recorded conversation that took place in March 1994 between Stamp and Vinny. Listening to the tape, Vinny sat thinking about how depressed he had been back then. Listening to his own voice reminded him that four short years ago, he'd not particularly cared if he lived or died. Closing his eyes, he tried to think of something else to block it out. The awful loneliness was unbearable, the jagged pain as brutal now as it had been then. He thought of his life now with Judy and how they first met. The thought of her bright smile, the color of her hair, and the absolute magic in her eyes when she looked at him comforted him. She had become everything that love is or could ever be. Well on his way to becoming a successful businessman, with plans to marry and start a family, he now wanted to live, to be free, and those desires made him want to fight this inconceivable act of revenge. Pulling himself out of it, he looked up and was back in the courtroom once again.

The questions Gonzalez was asking seemed like nitpicking, referring to whether or not Vinny spelled Gino's last name correctly for Agent Stamp or if Vinny had told him that Sabol and Gerry were making five grand a week the last time Sabol was out.

He began to question Stamp about the past threats to Vinny's wife. "Now, four lines from the top of the page." Gonzalez directed Stamp to the place in the transcript and said, "'That prick is still calling her up and threatening her at home.' Is the defendant referring to his soon-to-be ex-wife?" Gonzalez asked flatly.

"Yes," Stamp said.

"And he had described, consistently, what he told you in the past?"

Stamp looked puzzled, then replied, "Yes."

"Is your knowledge of these threats from Sabol to Debbie based on your conversations with the defendant?" Gonzalez asked, in the hopes that only Vinny had complained to him about the threats.

"No. I spoke to Debbie," Stamp insisted in a frigid monotone.

Gonzalez glared at him as if he were a misbehaved child. He then attempted to trivialize Sabol's past threats made to Sheri Stone and Debbie, but Stamp would not allow that to happen. After a few questions about how far he would go as an FBI agent to protect Sheri Stone, he gave up. "I have no further questions," Gonzalez said blearily.

Tommy felt cross-examination was in order. He stood and walked to the lectern, paused, thought a moment, then asked the million-dollar questions in rapid succession.

"The threats made to Debbie Davis by Richard Sabol, albeit old news in the prosecution's eyes, would you still consider them viable threats?"

"Yes," Stamp replied.

"Specifically, the threats that were made to you, an armed FBI agent, even though six years had passed, do you consider them to be viable threats?"

Agent Stamp's eyes brightened, and Tommy could feel his pulse quicken. "Yes," he replied in a deadpan voice.

"And when you made reference to Sheri Stone earlier, you said she related something about Sabol shooting a kid in the head and

'He'll do the same to me.' Did she, in fact, say that?" Tommy asked urgently.

"Yes, she did," Stamp said.

"And when you conducted your research into Sabol's criminal background, did you, in fact, learn that he had indeed shot a young man in the head?"

Agent Stamp hesitated a moment. There was dead silence in the courtroom.

"Yes, he did," Stamp replied vociferously.

Tommy paused for effect for the jury, then said with a huge, self-satisfied grin, "No further questions."

"You may step down," Schwartz said furiously. "Call your next witness," he ordered before Agent Stamp had exited the stand.

"The defense calls Vincent Davis, Your Honor," Tommy said in a confident voice.

This sparked immediate attention from the jury. All sixteen sets of eyes locked on Vinny as he rose and proceeded toward the witness stand.

Seated on the witness stand, Vinny patiently waited to give his testimony. Testifying in this trial was not an easy decision hastily made. He was afraid he might infuriate the jury by not taking the stand to prove his innocence. He remembered a moment of somber silence as his father and the defense team considered the ramifications. But the decision was ultimately his, and he did not want the jury to think he had anything to hide.

Vinny was sworn in, but before TC could begin, Schwartz was already on the attack. "Mr. Davis, you walked up here with a document. What is that?"

Vinny looked up. His eyes met the dangerous glare of Schwartz. "It's a time sequence of events that have happened since 1980."

"Whose is it? Is it in evidence?"

You know damn well it's not, you moron.

"No, sir, it's not."

Tommy interjected, "It is number 5 for identification, Your Honor."

The mad bull turned his glare at Tommy. "And what do you intend to do with that?"

"We're going to introduce it," Tommy replied cautiously. "We will use it as a tool to refresh his recollection, if necessary. The same way Mr. Gerry used a similar document that was prepared for him by the government."

He glared at TC with a look of disbelief and ordered, "Only if he needs it!"

He always glares. He shows us nothing but contempt. He's the contemptible one. By rights, he shouldn't even be sitting up there. I wonder if he ever smiles. I wonder how he behaves toward his wife and family. I wonder a lot of things about him, the prick.

Tommy wished Vinny a good afternoon and immediately had Vinny explain the document he was holding in his hand. "It's typewritten in boxes the same way that the document was prepared for by the government to assist Gerry Vittorio with his testimony. It is my recollection of the events that took place from 1980 to the present. It will help refresh my recollection as to the exact dates and events I intend to testify about here today."

"Your Honor," Tommy interrupted, "I have exchanged it with the government. At this time, I seek to move it in as evidence."

Gonzalez was on his feet. "I object!" he exclaimed.

Schwartz did not bother to hear the objection. "Sustain that objection! It's hearsay."

Tommy looked at Schwartz in shocked disbelief. He wanted to lash out at the judge. *How can it be hearsay for my client but not for Mr. Gerry?* Tommy looked toward the jury box with a quizzical look. The point was not lost with the jury; they saw this was not going to be a fair fight. Tommy stood scratching his head and attempted to recapitulate what the judge had just said. "Go ahead, please!" the judge instructed harshly.

Tommy began his questioning, beginning with Vinny's childhood, in a soft-spoken manner—where he was born, how old he was when he moved to Yonkers, his education, and his career choices. Tommy had Vinny explain how he met Debbie, his childhood sweetheart, at twelve years old, and later married her at the young age of twenty-one. The testimony was in no way as fascinating as Gerry's childhood, but the jury listened intently to what Vinny had to say. Tommy knew exactly what he was doing. The questions were serving a purpose. They were geared to humanize his client, in an attempt to show the jury that Vinny was not the evil man the prosecution had repeatedly suggested he was in their opening statement.

"Now, did the name Richard Sabol come up at any time subsequent to your beginning to date Debbie Manzo?" Tommy asked grimly.

"Yes, it did," Vinny answered earnestly. "Soon after I began dating and staying over my future in-laws' house, Debbie began receiving threatening phone calls from him. He found out she was dating me while he was locked away in prison. He threatened to cut off her fingers and mail them to her parents. He said he would throw acid on her face so that no other man would want her. He said, 'I'll kill your boyfriend, Vinny, and his whole family, and I don't care if his father is a cop.'" Tommy paused for effect.

The faces of the female jurors were that of bewilderment. "How old were you at this time?" Tommy asked.

"I was nineteen."

"Did there ever come a time when you yourself had contact with Mr. Sabol?" Tommy asked.

"Sabol would call my family's home, continuing his threats to not only me but my family members as well. It had gotten so bad that Debbie and I went to the prison. Debbie went in to explain to him that it was over while I waited outside in the car. For a while after that, the phone calls stopped. Debbie and I got engaged in October 1981 and set our wedding date for April 17, 1983. Life was perfect for the two of us. We were very excited about getting married and had thought we had heard the last of Richard Sabol."

"While you were engaged, did any other incidents occur relating to Mr. Sabol?" Tommy asked curiously.

"Yes. A few months before our wedding, Sabol was released from prison. One night, while I waited at my future in-laws' house for Debbie, she came home extremely late. She was crying, almost hysterical. When we asked her what happened, she informed us that Sabol abducted her with a shotgun outside of the office where she worked. He drove her around in a car, mocking the size of her engagement ring. Telling her if she married him, he would give her the world. She tried to tell him it was over. That was when he told her if she married me, he would kill her." Tommy paused another moment to let Vinny's words set deeply into the jurors' minds. A few jurors sat in shock and disbelief.

"Did you report it to the police?" Tommy asked.

"Her parents wouldn't let her. They said it was more trouble than it was worth. They were afraid Sabol might retaliate further against Debbie and their family."

"Did there come another time, when you were already married to Debbie?" Tommy asked.

"Yes," Vinny answered excitedly. "The wedding went on as planned in April 1983. Neither Debbie nor I had heard from Sabol before or after the wedding for quite some time. Then Debbie began receiving phone calls from him at her job. After months of attempting to reconcile with her over the phone and getting nowhere, he showed up at her office one day. She called me up at home, hysterical. I drove to her office in White Plains as fast as I could, but by the time I got there, he had already left."

Tommy then moved on to questioning Vinny about his employment with the police department.

"My father was a sergeant with the NYPD. Ever since I was a little boy and saw my dad in his uniform, I had wanted to be a cop. On January 21, 1985, my dream came true, and I was sworn into the New York City Transit Police Department. After graduating in the top 10 percent of my class, I was assigned to District 11, out of Yankee Stadium in the Bronx. I was assigned to Uniform Patrol and rode trains from the Bronx to Manhattan from 8:00 p.m. to 4:00 a.m."

"Now, after becoming a police officer, did there come a time when you again heard the name Richard Sabol?" Tommy asked.

"Yes, there had. A girlfriend of Debbie's told us that Sabol had gotten locked up by the feds on credit card fraud and was going to be sentenced in White Plains Federal Court in April 1986. I had never seen what he looks like, so I decided to go to his sentencing. When I got there that morning, the marshals handed me a presentence memorandum that described Sabol's entire criminal history. I read it in court as I watched the proceedings. The judge sentenced him to twelve years in federal prison. That night, I went home to Debbie and let her read the report about how evil her ex-boyfriend was. We were both elated that he would be in prison for the next twelve years and would no longer bother her."

"Now, after that day, when was the next time you gave any concern to Richie Sabol?" Tommy asked.

"There had been sporadic phone calls from him in prison to Debbie at her office. I didn't pay much weight to them because I knew he was in federal prison and wasn't going to harm anyone. That was until March of 1991, when I saw him driving a BMW on Central Avenue in Yonkers. He pulled up next to me in the car while I was stopped at a traffic light. He just smiled at me, waved, then threw a cigar in his mouth and drove off. I wrote down the plate number of the car, and as soon as I got home, I called the US Probation Department. I informed his parole officer who I was and that he had threatened me and my wife in the past. The officer asked if I wanted to have Sabol's parole violated, but he also warned me that Sabol would not do a lot of time on a parole violation. 'This Sabol character is a bad dude,' the probation officer told me. 'If you violate him, you might really piss him off and he would probably look for revenge. I know he's crazy, because he threatened to kill his last parole officer.' So on the parole officer's advice, I decided to pass on the parole violation. So instead I decided to notify my immediate supervisor, Sergeant Houston. The sergeant then notified the captain, and the Internal Affairs Division. Sergeant Houston, after reading Sabol's presentencing memorandum, notified the FBI in New Rochelle. As it turned out, Sergeant Houston knew Special Agent Stamp, who arrested Sabol on the credit card fraud case in 1986. Through Agent Stamp, Sergeant Houston was able to verify that Sabol was indeed a very volatile threat, even to law enforcement officers, and should be considered dangerous. The Transit Police was not used to dealing with threats against its officers, so they issued me a radio to keep in my house and alerted the Yonkers Police, who were to provide added patrols by my home."

The jurors looked at Vinny, pleading, anxious, believable in voice and expression. His testimony must have been compelling and dramatic.

"Now, around that time, did you take any steps to look into Mr. Sabol's activities?" Tommy asked, smiling at the jury.

"Yes," Vinny said. His tone was soothing, his face a mask of politeness. "I notified Sergeant Houston, who, in turn, notified all the agencies involved. He gave me the DEA agent's name and phone number. I placed a call to the agent and him. The agent assured me that Sabol would get no deals and was facing twenty years in prison. He also gave me the name of the prosecutor who was handling the case. The agent informed me that he would notify my captain at the case's conclusion."

"Now, after relaying that information down to Georgia, when was the next thing of importance that occurred regarding Sabol?" Tommy asked.

"On March 3, 1992, I received threatening phone calls at my home by who I believed to be Sabol. The voice said, 'I'm going to kill you and your family.'"

By the expressions on the faces of the jurors, Vinny and Tommy were scoring big points. Gonzalez sat patiently at the prosecution table, frantically scribbling notes on his legal pad.

Schwartz must have felt the tiniest bit of compassion of the jury and decided to intervene. "Mr. Davis," he said, with a tone of disgust, "are you reading off there?" Rage struck through his face like lightning as he pointed to the graph he would not admit into evidence.

"No, sir. Do you want me to flip it back over?" Vinny asked innocently.

Schwartz was unyielding. "I guess the court explained. Please don't read. Just refresh your recollection."

Vinny glared at him. His voice grew loud and defiant. "I'm not reading off the paper, because that's not on there." Vinny then smiled at the judge.

A snicker of laughter could be heard from the jurors, laughter brought on by Vinny's bravado.

Schwartz stared at the defiant, tough guy's face in front of him. He was fuming in his seat.

"Your Honor," Tommy interrupted bravely, "I have a document that I previously had shown Sergeant Houston. I believe we deemed it marked. I believe it's 2."

Schwartz turned his anger toward Tommy. "You know," he erupted, "you better have control of what your exhibits are! If that's what it is, fine."

"May I show the witness?"

"Sure," Schwartz answered through clenched teeth. Tommy approached the witness stand, smirked at Vinny, then handed him a copy of the Internal Affairs report that he had filed after receiving the threatening phone calls. Tommy had Vinny identify it as to what it was and its context.

"Your Honor," Tommy said, "at this time, I move the admission of the document as a business record."

"Objection!" Gonzalez exploded and was on his feet. "He's not the custodian!"

This is ridiculous! How the hell can I not be the custodian? I filed the goddamn report!

"Your Honor," Tommy protested, "I am moving it in evidence on a variety of theories I don't want to expound to the court."

"The objection is sustained," Schwartz declared.

Tommy looked genuinely amazed.

Not a qualified custodian? Is the judge insane?

Tommy looked at Vinny. He tried to smile, but his dark features only flinched uncomfortably. "You can put it down, Mr. Davis. It's not in evidence," Tommy said, the false heartiness dropped from his voice.

Vinny was furious as he looked contemptuously at Schwartz.

How can this bastard not let a police report of threats to a police officer in as evidence?

Tommy continued his questions in an attempt to get in as much information in the inadmissible police report as possible.

"After all these notifications that you made to local and federal law enforcement agencies in regards to threats against you and your family, did there come a time when you were informed that Mr. Sabol will be doing twenty years in prison?" Tommy asked confidently.

"Yes, there did. My captain called me into his office and informed me that Sabol was sentenced to twenty to life. He stated he was notified by Internal Affairs that if Sabol was ever released for a reason, that the department would be notified, and in turn I would also be notified. Other than that, Internal Affairs considered the case closed."

"Knowing that information, did you have any further concerns about Richard Sabol?" Tommy asked emphatically.

"No. I slept good at night."

Tommy moved on to new ground, asking questions about Vinny's divorce, his apartment burning down, and his bout with depression and alcohol. Vinny explained how depressing it was for his wife not to be able to conceive a child and how that depression affected her so deeply that she began abusing alcohol and eventually began using cocaine. He explained how he no longer knew the woman he once loved. He told the court that he didn't want a divorce but that his wife was out of control and did not want his help, or him, for that matter. Within three months of his separation, the apartment in which they lived was destroyed by fire. Vinny was forced to move in to the home he grew up in and began his own bout with depression and alcoholism. The jury listened sympathetically as Vinny's voice was choking with emotion as he explained that he had somehow failed his wife.

It was nearing the end of the day when Judge Schwartz interrupted. "Is this a good time to stop?"

Tommy nodded, as if considering the question. He then looked at the jury. They were captivated. Tommy then looked back at the judge, giving him a wry smile, and said, "This is a perfect time."

The air outside the courthouse was cold, but Vinny took a deep breath and rejoiced in its sweet smell of freedom. Tonight, he decided, he would get some rest. Vinny had been a wreck since the trial started, torn with ambivalence about spending night after night in strategy session after strategy session at the conclusion of each day of trial. Weekends were spent brainstorming. It had been an enormously traumatic experience for the both of them. But if Vinny was going to make it through Gonzalez's cross-examination, which might be tricky in every sense, he must rest.

CHAPTER 36

As Vinny took the stand for the third day, he looked weary. Exhaustion and stress were etched on his face. It was creased with expectation.

It had been a long, anxious wait for him to tell his side of a story too bizarre for even him to figure out, to comprehend fully. Here was his chance to let the jury hear the truth of the case and decide for themselves who was innocent and who was guilty. Gonzalez had proved to be a savvy prosecutor, beginning his case in a very slow, methodical manner. He structured his facts and theories in a way he saw as a firm foundation of guilt. It was obvious how clever he was to organize his case with a definite, slow beginning, middle, and then ending with enough speculation to lure Vinny onto the stand to defend himself. He knew Vinny was the only person who could fill in the gaping holes for the jury. What the defense team didn't anticipate was this: by Vinny taking the stand, Gonzalez would have a chance to dump a ton of shit on his head.

Vinny's direct examination by Tommy ended midmorning. Tommy had disassembled Gonzalez's case piece by piece. Tommy and Vinny were in perfect harmony. His testimony was alternately gracious and frustrating, solemn, and sometimes humorous. It was a phenomenal performance. It had the jury spellbound.

But all that changed when Gonzalez got his chance to cross-examine. Vinny's testimony began innocuously. Although Gonzalez operated in the courtroom with frightening efficiency, Vinny was undaunted. Gonzalez would fire questions like bullets, and Vinny would nonchalantly dodge them. The jury box was filled with bulging eyes as they listened. Gonzalez became agitated and irritated with the responses Vinny was giving to his questions. He let his frustration get the best of him when he asked a question in a dark, threatening tone.

"Now, I am going to ask you the question I know you have been dying to get."

Tommy was out of his chair as if he were sitting on hot coals. "Objection!"

Schwartz worked up a pretty good sadistic grin. "Overruled," he rumbled as he sat back in his chair defiantly.

Tommy bit his lower lip, reining himself in, holding back his temper. He could not believe this lunatic was a judge.

Gonzalez continued to prod with question after question of the "you know who" and "you know what" variety. It was an attempt to make Vinny change his testimony. Gonzalez desperately wanted the "you know what" to be a gun, but Vinny was insistent and could not be swayed. He was rock-solid.

The second eruption occurred when Gonzalez handed Vinny a taped transcript conversation between Sabol and Debbie. A transcript Gonzalez knew full well was ruled inadmissible before the beginning of the trial. "Your Honor," Gonzalez said vaguely, "may I show the witness some transcripts? I have them marked as government's exhibit 301, 302, and 303."

"All right," Schwartz said agreeably.

Gonzalez glided toward the witness stand and smiled at the jurors as he passed. The look on his face was one of "wait until you see this!"

"Do they look familiar to you?" Gonzalez asked as he strode to the podium.

"Yes," Vinny answered, with a hint of confusion in his voice.

I thought these fucking things were ruled inadmissible. What the fuck's going on here?

"In fact, they look familiar to you because they are transcripts of three tape-recorded conversations—"

"Objection!" Tommy shouted. Rage surged through him, now realizing what the transcripts actually were.

"Overruled!"

Anguish was flaming out of Tommy's face. "But, Your Honor, I object to characterization of something not in evidence. It's used to—"

"Overruled," Schwartz said harshly.

Tommy was fuming as Gonzalez resumed. "Now, as Mr. Cascione pointed out, they're not in evidence. I'm not going to ask you to read them, but could you look through them and tell us whether at any point during any of those three conversations, or if you can do it from memory, if there is any reference to Ms. Manzo calling Sabol an 'AIDS-carrying animal'?"

"Objection!" Tommy was on his feet again, his voice louder and more defiant.

"Overruled!" Schwartz thundered. He turned livid. "Don't prompt the witness! If you have an objection, say the word objection. If I need more, I'll ask for more. Do we understand each other?"

"Yes! But I don't think it bears—"

Schwartz silenced Tommy with a hand gesture and intense glare. His eyes glowed like blazing coals.

Tommy raised his eyebrows questioningly, as if he were asking the jurors what to do. He then sat down with a look of horror and disbelief. He knew what the judge was doing was legally inappropriate, unfair, and highly prejudicial. But what could he do except sit, smoldering?

At the end of the day, what the transcripts were most notable for was the curious insights they presented about Debbie and Sabol's relationship. In fact, the transcripts portrayed a contradiction to Vinny's testimony. It had become incontrovertibly clear that Gonzalez had done what he set out to do. He didn't need to elaborate for the jury. Debbie was not in fear of Sabol—she was his lover. And now Vinny was the scorned, jealous husband out to destroy Sabol at all costs.

But how the hell could I be jealous of something I knew nothing about? The fucking bitch sure covered her ass well. I had no idea until she told me. Gonzalez is insane! It doesn't make sense. It doesn't add up. Oh, yes, it does! He's trying to paint me the jealous husband to the jury! God, is there no limit as to how low he'll sink to win this case?

When court broke for lunch, chaos and pandemonium erupted. Tommy had been sitting, steaming, since the judge's last series of rebukes, sanctimonious lectures, and blatant manipulation of the law against his client, his friend.

As soon as the jury was cleared, he was on his feet. "Your Honor! The defense respectfully moves for a mistrial at this time, and I can be heard whenever is convenient for the court." There was no respect in his voice.

"Now is fine," Schwartz replied. His face puckered in an expression of disdain.

"Your Honor, two points I would like to make to the court. One is that—and I objected to it in a timely fashion—Mr. Gonzalez made a colloquy to my client. 'I'm going to ask you the question that you have been dying to hear.' I believe, and this was on an essential point in the case, that he was attempting to denigrate whatever answer my client would give and pointed it out to my client. I note to the court that I made a colloquy, an innocent one, and I was severely chastised before the jury."

Schwartz's face was red, but he managed a smile, a smile of disbelief, of total amazement. "This is utter nonsense! New York City utter nonsense!"

"I understand that the court feels differently about our practice," Tommy shot back belligerently.

Schwartz became enraged. "Don't interrupt me! Do you know how it works here?" Schwartz shrieked, pointing a finger at Tommy.

"I'm learning, Your Honor, I am learning," Tommy declared angrily, waving his hands in frustration as he spoke.

"Don't give me any guff!" Schwartz screamed, his face flushed with anger.

"I won't," Tommy countered angrily, "but I have to represent my client to the best of my ability."

"You do whatever you need! But don't you dare give me any guff. Do I make myself clear?"

Tommy was conciliatory. "May I finish my application?"

"No!" the mad bull barked back. "You will listen to me!"

It was clear to those watching the spectacle that Schwartz was out of control and the courtroom was in chaos. Vinny's mother let out a mournful, shuddering sigh of disbelief at his behavior. "Marshal! Remove that woman from the courtroom!" Schwartz bellowed, pointing angrily at her.

As Vinny's mother was escorted out by the US Marshals, Schwartz turned his glare back at Tommy. "Your objection is overruled," he said contemptuously.

"I have a second part of my objection," Tommy insisted.

"Your first objection is overruled as utterly baseless nonsense! Now, what's your second objection?" he asked suspiciously.

Tommy took a deep breath to cool down, then began calmly. "The second objection is that my client has been cross-examined for a lengthy period with a transcript of a conversation between Sabol and his ex-wife. This was a conversation that we all know my client was not privy to. Furthermore, it's a conversation that you yourself, Your Honor, ruled not admissible in evidence for various reasons. It's now being brought into evidence in the back door, and it cannot possibly impeach my client since he was not privy to it at the time it took place. It's giving the jury improper impressions that, somehow, he knew all these facts that were going on between third parties. Now they are hearing a lot of things that weren't admitted in evidence. I understand that the government has the absolute right to impeach his testimony with anything they see fit, whether in evidence or not. However, it is improper to have him reading from a transcript not in evidence and asking these questions regarding things that we all understand he was not privy to at the time."

"He was not reading the transcript," Schwartz proclaimed. "He was using it to refresh his recollection."

Tommy lowered himself into his chair. He massaged his forehead with his hand in disbelief.

How can you refresh your recollection to a conversation you were never involved in?

"Is there anything further?"

Tommy raised his eyes to Schwartz. "No," he said disgustedly.

"That woman will not be allowed back in this courtroom during the pendency of the trial." Then he stormed out.

Tommy turned to Vinny, a look of utter devastation on his face.

"Listen, TC. I can't believe a judge would scold an attorney, publicly humiliating him with intemperate outbursts the way he did. Even a psychotic like Schwartz should know we live in more temperate times, where winning isn't everything."

Tommy sat silently for a moment, then said somberly, "New York *asshole* is what he meant to say."

He studied TC's face. It showed weariness and dazed incomprehension. "The only asshole is the judge sitting up there, and he's in charge of this crucifixion. So what do you say we get some lunch?"

"Oh, yeah. He's an asshole, all right." Tommy rose and heaved a deep sigh.

Gonzalez spent the morning session grilling Vinny relentlessly about his personal life. Gonzalez found it inconceivable that he continued a sexual relationship with his wife after their divorce. He depicted Vinny's going to cocaine hangouts to obtain criminal information about Sabol as an obsession. Vinny remained impassive as Gonzalez continued to go for his jugular. It was obvious to everyone in the courtroom. The ingrained hostility toward the enormously calm Vinny as each question came with staccato regularity, always negative, and repelled by Vinny, who had carefully testified in numerous trials during his career. He was precise and meticulous while testifying, but he was growing increasingly intolerant of Gonzalez and his game playing while he continued to focus on his personal life instead of the evidence of the case. Gonzalez stood rigidly at the podium, turning pages of his notes. He stopped to stare at a page. He looked up at Vinny with a devious smile on his face, as if he had already won a guilty verdict.

"You testified yesterday that you kept a file on Sabol?"

"Yes."

"And within that file, you had a photograph of Richard Sabol?"

"Yes."

"And you testified yesterday that the reason you kept the photograph was to know what Sabol looked like?"

"That's correct."

Where's this slimy bastard going with this line of questioning?

"You don't think it's a little odd, Mr. Davis, that a married man keeps a photo of his wife's ex-boyfriend wrapped in a towel?" Gonzalez asked sarcastically.

"I'm not the jealous type, Counselor. It doesn't really bother me," Vinny replied coolly.

"Isn't it true that your wife would tell you from time to time that friends of hers would confuse you with Richard Sabol?"

Huh? I'm taller, bigger-framed, and outweighed Sabol by thirty pounds.

"You mean saying that I look like him?"

"Yes," Gonzalez said flippantly.

"Well, he has blond hair and blue eyes, so I can't see it. As you can see, I have dark-brown hair and hazel eyes."

Now the jury looked perplexed while taking a closer look at Vinny.

"The question was," Gonzalez said, raising his voice an octave, "isn't it true that, from time to time, your wife's friends would say or confuse you with Richard Sabol? In other words, saying, 'I saw you with Richard,' when, in fact, she was with you? Didn't she tell you about that?" Gonzalez pressed.

"Maybe, I don't recall," Vinny replied.

What the fuck do my looks, or Sabol, have to do with this case?

"In fact, isn't it true that you bear some resemblance to Mr. Sabol?"

This guy's a fucking joke! Asshole! I've had enough of his games. Now it's my turn. Antagonistic prick!

He put a contemplative frown on his face, as though he were pondering the question. The jurors sat waiting intently for his reply.

That's it. Make 'em wait.

"Oh!" Vinny finally replied, as though the thought just occurred to him. "I have been told that we have the same teeth, that we have Donny Osmond teeth, I think, was the exact quote."

The courtroom exploded with laughter. It was uncontrollable laughter by everyone except Schwartz and Gonzalez, who were both enraged by the outbreak.

Good. The jury's laughing and those two pricks are pissed off.

Gonzalez recovered and smiled, trying to appease the jury. But he wasn't about to give up.

"And the person who told you that was your wife?" Gonzalez asked calmly.

"Quite a few people, including friends of hers," he responded, as nonchalantly as possible.

"And that bothers you, doesn't it?" Gonzalez asked indignantly.

Vinny, not wanting to miss his chance for another laugh, was quick with a retort. "To have Donny Osmond teeth?"

Laughter roared like thunder in the courtroom. Even the mad bull managed to crack a brief smile.

The asshole probably doesn't even get the joke. He's just laughing because everyone else is and doesn't want to be taken for the fool he is.

Before the laughter subsided, Gonzalez exclaimed, "No! To look like Richie Sabol?"

Vinny was still laughing as he replied, "No, it doesn't bother me at all!"

Gonzalez held back his anger and kept it lodged, bitter, in his throat. It was a culmination of four years of pent-up frustration, and Gonzalez would not stop until he had his revenge. He would not be made a fool of. The hard evidence in the case was almost nonexistent. What Gonzalez had thought to be his one solid piece of evidence to support his contentions was blown to bits by Vinny's brother-in-law, Michael. Now Gonzalez's theory that Vinny had a more nefarious motive than to keep his family safe from Sabol was falling at the wayside. Gonzalez, though visibly frustrated, ploughed on.

After two more hours of eliciting Vinny's testimony, Gonzalez ran out of questions.

Vinny was not derailed. He remained smiling, soft-spoken, and immensely reasonable. His testimony was extensive, yet it remained factual, complete, and accurate. He was able to convey the impression to the jury that, if nothing else, Gonzalez's theory was, at best, amusing. The prosecution was in trouble, and the man on the bench knew it. Schwartz shook his head, looking at the expressions of boredom on the jurors' faces. Some were sleeping, while others yawned openly.

"If you are moving off this conversation," Schwartz said cautiously, "we will break for lunch."

An exhausted Gonzalez looked at the judge and said, "Yes, sir."

While court was adjourned for lunch, Vinny and TC were hit with another damaging blow to their case. TC observed one of the jurors reading a newspaper. The page 1 headline: NEW YORK CITY NONSENSE. And below that: FEDERAL JUDGE SCOLDS NEW YORK ATTORNEY IN OPEN COURTROOM.

Gonzalez was upset over the tone the trial was taking. He wanted to change it and was visibly frustrated when he didn't get the answers he wanted from Vinny's brother-in-law. Gonzalez had failed to produce clear and convincing evidence of Vinny's guilt. There were no startling revelations or admissions being made by Vinny. The three tape transcripts that were not in evidence, which Schwartz let in through the back door, were effectively blocked by Vinny. Most of the evidence presented was circumstantial, or hearsay, what somebody told somebody else. The prosecution was in trouble, so Gonzalez fired up the flames of journalism by feeding them the story. He resorted to cheap emotionalism to distort the public's view, in an attempt to remove the court of its proper function. Anyone who read the article now had the reporter's ideas, theories, feelings, and perceptions. By the end of the article, one would conclude Vinny appeared guilty.

Vinny looked at his friend. TC was smoldering, red-faced with anger. "I can't believe this shit!" He threw the paper down on the table. "Can you believe he did this?"

I can. He's been out to fuck me over right from the beginning. He's playing by no-holds-barred rules. Motherfucker.

Vinny sat back in his chair. The usual sparkle of humor in his eyes was gone. *I hate the way Gonzalez's cynically manipulating the media, and my case. He's showing cleverness for which I wasn't willing to give him credit. I underestimated him. Let that be a lesson for me. Gonzalez may be an asshole and a cocksucker, but he's not stupid.*

"Don't you see?" Tommy asked, his voice shaky. "If you're found guilty, then Juan Gonzalez would be the crusading 'personification of justice,' a prosecutor who has the tenacity to do whatever's necessary to put a crooked cop in prison. This article," Tommy proclaimed, pointing to the headline, "in no uncertain terms, insinuates that you are no different from the informants Gonzalez's exonerated. What the jury's seen, up until now, was a convicted criminal admitting to a vast array of crime seemingly far worse than those attributed to the man on trial before them. You've never committed a crime or harmed anyone in your life. Yet Gerry was the witness and you are the one on trial. This is an obstruction case, which the media has now turned into a murder conspiracy."

Vinny sat speechless, shell-shocked. When he managed to speak, it was in a terrified monotone. "Do you think the jury will believe what they read in the article?"

"The truth doesn't always sell to a jury. All I know is that it will now come down to a credibility contest, as to who the jury believes."

"You can't tell me you think the jury is going to believe Gerry over me?"

"I don't know how far Gonzalez will delve into your character, with past acts of indiscretion not related to this case—"

"Wait a minute! You said he's not allowed to go into my character."

"He's not, unless we open the issue ourselves by your own testimony! But look what's happened so far—the judge has let Gonzalez get away with doing whatever he wants." Tommy's voice was going up a few octaves, a sure sign of anxiety registering. "I swear to God, Vinny, if Mickey Mouse and Goofy came marching through that courtroom yesterday, I would not have been surprised. In fact, I was almost expecting it! This has not been a court of law we've been in— it's Disneyland!"

The expression on Vinny's face was that of a thousand unanswered questions, yet none of them plausible to justify words.

"Listen, Vinny. You know there's a lot at stake here for Gonzalez. If he loses and you're found innocent and he'd led the rush judgment, he will look like a fool who was seeking a scapegoat to cover up the tremendous error he made by making a deal with Gerry for his testimony. He can't let you be found innocent, because he has invested too much in your guilt. Gerry's testimony proved that he lied about firing your gun out the window of your car. Don't you think the FBI knew Gerry lied about that incident long before the agents testified at your department trial?"

Vinny remained speechless, still in a state of disbelief, unable to answer.

"At your trial, you were placed in a bureaucratic coffin. All Gonzalez had to do was carefully screw the lid close. The FBI agent he sent to testify was the messenger of death, who did just that. They went out of their way to get you fired in the hopes that you would flip and work for them. When that backfired, he was forced to arrest you because he'd already indicted you last January. He was covering his ass, knowing full well your appeal, to get your job back, went to the State Supreme Court. Gerry's lie would have come out, and the agent that testified, and Gonzalez knew about it!"

When court was brought back into session, Tommy sprung up to address Schwartz about the newspaper article.

"Your Honor," Tommy said impatiently, "we were apparently reported in the *Bergen Record* yesterday. There's a fresh article out there that the jury needs to be instructed on."

Schwartz looked up from the bench with a self-satisfied look on his face. He almost cracked a smile as he spoke. "I didn't know there were any articles, but I'll instruct them at our next break."

Liar. He knows. Someone would have brought it to his attention first thing this morning.

Tommy sat flushed with anger, but he had to bite his tongue. There was nothing he could do.

Vinny took the stand. He had gotten little to no sleep since the trial began. Fatigue was weighing him down. He was visibly exhausted from the long, fruitless nights spent at Tommy's house reviewing testimony, in preparation to do another eight hours the following day. He knew that with each indecorous question Gonzalez asked, the strands of his temper were beginning to fray, and his answers were suffering. When he spoke, it came out husky and strained with fatigue, uncharacteristic of the positive voice he had maintained up until now.

Gonzalez was noncombative as he continued his questioning.

"Mr. Davis," Gonzalez said softly, "let's see if we agree on some things. You agree that on December 25, you learned Richard Sabol was out of prison on a work release program? You agree you learned this from your brother-in-law? You agree that you told your brother-in-law and Gerry that Sabol was supposed to be doing twenty years in prison? You agree that you told Gerry that Sabol had him on video and audio tape and that you made all that information up so that you could find out what illegal activities Sabol was up to?"

Vinny answered yes to each of Gonzalez's probes.

Watch out! He's using a new tactic. He's stringing together a series of questions he knows I'll say yes to. Yes. Yes. Yes. Then he'll try to slip in a trick question. Careful.

"You also agree that after a second meeting with Mr. Gerry, you notified your supervisors and the FBI of illegal activities being conducted by Sabol and Mr. Gerry?"

"Yes."

Again. I'm ready for you, you scumbag.

"Now, on March 2, after Ms. Manzo told you, for the second time, that Richard Sabol had complained that you were causing him grief, saying that you were interfering with his plans to get out of prison, you had still not concluded that Richard Sabol was an informant?" Gonzalez asked sarcastically, a cunning smile on his face.

So soon? Heh! Bastard. Lemme play with him again, but just for a second.

He put a confused look on, as though he didn't understand the question, then blurted out his answer.

"I never pictured in a million years that any agency of the United States government would give Richard Sabol a fully loaded machine gun with a silencer!"

Gonzalez looked at Vinny as if to say, "Oh, shit!"

Heh! Keep a straight face. Gotcha, you prick. Schwartz, too. Pricks. I love it! Both had startled looks on their faces. *What the fuck can he say to that? The jury picked up on that, too. Good. They're waiting intently for the next question.*

Gonzalez paused, recomposed himself, then smiled slyly before trying again.

"So you were in sort of denial, weren't you?" Gonzalez asked, contempt in his voice.

Stupid fucking question. This guy's getting on my nerves. Stay calm.

"Call it what you want, Counselor. After hearing that, I said, 'There's no way my government is going to do that.' I didn't believe it!"

"It troubled you that Debbie was speaking to Sabol. You were jealous about her seeing him again. So jealous, in fact, that you wanted Gerry to kill him. Didn't you?" Gonzalez asked heatedly.

Persistent bastard. He's like that posse in Butch Cassidy and the Sundance Kid. *He's insane if he thinks that. My God! Where the fuck did he come up with this theory? Make him wait. Stay calm. You want an answer? Well, here's the truth.*

"At that time, if I knew my wife was seeing Richard Sabol, it would not be out of jealousy that I would act. It would be out of concern that she was hanging out with a man with a machine gun, and his friend Gerry with heroin and stolen property. She had just gotten out of a drug rehab, and I didn't want her mixed up in the middle of it. That's what I am trying to get across."

Gonzalez stood stone-faced, bewildered.

Another point not lost to the jury. Good. I hope they see he's just cooking this up to try to discredit me.

Gonzalez took a step back and shook his head. "Let's talk about your divorce. Now, you testified that it was Debbie who filed for divorce, correct? Did she file for divorce on the grounds of abuse by you?"

"Objection, Your Honor!" Tommy was on his feet.

"Overruled!" barked Schwartz, motioning Tommy with his hand to sit down.

Son of a bitch! He hasn't granted even one of our objections. It's one against two. Shit. This is America, the land of blind justice, fair justice. This is anything but fair.

Vinny shook his head in a gesture of disgust.

Some justice system! How'd a fucker like him get to be judge? Sit tight. It's almost over. We're ahead, we're winning. The jury's just got to be with me on this.

However, Tommy's fears were about to come true as Gonzalez, desperate to win, dived headfirst into Vinny's character. To this point, it was clear Gonzalez was losing. He'd run out of what little circumstantial evidence he had. His own witnesses had destroyed his false theories and wild-assed speculation about Vinny's evil intent. Now, his one last chance was to mislead the jury, and a prick of a judge was giving him all the leeway he needed to do just that.

When Gonzalez was finished turning Vinny's marriage into a life of mental, physical, and verbal abuse, two of the female jurors had looks of disgust on their faces. Gonzalez didn't stop there. He moved quickly into what he described as Vinny's blatant disregard of authority. He even tried to turn minor infractions of the police manual, which Vinny received reprimands for, into civil rights violations.

"You pulled your gun on a black woman and placed it to her head, did you not?" Gonzalez asked harshly.

"She was armed and just committed a robbery. We lost the complainant, so we had to let her go. I forgot to fill out the Stop and Frisk Form. I was a rookie cop, so I got in trouble for it." Vinny fashioned an expression of somber benevolence on his face, but as he scanned the jury, he knew he was in trouble.

"Objection, Your Honor!" Tommy exclaimed.

"Overruled!" Schwartz said brusquely. "He can impeach him."

Shit.

Gonzalez might not be able to shatter the rock with one almighty blow, but he intended to chip away at it till nothing remained of it.

"In 1985, there was another instance in which you did not follow proper procedure," Gonzalez said confidently. It was like shooting fish in a barrel for Gonzalez, as he had Vinny recite every mistake he ever made on the force. Although Vinny was not portrayed as a menace to society like Gerry was, Gonzalez was out to destroy his good character in the eyes of the jury. However, Gonzalez was just warming up. All that had just passed was but a prelude to his climax.

"Let's go back to 1985," Gonzalez said, his voice loud, his expression determined. "When you joined the force, did you fill out an application?"

"Yes, I did."

Gonzalez approached the witness stand and handed Vinny a copy of the application he filled out when he was eighteen years old. He began to tremble.

What's he going to try to nail me on here? Stay calm. Stay calm!

"You lied on that sworn application when you answered no to the question 'Have you ever tried drugs?'"

The jury was listening carefully.

Tell the truth. Try to explain.

In a low, barely audible voice, he answered. "Yes. Look," Vinny said softly, "I was eighteen years old, a kid. Who here hasn't lied on a job application?" Vinny asked desperately.

"You lied to get what you want!"

"Yes."

Tommy rubbed his face and rolled his eyes. He couldn't believe Schwartz was letting this take place, but he should have.

Gonzalez paused and smiled slyly at the jury.

This is surreal. I'm helpless. I'm nailed down here.

"Now, let's go forward in time to the department hearing on the underlying matter. You were charged with obstruction of justice, were you not?"

"Objection!" Tommy rumbled and was out of his chair, ready to punch Gonzalez in the face. "I believe it's an outside finding of law that's not binding on this court!" Tommy demanded, his voice filled with fire.

Schwartz glared angrily. "He's doing it to impeach at this point, not offering it to prove the truth of the matter asserted. He's got foundation. Overruled!"

Vinny gritted his teeth and stuck his chin out at Gonzalez.

Why don't you just shoot me? Why not shoot me right here? I deserve it. I fucked up your investigation. I'll fall down. I'll bleed. I'll die. It's better than going to prison in disgrace.

"Yes, I was."

It was Gonzalez's ace in the hole, getting Vinny to admit he was found guilty of each and every charge at his department hearing, almost identical charges now before the jury.

The rock was no more.

On redirect, there was nothing Tommy could do to undo what had just been done.

It's over. Yes, it's over. If I hadn't gone through this myself, I wouldn't have ever believed something like this could happen, today, in America. Gonzalez accomplished what he set out to do—to fuck me, fuck me royally. He got further with my testimony than he anticipated. I know. Look at him, sitting with a self-satisfied, shit-eating smile. He's glowing at the jury box, a victorious look in his eyes. He just showed them that I, Vinny Davis, a man who held a position of trust, a police officer sworn to uphold the law, betrayed my oath of office by lying.

But who doesn't lie? Little lies. Big lies. God doesn't, but He's the exception. Priests lie. Presidents lie. Wives, husbands, lovers, mothers, fathers, sisters, brothers—they all lie. Show me the man who's never lied. He doesn't exist. Gonzalez lied. Schwartz lied. They both broke their oaths of office. They transgressed ethical standards to fuck me. So have some jury members, and they haven't even deliberated yet.

Gonzalez, Gonzalez, Gonzalez. Damn him! He poisoned the jury against me by implying I was fired for violating my sacred oath of office, on the same charges I'm now being tried for. He's managed to destroy my credibility. The elements of deceit and betrayal of trust now place high among the jury as sins I've committed. It gives them good reason they should ignore the evidence and send me to prison. The sense that was my credibility—me, myself! I dedicated my life to truth, honor, justice, and the preservation of human life. Now I'm destroyed, bound tight by the angel of death. Take me. Better that than prison.

CHAPTER 37

Tommy and Vinny worked rigorously through the weekend. Tommy concentrated on his closing arguments and jury charge, while Vinny assisted in the legal research. If they weren't found locked in the seclusion of Tommy's basement, hard at work, they could be found at the law office of Iacullo and Salutti in Nutley, New Jersey. There, all three lawyers worked like a well-oiled machine until the work they prepared was flawless. Even the scrupulous eye of the Honorable Judge Schwartz would not be able to raise an objection or disallow one of their briefs. There had been no stone left unturned, every *T* was crossed and every *I* was dotted. They were ready.

By the late hours of Sunday night, they were exhausted. Tommy noticed Vinny had been in a bad way since he had testified. He looked at his friend sitting on the couch, hunched over, just staring at the floor. He was expressionless, and his eyes seemed unnaturally bright. The sight of him this way shocked Tommy, who had always seen him grief-stricken yet tough, composed, and inwardly strong. Now there was nothing radiating from his body but panic and fear. The trial had been more painful and debilitating to Vinny for the fact that he was guiltless. The sight of his name in the newspapers, depicting him as a rogue cop, was devouring his insides with each passing day. TC looked at Vinny, wondering what to say. For Tommy, it was very disconcerting. He was a man who measured his words carefully, as so many lawyers do. He had great instincts for compassion and morality, with a heart of gold, but still he remained speechless.

After another moment of silence, Vinny looked up to his friend. "Let me ask you something." His voice trembled with fear. "Do you think the jury will buy into the prosecution on this?"

"I don't know. It's hard to tell right now."

"It's insane, TC. On one hand, he wants the jury to believe that I am a genius, that I was some kind of supercop who has ESP, a clairvoyant, who'd figured out the impossible. On the other hand, he wants the jury to believe that I am a moron, that I was stupid enough to tell Gerry to kill Sabol, even though I knew he was protected by the feds. And to boot—this is the real kick in the ass—I then called the FBI and told them exactly what I did. Now, what am I, a genius or a moron?"

Tommy looked perplexed—it was a somber thought. "It is an incongruous duality."

Vinny lowered his head again as he fought back his emotions. "You know as well as I do," Vinny said solemnly, speaking with his head down, "the effect that article's going to have on the jury's ability to render a decision in accordance with the law. They might have been instructed by that asshole not to read the papers, but even if they strictly obeyed the court's order, nothing is going to stop family members from swaying them as to my guilt. And this judge!" Vinny's voice was rising in frustration. "Every single one of your objections fell on deaf ears. He runs that courtroom like a Nazi, for Christ's sake!"

Tommy walked over and placed a reassuring hand on his friend's shoulder. "It's not over yet," he said, his voice radiating confidence. It didn't help.

Vinny looked up; his eyes were glazed as they locked onto Tommy's. "What about the juror we lost today?" he asked worriedly. "She was on our side. Did you see the smile she gave me after the judge excused her? Now we have an alternate that I don't even think understands English," Vinny insisted without giving Tommy a chance to speak. "And while I'm speaking about jurors, what about the woman whose father is on life support down south? She told the judge she has to fly down there to take him off life support this week! How anxious do you think she is going to be to fight with the other jurors for my freedom with that hanging over her head? Do you really think she'll give a shit about me?" Vinny asked incredulously. His entire body filled with anger.

"We can't give up now!" Tommy said enthusiastically. "I've known you all my life, and you have never quit or given up on anything. We still have my closing arguments to raise more than enough doubts for an acquittal. We also have your intoxication defense. The judge will instruct them if they believe you were intoxicated, which their own witnesses said you were. They will have to find you not guilty by reason of intoxication."

Vinny's face brightened a bit, and he managed a smile to crease his lips.

"You really think so, Tommy?" Vinny asked admiringly.

"Yes, I do," Tommy said confidently. "Now, go home and get some rest. We have a big day tomorrow."

Two weeks of sleepless nights, decisions, and worries would soon be over.

The final act of this charade was about to begin.

There was an air of anticipation in the packed courtroom. Swarms of Vinny's and TC's friends and family had come to see the dramatic conclusion. The evidence had been presented. Countless audiotapes, with faceless voices, had been played. The videotapes had been shown, and the witnesses had testified. All that remained to do were the closing arguments.

The jury looked rested as they filed in. Vinny tried to read their faces or thoughts, but he couldn't. He was praying for a wink, a nod, a hand gesture. He would have settled for any positive subliminal message. He still was extremely nervous after the charge conference that took place at eight thirty that morning. It was then that Tommy and Vinny received the shocking ruling from Schwartz that he would not instruct the jury on intoxication. The judge ruled that the defense did not make its intoxication submission in a timely fashion. He also stated that he did not see a basis for an intoxication charge. It was another blatant misuse of his judicial powers, which infuriated Tommy most.

"Stevie Wonder could see intoxication in this case!" Tommy shouted when Schwartz left the courtroom.

Gonzalez gazed at Tommy coolly, as though amazed by his outburst. Smirking, he rolled his eyes and turned his back on him.

Tommy's blood boiled. His cheeks were flushed, and his eyes were filled with rage. Yet when he spoke, it was without a trace of passion, without a sign of any feeling at all. "This is what you call justice?" It was all he said. He then looked at the FBI agents. Then he looked at Gonzalez again. A silence followed. None of the agents or Gonzalez said a word. Tommy let out a low moan, shook his head, and walked out of the courtroom with Vinny in tow.

The second blow of the morning for the defense came when Tommy was informed that juror 1, who was thought to be the strongest juror for the defense, had mysteriously taken ill and would be replaced by an inattentive alternate. The morning turned into a disaster.

Vinny felt numb. So many conflicting emotions surging through him that he lost rational thought.

Schwartz entered the courtroom and addressed the court in a low, judicial voice. "Folks, this morning we are going to begin with summations. We will hear from the government first, then we will hear from the defense." Looking at the rabid prosecutor, Schwartz motioned with his hand for him to rise. "If you would, please."

Gonzalez took a moment to settle himself at the lectern before he began. He spoke softly, but quickly, and there was the slightest nervous tremor at the bottom of his voice. He began with his pleasantries, thanking the jury for their time.

He then began to proclaim, "Ladies and gentlemen, I said during my opening statement to you that the evidence in this case was going to show beyond reasonable doubt that the defendant, Vincent Davis"—Gonzalez paused for effect, pointing his accusatory finger at Vinny yet again—"has committed the crimes that were charged in the indictment." He warned the jury not to leave behind their good judgment, their life experiences, and most of all, their common sense when they retired to the jury room for deliberations.

"Now, I'd like to discuss with you the evidence in this case, and I may be, from time to time, referring to a timeline that I created." As Gonzalez said the word *created*, he magically unveiled an easel, covered with a white sheet, that was placed before the jury box.

A look of exasperation appeared on their faces.

Vinny nudged Tommy in the ribs and asked grimly, "Is he going to review the entire case all over again?"

"It looks that way. And by the looks of it, the jury does not seem too pleased."

Gonzalez began back in 1980, when Vinny met Debbie. He continued to explain his theory that Vinny was driven by an obsessive type of jealousy of Richard Sabol. He insinuated that Vinny was never driven by justice, to see justice done. "His main concern was not out of fear of Richard Sabol. He was motivated to see Richard Sabol stay in prison to keep him away from his wife, out of pure jealousy. The defendant was so obsessed with jealousy that he wanted Gerry to kill Richard Sabol. That was his only motivation for him to inform the Lucchese crime family that Sabol was a rat."

Vinny felt anger rushing through him, yet his smile remained fixed as he listened intently to Gonzalez's wild speculations.

As time passed, Gonzalez moved his attention off Vinny, returning to his trusty timeline creation. He then began to narrate every piece of useless information the jury had ingested over the last two weeks. For almost one hour, Gonzalez continued to prattle relentlessly.

Vinny looked toward the jury box to see the jurors' expressions. It was of no surprise to see juror 2 fast asleep. Only this time, five others had joined her. The waves of rage came over him.

What the hell is wrong with these people? he thought. Without thinking, Vinny pounded his fist onto the defense table.

The mad-dog judge, the Honorable Harold Schwartz, peered at Vinny with contempt, but Vinny didn't blink. They were locked on his piercing eyes. Vinny then casually glanced toward the jury box, bringing Schwartz's eyes with his to rest on the sleeping jury. Schwartz looked like he was going to explode. His face turned red.

"Counsel, members of the jury!" he bellowed in a voice that could be heard in downtown Newark. "It's important to pay attention! I realize it's early in the morning, but if you think you need a break, if you feel drowsy, let me know. I have to insist that you pay attention on the summations from the government, defense attorneys, and any rebuttal that's in this case. Do you want a break? Let me know, or we'll continue." His expression and voice must have scared them into compliance. They didn't want a break.

Gonzalez thanked the court, then continued his recital unfazed. Another twenty minutes had passed before Gonzalez moved on to explain the charge of witness tampering. The reading of the charge infuriated Vinny.

"Now, on witness tampering," he continued. "There is no requirement that there be an investigation going on, a federal investigation, something involving a grand jury, or a wiretap. All that's required is that the defendant corruptly persuaded or misled another person with the intent to hinder or prevent communication to law enforcement officers of possible federal criminal violations."

Vinny looked at TC quizzically, but before he could utter a word, Tommy motioned Vinny to wait. He sat patiently.

His blood boiled over the ridiculousness of Gonzalez's interpretation of the law. But Gonzalez didn't stop there. He moved on to Vinny violating his duty as a public servant. "He violated his department manual by associating with known criminals. He failed to take police action. He failed by conducting himself in a manner prejudicial to good order and against violating the laws."

Vinny sat completely helpless as Gonzalez continued his indecorous rhetoric.

"Final points I'd like to point out!" he exclaimed, raising his voice triumphantly. "Ladies and gentlemen, the defendant wants you to believe a lot of things. He wanted very much for the New York Police Department, when he applied on that application, to believe him when he swore that he hadn't tried drugs. He wanted them to believe that. He wanted Internal Affairs to believe he hadn't ripped up that school pass he had taken from a kid. He told them he didn't do it. That wasn't true. He wanted Internal Affairs also to believe he didn't do anything improper by logging that gasoline. He wanted them to believe that. In each case they didn't believe him, and he wound up getting disciplined."

Vinny was getting sick to his stomach, swallowing back the bile that came up his throat. Gonzalez watched Vinny, smiling, feeling the waves of rage coming out of his own body. He was enjoying the fact that he could poison a jury, misdirecting their attention from the facts and the evidence, and turn it into a character case.

Vinny was helpless. Gonzalez knew it. He continued, "He wants a lot of people to believe things that aren't true. I submit to you that you should not allow that to happen."

His voice was getting louder and shriller by the moment.

"You should look at the evidence without prejudice, impartially and fairly, I submit to you. When you do, you will find that the evidence supports a finding beyond reasonable doubt that the defendant is guilty of the charges in the indictment. He is guilty of obstructing justice, of conspiracy to obstruct justice, of witness tampering, and he's guilty of using telephones to promote his unlawful activity for having violated his duty as a public servant. Thank you very much."

Gonzalez could not help but smile smugly with satisfaction. Vinny smiled back with only a slight trace of bitterness.

The second the jury had cleared the room for the morning recess.

Tommy rose to the occasion. "Your Honor, I would ask the court for curative instruction to the jury."

Schwartz glared at Tommy. His face was ugly, distorted with venom. Tommy smiled firmly, refusing to be rattled. "Mr. Gonzalez," Tommy roared defiantly, "has said my client is not worthy of belief, referring to his department disciplinary matters. That someone else has concluded that he is not truthful, by being found guilty at his department trial, doesn't have any bearing on this jury or any reference to it!"

Schwartz smiled maliciously, knowing full well that Tommy was absolutely correct.

"Draw it up! I'll instruct the jury!"

Tommy smiled back with equal malicious satisfaction. It was a point well deserved for the defense, yet the damage had already been done. Gonzalez had poisoned the jury with his inappropriate reference. Even when Schwartz instructed the jury to forget what they heard, it would be too late—they had already heard it.

The jury returned and took their seats. The judge entered and took his. He was as pompous and tight-assed as the first time Vinny had set eyes on him. He stared at the defense table with an intensity that burned the air between them. Tommy knew he had to restore what credibility might have been lost, rapidly, since Gonzalez clearly demonstrated a total lack of compunction about attacking Vinny's character. There was also the collateral worry about Sabol not being called to testify. Tommy didn't know what to think about the jury. He had no idea of their state of minds. All he knew was, he would now be making up for the ignominy of the previous day's defeats.

On Schwartz's command, Tommy rose to address the jury. Tommy Cascione might not have had much time for sleep last night, but his step was elastic, his eyes full of light, his face alive with the excitement of the fight. His smile was confident, almost smug. But that was fine. All he had to do was be himself.

"Mr. Gonzalez did a very good job just now of laying out the case," Tommy began calmly. "Although he could not, as a partisan for his side, admit there is much here that is confusing. When trying to make sense of it, why this case, a case against one man, should take so long to come to fruition, we realize now, because it has become crystal clear, that the government had no case until Gerry decided that he wanted to trade something for his liberty. The government had no case without Gerry Vittorio!" Tommy proclaimed.

Tommy went on to explain how he was a big fan of classic science fiction, *The Twilight Zone*, *The Outer Limits*. He referred to a particular plot in which an evil being, or ghost, gets trapped behind a mirror in some other dimension. He elaborated how Sabol, an evil person by all accounts, got trapped behind the mirror by getting sentenced to a heavy federal prison term.

"What he did was reach out through that mirror and pulled Gerry in so he could get out. Now Gerry is trapped behind the mirror, and he doesn't like it much. So whom does he reach out for? After a couple of years in prison thinking about what he has got to sell, he goes for Vinny Davis. Now, to trade Gerry Vittorio for Vinny Davis is, I submit, not a good deal for society. Let's talk about Gerry Vittorio," Tommy said brusquely as he then proceeded to remind the jury that Gerry was an admitted thief, a professional bully, a gunslinger, a drug dealer, a mobster, a convict. He reminded the jury that Gerry had shot people, beat people almost to death, and threw them out of moving cars on the highway without remorse. "He has lied to you by saying he fired Vinny Davis's gun out a car window. He lied to you about Vinny Davis not being drunk when he had his meetings with him. Gerry calls it posturing, but the plain, simple truth is, he lied!" Tommy declared, pausing for effect for the jury.

Gonzalez sat shaking his head in amazement. Smiling, soft-spoken, and immensely reasonable, Tommy pressed on. "Now, we have learned more about Vincent Davis than we ever wanted or needed to know. He was a hardworking, active cop. He was married, in a relationship for almost ten years, with a wife who was a bit of a screwball." The remark brought vague smiles on the faces of some of the jurors. "But he stuck with her for a long time, and he helped her ride it out right through to the end, and he still does. Now," Tommy said as he brought up his next potentially telling point. "Vinny Davis never had to testify. In fact, he has an absolute right as the accused not to testify, and you could not have held this against him. His whole defense was already laid out clearly in his prior taped statements. He wanted to tell you his side of the story and let you judge him. Let you look into his eyes, hear his voice, and judge him. He felt you deserved that. You spent the time, and now you have to judge this man's life."

Tommy turned toward the defense table, where Vinny sat somberly.

"But what do we judge him on?" Tommy asked broadly, playing to the jury. "Did anything you hear about his teenage transgressions, about his sex life with his wife, about whether or not he had the same teeth as Richie Sabol, give you a really good-faith reason to dispute his testimony? Those things are trivialities. They don't negate the way he testified and how honest he was. He told you the whole story, warts and all." Tommy's voice had rose a few octaves as he continued. "The only thing he wouldn't put up with was the prosecution putting words in his mouth. If he says 'I remember it this way' and somebody doesn't like the answer, he's not going to change it to make them happy. That's honest testimony!" Tommy proclaimed.

Tommy was operating with excitement-charged electricity as he argued quite successfully for the jury about the insurmountable evidence problems the prosecution faced regarding Vinny's knowledge of any ongoing federal grand jury or wiretap investigation. Each and every witness for the prosecution testified that Vinny knew nothing of any federal investigation. Vinny watched his friend, whose eyes were riveted on the jury. Gonzalez wore a vague, bemused smile, and his eyes, too, were on the jury. Tommy took a step back and picked up a copy of the indictment off the defense table.

The jury watched closely as Tommy prepared to do the pièce de résistance. "I'm going to look at this indictment real fast," he explained to the jury. "Page 1 talks about the Lucchese crime family," Tommy said harshly. "The evidence proves this has nothing to do with my client." Tommy crumbled the page in his hand and threw it on the floor, a dramatic move that caught the jury's attention. "Page 2, more talk about the Mafia." Another crumbled page. "Page 3, conspiring, knowingly and willfully. In other words, he knew there was an ongoing federal investigation. Ladies and gentlemen, there is no proof," Tommy said flatly as he destroyed another page of the indictment and tossed it away. "Here's one," Tommy continued, holding up a page for the jury to see. "By threat of force and threatening communication?" Tommy said suspiciously. "You heard all the tapes, ladies and gentlemen. You heard tapes you didn't want to or need to hear, but you heard them all the same. Is there any tape that you have heard where Richard Sabol was threatened? Unless you threaten somebody, it's not a threat. It's a statement!" Tommy exclaimed as another page of the crumbled indictment hit the floor. "By the way," Tommy said, smiling maliciously at the jury, "where is Richard Sabol? Who is the tampered witness? Richard Sabol, who has been bought and paid for by the US government on taxpayer dollars, is living somewhere in relative comfort and needs. The intimidated witness is clearly meant to be Richard Sabol, and where is he?" Tommy's voice was harsh and accusatory as he threw up both his hands in exasperation, looking around the courtroom for Sabol to magically appear. "Ladies and gentlemen, you heard everything that was said to Sabol on tape. Did anyone of you hear anything said that would hinder him from reporting it to a law enforcement official? Everything that was said to him was taped by law enforcement. Agents were sitting right next to Sabol while he was on the phone. So how did my client hinder Sabol from communicating to law enforcement? You can't!" Tommy proclaimed. "This is an untamperable witness, and you know what they mean by witness tampering. This charge is something you can understand, and it's not what happened here. It never happened in this case!" Tommy demanded as one more page of the indictment made its way to the ground to lie beside the rest of the dead charges.

Not only the jury but the entire audience as well was mesmerized. Vinny saw Tommy and Gerry exchange significant glances at Juan Gonzalez's sweat-covered face, as if he yielded to the intense heat and excitement emanating from the jury box. Underneath all his bravado and flash, he was scared. And people who are scared do unscrupulous things.

"Now, that's the indictment," Tommy said, full of confidence, facing the jury with a bright smile on his face. "Not a single charge in there is proved by any standard. I don't mean to belittle any charge there." Tommy's voice was now extremely serious. "Because each and every charge is a serious, serious offense. There are no throwaways," he added while pointing to the crumbled remains of the indictment lying on the floor by his feet. "There are no give-mes. Each one of those charges is something that would tar someone for life, which would hang around his neck like an albatross and say, 'This guy was bad.' That's why we oppose each and every one of those charges."

Tommy paused for a moment. It was a somber thought, and he wanted it to sink in to the jury. A moment passed. Tommy looked up at the faces of the jury. Tommy then said somberly, "A quick review. Conspiracy: Vinny acted alone, therefore no matter how hard you try, you cannot conspire with yourself. Obstruction: Knowingly and willfully. What Vinny knew was what you heard from the government's own witnesses. He was told Sabol was not working for the government. Fellow law enforcement agents told him this, and he believed them. Witness tampering: The only credible threat here in evidence is a tape in which Richard Sabol tells Gerry Vittorio, 'I should have killed Vinny Davis years ago!' This guy's not posturing—he means it! This is a guy that shoots people for fun, and our government put a fully loaded machine gun in this maniac's hands!" He paused. "Ladies and gentlemen," he concluded, his voice now filled with emotion, "you have all the evidence and all the testimony. You cannot walk away from this case. You cannot go home, go to bed, and say in your hearts, 'I did the right thing,' unless you give this evidence a real hard look and realize that none of these charges stick, none of them have been proven, and what happened here was a bad thing for everybody. Nobody won here. If Vincent Davis walks out of this courtroom not guilty of all the charges, he didn't win. He lost the job he wanted his entire life. He has been humiliated and under a black cloud for years. You can't give that back to him. But you can find him not guilty of each and every charge because you have doubts to what you can give a reason. I know whatever you do, you will do for the right reasons from your head and from your heart. Thank you."

When Tommy stopped talking, there was dead silence. It was a powerful performance. The courtroom audience was captivated.

Outside the courthouse, Tommy accepted the accolades and compliments for the show that were due him. Family and friends who had watched his masterfully performed closing arguments gathered around him in a tribute to his talent. His performance should be persuasive enough to the jury, raising enough doubt to return a not-guilty verdict.

Tommy was extremely happy—jubilant, in fact. With all Tommy had been through, he was remarkably gracious. The nervousness was all gone, not a trace of doubt.

However, Vinny stood rigidly, with his hands in his pockets, his face a stone. His gaze was flat, without expression. There was sadness in his face. His eyes were bloodshot. This was by far the most traumatizing experience of his life. Vinny thought incredulously, *The laws tell the people if you don't take the law in your own hands, our system of justice will make sure the guilty party is found, and that system is going to carry out justice for us.* But of course, he was too incredibly stupid to have thought that. He couldn't believe his own brain had failed him so badly. But Vinny had no illusions; he knew anything could happen in that jury room, and he would not be totally at ease until he is vindicated.

"A celebration is in order!" someone from the crowd exclaimed.

"Let's go to Carlos's!" Tommy replied excitedly.

"It's on me."

The preverdict celebration was in full swing at Carlos's Restaurant, a small Italian restaurant directly across the street from Roosevelt High School, where Vinny had graduated. Tommy ordered appetizers, clams oreganata, hot and cold antipastos, and a variety of pizzas. Vinny was emotionally drained. He did not want to eat, he did not want to drink, and he did not feel like celebrating. He did not want to hear about the strategy of his defense or about what was in store for his future.

What he really wanted to do was go home to Judy. Vinny had called her earlier at her office from Tommy's car. She was elated to hear the good news and told him to meet her at her apartment at five thirty sharp.

"I have a surprise for you," she had said provocatively. As the time neared, Vinny made his rounds of thank-yous and goodbyes to his well-wishers. He needed to see Judy. He was consumed with the need to see her. Vinny embraced Tommy, thanking him for everything he had done. "You are truly a best friend," Vinny said appreciatively.

"Tell Judy I said hello," Tommy said by way of goodbye.

Vinny nodded an indeterminate promise and said, "I'll swing by your house in the morning," while making a dash to the exit door.

He got in his car and made his way as quickly as he could to Judy's. He looked at his watch as he put the key in the lock; it was five thirty on the dot. He opened the door and said enthusiastically, "Baby, I'm home!"

She responded from the living room in a sultry, seductive voice, "I'm in here, baby." At thirty years old, she was in perfect shape. Looking extremely beautiful reclining naked with her legs spread on the couch, her fingers softly stroking herself. "If you want me, come and take me," she said in a most seductive voice.

This, he thought, was exactly what he needed at this very moment. His adrenaline was pumping as he began to tear the clothes off his body. The week had been lonesome, and he had longed for her with each passing minute. He loved the fact that Judy was the type of woman to take charge and do whatever she deemed necessary to relieve the pressure.

"I've missed you so much," she sighed as he entered deep inside of her. Her luscious eyes were wide open, a friendly smile on her face. He embraced her tightly in his arms and kissed her, a long, lingering kiss that excited her. Fast, pure, exciting passion took over their bodies as they made love. She lost herself in his rhythm, in the passion of his arms, holding him in every way.

"I love you, so much," she cried before losing herself in an orgasm that seemed to never end.

Simultaneously, Vinny released himself inside of her, collapsing into her loving arms, exhausted, unable to move.

She looked at him. They gazed into each other's eyes. A smile creased her lips, relief, joy, with him again. The look in her eyes told how much she loved him. It was everything he wanted in the world.

CHAPTER 38

V inny and TC had made it through the third day of jury deliberations.

However, before leaving the courtroom, Vinny had a terrible feeling that he was lucky to have escaped. TC, on the other hand, was extremely confident. That was one thing Vinny admired about Tommy—his unbridled enthusiasm.

Too bad it's not infectious, Vinny thought to himself, gazing out the window at the approaching George Washington Bridge *God, how I fucking hate New Jersey. Everything about it turns my stomach. The place is a shithole. It stinks! God, how the chemical plant stink, and the fucking people can't drive. They shouldn't even have licenses! I'd make them walk. Assholes! All they do is cause traffic jams and accidents. After this trial's over, I may never cross this bridge again, not even to visit my parents. They'll have to come to New York if they want to see me.*

As Tommy drove in silence, obviously reflecting on the day's events, Vinny took out his cell phone and called Judy at work. "Hi, baby," he said enthusiastically as she answered.

"Where are you? You're not in the big house?" she asked sarcastically.

"No, monkey feet, I'm not," he answered playfully, referring to a nickname he had given her one night as they drove in the back of a stretch limousine on the way to the city to see the Broadway play *Les Misérables.*

He remembered back to that night the two of them all dressed up for a night on the town. A dozen long-stemmed yellow roses delivered to her office along with a card that read, "Be at my house at

six thirty sharp. Special surprise for you. I love you so much. Vinny."
When she arrived at Vinny's house and saw the long white limo
parked in front, she had wondered what her insanely romantic man
was up to.

When she entered the house, Vinny greeted her with a glass of
champagne and a passionate kiss.

"What's going on, Vincent?"

"Your chariot awaits outside, my lady. We have seven thirty reservations at Sardi's Restaurant in Manhattan. It's a famous restaurant
frequented by Hollywood movie stars and celebrities. Then afterward, we have front-row orchestra seats to *Les Misérables*. Afterward,
a romantic, roaring fire, some Luther Vandross, and who knows?"

"I could kill you! What am I supposed to wear? I can't go like
this!"

Vinny smiled and calmly said, "Follow me." He led her to the
bedroom and opened a closet he'd emptied for her to store clothes
she might need for work when she slept over, which had been quite
frequently.

"I can't wear anything in there for a night like tonight," she said
grimly.

Vinny reached in and withdrew a Versace dress she had fallen in
love with in a store on their latest trip to Atlantic City.

"Oh my God! How did you—"

"Miracles never cease when you are in love with a princess."

She had to laugh as she threw her arms around him. "Wait a
minute," she said, slowly withdrawing from the embrace. "None of
the shoes I have in there are going to match the dress."

"What would Cinderella do with her glass slipper?" He again
reached into the closet and handed her a box. Inside was a pair of
shoes she had unknowingly selected from a catalog, a catalog in
which she'd marked items she wanted to purchase at a later date, a
catalog Vinny swiped without her knowledge.

"You are more than any woman could ask for, Vincent Davis!"

"All I want to do is to make you the happiest woman in the
world."

"You, my love, always do. And I know you always will."

"Good," Vinny said, handing her a glass of champagne. "Now take your time and get changed. I'll wait for you downstairs."

She came down in less than five minutes.

She looked ravishing. It doesn't take long to put the finishing touches on perfection. On the ride in the back of the limo, the two of them were intoxicated with excitement. The two of them staring into each other's eyes, sipping champagne, and giggling like two schoolkids playing hooky. Judy's playfulness came out as she began to run her long manicured nails up and down Vinny's thigh. Giving him an instant erection, which Judy took as a sign to continue. She eagerly undid the zipper to his Armani slacks and removed his swollen member. She then kicked off her new shoes and began to caress his cock with her feet. The silk of her stockings was driving him wild as she moved her feet up and down the shaft.

He reached for her, pulling her forcefully by the back of the hair. They kissed passionately, entwining each other's tongues. He moved into position between her legs. She had never wanted him with such ravening intensity. He was helpless, captured by her spell. The phone rang. "What's that?" she said, embarrassed. Pushing him away. Repositioning herself in a ladylike pose.

Vinny picked up the limo phone despairingly and said yes.

"Mr. Davis," Marco, the driver, said mischievously.

"I just wanted to inform you that we are about to pull up in front of the restaurant."

"Thank you," Vinny said. Knowing full well the obviously experienced driver didn't want his customers to literally get caught with their pants down in front of Sardi's. Vinny looked at her. She was still glowing with lust in her eyes.

"We have to continue this later," he said, disappointed.

"That's a promise," she said with a devilish smile on her face.

"Are you still there?" Judy's voice demanded furiously.

"I'm here, baby," Vinny said, realizing he had become lost in a fantastic daydream.

"What happened?" she demanded. "I thought we got disconnected."

"I was just thinking about our trip to the city to see *Les Misérables*, and I got lost."

"Monkey feet, huh?" she said, laughing. "What a night to remember! Listen," she said impatiently, "as soon as you're done with Tommy, come right over my house. I have a surprise for you."

"I'll be there by 6:00 p.m.," he said.

"I love you, Vinny."

"I love you too, princess. I'll see you at six."

After hanging up the phone, Vinny looked at TC, who was smiling from ear to ear.

"What?"

"You have got it bad, my friend," Tommy said sarcastically.

"You don't have to tell me," Vinny said. "Falling in love for me," Vinny continued, "was like getting hit by a Mack truck. The air was knocked right out of me. I feel sick to my stomach and cannot eat. I break out in cold sweats, and I'm forever horny to the point where I can't get enough of her. Since I met her, my life has become full of hope and enthusiasm. And for the life of me, it is impossible to remove the smile from my face. Love had appeared without any warning signs. It is an uncontrollable emotion. You fall into it as if you were thrown off a high-rise building. You don't stop to think about what's happening. It's inevitable. An emotion you just can't control."

"I told you that you got it bad, but if it's any consolation to you, my friend, everybody knows she feels the same way about you. I have never seen two people more in love than you and Judy. Together, you radiate love. And no matter what happens with the outcome of this trial, she will always be right by your side. And to have that kind of love, you are truly blessed."

Vinny knew this. He thought Judy to be the kindest, most beautiful woman in the world. He trusted her implicitly, something he had never been able to do before. She was the one and only woman he thought he could spend the rest of his life with. Vinny also knew how lucky he was to have a friend like Tommy. Tommy had tenacity and determination, and even more importantly, he knew he would win.

Vinny arrived at Judy's apartment and was greeted with a passionate kiss. Her apartment smelled like an Italian restaurant. "What smells so good?"

"I have cooked you a fantastic dinner. Homemade chicken soup, a fine tossed salad with my special dressing, and pasta surprise."

His face lit up with expectation. He remembered the first night she had prepared a pasta dinner for him. After his first mouthful of the pasta dish she had prepared, he found it to be filled with the king of delight usually associated with sex and ate until he was stuffed.

"I bought a bottle of Chianti Classico, baby," she said.

"Why don't you open it and pour us a glass while I tend to our dinner?"

Vinny opened, poured, and made a toast. "To the most beautiful woman I have ever met."

She touched her glass with his. "To the sexiest and most generous man I've ever met!" They kissed gently.

Then she instructed him to get out of her kitchen and to sit down in the living room and relax. "Tonight, I take care of you," she said, gently pushing him out of the kitchen.

He sat peacefully, looking around her apartment, thinking of all the fond memories they had made there. Her apartment was beautiful, comfortable and very tasteful, a true reflection of her stylish personality. The memories they shared were not just sexual in nature. Although there was not one inch of that apartment they hadn't made love in. The memories ranged from spending quiet weekends lounging around, just enjoying each other's company, to semimajor construction such as installing a new sink and in the bathroom or replacing an old kitchen sink with a nonstop leak. He remembered a business trip she took to Atlanta. While she was gone, Vinny took that opportunity to regrout her bathroom. She was so surprised when she came home to find that done. Vinny remembered the fond memory of sitting on the floor in her living room as she carefully removed pieces of fine china from her wall units as Vinny sat attentively, listening to her explain the craftsmanship of each piece. It was the only thing of her mother's that she received when her mother passed away. It was a lasting memory of a mother she cherished. She reminded him so much of a little girl as she sat explaining how she could not wait until they married so she could display the china in their dining room. My God, how he loved everything about this woman! They were two soul mates who had found each other, two passionate people filled with an unusual lust for living.

"Dinner is served!" Judy said with her usual enthusiasm.

"Great. I'm starved!"

Over dinner, they discussed the trial. Vinny answered questions obliquely, so as not to worry her, but inside he was burning with horror and frustration.

She must have felt in her heart she might lose him forever, and she wanted to be as close to him as possible. Her eyes were filled with mixed emotions. She gazed up at him and said, "I adore you, Vinny. Please don't ever leave me."

"I adore you too, princess. I am never going to leave you. You are my soul mate." He began to kiss her, slowly at first, and as things heated up, he lost all control.

They had made love a hundred times since they had been dating, and each time seemed to be better than the last.

The next morning, he made coffee and a lunch for her to take to work. It was something he very much enjoyed doing. As he watched her get dressed, he couldn't help but wonder. What sort of woman was Judy? Was she a goddess? Did she have magical power? How did a woman penetrate a man's soul deep enough to change him? In the parking lot, they exchanged a long, passionate kiss goodbye, and her eyes began to fill with tears. She looked lost, bewildered, horrified.

"Oh my God, Vinny!" she sobbed, her head falling to his chest. "I've waited my whole life to find you, and I am not going to let them take you away from me!"

He held her close in his arms. Minutes passed. Finally, her tears subsided and Vinny tilted her chin up. He felt a heavy sadness come over him. "I love you, princess. Nothing on this earth is going to stop us from spending the rest of our lives together." He then looked into her magical eyes and said sarcastically, "Now, get your mangy ass to work!" They both burst out laughing.

He then watched her drive away until he could no longer see her car. He stood a moment longer, hoping that this was not the last time he'd see her. For today he knew there would be a verdict.

Tommy and Vinny made their way back across the George Washington Bridge, headed to Newark, an event that became an uneventful routine. There was little to talk about since the jury began deliberations. Tommy sensed an unusual fear in Vinny and decided to let him slip into a deep sleep. Vinny couldn't stop thinking of Judy. He couldn't overcome the fear of possibly losing her if he were convicted and sentenced to prison. Vinny sat and wondered if he had made the right decision about not going overseas as ordered by the government. He remembered emphatically the night he confided in Judy and disclosed everything to her. It was two weeks before her surprise party. The two of them were relaxing in Vinny's living room, drinking wine by a roaring fireplace. The *Grease* soundtrack was blaring on the stereo, a personal favorite of both of them. They each took turns doing their own renditions of "Hopelessly Devoted to You," "Greased Lightning," followed by a duet of "Summer Nights."

Vinny had gone off to the bathroom, and upon his return, he observed Judy staring at the wall above his desk. The wall was loaded with commendations for bravery, along with photos taken of Vinny at awards ceremonies with Mayor Koch, Mayor Dinkins, Mayor Giuliani, and Governor Cuomo. There was also a photo taken of him on the front page of *The Daily News* in which he was crouched behind a patrol car, gun drawn, preparing to open fire. She hadn't noticed Vinny enter the room. And when she did, she asked, "Why did they fire you from the force?" He knew the time had come. Their relationship was obviously headed toward marriage at an alarming rate, and she did have a right to know.

"Come sit next to me," he said as he lowered the volume to "Blue Moon" playing on the stereo. Vinny knew it was better to live in truth, no matter how terrible, than destroy yourself by living a lie.

Judy sat beside him on the couch and gazed into his loving eyes. The eyes of the man she had grown to trust and adore.

Vinny spoke seriously. "I feel I must tell you first that I truly love you, and from that, I want you to someday be my wife, and you deserve my confidence. You are also a compassionate and intelligent woman, so I know you will understand what I am about to tell you." Vinny explained the entire story, which started back in the summer of 1980, right to the present. The only information he chose to delete from the story was pertinent information regarding the ongoing investigation in which he was now involved. He deliberately left that out for her own safety. Knowing all too well what the feds were capable of if they found out she knew.

When he concluded the story, she looked at him and said, "You did nothing wrong. What's the matter with these people?" Then she continued, "Look at all these medals. You're a hero, and this is the way they treat you?"

"Listen, baby," he said warmly. "They want me to go overseas for a while—"

She quickly interrupted him midsentence. "Wait one minute," she demanded furiously. "You are not going anywhere for these people, and that's final. I have waited all my life for you, the man I want to spend the rest of my life with. There is no way you are going over there to get your head blown off for these ungrateful, mangy sons of bitches!"

Vinny had observed small outbursts of jealousy when she referred to the past women in his life, and she had expressed anger at the way his ex-wife had treated him. But he had never seen her become hysterical about anything. She must truly love him to become this emotional. Vinny held her close in his arms and convinced her to calm down by saying he wouldn't do or go anywhere without her approval. They sat back down on the couch. After a couple sips of wine and a few deep breaths, she appeared calm again.

"They will arrest me if I don't do what they say," Vinny said grimly.

"No, they won't," she said confidently, grabbing him into her arms.

"Baby," Vinny said, "you don't know these people. They are ruthless, manipulative, vindictive people who are used to getting what they want, whatever the cost."

"I don't care," she said. "They are not worth getting yourself killed for. The hell with your old job, your pension, and these people! You have almost been killed more times than I care to imagine. Everything happens for a reason, Vinny. You lost a job that could have cost you your life if you stayed on it. Maybe your being fired saved your life. We don't know that. But enough is enough. The past is the past. Just let it go, and we can start a new life together. And if God forbid they arrest you and it goes to trial, Tommy will defend you. Jesus, I think he loves you almost as much as I do. He would never let you go to prison."

She was absolutely right. Nothing in this world was worth the risk of losing this woman, let alone his life.

"We're here!" Vinny heard a voice saying. "Did you have a nice nap?" the voice asked.

Vinny opened his eyes and saw Tommy looking over at him from the driver's seat of his Lincoln Town Car.

"I must have passed out," Vinny said, now looking out the front window of the car parked facing the rear of the courtroom.

"You were tired, so I let you sleep. Did you get any sleep last night?"

"Not really. Judy cooked me dinner last night, and I spent the night."

"A last meal for a condemned man?"

"As a matter of fact, that was exactly what it felt like," Vinny responded.

"Did she grant you any last requests?" Tommy asked sarcastically, with a devilish look on his face.

"Every last one!"

Tommy laughed and said, "I knew there was something about that woman I liked."

They both laughed and began walking toward the courthouse.

CHAPTER 39

T he hours slowly passed as Vinny and his family sat waiting for the jury to return its verdict. He didn't stir. He couldn't think. He was just there, a pile of cells at the defendant's table. The madness seemed to be dissipating; it was moving toward its conclusion.

I pray to God this nightmare ends. Even TC's talked out. When was the last time that happened? He's got nothing to say. I've got nothing to say. There is nothing to say!

Gonzalez's assistant, a petite, attractive Hispanic female in her early twenties, entered the hallway.

"The jury has another note for the judge." She was disappointed, knowing it wasn't the verdict.

"I wonder what it is this time," TC said sarcastically. "May we order pizza? Kentucky fried chicken? Can we use the phone?" He was mocking the jury. Because of their stupid requests, they'd been summoned back to the courtroom several times. This was the seventh time in four days. Once again, they collected themselves, buttoned their suit jackets, entered the courtroom, and waited for the jury to file in. Vinny observed the jurors' faces as they marched in single file to their respective seats. They all wore the same tired look they'd had for the past four days. Not one showed a positive sign.

I wonder what the fuck it is this time.

The court clerk handed the judge the note. He glanced at it. He looked up, his eyes filled with amazement. Then a self-satisfied smile crossed his face. It was a look of a man who suddenly realized events were breaking his way. For effect, he glared at Vinny as he read their note. "Could you please read *willful blindness* to us?"

Vinny's heart skipped a beat; panic raced through his body.

Judge Schwartz continued to glare at Vinny with ice-cold eyes. His hatred and contempt were obvious. As he instructed the jury on the meaning of *willful blindness*, a cynical smile emerged on his face. He appeared immensely pleased.

Look at that prick. He's grinning like a Cheshire cat. The bastard knows it's in the bag. He had it in for me before he even laid eyes on me. Shit, I really, really need one sympathetic juror. Just one. Father, oh, father! What humiliation and embarrassment you must be enduring! I'm sorry. I only wanted to make it all up to you, make you proud of me, and now this. And, Mother, dearest Mother, looking down, watching this travesty. I know you're crying, Ma. This ain't the America you taught me to love, is it? Here was confirmation the judiciary is still the one place in our legal system where a judge can abuse his power and authority with almost certain immunity. Honorable and good men know revenge is not noble emotion, yet this judge seems to revel in it.

Judge Schwartz finished his instructions and asked the jury to return to their room for further deliberations.

Vinny looked at Tommy. From the look in his eyes, Vinny knew he recognized the dilemma.

Tommy looked over at Gonzalez, who was undoubtedly aware that Judge Schwartz, in his zeal to please the prosecution, was abusing his authority and undermining the American justice system by not charging the jury with intoxication. Nor did this seem to bother Gonzalez, the career prosecutor. He believed Vinny, and every other defendant on the planet, was certainly guilty of something.

Fool! Can't he see? No, he can't. The truth's so clear, yet he can't see it. He won't let himself see it, so I get fucked in the process.

Vinny suddenly became claustrophobic, dashing from the courtroom with Tommy on his heels. When they reached the men's room, Vinny felt nauseous. Faced with the horrible, ugly, unbelievable reality that he was now in serious trouble, that something had gone terribly wrong inside the jury room.

Tommy turned toward Vinny, an apologetic look on his face. "We have been royally screwed by this judge," he said, shaking his head in despair.

"The jury thinks I'm guilty," Vinny said, his voice tremulous. "They didn't listen. The stupid fools didn't listen to what really happened!"

"Try to calm down," Tommy said with perspicacity.

"How can you tell me to calm down, TC?" His voice was bitter as bile. "The jury just asked the judge to read *willful blindness* to them. I'm a fucking dead man!" Vinny cried out in agony. He rushed on, not giving Tommy a chance to stop him. "Did you see the look on the face of that miserable bitch juror 7 after the judge finished reading *willful blindness* to them? She looked at juror 1, the lawyer, with an I-told-you-so look—a lawyer, the son of a cop! With my luck, his fucking father works for Internal Affairs and thinks every other cop is dirty. He's the jury foreman, for Christ's sakes! Right now he is in that jury room, playing Perry Mason, showing off his newly acquired legal skills to the simple laymen on the jury. He is going to lead them to a guilty verdict like the pied-fucking-piper!"

Tommy put a calming hand on his shoulder, but his eyes showed anxiety from the intensity of Vinny's reaction. It had no effect, as Vinny continued to erupt like Mount Saint Helens.

"Let's see what else we have here," Vinny said. His voice bordered on the hysterical. "How about prosecutorial misconduct? That little twerp tried to extract testimony from me about the three recorded conversations between Sabol and Debbie. I can't refresh my recollection about a conversation I wasn't privy to. It's impossible!"

Vinny paced the bathroom floor, pondering. Fire raged in his eyes.

"What about Gonzalez recommending a sentence reduction for Gerry Vittorio if he testified truthfully? The wording made it clear that Gonzalez's recommendation hinged on whether he personally believed Vittorio's testimony, which could lead a reasonable juror to infer that Gonzalez had a special ability or extraneous knowledge to assess credibility. What about his bolstering in his opening statements? Implying that a witness's testimony had been corroborated by evidence that was available to the government but never presented to the jury.

"This case has been in trouble ever since the judge told you, 'This is New York City nonsense!' By Gonzalez having the media sensationalizing the case, they've made things worse. The mere mention of the words *rogue cop* is enough to make them convict me. You saw how the jurors looked at me after reading that article in the newspaper. The jurors that liked me are all gone! Juror 1, the construction worker who hated Vittorio, gets a toothache and gets removed with the judge's blessing, because he knew he was for the defense. Juror 5, that attractive female, has an important business trip. She gets excused. You saw the way she looked at me when they sent her home. It was almost as though she said she was sorry she had to leave. Then, this morning, juror 6 informs us she has to fly south tomorrow to take her father off life support. Do you really think she will fight for my vindication? I don't think so! She'll vote with what the rest of them decide just to get on a plane by tonight. Now, let's see. Who does that leave us with? Maybe juror 2, the schoolteacher, who waltzes into court every day reeking of booze and can't keep her eyes open, even behind the dark sunglasses she wears. Or maybe the alternate they put in from the Philippines, who doesn't speak a fucking word of English. He doesn't have a clue what's going on!

"Let's face it, TC, I'm fucked, and you know it! That lowlife, bastard judge didn't charge the jury with intoxication because he knew it was my only real defense beyond the fact that I didn't do it in the first place! If he had, that scumbag lawyer-juror would have been informing his flock in the jury room that they would have to find me innocent because of my intoxication. Instead, he's in there right now, telling them they must, by law, convict me on the grounds of willful blindness. I love that one! Where it can almost be said that I actually knew, by having my suspicions aroused, but that I deliberately looked the other way to remain ignorant! Some fucking legal concept. Theoretically, they can nail anyone on that. The only 'blindness' I'm guilty of is drunken blindness. Can't they see that?"

TC looked at him with concern. He could see the rage and fear on Vinny's face. He was clearly troubled. There was nothing he could say or do to make it better. His situation was bad, and they both knew it. But it was his duty, both as Vinny's friend and lawyer, to buck him up as best he could.

"Listen, Vinny. If they have anything, it's the obstruction charge. There's no way they'll convict on the other ten counts. It's totally impossible. If they get the one obstruction charge, we'll file an immediate appeal and continue bail pending appeal. So try not to worry. We will come out of this all right. Just don't say or do anything stupid when the jury comes back. We don't want to give Judge Schwartz any reason to deny bail."

Vinny was petrified. The thought of spending even one night in jail was horrifying. He saw comfort and strength in his best friend's eyes.

There's still hope. I mustn't give up hope. I pray TC's right. I've trusted him all my life.

"All right, TC. I'm in your hands, and I trust you with my life."

"Good!" TC brightened. "Now, splash some water on your face and regain your composure."

Vinny leaned on the edge of the sink and splashed water on his face as he tried to calm himself. He knew exploding at TC was unreasonable, like blaming the messenger for the message, but he had to purge his system of his frustration, anger, and fear somehow. He had no one but TC to whom he could explode, and God knows he had to explode or he'd go insane.

What a friend! I owe him. Now's not the time for saying I'm sorry. Later.

As they walked out of the bathroom, Gonzalez's secretary approached them and exclaimed, "They've reached a verdict!" The sound of excitement in her voice—her overenthusiasm—sent chills down Vinny's spine.

"Let's get in there. Remember, Vinny, stay calm no matter what happens."

Although he was speechless, he managed a smile and gave TC an encouraging nod.

As soon as the courtroom doors closed behind him, Vinny knew those in attendance also knew a verdict had been reached. A nervous bustle was apparent. Court personnel and marshals were posted at the exits to prevent any possible escape attempt.

Vinny approached the defense table, frowning, uncertainty mixed with bewilderment and sadness.

The jury filed silently into the courtroom. None looked at Vinny. He knew that was a bad sign. He had witnessed enough trials to know that if the verdict was in favor of the defense, some of the jurors would pass a reassuring glance at the defendant.

The judge made his grand entrance a moment later with a look of arrogance on his face, as if he already knew the verdict. A hiss of expectation raged through the courtroom. Vinny stared straight ahead. He stood with a dignity that no one, including the miserable son of a bitch sitting on the bench, could take from him. In spite of everything, he still had his dignity and his pride.

The judge took his place of honor and cleared his throat. "Ladies and gentlemen of the jury, have you reached your verdict?" he asked tensely.

The jury foreman stood up.

It was as Vinny suspected, the pissant lawyer. The butterflies in Vinny's stomach were now wearing roller skates.

"Yes, Your Honor," he said very distinctly.

"Then pass your verdict to the court clerk, please," the judge said with an air of arrogance.

The foreman did as instructed.

The clerk accepted the folded piece of paper and handed it directly to the judge. As he peered at it intently, a smirk spread across his miserable face.

An expectant silence hung over the courtroom. It was so intense Vinny thought everyone could hear each rapid, pounding heartbeat in his chest. It was so loud in his ears.

Holy shit! This can't be happening to me. Not after all the good I've done and the lives I've saved. Please, God, no. Don't let this happen to me.

The jury foreman read the verdict. "Guilty!"

I'm fucked. Dammit. How could they?

An outbreak of barely audible sighs came from behind Vinny where his family and friends sat. The sighs turned into a roar, and then tears, as the foreman continued to repeat the word *guilty* ten more times.

The sheer unreasonableness of their decision made Vinny momentarily forget to breathe. For what seemed an endless succession of seconds, he couldn't speak. He could not even move.

The decisive old man sat on the bench before him, grinning ominously, talking in the effect of the verdict with delight. He'd waited four years for this moment. He was going to savor every second of Vinny's grief as he stood, helpless and alone, before the sorry excuse of a judge—no!—of a man.

Steeling his resolve, Tommy looked at Vinny and, with deeply felt reluctance, said, "I don't know how to tell you this, but your grandfather passed away this morning."

What did he say? Gran? Passed away? Dead? No! Dead? Vinny felt as if a knife had been plunged through his heart.

Tommy continued to speak to him, but he could not hear a word. All he saw was Tommy's lips moving. For several moments, Vinny could not speak. Speech was beyond him. He was capable only of lowering his eyes and doing his best to simulate normal breathing.

When the armed US marshals stood guard behind him, he knew what to expect next. Instinctively, almost involuntarily, he began to remove his tie, belt, wallet, and cash, then took off his watch, and lastly, he removed his ring from his right ring finger: his gold "shield" ring, in the shape of his badge, with his patrolman's number on it. He had worn it proudly, almost religiously, every day for the past thirteen years. He handed it to his father, who stood rigidly, his face full of shock and disbelief as he watched the marshals handcuff and shackle his son like some violent criminal.

For a moment, Vinny stared at his family with a blank expression on his face.

He was so numb nothing inside him could escape.

The marshals started to lead him away. Suddenly, he felt an overwhelming gush of relief.

It's over. How fucking ironic! Sabol and Vittorio were the ones who committed all the heinous crimes presented to the jury, yet they're free and I'm going to jail!

"Some justice, huh?" he snickered on the way out, then with his head bowed, his body started to shake from fear and anticipation of the unknown that awaited him.

Vincent Davis was still in shock as he sat in the back seat of the United States Marshal's car, stunned, unable to formulate his thoughts. He was handcuffed and shackled like a dangerous criminal. Inside, he was burning with horror and frustration. The combined realization that he'd lost his grandfather and was going to prison was devastating. It was such crushing news that, for the moment, he was beyond tears. He was numb.

The marshals escorted him to Union County Jail, where he would now be treated as a common criminal. He thought of AUSA Gonzalez, who was, no doubt, out celebrating a victory he surely did not deserve.

How could the jury do this to me? The government's whole case was a tenuous, speculative, circumstantial mass of absolutely nothing! Did juries regularly convict in federal court cases on the basis of inferences from circumstantial evidence?

Vinny knew from experience that they didn't in State Supreme Court. He also knew no district attorney in the state of New York would bother indicting a case such as this, let alone take it to trial. But Vinny knew the reason for this circus. It was revenge.

Gonzalez is celebrating his victory, but really, what has he won? Nothing but bitter revenge. Yet there's no revenge sweeter than revenge long awaited. Prison will be more difficult and scary than anything I've ever done or experienced.

Summoned from the back seat of the car, he was marched to a solid steel door, where they were buzzed in electronically. They were greeted by a rather-large uniformed correction officer (CO), who took one look at Vinny and barked, "Stand over there and strip!" pointing to a space by the wall, in full view of everyone.

Vinny was full of fear and dread, yet he began to strip as ordered, as one of the marshals took Vinny's paperwork to a desk, where the supervising officer sat patiently. One of the escorting marshals was a very pretty Hispanic female. The embarrassment Vinny felt standing completely naked in front of her was nothing compared to the fear he felt if he did not do as he was told. The burly-looking officer walked over, stood in front of him, and began a series of instructions that were obviously routine. "Hold your hands out to your side," he said. "Palms up, palms down. Run your fingers through your hair. Open your mouth. Lift up your tongue. Lift up your balls. Turn around and face the wall. Lift up your left foot and let me see the soles of your feet. Now your right foot. Bend over and spread your cheeks. Good!" He was finally done.

He then threw an orange jumpsuit at Vinny and commanded, "Now, put this on!"

He quickly did so.

As he did, he overheard the female marshal say to one of the officers, "What a waste of a perfectly good man."

The jumpsuit was tremendously oversize, so he asked the CO politely if they had a smaller one.

He looked at Vinny and said emphatically, "The marshals told us who you are and what you did. Personally, I think it sucks. We just had a few of our own officers convicted last week. It's open season on law enforcement. I'm personally going to take you to our Protective Custody Unit and make sure the officers are aware of your situation. We take care of our own. You'll be safe here."

Vinny felt a sigh of relief. At last, he would be protected and looked upon as a brother officer in trouble.

"Thank you very much, Officer," Vinny said despairingly. "You have no idea how much better your reassurance makes me feel."

"No problem, brother," he replied.

"But that tent-size jumpsuit is for your own protection. A guy with your looks and shape can't walk around in no formfitting, tight-assed jumpsuit, if you get my drift!" he said humorously.

He now knew exactly what he meant and was petrified again.

The CO escorted him through what seemed to be a maze of dark, filthy corridors until he reached his designated area, where a friendly-looking face greeted him.

The CO was smiling and shaking his head in disgust as he spoke to the officer who had escorted him up. The escorting officer turned to face Vinny. He held out his hand to shake his and said, "Everything will work out. Officer Slater here will see you are taken care of."

"Thanks," Vinny said in a confident voice.

"My name is Jimmy Slater." He extended his hand to Vinny. They shook. "We do our best to take care of our own in here," he continued. "We don't have much here, but at least you'll be safe."

"Thanks very much," Vinny responded. "It means a lot to me."

Jimmy pushed a button that electronically opened a steel door leading to the cell area.

He then pushed another button that opened cell 12.

Vinny followed Jimmy into the cell as instructed and immediately observed the look of curious faces peering out of the tiny cell windows. Several of the prisoners began yelling obscenities. Vinny tuned them out.

"This is your cell," Jimmy said, motioning Vinny to enter. "I'll leave the door open for a while so you can get used to it. This is going to be hard for you to get used to, but trust me, you will. Do you want to make a phone call?" he asked nonchalantly.

"Could I?"

"Stay here. I'll bring it to you." In less than a minute, Jimmy returned with the phone and plugged it into a jack outside the cell. He picked up the receiver and held it to his ear to check that it was working. "It's all yours," he said, handing the phone to him. "Use it as long as you want."

"Thanks for everything, Officer," Vinny said. He was thankful for the opportunity and excited by the thought of hearing Judy's voice.

It had been hours since the verdict. He hoped that by now someone had called her with the bad news. He frantically dialed her number. She answered on the first ring, as though she were sitting by the phone, waiting for his call.

"Oh my God, baby!" she said. She was crying hysterically. "What happened?"

He fought back tears. The sound of desperation in her voice was tearing the heart out of him.

"It was a runaway jury," Vinny said anxiously. "One minute they were arguing so loud you could hear them through the walls of the courtroom, and the next minute they asked the judge to read back *willful blindness* to them. Then the next minute, I was in handcuffs and shackles and whisked away to jail."

"Willful blindness! What the fuck is *willful blindness?*"

Vinny took a deep breath and began to recite what the judge had read to the jury.

"It's where it can almost be said that the defendant actually knew, like when a person has his suspicion aroused, but then deliberately omits to make further inquiries because he wishes to remain in ignorance."

"That's insane!" Her voice was loud as thunder. "If anyone's blind, it's the jury. Couldn't they see that those bastards tried to use you? Couldn't they see how ludicrous the government is by letting Sabol and Vittorio free to roam the streets? Those two are murderers, career criminals who belong behind bars for the rest of their lives! Couldn't they see that you have suffered enough for one act of drunken stupidity? They are the ones that are willfully blind, not you!"

He had held back as long as he could, but the anguish in her voice pushed him over the edge.

He began to cry.

"I'm so sorry, princess."

"Oh, baby," she said affectionately, "try not to get upset. I spoke to Tommy on the phone, and although he's devastated, he promises he'll get you out of there. He's already filed a notice of appeal so you can get bail pending your sentencing. He said it will take a couple of weeks, but you should be home before Easter Sunday."

"I know," Vinny said, fighting back tears. "I'm more worried about you than I am about me right now. I hate having you upset by this, and if I lose you, I will surely die!"

"Don't worry about me, baby," she said soothingly. "As long as I know you're all right, I'll be fine. And don't worry, you'll never lose me. I adore you. Now, try to relax. Tommy will get you out, and you'll be back in my arms before you know it."

Vinny looked over and saw the CO at the doorway of his cell. "Hold on a second, princess," he said.

"I have to take the phone and close the cell. The boss is on his way up."

"Thanks, Officer," Vinny said. "Listen, honey, the CO has to take the phone. I'll call you as soon as I can. I love you so much."

"I love you too, baby. Call me as soon as you can, and be strong for me!"

"I will." He hung up the phone and handed it to the CO.

The moment the CO exited his cell, the solid steel door began to close automatically. When it slammed shut, the piercing sound of metal on metal drove right through his heart. Although he was not claustrophobic, his heart raced. Momentarily unable to breathe, he had to force himself to calm down.

Now I'm alone in the world. The cell isn't what I thought it'd be— no bars. Until I get out, I'm going to eat, sleep, and shit behind solid steel doors in a six-by-ten room. Fucking Sabol should be here, not me. Walls, floors, and ceiling, concrete. There're the air ducts high up in the walls. There's certainly no escaping this place. Escape? Fuck, that'd only get me deeper in shit. This is hopeless. Shit, I don't even know how long I'm going to be in here!

He lost all his strength and reason and wept in panic and despair. Minutes seemed like hours, hours like days, and days like weeks. Waiting seemed interminable. But as the months passed and he adjusted to prison life, Vinny was reasonably content. He was extremely lonely, yes, but he had learned to be satisfied keeping his own company.

The Third Circuit Court of Appeals denied his bail appeal because he was a flight risk, and because of his position as an ex-law enforcement officer, he might harm himself in an effort to avoid a lengthy prison sentence. He had been locked in a cage like an animal for almost four anguish-filled months.

As the sentencing date drew nearer, Tommy worked feverishly with the Federal Probation Department in an attempt to make sure

Vinny got everything he was entitled to according to the Sentencing Guidelines Commissions. His presentence report revealed that he could receive a sentence of thirty months, being a first-time offender convicted of a nonviolent crime. He might be placed in the Bureau of Prison's Shock Incarceration Program. That meant he might do six months in a military-style boot camp. Upon satisfactory completion of the program, he would be eligible for release.

TC and Vinny both agreed that Vinny should be a candidate for leniency—a mentally frail man who'd crossed the line at a moment of extreme weakness, but he would never err again.

Vinny did some research, and for the most part, commentators had been critical of strict liability crimes. The consensus can be summed up this way: To punish conduct without reference to the actor's state of mind is both inefficacious and unjust. It is inefficacious because conduct, unaccompanied by an awareness of the factors making it criminal, does not mark the actor as one who need be subject to punishment in order to deter him, or others, from behaving similarly in the future. Nor does it single him out as a socially dangerous individual who needs to be incarcerated or reformed.

The only fear Vinny had now was Gonzalez and the Honorable Judge Schwartz, who, he believed, would have him shot in a public forum if it were within his powers. But Tommy remained forever optimistic. His feelings were that the government got their pound of flesh and would remain content.

However, all the optimism in the world could not put his fears to rest. His fear of the unknown expressed itself internally—in nightmares, stomach problems, depression—and externally, as sudden explosions of temper. The latter was usually directed toward his family, who were trying desperately to help him deal with the helpless position in which he found himself.

His parents, brothers, and sister had come to visit him on numerous occasions. But the pain, despair, and disappointment he saw in their eyes each time was devastating to him. No longer could he deal with the people he loved seeing him in jail. The letters, cards, photos, and phone calls would have to suffice until such time as he would be transferred to a prison. Only then would he be afforded the opportunity to embrace his family, whom he loved and missed so dearly.

Judy remained a real trooper. Although she was furious that the court wouldn't let him out on bail pending appeal, she remained optimistic, loving, and extremely supportive. She had vowed to stand by and wait for her man, no matter how terrible the outcome might be. Their Sunday-night telephone calls, which she never missed, were the worst illusions of all for him. With the sound of her voice whispering softly in his ear, he imagined he could touch the woman he wanted so desperately, but he couldn't. She had only disappointed him once since his conviction, when she didn't show up for a visit. He insisted he didn't want her to come. He had seen the pain it cost his family to see him like that and did not want to subject her to that horror. But her persistence paid off, and he relented.

He waited all day, but she never showed up. When he spoke to her, more than a week later, he was upset, but he understood when she explained how afraid she had been to see him like that.

"As badly as I miss you, I couldn't bear the thought of seeing you in that much pain."

Okay, okay. Perhaps it's best she didn't come, after all. Seeing her beauty through a glass window without being able to throw my arms around her would be too much for me to bear. Yeah, I forgive her. Why not? We'll be together soon enough for the rest of our lives.

Meanwhile, Debbie, his long-forgotten, deceitful, adulterous bitch of an ex-wife, had returned to her life of alcohol and drug abuse. She was interviewed by a probation officer as part of the pre-sentence investigation being prepared for the judge. Vinny could not believe the things she said about him and their marriage, after all he had done for her, even after their divorce. He had arranged, through a friend, to send her to a rehabilitation center upstate for three months, free of charge. He had answered desperate phone calls in the middle of the night, forcing him out of bed to drive to some coke bar or police station to return her safely home to her parents. Thank God the probation officers noticed Debbie was crazy and added to the end of the report, "In our conversation with Ms. Davis, she indicated that she has a history of fighting with men." During this conversation, it appeared to the probation officer that she was under the influence of either alcohol or drugs. Vinny was thankful the officer got a chance to see Debbie for what she really was.

If only I'd known this woman would be an albatross around my neck. She's brought me nothing but bad luck.

Bad luck she continued to bring that had gotten worse. After Vinny's conviction, Debbie decided that she wanted everything Vinny owned that she had not gotten her hands on in the divorce settlement four years ago. First, she called Tommy, petulantly, demanding all the furniture, stereos, TVs, and jewelry left behind in the house Vinny and Michael shared. Fortunately, he was still living there.

Several times Tommy managed to stay civil with her. He explained that once a divorce was final, she no longer had a legal right to Vinny's personal belongings. But she was insistent and became belligerent, telling Tommy, "He's going away for ten years, so he doesn't need that stuff. I deserve it. He's my husband!"

This enraged Tommy, who accusingly told her, "If it weren't for you, filthy slut, Vinny wouldn't be in jail in the first place!"

However, this far from discouraged the ex-Mrs. Davis. She was determined to get what she reasoned, in her drug-addicted mind, was rightfully hers.

Her next plan of action was to call the FBI agents who investigated Vinny. The same agents she knowingly lied to about him. After getting the bureaucratic runaround from them, they considered her to be nothing more than a liar and a lush. She turned her sights to AUSA Gonzalez, whom she told, "I helped you put him away behind bars. You owe me!"

Gonzalez had the good sense to ignore her and referred her back to Tommy, which she knew was a dead end.

Still determined, she decided to break into Vinny's house one afternoon while Michael was at work and proceeded to take as much as her greedy little hands could carry. The thing that broke Vinny's heart the most was the sentimental value that she knew was attached to certain items.

Vinny's grandfather, who had died on the day of his conviction, had given him an antique solid-gold watch and a gold sapphire ring. He wore them on special occasions, which was something his grandfather loved to see. She also took the three-carat engagement ring that Vinny had planned to put on Judy's finger the day of his sentence. That was the day he finally decided he would propose to her, no matter what the outcome of his sentencing. Not content with that, she also took his "shield ring," which he wore every day since he got it after his rookie year, then a four-carat diamond-and-sapphire tennis bracelet, and a two-carat set of diamond earrings he had bought for Judy over the summer. In comparison, the rest of the jewelry—his old wedding band and Rolex watch—meant nothing to him. This woman he once loved now brought out an absolutely pathological hatred for her in Vinny.

Here I sit in jail, a highly decorated police officer. I dedicated my entire life helping other people, while my cheating, junkie ex-wife steals everything I own. Not only that, she's been carrying on an affair, for the past ten years, with the most evil, murdering criminal, who is now free from a twenty-year prison sentence! Even if the pope told me this story, I'd call him a pathological liar. This is too bizarre to be true, but fucking true it is!

Vinny rose from his bed, walked two paces to the small sink mounted to the wall, and looked at himself in the mirror. The reflection he saw was no longer that of a young man proud of himself and his accomplishments; he now saw a failure, a coward, and a fool.

CHAPTER 40

Vinny was awakened by the deafening sound of his cell door opening. He reached with the same instinctive reaction as an animal instantly alert for trouble. It was still dark.

A guard's voice said, "It's court day."

He suddenly remembered where he was. After four months of waiting, Vinny should be used to the system, but he was not.

A cop's supposed to be on the outside, not inside in the solitude of his cell.

After all the hours Tommy's put into research and motions, the result will come to a semiconclusion today. I will be face-to-face with a judge who's the reincarnation of Judge Roy Bean. His open hostility toward my lawyer and me is beyond logic. Damn. I feel sick in my stomach. Going before a judge to be sentenced for a crime you unknowingly commit is bad, but it's worse when you feel the judge has taken it personally, which the prick has. No matter what's said in court today on my behalf, I know I won't be judged fairly. Time to face the music.

By 7:30 a.m., Vinny was loaded in a van with other prisoners and driven to Newark Federal Court.

Today, judgment day, I'll learn my fate. I'm not optimistic. Only a fool would be optimistic with this judge and jury. The system's fucked, and now it's going to fuck me.

It was a system for which he'd been prepared to lay down his life, just as many other policemen had done. He'd been to too many funerals of policemen who had to think otherwise. But he now thought differently.

Since his conviction, since the moment the jury foreman proudly stood and announced the guilty verdict eleven consecutive times, he had lost all faith and hope in the federal justice system. Here was another blemish on America's justice system, the system that binds us together as law-abiding citizens. For us to function as a society, citizens must respect and obey not just the law but also the system that administers it. But the pact between the people and the government is a two-way street. The government's side of the bargain is that it should administer the law fairly, both in fact and in spirit. When either side breaks its responsibilities to the other, the system breaks down.

For the first time in four months, he finally would see his family and friends. He had missed them dearly. Although he would be totally humiliated, dressed in an orange jumpsuit and shackled hands and feet, he still was looking forward to seeing the people he loved, if only for a short while. From the holding cell, where he waited, he heard his name called. A sudden wave of fear and panic hit him. For Vinny, a man who faced many dangerous situations in his thirteen years as a cop, he suddenly was paralyzed and afraid to move. He began to pray, "Yea, though I walk through the valley of death, I shall fear no evil."

God, please help me. I'd rather be in a fierce gun battle than face my fear of the unavoidable unknown I'm about to face.

The Probation Department had done an extensive presentencing report, which recommended to the judge what they considered a lenient sentence of thirty to thirty-seven months. He was sure the judge would find a way to sentence him to more time. Vinny had been told numerous times by Tommy and his defense team that a judge would never sentence him outside the guideline range recommended by the Probation Department.

"Not even Schwartz would run the risk of looking like a fool in the Third Circuit Court of Appeals," Tommy encouragingly had told Vinny.

Even so, Vinny knew he was not dealing with a rational human being. He was dealing with a man who did not know the meaning of the word *compassion*, a ruthless and evil man who dispensed his own warped, self-serving version of justice, a man who somehow came to believe he was godlike and that he was the only judge who could properly dispense justice. Vinny thought it ludicrously ironic that the very man who freed two career criminals would sentence him to prison. *Illogical* was stamped all over this case from its beginning. No matter how many times he analyzed it, the exchange made no sense to him.

But wait! The judge didn't start this. He's finishing it. He's putting the nails in my coffin. Fucking Gonzalez! He's the one who opened the coffin, bound me hand and foot, and placed me, still alive, in it! How the fuck did he become a federal prosecutor?

As Vinny was escorted through a mazelike corridor in the basement of the courthouse, he continued to ponder on the ironic chain of events that had led him to this point. It made no sense to any person who knew what happened.

How does a federal judge justify releasing the criminal Sabol from a twenty-year sentence? An animal! Well-dressed scum, but scum nonetheless! The judge knows he's spent most of his adult life either in prison or concocting new criminal enterprises. He'll never change his spots, yet they've done a deal with him just to fuck me. But that's the system now: the feds buy and sell testimony from criminals in exchange for reduced sentences. Why? So they can chalk up convictions on their résumés. Pigs at the trough! If it weren't for the bought-and-paid-for testimony of criminals and conspiracy charges, the federal justice system would collapse. Meanwhile, the criminals are freed to commit more crimes. What do they fear? Not much, so long as they have information to sell the feds in exchange for yet another deal.

Vinny prepared himself to enter the court, a court he'd held in utmost respect his entire life, but now a court in which he'd lost all respect. He was physically sick as he thought about what was going to happen to him, something impossible to stop. He was about to be sentenced for crimes he unknowingly and unintentionally committed. It boggled his mind. Two career criminals were about to be sprung, surely to return to their lives of crime. And just as surely as Vinny knew it, so did the feds. They were pieces in a real-life game of Monopoly. Sabol and Vittorio were about to get "get out of jail" passes, and Vinny was about to lose a turn in life. He'd already lost everything he'd worked so hard for. Being an NYPD cop was not just a job to him—it was his way of life. He worked to protect and save people, while Sabol and Vittorio worked at hurting them. Vinny never feared an assignment given him, no matter how dangerous it was. He always thought, if he was injured or killed in the line of duty, some good would still result.

As he was escorted, handcuffed and shackled, down the dark and eerie hallway by marshals, he thought about how he might possibly relay his feelings to a judge who saw only the things he wanted to see, a judge who didn't believe in mitigating circumstances, a judge who believed only he, without error, knew what was right or wrong. How could he make a man like that see that he had made a colossal mistake by buying the bill of goods Sabol was selling the judge and the prosecutor, as he had done to numerous others in the past to escape from paying for his crimes?

How could Vinny relay his feelings to an egotistical maniac hell-bent on nailing him to the cross for all to see? He didn't see any way to do that.

He could never admit he made the mistake for which he'd been convicted. Such an admission would tar the rest of his life. Yet if he tried to explain, what would stop the judge from taking out his anger and frustrations on him and, in turn, sentence him to an even longer term of imprisonment?

Tommy and his parents told him to put aside his own personal feelings and throw himself at the mercy of Schwartz. But Vinny knew he had none.

He still hadn't decided what he would say. He'd wait until it was his turn to stand and address the court before committing himself to any decision. They brought him to the courtroom by the rear door. After being escorted through a labyrinth of corridors, Vinny hadn't spoken on the journey. Neither had the several marshals who escorted him. He was in shock, buried in thought. Thankfully, they were tactful. He felt chilled as he made his grand entrance, immediately making eye contact with Judy. She broke into an excited smile when she saw him holding her eyes with his. The hollowness in them as she tried desperately not to cry. Vinny wished he had more time to brace himself for this. He had had his share of doubts about whether or not she'd even attend.

He sat paralyzed at the defense table next to Tommy as they waited for the coup de grâce to be administered.

The Honorable Harold Schwartz was already perched in his place of honor. He stared down at Vinny like a vulture, just waiting for him to take his last breath before he swooped down to eat his carcass, tearing away at him until nothing but bones remained.

"Mr. Cascione, I'll hear from the defense first," Judge Schwartz said. His voice was deep and vaguely unnerving. He was ever so calm yet showed signs he wanted to end these proceedings as quickly as possible.

Tommy stood and read his appearance for the record and began strategically taking apart the probation report, which was prepared to assist the judge in his sentencing. In the report, probation recommended a sentence guideline range of thirty to thirty-seven months of imprisonment. Tommy had already responded in writing why Vinny should receive a lesser sentence.

Gonzalez also submitted his response as to why Vinny should receive a greater sentence. This was an unexpected move Vinny and Tommy never thought he would make after a meeting on May 1, 1998, between Probation, Gonzalez, Tommy, and Vinny—a post-conviction meeting that was unprecedented. Vinny explained to those in attendance that although he was drunk on the nights he committed the crimes for which he stood convicted, he should have known that Sabol was, in fact, working for the government in some capacity. Tommy and Vinny were led to believe that, based on that explanation, Vinny, therefore, accepted responsibility for his actions and the government would not seek a sentence higher than the Probation Department recommended.

According to the government, the evidence at trial established that the conspiracy to obstruct justice involved at least four individuals: Vinny; his brother-in-law, Michael; Maria, Michael's wife; and Gerry Vittorio. The defendant was the architect, organizer, and leader of the conspiracy. The probation officer refused to raise

Vinny's sentencing guideline range, stating the defendant's actions did not rise to the level of warranting an aggravating role. Based on the information provided by the government, the defendant's sister and brother-in-law might not have been criminally responsible. Even if they were, Probation saw little to suggest the defendant actually managed or supervised their activities. As for Vittorio, who was also involved in the conspiracy, he was not managed or supervised by the defendant and, if anything, had more to gain than the defendant by harming Sabol. However, Judge Schwartz must rule on this contested issue. Should Schwartz agree with the government, the total range of imprisonment would rise to thirty-seven to forty-six months. No doubt Schwartz would save the government's objection for last.

"Mr. Cascione! I will hear you in regards to the presentence report."

"Your Honor, defense counsel argues that the defendant is worthy of a reduction in sentence for acceptance of responsibility. Counsel indicates that the defendant voluntarily assisted in the investigation and gave a factual account of his responsibility."

"I am going to reject the application, Mr. Cascione!" Schwartz exclaimed. "As stated in the presentencing report, the timeliness of the defendant's acceptance of responsibility is a factor to consider in evaluating whether or not a reduction in sentence is appropriate. Although conviction by trial does not automatically preclude a defendant from consideration from this reduction, a determination that a defendant has accepted responsibility will be based primarily upon pretrial statements and conduct. Next application, Mr. Cascione," Judge Schwartz said with irritation.

"I object at a two-level enhancement for the defendant's abuse of a position of trust. Counsel argues that the fact the defendant was a police officer at the time of the offense had nothing to do with the crime. My client obtained public information on Sabol that any private citizen could have easily obtained."

"I am going to deny that application for reduction, Mr. Cascione," Schwartz said harshly. "Your client surmised through his police training that Richard Sabol was an informant, and then contacted at least two FBI agents and Sabol's prosecuting assistant

US attorney in Atlanta, Georgia, in an attempt to learn why Sabol was released from prison. Although the defendant was only provided with public information, he did not contact these individuals representing himself as an ordinary citizen. His responsibility as a police officer was to advise authorities of known illegal activity as soon as he learned of it. The defendant kept this information to himself, hoping to convince Vittorio to take action against Sabol. Until he was ultimately forced to go to authorities as Sabol had learned it was he who leaked the information to Vittorio. The fact the defendant was a police officer facilitated the commission, or concealment, of the offense. I'll hear your next application, Mr. Cascione," he said hurriedly.

"Your Honor, my next objection addresses my client's exposure to double charging and how that relates to the scoring of the offense. As of this point, we all understand that the full thrust of my client's conduct was aimed toward harming Richard Sabol. He was not trying to save anyone from prosecution or avoid arrest or do anything other than harm Sabol. The collateral result of my client's conduct was an obstruction of justice. The witness tampering charge refers to my client's attempt to harm Richard Sabol, who turned out to be a federal witness. I also argue that the three-level enhancement produces the same collateral effect, as does the two levels added for obstruction of justice. The government is adding obstruction to obstruction to obstruction to turn the same acts into years of imprisonment."

"I'm going to deny that application for reduction, Mr. Cascione," Judge Schwartz said belligerently. "Firstly, you argue that a base level of 12 is double the points that might otherwise have applied. A violation of obstruction of justice begins with a base level of 12. The fact your client was charged with and convicted of witness tampering had no bearing on the guideline computation, as all counts were grouped together to form a single offense level. Your client would have netted the same guideline score had he been convicted of only one count of obstruction of justice and nothing else. Secondly, the three-level enhancement is the lesser of the two alternatives under the specific offense characteristics and was appropriately applied in this case, as the exact consequence of your client's action did cause substantial interference with the administration of justice. Lastly, the two-level enhancement, for obstruction of justice, stems from a Chapter 3 adjustment for perjury at trial and is wholly separate from the scoring of the obstruction of justice offense under Chapter 2. Do you have any more applications, Mr. Cascione?" asked Schwartz, courteously, thinking there were no more.

"Yes, Your Honor," Tommy said, despair in his voice.

"Very well. Let me hear it." He was clearly frustrated.

"Thank you, Your Honor. I argue that it is warranted under 'Victim-Related Adjustments,' as the intended victim was Sabol, not the government, and my client took action, albeit unlawful, to end Sabol's reign of crime: a man who is a monster, thief, drug dealer, woman beater, con artist, and hopeful murderer."

"Again, Mr. Cascione, I'm going to deny your request. Chapter 3, part A, 'Victim-Related Adjustments,' addresses hate-crime motivation, vulnerable victims, restraint of victims, and terrorism, none of which is applicable in this case. Should you be inclined, a downward departure motion, under 5K2.10, 'Victim's Conduct,' you can present it to me. However, as stated by you, Sabol was not the victim of this offense. Do you have anything else that need be addressed by this court?"

Yep, this is a fuck-job. He's denied us everything, just as I thought. I had him pegged as a prick right from the beginning.

"Yes, Your Honor, one more thing."

"Proceed!" Schwartz exploded and, in doing so, made it clear to everyone that Tommy was wasting the court's time. Schwartz's mind was made up, and there was nothing he could say that could change it.

"Defense counsel takes issue with the financial condition of the presentence report. The defendant is quite broke. My client liquidated securities to pay for his legal defense, titled his car to his brother, and quitclaimed his equity in his home to his father to cover legal costs. My client will have to file for bankruptcy due to outstanding credit card bills in excess of $12,000 and has no means to make payment while incarcerated. He, therefore, will not be able to pay any fine imposed by this court. Thank you, Your Honor."

"Mr. Cascione, do you have anything else for this court, in regards to this sentencing, before I hear from the prosecution?"

"No, Your Honor."

The courtroom was mysteriously silent. There were no yells or sighs of frustration from any of Vinny's friends or family. They'd been warned about the judge and the fact that he would love nothing more than to jail anyone of them on a contempt of court charge. As for Vinny, Tommy had warned him to remain calm.

Tommy and Gonzalez had talked about the possible sentence before Vinny entered the courtroom. Gonzalez had agreed that if the judge went with the higher end of the sentencing recommendation, he would only seek the low end. With his lower recommendation, Vinny would only have to serve twenty-eight of the possible thirty-seven-month sentence.

Stay calm, stay calm. Even though my blood's boiling, I promised everyone I'd stay calm no matter what happens. After everything my family's been through for the past five months—has it really been five months?—I owe them that. I'm going to stand tall and take it like a man, whatever that bastard dishes out. I'm not going to embarrass my family anymore. I'm not going to let that black-robed bastard break me. I won't give him that satisfaction.

"Mr. Gonzalez, I'll hear you now." Now Schwartz was courteous. He smiled.

"Thank you, Your Honor. It is the government's position that the court should agree with the government, for the reasons I've outlined in a brief to Your Honor, on page 17 of the addendum to the presentence report, thereby raising the offense level to 21, yielding a guideline imprisonment range of thirty-seven to forty-six months."

What the fuck is this? He just stabbed us in the back again!

"The government firmly maintains the position that the defendant was the architect, organizer, and leader of the conspiracy. The government also believes the defendant should be sentenced to the upper two-thirds end of the thirty-seven to forty-six months."

Tommy's face filled with rage. Gonzalez had once again lied to him, and it was too late for him to do anything about it. He had been tricked.

"Anything else from the government, Mr. Gonzalez?" He was asking Gonzalez to add more fuel to the fire.

"No, Your Honor."

"Mr. Davis! I'll hear from you now!" Contempt and anticipation were on his face. The tiger had his quarry right where he wanted and was ready to pounce.

"First, Your Honor, I would like to apologize to the agents of the United States Customs Service for unknowingly and unintentionally placing them in harm's way."

He spoke the words he felt he had to, in a tone of compassionate necessity. He nodded at Tommy and smiled blandly, yet his eyes were bright, so full of desperate pleading that he drew a reassuring smile in return.

"I think my department record, both on and off duty, clearly shows that I would have given my own life to protect not only fellow law enforcement officers but innocent civilians as well. I would also like to apologize to my family for the humiliation I have caused them. Now, I would like to know when I will get my apology. Who will be the one to come forward and apologize for lying to me? I was promised by the DEA, the FBI, and the Assistant United States Attorney that Richard Sabol will be in prison for twenty years, that my family and I will never again be in fear of Richard Sabol, a man whose criminal record has spanned over two decades, a man I've had to spend the past twelve years having to track every move and whereabouts of to ensure my family's safety. For twelve years, I have made proper notifications to every federal law enforcement agency about his criminal activities. I played by all the rules!"

His indignation and anger began to show through.

"However, he has become so deeply involved in the commission of crimes over his life that he has become acutely aware of how to manipulate the system. He has it down to a science, and as usual, he got what he wanted. His one error of judgment was to threaten my family and me. Cops have long memories, and that one error has haunted him his entire criminal career. I would have done anything, within the law, to see that animal rot behind bars, where he rightfully belongs. But today he walks the streets a free man. Today, as I wait before you to be sentenced to prison for a crime I unknowingly committed, he is laughing. He is laughing in the face of justice. But then again, this is not about justice. This case has never been about justice. This case has been about vengeance. I can only hope that Mr. Sabol, while free on the streets, doesn't take the life of some poor, unsuspecting victim. For if he does, I will be able to sleep at night knowing that I did my best to help put him away for good. If God forbids he does kill someone, maybe a cop, or a federal agent, I can only wonder how well you and Mr. Gonzalez will sleep. My family has suffered greatly by this ordeal, and I beg you to show mercy on me. Thank you, Your Honor."

As he sat down, he was disgusted by his exhibition of weakness and humiliation by his loss of self-control. For Vinny, groveling before this man, in front of his family, was the ultimate humiliation.

"Mr. Cascione, do you have anything further to add?"

"No, Your Honor!"

"Mr. Gonzalez, do you?"

"Yes, Your Honor. I just want to reiterate to the court that the defendant did violate his oath as a police officer, and the government strongly believes he should receive the upper two-thirds of the guidelines range for his involvement in this crime. Thank you, Your Honor."

Tommy saw red again. If looks could kill, Gonzalez would be dead.

"Will the defendant please rise?" Schwartz looked amused. The moment he could finally savage his prey was at hand. He lived for such moments.

As Vinny stood, fear overcame him.

A hostile judge can kill you a thousand ways. He's already shown that a thousand times during my trial. His rulings have been an arbitrary exercise of authority. Today he's denied every one of TC's motions for a reduction of my sentence in a naked display of abuse of power. It's been a grim spectacle, but we ain't seen anything yet.

"This trial has proved you to be a crooked cop!" Schwartz shouted contemptuously. "You betrayed the trust allotted to you by the position you held. A position of trust has been violated by you."

The judge was pontificating, shouting like thunder, filling the courtroom with his voice.

"You are a dirty cop, as the evidence of this trial has proven. Thanks to you, the mobsters, who were the targets of the investigation you compromised, were given light sentences. I know that, because I was the judge who sat on the original trial, and upon their convictions, I was forced to give them light sentences. That is why I am going to grant the prosecution's request to up your sentencing level to 21, level A, and sentence you to forty-five months of a possible forty-six months, within that range!"

Several members of Vinny's family let out half-suppressed screams that made his blood run cold.

"You are a crooked cop who endangered the lives of federal officers. There have been numerous mentions as to your on- and off-duty accomplishments and the medals and commendations you received for your efforts. In response to that, all I have to say is this: It was your sworn duty to take the police actions, whether on or off duty. Your department acknowledged you by commending you in a way they saw fit. Therefore, I have not given them any additional consideration. The defendant is hereby remanded!"

Schwartz was barking.

"Marshals, remove the convict from my court!"

Vinny glanced around the courtroom. He took solace in the fact that no one had panicked.

He was astonished, humiliated, and shocked by what the judge had just said. For an instant, while he was infuriated, his body shook with anger and fear. Then, just as suddenly, his fury lessened. He continued standing, staring and grinning at the Honorable Judge Schwartz, never taking his eyes off the disturbing face of evil incarnate sitting above him. He knew he shouldn't be shocked or sad. It was something for which he'd been preparing himself for months.

He broke off his stare at the judge and looked around at his family and friends.

He despaired at the disappointment he saw in their faces.

Then it was Judy. His eyes locked onto hers. He continued to stare at her, studying her, searching her eyes and the expressions on her face. Fearfully, he noticed she had looked so different to him. It was at that moment that he realized the intimacy they once shared was gone. They were no longer a part of each other. He looked into the eyes of a total stranger. Her eyes no longer held the warmth and love he once cherished.

As the marshals prepared to escort him out the rear of the courtroom, he looked back at her, as though he was trying to fix her image in his mind forever. For a moment, he just stood there, then finally, he turned and was led away. He realized that this day he lost not only his freedom but also what he once thought was his one and only true love.

Back at Union County Jail, he somehow reveled in the solitude and loneliness, because he knew everything would change.

He picked up the phone and quickly dialed her number. The ringing stopped, replaced by a recorded voice. "The number you have reached has been changed. At the customer's request, no further information is given."

Vinny stood rigidly, swallowing back tears that wet his eyes. He began to tremble. He felt so helpless, so inadequate. But he knew in his heart the mechanical voice on the phone was right: no further information was necessary.

ABOUT THE AUTHOR

Vincent Davis was born in Bay Ridge, Brooklyn, and is the oldest child of Vincent and Jean Marie Davis. He attended Our Lady of Angels School until the tragic death of his mother at only thirty years old. The son of a New York City police sergeant, his family was relocated to Yonkers, New York, and was raised by his loving stepmother, Mary, and his grandmother Margaret. Vinny graduated from Roosevelt High School, where he played on the varsity baseball team and swim teams. He graduated from the New York City Police Academy in 1985 at the top ten percent of his class. He was assigned to uniform patrol where his abilities to make high-profile arrests earned him a position in plainclothes as an anti-crime cop. Patrolling the most dangerous neighborhoods in the Bronx, he is credited with hundreds of violent felony arrests. He earned a total of thirty-seven commendations for bravery and was decorated on Valor Day by Mayors Koch, Dinkins, and Giuliani. He received the PBA Cop of the Month Dinner Awards on two separate occasions by Governors Cuomo and Pataki.

CPSIA information can be obtained
at www.ICGtesting.com
Printed in the USA
FFHW020937071219
56783220-62467FF

9 781645 841913